SAINTS AND SINNERS

A History of the Popes

Saints & Sinners

A HISTORY OF THE POPES

Eamon Duffy

Yale Nota Bene
Yale University Press
New Haven and London

FOR JENNY

Published in association with S4C (Wales)
First published as a Yale Nota Bene Book in 2002

For information about this and other Yale University Press publications, please contact
    U.S. office: sales.press@yale.edu
    Europe office: sales@yaleup.co.uk

ISBN 0-300-09165-6

Library of Congress Catalog card number for the cloth edition 97–60897
A catalogue record for this book is available from the British Library

Printed in the United States of America

10   9   8   7   6   5   4   3   2   1

CONTENTS

ACKNOWLEDGEMENTS

I owe debts of gratitude to many people: to Harri Pritchard Jones, 'onlie begetter', and to his wife Lenna, for their friendship and truly Celtic hospitality. To Opus Television and its staff, in particular to Mervyn Williams, for the invitation to write this book, to Heyden Denman, cameraman, and to Amanda Rees, who directed the television series to which this book is the companion volume. To John Gillanders of Derwen, for endless patience and technical wizzardry. To Yale University Press and especially to Peter James, the copy-editor, to Sheila Lee, who researched the pictures, to Sally Salvesen, who designed the book and nursed it, (and me), through its final stages, and to John Nicoll, prince of publishers. Once again, Ruth Daniel read the proofs out of the goodness of her heart.

PREFACE TO THE NEW EDITION

For this new edition of *Saints and Sinners*, I have taken the opportunity to correct a (thankfully small) number of errors, to expand
and revise parts of all but the first two chapters, and to update the
Bibliographical Essay. The account of the papacy of John Paul II has
been extensively rewritten and augmented, and vigilant readers
will detect the modification of some earlier judgements. I have also
added a brief appendix explaining the procedures for the election
of a new Pope set in place by Pope John Paul II in 1996. The
process of revision has greatly benefited from the insights and criticisms of the reviewers of the first edition: I would like to express
my particular thanks to Patrick Collinson, T. F. X. Noble and Simon
Ditchfield. The illustrations to the first edition elicited much
favourable comment, and though it is flattering to the author of a
lavishly illustrated book when his publishers reckon his text worth
reproducing in its own right, there is inevitably some loss. This edition is less sumptuous than the first, but I hope that the large number of pictures and captions we have retained will continue to
extend and deepen the narrative in the text, rather than simply decorate it. I am greatly indebted to Sally Salvesen and to Ruth Applin
who designed the new edition. Finally, I renew the heartfelt dedication of this book to my wife Jenny.

Eamon Duffy

Feast of St Mary Magdalene 2001

PREFACE

Nearly 900 million human beings, the largest single collective of people the world has ever known, look to the Pope as their spiritual leader. His office symbolises the rule of God himself over their hearts and minds and consciences. The words of the popes weigh in the halls of power, and in the bedrooms of the faithful. And the papacy is the oldest, as well as arguably the most influential, of all human institutions. The Roman empire was new-born when the first popes ascended the throne of St Peter almost two thousand years ago. When Karol Wojtyla became the 261st Pope in 1978, the dynasty he represented had outlived not merely the Roman and Byzantine empires, but those of Carolingian Gaul, of medieval Germany, of Spain, of Britain, and the Third Reich of Hitler. Wojtyla himself was to play a not inconsiderable role in the collapse of the latest of these empires, the Soviet Union.

In the flux of history, the papacy has been, not a mere spectator, but a major player. As the Roman empire collapsed, and the barbarian nations arose to fill the vacuum, the popes, in default of any other agency, set themselves to shape the destiny of the West, acting as midwives to the emergence of Europe, creating emperors, deposing monarchs for rebellion against the Church. Popes have divided the known and yet to be discovered world between colonial powers for the sake of peace, or have plunged nations and continents into war, hurling the Christian West against the Muslim East in the Crusades.

The history of the papacy is therefore the history of one of the most momentous and extraordinary institutions in the history of the world. It has touched human society and culture at every point. From contemporary concern with issues of life and death, the morality of abortion or the death-penalty, of capitalism or of nuclear war, to the history of Western art and the major commissions of Michelangelo and Raphael, Bramante and Bernini, the papacy has been and remains still at the heart of many of the most urgent, the most profound and the most exuberant of human concerns.

This book, which is linked to a series of six television programmes, attempts to provide an overview of the whole history of the papacy from the Apostle Peter to Pope John Paul II. It traces the process by which Peter, the humble fisherman of Galilee, became the figurehead and foundation stone of a dynasty which has been able to challenge the most powerful secular rulers, and which commands the religious allegiance of more than a fifth of the world's population. The book is not a work of theology, though no history of the papacy can or should altogether avoid theology. I have tried to include enough theological explanation to enable the non-specialist reader to understand the milestones in the emergence of the papacy as a religious and political institution, but I have not thought it my business to justify or defend that evolution. For Roman Catholics, of course (of whom I am one), the story of the popes is a crucial dimension of the story of the providential care of God for humankind in history, the necessary and (on the whole) proper development of powers and responsibilities implicit in the nature of the Church itself. But by no means all Christians accept such a claim, and for some the papacy, at least in its modern form, is a disastrous cul-de-sac, and a prime cause of Christian disunity. For non-Christians the story of the popes is simply one more of the myriad stories of humanity, another of the multiple forms in which human hope and human ambition have expressed themselves. Whatever the reader's convictions, however, I hope that the narrative offered here provides a framework for understanding one of the world's longest-enduring and most influential institutions.

This is *a* history of the popes: it cannot claim to be *the* history of the popes. No one-volume survey of an institution so ancient and so embedded in human history and culture can be anything

more than a sketch, just as no historian can claim equal competence and grip across a 2,000-year sketch. There is no single story-
line, for history does not evolve in lines, and the papacy has been
at the centre of too many different human stories and enterprises
for it to have a single story of its own. Themes do of course recur.
In writing the book I have been struck by the extent to which
the mere existence of the papacy, and even its most self-aggrandising claims, have again and again helped ensure that the local
churches of Christendom retained something of a universal
Christian vision, that they did not entirely collapse back into the
narrowness of religious nationalism, or become entirely subordinated to the will of powerful secular rulers. From Barbarian Italy
or Carolingian Europe, to the Age of Enlightenment, or the Age
of the Dictators, the papacy has helped keep alive a vision of
human value which transcended the atavisms of history and the
rule of mere force, and has borne witness to the objectivity of
truths beyond the shifts of intellectual fashion. For all its sins, and
despite its recurring commitment to the repression of 'error', the
papacy does seem to me to have been on balance a force for
human freedom, and largeness of spirit.

I have tried to ensure that the narrative offered here is reasonably comprehensive, and that it accurately reflects the current
state of knowledge of the issues and events it covers. Inevitably,
however, the attempt to compress so much into so small a space
has involved drastic and painful decisions about what to omit, as
well as what to include: I do not expect my judgement about
what is central and what marginal to be agreed with by everyone.

Nor is every stretch of papal history equally easy going. Some
readers may be daunted by the theological complexities and the
historical unfamiliarity of some of the material covered in Chapter Two, which deals with the popes of the so-called 'Dark Ages'. I
have dealt with them in some detail, however, because the fundamental orientation of the papacy towards the West and away from
the East was decided in those centuries. Similarly, in the section
on the Renaissance popes, readers may be surprised to find far
more about the relatively obscure Nicholas V than about the far
more notorious Alexander VI, the 'Borgia Pope'. This is not

because Nicholas was respectable and pious, and Alexander scandalous and debauched (though both these things are true), but because in my view the career of Nicholas V tells us far more about the nature and objectives of the Renaissance papacy than the more colourful and better-known escapades of Alexander. Readers must judge for themselves. And finally, it is of course too soon to form a mature assessment of the nature or importance of the pontificate of John Paul II, or indeed those of his immediate predecessors. More than any other part of the book, the final chapter is offered as a tentative interim report, and a personal perspective.

I have tried not to clog the text with too many technical aids. A light sprinkling of reference notes identifies extended or contentious quotations, while more detailed guidance to the literature on any given subject will be found in the chapter-by-chapter and topic-by-topic Bibliographical Essay at the end of the book. A Glossary provides brief explanations of technicalities; I have included also a numbered chronological list of popes and antipopes.

Eamon Duffy
College of St Mary Magdalene, Cambridge
Feast of Sts Peter and Paul, 1997

CHAPTER ONE

'UPON THIS ROCK'

c. AD 33–461

I FROM JERUSALEM TO ROME

Round the dome of St Peter's basilica in Rome, in letters six feet high, are Christ's words to Peter from chapter sixteen of Matthew's Gospel: *Tu es Petrus, et super hanc petram aedificabo ecclesiam meam et tibi dabo claves regni caelorum* (Thou art Peter, and upon this Rock I will build my Church and I will give to thee the keys of the Kingdom of Heaven). Set there to crown the grave of the Apostle, hidden far below the high altar, they are also designed to proclaim the authority of the man whom almost a billion Christians look to as the living heir of Peter. With these words, it is believed, Christ made Peter prince of the Apostles and head of the Church on earth: generation by generation, that role has been handed on to Peter's successors, the popes. As the Pope celebrates Mass at the high altar of St Peter's, the New Testament and the modern world, heaven and earth, touch hands.

The continuity between Pope and Apostle rests on traditions which stretch back almost to the very beginning of the written records of Christianity. It was already well established by the year AD 180, when the early Christian writer Irenaeus of Lyons invoked it in defence of orthodox Christianity. The Church of Rome was for him the 'great and illustrious Church' to which, 'on account of its commanding position, every church, that is the faithful everywhere, must resort'. Irenaeus thought that the Church had been 'founded and organised at Rome by the two glorious Apostles, Peter and Paul,' and that its faith had been reliably passed down to posterity by an unbroken succession of bishops, the first of them chosen and consecrated by the Apostles themselves. He named the bishops who had succeeded the Apostles, in the process providing us with the earliest surviving list of the popes – Linus, Anacletus, Clement, Evaristus, Alexander, Sixtus, and so on down to Irenaeus' contemporary and friend Eleutherius, Bishop of Rome from AD 174 to 189.[1]

All the essential claims of the modern papacy, it might seem, are contained in this Gospel saying about the Rock, and in Irenaeus' account of the apostolic pedigree of the early bishops of Rome. Yet matters are not so simple. The popes trace their commission from Christ through Peter, yet for Irenaeus the authority of the Church at Rome came from its foundation by two Apostles, not by one, Peter *and* Paul, not Peter alone. The tradition that Peter and Paul had been put to death at the hands of Nero in Rome about the year AD 64 was universally accepted in the second century, and by the end of that century pilgrims to Rome were being shown the 'trophies' of the Apostles, their tombs or cenotaphs, Peter's on the Vatican Hill, and Paul's on the Via Ostiensis, outside the walls on the road to the coast. Yet on all of this the New Testament is silent. Later legend would fill out the details of Peter's life and death in Rome – his struggles with the magician and father of heresy, Simon Magus, his miracles, his attempted escape from persecution in Rome, a flight from which he was turned back by a reproachful vision of Christ (the 'Quo Vadis' legend), and finally his crucifixion upside down in the Vatican Circus in the time of the Emperor Nero. These stories were to be accepted as sober history by some of the greatest minds of the early Church – Origen, Ambrose, Augustine. But they are pious romance, not history, and the fact is that we have no reliable accounts either of Peter's later life or of the manner or place of his death. Neither Peter nor Paul founded the Church at Rome, for there were Christians in the city before either of the Apostles set foot there. Nor can we assume, as Irenaeus did, that the Apostles established there a succession of bishops to carry on their work in the city, for all the indications are that there was no single bishop at Rome for almost a century after the deaths of the Apostles. In fact, wherever we turn, the solid outlines of the Petrine succession at Rome seem to blur and dissolve.

That the leadership of the Christian Church should be associated with Rome at all, and with the person of Peter, in itself needs some explanation. Christianity is an oriental religion, born in the religious and political turmoil of first-century Palestine. Its central figure was a travelling rabbi, whose disciples proclaimed him as the fulfilment of Jewish hopes, the Messiah. Executed by the Romans as a pretender to the throne of Israel, his death and resurrection were interpreted by reference to the stories and prophecies of the Jewish scriptures, and much of the language in which it was proclaimed derived from and spoke to Jewish hopes and longings. Jerusalem was the first centre of Christian preaching, and the Church at Jerusalem was led by members of the Messiah's own family, starting with James, the 'brother' of Jesus.

Within ten years of the Messiah's death, however, Christianity escaped from Palestine, along the seaways and roads of the *Pax Romana*, northwards to Antioch, on to Ephesus, Corinth and Thessalonica, and westwards to Cyprus, Crete and Rome. The man chiefly responsible was Paul of Tarsus, a sophisticated Greek-speaking rabbi who, unlike Jesus' twelve Apostles, was himself a Roman citizen. Against opposition from fellow Christians, including Jesus' first disciples, Paul insisted that the life and death of Jesus not only fulfilled the Jewish Law and the Prophets, but made sense of the world, and offered reconciliation and peace with God for the whole human race. In Jesus, Paul believed that God was offering humanity as a whole the life, guidance and transforming power which had once been the possession of Israel. His reshaping of the Christian message provided the vehicle by which an obscure heresy from one of the less appetising corners of the Roman Empire could enter the bloodstream of late antiquity. In due course, the whole world was changed.

Paul's letters to the churches he founded or visited make up the largest single component of the New Testament, and the story of his conversion and preaching dominates another major New Testament text, the Acts of the Apostles. He was, without any question or rival, the most important figure in the early history of the Church. But he was never its leader. From the start, the Church had no single centre: it was founded at Jerusalem, but Jerusalem was destroyed by the Romans in AD 70, and already there were flourishing churches throughout the Empire at Antioch (where the disciples of Jesus were first called 'Christians') at Corinth, at Ephesus and at Rome itself. Paul's authority was immense, even beyond the churches he himself had founded. But he had never known Jesus, and did not feature in the foundation stories of Christianity. Though he claimed and was conceded the status of 'Apostle', he was not one of the 'Twelve', and had not walked the roads of Palestine with the Son of God. With Peter, however, it was a different matter.

The New Testament speaks with many voices. It is not a single book, but a library, built up over half a century or so from traditions of the remembered sayings and actions of Jesus, early Christian sermons, hymns and liturgies, and the letters of the great founding teachers of the early Church. Despite that, the Gospels do offer a remarkably persuasive portrait of Peter the Apostle, a Galilean fisherman whose original name was Simon Bar Jonah. Warm-hearted, impulsive, generous, he was, with his brother Andrew, the first to respond to Jesus' call to abandon his old life and become 'fishers of men'. Ardently loyal and constantly protesting his devotion to Jesus, Peter is just as constantly portrayed in all the Gospels as prone to misunderstand Jesus' mission and intentions, angrily rejecting Christ's prophecy of his Passion, refusing to have his feet washed at the Last Supper, snatching up a sword in a misguided attempt to protect Jesus when the Temple police come to arrest him in Gethsemane. Peter acts first and thinks later. His denial of Christ in the courtyard of the High Priest – and his subsequent bitter repentance – are all of a piece with the other actions of the man as he emerges from the sources.

In all the Gospels he is the leader, or at any rate the spokesman, of the Apostles. Throughout the Gospels of Matthew, Mark and Luke Peter's name occurs first in every list of the names of the Twelve. In each Gospel he is the first disciple to be called by Jesus. At Caesarea Philippi, at the turning-point of Jesus' ministry, it is Peter who recognises and confesses him as the Messiah, thereby explicitly expressing the Church's faith in its Lord for the first time. Peter is the first of the inner circle of disciples permitted by Jesus to witness his transfiguration on the mountain, and it is Peter who (foolishly) calls out to Christ in wonder and fear during it.

Of all the evangelists, it is Matthew who insists most on the centrality of Peter. In particular, Matthew elaborates the account of Peter's Confession of Faith at Caesarea Philippi. In his version, Jesus declares Peter's faith to be a direct revelation from God, and rewards it by renaming Simon 'Kephas', Peter, the Rock. He goes on to declare that 'upon this Rock I will build my Church, and I will give to you the keys of the kingdom of heaven, and whatever you bind on earth shall be bound also in heaven', the text that would later come to be seen as the foundation charter of the papacy (Matthew 16:13–23). There is an equivalent scene in the final chapter of the Gospel of John. Christ, in an exchange designed to remind us of Peter's threefold betrayal of Jesus during the Passion, asks Peter three times, 'Do you love me?', and in response to the Apostle's reiterated 'You know everything, you know that I love you,' Jesus three times commands him, 'Feed my lambs, feed my sheep.' For John, as for Matthew, Peter is the privileged recipient of a special commission, based on the confession of his faith and trust in Christ (John 21: 15–17). The special status of Peter in the Gospels, his commission to bind and loose, to feed the sheep of Christ, flow from his role as primary witness and guardian of the faith. In the subsequent reflection of the Church that complex of ideas would decisively shape Christian understanding of the nature and roots of true authority. The office of Peter, to proclaim the Church's faith, and to guard and nourish that faith, would lie at the root of the self-understanding of the Roman community and their bishop, in which it was believed the responsibilities and the privileges of the Apostle had been perpetuated.

Unsurprisingly, the relationship between Peter and Paul seems to have been uneasy, and Paul's attitude to Peter prickly and defensive. Paul himself provides the evidence for this unease in the earliest New Testament document to mention Peter, the Epistle to the Galatians. Anxious to vindicate his independent claims, he seems determined to concede as little as possible to the senior Apostle. Nevertheless, he recognises Peter's special place. It is to Peter, he tells us, that he went for information after his conversion, staying with him for fifteen days and seeing no other Apostle except James, the Lord's brother. He tells us also that Peter was charged with the mission outside Palestine to the Jews of the diaspora, while he, Paul, was sent to the Gentiles. In chapter two of the Epistle, Paul tells of his famous rebuke to Peter at Antioch, when he 'withstood Peter to his face', protesting against the fact that the leader of the Apostles had tried to conciliate hard-line Jewish Christians worried about breaches of the kosher laws, by abandoning his previous table-fellowship with Gentile converts. Paul tells this story to vindicate his own independent authority, and maybe his superior fidelity to Gospel teaching, over against Peter's notorious proneness to cave in to hostile criticism. The whole account, however, derives its rhetorical power from Paul's awareness of the shock-value for his readers of his temerity in 'withstanding [even] Peter to the face'. If Peter's authority were not recognised by Paul's readers as being especially great, Paul's rebuke would not have carried the *frisson* of daring which the passage clearly intends.

The picture of Peter which emerges from Paul's writings, as the most authoritative Apostle and head of the mission to the Jews of the

Mediterranean diaspora, is developed and elaborated in the first half of the Acts of the Apostles. Though other disciples play important roles, here in these early chapters of Luke's continuation of his Gospel Peter is the dominant figure. He leads the Pentecost proclamation of the resurrection, presides over the meetings of the young Church, works many miracles, is rescued from prison by an angel, and even pre-empts Paul's later role as Apostle to the Gentiles by baptising the centurion Cornelius, having received a vision from heaven revealing that this was God's will. Mysteriously, however, Peter fades out of the Acts of the Apostles, and of the New Testament, after his escape from prison in chapter twelve. Luke tells us enigmatically only that Peter sent word of his escape to James, now the leader of the Jerusalem church, and then 'departed and went to another place'. Of his subsequent career the New Testament has nothing at all to say.

Neither Paul, Acts nor any of the Gospels tells us anything direct about Peter's death, and none of them even hints that the special role of Peter could be passed on to any single 'successor'. There is, therefore, nothing directly approaching a papal theory in the pages of the New Testament. Yet it is hard to account for the continuing interest in Peter in the Gospels and Acts unless Peter's authority continued to be meaningful after his death. Matthew, whose Gospel was probably written for the church at Antioch, clearly thought so. He follows his account of the giving of the keys of the kingdom to Peter, the commission to bind and loose, with an extended section of instructions about the ordering of Church life. In it the authority of the community is backed up with the promise that 'whatever you bind on earth shall be bound in heaven, and whatever you loose on earth shall be loosed in heaven' (Matthew 18:18). Peter was widely believed to have founded the church at Antioch, and this unmistakable echo of Christ's words to him about binding and loosing in Matthew 16:18–19 seems to imply that, for Matthew, Peter's authority continued within his community.

The same sense that Peter's authority is perpetuated within the Christian community is in evidence in the New Testament writings attributed to Peter himself. The First Epistle of Peter claims to have been written by the Apostle, in a time of persecution, from 'Babylon', an early Christian code-name for Rome. Many scholars have detected an early Christian baptismal sermon buried under the letter format, however, and the elegant Greek style of the letter makes it very unlikely indeed that it is Peter's unaided work. Possibly it represents Peter's teaching mediated through an educated amanuensis. Whether he wrote it or not, however, Peter is presented in the letter not merely as an apostle and witness of the saving work of Christ, but as a source for the authority and responsibilities of the elders or governing officials of the Church. He writes to 'the elders among you', uniquely for an apostle, as 'a fellow elder', thereby underlining the continuity between the authority of the Apostles and that of the elders who now lead the Church which the Apostles had founded. The other hearers of the letter are urged to submit to the elders, whose role is presented as that of shepherds, tending the flock of Christ, the Chief Shepherd, and leading by humble example. This imagery might of course be derived directly from any number of Old Testament passages in which God is depicted as the Shepherd of his people, but its similarity to the Johannine commission to Peter, 'feed my lambs, feed my sheep', is very striking, and can hardly be a coincidence.

A general belief in the precedence of Rome emerged in the Christian writings of the second century, and was accepted apparently without challenge. From its beginnngs, this was rooted in the claim that both Peter and Paul had ended their lives in martyrdom at Rome under the Emperor Nero. On this matter, the New Testament is not much help. The last chapter of John contains a mysterious reference to Peter in old age having to 'stretch out his arms' and being led where he does not wish to go: the early Church believed this referred to his crucifixion (John 21:18). As we have seen, I Peter places Peter in Rome, and is very much a letter of comfort in the face of persecution. It is shot through with references to the 'fiery ordeal' and sufferings which its hearers are enduring, but it says nothing direct about Peter's own death. The Acts of the Apostles, similarly, ends with Paul in Rome, preaching 'quite openly and unhindered', with no hint of a coming martyrdom.

Nevertheless, there is no reason to doubt the ancient tradition that both Peter and Paul were put to death in Rome during the Neronian persecution of the mid 60s AD. The universal acceptance of this belief among early Christian writers, and the failure of any other Church to lodge competing claims to the possession of the Apostles' witness or their relics, is strong evidence here, especially when taken together with the existence of a second century cult of both saints in Rome at their 'trophies' – shrines at their graves or cenotaphs over the sites of their martyrdoms. These monuments were mentioned by a Roman cleric around the year AD 200, and their existence was dramatically confirmed by archaeology in this century. Building-work in the crypt of St Peter's in 1939 uncovered an ancient pagan cemetery on the slope of the Vatican Hill, on top of which Constantine had built the original Christian basilica in the fourth century. As excavation proceeded, it became clear that Constantine's workmen had gone to enormous trouble to orientate the entire basilica towards a particular site within the pagan cemetery, over which, long before the Constantinian era, had been placed a small niched shrine or trophy, datable to c. AD 165. This shrine, though damaged, was still in place, and fragments of bone were discovered within it, which Pope Paul VI declared in 1965 to be the relics of St Peter. Unfortunately, controversy surrounds the methods and some of the findings of the excavations, and we cannot be sure that the shrine does in fact mark the grave of Peter. The fragments of bone discovered there were at the foot of the wall and not in the central niche. We cannot be certain that they are his, especially since executed criminals were usually thrown into unmarked mass graves. It is possible that the excavation uncovered the site of Peter's execution, rather than his burial. Whether it is Peter's grave or his cenotaph, however, the mere existence of the shrine is overwhelming evidence of a very early Roman belief that Peter had died in or near the Vatican Circus.

The early written sources support this tradition. A letter written around AD 96 on behalf of the Roman church to the Christians at Corinth speaks of Peter and Paul as 'our Apostles', suffering witnesses of the truth who, 'having born testimony before the rulers', went to glory. Writing to the Roman Christians about the year 107, Ignatius, Bishop of Antioch, declared that 'I do not command you, as Peter and Paul did,' a clear indication that he believed that the Apostles had been leaders of the Roman church. Two generations further on, Irenaeus wrote that the Church had been 'founded and organised at Rome by the two glorious Apostles, Peter and Paul.'[2]

For all these reasons, most scholars accept the early Christian tradition that Peter and Paul died in Rome. Yet, though they lived, preached and died in Rome, they did not strictly 'found' the Church there. Paul's Epistle to the Romans was written before either he or Peter ever set foot in Rome, to a Christian community already in existence. First-century Rome had a large and thriving Jewish population, perhaps as many as 50,000 strong, scattered throughout the city but especially concentrated in Trastevere, across the river from the city proper, and organised in over a dozen synagogues. The Roman Jews were an expansive and self confident group, eager to make converts, and they had strong links with Palestine and Jerusalem. Jerusalem was the first centre of the Christian mission, and so it is not surprising that Jews believing in Christ found their way to Rome by the early 40s. By AD 49 they had become a significant presence in the Roman synagogues, and their beliefs were causing trouble. According to the pagan historian Suetonius, the Emperor Claudius became alarmed by the constant disturbances among the Jews over 'Chrestus' (a common early form of the name Christ), and expelled them from the city in AD 49. This expulsion can hardly have included all 50,000 Jews, but Jewish Christians certainly were obliged to leave the city, for two of them surface in the pages of the New Testament. The Jewish Christian tent-maker Aquila and his wife Priska or Priscilla were among the victims of Claudius' purge. They moved to Corinth, where they befriended the Apostle Paul (Acts 18:2), accompanying him when he moved on to Ephesus. They eventually returned to Rome, however, where their house became the meeting place of a church (Romans 16:3–5).

Of *a* church, notice, not of *the* Church, for Christian organisation in Rome reflected that of the Jewish community out of which it had grown. The Roman synagogues, unlike their counterparts in Antioch, had no central organisation. Each one conducted its own worship, appointed its own leaders and cared for its own members. In the same way, the ordering of the early Christian community in Rome seems to have reflected the organisation of the synagogues which had originally sheltered it, and to have consisted of a constellation of independent churches, meeting in the houses of the wealthy members of the community. Each of these house churches had its own leaders, the elders or 'presbyters'. They were mostly made up of immigrants, with a high proportion of slaves or freedmen among them – the name of Pope Eleutherius means 'freedman'.

To begin with, indeed, there was no 'pope', no bishop as such, for the church in Rome was slow to develop the office of chief presbyter, or bishop. By the end of the first century the loose pattern of Christian authority of the first generation of believers was giving way in many places to the more organised rule of a single bishop for each city, supported by a college of elders. This development was at least in part a response to the wildfire spread of false teaching — heresy. As conflicting teachers arose, each claiming to speak for 'true' Christianity, a tighter and more hierarchic structure developed, and came to seem essential to the preservation of unity and truth. The succession of a single line of bishops, handing on the teaching of the Apostles like a baton in a relay race, provided a pedigree for authentic Christian truth, and a concrete focus for unity.

A key figure in this development was Ignatius of Antioch, a bishop from Asia Minor arrested and brought to Rome to be executed around the year 107. *En route* he wrote a series of letters to other churches, largely consisting of appeals to them to unite round their bishops. His letter to the Roman church, however, says nothing whatever about bishops, a strong indication that the office had not yet emerged at Rome. Paradoxically, this impression is borne out by a document which has sometimes been thought of as the first papal encyclical. Ten years or so before Ignatius' arrival in Rome, the Roman church wrote to the church at Corinth, in an attempt to quieten disputes and disorders which had broken out there. The letter is unsigned, but has always been attributed to the Roman presbyter Clement, generally counted in the ancient lists as the third Pope after St Peter. Legends would later accumulate round his name, and he was to be venerated as a martyr, exiled to the Crimea and killed by being tied to an anchor and dropped into the sea. In fact, however, Clement made no claim to write as bishop. His letter was sent in the name of the whole Roman community, he never identifies himself or writes in his own person, and we know nothing at all about him. The letter itself makes no distinction between presbyters and bishops, about which it always speaks in the plural, suggesting that at Corinth as at Rome the church at this time was organised under a group of bishops or presbyters, rather than a single ruling bishop.

A generation later, this was still so in Rome. The visionary treatise *The Shepherd of Hermas*, written in Rome early in the second century, speaks always collectively of the 'rulers of the Church', or the 'elders that preside over the Church', and once again the author makes no attempt to distinguish between bishops and elders. Clement is indeed mentioned (if Hermas' Clement is the same man as the author of the letter written at least a generation before, which we cannot assume) but not as presiding bishop. Instead, we are told that he was the elder responsible for writing 'to the foreign cities' – in effect the corresponding secretary of the Roman church.

Everything we know about the church in Rome during its first hundred years confirms this general picture. The Christians of the city were thought of by themselves and others as a single church, as Paul's letter to the Romans make clear. The social reality behind this single identity, however, was not one congregation, but a loose constellation of churches based in private houses or, as time went on and the community grew, meeting in rented halls in markets and public baths. It was without any single dominant ruling officer, its elders or leaders sharing responsibility, but distributing tasks, like that of foreign correspondent. By the eve of the conversion of Constantine, there were more than two dozen of these religious community-centres or *tituli*.

Rome was the hub of empire, the natural centre for anyone with a message to spread – which was of course why the Apostles Peter and Paul had made their way there in the first place. Early Christianity jostled for space cheek by jowl with the other blossoming new religions of empire, a fact graphically illustrated by the presence of Mithraic shrines under the ancient churches of San Clemente and Santa Prisca (the reputed site of the house of Paul's friends Aquila and Priscilla). Late into the second century the language of the Christian community in Rome was not Latin but Greek, the real lingua franca of an empire that increasingly looked east rather than west. The Christian congregations in Rome themselves reflected the cosmopolitan mix of the capital city, and many had strong ethnic and cultural links back to the regions from which their members had migrated. As a result, the life of the Roman Church was a microcosm of the cultural, doctrinal and ritual diversity of Christianity throughout the empire. By the early second century, for example, the churches in Asia Minor had begun to keep the date of the Jewish Passover, fourteenth Nisan, as a celebration of Easter, whether or not it fell on a Sunday. Those Christian congregations in Rome who came from Asia Minor naturally maintained this regional custom, and this marked them off from 'native' congregations, who celebrated Easter every Sunday, and had not yet evolved a separate annual commemoration. Despite these differences, the governing elders of the 'native' Roman congregations maintained friendly relations with these foreign communities, sending them portions of the consecrated bread from their own celebrations of the eucharist as a sign of their fundamental unity.

This variety in the customs of Roman Christians was not confined to their calendar. Christianity all over the Roman world in the
first and second centuries was in a state of violent creative ferment.
What would come to be seen as mainstream orthodoxy coexisted
alongside versions of the Gospel which would soon come to seem
outrageously deviant, 'heretical'. But the *outré* and the orthodox were
not always easy to distinguish at first sight, and the early Christian
community in Rome had more than its fair share of competing
versions of the Gospel. For Rome was a magnet, attracting to itself a
stream of provincial elders, scholars and private Christians, eager to
see and learn from so ancient a church, above all eager to visit the
resting place of the two greatest Apostles.

Among them came a succession of teachers and thinkers determined to make their mark in the greatest city of the empire. They
included the arch-heretic Marcion, who arrived in the city in AD
140. Marcion denied that matter could be redeemed, rejected the
whole of the Old Testament and most of the New Testament scriptures, and taught a radical opposition between the angry Creator
God of the Old Testament and the loving God and Father of Jesus
Christ. He was a wealthy shipowner from the Black Sea, and by way
of credentials presented the Roman church with a handsome sum of
of money (22,000 sesterces, roughly the annual income of a noble
citizen). For a largely lower-class urban organisation with its own
overstretched social welfare system for widows, orphans and the elderly, and with an expanding aid-programme to needy churches elsewhere in the empire, wealth on this scale was an eloquent testimo-
nial. Marcion was able to function as an accepted Christian teacher
in Rome for several years before his expulsion from communion by
the elders of Rome in AD 144: his money was returned.

But Marcion was merely the most influential of a succession of
such deviant teachers round the mid century – men like Tatian, the
Syrian philosopher who came to reject the whole of Hellenic civilisation as incompatible with the Gospel, or Valentinus, who taught a
bizarre *gnostic* system (from the Greek word for *knowledge*) in which
thirty 'aeons' or spiritual powers emanate from the Supreme God, in
male and female pairs, Christ and the Holy Spirit forming one such
pair. All these men to begin with at least operated within the loose
framework of the Roman church, and Valentinus for a time even
entertained hopes of election as bishop or ruling elder.

II THE BISHOPS OF ROME

It was against this mid-century background of ritual and doctrinal confusion that the 'monarchic episcopate', the rule of the church by a single bishop, was accepted in Rome. Throughout the Mediterranean world the rule of bishops came to be seen as a crucial defence against heresy. As Irenaeus wrote in his *Treatise against the Heresies*, 'It is within the power of anyone who cares, to find the truth and know the tradition of the Apostles . . . we are able to name those who were appointed bishops by the Apostles in the churches and their successors down to our own times.'[3] There is no sure way to settle on a date by which the office of ruling bishop had emerged in Rome, and so to name the first Pope, but the process was certainly complete by the time of Anicetus in the mid-150s, when Polycarp, the aged Bishop of Smyrna, visited Rome, and he and Anicetus debated amicably the question of the date of Easter. Polycarp, then in his eighties, had known John, the 'beloved disciple,' in *his* old age. He therefore strongly urged direct apostolic authority for the practice of the churches from Asia Minor (and their satelite ethnic congregations in Rome itself) of keeping Easter at Passover. Anicetus contented himself more modestly with defending the practice of 'the presbyters who had preceded him' in having no separate Easter festival.

By now the pressure of heresy and the need for a tighter organisation was forcing the Christian movement as a whole to sharpen and refine its self-understanding, to establish its boundaries and clarify its fundamental beliefs. As part of that process of development and self-analysis, the Roman church began to reflect more self-consciously on its apostolic pedigree. It was in the time of Anicetus that the earliest attempts were made to compile a succession-list of the Roman bishops, drawing on the remembered names of leading presbyters like Clement. It was probably under Anicetus, too, that the shrine-monuments to Peter and Paul were first constructed at the Vatican and the Via Ostiensis. This architectural embodiment of the church's claims to continuity with the Apostles would continue into the next century, and from at least AD 230 onwards successive bishops were buried in a single 'crypt of the popes' in the Catacomb of San Callisto, the burial-ground on the Appian Way which the Church had acquired some time in the late second century.

Such monuments were the architectural equivalent of the succession–lists, expressions of the increasingly explicit sense of continuity between the contemporary Roman church and the Apostles. The earliest list to survive for Rome is the one supplied by Irenaeus, and in it this symbolic function is very clearly at work. Irenaeus underlines the parallels between Apostles and bishops by naming precisely twelve bishops of Rome between Peter and the current incumbent, Eleutherius. The sixth of these bishops is named Sixtus. It all seems suspiciously tidy.

The list is certainly a good deal tidier than the actual transition to rule by a single bishop can have been. The bishops laboured steadily to extend their authority and to regulate the life of the church in the city – Pope Fabian's division of the city during the 240s into seven regions, each under the supervision of a deacon, looks like part of this long-term effort at better order. But well into the third century Christianity in Rome would remain turbulent, diverse, prone to split. We know of several such dissident groups, such as the Theodotians, active at the end of the second century in the time of bishops Victor and Zephyrinus. Financed by a wealthy Byzantine leather–seller and a banker (both called Theodotus), these 'Theodotians' taught that Jesus was merely a very good man who had been adopted by God at his baptism and then raised to divinity at his resurrection. They failed to secure official acceptance of their views, but their economic clout meant that they were able to form a separate church and to pay the salary of their own rival bishop. In the next century, other dissidents like Hippolytus or Novatian, more orthodox than Marcion or Valentinus but all the harder to deal with on that account, would also find backers for a challenge to the authority of the official bishop of Rome.

From the start, then, the Roman bishops had to face difficult problems of unity and jurisdiction. The consequences of that preoccupation for the future were already becoming clear in the time of the last Bishop of the second century, Victor (189–98). Victor was the first Latin leader of the Christians of Rome, a sign that the church was spreading out of the immigrant milieu in which it had first taken root. He brought a Latin rigour to his office. He was a disciplinarian, determined to kick the dissident elements in the Roman church into line, and he adopted stern measures. It was Victor who excommunicated the Theodotians, and he also deposed a number of clergy who had been spreading gnostic teaching within the 'mainstream' communities in the city. But his most momentous exercise of authority was provoked by the perennial problem of the date for the celebration of Easter.

Our information about this incident comes from the extended account in Eusebius' *Church History*, written more than a century after the event. As Eusebius tells it, Victor picked a fight with all the churches outside Rome which were celebrating Easter at Passover, fourteenth Nisan (the so called Quartodecimans) instead of on the Sunday after Passover, which by now had been adopted in Rome and the West more generally. According to Eusebius, this developed into a full-scale confrontation between Victor and the churches of Asia Minor, whose position was vigorously defended by Polycrates, Bishop of Ephesus. After a series of regional synods all over the Mediterranean world had been held to debate the issue, Victor solemnly excommunicated all the Quartodeciman churches. He was respectfully rebuked by Irenaeus, who reminded him of the more tolerant attitude of earlier Roman presbyters, who, despite their disagreement, used to 'send the eucharist' to the churches which kept the Quartodeciman date for Easter.

This is a baffling incident, not least because any fragments of eucharistic bread sent on the long sea journey to the churches of Asia Minor would have gone mouldy or hard long before they reached their destination. It has become the focus for centuries of debate about papal authority, for both the friends and the enemies of the papacy have seen in Victor's high-handed actions an assertion of Roman jurisdiction over the whole of Christendom, as the Pope tried to make Roman custom the norm for all the churches. In fact, it is far more likely that Eusebius misunderstood his source materials. He wrote in the fourth century, at a time when his hero, the first Christian Emperor Constantine, was trying to impose uniformity on the Church on this very issue of Easter. Eusebius tells the story of the Quartodeciman controversy as a sort of rehearsal for Constantine's concerns. The tell-tale detail of the sending of the morsels of eucharistic bread, however, suggests that the dispute actually arose in the first instance within the city of Rome, and should be seen as primarily an internal affair. Victor was not brawling randomly around the Mediterranean spoiling for a fight, but trying to impose uniformity of practice on all the churches within his own city, as part of a more general quest for internal unity and order. The churches of proconsular Asia may well have protested at this condemnation of a custom which they believed they had derived from the Apostle John, but Victor's excommunication was aimed at Asian congregations in Rome, not fired broadside at churches over which he had no direct jurisdiction.[4]

Bishop Victor, then, was probably not taking the first steps towards universal papal jurisdiction. All the same, some notion of the special authority of the Roman church was already widespread. At the beginning of the second century, Ignatius wrote extravagantly about the Roman church as 'she who is pre-eminent in the territory of the Romans . . . foremost in love . . . purified from every alien and discolouring stain'. Ignatius admonished other churches, but for the church at Rome he had only praise. As the century advanced, that note of deference was echoed by others. We have already met in Irenaeus the claim that 'it is necessary that every Church, that is, the faithful everywhere, should resort to this Church [of Rome], on account of its pre-eminent authority, in which the apostolical tradition has been preserved continuously . . .'[5]

This 'pre-eminent authority' sprang, above everything else, from the fact that Rome preserved the witness of not one but both of the greatest Apostles; as Irenaeus' contemporary, the African theologian Tertullian, wrote, Rome was the 'happy Church . . . on which the Apostles poured forth all their teaching, together with their blood'. It was a 'happiness' that Roman Christians themselves were increasingly proud of, and devotion to Peter and Paul deepened in the third century. A new cult centre based at what is now the church of San Sebastiano emerged in the mid century, and hundreds of surviving graffiti there, invoking Rome's two great patron saints, convey the fervour of Roman popular devotion to them: 'Paul and Peter, pray for Victor,' 'Paul, Peter, pray for Eratus,' 'Peter and Paul, protect your servants! Holy souls, protect the reader.' From the year 258 a joint feast of Peter and Paul was celebrated at Rome on 29 June, a sign of the centrality of the two Apostles in the Roman church's self-awareness.[6]

To this apostolic prestige was added the fact that the church at Rome sat at the hub of empire. This was not necessarily a short-cut to stardom in early Christian eyes, for there was a strong anti-Roman tradition in the early Church. Rome was the harlot city soaked in the blood of the saints, the centre from which spread out wave after wave of persecution. The Book of Revelations' gloating vision of the coming ruin of Rome, 'Fallen, fallen, is Babylon the great' (Revela-

tions 14:8), remained a persistent strand so long as the empire continued to persecute the church, and survived even into the Middle
Ages. But by the same token, the church at Rome bore the brunt of
persecution, as the deaths of Peter and Paul under Nero showed, and
its witness was all the more glorious for being in the eye of empire.
The conviction that the Apostles had 'founded' the church at Rome
sprang above all from the fact that the shedding of their blood there
was the ultimate witness, *marturion*, to the truth of their Gospel.

But Christianity's rapid growth in the capital had more mundane
consequences. The church in Rome, even under persecution, was
wealthy. Because of the cosmopolitan nature of the Christian community there, the Roman church was especially aware of the ecumenical
character of the faith, its spread through the whole Roman world.
That awareness lay behind the Epistle of Clement to the Corinthians
in AD 96, which was a demonstration of the Roman church's sense of
responsibility for other churches. The Roman community continued
to show that broad concern in practical ways, by sending money as
well as advice and reproof to churches in need. In the mid second century, Dionysius, Bishop of Corinth, wrote a letter of grateful acknowledgement for financial aid sent by Pope Soter. He went on to say that
Soter's accompanying letter was being read out during services in
Corinth, as the Epistle of Clement still was from time to time.[7] As aristocratic converts entered the Church, moreover, the Bishop of Rome,
even in the age of persecution, was an increasingly influential person.
Pope Victor was able to use the fact that the Emperor Commodus'
mistress, Marcia, was a Christian, to get Christian prisoners released
from the penal colony of the Sardinian mines. The habit of appealing
to the Bishop of Rome in doctrinal disputes, which in later controversies would become a crucial lifeline for embattled supporters of
orthodoxy, sprang both from the sense of the dignity of a community
which had inherited not only the teaching but the eloquent blood of
the two Apostles, and, more mundanely, from the fact that the Pope
was an important grandee, a patron.

But the prestige of the church of Rome was not at this stage primarily a matter of the bishop's status or authority. It was the church
of Rome as a whole which basked in the glory of the Apostles and
commanded the respect of other second- and third-century Christian communities. About the year AD 200 the allegorical epitaph of
Abercius, Bishop of Heropolis in Asia Minor, recorded that he had

gone to Rome at Christ's command, 'to behold an empire and to see a queen in a golden robe and golden shoes; I saw there a people with a shining seal.'[8] The honourable status of the Roman church, the 'people with a shining seal', persisted even when there was no bishop in charge. In the long vacancy in the bishopric after the death of Pope Fabian in the Decian persecution (AD 250–1) , the presbyters and deacons of Rome went on exercising the oversight and care for other churches which had become characteristic of their church, sending four letters of advice and encouragement to the churches of North Africa, letters which were copied, circulated and read aloud during worship just as the letters of Clement and Soter had been. The letters breathe the distinctive sense of dignity and responsibility which was becoming the mark of the Roman church: 'The brethren who are in chains greet you, as do the priests and the whole Church which also with deepest concern keeps watch over all who call on the name of the Lord'.[9]

By the beginning of the third century, then, the church at Rome was an acknowledged point of reference for Christians throughout the Mediterranean world, and might even function as a court of appeal. When under attack for teaching heresy, the great Alexandrian theologian Origen would send letters appealing for support not only to the bishops of his own region, but to faraway Bishop Fabian at Rome, where he himself as a young man had made a pilgrimage. For the earliest Christians apostolic authority was no antiquarian curiosity, a mere fact about the origins of a particular community. The Apostles were living presences, precious guarantors of truth. The apostolic churches possessed more than a pedigree, they spoke with the voices of their founders, and provided living access to their teaching. And in Rome, uniquely, the authority of two Apostles converged. The charismatic voice of Paul, bearer of a radical authority rooted not in institution and organisation but in the uncompromising clarity of a Gospel received direct from God, joined with the authority of Peter, symbol of the Church's jurisdiction in both heaven and earth, the one to whom the commission to bind and to feed had been given by Christ himself.

Yet we should also bear in mind that all these signs of the special status of the church and Bishop of Rome were a matter of degree, not of kind. No other community could claim succession to two Apostles, but apostolic authority and the responsibilities and status it brought could be matched elsewhere. Other bishops and other churches sent gifts abroad, wrote letters of advice, rebuke or encouragement, and broke off communion with churches which were believed to have fallen into grave error. Irenaeus and Tertullian, in praising the glory of the Roman church, were praising the most notable example of a wider phenomenon. Come, urged Tertullian, 'recall the various apostolic churches . . . Achaia is very near you, where you have Corinth. If you are not far from Macedonia, you have Philippi, if you can travel into Asia, you have Ephesus. But if you are near Italy, you have Rome, whence our authority [in Africa] is derived close at hand.'[10]

Africa, in the person of its greatest theologian before Augustine, acknowledged the weight of Rome's authority. Yet even Africa might qualify and withdraw that allegiance. One of the most divisive issues in the life of the Church of the third century was the question of the treatment of those who lapsed from the faith during periods of persecution. Christianity had prospered within the empire, and by the early third century was a force to be reckoned with. In Rome, it was already a substantial property-owner, and by AD 251 the church employed forty-six elders, seven deacons, seven subdeacons, forty-two acolytes and fifty-two lesser clerics, readers and door-keepers: it had over 1,500 widows and other needy people receiving poor-relief. Its total membership in the city may have been as many as 50,000.

In an empire which was now threatened by internal breakdown and by the external pressure of the Gothic hordes, the visibility and expansion of Christianity provided an ideal scapegoat. Pope Callistus (c. 217–22) was murdered in Trastevere by a lynch-mob who were probably angered by recent Christian expansion in the crowded district. Rome celebrated a thousand years of prosperity under its ancestral gods in 247. The ills of the empire were now laid at the door of the growing numbers of those who refused to honour those gods. Riots against Christians became commonplace, and in 250 the Emperor Decius launched an official pogrom against the Church. Leading Christians were rounded up, and forced to offer sacrifice, in return for which they were given a certificate of compliance. Bishops and other leaders were specially targeted, and many of these behaved with great courage. Pope Fabian (236–50) was among the first to be arrested, and died from brutal treatment in prison. But there was also mass surrender – the Church's very success in recruiting huge numbers of the superficially committed backfired, and all over the empire Christians queued up to comply with the law. The overworked officials in charge of the sacrifices had to turn crowds away, telling them to come another day.

Christianity laid immense weight on the value of suffering for the faith. The word martyr means 'witness', and the martyr's death was the ultimate witness to the truth. By contrast, those who broke under persecution, offering the pinch of incense or the libation to the gods which the Roman state made the test of good citizenship, or those who simply surrendered the holy books or vessels of the Church – these people were considered apostates who had sacrificed their salvation. Opinion was bitterly divided about their ultimate fate and, more pressingly, about whether they could ever again be restored to membership of the Church. In Africa, the Christian community would eventually split down the middle on the issue. A hard-line party emerged in the fourth century, called Donatists after one of their leaders. They believed that any contact with lapsed clergy, including those *traditores* or traitors who without offering pagan sacrifice had nevertheless handed over books or Church goods, contaminated a church and all its members, and invalidated the sacraments which were administered in it. The Donatists formed a separatist pure Church, with their own elders and bishops.

The Roman church had its own bitter experience of persecution, and of both heroism and failure under persecution. Both experiences were manifest in its bishops. To the heroism of Pope Fabian was added that of Pope Sixtus II (257–8), arrested in 258 while presiding over worship in one of the funerary chapels in the catacombs. To avoid reprisals against his congregation he surrendered himself to the officers in charge of the raid, and was summarily beheaded with his deacons. By contrast, in the later persecution under Diocletian in 303, Pope Marcellinus (296–304?) would cave in to pressure. He surrendered copies of the scriptures and offered sacrifice to the gods. He died a year later in disgrace, and the Roman church set about forgetting him.

In Rome as in Africa, hard- and soft-line responses to the problem of the lapsed developed. In the wake of Pope Fabian's death, the church in Rome delayed electing another bishop till persecution eased. In the interim, the brilliant presbyter Novatian played a leading role in running the church, and all the indications are that he expected to become bishop in due course. Instead, the majority of the clergy and their lay supporters elected a far less able man, Cornelius (251–3). Novatian refused to accept the election, and his supporters had him consecrated by three bishops from the south Italian countryside: he set up as a rival to Cornelius. The key to this fiasco almost certainly lay in the two men's attitudes to the lapsed. Novatian was a hard-liner, believing that those who had denied the faith could never again be received into the Church, while Cornelius favoured the restoration of the repentant after they had done appropriate penance. It seems likely that the less able man was elected to implement this more realistic and humane pastoral policy.

Cornelius was a mild and unambitious man, who basked in the support of his fellow bishops – he gathered sixty of them at Rome to back his claims over those of Novatian, and collected letters of communion from those further afield. In particular, he won the approval of Cyprian of Carthage, the leading African Bishop. Cyprian had a very exalted view of the episcopal office, and emphasised the dignity of every bishop in his own church. He accepted the special standing of the see of Rome, 'the chair of Peter, the primordial [or "principal"] church, the very source of episcopal unity'. But Cyprian did not mean by this that other bishops were subordinate to the Pope. He himself, like many other bishops in the early Church, used the title 'Pope', which only came to be confined to the Bishop of Rome from the sixth century. Christ had indeed founded the Church on Peter, but all the Apostles and all bishops shared fully in the one indivisible apostolic power. There were, therefore, limits to Cyprian's deference to Rome, and that deference was to be stretched to its limits within a couple of years, with the election as pope of an aristocratic Roman, Stephen.

Stephen (254–7) was a member of the Julian family, and he was a bishop in the mould of Pope Victor, not Pope Cornelius. He was imperious, impatient, high-handed. He quickly got himself into Cyprian's bad books by rashly readmitting, not merely to communion but to office, a Spanish bishop who had been deposed for lapsing into paganism during the Decian persecution. Further provocation came when Stephen failed to take action against a Novatianist Bishop of Arles who was refusing the sacraments to the repentant lapsed even on their deathbeds. The Bishop of Lyons reported the matter to Cyprian – an interesting comment in itself on their understanding of shared episcopal responsibility for all the churches, as opposed to an exclusively papal role. Cyprian had then vainly pleaded with Stephen to excommunicate the Bishop of Arles. The request was of course also a tacit acknowledgement of Rome's superior jurisdiction. Nevertheless, the Pope evidently resented Cyprian's interference. The final breach came when Stephen intervened directly in Africa, and challenged Cyprian's practice about the rebaptism of heretics. Though Cyprian was a moderate in his willingness to receive back the repentant lapsed, he refused to recognise any sacraments administered in the hard-line breakaway churches of the Novatianists, who had established themselves in Africa. Converts baptised by Novatianist clergy were now seeking admission to Catholic communion: they were rebaptised as if they were pagans.

Behind Cyprian's practice here was a stern doctrine which denied that any grace could flow to human beings outside the visible communion of the Catholic Church. Rome took the milder view, which would eventually become the accepted teaching, that every baptism was valid provided it was duly performed in the name of the Trinity, whatever the status of the minister, and whether or not he was in heresy or schism. Stephen therefore ordered that returning schismatics should not be rebaptised, but simply admitted again to the Church by the laying on of hands.

Cyprian, however, refused to accept this ruling, and organised two synods of African bishops to condemn it. The Pope was not mentioned, but it was obvious who was the target of Cyprian's remarks in his preamble that 'none of us sets himself up as a bishop of bishops or exercises the powers of a tyrant to force his colleagues into obedience'.[11] Not surprisingly, the clergy he sent to Rome to inform the Pope of these moves were turned away unheard. Enraged by the African bishops' temerity, Stephen wrote to the churches in Asia Minor who followed Cyprian's tougher line on rebaptism of heretics, threatening to cut off communion with them, though he died before he could carry out this threat.

The incident had a broader significance. Though his letter does not survive, we know from Cyprian's comment on it that Stephen had backed up his condemnation of the African churches with an appeal to Matthew 16: 'Thou art Peter, and upon this rock I will build my Church.' During Pope Cornelius' lifetime, Cyprian had written a treatise on the *Unity of the Catholic Church*, in which he had bolstered his own authority and that of the Pope against the Novatianist schism by stressing the unique role of the See of Peter as the foundation of unity. He now rewrote the treatise, editing out these passages and denying that the Bishop of Rome had any special claim on Christ's promise to Peter. It was indeed the foundation of the See of Rome – but it was also the charter for every other bishop, all of whom shared in the power of the keys given to Peter. For Cyprian, therefore, it was folly for Stephen to 'brag so loudly about the seat of his episcopate and to insist that he holds his succession from Peter'.[12] Significantly, however, even at the height of his confrontation with Stephen, Cyprian avoided open attacks on the authority of Rome, and he suppressed the details of the Pope's maltreatment of his envoys. Rome remained a fundamental symbol of the unity of the episcopate, with whom an absolute breach was unthinkable.

The death of Stephen in 257, and the heroic martyrdom in the following year of his successor the Greek Pope Sixtus, followed six weeks later by Cyprian's own execution, defused this potentially disastrous confrontation – Sixtus, Cornelius and Cyprian would all in due course be commemorated together in the most solemn prayer of the Roman Church, the Canon of the Mass. But in many ways this was the first major crisis of the papacy, and it was charged with significance for the future. Stephen's invocation of Matthew 16 is the first known claim by a pope to an authority derived exclusively from Peter, and it is the first certain attempt by a pope to exert a power over other bishops which was qualitatively different from, and qualitatively superior to, anything they possessed. Till the reign of Stephen, the Roman church's primacy had been gladly conceded, rooted in esteem for a church blessed by the teaching and the martyrdom of the two great Apostles to the Jews and to the Gentiles, and augmented by the generosity and pastoral care for other Christian communities which had marked the Roman church in its first two centuries. With the confrontation between Stephen and Cyprian, the divisive potential of papal claims became clear.

III   THE AGE OF CONSTANTINE

The Roman empire in the third century was divided by civil war, and swept by plague and disease. It was ruled by a bewildering succession of emperors (twenty-five in forty-seven years, only one of whom died in his bed) thrown up by an army increasingly staffed by terrifying foreigners. In the ferment of oriental religions and new philosophies, old certainties were dissolving: it was for many an age of acute anxiety. For the Church, by contrast and partly in consequence, it was an age of growth and consolidation. In the melting-pot of empire, Christianity alone seemed to offer a single overarching intellectual and moral frame of reference, a simple code conveyed in vivid stories by which men and women could live. The parables of Jesus struck home where the arguments of the philosophers faltered. The Church's episcopal framework provided a remarkable network crossing the whole civilised world and a little beyond, and its charitable activities offered a life-line to the (Christian) poor in a state which no longer had the resources or the will to help them. In the Decian persecution, the resolution of the martyrs had offered an example of certainty and courage in sharp contrast to the weary routine which characterised much official pagan religion. In the freedom from persecution which descended on the Church for the last forty years of the century, Christianity became a dominating presence in many of the cities of the empire, especially in the East. The steps of the Emperor Diocletian's favourite palace at Nicomedia commanded a fine view of the Christians' new basilica in the town.

It was Diocletian, tough Dalmatian career-soldier and great reforming emperor, who launched the last great Roman persecution of the Church. Diocletian had been content to tolerate Christianity for twenty years (his wife and daughter were probably Christians) but his Caesar (military second-in command), Galerius, was a fanatical pagan, and Christianity was clearly an obstacle to Diocletian's vision of a reformed empire based on a return to traditional (that is pagan) values. In 298, pagan priests conducting the auguries at Antioch complained that the presence of Christian officials was sabotaging the ceremonies (the Christians had defended themselves from demons during the ceremony by making the sign of the cross). This was enough to trigger a confrontation which had been long brewing, and the persecution commenced. The aim at first was to oust Christians from the civil service and army, to close down and destroy churches, and to compromise the clergy. Under Galerius' influence, the persecution escalated and became a bloodbath. The toll was worst in the East and in North Africa, with most of the West relatively unscathed, but Rome was scandalised by the cowardly surrender of Pope Marcellinus, and the legacy of the persecution was to be a permanent schism in the African church over the question of communion with the lapsed. Christianity, however, was now too entrenched in the empire to be stamped out in this way. Galerius, who had succeeded Diocletian on the latter's retirement in 305, died in 311. He detested Christianity, but he was forced to issue an edict of toleration for Christians on his deathbed. And in the following year the fortunes of the Church changed irrevocably with the accession of Constantine as emperor.

Constantine had been declared emperor by the troops at York in 306 on the death of his father, Constantius, commander in-chief of the imperial armies in the West. Like his father, he had originally worshipped Sol Invictus, the Unconquered Sun, but his mother Helena was a Christian, and his sister Anastasia's name means 'Resurrection'. Constantine himself now moved towards Christianity. He achieved mastery of Rome in October 312, defeating the rival Emperor Maxentius at the Milvian Bridge outside Rome. Constantine attributed this improbable victory to divine intervention, but just which divinity he credited is a matter of debate. Years later he told the historian Eusebius that while still in Gaul he had prayed before battle to Sol Invictus for help. Next day he had seen in the sky a cross of light, and the words 'In this [sign] conquer.' For his struggle with Maxentius Constantine had banners made bearing this 'labarum', the cross being formed by the Greek monogram for Christ, the Chi Ro: the emblem was painted on the shields of his soldiers.

Constantine was not a sophisticated man, and this identification of the Unconquered Sun with Christ seems to have presented him with no problems. By 312, however, Constantine was certainly widely believed to be a Christian. When the Arch of Constantine was erected to commemorate his victory over Maxentius the inscription prudently omitted any mention of the 'Immortal Gods', vaguely attributing his triumph to the 'prompting of the Divinity'. His conversion to Christianity was probably gradual. The Chi Ro symbol would not appear on his coins until 315, and for five years after his accession Constantine continued to issue coins depicting himself as a devotee of the Unconquered Sun, or carrying images of the pagan gods.

From the moment of his accession, however, the fortunes of Christianity throughout the empire changed for ever. Whatever the state of his private conscience, Constantine had identified the Church not as the principle obstacle to unity and reform, but as its best hope. Christianity would provide imperial Rome with the common set of values and the single cult which it so badly lacked. From a persecuted sect, Christianity became the most favoured religion. A stream of edicts granted religious freedom 'to Christians and all others' (the order of the words here was crucial). Confiscated Church property was returned (without compensation to the purchasers), Christian clergy were exempted from the responsibilities of public office, and public funds were allocated for the work of the Church.

For the church in Rome, it was a bonanza beyond their wildest imaginings. The meagre early entries of the official papal chronicle, the *Liber Pontificalis*, based on scraps of half-remembered information or simply invented, suddenly explode into lavish detail in the entry for Pope Sylvester (314–35). Page after page lovingly enumerates Constantine's benefactions, above all, the great basilican churches he would build in and around the city: a cathedral, baptistry and residence for the Pope at the Lateran, raised partly in the palace of his wife Fausta and partly on the ruins of the barracks of the imperial horseguards, who, unluckily for them, had fought for Maxentius; the church of Santa Croce in Gerusalemme in the old Sessorian Palace; the great cemetery churches on the Vatican over the shrine of Peter, and at the third-century site of the joint cult of Peter and Paul, San Sebastiano. But the buildings were only the tip of the iceberg. To maintain them, massive grants of land and property were made — estates in Numidia, Egypt, in the Adriatic islands, on Gozo, farms in Tyre, Tarsus, Antioch, gardens, houses, bakeries, and baths in Rome itself. And then there was the avalanche of precious metals: for the Lateran, seven silver altars, weighing 200 pounds apiece, over a hundred silver chalices, a life-sized silver statue of Christ enthroned, surrounded by the twelve Apostles and four angels with spears and jewelled eyes, a chandelier of gold hung with fifty dolphins; in the baptistry, a golden lamb and seven silver stags from which water poured into a porphyry font.[13]

These benefactions were intended to establish the worship of Christ on a properly imperial footing. The Lateran basilica was immense, bigger than any of the secular basilicas in the Forum, capable of accommodating crowds of up to 10,000. But Constantine drew back from the symbolic imposition of Christianity in the historic heart of Rome. His two main city churches, at the Lateran and at Santa Croce, were on the fringes, near the walls, not at the centre, and, like St Peter's, they were built on imperial private property, not on public land. Rome remained pagan still, and Constantine's departure in 324 for his new capital, Constantinople, at Byzantium on the

Bosphorous and closer to the heartlands of empire in the Eastern and Danube provinces, left the city to the domination of conservative senatorial families. Their hereditary paganism was as precious to them as Protestantism would be to the Cabots and Lowells in nineteenth-century Boston, a mark of true *Romanitas* and of old money, and a witness against the vulgarity and populism of the Emperor's unpleasant new religion.

For Constantine, Christianity meant concord, unity in the truth. God had raised him up, he believed, to give peace to the whole civilised world, the *oecumene*, by the triumph of the Church. As he rapidly discovered, however, the Church itself was profoundly divided. The providential instrument of human harmony which God had placed in his hand turned out to be itself out of tune. Undaunted, he set himself to restore the unity of Christians, confident that for this, too, God had given him the empire. It was an aim and a confidence which his successors would share, and the imposition of unity on the churches at all costs became an imperial priority: ironically, it was a priority which set them on a collision course with the popes.

Constantine's first encounter with Christian division was not long in coming. In North Africa a new bishop of Carthage, Caecilian, had been consecrated in AD 311, and one of the officiating bishops was suspected of having handed over copies of the Scriptures during the great persecution. In a now familiar move, hard-line Christians announced that Caecilian's ordination was invalid because of the involvement of this *traditor*, and they set up their own bishop. Neighbouring bishops and congregations took sides, the hard-liners soon earning the name Donatists from their leading bishop, and once again the church in North Africa found itself deeply divided. Within six months of his seizure of power, Constantine had been approached by the Donatists, asking him to appoint bishops from Gaul (where there had been no *traditores*) to decide who was the true Bishop of Carthage.

This extraordinary appeal to an unbaptised emperor, whose conversion to Christianity may well not yet have been known in Africa, was highly significant. It had long been the custom for disputes in the African church to be referred to the bishops of Rome for arbitration or judgement, but this was an unattractive option for the Donatists, since Roman theology denied that the involvement of a 'traitor' bishop could invalidate a sacrament. Whether Constantine appreciated the politics of the appeal to himself, rather than to Pope Miltiades (311–14), is doubtful, but he wrote to the Pope, commanding him to establish an inquiry in collaboration with three bishops from Gaul, and to report back to him. It was the first direct intervention by an emperor in the affairs of the Church.

Caecilian and Donatus both came to Rome for the hearing, but in the meantime Miltiades had taken steps to transform the commission of inquiry into a more conventional synod, by summoning fifteen Italian bishops to sit with him and the Gallic bishops. Predictably, the synod excommunicated Donatus and declared Caecilian the true Bishop of Carthage in October 313. Miltiades set about coaxing Donatist bishops back into mainstream or 'Catholic' communion by promising that they would be allowed to retain episcopal status. Doggedly, the Donatists appealed once more to Constantine, and once more he responded with scant respect for papal sensibilities. He summoned a council of many bishops to Arles, appointing the bishops of Syracuse and Arles to oversee its proceedings. Miltiades had by now died and the new Pope, Sylvester I (314–35), did not travel to Arles. Nevertheless, with a better sense of the Pope's prerogative than the Emperor, the synod duly reported their proceedings in a deferential letter to Sylvester, lamenting that he had been unable to leave the city 'where the Apostles to this day have their seats and where their blood without ceasing witnesses to the glory of God'. They asked the Pope to circulate their decisions to other bishops, a clear recognition of his seniority.

Constantine's dismay at the divisions of Christian North Africa was to be redoubled when, having overthrown the pagan rival Emperor in the East, Licinius, he moved to his new Christian capital, 'New Rome', Constantinople. For the divisions of Africa were as nothing compared to the deep rift in the Christian imagination which had opened in the East. It was begun in Egypt, by a presbyter of Alexandria, Arius, famed for his personal austerities and his following among the nuns of the city. Arius had been deposed by his Bishop for teaching that the Logos, the Word of God which had been made flesh in Jesus, was not God himself, but a creature, infinitely higher than the angels, though like them created out of nothing before the world began. Arius saw his teaching as a means of reconciling the Christian doctrine of the Incarnation with the equally fundamental belief in the unity of God. In fact, it emptied Christianity of its central affirmation, that the life and death of Jesus had power to redeem because they were God's very own actions. But the full implications of Arianism were not at first grasped, and Arius attracted widespread support. A master-publicist, Arius rallied grass-roots support by composing theological sea-shanties to be sung by the sailors and stevedores on the docks of Alexandria. Theological debate erupted out of the lecture-halls and into the taverns and bars of the eastern Mediterranean.

The theological issues were mostly lost on Constantine, though many of the clergy he surrounded himself with were supporters of Arius, including the fluffy-minded Bishop Eusebius of Caesarea, historian of the Church and Constantine's chosen official biographer. It was obvious, nonetheless, that something had to be done to settle a dispute that threatened to wreck Constantine's vision of Christianity as the cement of empire. In 325 he summoned a council of bishops to meet at Nicaea to resolve the issue. Only a handful of Westerners attended, including the bishops of Carthage and Milan. Pope Sylvester sent two priests to represent him.

The Council of Nicaea, summoned by the Emperor, who presided over some of the sessions, was an event of enormous significance for the Christian Church. In due course, 'ecumenical' or general councils, of which this was the first, would come to be recognised as having binding authority in matters of faith. The Council was an unqualified disaster for the Arian party. Arius and his followers were condemned, and the Council issued a Creed containing the statement that Christ was 'of the same essence' (homoousios) with the Father, a resounding affirmation of his true divinity.

Nicaea was the beginning, not the end, of the Arian controversy. The defeated Arians had been frogmarched into agreement by an emperor determined to sew things up quickly. They were silenced, not persuaded, and after the Council was over, they regrouped and returned to the attack. Modified forms of Arius' teaching would win support throughout the Eastern empire for the next three generations, and Constantine's son and successor in the East, Constantius, himself adopted Arian beliefs. Constantine remained firmly committed to the Nicene faith – it was, after all, *his* Council. But he longed for a settlement of the disputes, and never abandoned hope that some form of words could be found which would paper over the differences between the two sides. Constantine himself was finally baptised on his deathbed in 337 by his Arian chaplain, Eusebius of Nicomedia. His body lay in state in the white robe of the newly baptised, and all around him his Empire began to fall to pieces.

The chief defender of the orthodox faith at Nicaea had been the deacon, Athanasius, from 328 Bishop of Alexandria. Athanasius was the greatest theologian of his age and a man of epic stamina and courage, but he was undiplomatic to the point of truculence, and as bishop he was not above strong-arm methods of enforcing discipline. In 335 his enemies, who were many, took the opportunity of the forthcoming anniversary celebrations of Constantine's thirty years as emperor to call for the renewed pacification of the Church. They persuaded Constantine that Athanasius had threatened to cut off Egyptian corn supplies to Constantinople if the Emperor interfered with him, and they succeeded in having Athanasius deposed, excommunicated and exiled to Gaul. One by one, his supporters were then picked off.

These struggles convulsed the Christian East: the fierce monks of the Egyptian deserts, led by St Anthony of Egypt, rallied to Athanasius and the Nicene faith. But for a generation all this was heard in the West only as a faint echo. Western theologians did not trouble themselves with Greek subtleties, and Latin, which had replaced Greek as the language of the Roman church relatively late in the third century, did not yet even possess adequate technical terminology to handle the debate properly. The Pope had played no part at Nicaea, though as a matter of honour his legates signed the Conciliar decrees before all the bishops, immediately after the signature of Hosius of Cordoba, president of the Council. But successive bishops of Rome endorsed the teaching of Nicaea, and saw support for Athanasius as support for the apostolic faith. As a stream of Athanasius' supporters made their way as refugees into the West, they were received with open arms at Rome, sometimes without much scrutiny of their theological views. In AD 339 Pope Julius (337–52) publicly received Athanasius himself into communion, and summoned his Arian enemies, gathered at Antioch, to come to Rome for a council to resolve the issue. He received a stinging reply, delayed till the date he had set for the meeting in Rome had passed, challenging his right to receive into communion a man condemned by a synod of Eastern bishops. Rome, they conceded, was a famous church, well known for its orthodoxy. Nevertheless, all bishops were equal, and the basis of Rome's spiritual authority, the Apostles Peter and Paul, had come there in the first place from the East. The Pope must choose the communion of a handful of heretics like Athanasius, or the majority of the bishops of the East.

This was a direct challenge to the Pope's authority. The gap between Eastern and Western perceptions of the place of Rome in the wider Church was clearly growing. Just how wide that gap might become was revealed three years later in 343, at the disastrous Council of Sardica. There had been a bloodbath in the imperial family as rivals scrabbled for power on the death of Constantine, and the empire was now ruled by his two surviving sons. Constantius, in the East, was a declared Arian. Constans, who ruled the West from Milan, was an ardent Catholic, and a strong supporter of Athanasius and Pope Julius. Worried by the theological rift which threatened the fragile unity and stability of empire, the brothers agreed that a joint council of East and West should be held at Sardica (modern Sofia in Bulgaria). Eighty bishops from each side attended, and the assembly was to be chaired by the leader of the Western delegation, Hosius of Cordoba, veteran president of the Council of Nicaea.

Sardica was a fiasco, which widened the rift it had been called to heal. For a start, Athanasius and his friends were allowed to sit as equals among the Western bishops, despite the fact that the Arians now wanted their case reviewed by the Council. The enraged Easterners refused to enter the assembly, and set up their own rival council, which excommunicated Hosius, Athanasius and the Pope. In retaliation the Westerners restored Athanasius, excommunicated his leading opponents, passed a series of canons defining Rome's right to act as a court of final appeals in all matters affecting other bishops throughout the empire, and sent a dutiful letter to Julius as their 'head, that is to the See of Peter the Apostle'.[14] The Canons of Sardica became fundamental to Roman claims to primacy. They were inscribed in the records of the Roman church in a place of honour immediately after those of Nicaea, and in the course of time they were mistakenly believed to have been enacted at Nicaea. The claim of Rome to be head of all the churches was thus thought to have the strong backing of the first and greatest of all the general councils.

Over the next few years, the unwavering support of Constans bolstered the Catholic party, and Constantius was even pressured into restoring Athanasius (briefly) to his see. But Constans was killed in 350, and Constantius became master of the whole empire. It was a disaster for the Nicene faith, and for the papacy. Like his father, Constantius saw Christianity as an essential unifying force within the empire. The debates about the person of Christ had to be solved, and he set about solving them by suppressing all support for Athanasius and the creed of Nicaea. Pope Julius died in 352. He had handled the Arian troubles with a firm and steady courage, but also with tact and courtesy to his opponents. His successor, Liberius (352–66), a cleric with an enthusiastic following among the pious matrons of Rome, was equally committed to the Nicene cause, but was a man of less steadiness and skill. Lobbied by Eastern bishops to repudiate Athanasius, Liberius unwisely appealed to Constantius to summon a general council to reaffirm the faith of Nicaea. Instead, at two synods, held at Arles in 353 and Milan in 355, Constantius arm-twisted the assembled bishops into condemning Athanasius. The handful who refused were exiled from their sees.

Liberius was appalled, and repudiated his own legates, who had caved in to pressure and subscribed to the condemnation of Athanasius. The influential court eunuch Eusebius (not to be confused with Eusebius of Caesarea) was sent to Rome to put pressure on the Pope. Liberius turned him away and, when he discovered that he had left an offering from the Emperor at the shrine of St Peter, he had the gift cast out. To the Emperor he wrote that his opposition was not to uphold his own views, but the 'decrees of the Apostles: ... I have suffered nothing to be added to the bishopric of the city of Rome and nothing to be detracted from it, and I desire always to preserve and guard unstained that faith which has come down through so long a succession of bishops, among whom have been many martyrs'.[15] The enraged Emperor had the Pope arrested and taken north to Milan, where he confronted him. Arian clergy round the Emperor suggested that Liberius' resistance was nothing more than a hint of old Roman republicanism, designed to curry favour with the Senate. The Emperor rebuked the Pope for standing alone in support of Athanasius, when most of the bishops had condemned him. Liberius reminded the Emperor that in the Old Testament Shadrach, Mesach and Abednego had stood alone against the idolatrous tyrant Nebuchadnezzar, and scandalised courtiers accused the Pope of treason – 'You have called our Emperor a Nebuchadnezzar.' The Pope remained firm, and was exiled to Thrace. In a final act of defiance, he sent back the 500 gold pieces the Emperor had allocated for his journey expenses, suggesting, with a nod in the direction of Judas, that they should be given to the Arian Bishop of Milan.[16]

Liberius' courageous conduct in the face of imperial pressure prefigured the struggles between papacy and empire which would dominate the history of medieval Europe. But his resolve did not last. Constantius detested Liberius, but knew he could not long retain control of the Church without the support of the Pope: the pressure was kept up. In the misery of exile, surrounded by imperial clergy and far from home, Liberius weakened. He agreed to the excommunication of Athanasius, and signed a formula which, while it did not actually repudiate the Nicene Creed, weakened it with the meaningless claim that the *Logos* was '*like* the father in being' and in all things. In 358 he was finally allowed to return to Rome.

He found the city deeply divided. On Liberius' exile in 355, the Emperor had installed a new pope, Liberius' former archdeacon Felix. Consecrated by Arian bishops in the imperial palace in Milan, Felix was an obvious fellow traveller, but imperial patronage was a powerful persuader, and many of the Roman clergy had rallied to him. Constantius was now unwilling simply to repudiate Felix, and commanded that Liberius and he should function as joint bishops. The populace of Rome would have none of it. There was tumult in the streets in support of Liberius, the crowds yelling 'One God, one Christ, one bishop', and Felix was forced to withdraw. He built himself a church in the suburbs, and lived there in semi-retirement, retaining a following among the city clergy and people. Liberius' credibility had been badly damaged by his ignominious surrender in exile, but painfully he rehabilitated himself, helping to organise peace-moves among the moderates on both sides of the Arian debate while insisting on loyalty to the Nicene formulas. Athanasius, if he did not quite forgive him, attributed his fall to understandable frailty in the face of pressure.

Liberius' successor Damasus (366–84), who had served as deacon under both Liberius and Felix, would inherit some of the consequences of his predecessor's exile. His election in 366 was contested, and he was confronted by a rival pope, Ursinus, whom he only got rid of with the help of the city police and a murderous rabble. Damasus was a firm opponent of Arianism and, with the support of a new and orthodox emperor, would resolutely stamp out heresy within the city. But the street battles and massacres of Ursinus' supporters with which his pontificate had begun left him vulnerable to moral attack, and very much dependent on the goodwill and support of the city and imperial authorities.

Damasus was also wary of taking sides in the quarrels which were still tearing apart the Church in the East. Hard-pressed supporters of Nicaea in the East like Basil the Great repeatedly begged his support. Damasus stalled, and sent a series of lofty letters eastwards, addressing his fellow bishops there not as 'brothers', the traditional formula, but as 'sons', a claim to superiority which was noticed and resented. With no intention of embroiling himself in the nightmare complexities of the Eastern theological debates, he thought the right procedure was for the bishops of the East to establish their orthodoxy by signing Roman formulas. His position was enormously strengthened by the accession as emperor of the Spanish General Theodosius, a devout Catholic who detested Arianism and who in February 380 issued an edict requiring all the subjects of the empire to follow the Christian religion 'which Holy Peter delivered to the Romans . . . and as the Pontiff Damasus manifestly observes it'. In the following year Theodosius summoned a general council at Constantinople – the first since Nicaea – and this Council, at which no Western bishops were present and to which Damasus did not even send delegates, succeeded in formulating a creed, incorporating the Nicene Creed, which provided a satisfactory solution to the Arian debates. This Constantinopolitan/Nicene Creed is still recited every Sunday at Catholic and Anglican eucharists.

But, in addition to its doctrinal work, the Council of Constantinople issued a series of disciplinary canons, which went straight to the heart of Roman claims to primacy over the whole Church. The Council decreed that appeals in the cases of bishops should be heard within the bishop's own province – a direct rebuttal of Rome's claim to be the final court of appeal in all such cases. It went on to stipulate that 'the Bishop of Constantinople shall have the pre-eminence in honour after the Bishop of Rome, for Constantinople is new Rome'.[17]

This last canon was totally unacceptable to Rome for two reasons. In the first place it capitulated to the imperial claim to control of the Church, since Constantinople had nothing but the secular status of the city to justify giving it this religious precedence. Worse, however, the wording implied that the primacy of Rome itself was derived not from its apostolic pedigree as the Church of Peter and Paul, but from the fact that it had once been the capital of empire. Damasus and his successors refused to accept the canons, and the following year a council of Western bishops at Rome issued a rejoinder, declaring that the Roman see had the primacy over all others because of the Lord's promise to Peter – 'Tu es Petrus' – and because both Peter and Paul had founded the see. The bishops went on to specify that if Rome was the first See of Peter, then the second was not Constantinople, but Alexandria, because it had been founded from Rome by St Mark on the orders of Peter, and the third in precedence was Antioch, because Peter had once been bishop there before he came to Rome.

Damasus's pontificate exposed the growing rift between Eastern and Western perceptions of the religious importance of Rome. The troubles of Liberius had made it clear that imperial oversight of the Church, and the overwhelming imperial priority of unification, might put Pope and Emperor at odds. But Rome itself was increasingly remote from the centre of imperial affairs. No emperor since Constantine had lived in Rome, and even the Western emperors based themselves in the north – at Trier, Arles and especially Milan. Milan had been the centre of Constantius' attempts to impose Arianism on the West, and an Arian bishop, Auxentius, remained in office till his death in 374.

Auxentius was succeeded as bishop by an impeccably orthodox career civil servant, the unbaptised Governor of the city, Ambrose, and it was Ambrose, not Damasus or his successor Siricius (384–99), who would become the dominant figure in the life of the Western Church in the last quarter of the fourth century. Ambrose set himself to increase the influence of the see of Milan, taking on the metropolitan role over the north Italian bishoprics formerly exercised by Rome, involving himself in episcopal appointments as far away as the Balkans, attracting clergy and religious to the city from Piacenza, Bologna, even North Africa. He presided over the creation of a series of great churches which would establish Milan as a Christian capital, in a way which Rome itself, still dominated by paganism, could not hope to do. The Basilica Nova at Milan, now buried under the present Duomo, was a gigantic church, almost as big as the Pope's cathedral church of St John Lateran, and unique outside Rome. Inheriting a bishopric in which Arianism was deeply entrenched, Ambrose set himself at the head of a movement to restore Nicene orthodoxy, mobilising the bishops of the West behind the Catholic cause. Above all, in a series of confrontations with the imperial family he marked out the boundaries of secular and ecclesiastical power, refusing to surrender any of the city churches for the use of Arian troops in the imperial army, denying the right of the imperial courts to judge in ecclesiastical cases, preventing Church funds being used to rebuild a synagogue destroyed in a religious riot, and finally excommunicating the Emperor Theodosius for having ordered the punitive massacre of civilians at Thessalonica after the murder of an imperial official. Ambrose was the real leader of the Western Church, and his biographer Paulinus significantly remarked of him that he had 'a concern for all the churches', a Pauline text often invoked by the popes.

The career of Ambrose is a salutary reminder of the limits of the papal primacy in the age of the great councils. But Ambrose's dominant position in Italy was built on a high doctrine of the papacy, not on an attempt to erode it. He had been brought up as a child in Pope Liberius' Rome. A sister had taken the veil as a nun from Liberius' hand in St Peter's, and the Pope was a familiar visitor to the house. Ambrose had been fascinated as the women of the family clustered around Liberius, kissing his hand, and the boy had amused and infuriated his relatives by imitating the Pope's stately walk and offering his own hand to be kissed by the womenfolk. It was from Liberius' career that he had his first lessons in resistance to imperial diktat, and there was nothing anti-papal about Ambrose's campaign to increase the influence of Milan. Indeed, the high prerogatives of the papacy were vital to Ambrose, for he frequently justified his activities as being carried out on behalf of the Pope. In 381 he masterminded the Council of Aquilea, which had despatched a letter to the Emperor in support of Damasus against the antipope Ursinus, in which Rome was described as 'the head of the whole Roman world'. From Rome flowed 'the sacred faith of the Apostles . . . and all the rights of venerable communion'.[18] Not surprisingly, Ambrose's Arian enemies saw him as Damasus' toady, obsequiously buttering up the Pope to increase his own influence. For his part, Ambrose promoted the cult of Peter and Paul in Milan as a pledge of shared religious loyalty to the Apostles, and Damasus encouraged him by sending him relics of the Apostles – the silver casket in which they came to Milan from Rome survives in the church of San Nazaro. Ecclesiastically, Ambrose's northern Italy was as yet a raw frontier. Its handful of bishoprics were scattered over vast, largely pagan areas, and nothing bound them together, or to Milan, except their common allegiance to Rome and Rome's Apostles. Ambrose's dominance in the region reminds us of the limitations of the papacy's leadership in the West, but it also reminds us of the powerful symbolic and practical need for that leadership. If the fourth-century papacy had not existed, it would have had to be invented.

IV THE BIRTH OF PAPAL ROME

The conversion of Constantine had propelled the bishops of Rome into the heart of the Roman establishment. Already powerful and influential men, they now became grandees on a par with the wealthiest senators in the city. Bishops all over the Roman world would now be expected to take on the role of judges, governors, great servants of state. Even in provincial Africa Augustine would complain bitterly of the devouring secular responsibilities of the bishop. In the case of the Bishop of Rome, those functions were complicated by his leadership of the Church in a pagan capital which was the symbolic centre of the world, the focus of the Roman people's sense of identity. Constantine washed his hands of Rome in 324, and departed to create a Christian capital in the East. It would fall to the popes to create a Christian Rome.

They set about it by building churches, converting the modest *tituli* (community church centres) into something grander, and creating new and more public foundations, though to begin with nothing that rivalled the great imperial basilicas at the Lateran and St Peter's. Over the next hundred years their churches advanced into the city – Pope Mark's (336) San Marco within a stone's throw of the Capitol, Pope Liberius' massive basilica on the Esquiline (now Santa Maria Maggiore), Pope Damasus' Santa Anastasia at the foot of the Palatine, Pope Julius' foundation on the site of the present Santa Maria in Trastevere, Santa Pudenziana near the Baths of Diocletian under Pope Anastasius (399–401), Santa Sabina among the patrician villas on the Aventine under Pope Celestine (422–32).

These churches were a mark of the upbeat confidence of post-Constantinian Christianity in Rome. The popes were potentates, and began to behave like it. Damasus perfectly embodied this growing grandeur. An urbane career cleric like his predecessor Liberius, at home in the wealthy salons of the city, he was also a ruthless power-broker, and he did not hesitate to mobilise both the city police and the Christian mob to back up his rule. His election had been contested, and he had prevailed by sheer force of numbers – as the *Liber Pontificalis* put it, 'they confirmed Damasus because he was the stronger and had the greater number of supporters; that was how Damasus was confirmed'.[19] Damasus' grass-roots supporters included squads of the notoriously hard-boiled Roman *fossores*, catacomb diggers, and they massacred 137 followers of the rival Pope Ursinus in street-fighting that ended in a bloody siege of what is now the church of Santa Maria Maggiore.

Damasus and Ursinus were competing for high stakes: as the pagan historian Ammianus Marcellinus commented sardonically,

> I do not deny that men who covet this office in order to fulfil their ambitions may well struggle for it with every resource at their disposal. For once they have obtained it they are ever after secure, enriched with offerings from the ladies, riding abroad seated in their carriages, splendidly arrayed, giving banquets so lavish that they surpass the tables of royalty...[20]

Ammianus' gibe about gifts from rich women was no random shot. An imperial decree in 370 forbade clerics from visiting the houses of rich widows or heiresses, and Damasus himself was nick-named *matronarum auriscalpius*, 'the ladies' ear-tickler'. But the new worldliness of the Roman church and its bishops was not the sole invention of its clergy. Since the mid third century there had been a growing assimilation of Christian and secular culture. It is already in evidence long before Constantine in the art of the Christian burial-sites round the city, the Catacombs. With the imperial adoption of Christianity, this process accelerated. In Damasus' Rome, wealthy Christians gave each other gifts in which Christian symbols went alongside images of Venus, nereids and sea-monsters, and representations of pagan-style wedding-processions.

This Romanisation of the Church was not all a matter of worldliness, however. The bishops of the imperial capital had to confront the Roman character of their city and their see. They set about finding a religious dimension to that *Romanitas* which would have profound implications for the nature of the papacy. Pope Damasus in particular took this task to heart. He set himself to interpret Rome's past in the light not of paganism, but of Christianity. He would Latinise the Church, and Christianise Latin. He appointed as his secretary the greatest Latin scholar of the day, the Dalmatian presbyter Jerome, and commissioned him to turn the crude dog-Latin of the Bible versions used in church into something more urbane and polished. Jerome's work was never completed, but the Vulgate Bible, as it came to be called, rendered the scriptures of ancient Israel and the early Church into an idiom which Romans could recognise as their own. The covenant legislation of the ancient tribes was now cast in the language of the Roman law-courts, and Jerome's version of the promises to Peter used familiar Roman legal words for binding and loosing – *ligare* and *solvere* – which underlined the legal character of the Pope's unique claims.

For Damasus, the glory of the saints had to be naturalised as Roman. Many of Rome's martyrs had come from elsewhere, but their deaths in the city had made them honorary citizens. He collected and reburied the bodies of the great saints, composing verse inscriptions for the new tombs which were carved in a specially devised lettering based on classical models. His inscription for the joint shrine of Peter and Paul at San Sebastiano is typical, and it directly tackled the claim made by the Eastern bishops in Pope Julius' time, that Peter and Paul belonged to the Christian East just as much as to Rome: 'Whoever you may be that seek the names of Peter and Paul, should know that here the saints once dwelt. The East sent the disciples – that we readily admit. But on account of the merit of their blood . . . Rome has gained the superior right to claim them as citizens. Damasus would thus tell your praises, you new stars.'[21] The pagan love of Roma Aeterna, the Eternal City, took on a new and specifically Christian meaning, which attached itself to the papacy, and its inheritance from Peter and Paul. This was not achieved without struggle, most famously the confrontation with the pagan senators led by Symmachus in 384 to preserve the pagan Altar of Victory in the Senate. Damasus mobilised Ambrose to lobby on his behalf in Milan, and the altar was abolished, leaving the statue of the Goddess to be reinterpreted by later ages as an angel. Prudentius, the great Latin hymn-writer, though well aware of the persistence of paganism among the conservative senatorial families, celebrated Rome as the capital of a world united in the Christian faith: 'Grant then, Christ, to your Romans a Christian city, a capital Christian like the rest of the world. Peter and Paul shall drive out Jupiter.' In the visual equivalent of Prudentius' prayer, the Apostles appear in the togas of Roman senators in the apse-mosaic of the church of Santa Pudenziana, built at the end of the fourth century.[22]

The Romanisation of the papacy was more than a matter of external decoration. Self-consciously, the popes began to model their actions and their style as Christian leaders on the procedures of the Roman state. In the last months of Damasus' life the Bishop of Tarragona in Spain wrote to the Pope with a series of queries about the ordering of the day-to-day life of the Church. Damasus died before the letter could be answered, and it was one of the first items across the desk of his successor, Pope Siricius (384–99). The Pope replied in the form of a decretal, modelled directly on an imperial rescript, and, like the rescripts, providing authoritative rulings which were designed to establish legal precedents on the issues concerned. Siricius commended the Bishop for consulting Rome 'as to the head of your body', and instructed him to pass on the 'salutary ordinances we have made' to the bishops of all the surrounding provinces, for no 'priest of the Lord is free to be ignorant of the statutes of the Apostolic See'.[23]

Siricius quite clearly had no sense that he was inventing anything, as his references to the 'general decrees' of his predecessors show: it may be that this form of reply to enquiries had already become routine. Yet his letter is a symptom of the adoption by the popes of an idiom and a cast of mind which would help to shape the whole mental world of Western Christendom. The apostolic stability of Rome, its testimony to ancient truth, would now be imagined not simply as the handing on of the ancient *paradosis*, the tradition, but specifically in the form of lawgiving. Law became a major preoccupation of the Roman church, and the Pope was seen as the Church's supreme lawgiver. As Pope Innocent I (401–17) wrote to the bishops of Africa, 'it has been decreed by a divine, not a human authority, that whatever action is taken in any of the provinces, however distant or remote, it should not be brought to a conclusion before it comes to the knowledge of this see, so that every decision may be affirmed by our authority'.[24]

This serene confidence in the Roman see was maintained in part by the immersion of the Roman clergy in a distinctive mental world. Round the papal household there developed a whole clerical culture, staffed by men drawn often from the Roman aristocracy, intensely self-conscious and intensely proud of their own tradition – Jerome dubbed them 'the senate'. Damasus himself was a product of this world, the son of a senior Roman priest who had himself founded a *titulus* church. Pope Boniface was the son of a Roman priest, Innocent I was the son of his predecessor as pope, Anastasius I (399–401), and had served his father as deacon. Indeed it was routine for the Pope to be elected by the senior clergy from among the seven deacons . The deacons dressed like the Pope himself in the distinctive wide-sleeved dalmatic with its two purple stripes, and they formed the heart of the papal administration – Boniface I (418–22) Leo I (440–61), and Felix III (483–92) were all succeeded by their archdeacons. In this clerical world, memories were long, and records were carefully kept. The tradition of Rome was thought of as part of the law of God, and preserved accordingly. 'The rules rule us,' declared Celestine I (422–32), 'we do not stand over the rules: let us be subject to the canons'.[25]

These claims went largely unchallenged in the West, and even in strife-torn Africa, though interventions there by the inexperienced and clumsy Greek Pope Zosimus (417–18) caused a good deal of resentment. By and large, Innocent I's conviction that the faith had been sent from the Apostles at Rome to the rest of Italy, Gaul, Spain, Africa and Sicily was accepted, and Rome's theoretical and practical primacy acknowledged in consequence. In practice, however, that primacy was experienced, and understood, quite differently in different regions of the West. In most of peninsular Italy, the Pope was in effect the sole Archbishop, and his power was wide-ranging and very direct. The popes called and presided at synods, ordained the bishops, intervened to regulate discipline and enforce the canons. Outside Italy, this metropolitan authority obtained directly only in those parts of the West where the popes had succeeded in establishing and maintaining vicariates, a succession of local episcopal representatives through whom they exercised supervision – at Arles in Gaul in the fourth century, revived in the sixth century under Pope Symmachus (498–514), in Illyria (the Balkan region) from the late fourth century, and briefly for Spain at Seville under Pope Simplicius (468–83). These apostolic vicars were thought of as sharing the papal 'care for all the churches', and the popes permitted them to wear the distinctive papal white woollen stole or 'pallium' as a sign of their co-operation in the papal ministry.

Elsewhere, the Pope's authority was that of the Patriarch of the West, on a par with that of the patriarchs of Alexandria, Antioch and, eventually, Constantinople and Jerusalem, over their regions. The

Pope's patriarchal authority was uniquely enhanced by the added prestige of Peter's authority. That prestige, however, was a matter of moral authority rather than of administrative power. It was occasional rather than constant, for the regional churches governed themselves, elected their own bishops without reference to Rome, held their own synods, ordered their own life and worship. Rome was important not as a daily presence, but as a fundamental resource, the only apostolic see in the West, above all functioning as a court of appeal in special circumstances. This last function was to be crucial in the emergence of papal theory: the 'case-law' built up in the course of such appeals was formalised in the decretals or letters containing the decisions of successive popes. In due course the decretals would be collected, and would play a key role in shaping Western thought about the Church, and the central place of the papacy in it.

For the churches of Gaul, Africa and Spain, therefore, the characteristic expression of papal primacy was not a matter of executive rule from Rome, which they would certainly have rejected. Instead, the Petrine ministry was experienced in the form of occasional interventions, almost always in response to local requests, designed to give the added solemnity of apostolic authority to the decisions and actions of the local churches. During the controversy over the teachings of Pelagius on free will and grace, for example, St Augustine and his fellow African bishops sent an account of the synodal decisions to Pope Innocent I. In pouring 'our little trickle back into your ample fountain', Augustine wrote, 'we wish to be reassured by you that this trickle of ours, however scant, flows from the same fountain-head as your abundant stream, and we desire the consolation of your writings, drawn from our common share of the one grace'.[26] The African bishops, it should be noticed, had asked not for guidance, but for a clinching final endorsement of their own decisions, a recognition that the doctrinal question had in fact been settled – that, in Augustine's words, *causa finita est* ('the debate is over'). Revealingly, however, Pope Innocent treated their letter as a request not for a seal of approval, but for an authoritative decision. Where the strongly collegial language of the African bishops spoke of the stream of their authority and that of Rome issuing from the same source, Innocent spoke of *all* streams as issuing from Rome. It was a difference of emphasis full of significance for the future claims of the papacy.

In the East it was yet another matter. There the papal primacy of honour derived from the succession to Peter, was indeed acknowledged, but the practical consequences the popes deduced from it were ignored or denied outright. Rome was seen as the senior patriarchate, one of five, the Pentarchy, whose harmony and agreement was the fundamental apostolic underpinning of the Church's authority. In Eastern thought, for example, the recognition of a council by the Pentarchy came to be seen as the decisive mark of a 'general' council, whereas, in the West, recognition by the Pope alone was the crucial criterion. Above all, the claim of Constantinople to be 'New Rome' was a constant threat to papal primacy, which the popes actively tried to counteract. From the 380s onwards the popes established a vicariate at Thessalonica, giving the Bishop extensive delegated powers in the appointment of new bishops and related matters, to prevent traditional papal influence in the Balkans passing to Constantinople. This vicariate was threatened in 421 when the Eastern Emperor transferred ecclesiastical jurisdiction in the area, now an official part of the Eastern empire, to the Patriarch. Pope Boniface fought a successful rearguard action to preserve his rights there, asserting papal oversight of all the churches, even in the East.

All these developments came together in the most remarkable Pope of the early church, Leo the Great (440–61), elected after acting as an extremely influential deacon under Celestine and Sixtus III (432–40). Leo, though not a Roman by birth, took on himself the mantle of *Romanitas* which had become the distinctive mark of the popes of late antiquity. He kept the anniversary of his consecration, 29 September, as his 'birthday', and in a series of sermons preached then and on the feasts of Peter and Paul he hammered home the identity of the papacy with Peter. Leo's sense of this identity was almost mystical. Peter was eternally present in Peter's see, and Leo, though an 'unworthy heir', was the inheritor of all Peter's prerogatives. Indeed, Peter himself spoke and acted in all that Leo did – 'And so if anything is rightly done and rightly decreed by us, if anything is won from the mercy of God by our daily supplications, it is of his work and merit whose power lives and whose authority prevails in his See.' To be under the authority of Peter was simply to be under the authority of Christ, and to repudiate the authority of Peter was to put oneself outside the mystery of the Church.[27] For Leo, the coming of Peter to the centre of empire had been a providential act, designed so that from Rome the Gospel might spread to all the world. Christian Rome, refounded on Peter and Paul as ancient Rome had been founded on Romulus and Remus, was the heart of the Church.

Leo acted on these convictions, harnessing his immense talents to strengthening papal authority throughout the West. His surviving correspondence reveals the sheer range of his activities – long letters of admonition to the bishops of Africa, Gaul and Italy, combating heresy, rebuking deviation from Roman customs, prescribing remedies for schism, disorder and irregularities in clerical appointment and conduct. He strengthened papal control over Milan and the north Italian bishoprics. When Hilary of Arles stepped out of line by assuming patriarchal powers over the bishops of Gaul, he confined him to his own diocese, and mobilised the Emperor of the West into a formal recognition of papal jurisdiction over all the Western churches. Leo was intensely conscious of his own responsibility for ensuring the teaching of the orthodox faith. He took vigorous measures against the Manichees in Rome, using the police against them as well as ecclesiastical censures, and he organised the bishops of Spain against the Priscillianist heresy there.

Leo had not a word of Greek, but he had made many Eastern contacts while still a deacon. As pope he worked to extend papal influence in the East, though he was conscious of the need to tread carefully. He savagely rebuked Anastasius, the Bishop of Thessalonica, his vicar in Illyricum, for overstepping his powers, invading the rights of the local metropolitans (archbishops with jurisdiction over the other bishops of a province), and generally offending the local bishops. Anastasius was merely a representative, he insisted, and did not have the *plenitudo potestatis*, the fullness of power, which was Peter's, and Leo's.

Leo's extensive use of the language of intervention and of authority, however, was not a matter of domination, nor of the simple exertion of power. His writings are also characterised by a language of service, and in them the Petrine ministry is seen as a vocation to vigilance on behalf of the whole Church, a commission to ensure that all is according to the traditions of the Apostles and the canons of the Church. 'If we do not watch with the vigilance which is incumbent upon us,' he declared, 'we could not excuse ourselves to Him who willed that we should be the sentinel.' The prerogatives of Rome are gifts for the building up of the whole Christian community: 'The Lord shows a special care for Peter and prays in particular for the faith of Peter, as if the future situation would be more secure for oth-

ers if the spirit of the leader remains unconquered. Thus in Peter the
courage of all is fortified and the aid of divine grace is so arranged
that the strength which comes to Peter through Christ, through
Peter is transmitted to the Apostles'.[28]

It was heresy in the East which provided the opportunity for the
greatest single exercise of papal ministry as Leo understood it. In 431
a general council at Ephesus had affirmed the divinity of Christ by
declaring that Mary his mother was not merely the mother of Jesus,
but 'the God bearer', 'Mother of God'. In the wake of Ephesus, dispute had arisen about the precise nature of the union of the divine
and human in Christ. Was Jesus' human nature absorbed into his
divine nature? Were there two natures in him after the incarnation,
human and divine – in which case was Christ really divine – or just
one – in which case was he really human? The disputes became as
fraught as the Arian problem had ever been, and combatants on both
sides looked to Rome for support. One of them, Eutyches, taught
that there was only one nature in Christ after the Incarnation, and
that as a result his humanity was fundamentally different from ours.
When this man appealed to Leo, the Pope was horrified. He composed a treatise on the Incarnation, refuting Eutyches and teaching
that in Christ there are two natures, human and divine, unmixed and
unconfused, yet permanently and really united in a single person, so
that it is possible to attribute to the humanity of Jesus all the actions
and attributes of his divinity, and vice versa.

This 'Tome', which took the form of a letter to Flavian, Bishop of
Constantinople, was not particularly original, but it was clear, precise
and strikingly phrased, and it became the basis for the settlement of
the question at the General Council of Chalcedon in 451, at which
Leo's legates presided. The Council Fathers greeted the reading of
Leo's document with enthusiasm, declaring that 'Peter had spoken
through Leo.' This was no more than Leo's belief about *all* papal
utterances, and he took the view that the Council adopted his teaching because it was the teaching of the Pope. Since the time of Damasus, Roman theologians had considered that it was papal endorsement which gave general councils their special authority and marked
them off from other assemblies of bishops. The bishops at Chalcedon, however, made no such assumption. They acknowledged the
special dignity and honour of the apostolic see, but they did not
therefore assume that whatever its bishop said must be true, and

seemed to have believed that *on this particular occasion* Peter had spoken through Leo. They had adopted his solution to the problem, therefore, not merely because it was his, but because they judged it true. To underline this, in canon 28 of the Council they restated the teaching of the Council of Constantinople that Constantinople took precedence after Rome 'because it is new Rome'. There could not have been a clearer demonstration of the gap between Eastern and Western views of the papacy, and Leo delayed his acceptance of Chalcedon for two years on the strength of it.

Leo the Great gave the papacy its definitive form in the classical world, and set the pattern of its later claims. Already around him the ruin of ancient Rome was visible, as barbarian armies, once viewed as potential recruits for the Roman legions, ravaged Italy. He had witnessed the sack of Rome by Goths in 410, an event which had rocked the civilised world. Jerome, far away in his hermitage in the Holy Land, thought it the end of the world. When he tried to dictate a letter on the subject, he could not speak for tears: *capta est urbs quae totum cepit orbem* – captured is the city which once held the whole world captive. Worse was to come, however. In 452 'for the sake of the Roman name', as the *Liber Pontificalis* expresses it, Leo had to travel to Mantua to persuade Attila the Hun to turn back his armies from Rome, and, miraculously, he succeeded. In 455, however, the best he could manage was to persuade the armies of Gaiseric the Vandal to content themselves with looting the city, and not to put it to the torch. For fourteen days, Rome lay at their mercy. When they had gone, he set himself to patch up the damage, melting down silver ornaments at St Peter's from the great days of Constantinian Rome to make chalices for the devastated city's churches.

Rome, for Leo, was indeed the *caput orbis*, the head of the world. But it was Christian Rome which was the Eternal City, not the thousand-year old wonder that he saw dissolving around him. The empire had been born so that Christianity might triumph. The spiritual Rome, built on the blood of the Apostles and alive in Peter's heir and spokesman, could not be ruined. Even in the palmy days of Constantine's conversion, the popes had had to make a distinction between Church and empire, for all around them the signs of empire were pagan. The trials of Pope Liberius and the defiance of Ambrose had taught the churches of the West that God and Caesar, allied as they might be, were not the same. In Leo's vision of the papacy as the head of an *imperium* which was not of this world, the Church had found an ideal which would carry it through the collapse of the classical world, and into the future.

CHAPTER TWO

BETWEEN TWO EMPIRES

461-1000

I UNDER GOTHIC KINGS

In the year 476 the last Emperor of the West was deposed by the Germanic General Odoacer the Rugian, and Italy became a barbarian kingdom. The change from empire to kingdom, from toga to trousers, however, was to take generations to make its full imaginative impact. The barbarian kings of Italy pursued their own interests, but they ruled, to begin with at least, in the name of the distant Emperor in Constantinople, maintaining and honouring the Roman Senate, and accepting the honorific title 'Patrician of the Romans'. Even Odoacer's ferocious successor Theoderic, a man who could sign his own name only with the help of a stencil cut from a plate of gold, accepted and exploited the fiction of empire. Theoderic adopted Roman dress, and his coinage carried the image of the Emperor. The Gothic kings based themselves on the Adriatic coast, in the old capital of the Western empire at Ravenna, and the glamour of Rome persisted. As Theoderic himself declared, 'Any Goth who can, wants to be a Roman: no Roman wants to be a Goth.'

The papacy was the West's most concrete link with the Roman past and with the living empire. Inheritors of Leo's vision of Christian Rome as the providential instrument of God, first citizens of the ancient capital and the most powerful men in central Italy, the popes led the Senate in honouring the Emperor's image at the inauguration of each new reign. The popes looked east, and their loyalty to the Emperor was increased by the fact that the kings of Italy were Arians, heretics who denied the divinity of Christ. Gothic supremacy in northern Italy decimated the Catholic hierarchy there, and the Popes' authority cut no ice with Theoderic's Arian bishops.

In such a situation the papacy might easily have come to seem no more than a Byzantine chaplaincy within barbarian Italy. But all was not well between Pope and Emperor, for in the late fifth century Constantinople and Rome were in conflict over fundamental Christian beliefs. The Council of Chalcedon owed its fundamental teaching to the Tome of Pope Leo, and the Church of Rome took the teachings of the Council of Chalcedon as the definitive expression of the Christian faith. Chalcedon had asserted both the full divinity of Jesus Christ, and his full humanity, two natures joined without confusion in one person. For Western theologians this 'two natures' formulation was an essential safeguard of Christ's solidarity with the human race he had come to redeem – it proclaimed the real involvement of human nature in the process of salvation. For many Eastern Christians, by contrast, to emphasise a two-nature Christology was to deny the reality of Christ's divinity, and to threaten the overwhelming truth that in the man Jesus the eternal God himself had suffered and died. For Christians of this outlook, Christ's humanity was absorbed and overwhelmed within the majesty of his divine nature, like a drop of water mingled in a cup of wine.

Huge areas of the empire subscribed to this anti-Chalcedonian one-nature (in Greek, 'monophysite') theology, especially Egypt, where it had the backing of many of the desert monks. The Eastern emperors, struggling to hold their scattered dominions together, could not afford to ignore or alienate monophysite feeling, least of all the cornfields of Egypt, the bread-basket of the whole empire. And so successive emperors pursued a desperate search for compromise. In 484 Acacius, Patriarch of Constantinople, adopted a pro-monophysite theology. He was supported by the Emperor Zeno, and Rome and Constantinople broke off communion with each other. Outrageously, the papal writ of excommunication was actually pinned to patriarch Acacius' robes by pro-Chalcedonian monks as he celebrated Mass. This so-called Acacian schism, dividing East and West, was to last for thirty-five years.

The popes, therefore, might loathe the barbarian kings, and long for closer links with a Catholic empire. In practice, however, the emperors were suspect, supporters of heresy. This suspicion led the popes to make an increasingly sharp distinction between the secular and the sacred, and to resist imperial claims to authority over the Church. Pope Gelasius (492–6) saw himself as a loyal citizen of the empire, and declared that 'as a Roman born, I love, respect and honour the Roman Emperor'. But he did not bother to inform the Emperor Anastasius of his election, and he made clear the limits of his obedience:

> There are, most august Emperor, two powers by which this world is chiefly ruled: the sacred authority of bishops and the royal power. Of these the priestly power is much more important, because it has to render account for the kings of men themselves at the judgement seat of God. For you know, most gracious son, that although you hold the chief place of dignity over the human race, yet you must submit yourself in faith to those who have charge of divine things, and look to them for the means of your salvation. You know that it behoves you, in matters concerning the reception and reverent administration of the sacraments, to be obedient to ecclesiastical authority, instead of seeking to bend it to your will . . . And if the hearts of the faithful ought to be submitted to priests in general . . . how much more ought assent be given to him who presides over that See which the most high God himself desired to be pre-eminent over all priests, and which the pious judgement of the whole Church has honoured ever since?[1]

This was not the sort of language Anastasius was accustomed to hearing from the docile court bishops of the East. Gelasius, however, set the tone for imperial–papal relations in the decades that followed. Anastasius was a devout amateur theologian, and had once even been considered as a candidate for the vacant bishopric of Antioch. He did not take kindly to these papal harangues, and in 517 told Pope Hormisdas (514–23) , 'You may thwart me, reverend sir, you may insult me: but you may not command me.'[2]

For the Gothic regime at Ravenna, tension between Rome and Constantinople was good news. King Theoderic was an Arian, but he was also a wise and indulgent ruler to his Catholic subjects, and he cultivated good relations with successive popes. These overtures got a mixed reception in Rome, where the Senate and the wealthy Roman families longed for reconciliation with Byzantium and the restoration of the empire in Italy. Divisions between pro-Gothic and Byzantine factions within both Senate and the clergy came to a head after the death of Pope Anastasius II (496–8), and led to the election of rival popes. The Archpriest Laurence was the candidate favoured by the aristocratic laity, anxious at all costs for reconciliation with the

Emperor, and willing to make doctrinal concesssions to achieve it. The clergy's candidate was the deacon Symmachus, unusually at this late date a convert from paganism, and a stern upholder of Roman doctrinal purity and papal claims. The population of Rome took sides on the issue, and to end the ensuing bloodshed the rival candidates presented themselves for arbitration in Ravenna before King Theoderic. According to the papal chronicler, Theoderic 'made the fair decision that the one who was ordained first and whose faction was found to be the largest should hold the apostolic see', but it can hardly be a coincidence that this turned out to be the anti-Byzantine, pro-Goth Symmachus (498–514). Laurence was bundled off to a consolation bishopric at Nuceria. The spectacle of a heretical barbarian arbitrating a disputed papal election did not bode well for imperial authority in Italy.

But pressure was building at Constantinople for the resolution of the breach with Rome. Theology dominated the public imagination in fifth-century Constantinople, as football or baseball does that of modern Manchester or New York. Even the circus teams, the Greens and the Blues, adopted theological slogans. Though the Emperor was an ardent monophysite, most of the population of Constantinople supported the teaching of Chalcedon. When monophysite additions were made to the liturgy in the chapel royal and in the cathedral of Hagia Sophia, bloody riots broke out. Rampaging mobs terrorised the city in support of the two-natures theology. Anastasius was forced to seek a reconciliation with Symmachus' successor, Pope Hormisdas, inviting him to preside over a synod in Thrace to sort out their differences. Neither the Pope nor the Emperor was prepared to compromise, however.

The deadlock was broken by Anastasius' sudden death, and the proclamation of a Latin-speaking peasant soldier, Justin, as his successor. Justin was a no-nonsense Chalcedonian Catholic with a simple faith: he had little patience with fine theological distinctions. Riding a tide of popular support, he forced the Eastern bishops to accept a formula drawn up by Pope Hormisdas, condemning Acacius and his teaching and acknowledging the authority of Chalcedon. The formula, which cited Christ's words to Peter in Matthew 16, *Tu es Petrus*, recognised the primacy of Rome, as the apostolic see in which the true faith had always been preserved, and made communion with Rome the essential test of membership of the Catholic

Church. It was a tremendous coup for the papacy, and thirteen centuries later the 'Formula of Hormisdas' would be cited by the First Vatican Council as proof of papal infallibility.[3]

Predictably, this settlement caused consternation in the East, but it marked the beginning of a real reconciliation between empire and papacy. Justin, and his nephew Justinian, who dominated his uncle and succeeded him in 527, were determined to restore imperial direct rule in Italy. Reconciliation with the papacy was fundamental to this plan. Theoderic recognised what was happening, and in the years before his death in 526 became paranoid about anything that smacked of pro-Byzantine feeling, which he interpreted as treason. In 524 he had his trusted adviser the philosopher Boethius garrotted in prison for alleged treasonable correspondence with Constantinople.

Theoderic thought of himself as the protector of Arian Christians everywhere. He watched with rage as the Emperor Justin's zeal for the Catholic faith overflowed into a campaign against heresy in the East. The Emperor confiscated Arian churches and had them reconsecrated for Catholic worship. Arian Gothic populations under imperial rule were forcibly converted to Catholicism. Determined to stop this policy, the King summoned Hormisdas' pro-imperial successor, Pope John I (523–6), to Ravenna. The Pope was ordered to lead a deputation of senators and ex-consuls to Constantinople. He was to persuade the Emperor to end the persecution, return the confiscated churches and allow the forcibly converted to resume their Arian beliefs.

This mission was a deep humiliation for the Pope, who felt acutely the contradiction of his position, the teacher of orthodoxy forced to act as apologist for heretics. With considerable courage, John flatly refused to ask the Emperor to allow converts to revert to heresy. He did however agree to seek toleration for existing Arian populations, and to ask for an end to the confiscations of church buildings. Despite his great age and failing health, he set off for Constantinople early in 526, arriving there just before Easter (19 April), the first Pope to make the journey to Constantinople.

Once there, what had begun as a humiliation turned into a triumph, for the Pope was received as a hero. The whole city came out to the twelfth milestone to greet him, and the Emperor treated him with ostentatious reverence, prostrating himself on the ground before him in a gesture which would have gladdened the heart of

Pope Gelasius. On Easter Day John was installed in Hagia Sophia on a throne higher than that of the Patriarch, he celebrated Mass before the Emperor in Latin, not Greek, and using the ritual customs of Rome, not Constantinople: he was allowed to place the Easter crown on the Emperor's head, an honour normally reserved for the Patriarch. The clerks of the papal chancery, hardened to Eastern rejection of Rome's Petrine claims, recorded ecstatically the honours heaped on the Pope by the Emperor, and the gratitude of the Greeks for being able 'to receive in glory the vicar of St Peter the Apostle'.[4]

Justin agreed to suspend hostilities against the Arians and return their churches, but the Emperor refused to allow the forcibly converted Arians to return to their damnable errors. This, however, was the element of the embassy which mattered most to Theoderic. The Pope and senatorial party returned to Ravenna to find the King convinced that they had not seriously attempted to secure real concessions from the Emperor, and maddened by accounts of the Pope's triumphant reception and the Roman party's delight in it. Worn out by the journey and shattered by the King's furious hostility, John died within days of his arrival in Ravenna. His body, carried in state back to Rome for burial in St Peter's, immediately became the focus of miraculous healings.

Yet popes retained their uses for the Gothic kings. As preparations mounted in Constantinople for a campaign to reclaim the West, the court at Ravenna looked for ways to buy time. The shortlived Pope Agapitus I (535–6) seemed a likely ally. Agapitus was an aristocrat from a distinguished Roman clerical dynasty, and a scholar deeply read in the Church Fathers. He was a stern disciplinarian, who risked offending the Emperor Justinian by taking a hard line over the rehabilitation of the Arian Goths of North Africa, now being forcibly recatholicised in the wake of Count Belisarius' triumphant imperial reconquest there. From Ravenna, Agapitus looked like a pro-Gothic pope, and Theodohad, the last Gothic King of Italy, sent him to Constantinople to try to deflect Justinian's preparations for the imminent invasion designed to restore imperial rule in Italy.

Justinian soon made it clear to the Pope that the reinvasion of Italy was not negotiable, and it is doubtful if Agapitus tried very hard to dissuade him. On the theological front, however, the Pope swept all before him. Justinian's forceful wife Theodora was an ex-actress with a lurid sexual reputation for wearing out relays of athletic young courtiers. She was also a devout monophysite, who kept a monastery of heretical monks in the imperial palace. Theodora exercised enormous influence over Justinian, and had secured the appointment of a monophysite, Anthimous, as patriarch of Constantinople. Pope Agapitus determined to have nothing to do with this man, refusing to hold communion with him, and, when threatened by the angry Emperor for his truculence, he was unintimidated. He had long wanted to meet the devout Justinian, he declared: instead, he seemed to stand before the pagan persecutor Diocletian. He demanded a public debate with the Patriarch, at which he had little difficulty in demonstrating Anthimous' suspect opinions. Overawed, Justinian 'abased himself before the apostolic see, prostrating himself before the blessed Pope Agapitus'. He agreed to the deposition and exile of the Patriarch, and invited the Pope to consecrate an orthodox replacement, who testified his faith by signing an expanded version of the formula of Pope Hormisdas. The Patriarch of Constantinople bowed to the superior doctrinal purity of the Pope of Rome.

Agapitus, however, did not survive long to enjoy his triumph. Six weeks into his visit to Constantinople he sickened and died: his body, wrapped in lead, was taken back to Rome for burial. But his mission to the imperial capital had demonstrated once again Rome's unflinching defence of orthodoxy, and, in the reverence of the Emperor and the papal consecration of a new patriarch, the Pope's primacy over the whole Church, East and West.

The suddeness of Pope Agapitus' death threatened to undo all these gains. Vigilius, the papal Apocrisiary (ambassador) in Constantinople, was an aristocrat whose father and brother were consuls. Consumed with ambition, he had lost no time in ingratiating himself with the real power in the court of Constantinople, the Empress Theodora. Posing as a monophysite sympathiser, he won her support for his candidacy for the papacy. In return, he promised to reinstate the banished monophysite Patriarch Anthimous, and even to repudiate altogether the teaching of the Council of Chalcedon. Laden with bags of Theodora's money for bribes, he raced Pope Agapitus' body to Rome. But he was too late. The Gothic King Theodahad had pre-empted any imperial candidate by forcing through the appointment of Pope Hormisdas' son, Silverius (536–7). The papacy seemed to have slipped through Vigilius' fingers.

Vigilius, however, was not a man to be trifled with. In December

536 the imperial General Belisarius 'liberated' Rome on Justinian's behalf, and established himself on the Palatine as governor. His wife Antonina was Theodora's closest friend and confidante, and together she and Vigilius persuaded Belisarius to arrest Pope Silverius, on a trumped up charge of plotting to open the gates of Rome to the Gothic army. Demoted to the status of a monk, the Pope was banished to an obscure town in Anatolia, and the see was declared vacant. The clergy now obediently elected Vigilius (537–55) as pope.

Worse was to follow. The bishop of the town in Anatolia to which Pope Silverius had been deported took up his cause. He secured an audience with Justinian and impressed on him the enormity of what had been done. There were any number of earthly kings, he pointed out, but only one pope. Rattled, Justinian had Silverius returned to Rome for a fair trial, to be reinstated if found innocent. Vigilius, however, now firmly in charge, was having none of this. The wretched Silverius was arrested again as soon as he arrived, and bundled off to a second exile on the island of Palmaria. There, a few months later, he died of malnutrition. To all intents and purposes, one pope, and he the son of a pope, had been deposed and murdered by another.

For Vigilius, however, chickens now began to come home to roost. Justinian badly needed to find ways of conciliating monophysite opinion in the empire, and in 543 his advisers came up with a scheme designed to do just that. They singled out for condemnation the writings of three long-dead writers, all of whom had supported a 'two-nature' Christology, and each of whom was a special target of monophysite loathing. The writings in question, known as the 'Three Chapters', provided Justinian with a way of distancing himself and his regime from Chalcedon, without actually repudiating the formal teaching of the Council.

With some reluctance, the Patriarch of Constantinople and the other Eastern bishops signed the condemnation of the Three Chapters. But feeling in the West was violently against anything which threatened the authority of Chalcedon, and Vigilius, whatever his private opinions, did not dare comply with the imperial demand. Here, with the imperial campaign to recapture Italy in full swing, was potential disaster. Justinian simply could not afford a pope at odds with the rest of the empire. In November 545 he had Vigilius arrested while he was presiding over the ceremonies for St Cecilia's

Day, a major festival in Rome, and put aboard a ship for Constantinople via Sicily.

There were few tears shed for Vigilius in Rome. According to the *Liber Pontificalis*, the crowd threw stones and yelled abuse at the Pope as his ship pulled away from the dock, for they blamed the many misfortunes of the city on the sordid way in which he had become pope. He was honourably received by Justinian on his arrival in January 547, however, and once again his ambition ran away with him. After a show of firmness, he resumed communion with the 'heretical' Patriarch Menas, and in April 548 he published a solemn *Iudicatum*, or judgement, condemning the Three Chapters, only preserving a fig-leaf of consistency by stating that this condemnation in no way impugned the authority of Chalcedon.

Reaction in the West was volcanic. Vigilius was universally denounced as a traitor to Roman orthodoxy. The bishops of Africa solemnly excommunicated him, and many of his own entourage repudiated him. In the face of this hostility, which threatened to pull the empire apart, Justinian allowed the Pope to withdraw his *Iudicatum*. He extracted a secret undertaking from him, however, to renew his condemnation of the Three Chapters at an opportune moment. Pope and Emperor agreed that a council was needed to settle the whole matter, but Justinian was not a man to wait on events. In 551 he published a long edict of his own once more condemning the Chapters.

Even Vigilius' capacity for accommodation to imperial pressure was now exhausted. He was determined to salvage whatever shreds of credibility remained to him in the West, and he organised resistance to the imperial decree. He summoned a synod of all the bishops then in Constantinople, and once more excommunicated the Patriarch. In the ensuing conflict, the Pope fled from imperial troops and sought sanctuary in the palace church of Sts Peter and Paul. Onlookers were treated to the sight of the elderly Pope clinging to the columns of the altar (which gave way and collapsed), while the palace guard attempted to drag him away by his hair, beard and clothing. The scandalised crowd forced the soldiers to leave the successor of St Peter alone. Public feeling obviously ran high, and next day the Emperor sent Belisarius himself to apologise. The Pope knew he was no longer safe, however, and, escaping by night across the Bosphorous, symbolically sought refuge in the church in which the Council of Chalcedon had met.

Had Vigilius died at this point, the scandals of his earlier career might have been forgiven him, for the sake of this heroic stand in defence of the Chalcedonian faith. Instead, he patched up a reconciliation with Justinian, and in May 553 the promised General Council, the fifth, met in Constantinople. Proceedings were dominated by imperial pressure, there were hardly any Westerners present, and no one was left in any doubt about what was required of them.

The Pope boycotted the Council, and issued a careful theological manifesto of his own, condemning some but not all of the writings included in the Three Chapters. Justinian, however, had no longer any need to walk on eggshells in respecting Western sensibilities. His troops had defeated the Gothic forces in Italy, and Rome was safe in Byzantine hands. He therefore decided to neutralise Vigilius once and for all. This he did by sending to the Council a dossier of Vigilius' secret correspondence with him, exposing for all to read the Pope's repeated promises to condemn the Three Chapters. Vigilius was totally discredited. The Council condemned not only the Three Chapters, but also the Pope, and Justinian formally broke off communion with Vigilius, while emphasising that it was the man Vigilius, and not the See of Rome, he was rejecting: *non sedem, sed sedentem* ('not the see itself, but the one who sits in it'). The disgraced Pope was put under house arrest, and his clerical entourage were imprisoned or sent to the mines. Broken in spirit, he published a series of humiliating retractions, before being finally permitted to leave Constantinople in 555. He never reached Rome, however, dying from gallstones on the journey at Syracuse.

The Vigilius affair dealt a series of shattering blows to the papacy. The prestige and leadership gained for Rome over the previous century had been frittered away, the papacy's reputation dragged through the mire. And the actions of Vigilius cast long shadows. His successor in Rome, Pelagius (556–61), was an elderly aristocrat, who had played a very creditable role in stiffening Vigilius' theological resistance to imperial pressure over the Three Chapters. He was, however, determined to become pope by hook or by crook, and turned his coat on Vigilius' death. To secure the Emperor's support, he suddenly accepted the Fifth General Council's condemnation of the Three Chapters.

Pelagius' conversion may just possibly have been genuine – he was perhaps influenced by the fact that both a general council and the previous Pope had ruled on the matter. His action, however, was universally denounced in the West as self-seeking treachery. His acceptance of the condemnation of the Three Chapters confirmed the failure of Vigilius, and left papal prestige in the West in ruins, especially in northern Italy and the Adriatic provinces. The sees of Milan and Aquilea, and all the bishops of Istria, broke off communion with Rome. It would be fifty years before communion was restored between Milan and Rome, and the Istrian schism was to persist for a century and a half. In Gaul, too, the Catholic bishops looked on him with suspicion, and the close links with Rome established through the papal vicariate at Arles were eroded. Fifty years later, the Irish monk Columbanus in a letter full of Irish wordplay would remind Pope Boniface IV (608–15) of the fall of Vigilius, and warn him of the need to preserve the orthodoxy of the apostolic see: 'Watch [*vigila*] that it does not turn out for you as it did for *Vigilius*, who was not *vigilant* enough.' Otherwise 'the normal situation of the Church will be reversed. Your children will become the head, but you . . . will become the tail of the Church; therefore your judges will be those who have always preserved the Catholic faith, whoever they may be, even the youngest.'[5]

The pontificate of Vigilius had also laid bare a fundamental difference of outlook between Emperor and Pope. In the hothouse atmosphere of Constantinople, a theology of empire had evolved which raised the person of the Emperor far above any bishop. Constantine had thought of himself as the thirteenth Apostle, and had made a bridle for his horse from of one of the nails with which Christ was crucified. The emperors of Byzantium proved themselves worthy successors of Constantine. Justinian, like Gelasius, believed that there were indeed two powers set over this world, the imperial and the pontifical, but unlike Gelasius he was certain that the senior partner in that alliance was the Emperor, not the Pope. It was the responsibility of the Emperor to see that bishops performed their share of the work. To the Emperor belonged the care of all the churches, to make and unmake bishops, to decide the bounds of orthodoxy. The Emperor, not the Pope, was God's vicar on earth, and to him belonged the title *Kosmocrator*, lord of the world, ruling over one empire, one law, one Church. Byzantine court ceremonial emphasised the quasi-divine character of the Emperor's office. His servants performed an act of solemn adoration, the *proskynesis*, on coming into his presence, and his decrees were received with divine honours, even the parchment they were written on kissed with reverence as if it carried holy scripture.

The bishops of the East saw no cause to challenge any of this. They accepted the Christian vocation of the Emperor as God-given, and they saw their role as that of obedient collaborators with the Lord's anointed. To a papacy nurtured in a high sense of apostolic dignity, and based in Rome with its civic traditions and recruitment from senatorial families, such values seemed increasingly alien. Pope and Emperor might have mutual interests, and emperors, when it suited them, might pay genuine homage to the senior Bishop and the successor of St Peter. Between the imperial vision of Byzantium, however, and the theological ethos of Rome, there was a great and growing gap. The experience of the popes as they set themselves to meet the needs of Italy and the West in the years after the imperial reconquest would see that gap widen to a gulf.

II THE AGE OF GREGORY THE GREAT

The imperial reconquest of Africa from the Vandals was achieved by Belisarius in one short and brilliant campaign launched in 533. The campaign to recover Italy from the Goths began the following year. It was to drag on for twenty years, but there would be no joy at its ending, for it left Italy depopulated and impoverished. Up to a third of the population had perished, and to the traumas of war and its attendant famines were added natural disaster, as successive waves of plague swept through the peninsula. Politically, too, the overthrow of the Gothic kingdom proved a disaster, not a liberation. The restoration of imperial rule brought no revival of the fortunes of the Roman aristocracy. Instead, every position of importance was filled by career administrators from the East: Italy became a Greek colony. It was expected, moreover, to pay handsomely for the privilege. The burden of imperial taxation proved far more oppressive, and far more efficient, than anything the Goths had imposed – Justinian's chief tax-collector in Italy was grimly nicknamed 'the scissor-man'. From the 540s onwards most of the surviving ancient families of Rome in a position to do so migrated east, to Constantinople, where it had become clear that all the opportunities and the fruits of empire lay.

Rome had a double share of the woes of Italy. Stripped of its traditional ruling class, separated by a long sea journey from the court at Constantinople, it had no real place in the new imperial order. Ravenna would remain the political centre of imperial Italy, as it had been of the Gothic kingdom. There, in the basilica of San Vitale, Justinian and Theodora set up their images behind the altar, unforgettable icons of the Byzantine convergence of regal and priestly authority. There the imperial governor of Italy, the Exarch, would rule in the Emperor's place. Rome was left to the crows and its own devices. Repeatedly besieged and plundered, it had been captured and devastated by Totila in 546. Its population, 800,000 in AD 400, had dropped to 100,000 by AD 500, and was down to 30,000 by the year of Totila's sack. Pope Pelagius, a man caught, as his epitaph declared, 'in a falling world', was reduced to begging clothing and food from bishops in Gaul for the poor – and even the former rich – of the city. The Senate was gone, and the wars had shattered the physical glory of Rome. Many of the great aqueducts which fed the city's baths, cisterns and fountains, and which had turned the cornmills on the Janiculum hill, had been deliberately cut by the Goths, or stripped by thieves of their lead linings. They leaked precious water from the mountains into the surrounding plain, beginning the long transformation of the Roman Campagna into the fever-ridden swamp which it would remain till the days of Mussolini.

By the end of the sixth century, the city's population was creeping up again, to about 90,000. Many of these, however, were refugees from a new invasion. For the imperial conquest, in destroying the Gothic occupiers, had removed the only real obstacle to a far worse scourge, the part-pagan and part-Arian Lombard tribes who descended in their tens of thousands from Austria in 568. In September 569 Milan fell to them, and their king Alboin took the title 'Lord of Italy'. By 574 the Lombards commanded half the peninsula, and had all but cut the connections between Ravenna and Rome. They were to remain in control for the next two centuries.

This was the inheritance of Gregory the Great (590–604). Gregory, who was born some time around the year 540, was a product of the patrician aristocracy which had suffered so much from the Gothic war. The family had a distinguished tradition of service to Church and city. Gregory was the great-grandson of Pope Felix III and a relative of Pope Agapitus I. He himself, while still in his early thirties, was to serve as prefect, the highest secular office in the city, as his brother would after him. Gregory's father, Gordianus, was one of the Church's regionaries, the lay officials responsible for administering the temporalities of the Roman see. In her widowhood his mother Sylvia became a nun, as did three paternal aunts. They followed a common Roman pattern of vowed life by living in retirement on their own property, where two of the aunts enjoyed visions of their papal ancestor, 'St' Felix, shortly before their deaths.

The retreat of the Roman aristocracy from the world into the Church was by no means confined to the womenfolk. In part it reflected the growing dominance of the Church in the life of the West. The call of monastic life, to contemplation instead of action, was powerful in a world in which all action seemed to lead to disaster, and in which the secular order seemed to be near its end. This was certainly so for Gregory: 'the world grows old and hoary', he was to write, 'and hastens to approaching death'. About 575 he resigned his city office, turned his parental home on the Caelian Hill into a monastery dedicated to St Andrew, and became a monk. The family's extensive estates in Italy and Sicily passed into the patrimony of the Roman Church, and on them too Gregory established a series of six monastic houses.

Gregory was to look back on the next few years, given over to prayer and reflection on scripture, as the happiest of his life. He was a dedicated monk, and was to destroy his health, and his stomach lining, by excessive fasting. His *Dialogues*, a set of miracle-encrusted lives of the early Italian monks, in particular the father of Western monasticism, St Benedict, was to become one of the most influential books of the Middle Ages (and the only work of Gregory's to find a Greek as well as a Latin readership). But above all, it was the contemplative dimension of monastic life he valued, and which as pope he missed:

> I remember with sorrow what I once was in the monastery, how I rose in contemplation above all changeable and decaying things and thought of nothing but the things of heaven ... But now, by reason of my pastoral care, I have to bear with secular business, and, after so fair a vision or rest, am fouled with worldly dust ... I sigh as one who looks back and gazes at the shore he has left behind.[6]

He was not left long in his retreat. In the crisis years of the late sixth century men of his abilities and experience could not be spared. He was ordained deacon against his will by Pope Benedict I (575–9), and placed in charge of the city's seventh district, with responsibility for administration and charitable relief. In August 579 the city was besieged by the Lombards, and a new pope, Pelagius II (579–90), was elected. Desperate for military help and relief for the beleaguered city, Pelagius sent Gregory as apocrisiary to Constantinople, to plead with the Emperor Tiberius. He was to remain there for seven years.

Even as deacon of the seventh region Gregory had continued to live in his monastery, and he took a group of monks from St Andrew's with him to Constantinople, turning the Roman embassy in Constantinople into a replica of his monastic home on the Caelian. He devoted himself to the spiritual life of this community, lecturing regularly to them on the Book of Job. But he also pursued his diplomatic duties with vigour, winning the trust of the royal family and becoming godfather to the eldest son of the new Emperor Maurice, debating theology with the Patriarch, and establishing a network of personal contacts which would stand him in good stead as pope. He remained, however, resolutely a Roman, refusing to learn Greek, suspicious of Eastern theology and liturgy, troubled by and disapproving of the Westerners in Constantinople who had gone native. As pope he would refuse to answer a letter from a woman-friend settled in Constantinople because she had written in Greek instead of her native Latin. Rome was the Eternal City, the dwelling-place of the Apostle – 'How anyone can be seduced by Constantinople,' he wrote, 'and how anyone can forget Rome, I do not know.'[7] The only aspect of Greek civilisation he seems to have valued was the retsina for which he formed a taste while Apocrisiary, and which he had specially shipped to Rome when he became pope.

Gregory was eventually recalled to assist Pope Pelagius II in attempts to resolve the Istrian schism, and so was in Rome during the dreadful winter of 589, when the Tiber rose and breached the city's war-damaged walls, flooding and demolishing churches and granaries, and decimating the winter food-supplies. In the ensuing plague Pope Pelagius was one of the first victims, and Gregory was at once elected by clergy and people to succeed him.

Gregory was a devout man, an unselfconscious participant in the unsophisticated popular Christianity of the West in his own day. The piety revealed in his *Dialogues* is colourful, receptive to miracles and marvels, readily moved to awe. Yet there was nothing fanciful about him: he had all the Roman virtues – practicality, realism, a passion for order. Despite his love of contemplation, he was no abstract thinker. He distrusted learning for its own sake, and he praised St Benedict for being 'skilfully ignorant and wisely unlearned'.[8] As pope, he was to need every shred of this practicality. Most of his letters survive, and they provide a window into the overwhelming scale and range of the tasks that confronted him, and the titanic energy with which, despite wretched health, he tackled them.

In the first place, he had to defend the city from the Lombards. Rome was now a military dukedom, with an imperial commander, based in the palace on the Capitol, nominally in charge. In practice, imperial resources were often diverted elsewhere – as Gregory complained bitterly to the Emperor Maurice, 'Rome is abandoned, that Perugia might be held.'[9] Gregory continued the policy begun by his predecessor, Pelagius II, of buying temporary truces from the Lombards 'without any cost to the republic' – that is, with bribes raised from the Church's own resources. He also found himself often obliged to pay the wages of the imperial troops or to provision the Roman garrison. He negotiated treaties, ransomed refugees and provided for their relief.

In many places, the Lombard advance drove out the Catholic clergy, and Gregory had to try to cobble together pastoral provision for the laity left behind. In imperial Italy, he used his primatial powers to try to secure decent episcopal appointments, imposing Roman clerics, when he could get away with it, in preference to unsuitable local candidates. He regulated the lives of existing monastic communities and encouraged new foundations. He tried to ensure that those in charge of the Church's lands and properties were good employers and used the revenues for the benefit of the needy. One cluster of letters show him disciplining a slack bishop who had tried to get rid of an overzealous archdeacon by forcibly ordaining him priest. Another shows him trying to rationalise the livestock holdings on the Church's properties in Sicily. In Rome itself he had a detailed register drawn up of every poor person in the city, where they lived, what their names and ages were, and allocated a weekly ration of corn, wine, cheese and oil to each. Food from the Pope's own table was sent to genteel folk fallen on hard times, an exquisitely tactful way of turning a charitable dole into a mark of respect. Twelve poor people ate with the Pope each day.

All this cost money, and one of the most remarkable features of Gregory's activity was his reorganisation and deployment of the patrimony of the Roman Church. The Church was by now the largest single landowner in the West, its property built up from imperial bounty in the Constantinian era, and then from the donations and legacies of great families like Gregory's own. The papacy had lands scattered in at least fifteen different regions, from Gaul to Africa, from the Balkans to Calabria. The rich Sicilian holdings were by far the most important – most of Gregory's own family properties were there – and Sicily had been untouched by invasion. This proved the salvation of Rome, for the papacy now took on the Roman state's traditional role of feeding the people. Gregory overhauled the whole working of these Church lands, replacing unsatisfactory 'rectors' – the chief officers of the patrimonies, who were often slack or corrupt local bishops or lay adminstrators – with hand-picked members of the Roman clergy and specially sworn lay assistants. He closely scrutinised their activities, and endlessly exhorted them to diligence and efficiency, scrupulous honesty, generosity to the poor, and fair dealing with tenants and employees.

There was more to this than money. The patrimonial organisation provided Gregory with a network of patronage, persuasion and liaison with the local churches and civic administration which enormously strengthened his grip over the churches of Italy and beyond. The channels of influence which they gave the Pope were exploited to maximum effect. The rector of the Ravenna patrimony functioned as papal ambassador to the Exarch, and kept a watchful eye on the Archbishop, who chafed at his subjugation to Rome and was angling for independent patriarchal status. This network, and the revenues which sustained it, laid the foundations for the role and influence of the medieval papacy.

Much of this activity was looked at askance in Constantinople. The Emperor resented Gregory's independent negotiations with the Lombards, and considered that he had no business making truces with the enemies of the empire. Gregory revered the empire as the one legitimate secular authority in Christendom, and he saw himself in civic matters as its servant – 'for the love of the empire, we have lost silver and gold, slaves and raiment'. But he in his turn resented armchair criticism levelled from the comfort and safety of Constantinople at those like himself who 'suffer in this place among the swords of the Lombards', and who were forced to watch 'Romans tied by the neck like dogs, to be taken to Gaul for sale'.[10]

Moreover, though he detested the 'unspeakable Lombards', he also thought of them not merely as the enemies of the Emperor and of Italy, to be bought or fought off, but as his pastoral responsibility, human beings with souls to be saved. The marriage of two successive Lombard kings to the Bavarian Catholic Princess Theodelinda gave the Pope a toehold in the Lombard court which he exploited to the full, showering Theodelinda with gifts, and being rewarded by the Catholic baptism of her son, Prince Adoloald. It was the first step in a process which would ultimately lead to Lombard renunciation of Arianism.

Gregory was also perfectly prepared to do battle with imperial officials in the localities when he thought they were oppressing the poor or infringing the rights of the Church. The authority of empire was rooted in responsibility. 'There is this difference between the kings of the barbarian nations and the Roman emperor,' he told Maurice, 'that the former have slaves for their subjects, the latter free men. And therefore, in all your acts, your first object should be the maintenance of justice, your second to preserve a perfect liberty.'[11] By the same token, he was ready to resist the Emperor when he encroached on matters of the spirit. In 593 Maurice issued an edict forbidding any serving soldiers to resign from the army in order to enter monastic life. In an empire at bay against armed enemies, it was not an unreasonable measure, but Gregory, who had himself abandoned public service to become a monk, would have none of it. He dutifully circulated the edict, but he wrote a blistering rebuke to Maurice, accusing him of abusing his power and locking up the way to heaven, reminding him of his humble origins and charging him with ingratitude to the God who had raised him to be emperor, before whose judgement seat, he pointed out, Maurice would soon have to stand. It is not a timid letter.[12]

Gregory was generally deferential in his dealings with the Emperor, but he was insistent on the primacy of the Roman Church. He told Maurice in 595 that 'the care of the whole Church has been committed to the blessed Peter, Prince of the

Apostles. Behold he received the keys of the kingdom of heaven; to him was given the power of binding and loosing, to him the care and principate of the whole Church was committed.' The issue of the primacy of Rome and its relation to Constantinople came to a head over the employment of the conventional title 'Ecumenical Patriarch' by Gregory's former friend, John the Faster, Patriarch of Constantinople. Gregory's predecessor, Pelagius II, had taken exception to the Patriarch's use of the word 'Ecumenical', understanding it to mean 'universal' and seeing in it a challenge to the universal authority of the Pope. This was in fact a misapprehension. The title meant no more than 'imperial' , and to begin with at least there was no larger agenda in its use. But Gregory remembered and revived Pelagius' objections, perhaps because they had been first raised by his ancestor, Pope Felix. He denounced John's continued use of the phrase, and tried to pressure members of the imperial family and the administration in Constantinople to put a stop to it. He also wrote to the patriarchs of Alexandria and Antioch, suggesting that, as bishops of the other two 'Petrine' sees, they shared in the Petrine office. They too were being insulted, moreover, since 'if one Patriarch is called Universal, the name of Patriarch in the rest is derogated'.[13]

Gregory cared greatly about order, but there was more at stake in this debate about the 'Universal Patriarchate' than petty worries about prestige. For him, precedence in the Church, and especially the papal primacy, was based on humility and service. His favourite title for his own office was *Servus servorum dei* (servant of the servants of God). One of his most influential writings was his treatise on episcopacy, *Pastoral Care*: in it he portrayed the bishop as one who prepares for rule by ruling himself in humility. The bishop must be a man of meditation, steeped in scripture, devoted to preaching, teaching, admonition, one who seeks 'to subdue himself rather than his brethren', 'a minister, not a master'.[14]

By contrast, he seems to have seen in the Constantinopolitan title an alternative, worldly understanding of ecclesiastical power, an attempt by the devil or Antichrist to corrupt the Church in the last days. In a devastatingly undiplomatic phrase, he told the Emperor that this demonic pride was one of the reasons why so many of the patriarchs of Constantinople had 'fallen into the whirlpool of heresy'.[15] His fellow patriarchs could not understand his concern.

Anastasius of Antioch sternly warned him against pride, while Eulogius of Alexandria, politely bewildered, promised never to call the Patriarch of Constantinople 'Universal Patriarch', in a letter in which he addressed Gregory as 'Universal Pope'. Like some later historians, Eulogius clearly thought that behind Gregory's rhetoric of humility and equality was a less attractive concern for his own dignity. Gregory was mortified:

> Here at the head of your letter I find the proud title of 'Universal Pope', which I have refused. I pray your most beloved holiness not to do it again, because what is exaggeratedly attributed to another is taken away from you. It is not in words that I would find my greatness, but in manner of life. And I do not consider that an honour which, as I know, undermines the honour of my brothers. My honour is the honour of the universal church. My honour is the solid strength of my brothers . . . Away with these words which inflate vanity and wound charity.[16]

Gregory's difficulties with the Emperor and the bishops of the East were more than matched in the West, for the authority of the papacy was fragile everywhere. Gregory longed to promote virtue, to eliminate corruption, to institute reform in all the churches of the West, but he could never simply assume he would be obeyed. Much of what he achieved, even with bishops traditionally under the direct jurisdiction of the popes, had to be done by coaxing, scolding and persuasion.

North Africa had always been an important sphere of papal influence, and had now been restored to Catholic rule for three generations, but Gregory had little success in his attempts to regulate church affairs there. He disapproved of the Catholic hierarchy's toleration of Donatist communities, and disliked the fact that the primacy among the African bishops moved round the senior sees, making it difficult for Rome to exert consistent influence or control. Gregory tried to have this system changed, but he was obstructed at every turn. The imperial Exarch in Africa refused to allow African bishops to take ecclesiastical appeals to Rome, and the bishops themselves were jealous of their independence and kept the Pope at arm's length. Even his unofficial vicar in Numidia, Bishop Columbus, complained that the frequency of the letters he received from Rome was making him unpopular with his colleagues.

Outside the *Imperium*, Gregory knew he had little control. He rejoiced at the conversion to Catholicism of the King of Visigothic Spain, Recarred, and wrote to congratulate him. He had no hand in the conversion, however, and made no attempt at direct control or even influence over the Spanish church, which went very much its own way. In Gaul he did attempt to work through the papal vicariate at Arles, but he concentrated his main efforts — for reform of episcopal appointments in Gaul, the abolition of simony, and Gallic support for the mission to England — on the cultivation of friendly relations with the royal family, especially the unsavoury Queen Brunhild. His correspondence with her is full of exhortation and advice, but is at least as deferential as his letters to the Emperor Maurice and his family, and he took the unprecedented step of bestowing the pallium on the Bishop of Autun, simply to please her. That she should demand the pallium for her bishop, and that Gregory should feel reluctantly obliged to concede it, illustrates both the prestige and the limitations of papal authority at the time.

And beyond Gaul there were Western churches over which Gregory had no real influence at all. Irish Christianity was a prime example of what has been called a 'micro-Christendom', which had evolved its own very distinctive institutions and style. Patrick and the other Irish missionaries of the fifth century had no doubt envisaged a church organised under the episcopal structure universal in the Mediterranean world, but the strongly tribal organisation of Irish society militated against this. The Irish, however, did take enthusiastically to monasticism, in a form quite unlike the orderly and regimented houses following the rule of St Benedict, and closer to the more idiosyncratic desert monasticism of the East. Irish monasteries, like the cluster of huts perched on a pinnacle of rock on the westernmost edge of Europe at Skellig Michael, had little in common with the urban decorum of monasteries like Gregory's St Andrew on the Caelian Hill. Increasingly, the Irish church formed a series of great monastic families, based within particular kin-groups, and radiating out from the founding houses.

We should not exaggerate the differences. The Irish church used a Latin liturgy, and respected the popes as the successors of St Peter. In the seventh century Irish church disputes, like those elsewhere, might be resolved by appeal to Rome. But in Gregory's day the Irish kept their own customs, and in particular they used an old-fashioned method of calculating the date of Easter which put them out of step with Rome. In his last years Gregory himself would be made painfully aware of the Easter question through contact with the great Irish monastic founder, Columbanus, whose monastery at Luxeuil, which kept the Irish date for Easter, was in trouble with the bishops of Gaul. Columbanus turned to Rome to strengthen his position, naively bombarding Gregory with a series of breezy letters soliciting the support of 'him who sits in the seat of Peter, the Apostle and bearer of the Keys', while at the same time lecturing him on the laughable inaccuracy of the Roman method of calculating Easter. Deference to Peter did not necessarily involve obedience to his successors.

Confronting so many challenges, there is no indication that Gregory had a single objective, a master plan. He responded to the material and spiritual needs of his world as he saw them, and was too concerned with the resulting avalanche of practicalities to have leisure for anything more. Almost two-thirds of his surviving letters are rescripts, replies to problems or queries posed by others, rather than initiatives sought by Gregory himself. In talking about his role as pope, he reverts again and again to the language of a mind coerced by circumstance.

The mission to Anglo-Saxon England, however, was one initiative by Gregory which cannot be explained in terms of response to the demands of others. It was to have the most momentous consequences for the papacy. No pope had ever before thought in terms of missionary outreach to the world beyond the empire. Celestine I (422–32) had indeed despatched a bishop named Palladius 'to the Irish who believe in Christ', but as the phrase suggests he was not thinking of a mission to pagans, and nothing very much happened as a result. The conversion of Ireland when it came was initiated as a private venture by the captured son of a Romano-British cleric: Patrick had no papal mandate.

Just why Gregory should have decided to evangelise England we do not know. The earliest biography, written in England a century after his death, tells how, while still a deacon, he saw handsome, fair-haired Anglo-Saxon boys in Rome. When told they were Angles, he replied, 'They are *angels* of God,' and immediately formed a desire to convert the nation from which they had come. The story is quite plausible in itself, and Gregory's interest in this people 'worshipping stocks and stones . . . at the edge of the world' may well have been aroused by seeing English slaves in the Roman market. Certainly by 595 he was instructing the Rector of the papal patrimony in Gaul to buy up seventeen or eighteen year-old English slave-boys, to be trained as monks in the Roman monasteries. He may already have been looking for interpreters for a mission to England.

One year later he despatched his mission, a party of Roman monks led by Augustine, prefect of Gregory's own monastery of St Andrew. They landed, forty strong, at Thanet, in Kent, which had probably been targeted because its king, Ethelbert, was married to a Christian, the daughter of the King of Paris. Though Gregory always spoke of England as the end of the universe, he had not forgotten that it had once been part of the empire. He hoped that in due course Augustine would establish two archbishoprics, each with twelve suffragan or subordinate bishops, in the old centres of Roman rule in Britain, London and York.

Some historians have seen the mission to England as a clear example of papalism, a pre-emptive strike by Gregory to prevent the evangelisation of the Anglo-Saxons by the Romano-British or the Irish, and to ensure that the English adopted Roman and not Irish customs and obedience. Conflict between Irish and Roman usage would indeed come to loom large in the early history of the English church. The eventual triumph of the Roman system, at the Synod of Whitby in 664, would form a major theme of Bede's great *Ecclesiastical History of the English People*, written more than a century after Gregory's death. But none of this was even on the horizon in 597, and Gregory was in any case not a man to fret unduly about uniformity in ecclesiastical customs. He told his friend Leander of Seville, who had enquired about the correct method of baptising, that 'where there is one faith, a diversity of usage does no harm to the Church'.[17] When Augustine, who did worry about such things, asked him whether he should use Roman or Gallican customs in the Mass in England , Gregory urged him to adopt whatever customs seemed likely to be helpful to the infant church in England, regardless of their source: 'My brother, you know the customs of the Roman Church in which, of course, you were brought up. But . . . things are not to be loved for the sake of a place, but places are to be loved for the sake of their good things.'[18]

In all probability we must attribute the English mission simply to Gregory's desire for 'an increase of the faithful'. He sought the spread of Catholic Christianity to the barbarian kingdoms of Britain as he had seen it spread in his own lifetime among the barbarians of Spain and Gaul, and as he hoped to see it spread among the Lombards. Whatever Gregory's motives, however, the Roman mission to England was to have an impact far beyond the bounds of Britain. The English church came to venerate the memory of Gregory as its founding father. The first biography of Gregory was composed not in Rome but in England, and his great treatise *On the Pastoral Office* and his letters were treasured there as precious sources of inspiration and guidance. A stream of Anglo-Saxon churchmen and kings made their way to Rome, to 'the localities sanctified by the bodies of the Apostles and martyrs'. They brought back with them a strengthened reverence for Roman ways, and for the Roman Bishop.

That reverence extended to all things Roman – building-styles, liturgy, even the tones to which the psalms were chanted in the Roman basilicas. But it focused itself on the person of the Pope, the inheritor, as even Columbanus had acknowledged, of the keys of Peter. Gregory was accustomed to send to select bishops and royalty, as marks of great favour, tiny reliquaries made in the form of a key, and containing a few filings from the chains of St Peter. These keys, which some of Gregory's successors also bestowed, were a potent symbol of the Pope's power to bind and loose. The imaginative power of the symbol was revealed at the Synod of Whitby in 664. King Oswiu, having heard the arguments for and against the Roman and Irish dating of Easter, ruled, with a smile, in favour of the Roman practice, because the keys of the kingdom had been given to St Peter, not to Irish leaders like St Columba of Iona. So, he declared, 'since he is the door-keeper, I will not contradict him; but I intend to obey his commandments in everything to the best of my ability, otherwise when I come to the gates of the kingdom, there may be no one to open them, because he who holds the keys has turned his back on me'.[19]

In the two centuries after the death of Gregory, English clergy – Willibrord, Boniface, Alcuin – would play a crucial role in the conversion and settling of Christianity in northern Europe. They would take with them the love and reverence for Roman books, Roman custom and the Roman Bishop which Gregory's English initiative had planted. For the newly Christian people of the barbarian north, the authority of the papacy would be understood, not as the contested precedence of the senior Patriarch in the ancient seat of

Empire, but as the charism of the key-bearer. Rome was the place where Peter had been buried, where he still dwelt, and where he spoke through the living voice of his successor. There was to be found the pattern of authentic Christian teaching and Christian worship, and the source of apostolic blessing and forgiveness. In turning north to the English, Gregory had unwittingly initiated a new phase in the development of the papacy.

III   THE BYZANTINE CAPTIVITY OF THE PAPACY

Gregory was unquestionably the greatest Pope of late antiquity and the early Middle Ages, and arguably the greatest Pope ever. His memory was venerated, as we have seen, in the Anglo-Saxon world and the churches with whom the Anglo-Saxons had contact, as 'the teacher of the English,' 'our Gregory.' A tenth-century Irish life of the Pope even claimed him as a Kerry-man, who had taught most of the Irish saints and who was finally buried on Aran.

In Rome itself, however, there were many who wished to forget or even to repudiate his legacy. His biography in the official papal chronicle, the *Liber Pontificalis*, is sketchy to the point of insult, and there are other signs of dissatisfaction with the direction in which he had taken the Roman Church. Gregory was the first monk to become pope. Determined to transform the Church by a spirit of monastic zeal and humility, he had chosen monks to fill key offices and lead key enterprises, like the mission to England. On his death, the Roman clergy's outraged *esprit de corps* and concern for career structure reasserted itself. Gregory's successor, Sabinian (604–6) was commended in the *Liber Pontificalis* for 'filling the Church with clergy', meaning that he had promoted city clergy in preference to monks. Sabinian's epitaph praises him for having worked his way up the ladder of promotion, an implied criticism of Gregory's rapid rise in a time of crisis. It would be seventy years before another monk was made pope, and successive papal elections swung back and forth between pro- and anti-Gregorian candidates.

These divisions in the Roman Church were highlighted by the rapid turnover of popes in the first half of the seventh century: there were ten elections between Gregory's death in 604 and Martin I's accession in 649. Recurrent elections had the effect of drawing attention to another striking feature of the period, the subordination of the papacy to the emperors at Constantinople. Many popes had already served as papal apocrisiary in Constantinople. Since the reconquest, it had been mandatory for the Pope-elect to seek confirmation of his appointment from the Emperor before he could be consecrated. The result was long and burdensome delay. Pope Sabinian had to wait six months for the imperial mandate, Boniface III (607) almost a year, Boniface IV (608–15) ten months, Boniface V (619–25) thirteen months. Some of these delays were due to the difficulties of travel and the elaborate bureaucracy of Constantinople, others to the preoccupations of the emperors with the growing crisis in the East.

For in the years immediately after Gregory's death, the empire was hemmed in by terrifying enemies. From north of the Danube, Slav hordes, above all the Avars, swept through the Balkans, driving the Greek-speaking population before them to the fringes of the Aegean and the Adriatic. At the same time, the Persian King Chosroes II was hacking out a Zoroastrian empire at the expense of Constantinople. In 613 Antioch was taken by Persian armies, in 614 Damascus and then Jerusalem. The Christian world watched in horrified disbelief as a pagan army destroyed the Holy Places and carried off the relic of the True Cross. By 619 all the Holy Land was under Persian control, and Constantinople itself was under siege in 626. The very survival of the Roman way of life seemed threatened.

With the help of massive gifts of silver and gold plate from the Eastern churches, the Avars were bought off, and the Byzantine armies rallied. The Persians were decisively defeated in 627, Chosroes murdered, and the True Cross recovered. It was a breathing-space, however, not an end. Eight hundred miles to the south of Constantinople, in the cities of Medina and Mecca, a new force was rising. It was the creation of a former merchant and camel-driver who in the 620s had become a visionary. His revelations, written in verse in the form of *Qur'an*, 'recitations', became the basis for a great new religious movement, Islam, which swept the Arab world. The Prophet Mohammed died in 632: by 637 Arab armies, fired by his vision of a world under the judgement of the one undivided God, had captured Antioch. By 642 Alexandria had fallen, by 698 Carthage. One by one, the ancient cradles of Christianity were wiped out, and the Mediterranean ceased to be a Christian lake.

Out of this continuing crisis in the East arose a closer identification

than ever between Church and empire. The battles of the emperors
were seen as holy wars, their victories the finger of God himself. In
highly charged ceremonies in 626 and 627 the Emperor Herakleios
processed with icons of Christ and the Virgin round the walls of Constantinople, and was blessed by the Patriarch Sergios with the recovered
relic of the True Cross. In such rituals, the distance between Church
and State disappeared, and the Emperor seemed as much priest as
prince.

As priest-emperor, Herakleios had to address the question of the religious disunity of his empire. The ambivalence of Christian attitudes to
the faith set out by Chalcedon persisted, and divided Christendom
when it had never more desperately needed to speak and act from a single heart and mind. Imperial support for the monophysite denial of the
two natures of Christ had proved a disastrous cul-de-sac, creating more
division than it resolved, driving wedges not only between East and
West, but within the churches of the East. Any solution to the problem
of the identity of the Saviour, it was clear, must start from acceptance –
or at any rate non-denial – of the teaching of Chalcedon.

Herakleios' Patriarch Sergios came up with just such a solution. He
suggested that the difficulties felt by many in confessing that Christ
possessed two natures, divine and human, would be eased if it could be
agreed that these two natures were united by a single energy. This
'monoenergist' theory was eventually refined to the notion that Christ
had indeed two natures, but only one will. This divine will, shared by
all the Persons of the Trinity, had dictated Jesus' human actions. This
theory had wide appeal, not least because Sergios suggested that it
offered an escape from the 'war of words' about Chalcedon which
threatened to tear the Christian empire apart. He urged that from now
on all discussion of Christ's natures should be banned. It was a suggestion that seemed to offer peace, and men of all parties rallied to his
solution.

They included the Pope, Honorius I (625–38). A gifted and energetic pro-Gregorian who took an active interest in the English mission, Honorius was also anxious to promote unity within the empire.
He was a loyal supporter of the Byzantine Exarch in Italy, and followed Gregory in managing the resources of the Church's patrimony for secular as well as strictly religious purposes, repairing aqueducts, paying for supplies of corn for the people, and helping fund
the imperial army in Italy. He was a vigorous church-builder and

restorer, and in an eloquent pro-imperial gesture he consecrated a church in Rome in honour of St Appolinarius, the patron saint of the exarchate at Ravenna.

Honorius was delighted by the apparent success of Sergios' attempts to secure unity among Christians, and immensely relieved that Eastern attacks on Chalcedon would now be banned. In his enthusiasm he wrote two letters to the East approving and elaborating the 'one energy' formula of Sergios, and speaking of Christ as having only one will. In 638, encouraged in part by Honorius' positive response, the Emperor issued a decree known as the 'Ekthesis', imposing 'monothelite' (one-will) teaching as the official doctrine of the empire.

The initial warm welcome for monothelitism, however, soon cooled down. It was rapidly realised by supporters of Chalcedon that the one-will doctrine, while appearing to preserve the Council's teaching on the unity of the divine and human in Christ, in fact subverted his human nature. What sort of human being could Christ be if he lacked a human will, and therefore could not make truly human decisions, take truly human risks? How could human beings be enabled to practise virtue, how could they be purified from a crooked and sinful will, if the Saviour who was their medicine and their model himself lacked a human will?

Anti-monothelite feeling rapidly took hold in Rome and the West generally, and it became clear that Honorius had compromised the doctrinal purity of the papacy. That conviction set Rome and Constantinople once more at odds. Honorius' successor, Pope Severinus (640), was elected in the autumn of 638, but he refused to accept the Ekthesis, and for twenty months the Emperor witheld the mandate necessary for his consecration. Roman opposition to imperial religious policy was maintained through the 640s, especially under the Greek Pope Theodore (642–9), who excommunicated and (in theory at any rate) deposed two patriarchs of Constantinople for supporting the Ekthesis. In retaliation, imperial troops looted the papal treasury in the Lateran, the papal Apocrisiary at the imperial court was arrested and exiled, and the altar of the papal residence in Constantinople was desecrated.

Theodore died in May 649. He was succeeded by a former apocrisiary in Constantinople, Martin I (649–53). Martin at once demonstrated his courage and his commitment to Theodore's policies by refusing to apply for the imperial mandate confirming his appointment as pope: he was consecrated without it two days after his election. Preparations had begun under Theodore for a synod at the Lateran to condemn monothelitism, and Martin went ahead with it. The Lateran synod was attended by 105 Western bishops, and by a crowd of Easterners resident in Rome, mostly monks, many of them refugees from monothelite persecution. One of the largest and, thanks to the Eastern presence, one of the most theologically sophisticated councils ever held in the West, it was a deliberate and formidable repudiation of the Emperor's religious authority. Pope Martin took steps to publicise the Synod's proceedings throughout the West, and to secure subscription to them by important absentees, like the Archbishop of Milan.

Not surprisingly, all this was intolerable to the court at Constantinople. The Exarch of Italy, Olympius, was ordered to persuade the bishops of the West to support the imperial moratorium on discussion of the question of the two wills. Failing that, he was to assassinate the Pope. Olympius was able to achieve neither part of his commission, and ultimately himself led an unsuccessful revolt against the empire. In June 653 his replacement, Theodore Kalliopis, succeeded in arresting the Pope in the Lateran basilica, where Martin had had his bed placed for sanctuary in front of the altar. Chronically ill and savagely maltreated by his gaolers (at one stage, while suffering from dysentery, he was held for forty-seven days without being allowed to wash), Martin was taken to Constantinople. There he was jostled by a hostile crowd, and charged with supporting Olympius' rebellion and even of corresponding with the forces of Islam. The real reason for Martin's arrest, his defiance of the Emperor over the monothelite question, was kept out of the show-trial proceedings, since the regime wanted to avoid raising dangerous issues of theological orthodoxy. With the whole weight of the empire against him, only one verdict was possible, and the Pope was duly found guilty of treason. He was stripped of his vestments, dragged in shackles through the streets and publicly flogged. Separated from the small band of clergy who had travelled with him from Rome, he was deported to the Crimea where he died in September 655 from the hardships he had endured.

Nevertheless, the imperial idea remained strong in the West. One of the worst elements in Martin's suffering was the knowledge that while he still lived the Roman Church had bowed to imperial commands, and had elected a new pope. Loyalty to the empire had been strained to the uttermost, however, and the relationship would never again be innocent or easy. Martin's successor, Eugenius I (654–7), was a saintly nonentity chosen for his readiness to please Constantinople. Despite that, he was shouted down and threatened by his Roman congregation when he tried to accept an ambiguous declaration of faith by the Patriarch of Constantinople on the monothelite question. Pope Martin's sufferings had not been entirely in vain, and Rome stood firm to the teaching of Chalcedon.

This underlying doctrinal hawkishness was softened by anxious deference to the Emperor's office. In 663 the Emperor Constans II himself spent twelve days in Rome. He was received with rapture, Pope Vitalian (657–72) tactfully saying nothing about Constans' brutal treatment of Pope Martin or the Emperor's continuing tacit support for monothelitism. Constans' visit was the occasion for an orgy of papal ceremonial, in which the Emperor and his soldiers were heaped with honours, and brought gifts in a candlelit procession to the tomb of Peter. The chanting in the Roman basilicas must have been drowned out, however, by the deafening clatter of Constans' workmen, who were busy stripping the bronze tiles and fittings from the great imperial monuments of the city, to be melted down or reused in Constantinople. This dismantling would hasten the decay of many of the noblest buildings in the city. Constans took Rome's imperial glory with him when he sailed away. Unsurprisingly, the *Liber Pontificalis* summarised his reign as one of oppression and disaster for the West: 'He imposed such afflictions on the people . . . by tributes, poll-taxes and ship-money, as had never before been seen . . . [He] also took away all the sacred vessels and equipment of God's holy churches, leaving nothing behind.' The papal chronicler's satisfaction in recording the Emperor's murder in his bath in 668 is undisguised.[20]

Constans' successor, Constantine IV, slowly came to recognise the futility of all this. Support for monothelitism had alienated the West, and it had not pacified the East. He decided therefore to reverse the religious policy of the last fifty years, and to abandon monothelitism. In 680 he summoned the Sixth General Council, which opened at Constantinople in November. Pope Agatho (678–81) was represented by a party of Greek clergy chosen from the many now resident in Rome. The Council was a complete victory for the Chalcedonian doctrine of two natures, and therefore for the papacy, though the victory was tempered from Rome's point of view by the Council's solemn condemnation of Pope Honorius among the other founding fathers of monothelitism. Rome prided itself on an unbroken record of fidelity to the truth, and papal claims gained credibility from the fact that Rome, unlike the great primatial sees of the East, had never fallen into error. Its orthodoxy was arguably partly due to sheer lack of imagination. Roman theologians were conservative, and had none of the sophistication and subtlety of their Greek counterparts, and so they were less vulnerable to the seductions of new ideas. Yet whether dullness or apostolic fidelity lay at its roots, Rome's proud tradition of dogged adherence to the ancient faith was acknowledged even in the East: a heretic pope was therefore a bitter pill to swallow. Honorius' condemnation was a price worth paying for the acceptance of Roman teaching in general, however, and the Council in its final address compensated by paying explicit tribute to Rome's age-old fidelity to the apostolic preaching.

Over the next ten years the benefits of reconciliation with the empire became apparent. The claims of the church of Ravenna to independent status, which had been endorsed by Constans, were now abandoned, the archbishops agreeing to submit to consecration by the Pope. The requirement that the popes should wait for confirmation of their appointment from Constantinople before they could be consecrated was waived, the Exarch at Ravenna being empowered to issue the necessary mandate. The crippling burden of imperial taxation on Church lands was eased.

But this accord was fragile, and the benefits of Byzantine rule were often less in evidence than its drawbacks. In 692 the Emperor Justinian II summoned a council to complete the disciplinary work of the Fifth and Sixth General Councils. This new Council, oddly known as the 'Quinisext' or 'Fifth–Sixth' Council, was an exclusively Eastern affair, and the 102 canons or regulations it eventually authorised contained a series of measures based on Eastern practice but absolutely unacceptable in the West. The Eastern Church, for example, permitted priests and deacons a normal married life, while the Western Church had long insisted on celibacy. The Eastern Church did not permit fasting on Saturdays, the Western Church required it. The Quinisext Canons also outlawed a number of devotional and iconographical conventions popular in the West, such as the symbolic representation of Christ as a Lamb. Finally, the Council re-enacted the 28th Canon of Chalcedon, giving the Patriarch of Constantinople equal privileges with Rome, and precedence over all the other patriarchs immediately after Rome.

All these measures were calculated to offend Westerners, and Constantine's successor, Justinian II, rubbed the Pope's nose in it by sending him the Canons, demanding his signature. Pope Sergius (687–701) refused, would not permit the Canons to be read or circulated, and instituted a number of pointed devotional gestures designed to underline the Roman Church's absolute rejection of the Council. He ordered the singing of the 'Agnus Dei' at the breaking of the bread at Mass. This was a series of petitions addressed to Christ as the Lamb of God, and he renovated mosaics at St Peter's and in the apse of the church of St Cosmas and Damian near the Forum, in which Christ was portrayed in the forbidden form of a Lamb.

This was war, and the Emperor retaliated by attempting a rerun of the affair of Pope Martin. The Pope's chief advisers were rounded up and deported to Constantinople, and Zacharias, captain of the imperial guard, was sent to Rome to arrest the Pope himself. It was a bad mistake, revealing the Emperor's failure to grasp the growing resentment of his authority in Italy. Italian-born troops from the imperial forces at Ravenna and the Duchy of the Pentapolis (the five cities of Ancona, Senigallia, Fano, Pesaro and Rimini) were brought to Rome to arrest the Pope: instead, they mutinied in his defence. Zacharias was forced to take refuge in the Lateran, and ended up actually hiding under the Pope's bed, while Sergius showed himself unharmed to the troops and the Roman crowds to calm their anger. Zacharias ignominiously fled the city, and soon afterwards Justinian was deposed in a palace coup. 'Thus, by Christ's favour' commented the papal chronicler, 'was God's Church with its prelate preserved undisturbed.'[21]

The truth was that Byzantine rule in Italy was now virtually confined to Sicily and the south. The emperors were increasingly pinned down by the Islamic threat on their eastern borders, and Italy mattered to them only as a fiscal milch-cow. The popes still thought of Constantinople as the source of legitimate authority in Italy, and each new pope dutifully requested – and paid handsomely for – the imperial mandate for their consecration. In practical terms, however, they were independent rulers, thrown back on their own resources in maintaining their place within the peninsula. From the early eighth century onwards, that place was increasingly precarious. The Lombard King Liutprand was determined to unite his realm by gaining control of the independent Lombard duchies of Spoleto and Benevento, which flanked Rome to north and south. This expansion threatened both imperial and papal interests, and the popes struggled to reconcile their loyalty to Constantinople with the brute realities of Italian politics. Resentment was focused on the growing burden of imperial taxation, for which Italy received in return no imperial protection. Pope Gregory II (715–31), as custodian of the Church's patrimony, was the largest contributor to the imperial revenue from Italy. He put himself at the head of this economic protest, forbidding payment of the unfair tax demands . The Lombards were now Catholics, and, though often effectively at war with them, the popes were able to exert a moral influence over them which could transcend politics. In 729 Lieutprand, acting in temporary alliance with an anti-papal exarch, besieged Rome: Pope Gregory II confronted the King and 'brought him to such remorse' that Lieutprand left his armour and weapons as offerings at the tomb of the Apostle, and abandoned the siege. Yet, despite a virtual breakdown in relations between papacy and empire, the popes were prepared to mobilise the prestige of Peter to buy Constantinople respite from its enemies. In 729 Gregory II helped the Exarch crush the rebellion of the pretender Tiberius Petasius, and in 743 and again in 749 Pope Zacharias negotiated Lombard withdrawals from imperial territory, and thereby saved the exarchate in Ravenna.

In 726, however, the Emperor Leo III set in motion a series of events which would snap the thin thread still connecting empire and papacy. For generations the Christian consciousness of the East had been increasingly concentrated on icons, painted images of Christ and the saints. Icons were held to mediate the abiding power and protection of the holy to the Christian community, in much the way that the relics of the saints, or the sacramental elements of bread and wine, had long been held to do. In the first year of his reign, during the Arab siege of Constantinople in 717, Leo himself had ordered the greatest miracle-working icon in Constantinople, the image of the Virgin *Hodegetria* (the Virgin 'showing the way'), to be paraded round the city walls, to comfort and reassure the people.

They needed all the comfort they could get, as the empire shrank under the Muslim advance. Theologians and preachers began to wonder aloud whether God was angry with his people, whether at the heart of the empire there lay some great sin, for which all were being punished. In 726 this speculation was given symbolic focus by a terrifying volcanic eruption: black ash settled like an omen all over the Aegean, and the Emperor acted. God was angry, he declared, because of the sin of idolatry. The Old Testament forbade the worship of images, yet the churches were full of them. He commanded the destruction of all images of Christ and his mother, and their replacement by the unadorned symbol of the cross, the sign in which Constantine, the founder of the Christian empire, had conquered.

Leo's edict was the product of profound social panic, several generations of theological reflection by bishops and theologians, and the cumulative impact of controversy about the person and natures of Christ. Whatever its causes however, the Emperor's attack on images, and the resulting wave of image-breaking or 'iconoclasm', fell like a thunderbolt in the West. The Exarch, who tried to enforce it in Ravenna, was lynched by an angry mob, and Pope Gregory II saw in it yet another example of the empire espousing heresy. Indignantly, he rejected Leo's decree, and warned him that as a layman he had no right to interfere in theological matters. The Emperor ordered the new Exarch to depose the Pope, provoking a series of uprisings which expressed Italian resentment of imperial rule: as the *Liber Pontificalis* commented, 'Romans and Lombards bound themselves together in the tie of faith, all of them willing to undergo a glorious death in the pontiff's defence.'[22]

Gregory did what he could to prevent this feeling escalating into revolution, urging loyalty to the imperial ideal, but the Iconoclastic crisis deepened under his successor Gregory III (731-41). The Emperor refused all papal offers of reconciliation, and so Gregory organised a synod in Rome in 731 which denounced Iconoclasm and excommunicated anyone perpetrating it. Significantly, the Archbishop of Ravenna took part in the Synod, a mark of the extent to which the Emperor's Iconoclasm had alienated even his supporters in Italy. Nevertheless, the Pope did the empire sterling service in 733 by negotiating the return of the exarchate of Ravenna from the Lombards. In gratitude, the Exarch donated six twisted columns of onyx to the shrine of St Peter. The gift was perhaps intended as an olive branch, but if so it did not disarm papal hostility to imperial religious policy. Pointedly, Gregory used the Exarch's columns to support a series of elaborate new images of Christ and the saints.

Gregory III's intervention to rescue the exarchate was all the more remarkable in that it coincided with a devastating imperial attack on the papacy. Realising that he had little chance of bringing Rome to heel behind his Iconoclast policies, Leo struck at both its spiritual jurisdiction and its material base. Some time in 732 or 733 he confiscated all the papal patrimonies in southern Italy and in Sicily, the main source of the Pope's income. He went on to remove from papal jurisdiction the bishoprics of Thessalonica, Corinth, Syracuse, Reggio, Nicopolis, Athens and Patras, in other words all the Greek-speaking provinces of Illyrica, Sicily and southern Italy. From now on, these would all be subject to the Patriarch of Constantinople. To hold the remains of the empire together, Constantinople was strengthening its grip on everything south of Naples, and ditching the rest. The exarchate at Ravenna would stagger on till its final destruction by the Lombards in 751, and the popes continued for a time to hanker after the old links with Constantinople. But Leo's actions had deeply embittered papal Rome. No pope had ever addressed an emperor in tones as defiant as those used by Gregory II during the height of the Iconoclastic disputes, and no pope had ever shown so clear a sense of the real source of the papacy's strength:

> The whole West has its eyes on us, unworthy though we are. It relies on us and on St Peter, the Prince of the Apostles, whose image you wish to destroy, but whom the kingdoms of the West honour as if he were God himself on earth . . . We are going to the most distant parts of the West to seek those who desire baptism. Although we have sent bishops and clergy of our holy church to them, their princes have not yet received baptism, for they wish to receive it from ourselves alone . . .
>
> You have no right to issue dogmatic constitutions, you have not the right mind for dogmas; your mind is too coarse and martial.[23]

Pope Gregory's contrast between the faithful West and the heretic East was laden with significance for the future of the papacy, and its final turn from East to West. It was to be less a matter of choice, however, than a recognition of realities: with Leo's confiscation of Sicily and the south, the papacy to all intents and purposes had been cast out of the empire.

It is one of the ironies of history that this long slow divorce between the Greek empire and the papacy should have taken place largely under Greek-speaking popes. Of the thirteen popes elected between 687 and 752, only two, Benedict II (684–5) and Gregory II, were native Romans, or even Latins. All the rest were Greek-speakers, from Greece, Syria or Byzantine Sicily. This extraordinary development, which could be said to have begun with the election of Pope Theodore in 642, reflected a profound transformation of the Roman clergy. Gregory the Great and Pope Honorius were the last representatives of a once-common papal type, of which Pope Vigilius was a less salubrious example – aristocratic bishops drawn from the Roman senatorial families. The calamities of the Gothic war and the imperial reconquest had put an end to that type, as the great families faded out or emigrated east. At the same time, Rome began to fill up with Greek-speaking clergy. Some came as a direct consequence of the restoration of imperial rule, in the wake of the Byzantine garrisons in Rome. Round the imperial quarter on the Palatine there sprang up a ring of churches staffed by Eastern clergy and dedicated to Eastern saints, most of them with military associations – Sts Cosmas and Damian, Sts Sergius and Bacchus, St Hadrian, Sts Quiricius and Giulitta, Sts Cyrus and John. To these camp-followers of empire were added wave after wave of the victims of empire, refugees from the monophysite, monothelite and eventually the Iconoclastic persecutions. And, thirdly, there came the refugees from Islam, as the ancient heartlands of Christianity – and of monasticism – went down before the Arab tide.

At precisely the moment when the supply of educated Latin clergy from which the popes were traditionally recruited was drying up, therefore, a flood of Greek clergy and monks arrived in Rome. By the end of the seventh century these Greek-speakers dominated the clerical culture of Rome, providing its theological brains, its administrative talent, and much of its visual, musical and liturgical culture. Greek monks were brought into the burgeoning relief work of the Roman Church, as small monastic communities were placed in charge of the ancient *diaconia*, distribution-points along the Tiber for corn and other doles to the poor. These centres were part of an emerging Byzantine quarter of the city, and the Greek churches of San Giorgio in Vellabro and Santa Maria in Cosmedin, at the foot of the Aventine, were formed out of such relief centres.

The impact of all this on papal Rome was far-reaching, sometimes daunting. In the reign of Pope John VI (701–5) the English Bishop

Wilfrid arrived in Rome. He came to appeal against the reorganisation of the church in England recently introduced by Theodore, the
gifted and energetic Greek Archbishop of Canterbury. Wilfrid's party
were honourably received, but were disconcerted to find the whole
papal entourage laughing and whispering among themselves, in
Greek. The entire papal delegation to the Sixth General Council in
680 was made up of Greeks. Even the native traditions of Roman
religious art were now transformed by Eastern influence, the monu-
mental realism of the Roman style, represented in the apse of Sts
Cosmas and Damian, being replaced by the delicate formalism of the
paintings in Santa Maria Antiqua, or the Byzantine-style icon of the
Virgin now in the church of Santa Francesca Romana. The worship
of the Roman Church itself was being transformed by Eastern influence. Round the person of the Pope there was growing up an
increasingly formal ceremonial, modelled on Byzantine court ritual,
which served to emphasise the sacredness of the person of the successor of St Peter. The austere, businesslike ceremonial of the Roman
rite was enriched and elaborated by feast-days, music and ritual
observances borrowed from Syria, Jerusalem and Constantinople.

None of this implied any watering down of the distinctive identity of the Roman Church. Pope Sergius I played a key role in introducing oriental observances into the Roman liturgy, like the Syrian
custom of singing the 'Agnus Dei', or the elaborate processions, with
Greek chant, which he introduced for the four major Eastern feasts
of the Virgin. Yet Sergius passionately resisted the Canons of the
Quinisext Council, which would have imposed alien Eastern customs on the Roman Church, and it was he who solemnly transferred
the relics of St Leo the Great, the great patron and formulator of the
papacy's Petrine and Roman claims, into a conspicuous new shrine
in St Peter's. Indeed, the Eastern popes, with their more learned and
sophisticated theological interests, brought a new, doctrinal edge to
the Petrine claims of the papacy, an emphasis which their confrontations with heretical emperors had sharpened and fixed.

Rome under the Greek popes, therefore, was a melting-pot. In it
many of the traditions of East and West were flowing together, to
create a vibrant and solemn religious culture which fascinated and
dazzled the newly Christianised peoples of Europe. A party of Irish
monks in Rome to discuss the Easter question met in their hostel
fellow pilgrims from Egypt, Palestine, the Greek East and southern

Russia. Kings, bishops, monks and the ordinary faithful travelled to Rome to beg the grace of the Apostle, to be near the relics with which Rome was full and which the Greek popes had gorgeously enshrined for their devotion. Whole quarters of the city were given over to them, like the Saxon Borgo near St Peter's, where the English in Rome were based.

Some, like the West Saxon King Caedwalla, came to be baptised and so 'spend their days ... that they might be more easily received into heaven', some, like Bede's Abbot Ceolfrid, to be buried, some, like Duke Theodo of Bavaria, simply to offer prayers. Others, like Boniface, the great English missionary to Frisia, came in quest of the prestige and backing they needed for a mission which would involve confrontation with the mighty of the earth, the captains and the kings. The Englishman Benedict Biscop, who made five visits between 653 and 680, came to Rome to find patterns of apostolic life. To his monasteries at Jarrow and Wearmouth, significantly named after Peter and Paul, Biscop took back Roman paintings, Roman books, even the arch-chanter of St Peter's to teach his monks the Roman tones for the office.

But none of these men sought a slavish replication of Roman ways, for Roman ways themselves were varied, caught in a rapid process of change. In imitation of Rome the English church quickly began to celebrate the four Eastern feasts of Mary, yet these had only recently been naturalised in Rome. The Gospel-book used at Mass in Bede's church at Jarrow was copied from an original brought back by Benedict Biscop, but the cycle of Gospel passages for the year which it contained followed the order of the church of Naples, rather than that of Rome. Biscop could have got his gospel book from Hadrian of Africa, who had been abbot of a Neapolitan monastery, and who travelled with Biscop and Theodore of Tarsus, the Greek appointed Archbishop of Canterbury by Pope Vitalian (657–72). But he might just as easily have got it from one of the monastic houses on the Aventine, filled as they were with monks from the south. Rome was not a rigid set of prescriptions, it was a loyalty, a dynamism centred on the presence of the Apostle, and the person of the Pope who sat in the Apostle's chair.

IV   EMPIRES OF THE WEST

The collapse of imperial power in Italy freed the popes from the oppressive attentions of Constantinople: it left them, however, exposed to enemies closer at hand. As Liutprand's push to extend and consolidate his kingdom crept ever closer to Rome, it became clear that the military resources of the former duchy, now in alliance with the popes, would not be enough to hold back the Lombard advance. In 739 King Liutprand laid siege to Rome itself, as he had done ten years earlier. Then, however, the remorseful King had left his armour as a votive offering to St Peter; this time, his soldiers looted the basilica and took away its ornaments, even its lights.

Gregory III looked north for help, to Merovingian Gaul, where Charles Martel had emerged as a Christian champion. Arab armies had overrun Visigothic Spain in 711, and had then pushed on into southern Gaul. In 732 Martel's troops defeated a Muslim raiding party in Poitiers; in retrospect, this defeat would come to seem the crucial halting-point of the hitherto unstoppable Islamic advance into Europe. Here, then, was a champion capable of rescuing the people of St Peter: the Pope sent emissaries to Charles' court. They took with them the keys of the shrine of St Peter, and a letter from the Pope designed to play on that northern reverence for the key-bearer which King Oswiu had exemplified so clearly at Whitby. 'Do not despise my appeal,' wrote the Pope, 'that the Prince of the Apostles may not shut the kingdom of heaven against you.'[24]

For the time being, his appeal fell on deaf ears, but the papacy did not give up on Charles or his successors, and under Pope Zacharias (741–52) the opportunity for closer ties presented themselves. Charles and his son Pepin were not monarchs in their own right, but mayors of the Palace to the Merovingian kings. This arrangement had long been a legal fiction, for the mayors in fact ruled, and the kings were feeble ciphers. In 750 Pepin sent a chaplain to the Pope with a theological question. Should not he who held the reality of royal power also hold the title? Pope Zachary agreed that he should, and, armed with this legitimation, Pepin was duly elected king by the nobility, and anointed and crowned in 751. The ceremony was performed by Boniface, the English missionary who had taken a special vow of loyalty to the Pope at his consecration as bishop in Rome by Gregory II.

It was a fateful moment, for in the same year the exarchate of Ravenna finally fell, and, having disposed of the Italian headquarters of the empire, the Lombards set about a mopping-up operation of other Byzantine towns in northern and central Italy. Within a year King Aistulf had laid siege to Rome, asserted his sovereignty over the duchy, and imposed an annual tribute on the people. Pope Zachary died before Aistulf's siege. He was the last of the Greek popes, and the last with any real loyalty to Constantinople. Over and above his political loyalty to Constantinople his real desire to keep open contacts between East and West is symbolised by the fact that he translated Gregory the Great's Dialogues into Greek. In his place the people elected a Roman aristocrat, Stephen II (752–7), an indication that what the times demanded was an expert local politician: for the next century, all but two of the popes would share this same aristocratic social background.

Stephen was immediately plunged into Rome's crisis, leading penitential processions through the city in which he shouldered a miraculous icon of the Virgin. As that action suggests, Rome remained very much at odds with the iconoclast emperors, but emperor Constantine V clearly felt the papacy remained a card in the imperial hand, and ordered the Pope to help secure the return of the exarchate. Stephen, remarkably, did travel to Pavia to see the King, but Aistulf forbade him to make any representations on behalf of the empire, and Stephen in any case had more pressing concerns than trying to salvage something for Constantinople from the wreckage of Italy. Instead of returning to Rome, he pressed on into Gaul, to seek the help of Pepin. On 6 January 754, the Feast of the Epiphany, Pope and King met at Ponthion.

It was the first of a series of symbolic encounters which went on into the summer of 754. These meetings helped shape the future of the papacy, and of Europe itself. Stephen's first objective was straightforward, to secure the help of the most powerful neighbour of the Lombards in restraining Aistulf's threat to the patrimony of Peter, and the populations under papal protection in central Italy. Pepin accepted the role of defender now offered him. In what would come to be called the 'Donation of Pepin', made at Quierzy, he undertook to recover and return to St Peter the duchy of Rome, the exarchate of Ravenna and the other cities and lands captured by the Lombards. In addition to this promise, which was what Stephen had crossed the

Alps to get, Pope and King outdid each other in a series of gestures which would prove almost as important for the future as the territorial guarantees. At their first meeting Pepin performed an act of ostentatious humility by walking alongside the mounted Pope, leading Stephen's horse like a groom. For his part, the Pope endorsed the legitimacy of Pepin's line by solemnly anointing the King, the Queen and Pepin's sons, giving the King and princes the title 'patrician of the Romans', and binding the Franks by a solemn vow never to recognise any other royal family.

Pepin rapidly fulfilled his undertaking, marching into Italy and defeating the Lombard armies in 754 and again, more decisively, in 756. The exarchate of Ravenna, the province of Emilia and the duchies of the Pentapolis and of Rome, freed of Lombard domination, were handed over to the Pope. The Emperor at Constantinople protested at once, demanding the return of these lands to him, since they properly belonged to the empire. Pepin replied that he had intervened in Italy not for the sake of the empire but for love of St Peter and for the forgiveness of his sins: the lands he had captured would belong to Peter. As a token, the keys of the cities and a document recording Pepin's donation were deposited on the grave of St Peter. A papal state had been created: it would endure, in much the form that Pepin gave it, for more than a thousand years.

This unprecedented situation was full of unresolved questions, the main one being that already raised by the protests from Constantinople: by what right, other than brute force, had Pepin given the recovered Italian territories to the Pope? It was perhaps to answer that question that there emerged at about this time an extraordinary forgery, known as the *Donation of Constantine*. This document purported to be a solemn legal enactment by the first Christian Emperor. In it, Constantine recounts the legend (accepted as historical fact in the eighth century) of his healing from leprosy during his baptism by Pope Sylvester I. In gratitude for this miracle, and in recognition of Sylvester's inheritance of the power of Peter to bind and loose, Constantine sets the Pope and his successors for ever above all other bishops and churches throughout the world. He gives him also 'all the prerogatives of our supreme imperial position and the glory of our authority'. Constantine tells how he had himself handed Sylvester his imperial crown, 'which we have transferred from our own head', but the Pope, in respect for his priestly tonsure, chose not to wear it.

Instead Constantine gave him a cap of honour, the *camalaucum*, and 'holding the bridle of his horse ... performed the office of groom for him'. Finally, 'to correspond to our own empire and so that the supreme pontifical authority may not be dishonoured', Constantine gave to the Pope and his successors not only the city of Rome, but 'all the provinces, districts and cities of Italy and the Western regions'.[25]

Nobody knows exactly when, where or why this document was assembled, though it is clearly closely related to Pope Stephen's dealings with Pepin. To some historians it seems likely that the *Donation* was cobbled together by someone in the Pope's entourage in preparation for his appeal to the King in 754, and that it represents a deliberate blueprint for the creation of a papal state to replace imperial authority in the West. Other historians believe the document is a later creation, composed piecemeal as much as two generations after Pepin's reign by clergy on the payroll of the Frankish royal family, and designed to justify the exercise of overlordship in Italy by Pepin and his successor Charlemagne, against the attacks of the Emperor in Constantinople.

On balance it seems more likely that the *Donation of Constantine* is the product of subsequent reflection on the events of Pope Stephen's momentous visit to the court of Pepin, than that the Pope or his advisers already had a clearly worked out papal claim to the sovereignty of Italy. Whatever its origin, however, it shows quite clearly that from 756 onwards the papacy believed that its safety in future lay not in token allegiance to the now powerless Byzantine empire, but in the creation of a territorial state within which the Pope ruled on behalf of St Peter, under the protection of Pepin's dynasty. Within this *sancti Dei Ecclesiae Respublica* – 'the republic [that is, state] of God's Holy Church' – Stephen seems to have dreamed of including all of imperial Italy and much of the Lombard kingdom. In the end he and his successors had to settle for much less – the duchy of Rome and part of southern Tuscany, and the territory of the old Ravenna exarchate, where the exercise of the Pope's sovereignty was often sabotaged by the ambitious archbishops of Ravenna.

Constantinople did not easily accept the new situation, and even formed an alliance with the Lombard King Desiderius to expel the Franks from Italy and to recapture the exarchate. The generation after Pepin's *Donation* was one of extreme anxiety for the popes. It was also a time of radical instability in Rome itself, for as soon as the papal state came into existence the ruling families of Rome plunged into murderous rivalry for control over it. Allying themselves to the Lombards, the Franks or the old empire, they jostled to have their candidates elected pope. The pontificates of Paul I (757–67) and Stephen III (768–72) saw challenges by the antipopes Constantine and Philip, and the papacy was sucked into a sordid whirlpool of internecine violence and betrayal, punctuated by blindings, torture and judicial murder.

The situation was changed dramatically by the emergence of Pepin's son Charlemagne (Charles the Great) as sole king of the Franks in December 771, and the election to the papacy in February 772 of Hadrian I (772–95). Charlemagne was to prove a colossus, whose imposition of political unity (of a sort) on much of western Europe captured the admiration and imitation of the kings and leaders of his own day, and has continued to haunt the European political imagination ever since. Hadrian was a tough-minded and devout aristocrat, renowned as a preacher and with a highly successful career in the papal administration behind him. These two strong men, at first wary but eventually admiring allies, gave substance to the association between Frankish crown and papacy which Pepin and Stephen had established. Charlemagne was a sincere son of St Peter, but he was also a man fascinated by the glamour of imperial Rome, which he was determined to recreate in his own realms. He took his role as patrician of the Romans seriously, and he was also intent on extending and strengthening Frankish influence in Italy. When the Lombard King besieged Rome in 773 and Hadrian turned to the Patrician of the Romans for help, Charlemagne decided to deal decisively with this thorn in his and Pope's flesh. He marched his army into Italy, captured the Lombard capital of Pavia, abolished the Lombard kingdom and added 'King of the Lombards' to his other titles.

He then decided to spend Easter 774 in Rome, a move which took the Pope by surprise, but which proved to be a huge success. Hadrian had Charlemagne greeted with all the honours formerly given to the Exarch: Charlemagne for his part showed a gratifying deference to the Apostle and his successor. Going to St Peter's to meet Hadrian (who had not himself come out of the city to greet him), he honoured the Apostle by kissing each of the steps up to the basilica, at the entrance to which the Pope was waiting. King and Pope took to each other, and five days into the visit Hadrian asked Charlemagne to reconfirm the Donation of Pepin. Charlemagne solemnly made over to him territories amounting to two-thirds of the peninsula, and deposited the document with his own hands on the tomb of Peter.

This was a blank cheque, issued at a point where Charlemagne's own ambitions in Italy had not yet clarified themselves. The Donation of Charlemagne represented what Hadrian hoped for, not what he or his successors were actually to achieve. Nevertheless, it was an auspicious beginning to a long friendship, and it became clear that each had a good deal to offer the other. Charlemagne believed that his realms would best be consolidated by imposing unity and uniformity on the churches within them: the Roman Church would provide the apostolic norms for that uniformity. Hadrian supplied Charlemagne with a model collection of canons, known as the 'Dionysio-Hadriana', to guide his Church policy, and, with some difficulty, given the liturgical diversity which prevailed in Rome, he also sent the King Roman liturgical books, to serve as models for Frankish worship.

The relationship with Charlemagne was not all roses. The King believed that his status as protector of the Roman Church gave him extensive rights of intervention – Hadrian thought of it as interference – in papal territory. In particular, Charlemagne heard legal appeals from citizens of the Ravenna exarchate, a matter which Hadrian thought infringed the rights of St Peter. Charlemagne also took a pugnaciously independent line on the question of Iconoclasm. One of the great successes of Hadrian's pontificate was his involvement in the Seventh General Council, convened by the Empress Irene at Nicaea in 787, to resolve the problem of Iconoclasm. Hadrian sent legates to this Council, together with a lengthy doctrinal treatise justifying the veneration of images. Both the legates and the papal treatise were warmly received, and the Council adopted the Pope's teaching, an echo of the triumph of Leo the Great at Chalcedon. Charlemagne, however, was alarmed by this rapprochement between Rome and Constantinople, and resentful that he had been treated as a barbarian king, not having been invited to send bishops to Nicaea. He commissioned his court theologians to produce the so-called 'Libri Carolini', a refutation both of Greek Iconoclastic teaching and of the Council's approval of the veneration of images. Pope and King found themselves badly at odds over an important matter of doctrine and worship. The Frankish opposition to the Council's approval of the use of images, however, was based on a mistranslation in the Latin text of the Conciliar decrees, which seemed to justify the unqualified adoration of images rather than, as in the Greek, their veneration. The resulting opposition between Hadrian and Charlemagne was successfully resolved at Charlemagne's Synod of Frankfurt in 794.

Hadrian's pontificate, however, involved far more than a successful collaboration with the King of the Franks. Though not a great innovator, Hadrian tackled the many problems confronting the papacy within the Patrimony of Peter itself. The most urgent of these was the need to replace the revenues lost by the imperial confiscations in Sicily, southern Italy and the Balkans. Pope Zacharias had made a start by creating a series of Church estates in the countryside around Rome. Hadrian continued this policy with vigour, extending existing holdings and creating six new *domuscultae*, as these estates were called, like the one at Caprocorum fifteen miles from Rome, the nucleus of which was land he himself had inherited from his family and to which he added by buying out the surrounding farmers. The produce from the Caprocorum estates – wheat, barley, beans, olives, wine and a hundred pigs a year – went to the Church warehouses at the Lateran, where there was a soup kitchen which fed 700 people a week. The *domuscultae* became the basis for the rebuilding of papal fortunes in the Middle Ages, and they provided the popes with more than their crops, for the tenantry were not only an easily deployed workforce, but a loyal militia in time of danger.

In addition to the building up of papal finances, Hadrian set about repairing the infrastructure and the outward face of the city itself. He rebuilt a series of crucial aqueducts, embanked the Tiber at St Peter's with 12,000 blocks of tufa, and extended the city's welfare system by creating new *diaconiae* and pilgrim hostels. Major rebuilding and repair projects were launched at many of the city's churches, including St Peter's, the Lateran, Santa Maria Maggiore, San Clemente. The huge roof-timbers needed were begged from Charlemagne's forests in the duchy of Spoleto; Frankish engineers were brought to Rome as consultants. The churches themselves were filled with lavish ornaments – silver-plated icons, embroidered coverings for the altars, veils to hang between the columns of the aisles. At St Peter's he paved the *confessio* before St Peter's tomb with plates of silver, and installed an immense chandelier of 1,365 lights. The relics of the saints, pillaged

during successive sieges, were moved in from the vulnerable subur-
ban cemeteries to the safety of newly constructed shrine niches in
churches like Santa Maria in Cosmedin, arranged in ambulatories
where the ever-increasing tide of pilgrims could venerate them.

The pontificate of Hadrian I was upbeat, assertive. But the air of
confidence was deceptive. To a great extent the apparent strength of
the papacy under Charlemagne depended on the character of the
Pope himself, and on Charlemagne's respect for him. Charlemagne's
biographer Einhard reported that he cried 'as if he had lost a brother
or a child' on hearing the news of Hadrian's death on Christmas Day
795. He had a magnificent Latin verse epitaph, composed by the
Englishman Alcuin, carved on a slab of marble and sent to Rome: it
records the King's tears for a lost father.

Hadrian's successor was another matter. Leo III (795–816) had
neither Hadrian's strength of character nor his aristocratic poise in
the presence of kings. He was a modest career cleric of Greek or perhaps even Arab ancestry, and from the outset Charlemagne took a
high line with him. The letter in which he acknowledged the news
of Leo's election set out the 'unbreakable treaty' which he desired
between himself as patrician and Leo as pope, in their joint responsibility for the 'Christian people' of Charles' realms. Its terms must
have caused some discomfort in the Lateran. 'My task,' Charlemagne
told Leo,

> assisted by the divine piety, is everywhere to defend the Church of
> Christ – abroad, by arms, against pagan incursions and the devas-
> tations of such as break faith; at home by protecting the Church in
> the spreading of the Catholic faith. Your task, Holy Father, is to
> raise your hands to God like Moses to ensure the victory of our
> arms. Helped thus by your prayers to God, ruler and giver of all,
> the Christian people may always and everywhere have the victory
> . . . and the name of Our Lord Jesus Christ resound throughout
> the world. May your prudence adhere in every respect to what is
> laid down in the canons and ever follow the rules of the holy
> fathers. Let the sanctity of your life and words be a shining exam-
> ple to all.[26]

Too much should not be made of this largely conventional compari-
son of the Pope's prayers to the raising of Moses' hands while Israel
fought the Amelikites. Nevertheless Leo doubtless noted that

Charlemagne restricted the Pope's role to saying his prayers and setting a good example by always sticking to the rules, while the King
both defended the Church from its enemies, and oversaw the spread
of the Catholic faith.

Leo, however, had more pressing problems than an overweening
king on his doorstep. Hadrian's long pontificate had ensconced a
number of his relatives and supporters in the Roman administration,
who may have resented the arrival of a parvenu pope with no pedigree. Strong factional rivalries developed in the city, and during a
procession of exorcism and blessing round the city in April 799 a
crowd led by Pope Hadrian's nephew Paschalis set upon the Pope
and tried to blind him and rip out his tongue. This was an attempt to
secure the Pope's deposition by making him unfit for office, but the
job was botched, and Leo recovered both sight and speech. He fled
to the protection of Charlemagne at Paderborn. The Patrician of the
Romans' protectorship of the Church was about to be put to the
test.

Leo's opponents also sent messengers to the King, accusing the
Pope of a whole series of crimes, including perjury and sexual mis-
conduct. Such serious charges could not be ignored, but it was by no
means clear what jurisdiction Charlemagne, or anyone else for that
matter, had over a duly elected pope. It was a long established principal that no power on earth could sit in judgement on the successor
of St Peter, and Charlemagne's advisers, including Alcuin, warned
him off any form of trial. Charles therefore sent Leo back to Rome
under honourable escort, with a Frankish commission of inquiry to
examine the charges. In December of the following year, 800, he
himself came to Rome to resolve the matter.

Charlemagne was received at Rome with imperial honours. In
marked contrast to his careful arm's-length reception by Hadrian in
774, Pope Leo came twelve miles out of the city to greet him and
escorted him to St Peter's in person. On 23 December the King
chaired a council of bishops, abbots and Frankish and Roman nobility in St Peter's, and when this assembly had disowned any intention
of judging the 'apostolic see, the head of all the churches', the Pope,
on oath, solemnly protested his innocence. Charlemagne would in
due course pass sentence of death on the Pope's opponents, commuted at Leo's request to exile. It was a victory of sorts for Leo, but
also a profound humiliation.

Two days later, on Christmas Day, Charlemagne attended Mass at St Peter's, and went with gifts to pray before the tomb. During Mass, the Pope placed a crown on his head, and the crowd, 'at the bidding of God and that of St Peter, keybearer of the kingdom of heaven' sang three times the 'Laudes' or praises reserved for an emperor: 'Charles, most pious Augustus, crowned by God, great and peace-loving Emperor, life and victory'. The Frankish accounts, but not the papal one, record that the Pope then performed the *proskynesis*, the solemn adoration customary before an emperor, kissing the ground before him. The papal chronicler adds that the Pope also anointed Charlemagne, 'his excellent son,' as king.

According to his biographer Einhard, Charlemagne later declared that his coronation as emperor had taken him by surprise, and that he would never have entered St Peter's if he had known what the Pope intended. This claim can certainly be discounted. It is inconceivable that Charlemagne stumbled unawares into the carefully choreo-graphed ceremony in St Peter's. The Pope's Christmas Day Mass was always said in the basilica of Santa Maria Maggiore. Its celebration at St Peter's instead was in itself a notable departure from custom, and a very public indication that something unusual was afoot. Charlemagne's court theologians had long since adopted the phrase *imperium chris-tianum* to describe Charlemagne's authority over his scattered realms. In his palace at Aachen, Charles had already created a complex of sec-ular and religious buildings deliberately conceived of as a 'second Rome'. It is unlikely that anyone in Charlemagne's entourage actually planned to establish a Western political empire before 800, but the Frankish court did take the view that the Eastern imperial throne, constantly allied to heresy in any case, was currently vacant (the Empress Irene had recently seized power from her son Constantine V). The papacy – and Christendom – was thus without any protector. The crisis of 799 therefore precipitated a decision. The exact nature of the authority by which Charlemagne, as 'patrician', had vindicated Leo and silenced his enemies had been in doubt. Charlemagne's imperial coronation settled the matter, once and for all.

Charlemagne's later protests, then, were probably designed to soothe the outraged sensibilities of the court in Constantinople, and to excuse his presumption in making himself emperor in the West.[27] If he had any real reservations about the events of Christmas Day 800, they almost certainly focused on the Pope's role. Thirteen years later, when Charlemagne passed his imperial title on to his son Louis, the ceremony consisted of Charlemagne's placing a crown on the altar of his palace chapel at Aachen. Louis then himself took the crown from the altar, and put it on his own head. For Charlemagne, imperial power came direct from God, not from any priest, not even the successor of Peter the key-bearer.

The ambiguities of Charlemagne's coronation were to haunt the history of both pope and empire during the Middle Ages. For the moment, however, they opened an age of renewed and optimistic co-operation between them. Leo celebrated this partnership in a series of mosaics installed in the new buildings he raised at the Lateran. In one scene Christ gives the papal pallium to Peter, while to Constantine he gives the labarum or sign of Christ's cross and name. In a corresponding picture, St Peter gives Leo the pallium, and hands Charlemagne a spear and banner. The mosaics may well predate the ceremony on Christmas Day 800, but they provide a clue to its significance for the papacy. Charlemagne was the new Constantine, anointed to protect and extend the faith under the guidance of St Peter – which for Leo meant under papal guidance.

Charlemagne, however, was unaware that he was the one to be guided. This became evident in a dispute in 810 over the addition of the *Filioque* clause to the so-called 'Nicene' Creed. This Latin phrase declared that the Holy Spirit proceeded from the Father 'and the Son', a belief well supported in scripture and widely held by Western theologians, but rejected in the East as an innovation, since it was not in the original text of the Creed. The *Filioque* seems to have originated in sixth-century Spain, but spread widely in the West. It was in general use in Charlemagne's realms, and he considered the Greek denial of it just another example of Eastern heresy. The Pope, however, while accepting the teaching implicit in the *Filioque*, rejected the right of the Frankish church – or indeed the Roman Church – to make additions to the Conciliar Creed which united East and West. He had the Creed, without the *Filioque* clause, engraved in Greek and Latin on two silver plaques, which, 'for the love and safeguarding of the true faith', he had fixed to the tombs of St Peter and St Paul. This eloquent affirmation of the unity of the Eastern and Western Churches in the faith of the Apostles declared in the ancient Creeds was a striking exercise of the papal office. Leo was guarding both the ancient teaching and the unity of the Churches. In the radical reordering of the political world which Charlemagne's new empire symbolised, the papacy continued to witness to an older unity, and to hold the bridge between East and West. Leo's urgent request to Charlemagne to suppress the use of the *Filioque* in his realms, however, was ignored. It was an ominous indication of the difference of vision, and the problem of demarcation between the authority of Pope and the Emperor.

In the years that followed the death of Charlemagne in 814, the problematic nature of that relationship became more obvious. Pope Leo's successor Stephen IV (816–17) travelled to Rheims in 816 to anoint and crown Charlemagne's son Louis the Pious. The Pope took with him what purported to be Constantine's own crown. This was an endorsement of the image of the renewed Constantinian age and empire which both Leo and Charlemagne had favoured, but the ceremony of anointing was a deliberate attempt by the papacy to stake out a role in the making of an emperor, which Louis' self-coronation in 813 had seemed to challenge.

Paschal I (817–24), who had himself hastily consecrated immediately after his election, to forestall any imperial interference, built on Stephen's gesture by extracting from Louis the so-called *Pactum Ludovicianum*. In this pact the Emperor reconfirmed the Pope in the papal patrimonies, but undertook not to interfere in papal territory unless invited, and agreed that newly elected popes need only notify their appointment after consecration. In 817 Paschal took the opportunity of a visit to Rome by Louis' son and heir Lothair, already crowned as co-emperor by his father, to anoint him, adding to the ceremony the gift of a sword to Lothair. This was perhaps a deliberate echo of St Peter's gift of a spear and banner to Charlemagne in Leo's mosaic at the Lateran, implying that the Emperor's office was bestowed on Louis by the Pope for the protection of the Church.

By contrast, Paschal's successor Eugenius II (824–7), elected with imperial influence, gave away most of these papal gains. He acknowledged the Emperor's sovereignty in the papal state, and he accepted a constitution imposed by Lothair which established imperial supervision of the administration of Rome, imposed an oath to the Emperor on all citizens, and required the Pope-elect to swear fealty before he could be consecrated. Under Sergius II (844–7) it was even agreed that the Pope could not be consecrated without an imperial mandate, and that the ceremony must be in the presence of his representative, a revival of some of the more galling restrictions of Byzantine rule.

Yet, if the revival of a Roman empire in the West created new challenges, there were also ways in which it enormously enhanced papal authority. Anointing by the Pope, carried out in Rome, was successfully established as an indispensable part of the making of an emperor. Pope John VIII (872–82) actually anointed two emperors in succession, Charles the Bald in 875, in preference to his brother Louis the German, and then Charles the Fat in 879. In strictly ecclesiastical terms, too, and despite extensive imperial control of Church affairs, papal authority grew. Charlemagne had organised the Frankish church under archbishops, subordinating the ordinary diocesan bishops to their 'metropolitans'. The Frankish bishops resented this extended metropolitan control, and the royal domination of the Church which it often mediated. Around the year 850 there appeared in France an elaborate forgery, allegedly the work of the early seventh-century Spanish scholar Isidore of Seville, but in fact designed as a very contemporary weapon against the authority of lay rulers and of metropolitan archbishops. These 'False Decretals' of 'Pseudo Isidore' were made up of a series of letters of early popes, all forged, a further series of papal letters from the time of Sylvester I to that of Gregory II, some of them spurious and many of them garbled, and a large collection of canons of councils, mostly authentic: the *Donation of Constantine* was also included. The point of the whole immense collection was to establish that the papacy was the real source of power in the Church, the Pope sharing his authority with the bishops at large as his vicars. The interference of metropolitan archbishops and synods in the affairs of other bishops was thus an infringement of papal authority, and bishops at odds with their metropolitans – or the crown – had a right of direct appeal to Rome.

The compiler of these False Decretals was not working for the papacy, but against the archbishops. The Pope was a safely remote figure in distant Rome, who could be relied on not to interfere in the regions. It was therefore safe to inflate his authority in order to limit that of the local archbishop. But the False Decretals survived the circumstances of their composition. Their systematic presentation of a massive body of authoritative ecclesiastical legislation (however dubious some of it might be) made the collection one of the most often cited reference-books of the medieval Church. The role of the papacy as the fountain of all jurisdiction in the Church, even that of councils, already widely accepted, gradually became axiomatic. Unwittingly, the authors had put a formidable weapon into the hands of the medieval popes.

Not that the affairs of Rome were totally dominated by the relationship with the Frankish empire. In the mid-ninth century the great threat to the papacy was the Muslim presence in Italy. Sicily was overrun in the 820s, and Arab forces were established on the Italian mainland by 838. In 846 a Saracen fleet carrying 500 horsemen sailed to the mouth of the Tiber, overran the weak coastal defences at Ostia, and attacked Rome; the graves of Peter and Paul were desecrated and stripped of all their riches. Between 848 and 852 the energetic monk Pope Leo IV (847–55), who had been consecrated in crisis conditions without imperial permission, set himself to make a repetition of the Saracen sack impossible. With financial help from the Emperor Lothair he raised a wall, forty feet high and twelve feet thick, with forty-four defensive towers, round St Peter's and the Vatican. The Leonine wall was both a demonstration of independent papal vigour, and an organisational triumph. Leo used labour-gangs supplied by the cities of the papal state, the larger monasteries and the *domuscultae*, to each of which was allocated a stretch of the work. For the first time, the Vatican was now safe behind walls. It was the first extension of the city since imperial times, and in some ways the most remarkable monument of papal Rome in the early Middle Ages.

There were others, less practical but just as eloquent. The appeal to the authority of the early Church and the popes of early Christian Rome which characterised the False Decretals also dominated the religious symbolism of the Church buildings of ninth-century Rome. The great new churches built by Paschal I, like Santa Prassede, filled with relics brought in from the catacombs and decorated with mosaics deliberately modelled on those in the Constantinian basilicas, played on that appeal. Both relics and images were designed to connect papal Rome, Rome of the pilgrims, to the heroic age of early Christian Rome. After the Byzantine cultural dominance of the seventh and eighth centuries, such buildings mark a recovery of confidence in the value of Rome's own past, and an eagerness to harness it to enhance the authority of Rome's bishop.

The pope who most completely embodied this renewed confidence was Nicholas I (858–67), the third and last Pope to be granted the title 'Great'. Nicholas was an aristocrat, saturated in the writings of his great predecessors Leo, Gelasius and Gregory, and totally committed to the exalted vision of the papal office they contained. His understanding of papal jurisdiction coincided closely with that of the False Decretals, which he had probably read. He considered that no synod or council had binding force unless approved by him, that no bishop might be deposed without his agreement, and that all his decisions as Pope had the force of law. The empire obliged the Emperor to protect the Church. In Nicholas' eyes, however, this responsibility gave emperors no rights to jurisdiction over the Church. Elected in his early forties, he set himself to translate a paper theory into concrete action.

Within Italy, this determination brought him face to face with the Archbishop of Ravenna. The old exarchate was officially part of papal territory and in Church law was subject to papal jurisdiction. For years, however, the work of papal officials there, the rights of papal tenants, and the free access of the inhabitants of the region to Rome had all been under attack from the archbishops. Renewed complaints by the local bishops about the tyrannical behaviour of Archbishop John of Ravenna gave Nicholas the grounds he needed for action. In 861 he summoned the Archbishop to Rome, and when John cited ancient precedents for the exemption of his see from this sort of summons, Nicholas excommunicated and deposed him. The Archbishop gave in, accepted a drastic reduction of his powers and swore obedience to Rome.

The same determination to bring upstart metropolitan archbishops to heel marked Nicholas' confrontation with Archbishop Hincmar of Rheims. Hincmar was the most distinguished of the Frankish bishops, and an imperial favourite. Like every other bishop in the West, he accepted the primacy of the Pope, but in practice he tried to minimise its impact on himself. He opposed the anointing of Charles the Bald as emperor, because of the direct jurisdiction he feared this would give the Pope in Charles' realms. A stickler for law, he saw the Pope as interpreter of that law and the final court of appeal within the Church, but he thought of him as judge, not legislator. No pope could change the established laws of local churches. In 861 Hincmar deposed a suffragan bishop with whom he had long been in dispute, Rothad of Soissons. Rothad appealed to Nicholas, but Hincmar and his allies tried to block him, invoking Frankish law to override the canonical right of appeal to Rome. This was a red rag to the Pope, who in any case believed that no-one had the right to depose any bishop without papal permission. Since he had never been consulted, he overruled Hincmar, and reinstated Rothad. When Hincmar fought his decision, Nicholas threatened to suspend him from celebrating Mass. Once again, the Archbishop gave way before the Pope, though after Nicholas' death Hincmar would go on resisting papal incursions into the Frankish church with undiminished vigour.

The most courageous demonstration of Nicholas' papal vision, however, came over the divorce of King Lothair of Lorraine. In 855 Lothair had made a dynastic marriage with Theutberga, daughter of the Duke of Burgundy. She proved unable to give him an heir, however, and Lothair divorced her on a trumped-up charge of incest, and married a concubine by whom he had already had three children. A synod of Frankish bishops meeting at Aachen obligingly recognised the divorce, but Theutberga appealed to the Pope. This case involved not only the role of Rome as a court of appeal, but the nature of Christian marriage in the tangle of Frankish and Germanic law. With characteristic decisiveness, Nicholas ruled in favour of Theutberga, and ordered Lothair to ditch his concubine and return to his legitimate wife and queen. When the archbishops of Cologne and Trier came to Rome with the decrees of a Frankish council recognising Lothair's divorce and remarriage, Nicholas excommunicated them for conniving at bigamy. The Archbishop of Cologne ignored the excommunication, the Frankish authorities supported him, and the quarrel snowballed. In February 864 Lothair's brother, the Emperor Louis II, marched on Rome to lay siege to the Pope. There were ugly confrontations, during one of which a procession into St Peter's was attacked, and the jewelled relic of the True Cross brought to Rome by St Helena was trampled and broken – it was rescued from the mud by a party of English pilgrims. Imperial bishops raged against the Pope 'who numbers himself as an apostle among the apostles, and who is making himself emperor of the whole world', but Nicholas' intransigence paid off. It became clear to the Emperor that the only way to make the Pope back down would be to kill him, and the moral weight of the papal office carried the day. The archbishops had to submit, and Lothair acknowledged Theutberga as his wife.

The Lorraine divorce case showed Nicholas at his courageous best, defying emperors, archbishops and regional councils in defence not only of papal prerogatives but of a friendless woman. The same determination marked his relations with the Emperor and churches of the East, but here the consequence was to be a tragic split between the Churches of East and West. Once again, the trigger was the deposition of a bishop.

In 858 the Byzantine Emperor Michael III was refused communion on the grounds of incest by Patriarch Ignatius of Constantinople. The Emperor deposed the Patriarch, and in his place appointed Photius, a brilliant and devout young layman from the imperial civil service. In breach of the canons, Photius was rushed through all the levels of the clergy in five days, and was duly installed as patriarch. Anxious to consolidate his position, he sent an announcement of his consecration to the Pope, justifying his uncanonical leap from layman to patriarch. Nicholas declined to recognise the appointment, however, till he had investigated the matter, and representatives of Rome duly travelled to Constantinople in September 860. They returned to Rome having agreed to the deposition of Ignatius, but Nicholas had meanwhile received an appeal from Ignatius. He repudiated his legates, and in 863 deposed and excommunicated Photius.

The Photius affair would rumble on long after Nicholas' death, but its significance was much greater than the rights or wrongs of Ignatius' deposition. Relations between Rome and Constantinople had been poor for generations, and since the creation of the Carolingian empire and the Iconoclastic controversy what little contact there was between the Latin and Greek Churches was charged with mutual suspicion. The Photius affair crystallised that hostility. When the Emperor Michael protested at Nicholas' excommunication of Photius, Nicholas unleashed a torrent of vitriol on him, denouncing the interference of the Eastern empire in matters that concerned only bishops, recalling the Greek Church's constant lapses into heresy and schism, challenging the credibility of a Roman emperor who could not speak Latin, and declaring that 'the privileges of this see existed before your empire, and will remain when it has long gone'. In a passage that clearly drew on the ideas found in the *Donation of Constantine*, he told the Emperor that the Roman Church was his mother, from whom he derived his imperial powers.[28]

The Photius affair was complicated by papal initiatives in Bulgaria. Under King Boris I, Bulgaria was a rising power in the Balkan region, a matter of immediate concern to the Emperor at Constantinople. Bulgaria had been evangelised by missionaries from the Greek Church, but Boris was anxious to maintain a political distance from Constantinople, and he had tried to get an independent Bulgarian patriarchate established, but had been blocked by Photius. He therefore turned to Rome, and asked Nicholas to send Latin missionaries to Bulgaria, and then to establish a Bulgarian archbishopric.

Nicholas welcomed Latin involvement in Bulgaria for several reasons. He was genuinely committed to missionary work, encouraging the activities of St Ansgar in Scandinavia, and of the missionaries to the Slavs in Moravia, Cyril and Methodius. But he was also intensely conscious of the lost jurisdiction of the papacy in Illyricum and the Balkans, and saw in the Balkan adventure an opportunity to recover and even extend it. Nicholas duly sent the missionaries Boris requested, together with a long and detailed instruction on the Christian faith, expounding Western belief and practice and, in the process, disparaging Constantinople. Photius responded to this with an equally harsh attack on the West, reminiscent of the Quinisext Canons and denouncing clerical celibacy, fasting laws, the Western use of unleavened bread in the Mass, and the intrusion of the *Filioque* clause into the Creed. The Photius affair had become a platform on which the long-term alienation of the Churches of East and West was acted out. In 867 Photius presided over a synod at Constantinople which excommunicated and deposed the Pope, though Nicholas was dead before news of this reached Rome. Rome and Constantinople were now formally separated.

The death of Nicholas I marks a watershed in the history of the papacy. Already Charlemagne's empire had been distributed among his quarrelling descendants. By the end of the ninth century it was no longer even a fiction. The papacy had acted as midwife at the birth of that empire because it needed a strong protector. With its dissolution the popes were left defenceless in the snakepit of Italian politics. Nicholas' feeble successor, Hadrian II (867–72), surrendered piece by piece all the high ground Nicholas had gained, backing down before Hincmar of Rheims, allowing Lothair of Lorraine, now once more cohabiting with his concubine, to receive communion, watching Bulgaria slip from Roman to Greek obedience.

Deprived of the support of empire, the papacy became the possession of the great Roman families, a ticket to local dominance for which men were prepared to rape, murder and steal. A third of the popes elected between 872 and 1012 died in suspicious circumstances – John VIII (872–82) bludgeoned to death by his own entourage, Stephen VI (896–7) strangled, Leo V (903) murdered by his successor Sergius III (904–11), John X (914–28) suffocated, Stephen VIII (939–42) horribly mutilated, a fate shared by the Greek antipope John XVI (997–8) who, unfortunately for him, did not die from the removal of his eyes, nose, lips, tongue and hands. Most of these men were manoeuvred into power by a succession of powerful families – the Theophylacts, the Crescentii, the Tusculani. John X, one of the few popes of this period to make a stand against aristocratic domination, was deposed and then murdered in the Castel Sant' Angelo by the Theophylacts, who had appointed him in the first place.

The key figure in both John X's appointment and his deposition was the notorious Theophylact matron, Marozia. She also appointed Leo VI (928) and Stephen VII (928–31), and she had been the mistress of Pope Sergius III, by whom she bore an illegitimate son whom she eventually appointed as Pope John XI (931–6). In 932 John deepened the Eastern Church's already almost limitless contempt for the West by granting a dispensation and sending legates to consecrate the sixteen-year-old son of the Emperor Romanus I as patriarch of Constantinople. It was, clearly, a period in which rulers liked to keep things in the family.

The collapse of the papacy after Nicholas I is reflected in a corresponding tailing away of the great papal chronicle, the *Liber Pontificalis*, the fundamental source for papal history from the sixth to the ninth centuries. This chronicle is made up of a series of papal biographies, begun in the Lateran chancery while their subject was still alive, and updated as necessary. The ninth-century lives are compiled on a lavish scale, but the life of Hadrian II is incomplete, and thereafter the chronicle effectively stops, each entry being no more than a line or two giving the Pope's name and regnal dates.

The reputation of the popes of the 'dark century' after the silencing of the *Liber Pontificalis* was low at the time, and has not improved with the years. Its symbol is the macabre 'cadaver synod' staged by Stephen VI in January 897, when he put on trial the mummified corpse of his hated predecessor but one, Pope Formosus. The corpse, dressed in pontifical vestments and propped up on a throne, was found guilty of perjury and other crimes, was mutilated by having the fingers used in blessings hacked off, and was then tossed into the Tiber. Stephen himself was subsequently deposed by the disgusted Roman crowd, and strangled in prison.

Yet not all these men were contemptible. Formosus himself, despite having at one time been deposed from his earlier bishopric of Porto by Pope John VIII for plotting to have himself made pope, was a very remarkable figure, a brilliant missionary in Nicholas I's Bulgarian enterprise, a key player in attempts to patch up relations with Constantinople after the Photius shambles, a gifted papal diplomat in the West, and a man of austere personal piety. Even the appointments made by relentless fixers like Alberic II, the secular ruler of Rome who was Marozia's son and eventual gaoler, included some admirable men. Ruthless politicians may be, indeed often are, conventionally pious, and Alberic was no exception. He appointed five popes, two of whom, Leo VII (936–9) and Agapitus II (946–55), were sincere reformers, promoting monastic revival and clerical reform in Italy and Germany. Leo in particular was the friend of the great Abbot Odo of Cluny, and, with Alberic's support, entrusted to him the reform of the Roman monasteries. Leo also encouraged the revived monastery of Subiaco, St Benedict's own house, and the reforming abbey of Gorze.

But even these relatively decent popes were in Alberic's pocket, and the dominance of the Roman ruling families made impossible any real papal initiative or consistency. In any case, Alberic more than compensated for these worthwhile appointments by securing a promise from the clergy and nobility of Rome to elect his son and heir Octavian as pope when Agapitus died, thereby uniting Church and state in Rome with a vengeance. Octavian was duly elected as Pope John XII (955–64) at the ripe age of eighteen. He was to die at the age of twenty-seven, allegedly from a stroke while in bed with a married woman.

The decision of Otto I of Germany in 962 to revive the empire of Charlemagne offered the papacy some hope of change. Otto I and his successors Otto II and III had an almost mystical vision of the Christian empire, and of the sacred responsibilities it placed on the shoulders of the Emperor. Already the stirrings of reform in the churches of Germany, especially in the monasteries, had formed a bond between Germany and the papacy. Monastic reformers, struggling against entrenched local interests, including unworthy bishops, looked to the papacy to provide support in the form of the privileges and exemptions they needed for survival. From the distance of Germany, the personal failings of the popes were less significant than the authority of their office. The re-emergence of the empire, now firmly centred on Germany, strengthened this link between papacy and reform.

Ironically, the Pope who anointed Otto I on the Feast of the Purification (2 February) 962 was the unsavoury twenty-five-year-old John XII. To him, however, Otto pledged the restoration of papal control of the lands promised by Pepin and Charlemagne, and the defence of the Church's freedoms. In return, papal elections had to be agreed by the Emperor's representatives, and popes would have to swear fealty to him. The Ottonian empire promised more than this to the popes, however. Otto's determination to replace Byzantine rule in southern Italy with his own held out the prospect of papal control of the churches there, which had long been subject to Constantinople. The German Emperor's power in northern Italy speedily resulted in the extension of papal influence there. Milan and Ravenna became more securely subordinate to Rome.

There was a price to pay. With the restoration of Charlemagne's vision came a return of Charlemagne's claims. The Ottonians expected to exercise tight control over the Church, and the popes appointed under Ottonian influence were expected to endorse Ottonian policies. Papal unease with these claims expressed themselves in the scaling down of the rite of imperial anointing. In place of the sacramental oil, chrism, used in the consecration of bishops as well as kings, a lesser oil was used, and the Emperor was anointed only on his arm and back, not his head, to symbolise that his office was to bear the sword for the defence of the Church. More practically, Ottonian policies were often unpopular in Italy, and the popes collected more than their share of the hostility those policies provoked. When Otto II died suddenly in 983, leaving the three-year-old Otto III to the regency of his Byzantine princess mother, Pope John XIV (983–4) was left friendless, and was soon deposed and murdered. Rome sank once more into the control of the Crescentii.

The imperial ideal was revived at the very end of the tenth century under the brief personal rule of Otto III. Of all the Ottonians, he had the most exalted view of Rome, and determined to establish his headquarters there. His understanding of his role as emperor, however, was perhaps influenced by his Byzantine mother. For Otto, the Pope was a junior partner, the chaplain of empire, whose first duty was conformity to the will of the Lord's anointed. To ensure that this was so, he looked first to his own family. His first papal appointment was a twenty-five-year-old German cousin (the first German Pope) who took the name Gregory V (996–9). But this move backfired, because Gregory was detested by the Roman ruling families, who were resentful of imperial interference. Without their support Rome became too hot to hold the Pope, and he was deposed temporarily in 996.

Gregory's death in 999 enabled Otto to try again, this time with the brilliant Frenchman Gerbert of Aurillac, one of the wittiest and most learned men in Europe, and an experienced ecclesiastical politician. Gerbert had once been archbishop of Rheims, replacing an unworthy predecessor who had been deposed without papal consent. To defend his own position, Gerbert had attacked papal rights of interference in local churches. At the time of his appointment to the papacy he was Archbishop of Ravenna. Gerbert took the name Sylvester II (999–1003) to symbolise the rebirth of early Christian Rome, the *Renovatio Imperii Romanorum* which had appeared on some of Charlemagne's seals, and which Otto had now adopted as his own. Gerbert would be Pope Sylvester to Otto's Constantine.

Otto had firm ideas about the nature of that partnership. Almost uniquely among leaders of the day, he realised that the *Donation of Constantine* was a forgery, and said so. The Emperor was not the creation of the papacy: rather, the papacy was an instrument in the hand of the Emperor. Yet Otto showered benefits on the Church of Rome, restoring to it the lost territories of Ravenna and the Pentapolis. On the theoretical front, too, papal fortunes revived. Sylvester's former hostility to papal claims evaporated once he was pope, and, ironically in view of his own earlier history, his vigorous assertion of the prerogatives of the Holy See, in Germany as well as Italy, now rivalled those of Nicholas I.

None of this was to last. Otto, still in his early twenties, died in 1002. Once more, the warring families of Rome reasserted their control of the papacy, with a corresponding decline in papal calibre. Imperial influence was not entirely eclipsed, however, and the Tusculan Pope Benedict VIII (1012–24) worked in close harmony with the

Emperor Henry II, whose attacks on Byzantine southern Italy he encouraged, in the hope of restoring papal authority there. This led to the breaking off of the fragile relations between the churches of Constantinople and Rome which had been patched up since the Photian schism. The situation was not eased by the fact that Benedict caved in to the Emperor's insistence that the Creed, containing the Filioque, hitherto excluded from the Roman liturgy, should be sung at every Mass. Pope and Emperor nevertheless collaborated on a number of reform measures, almost certainly initiated by Henry, such as the Synod of Pavia's stern measures in 1022 to stamp out clerical marriage and concubinage.

This imperial interlude, however, did not fundamentally alter the essentially local character of the papacy at the turn of the tenth and eleventh centuries. Whatever the grandiose theoretical claims of popes like Nicholas the Great, the reality was that the popes were harassed Italian prince–bishops, desperately struggling to preserve the territory of St Peter, sometimes responding to but never initiating reforms which were beginning to stir within Christendom. Even the imperial popes were desperately vulnerable – Leo VIII (963–5) had been exiled from Rome, John XIII (965–72) imprisoned and forced to flee, Benedict VI (973–4) murdered, Boniface VII (974, 984–5), twice banished, Benedict VII (974–83) exiled, John XIV (983–4) murdered, John XV (985–6) fled, Gregory V (996–9) exiled, Sylvester II (999–1003) driven out with his master Otto III. Ironically, the unavoidable price of papal security in the city seemed to be subordination to the rule of the local families, and the closing down of horizons.

Yet Rome retained its mystique. In 1027 King Cnut of England came on pilgrimage, 'because I heard from wise men that St Peter the Apostle has received from the Lord a great power of binding and loosing, and bears the keys of the kingdom of heaven; and therefore I deemed it useful in no ordinary degree to seek his patronage before God.' The Pope whom Cnut encountered on this journey, with whom he negotiated a series of privileges for the English church, and whom he watched crown and anoint Conrad II as emperor of the Romans, was John XIX (1024–32), the younger brother of the ruling Count of Tusculum. He was a typical representative of his age. He had bribed his way to the papacy, and had been elevated from the status of layman to pope in a single day. Yet Cnut, if he was aware of these things, was not scandalised, and evidently felt no sense of incongruity at the distance between the key-bearer and his earthly representative. The Pope, for Cnut, was not essentially a leader, a reformer or an exemplar. Like other priests, he was the guardian of mysteries so holy that his own merits or demerits hardly mattered. It was the office that counted, not the man who held it. The Pope, in the words of Louis Duchesne, was 'the high-priest of the Roman pilgrimage, the dispenser of benedictions, of privileges, and of anathemas'.[29] No one looked to him to be anything more, and many would have resented it if the popes had tried. All that, however, was about to change.

CHAPTER THREE

SET ABOVE NATIONS

1000–1447

I THE ERA OF PAPAL REFORM

At the opening of the eleventh century the papacy was a contradictory mixture of exalted theory and squalid reality. In theory the bishops of Rome were lords of the world, exercising a unique spiritual supremacy symbolised by their exclusive right to anoint the western or 'Holy Roman' Emperor. In practice, the popes were strictly and often humiliatingly subordinated to the power of the local Roman aristocracy, or to the German ruling house. Of the twenty-five popes between 955 and 1057, thirteen were appointed by the local aristocracy, while the other twelve were appointed (and no fewer than five dismissed) by the German emperors. The ancient axiom that no one may judge the Pope was still in the law-books, but in practice had long since been set aside.

The popes themselves were deeply embroiled in the internecine dynastic warfare of the Roman nobility, and election to the chair of Peter, as we have seen, was frequently a commodity for sale or barter. The Ottonian era had led to a temporary improvement in the characters of the popes, but by the second quarter of the eleventh century standards had crumbled once more. Benedict IX (1032–48), whose election was the result of a systematic campaign of bribery by his father, the Tusculan grandee Count Alberic III, was as bad as any of the popes of the preceding 'dark century'. Like his uncle and immediate predecessor John XIX, Benedict was a layman, and was still in his twenties at the time of his election. He was both violent and debauched, and even the Roman populace, hardened as they were to unedifying papal behaviour, could not stomach him. He was eventually deposed in favour of Silvester III (1045). With the help of his family's private army, he was briefly restored in 1045 amid bloody hand-to-hand fighting in the streets of Rome. He was evidently tired of the struggle, however, for he accepted a bribe to abdicate in favour of his godfather, the archpriest John Gratian. It was rumoured that Pope Benedict needed the money in order to marry.

Gratian was a man with a reputation for holiness and a genuine interest in religious reform. His choice of name, Gregory VI (1045–6), was probably a deliberate allusion to the purity of the papacy under Gregory the Great. His election was therefore greeted with delight by those who were looking for a clean-up of the Church. Peter Damian, the ex-swineherd who had become abbot of the monastery of Fonte Avellana, and was one of the leading voices of monastic and clerical reform of the day, hoped that Gregory's election might presage the return of 'the golden days of the Apostles', and prayed that religious discipline might flourish again under his guidance. Yet there was no doubt that money had changed hands to secure Gregory's election, both in setting up Benedict's pension and in providing financial sweeteners to the turbulent Roman crowd.

Into this delicate situation in 1046 strode the German King Henry III. Still in his twenties, he was a gifted warrior and a man of deep piety who saw his role as much in religious as in secular terms. Committed to the reform of the Church, he surrounded himself with bishops and men of learning. Henry had come to Italy to be crowned emperor. How much he knew about the circumstances of Pope Gregory's election before his arrival is uncertain, but on learning the facts he acted decisively. He would not be crowned by a pope whose authority was undermined by the sin of simony, the purchase of holy things. At a synod held at Sutri in December 1046, Gregory, Silvester and Benedict were all formally deposed, and Henry set about reforming the papacy. Over the next ten years he appointed a series of popes committed to the renewal of the Church in general, and of the See of Peter in particular. All were Germans, and the names they chose as pope are significant – Clement II (1046–7), Damasus II (1048), Leo IX (1049–54) and Victor II (1055–7). Marking a clear break with the Gregories, Johns and Benedicts of the 'dark century', these were the names of great popes of the early Church, and they symbolised a conscious aspiration to recover the purity of early Christian Rome. The greatest of these imperial appointments was an Alsatian count, Bruno, Bishop of Toul, the Emperor's distant cousin. Bishop Bruno signalled his exalted religious ideals by refusing the papacy unless Henry's choice was ratified by the Roman clergy and people, and he walked to Rome as a pilgrim for his installation as Pope Leo IX in 1049.

Leo represented the spearhead of a movement which had been stirring the Church in France and Germany for over a century. Though it aimed at the renewal of Christian life in general, it was intimately identified with reform of the monastic life. In the Frankish empire there had been a close connection between monasteries and monarchy, and successive emperors and kings had concerned themselves with the regulation and endowment of the great religious houses. Royal patronage enriched these communities, encouraged the proper keeping of the rule and the maintenance of a glorious liturgy, and protected the monasteries against interference.

The most famous of all the reforming communities of tenth-century Europe was the great monastery of Cluny, founded by Duke William of Aquitaine in 909. Like many other monasteries, Cluny was an aristocratic foundation, but one with a difference, for Duke William had decreed that the monks at Cluny 'shall be wholly freed from our power, and from that of our kindred, and from the jurisdiction of royal greatness'.[1] William placed his new monastery under the direct protection of the Holy See, and dedicated it to Sts Peter and Paul. This 'special relationship' with the papacy, ensuring Cluny's freedom from external pressure and contributing to its prestige, culminated in 1054 with the exemption of the monastery from all episcopal control except that of the Pope.

Cluny gradually became the centre of a great web of religious communities, some new, and some older foundations seeking reform. By the mid-eleventh century there were hundreds of Cluniac houses throughout Europe. In some ways Cluniac reform hardly strikes us now as a 'reformation' at all, and it certainly was not primarily associated with personal austerity of living, poverty, study and contemplation. What Cluny offered was the beauty of holiness, monastic life conceived of as an orderly and dignified observance of the monastic rule, the adornment of the monastic church with splendid architecture, rich vestments and beautiful books and the elaborate celebration of the liturgy of the hours and the Mass.

Cluny enjoyed excellent relations with the kings and emperors of Germany, and Cluniac houses everywhere basked in the favour of the European aristocracy: it was in no sense a revolutionary move-ment. But in one important respect Cluniac reform looked away from the Carolingian world in which monasticism had flourished under royal patronage, towards the papal future. For the German monasteries like Gorze, religious freedom meant freedom *under* the King. For Cluny, it meant, among other things, freedom *from* the King. This was a distinction which would come to dominate the very idea of religious reform, as more and more reformers came to see lay influence over the Church, however benevolent in intent, as the chief source of its corruptions.

In the mid-eleventh century, lay influence was everywhere in the Church. Monasteries and bishoprics were more than spiritual insti-tutions. They were enormously wealthy social and political corpora-tions, controlling vast revenues and carrying a corresponding weight in the calculations of kings. When William the Conqueror invaded England in 1066 he found there thirty-five monasteries, which between them controlled a sixth of the total revenue of the country. No ruler could afford to ignore such power, or to leave it unchecked. Everywhere in Europe rulers exercised close control over the choice of bishops and abbots in their realms. The monasteries and other churches founded by kings and princes belonged to them, and their revenues were often at the disposal of the lay 'proprietors'. Control by the ruler was symbolised in the ceremony of consecration of a bishop, in the course of which the King (or his representative) handed over the Bishop's staff and ring of office. This 'lay investiture' was to become the focus of the reform papacy's attack on lay inter-ference in spiritual matters.

The potential in all this for corruption is obvious. Since becoming a bishop made a man immensely wealthy and powerful, men were prepared to pay for the privilege. More often than not, new bishops were required to pay large sums of money to the ruler who had nominated them. Reformers denounced this as the sale of holy things, called the sin of 'simony' after Simon Magus, who in the Acts of the Apostles had offered the Apostles money for the power to work miracles. But simony was not always easy to distinguish from the reasonable levying of a tax by the ruler when the revenues of the bishopric were transferred to a new holder. The papacy itself exacted fees of this sort. When Benedict VIII established a new bishopric of Besalu in 1017, he stipulated that each new bishop should pay the pope one pound of gold. The papal clerk who recorded this provision carefully added that this payment was 'not for the consecration but in token of true obedience'.[2]

Cash payments as a condition for religious office were just one of the signs of the extent to which the Church was woven into the fabric of society. Clerical marriage and concubinage were another. In the Eastern churches, bishops were expected to be celibate: if they were married men on their election, they had to separate from their wives. In the West, this provision was applied to all clerics above the rank of subdeacon. Many popes and bishops had been family men, but in theory at least continuing sexual relations were ruled out by ordination. In practice, however, things were often very different. Clerical marriage or concubinage was routine all over Europe, and the laity may even have felt safer if their priest had his own wife. In England before the Norman Conquest many parish priests were married. The same was true in Milan and northern Italy generally, where married bishops were not uncommon, and clerical office might pass from father to son. Religious reformers in the West had always denounced this, but the reformers of the eleventh century were to place the attack on clerical marriage (known as 'Nicolaism') at the centre of their campaign for purity in the Church. The Tusculan Pope Benedict VIII had legislated against clerical marriage, but his concern was primarily with the dangers to Church property from greedy clerical families. In the reform era the concern was rather with the ritual purity of those who served the sanctuary, and with the symbolic separation of Church and world.

The early-eleventh-century papacy, for all its continuing theoretical claims, had been in many respects a local institution, trapped by geography and the politics of Rome. Leo IX determined to take the papacy out beyond Italy, and to make it the spearhead of a general reform. In a whirlwind pontificate of five years he travelled to Germany, France and northern Italy. Wherever he went he held a series of great reforming synods, which attacked the evils of simony, lay investiture and clerical marriage. The synod at Rheims, held in the year of his election, set the tone for later meetings. He had gone to Rheims to consecrate the new monastic church of St Remigius (the Apostle of the Franks), and to enshrine the saint's bones at the high altar. The French King, anxious about Leo's likely attacks on royal episcopal appointments, forbade his bishops to attend, and there were only twenty bishops present. Nevertheless, the Pope used the occasion to inaugurate a purge against simoniac bishops. Having placed the bones of St Remigius on the high altar, he demanded that the bishops and abbots present declare individually whether they had paid any money for their office. He evidently knew his men: the guilty majority were shamed into silence. The Archbishop of Rheims, who was host for the Council, was spared open humiliation, being summoned to Rome to account for himself. The Bishop of Langres fled, and was excommunicated and deposed. His defence counsel, the Archbishop of Besançon, was struck dumb while speaking on his behalf, a judgement held to have come direct from St Remigius himself. Bishops who confessed – a quarter of those present – were pardoned and restored, though one of them, the Bishop of Nantes, who had succeeded his own father in office, was stripped of his episcopal honours and reduced to the priesthood.

In one week, Leo had asserted papal authority as it had never been asserted before. Bishops had been excommunicated and deposed, a powerful and prestigious archbishop summoned to explain himself in Rome, and the whole system of payments for promotion within the Church had been earth-shakingly challenged. And Rheims was only the beginning. Leo launched an all-out attack on the financial traffic in ecclesiastical appointments, from village priests up to bishops and archbishops, deposing the guilty and even reordaining priests ordained by such bishops, for simony at the time was held to be a heresy which invalidated the sacraments celebrated by the simoniac. He enforced orthodox doctrine, condemning Berengar of Tours for heretical teaching on the eucharist, and he did what he could to reform practical abuses, like the appointment of bishops by the secular ruler without election by or with the consent of priests and people. He also began a campaign against married priests, insisting that all clergy must be celibate.

In a momentous step which foreshadowed a permanent change in the character of the papacy, he built round him a remarkable body of like-minded reformers as advisers and deputies, thereby beginning the transformation of the Roman Curia from a locally recruited to an international body of experts and activists. They included monks like the fiery Peter Damian, Humbert of Moyenmoutier (a learned zealot whom he made cardinal bishop of Silva Candida), Frederick of Liège, Abbot of Monte Cassino (later Pope Stephen IX), Abbot Hugh of

Cluny, and the energetic Roman monk Hildebrand, who, as Pope Gregory VII, would give his name to the whole reform movement.

Leo's determination to maintain the freedom of the papacy and to rid papal territory of political interference seemed compromised by a new development in Italy, the arrival of the Normans. Southern Italy was ruled by the Byzantine empire, Sicily by Muslims. But both regions were remote from the empires which claimed sovereignty over them, and were a paradise for landless adventurers. By the mid-eleventh century, Norman mercenaries, called in by local princelings struggling against Muslim or Byzantine overlords, had broken the Muslim power in Sicily and established themselves as a threat in their own right. They soon began to encroach on the southern reaches of the patrimony of Peter. Leo as a young man had led imperial armies in northern Italy. He now once again took to war, leading his own ram-shackle army in a disastrous attack on the Norman forces in southern Italy. He had hoped for help from the German Emperor, and had planned to join forces with the Byzantine armies of the south, to drive out this shared new enemy. In the event, no help was forthcoming. Leo was humiliatingly defeated in June 1053, and his Norman enemies kept him under polite but close arrest for nine months.

This shambolic military sortie into southern Italy was to have disastrous religious consequences. The Byzantine court and Church detested the Normans, but, even more deeply, they resented the Pope's interference in the south. Leo had characteristically taken the opportunity provided by the campaign to hold a reforming synod in the region, which was traditionally under the jurisdiction of the Patriarch of Constantinople. He had also appointed his closest adviser, Humbert of Moyenmoutier, as archbishop of Sicily. Leo probably had little choice in the matter, because the island was newly recovered from Muslim domination by the Normans, who sup-ported the imposition of a Latin church structure. Nevertheless, the Patriarch of Constantinople, Michael Cerularius, detested the West-ern Church, and responded by closing down all the Latin-rite churches in Constantinople. A deepening rift opened between East and West, with the Byzantine Church denouncing Latin liturgical practices like the use of unleavened bread in the Mass, and the Pope making ever stronger claims of papal supremacy. A long history of alienation and mutual suspicion lay behind this skirmishing, and nei-ther side was prepared to give an inch. Matters came to a head in July

1054 when Humbert, acting as papal legate, strode into the cathedral of Hagia Sophia and laid a bull of excommunication on the high altar. The Patriarch responded two weeks later by excommunicating the Pope, though Leo had in fact been dead for months. But the tragic and continuing schism between East and West, long brewing as the customs and beliefs of the two Churches had grown apart, was ominously prefigured in this confrontation.

Leo's startling reshaping of the papacy from the prime example of corruption into the chief instrument of reform was continued by his immediate successors. Victor II (1055–7), former Bishop of Eichstatt, was the last of the German popes appointed by Henry III. The reforming party in Rome at first suspected him of being over-committed to imperial interests. In fact, he proved a zealous defender of the Church's rights and property, and a keen promoter of reforming ideals such as clerical chastity and the campaign against simony. Victor's successor, Frederick of Lorraine, who took the name Stephen IX (1057–8), was no imperialist, being the brother of Godfrey of Lorraine, Henry III's most formidable rival in northern Italy. Because of this, he had left Rome for the life of a monk at Monte Cassino, in Norman southern Italy, when Henry came to Rome in 1055. Victor II, however, trusted him, and after Henry's death made him abbot of Monte Cassino in 1057, and shortly afterwards a cardinal priest. As pope, Stephen set about reforming St Benedict's own monastery at Monte Cassino, and entrenched the leaders of reform even more deeply in the papal establishment by making the reform propagandist Peter Damian bishop of Ostia, and appointing Humbert of Silva Candida as his chancellor or chief minister.

He also promoted the monk-deacon Hildebrand, whom he sent to Milan to establish links with the 'Patarini' movement there. Church and city in Milan were in the hands of a strongly aristocratic anti-reform elite. The Patarini, by contrast, were a populist opposition group who had taken up the reform campaigns against simony and clerical marriage. They looked for a clergy dedicated to poverty and chastity, and a renewal of the Church by a return to the apostolic pattern found in the Acts of the Apostles. Their nickname was a comment on their lower-class origins, for it meant 'rag-pickers', and the papal alliance with such a radical group was a portent for the future.

The Roman aristocracy were also opposed to the papal reform movement, which had robbed them of their control of papal territory and revenues. When Stephen IX died there was a long delay in electing his successor, caused by Hildebrand's absence in Germany. Seizing the moment, a group of nobles launched a lavish campaign of bribery, and succeeded in having John Mincius, Cardinal Bishop of Velletri and a member of the Tusculan clan, elected and enthroned as Benedict X in 1058. It was a shrewd choice, for Mincius had plausible reforming credentials and had been a friend of Stephen IX's. The reform party, however, refused to accept Benedict as pope. They fled the city, and Peter Damian, Cardinal Bishop of Ostia and therefore chief papal consecrator, refused to perform the ordination. In December that year the reform cardinals, meeting in Siena, elected the French Bishop of Florence, Gérard of Lorraine, as Pope Nicholas II (1058–61). Nicholas had the backing of the German court and, with the help of imperial troops and a lavish distribution of gifts to the population of Rome by Hildebrand, he drove Benedict out of the city. He was accepted as the true Pope early in 1059.

Nicholas' papacy was to be a further landmark on the road to reform. His determination to keep the initiative in the hands of the reforming party, and to prevent a repetition of the nobles' coup of 1058, manifested itself in a new procedure for papal elections. Popes in the past had been appointed in a bewildering variety of ways – elected by assemblies of clergy and people, hailed by acclamation at the funerals of their predecessors, nominated by local gang-bosses, appointed by emperors. A synod at the Lateran in April 1059 promulgated a new papal electoral decree, confining the actual choice to the seven cardinal bishops, with the subsequent assent of the cardinal priests and deacons, and then the acclaim of the people: vague and grudging provision was also made for imperial approval.

The 'cardinals' were simply the senior clergy of Rome. The word itself is probably derived from the term for a hinge or joint, and was first given to the twenty-eight parish priests of the titular churches of Rome, who also served the five papal basilicas which collectively formed the Pope's cathedral. This double role made these priests the 'hinges' between the See of Rome, and the parishes of Rome. The word lost this precise original meaning, however, and became an honorific sign of status. It was extended to the holders of the seven 'subarbicarian' bishoprics round Rome, and to the nineteen deacons of the city, and it was this group of fifty-four senior clergy which was now envisaged as the sole electoral body for the papacy, with the initiative and determining role going to the cardinal bishops. The decree was a clear attempt to exclude lay influence, whether from the Emperor or the Roman nobility, from the whole process.

The same synod made clerical marriage illegal, ordered the laity to boycott the Masses of priests who kept concubines, forbade the acceptance of churches from lay proprietors, and stipulated that the clergy serving a great church should live in common, a move towards a monastic pattern intended to improve clerical morals and discipline. But the most momentous development of Nicholas' pontificate was the reversal of previous papal policy towards the Normans, and the beginning of the papacy's consequent alienation from the German court. Here, practical necessity was the driving force. Since the death of Henry III Germany had been ruled by a minor, and the papacy had lost any real hope of effective German support against its enemies in Italy. The Pope determined therefore to form an alliance with the Normans of Sicily and southern Italy. The Norman hold on southern Italy had no legitimacy other than force of arms. The Pope now granted the Norman rulers there the duchies of Apulia and Calabria and the lordship of Sicily, as feudal fiefs under the sovereignty of St Peter. In return, they swore loyalty to him and promised military help when needed.

This was a daring move, for the popes had never been sovereigns of southern Italy or of Sicily, and in strict law had no right to give what did not belong to them. The *Donation of Constantine*, however, was used to justify the transaction, and its advantages for the popes were at once obvious. The establishment of Norman rule in these traditionally Byzantine areas meant the replacement of Greek by Latin ecclesiastical obedience, and a massive expansion of papal influence. Two years later Nicholas' successor, Alexander II (1061–73), would experience the practical benefits of this new relationship when the disgruntled Roman nobility persuaded the German Regent, the Empress Agnes, to flout the election decree of 1059 and install an antipope, Honorius II, in Rome. Honorius was driven out and the city forced into obedience by Norman troops.

This confrontation was part of the deepening alienation between the reform papacy and the German monarchy. Papal legates had been excluded from the court and a synod of German bishops had excommunicated Pope Nicholas. Alexander compensated for these worsening relations by strengthening his links with the Normans. In 1063

Norman warriors fighting Muslims in Spain and Sicily were granted the banner of St Peter as a mark of papal blessing, and in 1066 Alexander sent the banner to Duke William of Normandy for his invasion of England. Since the Normans enforced clerical celibacy and paid at least lip-service to the campaign against simony, the Pope could view the conquest as a means of furthering the reform of the Anglo-Saxon church. The reconquest of Spain further extended papal influence, for in 1068 the King of Aragon placed his country under the feudal protection of St Peter, and in 1071 ordered the clergy to use the Roman liturgy instead of the ancient Mozarabic rite.

By now, in any case, the dynamic of reform made conflict with the German court increasingly likely. Leo had identified the appointment of bishops and other clerics by secular rulers as one of the root causes of corruption in the Church. The Emperor Henry III had been the chief patron of the reform party, yet paradoxically as emperor he was also the chief offender in the matter of 'lay investiture', appointing and deposing popes and bishops. The issue came to a head in Milan, where the reform campaign against simony and clerical marriage had become the banner of the Patarini, and was therefore associated with social radicalism: reform and revolution became synonymous. On the death of the Archbishop in 1071, the young Henry IV promptly appointed an aristocratic new candidate from the anti-reform faction, investing him with staff and ring. A rival candidate favoured by the Patarini was recognised by Rome, and in 1073 Pope Alexander II excommunicated the King's advisers. Pope and monarch faced each other across the ditch of reform.

The man behind this stiffening of resistance to Henry's claims was the Cardinal Archdeacon of Rome, Hildebrand. Of Tuscan peasant stock, he had been educated from his early youth for service in the Roman Church, and had been a force within the reform movement for almost twenty years. As a young man he had become a monk of the monastery of Santa Maria on the Aventine, one of the Roman houses reformed under Cluniac influence. He had also been a member of the staff of John Gratian, the deposed Pope Gregory VI (whom he revered, and whose name he took when himself elected pope in 1073). Hildebrand followed Gregory into exile at the imperial court at Cologne, where he probably entered a Cluniac monastery. Recalled to Rome by Leo IX to manage papal finances, he became a key figure in the evolution of the programme of the reformed papacy, and after the death of Humbert of Silva Candida in 1061 was the leading 'hawk' among the reformers. He was elected pope by popular acclaim on the death of Alexander II.

Gregory VII (1073–85) was one of the most energetic and determined men ever to occupy the See of Peter, and he was driven by an almost mystically exalted vision of the awesome responsibility and dignity of the papal office. His views were in many respects no more extreme than earlier advocates of reform like Humbert of Silva Candida, but in the hands of a ruling pope, and a pope of such singleness of vision, they took on a new radicalism. The reform movement had been imposed on the papacy by a German emperor, but Gregory owed nothing to the empire, and had seen a pope and a loved superior deposed by a king. His whole pontificate was a repudiation of the right of any king ever again to do such a thing.

His view of the papacy itself was set out in a remarkable and somewhat mysterious group of twenty-seven propositions, known as the *Dictatus Papae* (the Pope's Memorandum), inserted into the papal registers in 1075. The eleventh century had seen a steady growth in collections of legal canons, textbooks designed to serve the new spirit of reform. The twenty-seven maxims which make up the *Dictatus Papae* were probably headings for a new compilation of canons designed to illustrate papal prerogatives.[3]

If so, the compilation was never completed, for although some of the maxims simply summarised long-standing claims of the papacy, the overall thrust of the *Dictatus* was revolutionary, going far beyond anything to be found in the textbooks and precedent collections. For example, the claims that the Pope can be judged by no one, that no one may be condemned while they have an appeal pending at Rome, or that 'major causes' arising in any church should be referred to Rome for judgement, were all widely accepted, at least in theory. The insistence that 'the Pope alone is called by right *universal*' shows how completely Gregory the Great's rejection of the Patriarch of Constantinople's use of the title 'ecumenical' had been forgotten. The claim that the Pope alone has the right to use the imperial insignia, or that princes shall kiss his foot, was derived from the *Donation of Constantine*, and from the incorporation of the Byzantine ritual *proskynesis* or adoration of the Emperor into papal ceremonial. The West had long claimed that 'the Roman Church has never erred', conveniently forgetting Pope Honorius, and it was a claim that was often conceded in the East. Gregory or his compiler was only slightly stretching this claim, with the aid of Matthew 16: 18–19, by adding that it 'never will err to all eternity according to the testimony of holy scripture'. A similar stretching of generally accepted views is found in the claim that the Pope is supreme over all bishops and councils, and hence that his legates, even when only in minor orders (he himself had been only a subdeacon for most of his career) take precedence over all bishops.

On the other hand, the claims that the Pope alone has the power to depose or translate bishops, to call general councils and to authorise or reform canon law had all been vigorously contested in the Frankish church, and would go on being contested up to the Reformation. The most startling maxims in the *Dictatus Papae*, however, were more radical still, for Gregory claimed that the Pope can depose emperors, and that he can absolve subjects from their allegiance to wicked rulers. Everyone acknowledged the role of the Pope in the making of an emperor, but no one had ever before deduced from this that a Pope could *un*make an emperor. In the interests of an exalted vision of his own office, Gregory was here striking at the heart of contemporary belief about the nature of monarchy and the political community. The extravagance of that vision was evident in his claim that a duly ordained pope is automatically made a saint by the merits of St Peter, an assertion which, in the light of the popes of the preceding years, must have made his contemporaries blink.

Gregory's was a lonely vision of the papacy. Though he often spoke of other bishops as *confrater* or *coepiscopus* (brother and fellow bishop) in practice he saw himself as fighting a solitary battle, in a world which had turned its back on the demands of the Gospel. He told one correspondent in 1074, in language borrowed from the letters of Gregory the Great, that the Church 'is everywhere battered by stormy waves and through ill fortune and negligence has come near to being shipwrecked and submerged'. To Hugh of Cluny he wrote, 'I can find scarcely any bishops who were elected and live according to the canons, who lead the Christian people in love and not in worldly striving. And among the secular princes I know none who prefers God's honour to his own, or justice to gain.'[4] Unsurprisingly, therefore, he saw other bishops as, at best, assistants and servants, not as partners and equals. His critics among the German episcopate would complain that he ordered them about 'like bailiffs on his estate'.

To begin with at least, however, Gregory tempered these austere and lofty claims with commonsense, charity and a good deal of personal warmth. He soon challenged Henry's handling of Church appointments in northern Italy and Germany, and sent reforming legates to Germany to confront the problems there. Yet he was ready to absolve even grave offenders who demonstrated real penitence, he reversed harsh decisions made by his legates, and despite his horror of simony he did not make an issue over lay appointments to spiritual office, provided it was clear that there was no hint of a financial transaction involved.

Nevertheless, in the long run Gregory's uncompromising vision was bound to lead to conflict with the German King, and conflict duly came. In 1075 Gregory held a synod in Rome which formally condemned lay investiture as sinful, and in the same year the long-standing confrontation over Henry IV's appointments to Milan literally flared up, when tensions between the Patarini and the establishment led to the burning of the cathedral there. Determined to settle the matter once and for all, Henry deposed both claimants to the archbishopric of Milan, and installed his own candidate. Henry was responding to the urgent appeal of the city fathers, but his high-handed action directly challenged the Pope's vision of the rights of the See of Peter and the recent prohibition of lay investiture. A letter of rebuke and challenge from Gregory, accompanied by an oral threat of excommunication and deposition, provoked a drastic response. In January 1076 the King summoned a synod of his bishops at Worms, denounced the Pope as a 'false monk', and pronounced him deposed, a sentence later confirmed by the bishops of Lombardy.

Henry's letter of deposition betrays the resentment against the policies of the reform papacy which had been building up long before his accession, condemning the papal alliance with the Patarini, designed 'to gain favour with the vulgar crowd', and papal promotion of the lay boycott against the sacraments celebrated by married or simoniacal priests. The Pope, he declared, had 'incited subjects to rebel against their prelates' and 'given laymen authority over priests'. The King also challenged the right of the Pope to depose an anointed king, who can be judged by no one except God. Gregory had acted 'as if the empire and kingdom were at your disposal, and not in the disposal of God'.[5] This was the voice of outraged authority, scandalised by the revolutionary implications of the reform papacy's programme, and the challenge it opposed to the established monarchic order. These sentiments would have been applauded by Charlemagne.

Gregory replied by excommunicating all the bishops who had collaborated with Henry, and, in an extraordinary and impassioned document, cast in the form of an extended prayer to St Peter, he declared Henry deposed for rebellion against the Church, and released all Christians from their allegiance to him: 'On thy behalf I bind him with the bond of anathema ... that the peoples may know and acknowledge that thou art Peter and that on thy rock the Son of the Living God has built his Church and that the gates of hell shall not prevail against it'.[6]

Henry had in fact badly overplayed his hand. His father had deposed three popes, but times had changed, and the papacy had grown greatly in prestige since the days of the Tusculan puppet popes. The German bishops were loyal to the King, but most drew the line at deposing the duly elected successor of St Peter. Ecclesiastical support for Henry began to crack, a process hastened by the fact that Archbishop William of Utrecht, one of those who had excommunicated the Pope, died suddenly a month later, and his cathedral was struck by lightning immediately after Henry had celebrated Easter there. More urgently, many disaffected princes, especially in Saxony, had become used to independence during Henry's long minority. They now seized the opportunity to rise against him. An assembly of princes in August 1076 delivered an ultimatum. Henry must revoke his sentence against Gregory and swear religious obedience to the Pope, and he must obtain absolution within a year of the original excommunication. There was to be an assembly at Augsburg early in 1077 in the presence of the Pope to resolve the differences between Pope and King.

Henry's political position now became increasingly untenable: he was forced to a humiliating submission. Gregory had set out for the Augsburg assembly, but had trouble getting through Lombardy, where royalist bishops formed a strong anti-papal barrier. He took refuge in the castle of the loyal papalist Countess Matilda of Tuscany, at Canossa in the Apeninnes. There, in January 1077, with the ultimatum from the princes fast running out, Henry came to beg absolution, standing barefoot in the snow to beg the Pope's pardon. Gregory was reluctant to act before the many contested issues had been settled at Augsburg, but finally relented and gave Henry absolution.

Canossa was an astonishing victory for the papacy, with the most powerful monarch in Christendom a suppliant at its gate, and the political unity and stability of Germany in the Pope's hands. However much the royalist party in Germany and northern Italy might deny the Pope's claims to jurisdiction over kings, here was eloquent acknowledgement that the King could not rule in defiance of the Pope. But the victory rapidly turned to ashes. In pardoning Henry, Gregory saw himself as pardoning a repentant sinner, not as conceding the issues contested between Pope and King. He vigorously denied that he had intended to restore Henry unconditionally to the kingship. Events, however, now developed their own momentum. The Lombard bishops refused the Pope passage into Germany, and Henry was able to present the events at Canossa as an end to strife between him and the Pope. The rebellious princes believed that the Pope had betrayed them, and they went ahead with the election of an anti-king, Rudolf of Swabia. Gregory tried unsuccessfully to mediate between Henry and Rudolf, but Henry's truculent resistance to Gregory and Rudolf's genuine commitment to the papal reform movement in Germany made real neutrality difficult. In March 1080 Gregory once more solemnly excommunicated Henry, predicted his imminent death, deposed him from the throne and declared Rudolf king.

It was a disastrous move. Apart from anything else, the Pope had backed the wrong horse, for Rudolf was killed in battle later the same year, and Henry remained horribly healthy. But the mistake was worse than mere miscalculation. In 1076 moderate opinion everywhere had seen Henry as the aggressor, the Pope as defender of the right. The position was reversed now, for the papal deposition of Henry seemed no more than the thinnest of veils covering the naked ambition of the German princes: the papacy was sprinkling holy water on rebellion against the Lord's anointed. Gregory, more than ever, seemed a dangerous revolutionary, and a zealot determined to concede nothing. Slowly, support for the Pope began to ebb away.

Henry was therefore able to appoint an antipope, Archbishop Guibert of Ravenna, who took the name Clement III, though repeated attempts to capture Rome and install the Antipope came to nothing. The conflict reduced Gregory's finances to chaos, however, and he even contemplated mortgaging the lands of St Peter, a move vetoed by the Roman clergy. He got by on emergency supplies provided by friendly rulers like the Countess Matilda of Tuscany. In 1084, however, Henry was able at last to enter the city and hand St Peter's over to Clement. The Antipope crowned Henry emperor there a week later. Gregory watched helpless from the Castel Sant' Angelo, abandoned by most of his cardinals, and blamed by the Roman people for the disasters which had befallen the city. He was rescued by the army of the most powerful Norman in Italy, Robert Guiscard, with whom, ironically, Gregory had once been bitterly at odds. The rescue destroyed whatever credibility Gregory had left, however, for the Normans subjected the city to the worst sack it had experienced since the fall of the Roman empire. Gregory was forced to flee, pursued by the curses of the Romans, and he died in bitter exile in Norman territory at Salerno, defiant and free from self-doubt to the end – 'I have loved righteousness and hated iniquity: therefore I die in exile.'

Nineteenth-century historians liked to portray the confrontation between Pope and Emperor (or rather Pope and King, for in Gregory's eyes Henry was never Emperor) as a conflict between Church and state, with Gregory usurping the rights of the secular power. But no one in eleventh-century Europe thought of Church and state as separate or separable entities. There was only one Christendom, and the conflicts between Pope and Prince arose from conflicting claims to spiritual headship within that single entity. Gregory's achievement was to stake out, in the starkest of terms and with a new clarity, the spiritual claims of the Church. In the process, however, he shifted the foundations on which the relationship between Pope and monarch was believed to rest. Five centuries before, Pope Gelasius had declared that there were two powers, the pontifical and the royal, by which the world was chiefly governed. Gelasius had insisted that in things of the spirit the pontifical power took precedence, and that assumption had embedded itself in Western religious thinking. Yet pope and king remained twin sacred powers, ordained by God and each in his own sphere supreme.

Gregory brushed this venerable belief aside. Empire was pagan in origin, and belonged to an intrinsically lower order than the priesthood, above all the papacy. 'Shall not an authority founded by laymen,' he asked, 'even by those who do not know God, be subject to that authority which the providence of God Almighty for his own honour has established and in his mercy given to the world?' As for the reverence due to monarchy,

> Who does not know that kings and rulers are sprung from men who were ignorant of God, who by pride, robbery, perfidy, murders, in a word, by almost every crime at the prompting of the devil, who is the prince of this world, have striven with blind cupidity and intolerable presumption, to dominate over their equals, that is, over mankind? ... who can doubt that the priests of Christ are to be considered the fathers and the masters of kings and princes and all the faithful?'[7]

It is often thought that Gregory's claim to depose kings was rooted in a forgery, the *Donation of Constantine*. In fact, the precedent he liked to cite was Pope Zacharias' permission to Pepin to depose the last Merovingian King, Childeric III. This was far more radical than anything deducible from the *Donation*, for it was based on the notion not of rights, divine or otherwise, but of usefulness, fitness or suitability. Zacharias had deposed the King 'not so much for his iniquities, as because he was not fitted to exercise so great a power'. Gregory's view of kingship was profoundly desacralised, light-years away from the quasi-sacramental aura that hovered round the priest–kings of Carolingian Europe. It was for the Pope to decide who was or was not 'fitted' to exercise royal power, and the acid test was not birth, nor election by the people, nor anything except utility to the Church. This almost, but not quite, boiled down to obedience to the Pope. Gregory put up with the determined resistance of William the Conqueror to papal intervention in the English church, and his refusal to receive legates or allow English bishops to visit Rome, because the King, by embracing reform, preventing clerical marriage and abstaining from simony, had shown himself more honourable and more tolerable, more 'suitable', than other kings.

Gregory's pontificate represents the highest point of papal aspiration to dominion over the secular world. Later popes might refine his claims, but none would ever exceed them, and many would back away from their full implications. Paradoxically, he achieved startlingly little in concrete terms. Most of the bishops he excommunicated and deposed remained tranquilly in office, Henry long outlived him, and the papal reform changed direction after him, away from the attempt to rule the rulers, and towards the strengthening of its hold over the Church itself. Yet, if he was defeated in the short term, the spirit of papal reform owed everything to him, for after him the papacy never receded from its claims to freedom from secular and political control in spiritual matters. At the Council of Clermont, ten years after Gregory's death, Pope Urban II articulated once more the aims of the reform papacy, in terms borrowed from Gregory. The Church, he declared, 'shall be Catholic, chaste and free: Catholic in the faith and fellowship of the saints, chaste from all contagion of evil, and free from secular power'.[8] Because of Gregory, there would never again be another Charlemagne. No pope for a hundred years, perhaps no pope ever, would loom so large on the European scene as he had done.

II FROM PAPAL REFORM TO PAPAL MONARCHY

Gregory based his vision of papal supremacy on a total identification with the Apostle Peter: for him, as for all his predecessors, the Pope was the vicar of St Peter. But in the wake of the Gregorian era popes were increasingly dissatisfied with that way of stating their claims. The power they exercised over the Church, they believed, was not as deputies of Peter (for other bishops might claim apostolic origins for their sees) but, like Peter himself, as deputies of Christ. More than a century after Gregory's death Pope Innocent III (1198–1216) declared, 'We are the successor of the prince of the Apostles, but we are not his vicar, not the vicar of any man or Apostle, but the vicar of Jesus Christ himself.'[9]

It was a claim which was fleshed out in a multitude of ways. Throughout the eleventh and twelfth centuries reformers of every aspect of the Church's life turned to Rome for support, encouragement and spiritual heavy artillery. Monastic reformers like St Bernard of Clairvaux saw in the papacy a God-given power which could override the corrupt worldliness of local bishops and priests, and which could declare the God-given direction of the Church in its search for purity and holiness. The Pope was Moses, declaring God's law to his people. Bishops struggling against secular interference looked to Rome and the Pope's spiritual authority for protection. Above all, the development of a sophisticated system of canon law, over which the popes presided as judges and courts of final appeal, made the papacy the centre of every concern of Christendom.

System and order became the marks of the papal regime – this was the period, for example, in which the process of canonisation of saints, once a rule-of-thumb matter of local devotional recognition, was systematised and confined to the papacy. Papal business multiplied as litigants referred to the papal courts a multitude of matters once settled locally, such as dispensations for cousins to marry each other, appointments to lucrative ecclesiastical benefices, and the right to found a new monastery or to keep a private altar. Business grew like this not because popes insisted on their claims (though of course they did), but because Western Christendom found the papacy invaluable, a legal system which could be worked to everyone's advantage, and an external control over local vested interests. The expanding papacy, armed with the exalted spiritual claims for which Gregory had struggled, in a thousand practical ways oiled the wheels of Church life, bringing stability and order to everything from treaties between warring nations to the property rights of country curates.

The transformation of the papacy was, among other things, the transformation of its institutions. As Rome was increasingly perceived as the executive centre of the Church, machinery evolved to handle the increase of business. Leo IX had made innovatory use of regional synods of bishops and abbots, assembled wherever he went, and serving both to commit local hierarchies to the cause of reform and to publicise the reform programme. Under his successors, the Roman synod took on a particular importance. Gregory VII held a synod every year in Lent, and these functioned both as debating chambers within which doctrinal and disciplinary decisions were hammered out and as courts in which solemn judgements were pronounced. These assemblies consolidated the authority of the Pope by associating the bishops with him, and cemented a sense of common identity and commitment to reform under him. Despite Gregory's masterful way with other bishops, these synods were genuine deliberative assemblies, in which dissident voices were allowed. Under Urban II, whose synods were mainly held outside Rome, they increasingly functioned largely as rubber stamps, endorsing policies presented to the Council by the papal entourage.

In part this development reflected the growing numbers of those attending the synods. At the Council of Rheims in 1119, which excommunicated King Henry V and his antipope Gregory VIII, there were 427 participants, too large a forum for constructive discussion. The first three of the extraordinary series of four general councils held in the Lateran between 1123 and 1215 were platforms from which the fundamental emphases of the reform programme were reiterated, and delinquents condemned. Councils had become bodies in which the Pope proclaimed laws for Christendom. Indeed the mere calling of a general council by the Pope rather than the Byzantine Emperor was a novelty, and an eloquent expression of the massive growth in the stature of the papacy. Yet councils also served to consolidate a sense of episcopal identity and collegiality, and thereby to evolve a potential counterweight to the emerging papal monarchy – as the popes would one day discover to their cost. They helped also to educate bishops into a sense of the Church as an international and not merely a regional entity. At the Third Lateran Council, the prince-bishops of Germany and France rubbed shoulders with an Irish bishop whose sole income (as he explained) was derived from the milk from three cows, and the Pope consecrated two Scottish bishops, one of whom had walked to the Council with a single companion. Such encounters played an important role in the medieval reimagining of the Church not as a communion of local churches, but as a single international organisation, with the Pope at its head.

The transformation of synods and councils was possible because many of their functions were being taken over by the cardinals, in particular by the Consistory, the regular meeting of the cardinals with the Pope. The cardinals had been crucial to the success of the reform movement from the very beginning – Peter Damian had called them 'the spiritual senators of the Roman Church', and considered that the prerogatives of the cardinal bishops transcended those of patriarchs and primates. From 1059 the cardinals were the chief electors of the Pope, and the election decree of that year specified that the choice lay in the first place with the seven cardinal bishops. The rest of the cardinals refused to concede this, however, and the rules governing papal elections remained murky for more than a century. The exclusive right of the cardinals to elect was not in fact securely established till the mid twelfth century, and the requirement for a two-thirds majority, which still holds, was not fixed until Lateran III in 1179. Even so, a majority was not an inevitable guarantee of legitimacy. Innocent II (1130–43) was elected by a minority of cardinals, his opponent, the Antipope Anacletus II by a large majority, yet in the long run it was Innocent who was recognised as the true Pope.

In the course of the twelfth century the cardinals became the chief executive officers of the papacy, meeting regularly with the Pope – and sometimes without him – to hear legal cases, appeals and requests for canonisation, to discuss doctrinal issues and to issue judgements. There were in theory up to fifty-four cardinals at any one time. In practice, the cardinals themselves worked to restrict the number in the interests of conserving power in fewer hands. At the death of Innocent III in 1216 there were only twenty-seven, at the death of John XXI in 1277 there were only seven.

The cardinals gradually became much more than advisers. Initially their signatures to papal acts in Consistory were probably understood as those of witnesses, but they came to be seen as necessary for the legitimacy of papal decisions. As the papacy evolved towards being a spiritual monarchy, the cardinals took on some of the characteristics of barons. They developed their own strong sense of collegiality, which could often block papal policies or lead to indecisiveness and inconsistency. In the twelfth century most were Italians, but they were routinely recruited from outside Italy also for, as Bernard of Clairvaux asked his pupil Pope Eugenius III (1145–53), 'Surely they who are to judge the whole world must be chosen from the whole world?'[10]

The cardinals provided the pool from which the papal legates were selected. The popes from time immemorial had worked through locally based 'vicars' or agents, often the archbishops. These 'permanent legates', acting on behalf of the Pope in the localities, were gradually replaced by cardinals, especially cardinal bishops, despatched to deal with particular problems. The legates were ecclesiastical diplomats, travelling in a splendour calculated to overawe and outrank the local hierarchies, holding court and dispensing papal justice as they went, granting privileges, raising revenue to support the growing demands of the papal machinery. The legates could play a crucial role in the shaping of local churches along reformed lines, as Nicholas Breakspear, the future Pope Hadrian IV, did in Scandinavia in 1150, laying the foundations for the establishment of separate hierarchies in Norway and Sweden, till then subordinate to the Danish church. The system of legates institutionalised the mobile, proactive understanding of papal primacy over the churches of Europe which had been inaugurated by Leo IX's travels. Their role as the arms of the papal monarchy was crucial to its growing prestige and power. Of the nineteen popes in the century between Gregory VII and Innocent III, fifteen had been legates before their election.

As the Consistory increasingly became the supreme court of Christendom, the business heard before it became immensely varied, but often maddeningly trivial. Rome had originally been conceived as the court of final appeal: in the course of the twelfth century it took on the role of a court of first instance. With the journeying of Urban II in France and the sudden accessibility of the papal court outside Italy, business multiplied, and that trend intensified in the course of the next century. The Pope became the 'universal ordinary', exercising direct jurisdiction in every corner of Christendom, dispensing judgements which were built into the precedent books and became the basis of law.

The roots of this development were religious, based in the traditional Roman interpretation of the commission of Peter. Bernard of Clairvaux wrote: 'It is true there are other doorkeepers of heaven and shepherds of flocks: but you are more glorious than all of these . . . they have flocks assigned to them, one to each: to you all are assigned, a single flock to a single shepherd . . . You are called to the fullness of power. The power of others is bound by definite limits; yours extends even over those who have received power over others.'[11] For Bernard as for Gregory the Great this lofty commission was a call 'not to dominion, but to ministry through the office of your episcopacy'. Yet Bernard had no doubt that this ministry demanded that the Pope be exalted. 'Why should you not be placed on high, where you can see everything, you who have been appointed watchman over all?'[12]

It was the work of the twelfth-century papacy to transform this religious perception into legal reality. The great originator here was Pope Alexander III (1159–81), the first of a long line of lawyer-popes. About a thousand papal decretals, or formal papal letters embodying legal decisions, survive for the twelfth century. An amazing 700 of them are Alexander's, of which more than half concern English matters.

This flood of legislation was matched by a flood of legal codification. The study and practice of canon law had made a huge stride forward with the compilation by the Bolognese monk Gratian of the *Concordia discordantium canonum* ('the harmony of discordant laws') about the year 1140. This massive collection and systematisation of the whole body of canon law to the mid-century brought order and a dialectic method of resolving legal contradictions to a previously chaotic situation. It helped establish canon law as one of the principal fields of intellectual effort and advance over the next century. Gratian's work was the enterprise of a private scholar, as most medieval legal collections were: the papacy had no hand in it. But it drew heavily both on papalist forgeries like the *Donation of Constantine* and on papal decretals. Canon law was papal law, and the growing dominance of law within the Church was a key factor in the establishing of the papacy at the heart of the Church, as the monarch and his courts lay at the heart of secular legal systems.

All this had a negative side, which was much commented on. The right of any cleric to appeal to Rome, and the prohibition of local action against them while the appeal was pending, meant that culprits could fend off just punishment almost indefinitely by appealing to the Pope. The judgements given in the papal court on cases far away was often based on insufficient information, or the one-sided presentation of a party in a dispute. Ecclesiastical superiors could be harassed by mischievous accusations against them at the papal court, and Gregory's insistence in the *Dictatus Papae* that with papal permission 'subjects may accuse their rulers' seemed to many to subvert all order in Church and society. Bernard of Clairvaux would warn Eugenius III against undermining the hierarchy of the Church – 'You have been appointed to preserve for each the grades and orders of honours, not to prejudice them.'[13]

It is no accident that it was in this period that the papacy began to use the term 'curia' (court), to describe its administration. The term was introduced by Urban II, and he began a reorganisation of every aspect of the papal household, which over the next fifty years would evolve into a highly efficient working machine, at the head of which stood the cardinals. There was a price to pay for this increase of efficiency. This papal household developed a strong *esprit de corps*, and was perceived by outsiders as a closed shop – as indeed it might be. No fewer than nine of the cardinals created by Pope Paschal II (1099–1118) began their careers as chaplains and clerks within the Curia. All medieval bureaucracies financed themselves by exacting fees for their services, and the Curia was no exception. Round the judgement seat of Peter was thrown a *cordon insanitaire* through which gold was the only passport. Savage satire blossomed against the sale of grace at the papal Curia. The only saints venerated at Rome, it was said, were saints Albinus and Rufus, silver and gold. 'Blessed are the wealthy, for theirs is the court of Rome.'[14]

These criticisms were not confined to the Curia, but reached to the popes themselves. Papal finances in the Middle Ages were never secure. The bulk of the papal income came from the Patrimony of Peter, the territories ruled by the pope. But these were constantly being eroded by marauders like the Normans, and the recurrent conflict with the empire and the many papal schisms of the period meant that the 'real' popes were often cut off from the revenues of the Patrimony. In the last years of his life Gregory VII lived on hand-outs from his Norman allies and from friends of the papacy like Matilda of Tuscany, while his opponent, the imperial Antipope Clement III, enjoyed the revenues of the lands of St Peter. Similarly, Innocent II (1130–43) spent much of his pontificate in exile, while the Antipope Anacletus II commandeered the papal revenues.

The constant friction between the twelfth-century popes and the city of Rome itself, especially after the declaration of the Commune in 1143, when the city took its own government into its hands, made Rome unsafe for the popes, and they often had to take refuge else-where. Cut off from their patrimony, they were permanently strapped for cash. This meant they had to improvise, and successive popes looked for sources of funding which did not depend on the patrimony. Archbishops paid huge fees for the pallium, charges were made for papal privileges and exemptions, the monasteries and churches under papal protection paid a tax or 'census', kingdoms which were fiefs of the papacy, such as Spain and Sicily, paid feudal dues, and England and Poland paid Peter's Pence, a tax levied on churches throughout the land. In the course of the twelfth and thir-teenth centuries the papacy began to reserve to itself the right to appoint to an increasing number of benefices, such as those vacated by clergy promoted to bishoprics, or any benefices vacated by the death of a cleric while visiting the papal Curia. Such measures not only added to papal income, but vastly increased papal influence and control through a web of patronage. In 1192 Celestine III's chamber-lain Cencius compiled the *Liber Censuum*, an exhaustive listing of all sources of papal funding, designed to maximise revenue. It was far more than a financial tool, and became a powerful instrument of centralisation, a map of the institutions, churches and kingdoms over which the papacy exercised jurisdiction, and a means of consolidating and extending that jurisdiction.

From the beginning papal reform had gone alongside monastic reform, and monks remained central to the growing influence of the popes in the twelfth century. Papal protection defended reformed monasteries against the interference of hostile bishops or the depredations of lay proprietors and rulers. In return, the monasteries provided the papacy with a loyal and prestigious counterweight to recalcitrant local hierarchies. In the course of the eleventh century 270 religious houses had secured papal letters of exemption; in the course of the twelfth century, more than 2,000 would do so. To many observers, this development seemed subversive of the authority of bishops over religious houses in their dioceses, and this was something the papacy itself would become more sensitive to as the bishops themselves absorbed reforming ideals, and the confrontation between papacy and regional hierarchies eased.

Of the nineteen popes from Gregory VII to Innocent III, eleven were monks or canons regular. The reform popes had turned to the monasteries to find men free from the simony, corruption and unchastity which polluted so many secular clergy, so many of the bishops. Monks would be pure instruments for the cleansing of the Church. Gregory VII had written to Abbot Hugh of Cluny, asking him for 'some wise men from among his monks, suitable for him to appoint as bishops . . .' In the next two generations no fewer than eleven monks from Monte Cassino became cardinals. Gregory's sucessor Victor III (1086–7) had been Abbot of Monte Cassino, *his* successor Urban II (1088–99) was a monk of Cluny, and *his* successor, Paschal II (1099–1118) was Abbot of the monastery at San Lorenzo fuori le Mura. Urban consecrated the new church at Cluny, the largest in Christendom before the building of the new St Peter's in the Renaissance, while Paschal stacked the papal establishment with monks. He appointed seven monks of Monte Cassino as cardinals, and one third of all his sixty-six appointments to the college of cardinals were monks. Unsurprisingly, his successor, Gelasius II (1118–19), was a monk of Monte Cassino.

This extraordinary involvement of the monasteries with the papacy would outlive the great period of papal reform, and continue into the new age of monastic foundation represented by St Bernard and the Cistercians. Clairvaux produced eight cardinals in the course

of the twelfth century, and when Bernard's former pupil Bernardo
Pignatelli became Pope Eugenius III (1145–53) Bernard's influence
was so strong in the Curia that the cardinals grumbled that Bernard
was pope, not Eugenius.

Perhaps the most striking proof of the transformation of the
papacy into the greatest spiritual power in Christendom was the
extraordinary response to Urban II's call at Clermont in 1095 to
deliver Jerusalem from Muslim control, the launching of the First
Crusade. The Crusades were a revolutionary new phenomenon,
born out of the amalgamation of originally distinct elements – pilgrimage, holy war and, somewhat less certainly, the movement called
the Peace or Truce of God. The Peace of God movement had been
begun by the bishops of Burgundy and Aquitaine at the beginning of
the eleventh century. Revolted by the murderous wars of the aristocracy, they held peace councils, excommunicating the aggressors,
defending the rights of the poor who suffered because of war, and
imposing fixed periods or 'truces' during which all hostilities against
fellow Christians must cease. The movement spread to northern
Europe and to Italy, and was backed by the reform papacy.

An alternative to destructive wars between Christians was holy
war against the enemies of Christianity. There was a long tradition of
papal support for such 'holy wars', primarily those against the Muslims in Spain. Gregory VII had himself planned to lead a military
expedition to rescue the Christians of Constantinople from the
Turks. Urban may also have had in mind a rescue-attempt to help
Constantinople, but his prime concern was the liberation of the
Holy Places from Muslim rule. He called on the warriors of Europe
to channel their energies into an expedition to restore the Holy
Land to Christendom, and explicitly linked this warfare to the traditional spiritual benefits of pilgrimage – 'If any man sets out to free
the Church of God at Jerusalem out of pure devotion and not out of
love for glory or gain, the journey shall be accounted a complete
penance on his part.' So clear a link between salvation and holy war
was something new, and it caught the imagination of Europe. One of
the battlecries of the Crusade was *Deus lo volt* (God wills it!). Urban
made a cross of cloth sewn on to one's clothing the sign of the Crusade, and he bound those who agreed to go by a solemn vow. Failure
to honour this vow would bring spiritual condemnation, fulfilment
of it would bring remission of sins. He granted an indulgence, or free

pardon from the punishment due to sin, to all Crusaders, which was equivalent to a lifetime of hard penance. For hard-boiled and violent men in a world much preoccupied with sin and its consequences, this was a powerful incentive – as the Crusader Geoffrey of Ville-hardouin wrote, 'because the Indulgence was so great the hearts of men were much moved; and many took the cross because the Indulgence was so great'.[15]

The exact nature of Urban's promise is unclear, and the doctrine of Indulgences had far to go before reaching its full-blown form under Innocent III. But in any case, there were all the signs that popular enthusiasm here ran far ahead of papal intentions. The spiritual benefits which Urban promised boiled down to the substitution of the danger and effort of the Crusade for normal ecclesiastical penance. This was something distinct from the forgiveness of sins, which remained dependent on true repentance and sacramental confession. But all over Europe popular opinion seized on the notion that by virtue of involvement in the Crusade a man's sins were wiped away. Gradually the language of the popes about the Crusade dropped the early theological caution, and spoke of 'full remission of sins'. By the end of the twelfth century, theologians had begun to worry about this, and papal language returned to its earlier reticence. These fine distinctions, however, were lost on the majority of Crusaders, for the papacy had triggered a wave of popular religious feeling which took on a theological life of its own.

In 1095 all that lay in the future. In the meantime, from all over Europe, even from the fringes like Ireland and Scotland, men hurried to share in this great spiritual venture of arms. By 1099 Jerusalem had been taken and the Muslim population massacred. It was the beginning of an enterprise which would continue for centuries, and whose moral ambiguities would deepen with the passing years.

But for the papacy in the short term at least it was a triumph. Only the key-bearer could have aroused the imagination of Europe with a promise of sins unbound, of penances remitted by the act of holy war. Only the Pope had the moral authority to persuade Europe with unblinking certainty that 'God wills it'. The Crusade was led by the Bishop of Le Puy, appointed papal vicar by Urban, and the Pope placed the Crusaders themselves, their family, their property and lands under the protection of the Church – in effect the Crusader and his dependants became temporary clerics, and were thereby exempted from the jurisdiction of the secular courts. This legal protection was a very precious privilege, for no one could be sued or prosecuted for crimes or debt, for example, while it lasted. It was the material equivalent of the Crusading Indulgence, and like the Indulgence was a benefit only the Pope could have bestowed. Finally, the most telling aspect of the First Crusade was that this mighty wave of military enthusiasm owed nothing whatever to any king or emperor. The Pope had summoned the chivalry of Europe round the banner of the cross and St Peter, to overwhelming effect. No secular ruler could have done as much, and there could be no more eloquent demonstration of the centrality of the reformed papacy in the religious imagination of medieval Europe.

III   THE PINNACLE OF PAPAL POWER

The papacy at the beginning of the twelfth century was at an unprecedented height in its spiritual prestige, and in its own self-confidence. As the century progressed, it would gather round itself more and more of the trappings of monarchy. New popes were crowned with a distinctive cap and gold circlet, quite distinct from the episcopal mitre they wore during the liturgy. According to the *Donation of Constantine*, this cap or tiara symbolised their lordship of the West. The rebuilding and decoration of the churches of Rome which successive popes undertook made lavish use of imperial motifs. Papal thrones were embellished with lion arm-rests, and porphyry and gold featured large in the designs for the Roman sanctuary floors, altars and pulpits produced by the Cosmati workshops. St Peter, declared Bernard of Clairvaux, had received the whole world to govern, and it was the task of his vicar 'to direct princes, to command bishops, to set kingdoms and empires in order'. There were indeed two powers, 'two swords', the spiritual and the temporal, but both belonged to Peter, 'the one to be unsheathed at his nod, the other by his hand'.[16]

For Bernard this was a spiritual not a temporal claim, and he deplored the secular pomp and the secular business with which the popes were surrounded. Peter, he told Eugenius III, 'is not known ever to have gone in procession adorned in jewels and silk, nor crowned with gold, nor mounted on a white horse nor surrounded by knights . . . In these respects you are the heir not of Peter but of Constantine.'[17] In practice the distinction between what Peter had bequeathed to the papacy and what came from Constantine was not so easy to unpick, and the popes of the twelfth century did not try very hard. The burial of Innocent II in a porphyry tomb from the Castel Sant'Angelo, which was believed to have been the sarcophagus of Hadrian, and of Pope Anastasius IV in a porphyry coffin which had once held the bones of St Helena, demonstrated how closely the spiritual and temporal claims of the popes had converged.

It is hardly surprising, therefore, that the papacy remained at odds with the empire for much of the twelfth century. The Investiture Controversy became both the symbol of the reformed papacy's claims and the rock on which it seemed they might founder. The imperial Antipope Clement III died in September 1100, and his successors were men of straw who lacked imperial backing. The schism rumbled on till 1111, but was not a serious threat to the popes. But Henry remained determined to maintain his right to invest the bishops of his realm with ring and staff, and his overthrow and replacement by his son Henry V in 1106 changed nothing on this score: Pope and King remained at loggerheads. When Henry V came to be crowned emperor in Rome in February 1111, Paschal II offered a desperate solution. If Henry would renounce investiture and permit free and canonical election of bishops, the Church in return would renounce all the 'regalia' – land, property and income derived from the secular power. From henceforth, the clergy from parish clerk up to the archbishops would live on voluntary offerings and church dues like tithes.

Paschal was a monk, intent on separating the Church from the contamination of worldliness, but this solution had no chance of success. When the terms of the agreement were read out at the coronation ceremony, the German princes and bishops present rioted, refusing to consider so radical a dismantling of the structure of German landed society. The coronation could not proceed. Henry's response was to clap the Pope and cardinals into gaol, and to threaten to recognise the Antipope Silvester IV. Paschal caved in, crowned Henry, and in April 1111 granted the 'privilege of Ponte Mammolo', conceding the right of investiture to the Emperor.

Paschal bitterly regretted this betrayal of the reform cause, and he subsequently revoked the 'pravilege', as the 'depraved privilege' came to be called, in a dreadful twelfth-century pun. His frail and elderly successor, the Cassinese monk Gelasius II (1118–19), was to pay the price for this resistance, leading a harassed and persecuted existence, ousted from Rome by the antipope Gregory (VIII) and on the run from Henry V: he died and was buried at Cluny. It was clear that if the work of the papacy was to be conducted with anything like tranquillity, the issue of investiture had to be settled once and for all. Pope Callistus II (1119–24) was able to do this, in the Concordat of Worms he concluded with Henry V in 1122. The Worms agreement built on a compromise arrangement first worked out in Norman England, whereby newly elected bishops swore fealty to the ruler for the temporalities of their sees, but the King made clear that he claimed no spiritual jurisdiction over them by abandoning investiture with staff and ring. Instead, on receipt of their pledge of allegiance he conferred their lands on them with a tap from his sceptre. Canonical elections to the bishoprics and abbacies would be held in the Emperor's presence, and the Emperor was given power of arbitration in the event of disputed elections.

The settlement at Worms ended the conflict with the empire, at least for one generation, and the breathing-space it bought allowed the popes to turn their attention away from a sterile confrontation with the secular power to the implementation of religious reform within the Church at large. They had in any case other troubles closer at hand. Gregory VII had allied himself and the cause of reform with the Pierleoni family, wealthy bankers recently converted from Judaism, who threw the weight of their new money behind the Gregorian papacy. Their great rivals were the Frangipani, and the twelfth-century popes found themselves increasingly caught in the crossfire between these feuding families. There was no return to the papal captivity of the 'dark century'. Never again would a single family own the papacy, as the Theophylacts or Tusculani had done, but they could make Rome uncomfortable for the popes, and the elections of Honorius II (1124–30) and Innocent II (1130–43) were dogged and complicated by these dynastic tensions.

The popes were also threatened by the mounting hostility of the city of Rome to their rule. As the papacy became more international, it forfeited Roman loyalty. This distancing was already present in the 1059 papal election decree, which effectively excluded the people of the city from any real say in the process. Every new pope had to spend huge sums on lavish gifts to the citizens to ensure acceptance of his election, a use of Church funds which brought bitter criticism from reformers everywhere. The twelfth century also saw a revival of republican spirit in Rome, and a pride in the city's secular past, which culminated in 1143 with the setting up of a commune by the citizens and the establishment of an independent senate. All the mid-century popes had to contend with the threat of revolution in the city and the papal state round Rome. Lucius II (1144–5) died of wounds sustained while storming the forces of the Commune on the Capitol, and Eugenius III, Hadrian IV (1154–9) and Alexander III (1159–81) were all driven out of the city by the citizens.

Control of Rome was not everything, however. The Antipope Anacletus II, Pietro Pierleoni, elected by a majority of the cardinals in 1130, was securely in charge of Rome, backed by the family bank and the Normans of southern Italy. But his opponent, Innocent II, was widely perceived as the true inheritor of the papal reform movement. He received the support of the most influential propagandist in Europe, Bernard of Clairvaux, and of most of the monarchs and national hierarchies of Europe. These included the Emperor Lothar III, who signalled his recognition of Innocent by performing the stirrup service for him at their first meeting, leading his horse by the bridle, as Constantine was reputed to have done for Pope Silvester, and as Pepin had done for Pope Stephen. Though Anacletus held the Vatican and St Peter's till his death in 1138, almost no one in Europe believed him to be the true Pope, and his claims were set aside by the Second Lateran Council in 1139, attended by more than 500 bishops from sees as far apart as Lincoln and Jerusalem. The papacy was now more than ever an international, not a local, institution.

Many of the problems confronting the mid-twelfth-century papal monarchy are starkly revealed in the pontificate of the only English Pope, Nicholas Breakspear, Hadrian IV (1154–9). Breakspear was a native of St Albans, but had been refused entry as a monk to the monastery there (his father did enter the monastery, where he is buried). He pursued a monastic vocation abroad, and became canon and eventually abbot of St Rufus in Avignon. Talent-spotted by Eugenius III, he became cardinal bishop of Albano (prompting puns about failure in St Albans but success in Albano), and was a hugely effective papal legate in Scandinavia, where he restructured the church and established new hierarchies for Norway and Sweden.

Elected on a wave of triumph on his return from his Scandinavian mission, Hadrian was immediately confronted with attacks on papal territory in southern Italy from the Norman King William I of Sicily. The reform papacy's early support for the Normans had soured as their territorial ambitions had grown, and Norman support had helped prop up the Antipope Anacletus II. Hadrian was also under pressure from the Commune in Rome, now led by the radical monk Arnold of Brescia, who denounced all ecclesiastical wealth, and the papacy in particular as the head of a corrupt system. Hadrian had been a notorious disciplinarian as abbot in Avignon, and he was equally hard-boiled as pope. He put the city of Rome under interdict so that no sacraments could be celebrated there, expelled Arnold, and later had him arrested and executed by the German King, Frederick Barbarossa.

On this occasion Barbarossa featured as an ally of the Pope, but he soon revived the old hostility between Emperor and Pope, with all the bitterness of the earlier Investiture disputes. The citizens of Rome had tried to play Pope and King off against each other by offering Barbarossa the imperial throne. Frederick, a deep admirer of Charlemagne and Otto the Great, was indeed determined to restore the glories of their empire, but he considered that the empire came from God and his own strong right arm. He had no intention of accepting it from a bunch of middle-class radicals.

Hadrian therefore hoped for an alliance with Frederick which would simultaneously eliminate the danger from the Commune and provide him with protection against the Normans. Frederick, however, was not content to be the Pope's policeman, and profoundly distrusted the monarchic pretensions of the papacy. He had probably seen the Lateran mosaics depicting the Emperor Lothar receiving the crown of empire from Innocent II in 1133, with the inscription 'The king becomes the vassal of the Pope and takes the crown which he gives.' Barbarossa would be no man's vassal. He came to Italy to be crowned, but when he and Hadrian met in Henry's military camp at Sutri in June 1155, he refused to perform the stirrup service, which he took to be a sign of vassalage. His refusal was immediately interpreted as a declaration of hostility to the Pope, and Hadrian's terrified cardinals turned tail and ran, leaving the Pope alone. Agitated negotiations and consultation of ancient precedents persuaded Frederick to surrender on this issue next day, but he did so with a bad grace. It became clear that Hadrian could count on no help from him.

A further disastrous misunderstanding in 1157 led to a total break-down in relations. Hadrian sent legates to the Diet of Besançon with a letter to Frederick reminding him of the 'benefits' he had received from the Pope when he had been crowned. The German word used to translate the Latin 'Beneficia' meant feudal grants, and the legates were lucky to escape with their lives, as Frederick's court erupted at the Pope's apparent claim that the Emperor was his vassal. Hadrian may well have meant to imply just this, but, if so, he backed off rapidly. The damage was done, however, and at Hadrian's death Pope and Emperor were at odds over episcopal appointments in northern Italy (including Ravenna, that ancient thorn in the side of the popes) and Hadrian was plotting with discontented Lombards to rise against Frederick.

All this forced yet another papal change of heart about the Normans. Unable to beat them, Hadrian joined them. He recognised William as king of Sicily, and granted him sovereignty as a papal vassal over southern Italy, together with rights over the church there which would have made Gregory VII turn in his grave. He extended this favour to the Normans elsewhere, and in the bull *Laudabiliter* of 1156 he granted the English King Henry II the right to incorporate Ireland into his realms.

There was more to this snuggling up to the Normans than papal opportunism. The church in Ireland was already experiencing the stirrings of reform – St Malachy, Archbishop of Armagh, who died in 1146, introduced the Cistercians into Ireland, and Malachy himself died in the arms of St Bernard. In 1162 another great reformer, Lurchan ua Tuathail, would become archbishop of Dublin. But the permissiveness of Irish social and sexual customs, and the still partially tribal church organisation there, were deeply shocking to European convention. In the life of Malachy which he composed Bernard painted the Irish church and people in the most lurid terms, in order to highlight the Archbishop's reforming zeal and heroism. The Irish were not men but beasts, wallowing in vice, worse than any other barbarians. This jaundiced picture of the Irish was held pretty generally throughout Europe, especially in reforming circles, and it helps to explain the Pope's actions.

Henry did not at once act on *Laudabiliter*, and when the Normans did descend on Ireland in 1169 they did so at the invitation of a deposed king of Leinster (the eastern province of Ireland), Diarmuid

Mac Murchada, as defenders of the right. Mac Murchada himself was a leading patron of Church reform, a monastic founder and friend of the Cistercian movement, and the brother-in-law of Lurchan ua Tuathail. In 1162 he had presided as king at an Irish reform synod attended by papal legates. So the first round of the long and tortured relationship between England and Ireland began with papal blessing, and with a Norman force which could plausibly claim to be warriors for the Pope, commissioned by the vicar of St Peter to reform 'the barbarous enormities of the Irish'.

Hadrian's pontificate illustrated vividly the narrow room for manoeuvre, and the far reaching claims, of the twelfth-century popes. For all his decisiveness and vigour, none of the problems he confronted was resolved, and he left his successors facing an alienated empire and involved in an uneasy and dangerous alliance with the unscrupulous and land-hungry Normans. Alexander III (1159–81) would have to contend with a series of four imperial antipopes, the first of whom, Ottaviano of Monticelli (Victor IV), snatched the papal scarlet mantle from Alexander's shoulders at his installation, and placed himself on the papal throne.

Alexander was a vigorous reforming pope, whose legal expertise enormously contributed to the consolidation of papal authority. The Third Lateran Council, which he convened in 1179, was another milestone on the papal road to domination of the Western Church, enacting a wide-ranging papal programme against clerical corruption, heresy and in support of the blossoming of theology and canon law within the universities. The Council met in the wake of an accommodation between Alexander and Barbarossa, but for much of Alexander's pontificate the confrontation with a hostile emperor had hamstrung the papacy, as it would his immediate successors. Throughout the 1160s, for example, fear of tipping the English King Henry II into the arms of the Emperor and the Antipope Paschal III had coloured Alexander's dealings with England, and prevented him from supporting wholeheartedly Becket's resolute stand against royal encroachments on the liberties of the Church. Not till Becket's martyrdom and the King's consequent penance was Alexander in a position to call Henry to order.

By the end of the twelfth century, the finger of the papacy lay on every living pulse in the Church. The last Pope of the century, Innocent III (1198–1216), may stand as the greatest representative of this pinnacle of papal power and influence. One of the series of lawyer popes thrown up by the growing centrality of canon law within the papal system, Innocent was a Roman nobleman whose personal name was Lothar of Segni. He was only thirty-seven when elected in 1198. An uncle had been Pope Clement III (1187–91), Innocent's successor but one was his nephew Gregory IX (1227–41), while a great-nephew was to become Alexander IV (1254–61). But Innocent was elected pope on his merits rather than because of his family connections. Highly intelligent and a man of absolute personal integrity, he had studied theology at Paris and (probably) law at Bologna. As a student he had made the pilgrimage to the shrine of Thomas Becket at Canterbury, the great martyr for the spiritual rights of the Church against the claims of secular rulers, and this was a concern which would remain close to Innocent's heart.

Innocent was a small, handsome, witty man, fond of puns and ironic wordplay, keenly alert to the absurd in the events and people around him. His first biographer described him as 'strong, stable, magnanimous and very sharp'. He might have added that Innocent was also supremely self-confident. Certain that he enjoyed the direct guidance of God, he felt the full majesty of his own office. 'Others are called to the role of caring,' he declared, 'but only Peter is raised to the fullness of power. Now therefore you see who is the servant who is set over the household, truly the vicar of Jesus Christ, the successor of Peter, the Christ of the Lord, the God of Pharaoh.'[18] Armed with that conviction, he threw himself into the reform of the Church in every aspect.

He was himself the author of several enormously popular devotional treatises, written before he became pope. His *Mysteries of the Mass* became the basis of the standard liturgical handbooks of the later Middle Ages. His treatise on the *Misery of the Human Condition*, a conventional diatribe against the misery and vanity of the world, perhaps inspired by his long years in the corridors of power at the Lateran, survives in a stupendous 700 manuscripts. Though his health was poor, he was restlessly active, and his energy often exhausted his entourage. One of his chaplains has left a remarkable and attractive account of a summer encampment in August 1202 outside the walls of St Benedict's monastery at Subiaco, where Innocent had gone to get away from the heat of Rome. In the stifling heat the chaplains and clerks of the Curia choked on the smoke from the cook's fire, were devoured by gnats and were distracted by the noise of the cicadas and the pounding of the apothecary's pestle and mortar. They nodded asleep over their paperwork while, in a shabby tent to one side, the Pope, 'our most holy father Abraham', 'the third Solomon', worked on, emerging occasionally to bathe his hands and rinse his mouth in a small stream. The chaplains eventually forced him to stop, and sat at his feet chattering and swapping jokes.

For the last twenty years of the twelfth century the papacy had been overshadowed by the hostility of the Hohenstaufen dynasty in Germany, and for the last ten the papal state had been in danger of encirclement, because of the death without heir of the Norman King William of Sicily. The Emperor Henry VI claimed Sicily for his infant son, the future Frederick II, hoping to unite north and south Italy under a single dynasty. The popes, insisting that Sicily was a papal fief, backed another claimant, so as to prevent this imperial pincer-movement. But Henry himself died in 1197. His death brought a contested royal election in Germany, and the succession of the infant Frederick in Sicily, whom the Empress Regent quickly made a papal ward and placed under Innocent's protection. Henry's death also created a power vacuum in central and northern Italy, and Innocent determined to make the most of it by attempting to recover the papal territories which had been relentlessly eroded in the twelfth-century conflicts with the empire and the Normans. These included lands in the Campagna, in Tuscany, in Umbria and the Marches of Ancona, in Ravenna and in the scattered lands which Matilda of Tuscany had bequeathed to the reform papacy. He worked on Italian resentment of imperial taxation, making effective use of the text 'my yoke is easy, my burden light' to recommend papal overlordship. His eventual territorial gains were slight, but the campaign did result in an increase of tribute from cities which had previously paid little or nothing: Innocent used the new revenue to fund ambitious poor-relief programmes and the extensive renovation of the Roman churches.

Innocent based his campaign to recover the eroded patrimony on documented gifts by the Carolingian and German emperors, not on the contested generalities of the *Donation of Constantine*. There can be no doubt, however, that he took an exalted view of the lordship of the Pope over the Emperor. He believed that the Pope had ultimate authority over the secular as well as the religious sphere. Christ, he declared, had left to Peter 'the government not only of the Church but of the whole world'. He liked to quote Jeremiah: 'I have set you over nations and over kingdoms, to pluck up and to break down, to destroy and to overthrow.' The Pope, he believed, was set in the middle between God and man, 'lower than God but higher than man: one who judges all, and is judged by no one'. Yet he thought that papal intervention in secular matters should be *ratione peccati*, confined to cases where human sin and error threatened the fundamental purpose of secular government, which was the protection and furthering of the Church, and the extirpation of heresy.

Given these views, it is not surprising that when the partisans of Henry's brother Philip of Swabia tried to insist that Innocent *must* crown him emperor because he had been duly elected 'king of the Romans', Innocent replied that in contested elections the Pope was free to choose between the candidates. The only relevant criterion was the candidate's 'suitability' as a champion of the rights and interests of the Church.

Philip had strong support and was the better candidate: he would eventually have prevailed, but his murder in 1208 resulted in the victory of the papacy's candidate, Otto of Brunswick. He posed at first as a dutiful son of the Roman Church and a patron of reform, and Innocent rejoiced that at last Pope and Emperor might join forces to reform Church and world: 'If we two stand together, "the crooked shall be made straight and the rough places smooth", for the pontifical authority and the royal power (both of them supremely invested in Us) fully suffice for this purpose, if each helps the other.'[19] It was not to be. Otto soon revived all the imperial claims of Barbarossa and Henry VI, and Innocent transferred his hopes to Frederick of Sicily; he excommunicated Otto in March 1211. The German opposition to Otto seized on this signal and elected Frederick II in his place, and Innocent's political instincts seemed justified, for in 1213, in the 'Golden Bull of Eger' Frederick guaranteed free episcopal and abbatial elections throughout his realms, surrendered claims over vacant churches, and allowed the right of appeal to the Curia, formerly restricted in Sicily. In 1215 he was crowned at Aachen, and took the Crusade oath. In the same year, the Fourth Lateran Council confirmed him as emperor. To allay Innocent's fears about encirclement, he undertook to crown his infant son Henry king of Sicily, but to make him a papal ward and to allow the Pope to appoint a regent for Sicily. Frederick was to renege

on all this, but by the time of Innocent's death in 1216 the Pope's policy towards the empire seemed an unqualified success.

In his relations with other monarchs Innocent combined the same
exalted theory of papal supremacy with a practical willingness to
accommodate friendly rulers. He intervened energetically in succession disputes in Norway, Sweden, Bohemia and Hungary, but is most
famous for his excommunication of King John of England in 1209
because of the King's refusal to accept the appointment as archbishop
of Canterbury of Stephen Langton, an old friend of the Pope's from
their student days in Paris. After a bitter conflict John gave in, and
made England and Ireland feudal fiefs of the papacy, paying a tribute of
1,000 marks a year. He also asked Innocent to send a papal legate to
regulate Church affairs in England (English kings since William the
Conqueror had excluded legates) and he granted free elections to
bishoprics and abbacies; in 1215 he too took the Crusading vow. This
papal victory on all fronts, however, did not undermine royal power.
Instead the Pope subsequently gave almost unqualified support to the
King against his barons (including Archbishop Langton) and, in support of John, Innocent declared Magna Carta null and void.

But the keynote of Innocent's pontificate was practical, pastoral
reform. Theology at Paris when he was a student was dominated not
by high speculation, but by practical topics such as the morality of
the laity, the celebration of the liturgy, the reform of the Christian
life. These were the issues that recur throughout Innocent's own
writings, and that characterise his greatest achievement, the work of
the Fourth Lateran Council, which met in 1215. The Council tackled an enormous range of issues, all of them practical: the establishment of orthodox teaching, especially on the sacraments – this was
the Council which defined the doctrine of Transubstantiation – new
regulations requiring every Christian to go to confession and communion at least once a year, improvements in record-keeping in
Church courts, a tidying up and easing of the laws about marriage
within prohibited degrees of kinship, rules for the better discharge
of episcopal duties and especially preaching and catechising in the
language of the people, and reform of the monasteries. Behind much
of this the distinctive concerns of the Pope can be detected, and the
Council was the high point of the medieval papacy's involvement
with and promotion of the best reforming energies in the Church
at large.

Orthodoxy was one of Innocent's major preoccupations. It was an age of spontaneous and often alarming movements of religious enthusiasm. The wealth and worldliness of many churchmen and the embedding of the Church in the heart of the European establishment produced waves of revulsion among the devout, which often spun off into heresy. Innocent set about rooting out all such heresy – especially among the Cathars in Spain and southern France, a group whose religious imagination was haunted by the conflict between the powers of darkness and light. They identified the material world with evil, and so their leaders or 'perfecti' ate no meat, abstained from sex and denied the value of the Church's sacramental system.

Innocent encouraged secular rulers to stamp out such doctrinal deviance in their realms, and he sponsored preaching and teaching campaigns against Catharism, also known as Albigensianism, at first using Cistercian missionaries. Part of the attraction of the Cathar teachers, however, was their austerely 'apostolic' lifestyle. The Cistercian preachers, by contrast, mounted on horses and dressed in fine cloth, failed to impress. Innocent turned instead to a group of wandering priest–preachers led by the Spaniard Dominic Guzman. Dominic and his disciples, who would one day become the Order of Preachers, were skilled in theological dialectic, but they also lived the life of poor men, begging their bread and going as roughly clad as the Cathar apostles. Innocent's acceptance of such a group was characteristic of his freedom from a slavish imprisonment within bureaucracy and law. For all his own canonistic and administrative preoccupations, he possessed the imaginative ability to recognise and rise to the needs of the moment.

In all this Innocent did not shrink from the use of force, especially after the murder of Peter of Castelnau, the legate he had sent to organise the mission to the Cathars in the south of France, in 1208. He believed that the sword had been placed in the hand of the ruler for the protection of God's truth. He encouraged the Crusade against the Albigensians which climaxed in the appalling massacre of the inhabitants of the Cathar town of Béziers in 1209, offering an Indulgence to all who took part in the campaign and raising funds for it by a tax on the French clergy.

This forceful way with error, however, needs to be set alongside Innocent's sensitive handling of the many charismatic lay religious movements which characterised the time, and of which the Franciscans were the most orthodox expression. Innocent recognised that heresy could be effectively disarmed only if genuine religious zeal and reform were fostered: repression was not enough. Francis was introduced to Innocent by the Pope's nephew, Cardinal Ugolino, and the Pope was clearly exercised by Francis' eccentricity and uncouth appearance at their first meeting in the Lateran – according to Matthew Paris, he told Francis to go and play with the pigs, where he belonged. To his consternation, Francis chose to take him literally, and reappeared in the Consistory next day caked in pig-dung: the Pope hastily granted his requests.

Whatever the truth of that story, Francis and his companions did seek papal support for their movement of absolute poverty. Innocent would put nothing on paper, but he tonsured the little group, thereby extending to them the protection (and restraints) of clerical status, and he gave them permission to preach, provided they kept to moral exhortation and steered clear of theology. It was a characteristically shrewd response, cautious but supportive, and the Franciscans went on to become pillars of papal authority. It says a good deal about the centrality of the papacy that popular charismatic movements like Francis' should need and seek papal backing. It says much for the vision and genuine spirituality of Innocent and his immediate successors that the support was forthcoming.

Crusading in general had Innocent's full support. War against the infidel was 'the battle of Christ', and he shared the conviction of his predecessors that the recovery of the Holy Places from Muslim rule was the special responsibility of the Pope. This aspect of his activity, however, was almost uniformly disastrous. He first called for a Crusade to liberate Jerusalem in 1198, and imposed an income tax of 2.5 per cent on the clergy to fund it. In the event, the Fourth Crusade was not launched till 1202, and it had spun out of Innocent's control before any of the Crusaders left the West. The Crusading army was diverted to Constantinople by an invitation from the nephew of Emperor Alexius III to help overthrow his uncle and establish a regime in communion with Rome. This turned into the brutal sacking of the Eastern Christian capital, Constantinople, and the creation of a puppet regime with a Latin emperor, and a Latin patriarch. In theory, the schism between East and West was over. In reality, the outrage of the Fourth Crusade permanently poisoned relations between Greek East and Latin West.

Innocent certainly had not intended this outcome, and tried to turn the troops away from Constantinople, but he came to welcome it as a providential solution of the problem of the Eastern schism. 'By the just judgement of God,' he wrote, 'the kingdom of the Greeks is translated from the proud to the humble, from the disobedient to the faithful, from schismatics to Catholics.'[20] He never abandoned the Crusading ideal, however, and applied Crusading theory to the conversion of the remaining pagans of the north, encouraging the Christians of Saxony and Westphalia to take up arms against the pagans of Livonia, by granting them the same spiritual privileges as would be gained from a pilgrimage to Rome. To encourage crusading zeal he extended the Crusade indulgence not only to those who took part directly, but to those who merely assisted the Crusade with money or advice. One of the principal objectives of the Fourth Lateran Council was the launching of another Crusade to Jerusalem, which Innocent himself planned to lead from Sicily, though he was to die before the Crusade (in which, famously, Francis of Assisi took part) was launched.

IV EXILE AND SCHISM

The successors of Innocent III worked in his shadow. Most of the enterprises of Honorius III (1216–27) and Innocent's devout and energetic nephew Gregory IX (1227–41) were inherited from him. They continued his support for the new and controversial mendicant orders. Honorius formally established the Dominicans in 1216, and Gregory, who had acted as Francis' minder and protector in the Curia, canonised Francis in 1228, less than two years after the Saint's death. Honorius, Gregory and their immediate successors were all Bologna-trained lawyers, and they also developed further Innocent's work of legal codification. In 1234 Gregory promulgated the *Liber extra*, the first complete, authoritative collection of papal decretals, edited by the Spanish curial lawyer Raymond of Penafort. Almost a third of the decretals it contained were Innocent's, and the collection was to remain the fundamental canon law text until the First World War.

Honorius continued Innocent's missionary involvements in the Baltic region, and he also carried on and stepped up the campaign against the Albigensians. Gregory was equally committed to stamping out heresy, and he put the seal on the use of force against error in

1231, when he absorbed into canon law the imperial legislation which decreed the burning of convicted heretics by the secular power. In the same year he instituted the papal Inquisition, designed to supplement diocesan courts by providing an international tribunal to combat a heresy which itself paid no heed to diocesan boundaries. Gregory put the Inquisition in the hands of the friars, especially the Dominicans, whose sometimes relentless activities earned them the nickname *Domini canes* – the hounds of the Lord (the pope). The Inquisition, in fact, often supplanted the diocesan courts it had been founded to assist. It was soon active in France, Italy, Germany, the Low Countries and northern Spain, and under its fierce scrutiny Catharism shrivelled and faded away.

The most awkward legacy of Innocent III, however, was Frederick II. Frederick was one of the most forceful kings of the Middle Ages, a proud and ruthless ruler. He was half-Sicilian, and spent most of his life in the Mediterranean. His court was an exotic cultural, racial and religious mix and he displayed his pragmatism by tolerating both Jews and Muslims. He was, however, an unsatisfactory son of the Holy See. All his assurances about the preservation of papal lordship in Sicily, his respect for the rights of the Church and the integrity of the papal patrimony, and his vow to assist in the main papal enterprise by going on Crusade, proved false. In the hope of persuading him to set off for Jerusalem, Honorius crowned Frederick emperor in 1220, to no avail. In 1227 Gregory, disgusted by endless empty promises, excommunicated Frederick. In fact, in the following year, the Emperor, still under the papal ban, went to the Holy Land, and in a bloodless negotiation succeeded in recovering the Holy Places, but Gregory was not mollified, and fomented rebellion and the election of an anti-king in Germany.

An uneasy truce broke down again by 1239, when it became clear that Frederick planned to turn the empire and Sicily into an hereditary monarchy. This was to be the first step in the imperial capture of the whole of Italy, including Rome. Emperor and Pope exchanged insults like fishwives. Gregory denounced the Emperor as a heretic, an oath-breaker and a man who had gone native by adopting Muslim customs, including a harem guarded by eunuchs (which was perfectly true). Frederick denounced the extortion of the Roman curial system, claimed that attacks on himself were really attacks on all secular rule (in which there was also some truth) and denounced the

Pope, though not the papacy, as Antichrist. Confronted by Frederick's call to the princes of Christendom to unite against Rome, Gregory summoned a general council in 1241. In retaliation, Frederick invaded the Papal States. The council never met, because Frederick coolly waylaid the Genoese fleet and kidnapped 100 of the bishops arriving by sea, and the Pope died in August of the same year.

His death was the signal for the first formal papal Conclave (the word means literally, 'with a key', a reference to the fact that the cardinals were locked in till they produced a pope), which rapidly turned into a nightmare. The civil ruler of Rome, the Senator Matteo Orsini, determined to secure a strong and anti-imperial pope fast, had locked the ten cardinals then in Rome in the ancient Septizonium Palace, with armed guards to keep them inside. No candidate could gain the required two-thirds majority, and as the crippling heat intensified the primitive lavatories overflowed, and one cardinal died. In desperation they elected the elderly theologian Celestine IV: he survived his election only seventeen days, however, and the terrified cardinals fled the city. It was to be almost two years before they met at Anagni and elected the brilliant canon lawyer Sinibaldo Fieschi as Innocent IV (1243–54). Innocent completed the assault on Frederick which Gregory had begun. Excluded from Rome, he moved to Lyons, where in 1245 he summoned the Council Gregory had been unable to hold. The agenda he proclaimed at the opening of the Council on the eve of the Feast of Sts Peter and Paul included the healing of the five 'wounds' from which the Church suffered – the sins of the clergy, the loss of Jerusalem to Islam (since 1244), the troubles of the Latin kingdom of Constantinople, the Mongol invasion of Europe, and the persecution of the Church by Frederick. Of these, the last was the burning issue, and the Council duly excommunicated Frederick for perjury, peace-breaking, sacrilege, heresy and murder, declared him deposed, and encouraged the German princes to elect a new king.

This solemn deposition of an emperor by a general council was a remarkable sign of the authority of the Pope. No German bishop defended Frederick at the Council, and the deposition marked the beginning of the end for the Hohenstaufen dynasty. Frederick had been crowned in 1220, but there would be no further imperial coronation until 1312. After Frederick's death in 1250 the Hohenstaufen empire fell apart, and Germany descended into a long period of political chaos and contested successions. The papacy had called the empire into existence in 800 to protect it from its enemies. Four and a half centuries later, it presided over that empire's funeral rites. In the process, however, it had stirred fundamental questioning about the secular power of the popes and the wealth of the Church. Conflicting parties had come into existence and would dog the politics of Italy for generations to come. The Guelphs, who drew much of their support from republican sentiment in the Italian communes, supported the papacy in its opposition to German emperors. The Ghibellines, who included many of the older aristocracy, looked to a renewed empire which would restore unity and honour to Italy. The party labels, derived from German factions, soon ceased to have exact meanings, but it was an ominous sign for the papacy that some of the most penetrating and most Christian minds of the time, like that of the Florentine poet Dante Alighieri, should side with the Ghibelline and not the papal cause.

As the empire faded, the nations of northern Europe grew in importance, and most of them looked to the papacy for prestige and support. Henry III of England, insecure against his own barons, hoped for a share in the Hohenstaufen inheritance in the Mediterranean. He paid Pope Alexander IV (1254–61) to have his son Edmund declared king of Sicily, and tried to have his brother Richard of Cornwall made king of the Romans and so heir to the empire. Henry also summoned the symbols of Rome's secular and religious past to prop up his own shaky monarchy. In the late 1260s he imported Cosmati workmen from Rome to decorate Westminster Abbey in the Roman style. The Abbey, dedicated to St Peter, was under papal protection, and the shrine of St Edward, Henry's own tomb, and the great sanctuary floor with its imperial or papal circles of porphyry, became the only examples of Cosmati work outside Italy.

The popes themselves valued these links with the northern monarchies, and in 1263 Urban IV sent Cardinal Guy Foulques, the future Clement IV, as legate to England specifically to help Henry against his barons. Above all, however, the popes turned increasingly for protection to France and the Angevin dynasty. The holding of the deposition Council of 1245 at Lyons was a portent of future developments here, and much of the energies of the popes in the third quarter of the century, when two of the popes, Urban IV (1261–4) and Clement IV (1265–8) were French, were devoted to the struggle to replace Hohenstaufen control of the papal fief of Sicily – and hence of southern Italy – with that of Charles of Anjou. This dependence on Charles was to backfire, for just like his Hohenstaufen predecessors he set himself both to become master of Italy and to conquer the Byzantine empire. Papal independence was once more under threat, and the papacy cast yet again in the role of Frankenstein, having created a monster it could not control.

The danger from an overmighty French king in Sicily was not the only price the papacy had to pay for its victory over the Hohenstaufen. The struggle with Frederick and his sons placed ruinous strains on papal revenue, and forced the popes to work their financial machinery ever harder, relentlessly expanding their demands on the regional churches. From claiming the right to intervene in disputed episcopal elections, the papacy went on to claim the right to nominate to all bishoprics, however chosen. In effect this meant not that they selected all bishops, but that they exacted a fee from all of them. By the end of the thirteenth century every new bishop and abbot had to pay a tax of one-third of his first year's income, half to the Pope, half to the cardinals.

The papacy also hugely expanded its rights in the 'provision' of benefices. Clement IV began this process by reserving the right to 'provide' or appoint to all benefices whose incumbents died while they were in Rome. This was extended to all benefices whose incumbents died within two days' journey of Rome, which of course in due time became all benefices whatever within a two-day radius of Rome. Papal provisions benefited more than the Pope. Fortune-hunters all over the Church besieged the Curia with requests for preferment through the papal machinery, not least the crowned heads of Europe, who discovered that the cheapest way of paying their great servants of state (mostly clerics) was by securing bishoprics and abbeys for them by means of papal provisions. The system made enemies for the popes as well as friends. The Council of Lyons in 1245 heard a formal complaint from a group of English noblemen about papal provision of Italian and French clergy to English benefices, and the English anti-papal heretic John Wyclif owed at least some of his hostility towards the papacy to his own unsuccessful application for preferment through the papal court. Supply, inevitably, was never able to keep pace with demand.

Nor were escalating financial demands and provision to benefices the only factor which helped discredit the late-thirteenth-century papacy. Papal patronage of the Dominicans and Franciscans (first Dominican pope 1276, first Franciscan pope 1288) and the extension to them of privileges and exemptions enraged the secular clergy and the local hierarchies, and caused questioning of the whole principle of papal exemptions. From Innocent IV onwards many of the popes forfeited moral credibility by using some of the most solemn spiritual weapons of the reform papacy for purposes which were blatantly political. Innocent, for example, preached 'crusade' against Frederick and his successors, and Martin IV (1281–5) and Honorius IV (1285–7) supported as a 'crusade' what was blatantly a dynastic war waged by France against the kingdom of Aragon. The search for a counterbalance to the Hohenstaufens resulted in the unedifying spectacle of popes hawking the succession in Sicily, and eventually that of the kingdom of Germany, to almost anyone who would take it. In the hands of lesser men the lofty spiritual claims of Gregory VII and Innocent III came increasingly to look like a cloak for cynical political manipulation.

Institutionally, too, the papacy's authority was being eroded. Aristocratic factions within the city of Rome once again made it an insecure base for stable papal government. Innocent IV was exiled from Rome and even Italy for six years, and all but two of the papal elections of the thirteenth century had to take place outside Rome. The skyline of Rome itself was now dominated by the fortified war-towers of the aristocracy (a hundred were built in Innocent IV's pontificate alone) and the popes increasingly spent their time in papal palaces at Viterbo and Orvieto.

In the midst of these thirteenth-century struggles, a bizarre legend began to circulate which both highlighted and made mock of some of the papacy's most central claims. The story of Pope Joan first occurs in an anonymous Dominican chronicle written in 1250, the year of Frederick II's death: it soon spread throughout Europe via the international network of the Preaching Friars, endlessly repeated and embellished in chronicles and collections of sermon exempla. In its full-blown form the story tells of an Englishwoman, Joan, educated in Mainz, who passed herself off as a man, became a monk and was ultimately elected to the papacy, taking the name John. Sexually promiscuous with secret lovers, her fraud was dramatically exposed during a solemn papal procession to the

Lateran. The crowds blocked the papal progress in the narrow streets near the basilica of San Clemente, the jostling of the pope's horse triggered a premature labour and the 'popess' was publicly delivered of child: in most versions of the story the enraged crowd then lynch her.

The setting for this story was hazy in the extreme – always in the remote past, it was located first in the early twelfth century, but eventually in the year 854 (when in fact Leo IV was still Pope). Medieval storytellers were fascinated by it, for, in the manner of the scurrilous rituals of carnival, its mockery went to the heart of the sacred, turned on their heads all the central affirmations of the reform papacy, and played on some of devout men's worst fears – a sexually active pope, a woman in the place of the highest authority, deception at the heart of the Church, lawlessness and fraud in the seat of law and truth. No one during the Middle Ages questioned the historicity of the myth, and as the legend established itself it was pressed into service by people with axes to grind and points to prove. William of Ockham, the great fourteenth-century Franciscan philosopher, would use it as a weapon against Pope John XXII when the pope condemned Franciscan teaching on poverty: Ockham argued that the existence of Pope Joan demonstrated that false popes (like John XXII) could deceive almost everyone, yet be no true pope after all.

So 'the popess' became part of the accepted history of the papacy, and her portrait appeared in lists and galleries of past popes (like the one still to be seen in Siena Cathedral). It even came to be believed that every papal coronation contained a solemn verification of the pope's masculinity. When a new pope took possession of his Cathedral at the Lateran, ancient ceremonial required him to sit briefly on two ancient Roman chairs of porphyry, the 'sedia stercoraria', each seat of which was pierced with a hole (no one knows what these holes were actually for, but they were possibly imperial birthing stools or, more probably, ancient Roman bedroom commodes or bidets). By the mid-fifteenth century, travellers and humanist historians were apparently seriously repeating as fact the preposterous tale that when the new pope sat down in the first of these chairs, a junior cardinal approached and knelt in order to reach up under his robes and feel his genitals: the cardinal then cried out 'Testiculos habet', and the crowd responded joyfully 'Deo

Gratias' ('He does have testicles', 'Thanks be to God'). This ludicrous hotchpotch of legend and mis-read ritual was to prove a godsend to the enemies of the papacy, during the debates within the Franciscan order over poverty, in the Conciliar movement and during the Protestant reformation, when much was made of Pope Joan as the archetypical 'Whore of Babylon'. It would not be finally laid to rest until the mid-seventeenth century, when a Protestant historian, David Blondel, worked patiently through the successive versions of the legend and demonstrated its impossibility from start to finish. But the pull of the story, and its four centuries of survival, depended on the fact that it held a disturbing and distorting mirror up to the institution it satirised. 'Pope Joan' was a sardonic commentary on the apparently limitless escalation of the claims – and the reform programme – of the high medieval papacy.

The second half of the thirteenth century saw a rapid turnover of popes – thirteen between 1252 and 1296, as opposed to the four who reigned between 1216 and 1252. The influx of French cardinals into the college meant that some cardinals were in effect lobbyists for their monarchs. The consequent political polarising of the college into factions led to long and indecisive conclaves, and long vacancies between pontificates – almost three years between the death of Clement IV in 1268 and the election of Gregory X (1271–6). The best Pope of the later thirteenth century, Gregory X, tried to legislate against this at the Second Council of Lyons in 1274, by requiring the Conclave to meet behind locked doors within ten days of a pope's death, and by providing for the systematic reduction of the rations of the cardinals during prolonged conclaves. This produced a short-lived improvement, but meanwhile the cardinals became more and more conscious of their own power, and more concerned to bolster their oligarchy against the papal monarchy.

This is not to suggest that the popes of the later thirteenth century were without spiritual aspiration or real achievement. Gregory X genuinely longed for the healing of the schism with the East. This, together with the eagerness of the recently restored Eastern Emperor, Michael VIII Paleologus, for papal assistance against the expansionist ambitions of Charles of Anjou, led to a fragile reunion. Greek delegates attended the Second Council of Lyons, and professed their faith in the papal primacy, the Roman doctrine

1. Antonio Filarete, *The Crucifixion of St Peter*, from the bronze doors commissioned for Old St Peter's by Pope Eugenius IV: the papacy, like St Peter's and St Paul's basilica, was erected on the foundation of the burial-places of the apostles.

2. St Peter and St Clement, from the twelfth-century apse mosaic in S. Clemente, Rome. This medieval mosaic, created at the height of the papal reform movement, evokes the proud Roman heritage of the Papacy (Peter and Clement are wearing senatorial togas), and traces the pedigree of the popes back to the martyred Prince of the Apostles.

3. The Crypt of the Popes, Catacomb of S. Callisto. By the mid-third century the Roman Church was intensely aware of its apostolic pedigree. This crypt for the burial of the popes helped focus the community's sense of identity round its institutional continuity with the Apostolic age. The inscription on the altar is by Pope Damasus I, celebrating the 'bodies of the saints' buried here.

4. *Colossal head of Constantine*, Capitoline Museum, Rome. The accession of a Christian emperor altered the Church's relations with society. Constantine and his successors saw Christianity as vital to the unity of their Empire: their determination to dominate the Church set them on a collision course with the popes.

5. Sta Sabina, Rome, built during the pontificate of Celestine I (422-32) among the patrician villas on the Aventine, represents the Christian conquest of a proudly pagan city.

6. Alessandro Algardi, *The Meeting of Leo the Great and Attila*, St Peter's. This bas-relief marking the grave of Pope Leo the Great commemorates Leo's successful encounter with Attila the Hun at Mantua in 452, when the Pope persuaded the barbarian leader not to march on Rome. In the carving Peter and Paul, twin protectors of Christian Rome, threaten vengeance from heaven.

7. The emperor Justinian with archbishop Maximinian on his left, presents a golden paten for use in the celebration of the Mass, mosaic in S. Vitale, Ravenna. The emperor never set foot in Ravenna, but his image here is an overwhelming icon of Byzantine sacred monarchy, and the prestige of the bishop of the chief Italian centre of the divided empire. The popes would resist both these threats to their authority.

8. Claude Lorrain, the Arch of Septimius Severus, Christ Church, Oxford. This drawing of flooding around the Capitol captures the decay of the classical city. Similar sights would have greeted visitors to Rome from the sixth to the nineteenth century.

9. *St Gregory the Great at his Writing Desk*, Kunsthistorisches Museum, Vienna. This tenth-century ivory portrays Pope Gregory as the newly converted nations of the North would remember him, the inspired teacher and guide. The Holy Ghost whispers in his ear, while a bevy of scribes copy his works.

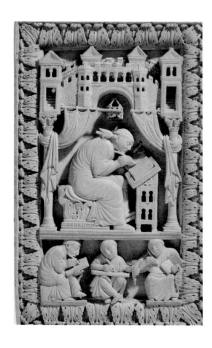

10. The Canterbury Gospels, Parker Library, Corpus Christi College, Cambridge. These scenes from the Life of Christ are part of a gospel-book believed to have been brought to England by Augustine of Canterbury in 597. It is used at the ceremony of enthronement of every new Archbishop of Canterbury.

11. A fighting faith: the rapid advance of Islam transformed the Christian geography of the Mediterranean.

12. The rejection of iconoclasm: the popes led the Latin West in rejecting Iconoclasm. In the apse mosaic of S. Maria in Domnica Pope Paschal I kneels before a Byzantine-style image of the mother of God, the culmination of a century of Roman church redecoration which was profoundly influenced by the religious art of the East.

13. Gold votive offering, excavated beneath St Peter's. This sixth- or seventh-century gold votive offering is one of the many tokens left behind by the stream of pilgrims to the tomb of the Apostle Peter.

14. S. Maria in Cosmedin, Rome. This church at the foot of the Aventine was created out of one of the ancient Diaconia, or food distribution centres, and assigned by Hadrian I to Greek monks fleeing from the iconoclastic persecutions in the East. It became the centre of the 'schola Graeca', the Byzantine quarter of Rome

15. The Monastery of the Santi Quattro Coronati. This fortress monastery, perched on the Coelian hill above the pope's ceremonial route to the Lateran, was safer than the exposed and vulnerable cathedral, and used as a refuge by successive popes. Leo IV built the tower c.850, after the invasion of Rome by Muslim raiders: further defenses were put in place in the thirteenth century, during the struggles between the popes and the Hohenstaufen emperors.

16. *The Donation of Constantine*, detail, fresco, Church of the Santi Quattro Coronati, Rome. In this thirteenth-century fresco, painted as part of a papal propaganda war against the Emperor Frederick II, all the main features of the legend of the Donation are represented: Constantine gives Pope Sylvester the tiara which symbolises temporal power over the West; behind the emperor is the saddled horse with which he will perform the 'bridle service' for the Pope.

17. Mosaic from the Lateran. In this scene, commissioned by Pope Leo III before Charlemagne's coronation, St Peter hands Leo the Pallium, symbol of his spiritual authority, while Charlemagne, protector of the Patrimony of Peter, receives a lance and banner.

18. Otto III, *The Munich Gospels*, Staatsbibliothek, Munich. Otto is enthroned between lords spiritual and temporal in this dedicatory miniature.

19. Cluny Abbey: the surviving south transept of the eleventh-century church

20. Henry IV from the Shrine of Charlemagne, Palace Chapel, Aachen.

21. The overthrow and death of Gregory VII, from the *Chronicle of Otto von Freising*, 1156, University of Jena. At the top of the picture, Henry IV is attended by the antipope Clement III, who crowned him emperor and Gregory makes good his escape from Rome. Below, Gregory is shown in exile and on his deathbed.

22. The Crusader Assault on Jerusalem, 1099, from the *Romans de Godefroy de Buillon et de Salehadin*, Bibliothèque Nationale, Paris.

23. Giotto, *The Dream of Innocent III*, Upper Church, Assisi. Innocent struggled to contain charismatic movements like the early Franciscans within the bounds of Catholic orthodoxy. In the legend of the pope's dream, he sees the 'little poor man' of Assisi holding up the crumbling Lateran Basilica, a symbol of Franciscan support for Church and Papacy.

24. *Boniface VIII inaugurates the Jubilee*, in this copy of a now ruined fresco in the Lateran. Boniface, wearing the elongated papal tiara which symbolised his claim to supremacy over every human authority, exercises the fulness of papal spiritual power by proclaiming the first Jubilee indulgence.

25. The Palace of the Popes, Avignon.

26. Donatello and Michelozzo, Tomb of John XXIII, Baptistery, Florence. This monument to the 'onetime pope' is the most magnificent surviving monument to the Conciliar movement and the papal schisms of the fourteenth and fifteenth centuries.

27. Melozzo da Forlì, *Sixtus IV nominates Platina Prefect of the Vatican Library*, 1476–7, Vatican Library. The Humanist Platina kneels; the pope is surrounded by favourites and nephews; the standing Cardinal facing the pope is Giuliano della Rovere, the future Pope Julius II.

28. Pietro Perugino, *Christ giving the Keys to Peter*, Sistine Chapel. The great Renaissance programme of paintings for the Sistine Chapel, of which this is one, defiantly asserted the spiritual claims of the Popes, even as the realities of Italian politics were eroding papal prestige and power.

29. Lucas Cranach, *The Papal Trade in Indulgences*, woodcut illustration to *Passional Christi und Antichristi*, 1521.

30. The Sack of Rome by Charles V's troops, 1527, private collection. The Pope is visible in the loggia of the Castel Sant'Angelo.

31. Titian, *Paul III*, Museo di Capodimonte, Naples. Paul III, father of three sons and an extravagant renaissance grandee, nevertheless appointed many reformers to the College of Cardinals, and called the Council of Trent, which dramatically transformed and purified the Catholic Church.

32. The Post-Tridentine papacy. In this propaganda print by Giovanni Pinadello, Sixtus V is surrounded by his achievements and building projects.

33. Bernini's Baldacchino. The self image of the Baroque papacy: Urban VIII commissioned this huge canopy over the papal altar and the tomb of Peter: later, Bernini added the grandiose shrine of the Chair of Peter, visible below the sunburst window. The relic of St Peter's Chair which it contained has been proved to be in fact the throne of the Frankish emperor Charles the Bald – an unintended ironic sidelight on the secular involvements of the papacy.

34. In this engraving Clement XIV's abject surrender to political pressure in dissolving the Jesuit order is portrayed as the result of Divine inspiration.

35. A new Sack of Rome: under the peace of Tolentino (1797) the papacy granted 100 art objects and 500 manuscripts to the French people. During the Napoleonic domination of Italy many of the Vatican's greatest treasures were taken as spoil to France.

36. Jacques-Louis David, detail from *The Coronation of the Emperor Napoleon and Empress Josephine*, in Notre-Dame, Paris, 2 December 1804, Musée du Louvre, Paris. Napoleon crowns himself and his consort, watched helplessly by Pope Pius VII, the courageous monk Napoleon sought to reduce to the status of an imperial chaplain.

37. Pius IX, Victor Emanuel II and Garibaldi: a dream of harmony. In this popular print the aspiration for an Italy united spiritually and materially finds expression. Garibaldi, the King and Pius IX link arms.

38. The First Vatican Council in session in St Peter's from *Illustrirte Zeitung*, January 1870.

39. *Il Papa-Re*: the court of the Pope-King, Leo XIII and his entourage in the Vatican garden.

40. Benedict XV as Noah. A German journalistic comment on the peace-efforts of the First World War pope Benedict XV: the pope, as Noah, sends a dove out of an ark on a sea of blood. The pope's attempts at neutrality earned him a reputation of being a 'Boche' pope.

41. Pius XI receiving the gift of a porcelain dinner service from the Ambassador of the Weimar Republic on the 50th anniversary of his priestly ordination in 1929. The position of the Catholic Church in Germany steadily improved in the decade leading up to the signing of the Concordat with Hitler in 1933.

42. Pius XII calling for peace in a radio broadcast, 1943. Second from the right is Giovanni Battista Montini, the future Paul VI.

43. Pope John XXIII blessing the crowds following his coronation, 4 November 1958.

44. A world council: the diplomatic corps and the representatives of the other Churches at the opening session of the Second Vatican Council, 11 October 1962.

45. Paul VI at the state funeral of Aldo Moro, S. Giovanni in Laterano, Rome, 1978.

46. Pope John Paul II kissing the ground on his arrival at Orly airport, Paris, 1980. Archbishop Marcinkus, head of the Vatican Bank, stoops protectively over him.

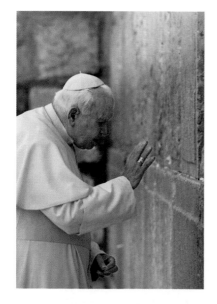

47. A frail John Paul II makes an historic act of penitence for Christian atrocities against the Jews at Jerusalem's Wailing Wall.

of purgatory and the *Filioque*. This reconciliation, however, was dictated on the Greek side by political necessity, not conviction, and the Emperor had the greatest difficulty persuading the Byzantine clergy to accept it. Gregory's less sympathetic successors tried to impose steadily more stringent and humiliating demands on the Greeks: the union did not last.

At the beginning of the thirteenth century, Innocent III embodied much of what was best in the high medieval theory of papal supremacy. At the end of the century Boniface VIII (1294–1303) encapsulated some of its contradictions. Benedetto Caetani was a career cleric, trained in law at Bologna and with a distinguished diplomatic career behind him. His immediate predecessor as pope was the saintly but hopeless monk–hermit Celestine V, elected after more than two years of deadlock in the hope that a saint might transform the Church. Instead the unworldly old man (eighty-five when elected) became the naive stooge of the Angevin King of Naples – seven of his twelve first cardinals were Frenchmen, four of them Sicilian subjects of Charles II.

Celestine was a visionary, the founder of a brotherhood of hermits with strong links to the radical Franciscans. He therefore represented precisely that dimension of the thirteenth-century Church which most detested the wealth, worldliness and legal and political entanglements of the papacy. His election fed apocalyptic hopes of a *Papa Angelicus*, a holy and unworldly pope who would cleanse the Church and prepare the world for the advent of Christ. The notion of an unworldly pope, however, was by now almost a contradiction in terms. Three-quarters of a century earlier, Innocent III had managed to hold together hierarchy and charism, but Celestine's election highlighted just how incompatible these two visions of the Church had become. Faced with political and financial complexities which prayer and fasting seemed powerless to untangle, Celestine resigned after six months. His abdication speech was written for him by Cardinal Caetani, whom he had consulted about the legality of his resignation, and who was elected in his place. Determined to avoid any danger of schism from the outraged 'spiritual' element in the Church who had looked to Celestine to redeem the papacy, Caetani tracked down his predecessor, who had returned to his old life as a hermit, and kept him a prisoner in miserably cramped conditions till his death at the age of ninety.

Boniface is a mysterious man, proud, ambitious, fierce. He achieved a good deal that is in line with the reforming acts of many of his predecessors, founding a university in Rome, codifying canon law and re-establishing the Vatican Archive and Library. Law did not exhaust his understanding of his office. It was Boniface who declared the first Jubilee or Holy Year in 1300, when tens of thousands of pilgrims converged on Rome to gain indulgences, adding enormously to the prestige of the papacy and the spiritual centrality of Rome (and in the process enriching the Roman basilicas, where the sacristans were said to have had to scoop in the pilgrim offerings with rakes). This promise of 'full and copious pardon' to all who visited St Peter and the Lateran after confessing their sins was the most spectacular exercise of the power of the keys since Urban II issued the first Crusade Indulgence, and it caught the imagination of Europe. At any one time throughout the Jubilee Year of 1300 there were said to be up to 200,000 pilgrims in the city, and the Leonine wall round the Vatican had to be breached to allow the crowds to pass through. The poet Dante made the Jubilee pilgrimage, and he set the *Divine Comedy* at its central point, in Holy Week 1300. In a famous passage in the *Inferno* he compared the traffic arrangements for the crowds in Hell to the one-way system he had seen in use for the pilgrims crossing the Ponte Sant' Angelo during this first Jubilee.

> In the chasm's bottom
> the naked sinners faced towards us as they came,
> and, on the other side, hurried faster along with us.
> In the same way the Romans, because of the great throngs
> In the Year of Jubilee across the bridge,
> Have worked out ways of getting the people over.
> So the people on one side face the Castel and move towards St
> Peter's,
> And on the other path they go towards the Mount.[21]

If Boniface displayed a commitment to the lofty spiritual claims of the papacy, he also displayed some of the worst traits of clerical careerism, enriching his relatives at the expense of the Church, and waging a relentless war against his family's traditional rivals, the Colonna family. Boniface even offered the spiritual privileges of the Crusade to anyone who joined in this vendetta against the Colonna. Both his personal character and his orthodoxy were later called into question, his enemies accusing him, in graphic and disturbing detail, of being a sodomite (sex with boys or women, he was alleged to have said, was no worse than rubbing one hand against another). Even more disturbingly, he was said to have been a non-believer, rejecting the resurrection and saying that heaven and hell were here.

These accusations, spread by the French crown during his lifetime and repeated after his death, have been generally regarded as motivated by malice. But, whatever Boniface did or did not believe about God, sex or the afterlife, he believed passionately in the papacy. His pontificate had begun auspiciously, with Charles II of Sicily and his son, Charles King of Hungary, leading the Pope's white horse by the bridle as he went to be crowned. Boniface determined to exert to the full the temporal sovereignty this symbolised, but in fact most of his political ventures backfired. He harnessed Angevin support to impose papal rule in Tuscany, but Charles II's brutal treatment of Florence and the exiling of the leading 'Black' or Ghibelline party, including Dante, embittered the region against the Pope. His attempts to secure Angevin rule in Sicily failed, as did his intervention with Edward I of England on behalf of Scotland, which he claimed as a papal fief. He had no better luck in his attempts to settle the succession in Hungary and Poland. It is a significant fact that among the hundreds of thousands of pilgrims to Rome in 1300, there was not a single crowned head.

His most disastrous venture into high politics, however, was in his confrontation with the King of France. Since the time of Innocent III it had become established practice to finance Crusading ventures by taxes on the clergy. Philip the Fair now imposed a similar tax to fund his war of conquest in Gascony. Boniface, who longed to unite the princes of Europe under his own leadership in a new Crusade, challenged the French crown's right to the property of the Church. In 1296 he issued the bull *Clericis Laicos*, forbidding the laity to take or the clergy to give away the property of the Church. The bull's opening sentence ('All history shows clearly the enmity of the laity towards the clergy') was based on scholastic textbook commonplaces, but it nevertheless accurately signalled the militant clericalism of Boniface's outlook.

That clericalism, and above all his lofty sense of the dignity of his own office, is represented by his remodelling of the papal tiara, elongating it to correspond to the biblical measure of the 'ell', a sign, for Boniface, of completeness and superiority. It became increasingly clear, however, that King Philip did not accept that supremacy, and that he aspired to a new Christian empire stretching from the southern Mediterranean to the North Sea in which the papal state would be swallowed up. Boniface was having none of this, and in 1302 he issued the bull *Unam Sanctam*, the culminating blow in a propaganda war against the French crown. In it the Pope notoriously claimed that 'it is altogether necessary for salvation for every human creature to be subject to the Roman Pontiff'. He insisted that the Pope wielded both the spiritual and secular sword, but gave the secular sword to princes to use for the good of the Church.[22]

Unam Sanctam was largely made up of a tissue of quotations from previous popes and from great theologians like Bernard of Clairvaux and Thomas Aquinas. Its claims were not in fact very different from those made by every pope since at least the time of Gregory VII. Certainly most of what Boniface asserted can be found in germ in the writings of Innocent III. In his confrontation with the French king, Boniface undoubtedly had both law and tradition on his side. Boniface, however, was reiterating these teachings at a time when his struggle with the King of France was going badly, and when everyone could see that his temporal claims in real terms were hollow. In the long run the insistence on so high a doctrine of the papacy, at a time when the Pope was at the mercy of his enemies, served not to strengthen but to cast doubt on the claims themselves. Boniface prepared a bull excommunicating the French King in September 1303, but before it could be promulgated French forces, accompanied by two of the deposed Colonna cardinals and their relatives, broke into the papal palace at Anagni and mobbed the Pope. Boniface faced his enemies with courage, in full papal regalia and shouting, 'Here is my neck, here is my head,' challenging them to kill him. The French troops drew back from that final atrocity, and were driven out of the town by the citizens the next day. Boniface never recovered from his ordeal, however. He returned to Rome a broken man, roaming round his apartments crying out in rage and humiliation. He died a month later. The 'outrage of Anagni' shocked Italy and Europe. Dante, who hated Boniface and placed him upside down in a subterranean furnace in hell, nevertheless saw the maltreatment of the Pope at Anagni as the recrucifixion of Christ. In a real sense, however, it called the bluff of the high medieval doctrine of the papacy, for it measured the distance between inflated religious rhetoric and cold reality.

Popes who understood themselves to be the vicars of St Peter were tied to Rome, for Peter's body was at Rome. The Pope's altar stood above the tomb of the Apostle. But popes who were the Vicars of Christ, however much they might insist on the possession of Peter's authority, were not bound by geography in the same way. The popes of the tenth, eleventh and twelfth centuries had been deeply involved in the local politics of Rome. In the thirteenth and four-teenth centuries the internationalising of papal power and papal claims made that involvement seem claustrophobic, limiting and, in the face of popular hostility and aristocratic intrigue, dangerous as well. In any case the popes were increasingly involved in the growing complexities of international politics. From Charlemagne to Freder-ick II it was the emperors with whom popes had to reckon. In the late thirteenth and fourteenth centuries other rulers, especially the kings of France, loomed on the papal horizon and posed a threat to papal independence.

For most of the fourteenth century, the bishops of Rome lived far away from Rome, in the fortified city of Avignon. The seventy-year exile of the popes at Avignon was a disaster for the Church, and came to be known as the Babylonian Captivity of the papacy. Yet it came about by accident. Boniface VIII's successor, the unworldly Domini-can Benedict XI (1303–4), survived only nine months. He died in exile at Perugia, and the Conclave to elect his successor met there. The Conclave was bitterly divided into two rival camps, one hostile to France and determined to exact revenge for the scandalous treat-ment of Pope Boniface at Anagni, the other, smaller group intent on reconciliation with France and anxious to mollify the French crown. The Conclave sat in deadlock for eleven months, till a split in the anti-French party allowed the election of the Archbishop of Bor-deaux, Bertrand de Got, as Pope Clement V (1305–14). Bertrand was not himself a cardinal, nor was he present at the Conclave. He was yet another Bologna-trained canon lawyer with a distinguished diplomatic career behind him and a good working relationship with Philip IV of France.

To please the King, he allowed himself to be crowned at Lyons, and he remained in France, partly because of the chaotic political sit-uation in central Italy, and partly in the hope of bringing about a peace between France and England, so that their energies could be directed into another Crusade to the Holy Land. In 1309 Clement settled at Avignon. It was a sensible choice, for it was not strictly speaking French territory. The surrounding region was part of the Papal States, and the city itself was subject to the kings of Sicily, until bought by the popes in the mid-century. It was near the sea, and far more centrally placed for most of Europe than Rome had been. The move was not at first intended to be permanent, the Pope camping in the Bishop's palace, his Curia billeted round the town, and only a minimum working archive being kept in the city.

Clement, first of the Avignonese popes, was a shameless nepotist (he made five members of his family cardinals), but he was also in many respects an impressive character, despite suffering from a recurrent cancer the pain of which kept him a recluse for months at a time. He was a good administrator, who revised and expanded the code of canon law, adding a valuable new section called 'The Clementines'. Deeply committed both to the Crusading ideal (which would continue to attract European rulers and their subjects, but was destined to disruption by the Anglo-French wars, the chaotic politics of Italy, and by the Black Death) and to the somewhat more positive ideal of preaching missions to the East, he strengthened the already crucial links between the papacy and the universities, founding chairs in oriental languages at the universities of Paris, Oxford, Bologna and Salamanca.

His greatest difficulty was resisting the domination of the French crown. King Philip pursued a relentless vendetta against the memory of Boniface VIII, and tried to force Clement to summon a general council to brand him as a heretic and a sodomite. Clement had no love for Boniface, but realised the devastating consequences such a condemnation would have for papal authority. He managed to resist the call for the condemnation of Boniface when the Council of Vienne, the last great papal Council of the Middle Ages, met in 1311. He was, however, forced to remove all Boniface's anti-French measures from the papal records, and to canonise Celestine V, whom Boniface had imprisoned. (Clement defused this by canonising him under his monastic name of Peter, not his pontifical name, and as a 'confessor', not, as Philip had wanted, as a martyr, with the implication that Boniface had had him murdered.) He was also obliged to dissolve the Knights Templar, a military order dedicated to crusade, whose wealth and power had earned them many enemies, and whom Philip accused of heresy, necromancy and sexual perversion.

The Knights were duly condemned and dissolved at Vienne. Clement did what he could to soften measures against the Templars, and to save their property for the Church, but many were burned at the stake on trumped-up charges, a measure of the weakness of the papacy in the face of royal pressure.

This continuing vulnerability of the papacy to the French crown under Clement's six successors at Avignon was not just a matter of external pressure from the monarchy. Inevitably the papacy itself was 'colonised' in the course of its long exile in France, and the papacy became French. We need, however, to beware of assuming too much about this 'Frenchness'. France was still a collection of regions, each with its own language, legal system and local culture. Pope John XXII (1316–34), a southerner, could not read letters from the French King without the help of a translator. Nevertheless, all the Avignon popes were Frenchmen of some sort, and, of the 134 cardinals they created, no fewer than 112 were French, 96 from the surrounding region of Languedoc alone. Seventy per cent of all curial officials during this period about whom we have knowledge were French. Of the twenty-two non-French cardinals, fourteen were Italian, two were English, none at all were German. Though the Avignon popes continued to maintain the universalist claims of their predecessors, and to see themselves as the Father of all Christians, this solid identification of the papacy with France affected perceptions of the papacy, and contributed to a growing questioning of its claims to supremacy in the Church.

Prominent among these was the emergence of secularised political theory, a development for which in some ways the papacy itself was responsible. Since before the time of Gregory VII the popes had encouraged the development both of canon law and of university theology and philosophy. The rise of Aristotelianism within the universities moved reflection on the nature of human society away from the Augustinian pattern inherited from late antiquity – within which the tensions between Pope and Emperor had arisen – towards the notion that the state had a natural autonomy and order separate from that of the Church. In the fourteenth century this line of thought reached its extreme in the teaching of Marsilius of Padua, whose secular account of society effectively reduced the Church itself to a department of state (the *Pars sacerdotalis*). Marsilius lodged the supreme power, delegated to kings, not in the Pope but in the people. Marsilius' theories took on concrete form when Lewis of Bavaria had himself crowned emperor in Rome in 1328 by a senior Roman layman, a member of the Colonna family.

The Pope whom Lewis defied by this act was John XXII, whose pontificate highlighted many of the best and the worst features of the Avignon papacy. Personally an austere and frugal character, he emphasised the grandeur of the papacy, insisting on his superiority over and right to appoint the Emperor. He was a financial and administrative reformer, increasing papal control over episcopal and monastic appointments, extending the system of papal taxation ('annates') throughout Europe, reorganising the papal Curia and the code of canon law. He was confronted by a major and long-standing division within the Franciscan order, a radical 'Spiritual' wing repudiating property and criticising many aspects of current Church life. These 'Spirituals' had always blamed the popes from Gregory IX onwards for permitting and even requiring the modification of the Rule from its primitive severity. John now entirely alienated them and even many moderate Franciscans by condemning outright the teaching that scripture proved that Christ and his Apostles were 'paupers', that is, that Christ had owned nothing. Even more catastrophic was his repudiation of the arrangement whereby the popes were the nominal 'owners' of the property of the Franciscan order, which only had the 'use' of it. This drastic abandonment of earlier papal policy split the order, and led to the election of a 'Spiritual' Franciscan as antipope in Rome in 1328. The 'Emperor' Lewis denounced John as a heretic, and his decidedly eccentric beliefs about the nature of the beatific vision eventually led to John's formal condemnation as a heretic.

As the administrative reforms of John XXII suggest, however, the exile was not entirely negative. The Avignon papacy was at least freed from its age-old and mostly disastrous involvement in the intricate family vendettas of the Roman nobility, and the papal court at Avignon became more than ever the administrative and juridical centre of the Church. The popes of the early Middle Ages had drawn their power from the relics of the Apostles, the popes of the Avignon period from their centrality in the legal systems of Europe. Unsurprisingly, therefore, the Avignon popes greatly refined and systematised the papal bureaucracy and the papal finances. The system of curial departments had its origins then, and the establishment of the

Rota in 1331 created the machinery for dealing with marital cases which though much modified is still in use.

These reforms carried their own problems, of course. The extension of papal 'provisions' from the papal claim to fill vacancies created by clergy who happened to die while at Rome to a multitude of additional cases, eventually including all bishoprics and archbishoprics, helped to eliminate local electoral quarrels and to improve the standard of those appointed. It also invaded many existing rights, and created a bottomless pit of hungry expectation and a scramble for jobs, which the popes could never hope to satisfy. At a time when France, Germany and England were at odds, the fact that a good deal of the papal income came from provisions and procurations in Germany and England led to resentment, and a sense that the resources of the churches of England and Germany were being devoured by France. This was an illusion, in fact, for probably more than half the income of the Avignon papacy came from France. Nevertheless, the impression persisted, and soured attitudes to the popes. The growing complexity of papal administration catered to real needs, but developed a top-heavy life of its own and strained goodwill towards the papacy itself. Already at the Council of Vienne William Durand, Bishop of Mende, had called for the reversal of the trend towards the centralisation of the Church around the pope, and had argued in favour of greatly strengthened local hierarchies and regional synods. Nothing came of Durand's proposals, but these dissatisfactions grew.

Nor were the vastly increased papal revenues wisely spent. Some of the Avignon popes were wildly extravagant. Clement VI was a charitable man who stayed in Avignon during the Black Death there which wiped out more than 62,000 of the inhabitants, supervising sick-care, burials and the pastoral care of the dying. But he was also a bon viveur and a lavish entertainer, who declared that 'a pope should make his subjects happy'. He spent money with reckless abandon, and once declared that 'my predecessors did not know how to be popes'. Much of it was poured into the black hole of internecine Italian politics and warfare, as the popes struggled to hold together from a distance the papal patrimony in Italy. It has been calculated that John XXII spent 63 per cent of his income on warfare, and two thirds of all the revenues raised by the Avignon papacy was spent on retaining mercenary armies and on the sweetening of allies in the snakepit of Italian politics.

The papacy's seventy-year exile at Avignon came to an end in January 1377 when Pope Gregory XI (1370–8), the last Frenchman to be elected pope, returned to Rome. A deeply religious man of mystical temperament, he believed Rome to be the only right place for the Pope, a view in which he had been encouraged both by the precarious state of the papal territories in Italy, which demanded his personal attention, and by more spiritual persuasions of the Dominican visionary St Catherine of Siena. In her letters she calls him 'dulcissimo babbo mio' (my sweetest daddy), but her advice was relentlessly demanding: 'Even if you have not been very faithful in the past, begin now to follow Christ, whose vicar you are, in real earnest. And do not be afraid . . . Attend to things spiritual, appointing good shepherds and good rulers in the cities under your jurisdiction . . . Above all, delay no longer in returning to Rome and proclaiming the Crusade'.[23] It says much for the spiritual stature of the Pope that such letters could be written to him, and that he was willing to act on them.

But Gregory died in March 1378, and the Conclave which elected his successor was mobbed by the Roman crowds, terrified that the French cardinals might elect a French pope who would return to Avignon. Under this pressure, the cardinals elected an Italian, though not a Roman, Bartolommeo Prignano, absentee Archbishop of Bari. He took the name Urban VI (1378–89). Urban as a cardinal had been a leading administrator, regent of the papal chancery at Avignon, and was much respected. As pope, however, he turned out to be violent, overbearing and probably clinically paranoid. Unable to manage or even to cope with him, the cardinals repudiated him. Less than six months after electing Urban, they fled Rome, declared Urban's election invalid because conducted under duress, and elected the Cardinal Bishop of Geneva as Pope Clement VII. The Great Schism had begun.

Clement made his way, with the entire Curia, back to Avignon, while Urban created a new curia by appointing twenty-nine cardinals from all over Europe. There were now two popes, two papal administrations, two self-contained legal systems. The countries of Europe would have to choose which Pope they would obey. It was an agonising dilemma. There had often been antipopes before, but the rivals had usually been elected or appointed by rival groups. Here, the very same cardinals who had by due process chosen the Pope, had by due process declared him no pope at all, and had solemnly elected his successor. Even saints were confused about the rights and wrongs of the situation. St Catherine of Siena supported Urban, St Vincent Ferrar supported Clement. Nations tended to choose their allegiance along dynastic and political lines. France, Burgundy, Savoy, Naples and Scotland submitted to Clement and the Avignon papal administration, while England, Germany, north and central Italy and central Europe obeyed Urban. The great religious orders divided on the issue. The popes excommunicated each other and placed their rivals' supporters under interdict.

In the long perspective of history, the Roman Catholic Church has accepted that the 'real' popes were Urban and the successors elected by his cardinals and their successors. At the time, however, and throughout the thirty-nine years during which the schism persisted, this sort of clarity was hard to come by. Certainly, there is no getting round Urban's near insanity, and his brutal treatment of opponents – at one point he had six cardinals under torture, five of whom eventually simply disappeared. Successive popes (five in all) and antipopes (four in all) expressed a wish to see the schism end, but in practice both sides put all their energies into consolidating their own support and undermining that of their rivals.

For the Church at large it was a trauma. The practical effects of the Great Schism were disastrous, for the rival popes created rival colleges of cardinals, and appointed competing bishops and abbots to the same sees and monasteries. The spiralling expenses of the papacy had now to be met from a divided constituency, rival popes scrambling for contested revenues. Here, ironically, the Roman obedience fared badly. The Avignon regime had never been fully dismantled, and had three generations of administrative machinery – and archives – behind it. The new Avignon popes managed to sustain much of the old jurisdictional and financial structures. By contrast the internal finances, administration and record-keeping of the Roman papacy seem to have collapsed under the strain, and as a result we know next to nothing about its running during the schism.

Yet the Pope was more than an administrative head. He was Christ's own Vicar, holding the keys of heaven. In him alone was the power to dispense in hundreds of complex spiritual difficulties, in his hands was the power to give or to withhold the precious indulgences which would speed the believer through the pains of purgatory. The source of the right of archbishops and bishops to exercise their spiritual powers, the final court of appeal in doctrinal uncertainty, the

Pope was necessary for the life of the Church, and obedience to the false Pope would deliver the deluded individual or community into the hands of the devil. As year followed year and the schism became a permanence, men began to ask themselves how it could be ended. Could it be that Christ had left his Church with no means of solving the problem of being a body with two heads?

It was out of this agonised questioning that the movement known as Conciliarism was born. Great popes of the high Middle Ages, like Innocent III, had regularly used synods and general councils as a means of promoting reform and addressing the needs of the Church. Could a council put an end to the schism, by calling on both popes to resign, and choosing a new pope who would thus be the choice not of this group of cardinals or that rival group, but of the whole Church? These were attractive ideas, a way out. But if a council could do this, what became of papal supremacy, of the doctrine taught by Gregory, by Innocent, by Boniface and their successors, that the Pope judges all, and is judged by none?

The Conciliar solution was tried in 1409, when a group of disillusioned cardinals of both obediences, despairing of a negotiated solution between the rival popes, summoned a council. This call received wide support, and the Council, meeting at Pisa, deposed Pope Gregory XII (1406–15) (the Roman Pope) and Pope Benedict XIII (1394–1417) (the Avignon Pope). The Council then elected a new pope, Alexander V (1409–10). Neither of the old popes accepted their deposition, however, and so the Church now had three popes. The situation was finally resolved by the Council of Constance, which deposed John XXIII and Benedict XIII, and offered Gregory XII the face-saving gesture of a dignified abdication. An electoral body composed of the cardinals and thirty representatives of the Council elected Cardinal Odo Colonna as Pope Martin V (1417–31). Benedict XIII held out against the decision, and his cardinals elected a successor in due course, but they had virtually no support, and to all intents and purposes the schism was over.

The high papal prestige and unchallenged papalist theory of the era of Innocent III, however, was gone for ever. There was now an important body of opinion in the Church which held that in emergencies even the Pope was answerable to the Church in council, and the Council of Constance solemnly decreed as much. At one level, this was merely a formalising of what had long been believed, that a heretical pope *could* be deposed by the cardinals or by a council, not because they possessed an authority above that of the Pope, but because by virtue of his heresy he automatically ceased to be pope: a council might therefore exercise authority over the person of an individual pope, leaving the office itself untouched. Even the theorists of the Gregorian papacy, like Humbert of Silva Candida, had conceded as much. But there were those who went further, and saw the decrees of Constance not as formulating emergency measures for dealing with papal apostasy, but as spelling out the underlying realities of authority and power in the Church. Taking their lead from the political theories of Marsilius of Padua and William of Ockham, they taught that true religious authority rested not in the Pope or even the college of bishops, but in the Church as a whole, which might delegate it to anyone at all. A general council was thus like a parliament, the nearest approach to a perfect expression of the authority of the whole Church, and popes and bishops, who held their power only derivatively, must obey a council, and could be deposed by a council at will.

These were genuinely revolutionary beliefs, which corresponded to nothing in the tradition, certainly not to the actual historical exercise of papal authority, or that of the episcopate. 'Representative' theories of this sort imagined the unity of the Church in terms of a political conglomerate, not as a communion of churches united in charity under pope and bishops. They were as subversive of the Church's tradition as the most extreme papalism. Such extreme theories were held by only a handful of theologians, but they clouded theological debate among sincere supporters of the councils, and they permanently prejudiced the papacy and the cardinalate against the whole notion of Conciliar reform.

For Constance was intended not merely to end the schism, but to reform the Church. All previous reform councils, however, had been papal councils, planned, convened and managed by the popes, and debate raged at Constance about whether the reform programme or the election of a new pope should be dealt with first. In the end the papal election was held before the reform decrees were promulgated. Since these included limitation of the numbers of cardinals (thereby restricting the papacy's freedom of appointment), reduction of papal power and restriction of papal rights of provisions and dispensation, there was widespread, and in the event justified, gloom about the prospects of the reform decrees being implemented. The Council attempted to tie the popes to reform and the scrutiny of councils, by decreeing that another council must be held within five years, another within seven years of that, and thereafter that there must be a council every ten years.

Apart from the solution of the schism and the election of Martin V, the Council of Constance is best remembered for the condemnation and burning of the Czech reformer John Hus. Hus held views on predestination and the membership of the Church, partly borrowed from the English heretic John Wyclif, which were heretical by the standards of the late medieval Church. His uncompromising moral fervour and denunciation of the corruptions of the clergy, however, echoed the convictions of many devout men and women. Many of the religious changes he called for – greater access to the Bible, more preaching and catechising, greater involvement of the laity in religious affairs (symbolised by the restoration of the chalice in communion, which for several centuries had been administered to lay people only in the form of bread) – were in no way heretical, and had widespread support among reform-minded intellectuals. Hus himself seems to have had no desire to challenge the fundamentals of Catholicism. His condemnation by a council intent on reforming the Church by restoring her unity did not bode well for the papacy.

The election of a universally recognised pope did not put an end to the Conciliar movement. The demand that councils should meet regularly was a nightmare prospect for a papacy struggling to reassert its authority, and one which Martin V and his successors were to resist vigorously. The Council of Basle (1431–9) was dominated by this conflict between Pope and Council. Only a small proportion of the participants in the Council were bishops, the rest being theologians and proctors appearing on behalf of absentee bishops. At the opening session, not a single bishop was present. Pope Eugenius IV (1431–47) therefore decided to dissolve the Council, but the members refused to accept his decision, and after two years of haggling the Pope gave way. The Council began to behave as if it collectively were pope, appointing its own officials, acting as judge in lawsuits, even granting indulgences. Its reform programme was wide-ranging and much needed, but it was dogged by an anti-papalism which was certain to bring it into conflict with Rome. The reform party worked on the belief that, if the head were reformed, reform of the members would follow. They therefore homed in on the corruptions of papacy and Curia, and decreed the abolition of the payment of clerical taxes to the Curia, a measure which would have deprived the Pope and cardinals of most of their income, without any form of compensation. Finally the Council declared itself superior to the Pope, and when Eugenius protested, declared him deposed, and elected the saintly Duke of Savoy as the Antipope, Felix V.

Felix V was never able to establish his authority outside his own dominions, and was eventually reconciled to Pope Nicholas V (1447–55), who made him a cardinal. The Council's action in resurrecting the papal schism, however, did much to discredit it and the Conciliar movement, even among the many clerical intellectuals who longed for reform. The papacy received a further boost from the success of Eugenius' rival papal Council of Ferrara/Florence, which in 1439 took advantage of the desperation of the Byzantine empire in the face of the Turkish threat to achieve a triumphant resolution, on Latin terms, of the schism with the Eastern churches. Attended by the Greek Emperor himself and by representatives of the ancient patriarchates, the Council succeeded in securing Greek acceptance of the *Filioque* and other Western doctrines like purgatory. Above all, it solemnly reiterated the doctrine of papal supremacy, in terms which made a nonsense of Conciliar attempts to subordinate the Pope to a council. Like the union of 1274 under Gregory X, this agreement was widely disowned in the East, and the fall of Constantinople in 1453 buried it, but at the time it was a tremendous coup for Eugenius and the restored papacy.

The Conciliar crisis posed in an acute form the question of the Pope's authority to teach. The jurisdictional primacy of the popes, and their function as centre of unity, had always been inseparable from their doctrinal authority. The tradition that the See of Rome had always preserved the apostolic truth, and would always do so, had been enshrined in 519 in the formula of Hormisdas. This freedom from error was never called 'infallibility' – only God was thought of as infallible. Nor was it thought to exempt individual popes from the possibility of error, for Honorius and Vigilius had erred. It was the fundamental and continuous teaching authority of the see, not individual utterances by particular incumbents, which was believed to be faithful and reliable. In the high Middle Ages the Decretalists had specifically excluded heretic popes from the universal principle that the Pope is to be judged by no one. And papal teaching authority was not thought of as being independent of the other teaching authorities in the Church. Scholastic theologians like St Thomas Aquinas recognised that the Pope could introduce new formulas of faith, but Thomas thought of this in the context of papal councils like the Lateran councils, and saw papal authority to determine the faith as being exercised as the head of such a council, not in opposition to it or independence from it. It became Dominican tradition that individual popes might err when speaking in their capacity as individuals, but that popes could not err when acting with the counsel of the Church. This Dominican teaching would be reiterated to good effect in the debates at the First Vatican Council.

A crucial influence in the development of the idea that the Pope himself might be free from error came from the Franciscan debates about poverty. Successive popes had ruled in favour of the Franciscan rejection of property. When Pope John XXII repudiated that teaching, and denied that Christ was a pauper, Franciscan theologians appealed against his judgement to the infallibility of other, earlier popes. They argued that the Church, in the person of those popes, had repeatedly accepted the Franciscan view of poverty as an evangelical form of life. John XXII, therefore, was in error in rejecting this infallible teaching – and since true popes do not err, this proved that he was no longer a true pope. Papal infallibility was here being invoked not to *exalt* the Pope's authority, but to limit it, by ensuring that a pope did not arbitrarily reverse earlier Christian teaching.

All these thoughts looked different in the light of the Great Schism and the Conciliar crisis. St Thomas' assumption that popes and councils were always in harmony no longer held good. Confronted with the struggle between Pope and Council, some Conciliarist theologians for the first time asserted the freedom of councils from error, while insisting that popes might err. Their papalist opponents, by contrast, asserted that Councils might err, unless approved by the Pope, but that true popes were always preserved in the truth. The debate polarised opinion, and set the prerogatives of the popes over against those of bishops and councils, though the early theorists of papal authority, like Leo the Great or Gregory the Great, had seen papal authority as serving and supporting that of other bishops. These polarities helped undermine Catholic theology of Pope and Church, and would dog thinking about these issues up to the twentieth century. A debate had been opened which would rumble on till 1870 and beyond.

The schism left the papacy wounded, suspicious of the whole notion of general councils, and dangerously resistant to the growing demand for reform. In political terms, too, it was drastically weakened. Though papal approval was still a card worth having in a monarch's hand, and papal hostility a problem for the ruler of a Catholic people, never again would a pope unmake emperors, or exercise real jurisdiction over the traditional feudal fiefs of the papacy. There would never again be an Innocent III. The restored popes of the fifteenth century were no longer the unchallenged arbiters of nations, and had as much as they could do to recover and hold on to the core of the Papal States. To undermine the claims of the councils to decide on their legitimacy, Martin V and Eugenius IV came to individual agreements or 'concordats' with many of the rulers of Europe. Such concordats relentlessly eroded many of the papal prerogatives wrested from the secular powers by the reform papacy, and drastically reduced papal control over local churches. In the process they also reduced papal income. In the aftermath of the schism, this was less than half what it had been before the move to Avignon, and the bulk of it came from the secular revenues of the papal state, as national churches ceased to pay the spiritual revenues which had funded the reform papacy. Conciliarism had placed a weapon against the papacy in the hands of the nation states, and they did not hesitate to use it. In 1438 the King of France unilaterally adopted twenty-four of the decrees of Basle and incorporated them into French law as the 'Pragmatic Sanction', asserting the supremacy of councils over popes, limiting papal rights of appointments to French benefices, abolishing many of the sources of papal revenue such as annates, and forbidding appeals to Rome.

It was hardly surprising that secular princes, keen to assert their authority over a Church which transcended national boundaries, were determined that the high medieval doctrine of papal supremacy should not be recovered and consolidated. In 1477 Lorenzo de' Medici declared that there were definite advantages, scandal apart, in having three or even four popes. After the arc of achievement on which Leo IX had set them, the popes were once again trapped within the politics of Italy, obliged to concede control of the local churches to kings and princes, under fire from the best informed and most devout churchmen of the age, and once again perceived as the chief obstacle to desperately needed reform. The papacy, it seemed, had come full circle.

CHAPTER FOUR

PROTEST AND DIVISION

1447–1774

I THE RENAISSANCE POPES

The Renaissance papacy evokes images of a Hollywood spectacular, all decadence and drag. Contemporaries viewed Renaissance Rome as we now view Nixon's Washington, a city of expense-account whores and political graft, where everything and everyone had a price, where nothing and nobody could be trusted. The popes themselves seemed to set the tone. Alexander VI (1492–1503) flaunted a young and nubile mistress in the Vatican, was widely believed to have made a habit of poisoning his cardinals so as to get his hands on their property, and he ruthlessly aggrandised his illegitimate sons and daughters at the Church's expense. Julius II (1503–13), inspired patron of Raphael, Bramante, Michelangelo and Leonardo, was a very dubious Father of all the Faithful, for he had fathered three daughters of his own while a cardinal, and he was a ferocious and enthusiastic warrior, dressing in silver papal armour and leading his own troops through the breaches blown in the city walls of towns who resisted his authority. Leo X (1513–21), son of Lorenzo the Magnificent of Florence, was made a cleric at seven and a cardinal at thirteen years old: as pope he ruled both Rome and Florence. He was the Pope whose Indulgence issued to fund the rebuilding of St Peter's led Luther to publish his Ninety-Five Theses, and so precipitated the Reformation. At his death Leo left the Church divided and the papacy close to bankruptcy. From the universal pastors of the Church the popes had declined to being Italian politicians: after 1480 even the business of the papal Curia was being conducted in Italian – not, as before, in the lingua franca of Latin.

All this presents a luridly one-sided picture of the Renaissance popes. It takes no account of the massive task of reconstruction which confronted the papacy in the wake of the Great Schism. The popes of the later fifteenth century had to reinvent Rome. Medieval pilgrims were, for the most part, interested only in the churches and the holy relics with which Rome abounded, caring little for the remains of ancient Rome which lay buried all around. Medieval Rome was in fact a series of linked villages clustered near the Tiber and the Ponte Sant'Angelo, surrounded by grassy wooded mounds from which the wreckage of the pagan past stood out. Most of the pagan city lay abandoned and overgrown, used as a quarry for modern jerry-building, its marble facings and statuary fed into lime-kilns to make cement, its windowless ruins squatted in by beggars and farm animals. Cattle grazed in the Forum, sheep wandered over four of the seven hills.

Rome had no industries except pilgrimage, no function except as the Pope's capital. The city and its churches were radically impoverished by the long absence of the popes in Avignon and the schism which followed. On his return to Rome in 1420 Martin V found it 'so dilapidated and deserted that it bore hardly any resemblance to a city ... neglected and oppressed by famine and poverty'. When Martin restored his derelict cathedral of St John Lateran in 1425, he constructed the magnificent decorated floor by the simple process of looting porphyry, marble and mosaic from the city's ruined churches.

The Renaissance popes were determined to change all that, and set about planning new streets and raising buildings to perpetuate their own and their families' names, buildings which would be worthy both of the centre of the Church and of the greatest of all earthly cities, the mother of Europe. The fifteenth and early sixteenth centuries in Rome were the age of Humanism, a great age of renewed classical learning, the rediscovery of the principles of classical art, the flowering of creativity in painting, sculpture and architecture, and of a delight in life and beauty which represented not just lavish extravagance, but a renewed sense of the glory of creation. It was a religious vision in its own right: to understand it, we need to consider the first and in some ways the most attractive of the Humanist popes, Nicholas V (1447–55).

Nicholas, who had been a cardinal for less than three months before his election, became pope at an auspicious moment. A month before his election the princes of Germany had abandoned their support for the Council of Basle and the Antipope Felix V, and had recognised Pope Eugenius IV (1431–47). The Conciliar movement was running out of steam, as European monarchs made their own advantageous arrangements for control of their national churches with the papacy, and withdrew their support for ecclesiastical rebellion. Within two years, with the help of France, Nicholas was able to win over Felix V. He was also able to consolidate the rapprochement with Germany, and to recover some of the papal rights and revenues forfeited during the previous hundred years. In 1452 he crowned the German King Frederick III as emperor in Rome, the last imperial coronation ever to take place there.

These pacific measures were symptomatic of his whole reign. The pontificate of Eugenius IV had been stormy, with the Pope at odds not only with the Conciliarists and with the kings of France, Germany and Naples, but also with the city of Rome itself, with towns and regions in the Papal States like Bologna and the March of Ancona which had achieved virtual independence during the Great Schism, and above all with the mighty Colonna family. Martin V had been a Colonna, and his family had rapidly acquired control of vast tracts of papal territory, ostensibly as a way of reclaiming it for the papacy, but in fact for their own enrichment. Eugenius' attempts to force them to disgorge these ill-gotten gains led to his own nine-year banishment from Rome, which ended only in the autumn of 1443.

Nicholas was a less confrontational personality, and was able to resolve all these conflicts. Neapolitan and German ambassadors took part in his coronation, and he told the Germans that the popes had 'stretched their arms out too far, and have left scarcely any power to other bishops ... It is my firm purpose not to impair the rights of the bishops who are called to share my cares.'[1] Before the end of his pontificate the principal rulers of Italy had signed the Peace of Lodi (1454) and an unaccustomed (if short-lived) peace had broken out. In the breathing space all this gained, Nicholas was able to turn his attention to his real love, the creation of a renewed Rome. As a student at Bologna and especially as a private tutor in the Strozzi household in Florence he had absorbed the love of antiquity, learning and the arts which was considered the mark of a civilised man. He became an ardent book-collector. While still a poor priest, supplementing his income by ringing the bells in the churches of Florence, he declared that books and buildings were the only things worth spending money on.

These had become unfamiliar sentiments for a pope. Martin V had himself made an energetic start on the repair of Rome's devastated churches and public amenities, but he profoundly distrusted Renaissance learning, especially its obsession with pagan authors. He had a low opinion of what Gratian had called 'the literature of the damned', and thought that everything worth preserving from antiquity was contained in the works of St Augustine. His suspicion was not entirely unfounded, for some of the work of the Humanists, as the leading thinkers of the Renaissance were called, was quite explicitly anti-papal. In 1440 the great scholar Lorenzo Valla used Humanist tech-niques of textual and historical criticism in a devastating demolition job on the *Donation of Constantine*, proving that it was an eighth-cen-tury forgery. Valla was a client of King Alfonso I, ruler of Sicily, who was currently the Pope's enemy, so he was not entirely without an agenda. Nevertheless, he found a ready audience when he argued that the temporal claims derived from the bogus Donation had made the popes not the Father of the Faithful, but the oppressor of Christians – 'so far from giving food and bread to the household of God . . . they have devoured us as food . . . the Pope himself makes war on peaceable people, and sows discord among states and princes.'[2]

These remarks summarised a long tradition of Christian unease at the worldliness which the establishment of the Church had brought. They were aimed at Eugenius IV, whose nine years in Tuscany had, nevertheless, brought him into contact with more appealing aspects of the Renaissance. When the Pope returned to Rome, he brought the great Tuscan Dominican painter Fra Angelico with him. It was left to Nicholas V, however, to put Renaissance concerns at the cen-tre of the papal programme. In the aftermath of the councils, reform was on everyone's lips. Nicholas believed that the literature, the buildings and the arts of ancient Greece and Rome could provide a source of renewal for the present. He determined to create 'for the common convenience of the learned, a library of all books both in Latin and in Greek that is worthy of the dignity of the Pope and the Apostolic See'. Papal emissaries were sent to the far ends of Europe in search of rare manuscripts, and the Pope made it a particular con-cern to commission good Latin translations of the Greek pagan and Christian classics. The rediscovery of Greek science, literature and philosophy was one of the most powerful engines driving Renais-sance thought and art. One of the fruits of the union between the Churches of East and West achieved at the Council of Florence was the arrival in the West of John Bessarion, former Archbishop of Nicaea, whom Eugenius made a cardinal. The 'Cardinal of Nicaea' became a magnet for Greek scholars seeking patronage in the West, and his protégés became crucial to Nicholas' project. In time, Nicholas created a library of over a thousand precious volumes in Greek and Latin, the core of the future Vatican Library.

Nicholas also inaugurated the physical transformation of Rome. He symbolised the recovery of papal control in the city by restoring the Castel Sant' Angelo and repairing the medieval Palace of the Senators on the Capitol. His major works were at the Vatican, however, which he now made the chief papal residence, abandoning the run-down Lateran. He added a new wing to the Vatican Palace, decorated with frescoes by Fra Angelico. He rebuilt and extended the Leonine walls. Most daringly of all, he planned the radical reconstruction of St Peter's itself. In the thousand years since Constantine, the basilica had shared in the city's dilapidation. According to the great architect Alberti, who worked in the Curia under Nicholas, collapse was only a matter of time. Nicholas planned to add transepts and a new apse round the shrine of the Apostle, to accommodate the crowds of pilgrims – the alterations would have extended the length of the church by a third. He also planned a new piazza for grand papal blessings in front of St Peter's, in which would be placed the obelisk from the Circus of Nero near which Peter had been crucified.

Nicholas did not live to complete his many projects, but in a speech to the cardinals from his deathbed in 1455 he emphasised the religious vision that underlay them. His buildings were to be sermons in stone, laymen's books. The learned who had studied antiquity could truly understand the greatness and authority of Rome, but:

> to create solid and stable convictions in the minds of the uncul-
> tured masses, there must be something that appeals to the eye: a
> popular faith, sustained only on doctrines, will never be anything
> but feeble and vacillating. But if the authority of the Holy See
> were visibly displayed in majestic buildings, imperishable memo-
> rials and witnesses seemingly planted by the hand of God himself,
> belief would grow and strengthen like a tradition from one gener-
> ation to another, and all the world would accept and revere it.[3]

These words in many ways provided the programme for the Renaissance papacy.

Nicholas' sensitivity to the 'uncultured masses' from 'all the world' was almost certainly shaped by his experience of the Jubilee Year of

1450. The Jubilee, a year during which truly penitent pilgrims to Rome could gain a 'plenary Indulgence' which wiped away all the penance incurred by their sins, had first been instituted by Boniface VIII in 1300. The Jubilee of 1450, however, was a landmark event. For the first time since 1300 Rome had a resident pope, unchallenged by any rival, and the Jubilee became a symbol of the restored unity and peace of the Church.

From its inauguration on Christmas Day 1449 it was a huge success. Tens of thousands of pilgrims flooded into Rome, so many that bands of volunteer militia armed with staves had to be organised to keep order in the streets. There were not enough beds in the city to accommodate everybody, and thousands camped out in fields and vineyards. The Pope, endlessly in demand for papal blessings, ordered that the great relics of Rome – the enshrined heads of the Apostles Peter and Paul, and the handkerchief with which Veronica was supposed to have wiped the face of Christ on the way to Calvary, – should be exposed every weekend, for the veneration of each new wave of pilgrims. Endless queues shuffled in and out of the basilicas till late into the night, and as provisions ran out the Pope was obliged to shorten the required stay in Rome from eight to three days.

The Jubilee had its disasters: in the summer a plague raged, the graveyards filled up, and the pilgrim routes of Italy were lined with corpses. The plague eventually cleared and the flood of pilgrims resumed, but on 19 December, in the last week of the Jubilee, a bucking mule caused a stampede among the crowds pressing home to their lodgings in the late afternoon across the Ponte Sant' Angelo. In the crush, at least 200 people were trampled to death or drowned in the swollen Tiber. The nearby church of San Celso became a makeshift mortuary, where the dead were laid out in rows for identification.

Despite these horrifying events, the Jubilee was a formative event for the Renaissance papacy. After the long traumas of the schism and the anti-papal propaganda of the Conciliar movement, it confirmed beyond argument the centrality of Rome and the Pope in popular Catholicism. With a sure instinct, Nicholas sealed this link by choosing the centre-point of the Jubilee year, Whit Sunday 1450, to stage the canonisation of St Bernardino of Siena, who had died only six years earlier. Bernardino was a highly controversial Franciscan, whose unconventional revivalist rallies and salty vernacular pulpit style had swept Italy and made him the best-known preacher of his day. His canonisation allied the papacy with the current of popular religious feeling and captured something of Bernardino's prestige for the institution. More mundanely, the Jubilee pilgrim offerings provided a bonanza which restored papal finances and funded Nicholas' various projects. The Pope is said to have lodged 100,000 gold florins in the Medici bank alone, more than a third of his normal annual income, and almost as much as his entire secular revenue from the Papal States.

The Jubilee also became an instrument of papal reform. The Conciliar movement had called for the reform of the Church, in 'head and members', in practice giving priority to the institutional reform – by which was meant reduction – of the role of Pope and Curia. Concern for the removal of other abuses, however, was widespread, and Nicholas extended the Jubilee and signalled his support for reform in 1451 by sending special legates through Europe to preach reconciliation and renewal. The legate for Germany was Cardinal Nicholas of Cusa, Archbishop of Brixen. Cusa had once been a pillar of the Conciliár movement, and his *De Concordantia Catholica* was probably its most enduring theological product. He had been appalled by the revolutionary proceedings of the Council of Basle, however, and had become an ardent defender of the papal cause. Alongside the revival of personal piety encouraged by the Jubilee Indulgence, he was to enforce clerical and especially monastic reform, and he launched a vigorous campaign to improve lay religious knowledge. All this was accompanied by elaborate ceremonial, including solemn processions in which Cusa carried the Blessed Sacrament through the streets, and presided over the veneration of local relics. He also concerned himself, however, with curbing superstition, preaching against the sale of indulgences, and attacking suspect devotions, such as the pilgrimage to the Holy Blood of Wilsnack. His activities in Germany were matched by the similar though shorter legatine mission of John of Capistrano to Austria. Capistrano was an observant Franciscan and had been a close friend of St Bernardino's, and the temperature of his preaching was correspondingly warmer. Crowds of the sick flocked to be touched with the relics of St Bernardino, and in the wake of Capistrano's vehement sermons 'bonfires of vanities', including backgammon tables and playing cards, were made outside the churches. Capistrano was also responsible for the return to Catholicism of many followers of Hus.

And everywhere, like Cusa, he was greeted 'as ambassador of the Pope and preacher of truth', and the people flocked to him 'as if St Peter or St Paul or some other Apostle were passing by.'[4] These attempts at papal reform were perfectly genuine, and achieved much good. To many people, however, they seemed no more than cosmetic tinkering, attempts to buy off more radical demands with a few piffling gestures. The call for a council, and the reform of the papacy and Curia, as the root of the Church's ills, continued.

The last years of Nicholas V were overshadowed by his grief over the fall of Constantinople to the Turks in 1453, and by the discovery in the same year of a Roman republican plot to murder the Pope. The marriage he had made between the papacy and Renaissance art and learning, however, endured. It survived his immediate successor, the elderly Spaniard Callistus III (1455–8), whose main preoccupation was the recovery of Constantinople from the Turks, and for whom everything else was a waste of money. Callistus called a halt to all Nicholas' building projects, and is reported to have cried out on walking into his predecessor's library, 'See how the treasure of the Church has been wasted.' He is said to have sold the precious bindings from Nicholas' books to finance the fleet he built against the Turks.

For the rest of the century, however, the popes were enthusiastic patrons of the Renaissance. Callistus was succeeded by one of Italy's most famous Humanists, the Sienese Aeneas Silvio Piccolomini, who took the name Pius II (1458–64). Aeneas was known throughout Italy and beyond as a connoisseur, an historian and the author of erotic plays and tales. His successor was the Venetian nobleman Paul II (1464–71), a man of lavish tastes who loved games, ceremonial and the Roman Carnival, and who was intensely proud of his own good looks – he had toyed with the idea of calling himself Pope Formosus II ('Formosus' means 'beautiful'). Paul was the nephew of Pope Eugenius IV, and used the status and wealth this brought him while still a cardinal as a typical Renaissance dilettante, building up a unique collection of antiques and artworks. As pope he launched a programme of restoration of ancient monuments such as the Pantheon, the equestrian statue of Marcus Aurelius, and the arch of Titus, and the first printing presses were established at Rome under him.

The culmination of this papal patronage of the arts came under Francesco della Rovere, the Franciscan theologian who became Sixtus IV (1471–84), and his nephew Giuliano della Rovere, who became

Julius II (1503–13). From the outset, Pope Sixtus belied his poor Franciscan origins by the lavishness of his patronage. His coronation tiara alone cost 100,000 ducats, more than a third of the papacy's annual income. Sixtus launched a lavish campaign of rebuilding which realised many of the aspirations of Nicholas V. They included the first new bridge across the Tiber since antiquity, the Ponte Sisto, built to relieve the pressure of pilgrims on the Ponte Sant'Angelo and ensure that the tragedy of 1450 never recurred. He rebuilt the foundling hospital of Santo Spirito in the Borgo, and the church of Santa Maria del Popolo, the della Rovere family mausoleum which dominated the entrance to the city used by pilgrims from the north.

His most famous commission, however, was the Sistine Chapel in the Vatican itself. This building was designed to provide a setting for papal elections, and more especially for the meetings and common worship of the 200 clerics who, with the Pope, formed the *cappella papale* or papal chapel. Sixtus was a passionate lover of music, and in addition to creating the chapel he established the Sistine choir to provide appropriately splendid music for the papal liturgy. The chapel itself was decorated with twenty-eight painted niches between the windows containing the portraits of the popes of the first three centuries, and with two matched fresco cycles of the lives of Moses and of Christ by the greatest painters of the day.

These frescoes were not simply pious decoration, but were carefully worked out ideological statements, laden with papal symbolism. In Botticelli's *Punishment of Korah*, for example, the theme is the dreadful punishments which befall those who rebel against Moses, God's priest, king and prophet. Moses here is a 'type' or prophetic symbol for the Pope, and the inscription reads: 'Challenge to Moses bearer of the written law'. Contemporaries would have picked up at once the allusion to the Conciliar movement and to the Italian princes currently at war with the Pope.

The matching scene across the chapel, Perugino's *Christ Consigns the Keys to Peter*, is similarly inscribed: 'Challenge to Christ bearer of the law'. In the background are portrayed the Gospel story of the tribute money, in which Christ's relationship to the temporal power of the Roman empire was questioned, and the story of the stoning of Christ after his sermon in the synagogue at Capernaum, in which his authority as a religious teacher was rejected. In the foreground, Christ hands the golden key of spiritual authority to Peter, from which hangs suspended the base-metal key of temporal power, a deliberate evocation of the papal version of the 'two-powers' theory inherited from Gregory VII and Innocent III, in which the Pope possesses both spiritual and temporal power, exercising spiritual power directly, and temporal power indirectly through obedient Christian rulers. The Pope, like Christ, is supreme in both spheres.

Alongside these artistic commissions, Sixtus developed other aspects of Nicholas V's programme, completing the establishment of the Vatican Library and appointing the Humanist Bartolomeo Platina as its librarian. Sixtus did all he could to claim the total credit for the library, but the foundation bull of the library echoes Nicholas in describing the library as being 'for the enhancing of the Church militant, for the increase of the Catholic faith, and for the convenience and honour of the learned and studious'.[5]

Sixtus IV's nephew, Julius II, continued his uncle's patronage of the arts in the service of the papacy, but on an even more awesome scale. In the Vatican Palace itself, he refused to live in the rooms which his hated Borgia predecessor, Alexander VI, had lavishly decorated. He moved upstairs, and brought in Raphael to decorate his new apartments with paintings which similarly celebrated both reason and faith, the glories of pre-Christian philosophy but also and especially the teachings of the Church. The results are among the greatest glories of European art – the *School of Athens*, with its triumphant celebration of intellect, the *Disputation on the Sacrament* and the *Miracle of Bolsena*, the latter an unexpected glimpse of Julius' perfectly genuine religious devotion – and a series of scenes which echoed the warrior Pope's own determination to free the Church from her worldly enemies: the *Expulsion of Heliodorus*, the *Liberation of St Peter* (Julius had been the Cardinal Priest of the church of St Peter in Chains), the *Repulse of Attila*.

Nicholas had planned the rebuilding of St Peter's: on 18 April 1506 Julius laid the foundation stone of the new church. It was to take 150 years to complete, for, where Nicholas had envisaged an extension of the existing building, Julius characteristically determined to make a clean sweep of the Constantinian church and the hundred or so altars, tombs and chapels it had acquired in the thousand years since it had been built. His architect, Bramante, planned a grandiose domed building centred on the shrine of the Apostle, but the new choir was also to contain an immense and vulgar tomb for the Pope. Had it been completed it would have been more appropriate for a pharaoh than a Christian bishop, and Julius' presence in the mother church of Christendom would have been hardly less visible than that of St Peter. Above all, it was Julius who coaxed, bribed and browbeat the greatest artist of the Renaissance, Michelangelo Buonarroti, to decorate the ceiling of the Sistine Chapel with frescoes which breathe the spirit of Humanist Christianity, the whole design a celebration of human beauty and of divine grace in creation and redemption.

By the turn of the sixteenth century, then, Rome had become the centre of the Italian Renaissance, and for two generations the Curia had been one of the major career routes for literati on the make. Famous Humanists competed for posts as papal secretaries, and eventually colonised the entire papal bureaucracy: at its height the Curia was employing up to a hundred Humanists at any one time. The popes harnessed the new educational skills of the Humanists, as they harnessed the skills of painters and architects, to create for the papacy an image of greatness.

In the process, the theology of the papal court underwent something of a revolution. The revival of interest in Greek literature and philosophy, and in antiquity in general, had led to a reassessment of the 'literature of the damned'. A Christianised Platonism became fashionable, which saw Christianity not in opposition to the religion of the pre-Christian world, but as the fulfilment of all that was best in it. In ancient Egypt, Babylon and Greece would be found poetic or allegorical traces of the truths fully revealed in Christ, and the wisdom of the ancient philosophers was God-given. Traces of this sort of thinking can be seen in Michelangelo's scheme for the Sistine Chapel ceiling, where the pagan Sybils sit alongside Old Testament prophets as foretellers of the Christian mystery. They are even more obvious in the decorations Pope Alexander VI had painted by Pinturicchio for the Borgia apartments in the Vatican in the early 1490s, where the mysteries of Osiris are used as types of the saving work of Christ.

This process could go too far. Alongside this 'poetical theology' went less benign forms of assimilation of the pagan past. The members of the Humanist Roman Academy visited the catacombs to see ancient inscriptions and frescoes, collected sculpture, and cultivated an elaborate Ciceronian Latin style. Some of them also flirted with a deliberate and provocative 'paganism' which included active republicanism and open homosexuality. Paul II, himself an ardent Humanist, was nevertheless alarmed by what he took to be an exaggerated respect for pagan authors and pagan values. He antagonised this group in the 1460s by a reorganisation of the Curia (partly designed to limit the influence of Cardinal Alessandro Borgia), which in fact reduced the number of curial posts open to Humanists. In 1468 a plot to assassinate the Pope was discovered, in which sixty members of the Academy were believed to be implicated.

Even where matters were not taken to these lengths, the self-consciously classical culture of the Renaissance Curia represented a radical break with many established Christian assumptions and attitudes. As a result it was both incomprehensible and highly offensive to many. The greatest of all the Humanists of northern Europe, Erasmus of Rotterdam, satirised the absurd Ciceronian mannerism of curial writing, which referred to God the Father as 'Jupiter Optimus Maximus', to the Virgin Mary as 'Diana', to the Apostles as 'legates' and to the bishops as 'proconsuls'.

For Erasmus such mannerisms were more than foibles. They were marks of a growing secularism within the papal court, and he was not the only one to comment on it. It was not Humanism which lay at the root of it, however, but the struggle of the popes to maintain the independence of the Papal States. Despite the 1454 Peace of Lodi, fifteenth-century Italy was a highly unstable place of shifting allegiances and ferociously contending states led by ruthlessly self-aggrandising families – the Medici of Florence, the Sforza of Milan, the Malatesta of Rimini. Behind these local forces loomed larger powers, for Spain had claims to Sicily, and France to Milan. After the French invasions of Charles VIII in 1494 and Louis XII in 1499, Italy would become the cockpit for a larger European struggle between contending powers.

Since the time of the Lombard invasions, the defence of the lands of St Peter had been one of the major concerns of papal policy: it had given birth to the Frankish empire. In this age of warring princes, however, it took on a new intensity, as the popes themselves increasingly became princes warring against other princes. Like so much else that was unattractive in the Renaissance papacy, this development can be traced back to the pontificate of Sixtus IV. Initially an ardent ally of Milan (the Duke of Milan had helped secure his election) and much under the influence of his bloodthirsty nephews Pietro and Girolamo Riario, Pope Sixtus was rapidly involved in a series of sordid wars — against Florence, Ferrara, Venice. In these, the Pope shifted alliances with all the untroubled cynicism of a secular prince in the age of Machiavelli. In 1478 he connived at the Pazzi conspiracy to murder Lorenzo and Giuliano de' Medici at High Mass in the Duomo in Florence.

The pattern established by Sixtus was adopted by his successors: Innocent VIII (1484–92) fomented rebellion in Naples, and allied himself to the ruling family of Florence, the Medici, by the simple expedient of marrying his illegitimate son Franceschetto to a daughter of Lorenzo the Magnificent. This dynastic note became a concerto under Innocent's Spanish successor, Roderigo Borgia, Pope Alexander VI, who was the father of at least nine illegitimate children. Alexander is arguably the most notorious of all the Renaissance popes. Magnetically attractive to women, he had a succession of mistresses with whom he lived quite openly, the last and youngest of them, Giulia Farnese, even after he became pope, in his sixties.

Throughout his career, disreputable legends blossomed round him. In a famous letter, which became the foundation for much of Alexander's later notoriety with historians, Pope Pius II rebuked the then Cardinal Borgia for hosting a debauched garden-party in Siena, to which the fashionable women of the town were invited, but from which their husbands, fathers, brothers and all other men were excluded. Sadly, as the Pope conceded, the rumours turned out to be greatly exaggerated, the garden-party socially not sexually exclusive, and most of the legends about Alexander are similarly unreliable. Stories of his debauched and extravagant lifestyle contrast starkly with the spartan and coarse diet (a good many sardines) which he himself preferred, and which he imposed on his household, with his precise and slightly stuffy piety and concern for orthodoxy, and with the meagre artistic and architectural patronage he dispensed. The sober truth about his sexual appetite and his single-minded devotion to his family, however, was scandalous enough. As pope he systematically used his children's dynastic marriages to form alliances with a succession of princes. He also alienated large tracts of the papal lands to create independent duchies for his sons Juan and Cesare. Cesare was the admired model for Niccolò Machiavelli's treatise on Renaissance statecraft, *The Prince*. His conquests in the Papal States were ostensibly designed to reduce to obedience rebellious local rulers, nominally papal vicars for territories which they had in fact appropriated. Cesare's activities as captain general of the papal armies, however, were little better, being impossible to distinguish from the settling of ancient feuds between the Borgias and rival Roman families like the Orsini. Cesare was not the champion of the papal cause, but lord of a personal fiefdom. In the same way, the Medici Pope Leo X (1513–21) pursued a war policy designed to further the interests of Florence and his family, rather than the interests of the papacy as such.

Papal diplomacy and papal warfare, however, were not inevitably linked to the aggrandisement of the Pope's family. The most ferocious Pope of the period – imperious, hot-tempered, manically active – was the della Rovere Julius II. Known to his contemporaries as *il terribile*, an untranslatable word that suggests a violent force of nature rather than a personality, Julius stormed up and down the Italian peninsula in his suit of silver armour at the head of his own troops: on one occasion he belaboured with his staff the quaking cardinals who were reluctant to follow him through snowdrifts breast-high on their horses. His wars, however, unlike those of Sixtus IV or Alexander VI, were designed to secure the position of the papacy itself, not the reigning Pope's family. He set himself to liberate papal territory which had been appropriated by the family of Alexander VI, to push back Venetian incursions into the papal territory of Romagna (the old exarchate of Ravenna). By the end of his pontificate he had driven the French out of Italy and had extended the Papal States to include Parma, Piacenza and Reggio Emilia.

Julius faithfully and spectacularly served the interests of the papacy as he understood it, including its financial interests. Though he was the most lavish of art patrons, and poured money into his wars, he left the papal treasury full. Yet there is no escaping the utterly secular character of such a pope. It was said of him that there was nothing of the priest about him but the cassock, and he did not always wear that. The last portrait by Raphael shows the fierce old man in a ragged beard, the first Renaissance Pope to wear one. Julius had grown the beard not for piety or fashion, however, but in imitation of his pagan namesake Julius Caesar, who had stopped shaving as a pledge of vengeance on the Gauls, for their massacre of his legions. Pope Julius' beard was a pledge of vengeance against his many enemies – the French, the Turks, the Bolognese, and even the Romans.

One of the most striking features of the Renaissance papacy was the extent to which successive popes promoted their own relatives.

This was not necessarily in itself a moral failing. The papacy was an elected monarchy, and newly elected popes inherited from their predecessors a labyrinthine bureaucracy and a college of cardinals who were often hostile and obstructive. The existence of such complex loyalties within the Sacred College was formally recognised and signalled at papal conclaves. During the election period, the rooms of cardinals created by the dead Pope were draped in violet, the rooms of others in green.

In such circumstances, the promotion of a kinsman to the cardinalate might be the only way to ensure colleagues and collaborators who could be relied on. In the sixteenth and seventeenth centuries cardinal nephews routinely took on the role of secretary of state. But the Renaissance popes pushed these things to extremes. The Spanish Pope Callistus III not only promoted two nephews to the cardinalate (one of them the future Alexander VI) but made a third nephew commander in chief of the papal armies, and he flooded the papal household and the Curia itself with Catalan officials. It may be that a foreign pope needed more in the way of family backing if he was to master the Curia than a native Italian did. At any rate, Pius II was more restrained, making just two nephews cardinals, one of whom later reigned for twenty-seven days as Pius III (1503).

Once again, however, Sixtus IV raised the stakes. He made six of his nephews cardinals, and married other nephews and nieces into some of the great Italian dynasties – Naples, Milan, Urbino. Not content with this, he heaped benefices on them, giving his cardinal nephews the incomes of princes. Giuliano della Rovere, the future Julius II, was Archbishop of Avignon, Archbishop of Bologna, Bishop of Lausanne, Bishop of Coutances, Bishop of Viviers, Bishop of Mende and Bishop of Ostia and Velletri, and Abbot of Nonantola and of Grottaferrata, and he had scores of lesser benefices.

The inevitable outcome of all this was the creation of a wealthy cardinalatial class, with strong dynastic connections. At Eugenius IV's election in 1431, half the twelve cardinals came from outside Italy. At Alexander VI's election in 1492, only one out of twenty-three cardinals (Alexander himself) was non-Italian. As the papal families intermarried with the princely houses of Italy, the Sacred College and the papacy itself came to resemble a rollcall of the great – Farnese, Medici, Gonzaga, Este. Innocent VIII, having married his son into the Medici family, obligingly made Lorenzo the Magnificent's son

Giovanni a cardinal – at the age of thirteen. In due course, as we have seen, this Cardinal Medici would be elected Pope Leo X. Aristocratic infiltration of the cardinalate was in part a function of the increasing politicisation of the papacy. The rulers of Italy, France and Spain needed tame (though mostly Italian) cardinals to exert pressure on papal policy, or at any rate papal elections.

For, paradoxically, this was also a period in which the cardinals were increasingly excluded from papal policy-making, and declined from being papal counsellors to being pensioned courtiers. Tensions between pope and cardinals had existed since at least the time of Gregory VII, and the custom of making electoral pacts had grown up during the Avignon papacy. These were agreements entered into by the cardinals in Conclave, which imposed restrictions on the new Pope's freedom of action – limiting the number of new cardinals he could create, or the types of decisions or policies he could make without the agreement of the Sacred College. Human nature being what it is, however, such pacts were easier to make than to enforce. A duly elected pope was a monarch, and could do more or less as he pleased. The first Pope after the Great Schism, the steely Colonna Martin V, had acted without the slightest pretence of consultation, and the cardinals were reduced to quivering, stammering children in his presence. Yet cardinals had played a crucial role both in beginning and in ending the schism – the Council of Constance had been convened by cardinals – and many hoped that some at least of the objectives of the Conciliar movement might be attained through the pressure placed by cardinals on successive popes.

All this was so much huff and puff, however, for the cardinals had no sanctions against the Pope, and depended on him for their security and wealth. Eugenius IV, Pius II, Paul II and Sixtus IV all accepted such pacts at the Conclave, but none of them kept them once they were elected. When in 1517 Leo X discovered a plot against him among the cardinals, he executed the ringleader and swamped the Sacred College by creating thirty-one new cardinals in a single day. In the process he not only overwhelmed his enemies by sheer numbers, but drastically reduced their income, much of which came from shares in a fixed pool of revenues.

The one place where the cardinals were supreme was in Conclave, when they elected the new Pope. Locked into the Vatican, the cardinals ate and slept in dark and airless wooden cells erected for the occasion, and were officially cut off from the outside world. Renaissance conclaves were hotbeds of intrigue, the outcome of which was rarely predictable. We have an eyewitness account of the 1458 Conclave from Aeneas Silvio Piccolomini, who emerged as Pius II. He recalled the endless plotting in the lavatory block – 'a fit place for such elections!'[6] Religious considerations alone seldom dominated the choice of popes. Rivalries between France and Spain, or between Milan, Venice and Naples, or more local rivalries like those of the Orsini and Colonna families, all played a part, as did internal tensions within the Sacred College. In 1458 Pius II was elected partly because of his personal amiability, but mainly because violent resentment of the Spanish domination of the previous pontificate combined with fear of French political influence to rule out any foreigner, and hence the likeliest candidate, the French Cardinal d'Estouteville. In 1464, a conclave at which the favourite candidate was the formidable Spanish Dominican defender of papal infallibility, Juan de Torquemada, the successful candidate was the worldly papal nephew Pietro Barbo, elected because he was felt to be a loyal member of the Sacred College, who would be pliant – as it transpired, a sadly misplaced assumption.

The spread of nepotism and of venal appointments to the cardinalate, in return for money or favours, made the outcome of elections towards the end of the century even less likely to reflect a simple search for 'God's candidate'. In the 1484 conclave which elected Innocent VIII (1484–92) there were a record twenty-five cardinals present, many of them scandalously secular men. Proceedings were stage-managed by Giuliano della Rovere, nephew of the dead Pope. When it became clear that he himself was unelectable, he saw to it that a manageable nonentity was chosen. The successful candidate, Cardinal Cibo, bribed electors by countersigning petitions for promotion brought to him in his cell the night before the decisive vote.

Roderigo Borgia's election as Alexander VI in 1492 was accompanied by even more naked bribery. A new pope had to resign all his benefices, and so had gifts to distribute. Borgia, a gifted administrator and diplomat with a long and successful curial career behind him, was one of the most spectacular of pluralists, and had at his disposal literally dozens of major plums – bishoprics, abbeys, fortresses, fortified towns. They were allocated in advance to consolidate the majority he needed. It is in fact quite likely that Alexander's political shrewdness and administrative experience would have won him the support he needed to become pope, and the bribery at his election was not much worse than at many others. Yet, for all his ability, Roderigo was a worldly and ruthless man, and at the time of his election was already the father of eight children, by at least three women. That such a man should have seemed a fit successor to Peter speaks volumes about the degradation of the papacy.

Before the Great Schism, the papacy had derived much of its funding from the vigorous exercise of its spiritual office – payments from suppliants at the papal court, revenues derived from papal provisions, annates on benefices, Peter's Pence. The erosion of papal prerogatives during the schism and Conciliar era, however, drastically reduced such payments, and the papacy was increasingly thrown back on the secular revenues derived from the Papal States – a fact which accounts for the papal wars in defence of those States. A major addition to papal income came in 1462 with the discovery of an alum-mine at Tolfa in the District of Rome. Alum was a vital chemical for both the cloth industry and the leather trade. Till 1462, however, there was no significant European source, and most supplies came from Muslim west Turkey. The popes were now able to forbid Christian use of Turkish alum, and to establish a monopoly of European supplies. The resulting income was officially earmarked for war to recover Constantinople and the Holy Places, and to turn back the Turkish advance in eastern Europe. By 1480 alum profits made up a third of the Pope's secular revenue.

Nevertheless, the mounting cost of papal wars, and the lavish building programmes of successive popes, made the search for new sources of revenue unending. The most notorious of these was the sale of indulgences, especially the indulgence for the rebuilding of St Peter's. More significant still, however, was the growing dependence of the popes on the sale of office. Essentially, this was a form of public funding by floating loans. Investors bought a position in the papal Curia for a large cash payment: they recouped their capital investment and a life interest in the form of the revenues of the post they now owned. This meant that in real terms a large proportion of papal income was mortgaged to repaying office-holders, and successive popes resorted to inventing new layers of bureaucracy to raise further capital: the conscientious Pius II did this to fund his Crusade. The result was the multiplication of virtually useless offices. Innocent VIII, for example, established fifty-two *pulumbatores*, officials responsible for fixing the lead seals on official documents. Each pulumbator paid 2,500 ducats for his post – about a hundred times the annual salary of a country priest.

The sale of office paralysed reform, for it created a huge class of officials with a vested interest in preventing the streamlining of the papal administration or any attempt at removing financial abuses within the Curia. It also edged out talent: from the 1480s it was increasingly difficult for low-born men of ability to secure a post within the Curia without the necessary purchase-price. More and more offices became soft billets for idle drones. By the time of the death of Leo X in 1521 it was calculated that there were more than 2,150 saleable offices in the Vatican, worth in the region of 3,000,000 ducats. They included even the highest offices within the papal court, like the post of Cardinal Camerlengo.

The secularising effects on the papacy of all this can be seen most clearly in the collapse of papal commitment to the Crusading ideal. Pope Urban II had invented the Crusade, and his successors placed Crusading high on the list of fundamental papal priorities. Papal leadership of a united Christendom launched against the enemies of the cross remained a seductive vision. In the fifteenth century, however, it was one that had less and less appeal to the rulers of Europe, who preferred to fight each other. The fall of Constantinople in 1453 horrified the popes – the future Pius II wrote that 'one of the two lights of Christendom has been extinguished' – and successive popes from Nicholas V onwards tried to galvanise the princes into action. Callistus III poured all the energies of his pontificate into the project, sending legates throughout Europe to preach a Crusading Indulgence, taxing the clergy, and turning the Tiber into a shipyard for a Crusading fleet. The main effect of all this was to antagonise the already resentful national churches, and to trigger calls for a general council to put a stop to unreasonable papal demands. Pius II, equally committed to the Crusade, had no better luck. Confronted with princely indifference and by Venetian reluctance to jeopardise trade by antagonising the Turks, the dying pope went himself to Ancona to lead an expedition. 'Our cry to "go forth"', he declared, 'has gone unheeded. Perhaps if the word is "Come with me" it will have more effect.' He died at Ancona waiting for support which never came or, in the case of Venice, which came too late.

Under Innocent VIII, however, four centuries of papal commitment to the pushing back of Islam was abandoned. In 1482 the Turkish Prince Cem, younger son of Sultan Mehmet II, the conqueror of Constantinople, presented himself before the Knights of St John at Rhodes. Naively, he asked their help in overthrowing his brother Bayezit, who had succeeded Mehmet II. Instead of helping him, the Knights negotiated a deal with Bayezit, who paid handsomely to have his dangerous brother kept under lock and key. In 1486 Innocent VIII placed Cem under papal protection (having bought the prisoner from the Grand Master of the Knights of St John by making the latter a cardinal), and three years later established him in some style in the Castel Sant' Angelo.

The Pope now became chief gaoler to the Sultan. Bayezit sent Innocent a gift of 120,000 crowns (almost equal to the total annual revenue of the papal state), and the relic of the Holy Lance which had pierced Christ's side on Calvary. A special shrine was built for it in St Peter's. Thereafter the Pope received an annual fee of 45,000 ducats to keep Cem in custody. These sophisticated proceedings were more than equalled by Innocent's successor, Pope Alexander VI. He actively discouraged the Crusade, and applied to Bayezit for a further subsidy of 300,000 gold ducats, which he explained would help him keep France out of Italy, and so prevent it being used as the launching-pad for a French Crusade against Constantinople, now renamed Istanbul. The subordination of religious zeal to political pragmatism could go no further.

II THE CRISIS OF CHRISTENDOM

The Renaissance papacy, for all its glories, had shown itself again and again chronically resistant to reform. Yet everywhere in the Christian world, ever more urgently, reform was being called for. In Italy, that call was sounded most emphatically at the end of the fifteenth century by the Prior of the Dominican house of San Marco in Florence, Girolamo Savonarola. A revivalist preacher in the mould of John Capistrano or Vincent Ferrar, Savonarola announced apocalypse, and saw in the French invasion of Italy and the expulsion of the Medici from Florence the purifying scourge of God. Under his preaching, a heady mixture of biblical prophecy, cloudy political comment and moral fulmination, Florence plunged into an extraordinary experiment in theocratic republicanism. Most forms of public amusement were banned, membership of the Dominican priory rocketed from 50 to 238 friars, married women left their husbands and entered convents, and outside the Palazzo Vecchio there were bonfires of vanities – jewels, lewd books, immodest clothing. With his own hands, the great Florentine artist Sandro Botticelli burned his own 'pagan' pictures.

Savonarola identified the Rome of Alexander VI with the forces of Antichrist, whose downfall he predicted: 'I saw in a vision a black cross above the Babylon that is Rome, upon which was written *Ira Domini* [the wrath of the Lord] . . . I say to you, the Church of God must be renewed, and it will be soon.' Rome was a moral pig-sty, where everything, including the sacraments, was for sale. And in what everyone recognised as a reference to the Pope he lamented that 'Once, anointed priests called their sons "nephews"; but now they speak no more of nephews, but always and everywhere of their sons . . . O prostitute Church.'7

Alexander excommunicated Savonarola in 1497, after two years of increasingly frustrating attempts to silence him by less drastic means. In 1498 the city, disillusioned by adversity, turned on its prophet, and he was hanged and burned in the square where he had presided over the bonfires of vanities. His attack on Alexander continued to resonate, however. At the height of their confrontation he had declared Alexander to be no true pope, because he was an immoral atheist, and had called for a general council to reform the Church, starting with the papacy. This revival of the demands of the Conciliar movement was widely seen as playing into the hands of the French, who would later try to convene just such a council to unseat Alexander's successor, Julius II (at Pisa in 1511). It touched a chord, nonetheless. Savonarola's memory continued to be venerated even by ardently pro-papal religious leaders like the English theologian Bishop John Fisher, who would go to the scaffold in defence of papal authority in Henry VIII's England. All good men recognised that something would have to be done about the popes.

From the north, a cooler voice than Savonarola's was calling for reform, the voice of Erasmus of Rotterdam. In northern Europe the Renaissance was a more sober and more exclusively Christian movement than in Italy, deeply influenced by late medieval religious movements such as the 'Devotio Moderna' and the search for a more authentic personal piety. For the northern Humanists, the quest for a return to the pure sources of human culture included Plato and

Cicero, but focused on Christian classics – the writings of the early Fathers of the Church, and above all the scriptures. Erasmus poured his energies into producing editions of the works of St Jerome, St Augustine, St Ambrose. Above all, his edition of the Greek New Testament with a modern Latin translation (1516) aimed to bring before his contemporaries 'Christ speaking, healing, dying and rising'.

Erasmus was more than a pious scholar. He was also Europe's wittiest satirist, and in a stream of lacerating comic works, like *The Praise of Folly* of 1509, he poked savage fun at the corruptions of the Church. He detested violence, and he had no desire to stoke the fires of revolution. He did want to use laughter to expose absurdity and corruption, however, to tickle the Church into reforming itself. He became the most celebrated man in Europe, and kings and cardinals competed for his friendship. Between 1506 and 1509 he lived in Italy, absorbing the glories of the Italian Renaissance, and casting a sardonic eye on the activities of Julius II.

Erasmus and the many reform-minded Catholics who thought like him hated the. belligerent and worldly Julius, for the warrior-pope represented everything they thought a priest should not be. After Julius' death an anonymous satire appeared entitled *Julius Exclusus*, which everyone assumed was the work of Erasmus, though he himself always resolutely denied it. Whoever its actual author was, it was saturated with the spirit of Erasmus' angry mockery, a devastatingly funny but deadly indictment, in which the late pope was accused of every crime from sorcery to sodomy. The heart of the satire was the encounter at the gates of heaven between St Peter and the dead Julius, still clad in his armour and accompanied by an army of noisy ghosts created by his wars. Peter refuses to recognise this murderous thug as his successor, or to admit him to heaven, and in the ensuing argument Julius unwittingly betrays the sordidly materialistic vision of the papacy which many men feared underpinned the glories of Renaissance Rome. In reply to Peter's demand whether he has been his true successor by teaching true doctrine, gaining souls for Christ, being diligent in prayer, Julius rebukes the presumption of the 'beggarly fisherman' and replies:

> You shall know who and what I am . . . I raised the revenue. I invented new offices and sold them. I invented a way to sell bishoprics without simony . . . I annexed Bologna to the Holy See. I beat the Venetians. I drove the French out of Italy `. . . I have set all

the princes of the Empire by the ears. I have torn up treaties, kept great armies in the field. I have covered Rome with palaces, and I have left five millions in the treasury behind me.[8]

This bitter satire was rooted in disappointment at the failure of reform, above all, the failure of the popes to call a reform council. In 1511 a group of disgruntled cardinals supported by Louis XII of France had tried to reinvent the Conciliar era by summoning a council against Julius at Pisa. Quite obviously a French political ploy, this assembly received almost no support, but it forced Julius to reply in kind. In May 1512 he opened the Fifth Lateran Council in Rome, destined to be the last papal Council before the break-up of Western Christendom. In terms of reform, Lateran V was toothless, composed mainly of Italian bishops, its officials appointed by the Pope, its agenda dictated by him, its decrees published in the form of a papal bull. The summary of its proceedings which Julius Exclusus put in the dead pope's mouth – 'I told it what it was to say . . . We had two Masses, to show we were acting under Divine Inspiration, and then there was a speech in honour of myself. At the next session I cursed the schismatic cardinals. At the third I laid France under an interdict . . . Then the Acts were drafted into a bull and sent round Europe' – is a caricature, but not all that far wide of the mark.[9]

Julius died before Lateran V had completed its work, and the advent of the new Medici Pope Leo X, young (he was only thirty-seven), cultivated, peaceable and free from the grosser vices, led to a surge of expectation. He had signed an electoral pact which bound him to continue the Council, but nothing happened. A few of the milder reform measures found their way into the papal bull *Supernae Dispositionis Arbitrio*, but nobody, least of all the Pope, paid any attention. From the Pope's point of view the most satisfactory outcome of the Lateran Council was the discrediting of the schismatical Council of Pisa, and the French monarchy's abandonment of Conciliar theory, a stick it had brandished over the heads of the popes for the best part of a century. While the Lateran Council was still sitting he signed the Concordat of Bologna (1516) with the French crown. This gave the King the right to appoint to bishoprics, abbacies and major benefices in his territories. But it restored the payment of annates to the Pope, permitted appeals to Rome (forbidden by the Pragmatic Sanction of 1438, which was now annulled), and formally acknowledged the Pope's supremacy over a general council. In practice, the Concordat made the French King master of a French national church, over which the Pope had little control. Leo considered this a price worth paying for the abandonment of the Pragmatic Sanction, the theoretical recognition of papal prerogatives and the actual restoration of a substantial part of papal revenues.

In the same year in which Erasmus published *Julius Exclusus*, in which the Lateran Council ended, and in which Pope Leo packed the College of Cardinals with thirty-one new creations, an unknown theology professor in Wittenberg, an obscure new German university, proposed an academic debate on the subject of indulgences. His name was Martin Luther, and he was reacting against the indulgence which Pope Julius and after him Pope Leo had issued to help fund the rebuilding of St Peter's. Raising donations for Church projects by dispensing spiritual blessings was a long-established practice, and few people questioned it. The preaching of this indulgence, however, was riddled with corruption. In Luther's part of Germany the profits were being shared between the Pope and Prince Albrecht of Brandenburg, Archbishop of Magdeburg, a twenty-three-year-old who had recently also bought the archbishopric of Mainz, and was using proceeds from the Indulgence to pay off the bribes and loans this had involved. The chief publicist for the Indulgence, the Dominican preacher Tetzel, was eager to rake in contributions, and was none too subtle about what he promised in return. The Indulgence, he claimed, would release loved ones from their sufferings in purgatory: he even set the promise to a German rhyme which roughly translates as:

> Place your penny on the drum,
> The pearly gates open and in strolls mum.

Devout minds everywhere were revolted by this sort of stuff, and there had been many protests before about such abuse of indulgences. But Luther was not protesting about the abuse of indulgences: he was protesting about indulgences themselves. Luther was a pious and scrupulous monk, who had recently passed through a profound spiritual crisis. Overwhelmed by a sense of his own sinfulness, he had found the idea of God's justice terrifying, and the Church's remedies through confession and acts of penance powerless to calm his fears. Release had come from a phrase in St Paul: 'The righteous shall live by faith.' For Luther, this one phrase turned the whole medieval system of salvation on its head. The saint was not, as the Church taught, a man or woman who no longer sinned: the saint was a sinner who put all his or her trust in God. Good works, penance, indulgences, contributed nothing to salvation. Faith, a childlike dependence on God, was everything. There was a place for good works in the Christian life, but as a thankful response for salvation achieved, not as a means of earning it. A phrase from one of Luther's lectures on Romans puts the matter in a nutshell. The Christian was 'always a sinner, always a penitent, always right with God'.

For Luther, then, the St Peter's Indulgence was a cruel and blasphemous con-trick, taking money for empty promises. He denounced it as a pious racket, and his protest was taken up on every side. This was the age of the printing revolution. For the first time a technology existed which could spread ideas rapidly across the whole of Europe, which could take theology out of the monastic cloister or the university lecture-room into the market place. Within a matter of months Luther was the most famous man in Germany. As the Church authorities moved against him, he abandoned the Indulgence issue and launched an attack on the whole range of Catholic teaching and practice. If faith was everything, and faith came from the Word preached and the scriptures read, then reliance on priests, sacraments, hierarchy, was all in vain.

These ideas spread through Germany like wildfire. Luther taught the priesthood of all believers, the right of the simple men and women of Germany to test for themselves the truth of what they were told by reading the Bible, which he proceeded to translate into German. To the poor, this seemed like a call to liberation from all that oppressed and impoverished them. It was a time of hunger and great social tension. In 1525 the peasantry of Germany rose against their masters, and many of them had slogans from Luther's writings written on their banners. Luther hastily disowned these revolutionary readings of his message, but for the rich and powerful, too, his message had its charms. Luther's denunciation of the racketeering of the medieval Church, his rejection of the monastic life as pointless and anti-Christian, meant that Church property was theft. Got by fraud, by right it belonged to the state. Luther called on the rulers of Germany to protect the Gospel. They responded by helping themselves to the property of the Church. His message was a stone thrown into a calm pond: the ripples spread and spread.

In Rome, Leo X failed utterly to grasp the seriousness of the crisis, the need for drastic action to hold the Church together and to meet the legitimate demands of the reformers. The sophisticated Roman and Florentine worlds of classical learning and artistic patronage, the convoluted game of Italian dynastic politics in which the papacy must be a player if it was to survive at all, simply had not equipped him to appreciate the more immediate and existential anxieties of the earnest north of Europe.

Leo tried at first to have Luther silenced by the authorities of his religious order, the Augustinians. When that failed, he tried to remove the political protection being extended to Luther by the local Prince, Frederick of Saxony. Finally, in June 1520, he issued a bull, *Exsurge Domine*, condemning Luther's teaching on forty-one separate counts. Luther responded by publicly burning the bull, adding that 'this burning is only a trifle. It is necessary that the Pope and Papal See should also be burned. He who does not resist the papacy with all his heart cannot obtain eternal salvation.' He was solemnly excommunicated, and took no notice whatever. A similar defiance of Alexander VI, a far worse pope than Leo, had undone Savonarola in 1498. Times had changed, however, and German hostility towards the papacy was of a different order from anything Italy knew.

For more than a century there had been a strong anti-Roman tradition in Germany, fuelled by memories of the struggle of Frederick Barbarossa with the twelfth-century papacy, by the ideas of the Conciliar movement, by the example of the Hussite schism in Bohemia, and by the financial and jurisdictional demands of the papacy in Germany. Luther and his supporters harnessed and exploited this groundswell of resentment, and reformation pictorial propaganda brilliantly homed in on images of a voracious and corrupt papacy — popes excreted from the anus of the devil, popes recrucifying Christ, popes as the seven-headed beast of the Book of Revelation, each head crowned with the papal tiara.

Leo's sudden death on 1 December 1521 left the papacy directionless and bankrupt. A strong faction among the cardinals wanted Leo's able nephew, Giulio de' Medici. Others, equally determined to exclude the Medici, were divided by fears of imperial or French influence in Italy. Out of the confusion emerged a surprise choice, a carpenter's son from the Netherlands, former tutor to the Emperor Charles V, Governor of the Netherlands and Grand Inquisitor of Spain, Hadrian of Utrecht. Hadrian had not even been present at the

Conclave, being absent in Spain. He was chosen to break the dead-lock because no one knew anything against him, and at sixty-three years old he was unlikely to be pope for long.

The election of Hadrian VI (1522–3) created consternation. Charles V, confident that he now had a tame pope, was delighted. Francis I, for the same reason, was appalled. The Romans were aghast at the idea of a northern barbarian pope with a reputation for per-sonal austerity verging on puritanism. His arrival confirmed these fears. He made it clear there would be none of the customary bonanza of papal favours, and instituted a programme of drastic economies which included a swingeing reduction of personnel in the Curia. He announced his intention of abolishing many of the offices invented and sold by his predecessors. An old-fashioned scholastic theologian (Erasmus had attended his lectures) he cared nothing for the Renaissance. The Vatican collection of classical sculp-ture was dismissed as so many 'heathen idols', Raphael's pupils were sent packing and the decoration of the Vatican apartments halted, and he also stopped the construction of the triumphal arches being put up by the city to welcome him, on the ground that they were pagan.

Hadrian was a devout man, and a reformer. He caused astonishment by celebrating Mass every day, something no pope in living memory – perhaps no Pope ever – had done before. He had witnessed and taken part in the movements towards reform – biblical studies, clerical edu-cation, improved preaching – which Erasmian Humanism was inspir-ing in Spain and northern Europe. Unlike Leo, he was also intensely aware of the need to tackle the religious turmoil in Germany. In November 1522 he despatched a legate to the German Diet of Nuremberg. In the Pope's name, the Legate acknowledged before the Diet that the evils in the Church had spread downwards from the papacy, and he announced Hadrian's intention of a thorough reform of the Roman Curia and the hierarchy generally. The limitations of Hadrian's vision, however, came in what he had to say about Luther. This 'petty monk' was a rebel against Catholic tradition. If he acknowledged his fault, he would be received back as an errant son. Otherwise the Diet must take severe measures to suppress him and his teaching – amputation was sometimes the only means to remove gan-grene from a body.

There was a strong element of unreality about all this. Though Hadrian had received detailed accounts of the wildfire spread of

Lutheran support in Germany, he responded as the Grand Inquisitor of an authoritarian state like Spain might have been expected to respond, with a mixture of stern admonition and threats of reprisals. Luther's protest had touched a nerve too sensitive to be anaesthetised by curial reform, however extensive, and the threat of ecclesiastical repression was pointless when it was unenforceable. Nothing in Hadrian's response suggests any grasp of the real power of Luther's message, the evangelical fervour and the sense of the radical and blessed simplification of religious life which it offered.

Hadrian died in September 1523, a disappointed man. Despite his close relationship with Charles V, he had struggled to keep the papacy neutral between France and the empire. He was a clumsy politician, however, and France's refusal to co-operate in a Crusade and a threatened invasion of Lombardy had in the end forced him into an alliance with Charles. His longing for a Crusade against the Turks, who had taken Belgrade in 1521 and threatened to overwhelm Hungary, came to nothing, and in December 1522 Rhodes fell to Turkish forces. His attempts to cleanse the Curia resulted in an indiscriminate clear-out which included crucial administrators. Papal business ground to a halt, and the inexperienced Pope wavered over urgent decisions, for lack of expert guidance. When he died Rome erupted in joy, and Europe heaved a collective sigh of relief. The late Pope, it was said, would have made a splendid monk. His tomb inscription quoted a bitter saying of his – 'How much depends on the times in which even the best of men are cast.' It was to be four and a half centuries before the cardinals took the risk of electing another non-Italian pope.

Hadrian's successor, Giulio de' Medici, Clement VII (1523–34) could not have been a greater contrast. He was a Renaissance aristocrat, the bastard son of Guiliano de' Medici. Acknowledged as his grandson by Lorenzo the Magnificent, he had been made a cardinal in 1513, and in due course had become his uncle Leo X's closest and best adviser. At the time of his election, Clement was universally respected. He was immensely hard-working and efficient, pious in a conventional way, free of sexual scandal. A connoisseur of painting and literature, he was patron to Raphael and Michelangelo, and commissioned the *Last Judgement* for the Sistine Chapel, though he did not live to see Michelangelo start work on it.

He was a disastrous pope. Raphael's portrait of him as a cardinal in the background to his portrait of Leo X catches the self-contained, secretive complacency which was the chief mark of his character, and which made him baffling to his advisers and his adversaries. He was also hopelessly indecisive. Highly effective as second-in-command, he was paralysed by the possession of supreme authority, and had no more sense than his uncle Leo X of the urgency and magnitude of what was happening in Germany. Like Leo, he seems not to have grasped the growing credibility gap between papal claims and cold reality. It was an age of growing assertiveness among the monarchs of Europe, and of the emergence of strong nation states dominated by powerful and frightening rulers – Francis I of France, Henry VIII of England, Charles V of Spain and the German empire. As the nations of Europe increasingly went their own way, Raphael's workshop decorated Clement's state rooms with frescoes glorifying the *Donation of Constantine* and the unchallenged supremacy of Rome.

While still a cardinal Clement had been an ardent supporter of the Emperor against the French. Everyone expected this policy to be continued, but in fact the Pope swung back and forth between France and empire. Up to a point, his indecision was understandable. Charles V was a far more devout Catholic than Francis I of France, but both men wanted to dominate northern Italy, where their armies were locked in conflict. From Clement's point of view (both as pope and as a member of the Florentine ruling house of Medici) Charles was a particular threat. Inheriting the sovereignty not merely of Spain (and therefore Naples) but also of the Netherlands, Austria and Germany, not to mention the Spanish New World, he was the most powerful man in Europe. He controlled Naples: if he were to control Milan and Lombardy also, the papacy (and the other north Italian and Tuscan states) would be caught in a pincer movement, which Clement dreaded. Charles' high sense of religious responsibility did not commend him in Rome, for he was heir also to the ancient imperial tradition of the Middle Ages, and he believed that he, rather than the Pope, was responsible for the well-being of the Church in his realms. Charles systematically eroded papal influence in the Church in Spain and southern Italy.

The years immediately after Clement's election, therefore, were marked by repeated shifts of papal alliance between France and Spain, and by opportunistic papal attempts in northern Italy to erode imperial rule there and maintain the independence of Milan, which increasingly exasperated the Emperor. There was talk of the Emperor deposing the Pope, and of the confiscation and redistribution of the Papal States. The smouldering factionalism of the great Roman families was fanned into flame by these uncertainties, and Cardinal Pompeio Colonna planned a coup to unseat Clement and seize the papacy. On Monday, 6 May 1527 all this came to a head. The imperial armies based in northern Italy under the command of the renegade French Duke Charles of Bourbon had pushed south to consolidate imperial power in central Italy. Their advance triggered a rebellion against Medici rule in Florence, and Clement's family were driven out of the city. Bourbon and his armies moved south to capture Rome.

None of the troops had been paid for months, and many of them were rabidly anti-papal Lutherans: from every point of view, the Eternal City was rich pickings. The Pope fled to the Castel Sant' Angelo, his white robes disguised by a purple cloak thrown over them by one of his staff. For eight days the German army rampaged through Rome, raping, stabbing, burning. Horses were stabled in St Peter's and the Sistine Chapel, Luther's name was scribbled over Raphael's painting in the Vatican Stanze. At least 4,000 citizens were killed, and every movable item of value was stolen. The Vatican Library survived only because one of the imperial commanders had set up his quarters (including his stables) there. Lutheran troops maddened with drink rampaged round Rome dressed in the robes of cardinals and popes. There were mock processions and blessings, and a troop of Lutheran soldiers assembled under the Pope's window at the Castel Sant' Angelo, insisting that they were going to eat him. Every cleric and citizen of means had to pay a ransom for their delivery, some as many as five or six times over, as gang after gang of soldiers repeatedly rounded up the same hostages. Cardinal del Monte, the future Pope Julius III, was hung up by his hair. The Pope's ransom was set at 400,000 ducats, more than his annual income. His goldsmith, Benvenuto Cellini, set up a makeshift furnace in the Castel, and melted down all the surviving papal tiaras, except that of Julius II, to try to make up the amount.

The Sack of Rome shocked the conscience of Europe. Imperial propagandists tried to present it as a cleansing of the Augean stable, a fitting judgement on a city in which Christianity had been mocked by worldliness. Few Catholics accepted this. Even Erasmus, who had written so scathingly about the worldliness of the popes, deplored the spoliation of the city which was 'not only the fortress of the Christian religion and the kindly mother of literary talent, but the tranquil home of the Muses, and indeed the common mother of all peoples'.[10] Clement, however, came to terms with Charles, crowning him emperor at Bologna in 1530, the last papal coronation of an emperor ever. The Papal States were restored to the Pope, his family re-established as rulers of Florence, and he returned to Rome.

But not to normalcy: it would take a decade for the city to recover from the trauma of the Sack. The population had halved, the artists had fled, building had stopped, house-prices plummeted. The spiritual ethos had shifted, too. Reformation was no longer a remote rumour from Germany. It had stalked with mailed boots through the streets of Rome, it had caroused from chalices, stripped the jewels from the bones of saints and from the covers of the Gospels. The golden bubble of the Renaissance had been punctured.

Meanwhile, Clement's pontificate drew towards its inglorious close. His uneasy relations with Charles V made concerted action against Protestants in Germany impossible. It became increasingly clear that if the religious divisions of Germany were to be resolved, then it would have to be by a general council. Luther had called for such a council as early as 1520: by the 1530s, everyone wanted one. Everyone, that is, except the Pope. Protestants demanded that such a council should be 'free' and 'Christian', which sounded fine, till it became apparent that 'free' meant independent of the Pope – and therefore neither convened by him nor taking place on Italian soil. By 'Christian' Lutherans meant that laymen should take part in the Council on equal terms with bishops, and that all the Council's decrees should be based exclusively on scripture. Agreement to these terms would be equivalent to conceding the whole Protestant case, and repudiating a view of the relation between Pope and Council which Rome had defended for a thousand years. Despite mounting pressure from Charles, Clement resisted. In the delay, the divisions of Western Christendom hardened and set. Germany and Switzerland descended into religious civil war, and Protestant teaching spread to the Netherlands, to France, even to Spain and Italy.

One country which had seemed impregnable to the new doctrines was England. Henry VIII was ardently orthodox, and had rapidly mobilised the best theologians in England to confute Luther and his associates. He himself published an able attack on Luther's teach-

ing on the sacraments, and was rewarded by Leo X with the title
'Defender of the faith'. Through the 1510s and 1520s, Erasmus had
publicised the triumphant reign of Catholic Humanists like Thomas
More at Henry's court. Henry, however, had no son, and wanted to
set aside his Spanish wife Catherine of Aragon in order to marry one
of the court ladies, Ann Boleyn. The current marriage was a dynastic
one, designed to unite Spain and England, and Catherine was the
widow of Henry's elder brother Arthur. Canon law forbade marriage
to a deceased brother's wife, so to marry her Henry had needed a
papal dispensation, which he got from Julius II. There were, however,
conflicting biblical texts, some of which seemed to forbid a man
from marrying his brother's widow, others which seemed to allow it.
If scripture did indeed forbid such a marriage, could the Pope permit
it? Theologians disagreed. Henry now announced that he believed
that the prohibition against such a marriage was God's law revealed
in scripture, not merely that of the Church, and from the written law
of God there could be no dispensation, not even from the Pope. His
and Catherine's inability to have a son was God's judgement on an
illicit union; the papal dispensation was clearly void.

The case was a knotty one, though on balance the best theological
opinion was against the King. Henry, however, seems to have
believed sincerely what he said, and popes had accommodated
princes on thinner grounds than this before. Through the 1520s Cardinal Wolsey worked to get Henry his divorce, and the Vatican must
have considered it, for the archives contain a draft papal bull granting
it. Whatever the rights and wrongs of the matter, however, the Sack
of Rome changed everything. After 1527 Clement was the Emperor's
prisoner, and Charles was the favourite nephew of Catherine of
Aragon. There was now no question of granting Henry what he
wanted. Rome first stalled, and then refused. Henry turned on the
Church in England, asserted his own supremacy over it, and repudiated the papacy. England, still, outside London and a few provincial
cities, relatively untouched by Protestant ideas, was lost to the papacy.

III THE COUNTER-REFORMATION

The choice of a new pope is often a signal of what has been disapproved of in the preceding regime, and the death of Clement VII
might have been expected to produce another pope in the mould of

Hadrian VI. The election of Alessandro Farnese as Pope Paul III (1534–49), however, seemed a determined gesture in the face of growing religious crisis towards the departed glories of Renaissance Rome. In some ways he was the obvious choice. At sixty-seven he was the oldest of the cardinals, and the most experienced. Enormously charming, he was also enormously intelligent, and Clement VII had repeatedly urged that he should be elected as his successor. Despite a long and highly effective career in papal diplomacy, he had managed to remain on friendly terms with both France and the empire, and neither Francis I nor Charles V objected to his election.

Yet there was plenty about him to worry earnest men. The first Roman nobleman to be elected pope since Martin V, he was emphatically a product of old corruption. His ecclesiastical career had got off to a flying start because his sister Giulia was Alexander VI's last mistress – Farnese was known in sarcastic Roman circles as 'Cardinal Petticoat'. To the end of his life he had Mass celebrated in his chapel annually for the repose of Alexander's soul. As cardinal he himself kept a mistress, by whom he had four children, and on the Via Giulia he built himself one of the most magnificent palaces in Rome, a treasure-house of art and opulence.

His early months as pope set a pattern he was to maintain for the whole of his long reign. His first cardinals were his two teenage grandsons, and he established a succession of cardinal nephews in splendour at the Palazzo Farnese. Like Alexander VI, he carved chunks out of the Papal States for his sons. After the tight-fisted regime of Clement VII, Rome erupted into firework displays, masked balls, *risqué* plays. He revived the Carnival in 1536, and it grew every year in extravagance, with elaborate floats laden with scenes from classical mythology, so massive they had to be drawn by teams of buffalo. The Pope delighted the people of Rome with lavish entertainments, bullfights and horse-races through the streets and piazzas. Deliciously shocked commentators noted that the Pope's dinner-guests included women, that he entertained his sons and their wives at banquets in the Vatican, that he unblushingly chose the third anniversary of his coronation for the christening of one of his grandsons (though he discreetly absented himself from the ceremony). He was an ardent believer in astrology, timing consistories, audiences, even the issue of bulls, according to the most auspicious arrangements of the stars.

Paradoxically, it was this unlikely Pope who gave the internal reform of the Catholic Church the impetus and direction it had till now so patently lacked. For all his worldliness and charm, he had himself been touched by the forces of reform. He had taken the decrees of the Fifth Lateran Council seriously, implementing them in his diocese of Parma, working (through a deputy) for an improvement in clerical standards. In 1513 he had ended his liaison with his mistress, and, though many curial cardinals were content to remain in minor orders all their lives, in 1519 he took the highly unusual step of seeking ordination to the priesthood. From that point onwards, despite the magnificence and display, he was associated with the party of reform.

At his election, Paul III knew very little about the state of Germany (a fair indicator of the lack of seriousness with which it had been treated under his predecessor). One of his earliest actions was to summon the Papal Nuncio from Vienna to brief him on what needed to be done. As a result, he became convinced that the call for a council could no longer be ignored. Against strong opposition from the cardinals, who feared that Conciliar reform was all too likely to begin with them, Paul began to press both the Emperor and the King of France to help convene such a council. It was a fraught issue, however. The Lutherans would not attend a papal council meeting on Italian soil, or presided over by the Pope. The Emperor wanted the Council to tackle practical reform, leaving him to negotiate a doctrinal settlement with his rebellious Protestant subjects. The Pope wanted the Council to tackle both doctrine and practical reform, and insisted it must be under papal presidency. Charles desperately needed a council to heal the internal divisions of Germany, but France thought that these divisions kept Charles usefully busy, and unable to attack France, and was quite happy to see them continue. Proposal after proposal for a council was vetoed by one side or another, and it was not until December 1545 that the Pope succeeded in launching the Council at Trent, in the Italian Alps, acceptable to Germans because nominally in imperial territory.

In the meantime, Paul maintained the forward pace of reform by a series of remarkable promotions into the cardinalate. One of the first was the devout Venetian layman Gasparo Contarini, who had undergone a conversion experience very like Luther's in 1510, and who had become the key figure in devout Humanist circles in Italy. His elevation was intended as a clear signal of seriousness about the reform question. Under Contarini's guidance Paul drew to Rome a remarkable circle of reformers, all of whom he made cardinals. They included Reginald Pole, Henry VIII's cousin: he was another devout Humanist who shared many of Luther's convictions about the nature of salvation and the need for reform. Paul also promoted Bishop Gian Matteo Giberti, a curial administrator and Humanist scholar who had undergone a profound personal conversion after the Sack of Rome, and had become a model reforming Bishop of Verona, and another Humanist, the former papal secretary Jacopo Sadoleto, Bishop of Carpentras. In contrast to these intellectuals was Giampietro Caraffa, a sixty-year-old Neapolitan nobleman who had been Archbishop of Brindisi and who had served as papal nuncio in England, Flanders and Spain. Summoned to Rome by Hadrian IV to help in reform, in 1525 he had renounced his various bishoprics, and had helped found the Theatines, an austere association of devout noblemen who embraced a life of poverty and apostolic service through the ordained priesthood.

This extraordinary 'ministry of all the talents' was shaped into a Reform Commission, to produce a report on the ills of the Church and to suggest remedies. Not a single member of the Curia was included. Its report, the *Consilium de Emendenda Ecclesia*, presented to the Pope in March 1537, was dynamite. In the bluntest of terms, it laid the blame for the ills of the Church, including the outbreak of the Protestant Reformation, squarely on the papacy, cardinals and hierarchy. It listed the evils of the Church, from papal sales of spiritual privileges, curial stockpiling of benefices, heretical or pagan teaching in universities, down to such matters as the ignorance of country curates or the poor spiritual direction in convents of women. It lamented the corruptions of the religious orders, recommended that all but the strictly observant religious orders should be abolished, and that novices in slack houses should be removed at once before they could be contaminated. This report was extremely unwelcome to the Curia, who did their best to block it. A copy was leaked to the press, however. In 1538 Luther published a German translation, with lip-smacking introduction and notes, and the resulting bad publicity meant that the report was shelved. The tide of reform, however, was too strong now to be turned back.

It was not a tide which flowed neatly in one direction. Contarini and Pole shared an understanding of reform which extended beyond the Church's practices to her doctrines. On the question of ecclesiastical authority and the sacraments, they believed that Luther was deeply and sinfully wrong. On the fundamental question of the nature of 'justification', the salvation of the sinner by faith in Christ rather than by good works, however, they were certain he was right, and was recalling the Church to her ancient faith. As Cardinal Pole declared, 'Heretics are not heretics in everything.' They therefore hoped and worked for reconciliation with the Lutherans. By contrast, Cardinal Caraffa believed absolutely in the urgent need for moral, institutional and spiritual reform in the Church, but rejected any approach to Luther's teaching as rank heresy. Churchmen might sin, but the Church could not err, and the right way to deal with obstinate heretics was not to talk to them, but to hunt them down and eliminate them. He came increasingly to distrust Contarini and Pole and their circle as feeble conciliators or worse, men with their libraries full of heretical writings, a crypto-Protestant fifth column within the Church.

Paul III was temperamentally more in sympathy with the outlook of the 'Spirituali', as Contarini and his associates were known, but he supported both versions of reform. The collapse of negotiations between Contarini and representatives of the Protestant cause at Regensburg in 1541, however, gave Caraffa his head. The way of negotiation had failed, and Paul III asked Caraffa, 'What remedy must be devised for this evil?' Caraffa suggested the establishment of a Roman Inquisition, 'to suppress and uproot error, permitting no trace to remain'. In July 1542 he was appointed one of six inquisitors general, with powers of arrest and scrutiny all over Europe, and a jurisdiction which overrode that of local bishops. Caraffa's enthusiasm knew no bounds; he used his own resources to set up a headquarters and prison in Rome. In the same year Contarini died, deeply discouraged, and his type of conciliatory reform was further damaged when two of his protégés, the preachers Peter Martyr Vermigli and Bernardino Ochino, became panicky about the growth of repression, abandoned the Catholic Church, and fled to join Calvin in Geneva. Peter Martyr in due course would find his way to England and become Regius Professor of Theology at Oxford under Edward VI.

Paul III, however, knew that repression was not enough. He pressed on with reforms of the Curia and of the administrative and financial machinery of the papacy itself, abolishing most of the more scandalous sources of revenue, compensating by stepping up taxation in the Papal States: he is said to have trebled the tax revenue during his pontificate. He needed every penny, for he was helping subsidise Charles V's wars against the German Protestant princes of the 'Schmalkaldic League'. He was also pressing ahead with the reconstruction of Rome, to reflect both the spiritual and the temporal glory of the Church and papacy. Julius II had laid the foundation-stone of the new St Peter's in 1506, but his death in 1513, and that of his architect Bramante in the following year, had left the project incomplete, and the greatest church in Christendom a building-site. It would remain so for more than a century, and though the work went forward under each succeeding pope, a series of chief architects (including Raphael) had deprived the scheme of the coherence and drive of Bramante's original design.

In 1547 Paul appointed Michelangelo as chief architect for the new St Peter's, and Michelangelo's scheme was an inspired simplification and development of the original 'Greek cross' plan proposed by Bramante. It was to be surmounted by a stupendous dome, 370 feet high inside, one of the most daring and one of the most beautiful architectural structures ever raised. Michelangelo worked on St Peter's for the rest of his life, refusing all fees since he considered it an offering to God and the Apostle. Seventy-two years old when he was appointed, he toiled on St Peter's for seventeen years, but lived to see only the drum supporting the dome completed: the dome itself was not finished till 1590. Paul also commissioned him to create a splendid new civic centre on the Capitol, with the equestrian statue of Marcus Aurelius as its centrepiece, and persuaded him to complete his great *Last Judgement* for the Sistine Chapel.

Alongside these papal ventures, other forces for change and renewal were making themselves felt in Rome. In the year of Paul's election a young Florentine layman named Philip Neri came to Rome, where he began an unconventional ministry among the clerks and apprentices who crowded Rome's inns and brothels, involving lay-preaching, individual spiritual direction, the traditional Roman pilgrimage to the seven basilicas and the catacombs, and the performance of sacred music. In the second half of the century popes and cardinals would compete to shower favours on Neri, who would be greeted as the 'Apostle of Rome'. In 1540 there arrived a group of Spanish priests and laymen led by the ex-soldier Ignatius Loyola. Originally hoping to be missionaries to the Holy Land, they now placed themselves at the disposal of the Pope for missionary work wherever he chose to send them. In 1540 Paul issued a bull approving this 'Society of Jesus', and Ignatius became its first general. The Jesuits would become the single most important force within the Catholic Reformation, and one of the principal bulwarks of the papacy.

In December 1545 the long awaited Council met at Trent. It would continue, off and on, through the next five pontificates, and it had many limitations. There were only thirty-one bishops at its opening, and only one of them was German. Even at its largest it never had more than 270 bishops present, and there were never more than thirteen Germans involved. To Protestant eyes it seemed a charade, populated by stooges on the Pope's payroll. Proceedings were carefully regulated by papal legates in constant contact with Rome, and even some of the bishops doubted the genuine freedom of discussion. If the Holy Spirit was present at all, it was said, he must come in the Pope's postbag.

Yet from its opening in 1545 the Catholic Church went on the offensive against the dangers which threatened it. Its mere existence was a triumph of papal diplomacy, and so was the fact that, despite Charles V's efforts to prevent it, the Council from the start dealt with both doctrine and practical reform. It began by clasping the nettle, tackling doctrines like justification by faith which lay at the heart of the Protestant revolt. In a sense Trent came a generation too late, a generation during which the split in the Church had widened and hardened. Yet the intervening years had helped clarify issues, and the Council's teaching on the contested points – justification, the seven sacraments, transubstantiation, purgatory – was uncompromising, but clear and cogent. It was not merely negative, however, and it eliminated a lot of dubious late-medieval Catholic interpretation as well as Protestant teaching. The Council's doctrinal statements gave the Catholic Reformation a clear, firm agenda to work to.

Out of Trent, too, came a whole raft of practical reforms. The Council adopted an entirely new system of training for clergy, in special colleges or 'seminaries' (the word means 'seedbed') designed to produce a better-educated, more moral and professionally conscious clergy. It made provision for more preaching and teaching, attacked abuses and superstition, insisted on more conscientious fulfilment of episcopal and priestly duties. The Church after Trent would be better organised, better staffed, more clerical, more vigilant, more repressive, altogether a more formidable institution. As its reforms took effect, the advance of Protestantism would be halted and then, slowly, reversed. None of this was instantaneous, and Paul III saw only its bare beginnings. But the process of reform was now unstoppable.

It survived the election of Giovanni del Monte as Julius III (1550–5), a man with all the worldliness of Paul but none of his greatness. Julius revolted everyone by his passion for onions, which he had delivered by the cartload. He outraged even the Romans by promoting his teenage monkey-keeper, Innocenzo, to the cardinalate, having first had him adopted by his brother. Innocenzo, who emphatically did not live up to his name, had been picked up by Julius in the street in Parma. The Pope visibly doted on him, and the charitably disposed told themselves the boy might after all be simply his bastard son. Julius reconvened the Council, but was incapable of leadership – one of the ambassadors at his court described him as a rabbit. Nevertheless, the transformation of Catholicism went on, for example in the founding of the Germanicum, a college staffed by Jesuits to train priests to recover Germany for the Catholic Church. Even under such a pope as Julius, the papacy had become the natural rallying point for the forces of Catholic recovery.

Reform was also to survive the election of the aged Cardinal Caraffa as Pope Paul IV (1555–9). Now seventy-nine, Caraffa had singlemindedly devoted his whole life to the reform of the Church. Yet he distrusted most of the other forces at work towards that reform. While Ignatius Loyola was still a theological student in Paris, Caraffa had denounced him as a heretic, and Ignatius 'trembled in every bone' when he heard of the Cardinal's election. He was not the only one. Caraffa's distrust of his former colleagues among the Spirituali had grown with the years to the point of obsession. At the previous Conclave, which had elected Julius III, Cardinal Pole had repeatedly come within a single vote of election. His chances had been dashed by Caraffa's hints that Pole was really a Lutheran. Pole was not at the Conclave of 1555, for he had become archbishop of Canterbury and papal legate in England, where the accession of the Catholic Queen Mary had temporarily halted the Reformation. Caraffa undermined the Catholic restoration in England by withdrawing Pole's legatine authority, and he summoned him back to Rome. Pole ignored this invitation, which was wise, since the Pope was rounding up the rest of the Spirituali, like the much revered Cardinal Morone, imprisoned on suspicion of heresy in 1557.

This terrifying old man set about implementing his version of reform, in an atmosphere of growing fear – it was said that sparks flew from his feet as he strode through the Vatican. He suspended the Council of Trent indefinitely, replacing it with a commission of cardinals, theologians and heads of religious orders, to steer practical reform – a measure reminiscent of the Roman synods of Gregory VII. The activities of the Inquisition were stepped up, and in 1557 he introduced the Roman Index of Prohibited Books. This was a ruthless document, banning anything that was not rigidly Catholic. All Erasmus' writings were included. Since his grammatical textbooks for schools were a staple of Jesuit education, this measure caused uproar.

No one was safe from suspicion. The impeccably orthodox Cardinal Primate of Spain, Archbishop Caranza, who had helped mastermind Mary Tudor's reimposition of Catholicism in England, was arrested by the Spanish Inquisition on suspicion of heresy. Paul had him brought to Rome and imprisoned. No issue was too piffling for the Pope's attention. He even became agitated about the presence of married men in the Sistine choir, a contamination of the purity of the papal chapel. No group was exempt. The Jews of Rome were herded into ghettos, forced to sell their property to Christians, and made to wear yellow headgear; copies of the Talmud were searched out and burned. There was a campaign to imprison prostitutes, and beggars were expelled from Rome.

Paul detested all things Spanish, resenting Spanish control of his native Naples and distrusting Charles V's religious policies. He never forgave Charles for the Sack of Rome, and he was convinced that the Emperor was not only a tyrant who treated all Italy as his own, but also a heretic and a schismatic who had systematically undermined papal authority. He was outraged by the Peace of Augsburg of 1555, which brought peace to Germany by conceding large tracts of the empire to the Lutherans, wherever there was a Lutheran ruler – *cuius regio, eius religio*. To Caraffa, this was apostasy, and he plunged the papacy into a disastrous war with Spain. Europe watched in disbelief as the Pope made war on the country which was the chief prop of the Catholic Reformation.

He was encouraged in all this by his unscrupulous nephews, Carlo, whom he made cardinal, and Giovanni, whom he made duke of Paliano. It is the supreme irony of Paul's papacy that he should have placed absolute trust in these nephews, both of whom abused his trust to line their pockets, a fact which everyone in Rome knew about except the Pope. When he finally grasped the true situation, in January 1559, it broke him. He stripped his nephews of all their offices and drove them from the city, but he never recovered his confidence or drive, and within a year he was dead.

Paul IV is a genuinely tragic figure, a man of unflinching courage and integrity, robbed of real greatness by a fatal narrowness of vision, and by his inability to apply to his own family the bleak and unwavering scrutiny he turned on everyone else. He was the most hated Pope of the century, and when he died no one mourned him. Joyful mobs rampaged through the streets of Rome, his statues were toppled and smashed, and the cells of the Inquisition broken open to release the prisoners.

The contrast between Paul III and Paul IV was more than the contrast between a bon viveur and a puritan. The two men embodied two different visions of reform. In Paul III reform was still recognisably part of the surge of positive energies which we call the Renaissance. It was pluralist, made up of many voices, it could accommodate the theological exploration of the Spirituali as well as the austere orthodoxies of Caraffa, and it harnessed daring religious experimentation, such as Loyola's Jesuits and their new intensely personal spirituality. Under Paul IV reform took on a darker and more fearful character. Creativity was distrusted as dangerous innovation, theological energies were diverted into the suppression of error rather than the exploration of truth. Catholicism was identified with reaction. The contrast was of course not absolute: Paul III encouraged the use of force against heresy, and Paul IV valued the work of the new religious orders. Yet there is no mistaking the establishment in these two pontificates of a dialectic of reform – creativity versus conservation. For the rest of the Tridentine era, Catholic Reformation would move between those poles, and it would be the task of the popes to manage the resulting tensions.

Indeed, the popes themselves were part of the dialectic, for there was no such thing as a 'typical' Counter-Reformation pope. Despite the growing seriousness of Roman religion, the Renaissance tradition which runs from Nicholas V through Julius II to Paul III did not die out. Caraffa was succeeded by just such a figure, Giovanni Medici (no relative of the great Florentine family), who took the name Pius IV (1559–65). A Bolognese lawyer, he was the father of three illegitimate children, and his career as a papal servant had taken off when his brother married into Paul III's family; as pope, he himself was a vigorous benefactor of his many relatives. These, as it happened, included a genius and a saint, his nephew Carlo Borromeo, who at the age of twenty-three became Pius' right-hand man and a crucial figure in the promotion of the work of Trent. Pius was conventionally religious and an affable, cultivated and able administrator, but, unlike his devout young nephew, no zealot in anything. Unsurprisingly, he had been under a cloud during Caraffa's papacy, and that fact stood him in good stead during the conclave that followed Paul IV's death.

He in turn was succeeded by Michele Ghislieri, Pius V (1566–72), a former shepherd who had entered the Dominican order and had served as grand inquisitor under Paul IV. Pius V was an austere saint who wore the coarse clothing of a friar under his papal robes and who lived mainly on vegetable broth and shellfish. Though he had briefly fallen foul of Paul IV for excessive leniency as inquisitor general, he revered Paul's memory and had to be dissuaded (by Carlo Borromeo) from calling himself Paul V. He revived many of his policies, including Caraffa's savage use of the Inquisition, his harsh treatment of the Jews, and his suspicion of Spanish religious policy. He also believed as fully as Gregory VII or Boniface VIII in the supreme authority of the papacy over secular rulers, and he excommunicated and deposed Elizabeth I of England, a measure which offended Catholic as well as Protestant rulers, and which achieved nothing except the stepping up of government persecution of the Catholics in England. Roman theologians themselves became increasingly cautious about this aspect of papal claims. In 1590, the Jesuit Robert Bellarmine would encounter papal wrath for arguing that the Pope had only an 'indirect' authority over secular rulers.

On Pius V's death the cardinals once again elected another man of the world, Gregory XIII (1572–85), a former law professor with a bastard son, whom he proceeded to make governor of the Castel Sant' Angelo. And Gregory in turn was succeeded by Felice Peretti, Sixtus V (1585–90), perhaps the most formidable of all the Counter-Reformation popes. Sixtus, like his patron and model Pius V, was a peasant's son and a friar – in his case a Franciscan – who lived in the

Vatican as if still in his cell. He loathed his predecessor, Gregory, whom he considered worldly and extravagant, and as pope he frequently disparaged his memory in public.

Sixtus seemed to many to combine the most daunting characteristics of Julius II and Paul IV. Violent-tempered, autocratic and ruthless, he ruled the Papal States with a rod of iron, introducing draconian legislation to deal with street violence in the city and brigandage in the surrounding countryside. It was said that there were more criminals' heads displayed on spikes along the Ponte Sant'Angelo in the first year of Sixtus' reign than there were melons for sale in the markets of Rome. He was equally fierce in his religious policies, encouraging the forces of Catholicism in France, Poland and Savoy to throw the weight of their armies behind the campaign against the Reformation, and offering to help finance the Spanish Armada against England. He instituted a moral purge in Rome, executing religious who broke their vows of chastity, and he attempted to impose the death penalty for adultery (a measure which, not very surprisingly, proved unenforceable). Indeed, many of Sixtus' reforms may have been less dramatic and effective than his publicity machine led contemporaries then, and historians since, to believe. His campaign against banditry was neither so innovatory nor so successful as he claimed, for it built on initiatives taken by previous popes, including his much despised predecessor Gregory XIII. Banditry would remain an endemic problem in the Papal States until the nineteenth century. However, Sixtus' conscious manipulation of a propaganda machine, which proclaimed the irresistibility of papal rule and the renovation at his hands of Rome and of the Church, tells us as much about the self-understanding of the Tridentine papacy as any actual successes. He was determined above all that the papal edict *plenitudo potestatis* should be asserted. He systematically reduced the power of the cardinals, and emphasised papal supremacy by requiring every new bishop, archbishop and patriarch throughout the Church to come to Rome before taking up their appointment, and thereafter to make regular *ad limina* visits to Rome, to report on the state of their diocese to the Pope.

In all this Sixtus V most resembles 'austere' popes like Paul IV and Pius V. Yet he also set about reconstructing the city of Rome on a scale which rivalled the most extravagant of his predecessors. Of all the popes of the century, he came nearest to fulfilling the programme of

Nicholas V, to make the external face of Rome mirror the spiritual greatness of the papacy. It was Sixtus who completed the dome on St Peter, a symbol of the overarching authority which he struggled to impose on the Church. The ancient pilgrimage to the seven great basilicas of Rome had been revived by Philip Neri, and had contributed to a renewed sense of Rome as a holy city. Sixtus built on this revived piety by reinstituting the ancient 'stational liturgy', in which the Pope during Lent solemnly processed to celebrate the liturgy in a different titular church each day. He constructed a series of great new roads to improve access to the basilicas and to link the city in a star-shaped plan focused on Santa Maria Maggiore, where he constructed a great funeral chapel for himself and Pius V. He deliberately reclaimed Rome's pagan imperial past for the papacy, moving the great obelisk which had originally been in the Circus of Nero into the centre of the Piazza in front of St Peter's (it took 800 men, forty horses and forty winches to do the job), and crowning the other obelisks and columns of Rome with Christian symbols. And, despite all this expenditure, he left behind him in the Castel Sant' Angelo a treasure of 5,000,000 ducats, which he bound his successors to leave untouched except for the defence of the Papal States. By the end of the century the population of Rome had risen to 100,000, which might leap by 500,000 in a Jubilee Year. Thirty new streets had been constructed, hundreds of fountains and ornamental gardens fed by the three restored aqueducts had sprung up (most famously Sixtus' own magnificent 'Aqua Felice') and Rome had become the leading city of Europe, and the artistic capital of the world.

Whatever the temperamental contrasts between the popes, the drive to concentrate authority and initiative in the hands of the papacy was a feature of the whole Counter-Reformation period. In many ways this was a surprising outcome. On many issues, the papacy seemed still to many an obstacle in the way of reform, rather than the best agent of reform. The final sessions of the Council of Trent in 1562-3 were stormy because many bishops, led by the Spaniards, wanted strong decrees on the 'divine right' of bishops. These were to emphasise that bishops derived their authority and their obligations direct from God, not merely by delegation from the Pope, as the Jesuit theologians at the Council argued. Therefore popes could not give bishops dispensations to live away from their bishoprics (for example in Rome, as cardinals in the Curia). Skilful diplomacy by the papal legates chairing the Council avoided a show-down on this issue, but the Pope had become extremely alarmed at the hostility of many bishops to papal claims, and even set a watch on the legates, in case they wavered. Many bishops were also uneasy about leaving the implementation of the reforms to the Pope, and called for the establishment of some permanent Conciliar body which would see that the Council's wishes were carried out. Once again, the Jesuits at the Council argued in favour of leaving imple-mentation to the Pope, including the reform of the Curia – but in private they considered that the Pope should be threatened with deposition by the Catholic powers if he failed to deliver.

Nevertheless, it was the papacy which in fact inherited the task of reform. When the Council of Trent finally ended in 1563 many of its reforms were incomplete, and all needed implementation. It was left to Pius IV and especially Pius V to confirm the decrees of the Coun-cil, to publish the revised Index of Prohibited Books (1564), to revise and reform the missal (1570), the breviary (1568) and other service books, to produce a catechism (1566) which would interpret the Council's work to the parish clergy, and to promote the foundation and proper staffing of seminaries.

The enhanced role of the papacy was in part the result of the col-lapse or abdication of other traditional agents of religious reform. Since large parts of Europe had become Protestant, the old reliance on Catholic rulers to care for (and to some extent finance) the work of the Church could no longer be taken for granted. It fell to the popes to organise and promote the missionary drive to recover the lost populations of Europe. Rome became, what it had never before been, the working headquarters of the most vital movements for reform and renewal in the Church. Papal seminaries like the Ger-manicum poured out new-style priests to reconvert Europe. Gregory XIII was particularly active here, establishing the Gregorian Univer-sity (1572), transforming the English pilgrim hospice into a seminary (1579) which sent a stream of missionaries – and martyrs – to Eliza-bethan England, and establishing Greek, Maronite, Armenian and Hungarian colleges. The clergy produced by these colleges became fundamental to the recovery of Catholicism in Europe and beyond, and wherever they went they carried with them a renewed sense of *Romanitas*, and loyalty to the Pope.

Most of these establishments were staffed by Jesuits, and new religious orders and congregations, like the Jesuits or the Oratorians, added to the prestige and centrality of the papacy by the simple fact that their headquarters were established in Rome, under the eye of the popes. In the later sixteenth century Rome became a beacon for a renewed Catholicism, a status symbolised in the rebuilding of its churches and streets, crammed with lavish imagery expressing the new dynamic spirit of orthodoxy, loyalty, activity for God. The Jesuit headquarters church, the Gesù, or the Oratorian Chiesa Nuova, still capture the exhilaration and upbeat confidence of this time, and the sense that the city of the popes was once again *Roma Sancta*, Holy Rome. In 1575 a Jubilee Year was declared, and tens of thousands of pilgrims from all over Europe flooded into Rome to gaze on the renewed city and to imbibe the spirit of the new Catholicism.

Reform of the Curia was a high priority at Trent, as it had been since the outset of the Conciliar movement. In the late sixteenth century it was also a papal priority, as the popes systematically sought to reduce the cardinalate to powerlessness and docility. The mere increase in numbers of cardinals, and the promotion of poor men among them, went some way to achieving this, as did the routine appointment of a cardinal nephew as private secretary to the Pope. But the decisive move was made by Sixtus V in 1588, when he established the number of cardinals at a maximum of seventy, and divided them into fifteen separate congregations, six with responsibilities for the secular administration of the Papal States, the other nine to deal with various aspects of the papacy's spiritual concerns – the Inquisition, the Index, the implementation of Trent, the regulation of bishops, matters of ritual and cult, and so on. This delegation to separate congregations was a tidying up and extension of existing arrangements. In itself it made for greater efficiency, but it also marginalised the Consistory, by taking most of its business away from it. It was plain that the cardinals now functioned as the Pope's agents and servants, and the Pope related to the cardinals in small groups on specific issues, rather than to the concerted might of the College as a body.

Everywhere, pressure was needed to ensure that the reforms were implemented; and that pressure had to come from the popes. To push the secular princes into co-operation, Gregory XIII developed the use of diplomatic agents, the nuncios, as the principal instrument of papal policy in every Catholic state. These papal representatives, usually given the dignity of a titular archbishopric, worked to secure practical reforms, to stir Catholic rulers to fight Protestantism, to establish seminaries, and to urge local hierarchies on to vigorous action. The post of papal legate, once the chief instrument of the reform papacy outside Italy, now became an honorific one bestowed on local grandees: the nuncios became the Pope's hands, eyes and ears all over Europe. Delegated papal powers now became a powerful tool in the hands of the local Catholic hierarchies. Zealous reforming bishops, such as Cardinal Borromeo in Milan, frequently found themselves resisted in their efforts to cleanse their diocese by recalcitrant religious houses, armed with ancient papal privileges exempting them from episcopal control. Nothing but fresh papal commands could override such exemptions, and the obstacles they had always placed in the way of episcopal inspection and oversight in the localities had long fuelled anti-papal resentments among conscientious men: they were prominent among the grievances against the pope and Curia aired in the early stages of the Council of Trent. In the wake of Trent however, Borromeo and his colleagues were able to call on those same papal powers, using delegated papal authority as legates in their own diocese to trump the older papal grants of exemption, and bulldoze away resistance to reform.

In all this, the drive towards centralisation in the organisation of the papacy resembled the aspirations of the strong national monarchies which dominated Europe. It was signalled accordingly. In an age of Absolutism, the popes more than any other rulers surrounded themselves with the trappings of absolute rule, rebuilt throne-rooms and ceremonial approaches, commissioned grandiose programmatic art and architecture which spoke of power. The century of rebuilding in Rome, which would culminate in the work of Bernini under the popes of the mid-seventeenth century, was designed to proclaim the untrammelled rule of the sovereign pontiff. But the sober reality was a good deal more complex. Central as the papacy now was to every major Catholic enterprise, the direct authority of the popes encountered even in Italy, and emphatically beyond it, a hundred drags and resistances: the political interests of the kings of Spain who governed southwards in Naples and northwards in Milan, the inertia or vested interest of the bodies which made up the local churches – religious orders and religious corporations, convents or colleges of canons – the non-cooperation of local bishops or priestly collectives excessively (or realistically) deferential to petty princes, regional aristocracies or city governments. Popes were elected monarchs, their reigns for the most part short, their freedom of action curtailed even in Rome by the presence of independent-minded cardinals – their wealthy families and clientages – who had been created by their predecessors, and who were often at odds with each other, jostling for influence or promoting the rivalries of the Congregations they headed or served in, and sometimes hostile or indifferent to the policies of new popes. The consistent formulation and promotion of long term strategies in such circumstances was dogged with difficulty. Even the best-intentioned papal attempts to forward the programme of Trent involved in practice a constant exercise in the art of the possible, and a hundred compromises.

Not least of these papal difficulties was the fact that popes often found themselves in conflict even with devout Catholic princes. In some cases, this was a matter of the jealous national defence of the 'liberties' of the local church. The French crown had got control of an almost separatist church in France by the Concordat of 1516. It resisted any moves on the part of the popes or the wider Church, however laudable in themselves, which might erode that control. France was by no means alone in this. It absolutely refused to accept the disciplinary decrees of Trent, Spain accepted them only after much delay, and then only with a restrictive clause 'saving the royal power'.

Resistance by the secular ruler might touch any number of 'spiritual' issues, large and small. In 1568 Pope Pius V prohibited bullfights as sinful, and ruled that no one killed in a bullfight might receive Christian burial. The Spanish crown refused to allow the decree to be promulgated in its territories, and found theologians to prove the Pope was wrong. The appointment of reform-minded clergy might be hindered, as in Spanish-ruled Sicily, by the crown's traditional monopoly on clerical appointments.

Such frictions arose in direct proportion to the zeal of the popes. The Counter-Reformation papacy saw itself as called to unite all Catholic princes in an effort to reform the Church internally, and to suppress the enemies of the Church, be they Turks or Protestants. The undoubted papal triumph in the latter of these endeavours was the Christian League between Spain and Venice which in October 1571 defeated the Turkish fleet in the Gulf of Corinth, at Lepanto. Clement VIII in the 1590s raised and paid for an army of 11,000 soldiers to help break the Turkish hold on Hungary, and Paul V and Gregory XV between them would pour more than 2,000,000 florins in subsidies to the Catholic armies in the opening years of the Thirty Years War (1618–48).

No pope, however, could now hope to act as arbiter over the fate of nations in the way that Innocent III had done, though the universal prestige of the papacy might still have an impact on the international scene. Popes or their nuncios might play a key role in negotiating peace between warring princes – as the future Gregory XV did between Spain and Savoy in 1616. The popes, however, were not content with such walk-on parts in the history of Europe. They believed that the princes should pursue Catholic policies in all things, and believed that the papacy was the divinely chosen instrument for shaping such policies.

Catholic princes rarely saw things so simply. The Habsburg emperors in the second half of the sixteenth century presided over a complex and ramshackle empire in which Catholics coexisted with every conceivable variety of Protestant, from high Calvinist to Unitarian. The popes thought that for the Emperor to tolerate religious error was to abdicate his imperial responsibilities as protector of the Church. They urged drastic measures to produce conformity, demanded that earlier concessions made to Protestant sensibilities, like marriage of the clergy or communion from the chalice, should now be withdrawn. The emperors, receptive enough to the idea of a strong state with only a single religion, knew that as things stood it was an unattainable ideal, and dreaded the rebellion such measures would provoke. They saw to it that their Church was staffed by men who shared their realism, and who could stonewall Roman centralism. Between 1553 and 1600, no Hungarian bishop set foot in Rome, and neither the Inquisition nor the Index was sanctioned in imperial lands.

Elsewhere in Europe, the popes pursued a similar aggressive policy towards heresy. Successive popes poured money into supporting the Catholic side in the French Wars of Religion, and worked to prevent the accession of the Huguenot (French Protestant) King Henri of Navarre as Henri IV of France. In 1572, after the St Bartholomew's Day Massacre in France, during which between 5,000 and 10,000 Protestants had been butchered, Gregory XIII ordered the celebration of a solemn 'Te Deum' of thanksgiving. Such policies threw the popes into alliance with extremist forces like the Catholic League in France, which in turn was being bankrolled by Spain. It was difficult in such circumstances for the popes to preserve the neutrality among Catholic princes looked for in the Father of all the Faithful. Under the saintly but realist Pope Clement VIII (1592–1605) better counsels prevailed, and the papacy came to terms with Henri IV, accepted (though after long hesitation) the toleration granted to Protestants by the Edict of Nantes, and thereby freed itself, for the time being at least, from its unhealthy dependence on Spain.

The frictions between the papacy and the Catholic powers were symbolised and rubbed to rawness each year by the annual proclamation of the bull *In Coena Domini*, which was essentially a solemn list of condemnations for crimes against the Church. In 1568 Pope Pius V expanded this bull with clauses listing the usurpations of secular authorities against the rights of the Church and the clergy. The new clauses excommunicated anyone who appealed to a general council against the Pope, any ruler who banished a cardinal, bishop, nuncio or legate, and any secular court or individual which instituted criminal proceedings against clerics. Spain and Austria both forbade the promulgation of this bull, the Viceroy in Naples confiscated and destroyed all copies, and Venice, which had recently expelled a cardinal, refused to allow it to be published on Venetian soil.

And it was in Venice that the conflict of the papacy with the Catholic states received its most spectacular expression. The Republic of Venice was an Italian Catholic state which fiercely guarded its practical independence of the papacy. It existed to trade: it had Protestant mercantile communities within its territory, it needed to maintain good relations with the Turks. Fierce Counter-Reformation papal policies, calling for Crusade against the Turks and persecution of Protestants, could not be adopted as Venetian policy. Venice was devout and orthodox, but it policed its own orthodoxy. Inquisitors functioned in Venetian territory (Sixtus V had been inquisitor for Venice under Paul IV), heretics were harassed, books were burned. But the inquisitors sat alongside secular officials appointed by the Signoria (governing council), and they did not have a free hand.

Moreover, Venice was a republic and (in this respect like Rome) elected its own rulers. Venetians disliked the monarchic character of the Counter-Reformation papacy, and they rejected the Pope's claim to be able to unseat rulers. The Republic considered all its citizens to be subject to its authority, whether they be clergy or laity, and reserved the right to tax the Church. In 1605 the election of Camillo Borghese as Pope Paul V (1605–21) precipitated a showdown. Paul had an exalted understanding of the secular authority of the popes: in 1606 he would canonise Gregory VII. Venice had recently passed laws forbidding the foundation of new churches or the leaving of legacies to the clergy. It was also proposing to put two priests on trial. For these blatant breaches of *In Coena Domini* Paul solemnly excommunicated the whole Signoria in April 1606, and placed the city of Venice under interdict, so that no sacraments could be celebrated there, no Masses said, no babies baptised, no corpse given Christian burial.

The Interdict was a bad mistake. Catholic opinion everywhere thought it a disproportionate reaction to the provocation, rulers everywhere were alarmed at this direct confrontation with a sovereign state. Worse, it simply did not work. Paul had been convinced that the deprivation of the sacraments would create a groundswell of opinion in Venice which would force the Signoria to come to terms. Instead, anti-papal feeling flared in the city, a damaging propaganda war was launched in which papal claims were put under the microscope, and the authorities remained defiant. The clergy were given an ultimatum. They must ignore the Interdict – and the Pope's authority – and go on providing sacraments and services, or they must leave Venice for ever. The Jesuits agonised, then left: it was to be fifty years before they were allowed back on to Venetian territory. Venice portrayed the Pope's action as an assault on the freedoms of every state, and the Pope began to fear that Venice might throw in its lot with the Protestants. In 1607 he was obliged to lift the Interdict, without having exacted any real concessions from the Republic. The ultimate papal weapon, excommunication and interdict, had been tried with maximum publicity, and found ineffective.

The Venetian Interdict revealed the hollowness of papal claims to universal jurisdiction in early modern Europe. The changing role of the popes in the history of missions in the sixteenth century, by contrast, demonstrates better than almost any other issue the enormously enhanced prestige of the papacy. The sixteenth century was a period of quite unparalleled European expansion, to both east and west. To begin with, however, this did not strike the popes as a matter of direct concern to them. In a series of bulls between 1456 and 1514 successive popes granted the Spanish and Portuguese monarchies the task of converting the peoples encountered in the course of exploration. In 1493 Pope Alexander VI had divided the world into two regions, east and west of the Cape Verde Islands, the Spaniards to rule in the west, the Portuguese in the east. The power over the personnel and revenues of the Church thus granted to the two Iberian crowns was among their most treasured prerogatives, and the Spanish crown in particular took seriously the missionary obligations which accompanied it. In the course of the first half of the century new hierarchies were planted in Mexico, Peru and central America, a constellation of new churches. It seemed that God had called a new world into existence to compensate for the souls being lost by the Church to Protestantism in Germany and elsewhere.

As the sixteenth century progressed, missions multiplied, and the papacy became more central to them. The popes of the first half of the century never initiated missionary enterprises, though their sanction was essential for their success. Only popes could establish new hierarchies, and only popes could adjudicate the theological conundrums thrown up by mission, such as whether or not pagan peoples might be enslaved by their Christian conquerors or (later) whether Chinese Christians might be allowed to continue to venerate their ancestors and to practise other traditional customs which looked as if they might imply pagan beliefs. The Jesuit order had been founded to promote mission, and its fourth vow of unquestioning obedience to the Pope was explicitly framed in terms of readiness for mission wherever the Pope might send them. The spectacular (and well-publicised) missionary successes of Francis Xavier and his Jesuit successors in the Far East contributed to a mounting sense of the unfolding of the Gospel through the whole world, for which the papacy provided the obvious and indeed the only focus.

It became increasingly clear, too, that the patronage exercised by Spain and Portugal over the missions might hinder as well as assist the spread of the Gospel, limiting the freedom of action of missionaries as much as royal authority limited the freedom of national churches in Europe. From the time of Pius V there were growing papal efforts to bring missionary activity under papal control. Pius established two congregations of cardinals to co-ordinate missionary activity both to Protestant Europe and to the pagan East and West. In the second half of the century Rome became the natural point of reference for all such ventures, for only the papacy had the universal concern and single point of vantage denied to the monarchies, however conscientious. Gregory XIII's seminary provision for missionaries to Germany, England and eastern Europe, mostly staffed by the Jesuits, were another stage in this development. It culminated under Gregory XV in 1622 with the establishment of a special Sacred Congregation for the Propagation of the Faith, fifteen strong instead of the more usual half-dozen, to oversee all aspects of mission, from Protestant England to China and Japan. *Propaganda Fide*, as the Congregation was known in Latin, under its energetic secretary Francis Ingoli, rapidly found itself backing native Indian and Chinese clergy against Portuguese racism, attacking royal delay in appointing bishops for mission territories and supplying the lack by appointing 'vicars apostolic', missionary priests in episcopal orders, directly responsible to the Pope. In its first twenty-five years Propaganda founded forty-six new missions. By 1627 it had its own multi-racial seminary, the Urbanum, and its own printing-press at Rome, fit symbols of the proactive and universalist papacy which had brought it into being.

The increased authority of the Counter-Reformation papacy triggered a corresponding surge of Protestant hostility. For many of the reformers, the popes were not merely the leaders of a corrupt Church, but the willing instruments of Satan himself. A revived interest in the prophecies of the Book of Daniel and the Book of Revelation led to the identification of the Pope as Antichrist, and of the Catholic Church as the 'Synagogue of Satan', which was to murder the saints and witnesses of Christ, and to make war against the true Church in the last days.

These fears were focused in 1582, when the vigorous reforming Pope Gregory XIII revised the existing hopelessly inaccurate 'Julian' Calendar, omitting ten days from October 1582 to correct the errors which had crept in over the centuries, and introducing a new method of calculating the Leap Years to prevent new inaccuracies arising. Gregory's reform was long overdue: the need for a reform had been discussed for centuries, and it was a huge improvement on the existing calendar. It was widely welcomed by astronomers and scientists, including the Protestants Johann Kepler and Tycho Brahe. The Gregorian Calendar, however, caused widespread anger and fear among Protestants, many of whom saw it as a device of Antichrist to subject the world to the devil. Gregory's coat of arms included a dragon, and this was seized on by opponents of the calendar reform as an omen. The Pope, it was claimed, was trying to confuse calculations of the imminent end of the world, so that Christians would be caught unprepared. The changes were an interference with the divine arrangement of the universe, and they would plunge Europe into a bloodbath. With the 'mind of a serpent and the cunning of a wolf', Gregory was attempting to smuggle idolatrous observances into the world under the pretext of more efficient calculation. The University of Tübingen decreed that anyone who accepted the new Calendar was reconciling themselves to Antichrist. It was outlawed in Denmark, Holland, and the Protestant cantons of Switzerland, and in many German Protestant states the civil authorities prevented the Catholic clergy from using it. The Emperor Rudolf II was able to secure its acceptance more widely in the empire only by omitting any reference to the Pope, and imposing the new calculations as an imperial secular decree. England, where anti-papal feeling was particularly strong, did not accept the new calendar till 1752, and Sweden not until 1753. The Pope had become the bogey-man of Protestant Europe.

IV   The Popes in an Age of Absolutism

On 8 November 1620, an international Catholic army routed the forces of the Protestant Elector Palatine, Frederick of Bohemia, on a hillock just west of the city of Prague. The Battle of the White Mountain, the first major Catholic victory of the Thirty Years War, had some of the trappings of the Crusade, and the password chosen for the day was 'Sancta Maria'. The battle marked the beginning of the end for the Protestant cause in central Europe, and represented a triumph of the confessional politics which the papacy had been advocating since the opening of the Council of Trent. Massive papal subsidies had helped equip the Emperor Ferdinand II's troops and those of the German Catholic League. Ferdinand himself was a representative of a new kind of Catholic prince, educated and guided by the Jesuits, determined to end the uneasy coexistence with Protestantism which had characterised imperial politics in the later sixteenth century, and to impose Catholicism everywhere. To celebrate the rout of Protestantism, the Lutheran church of the Holy Trinity in Prague was confiscated and rededicated to Our Lady of Victories, and the Emperor deposited there in thanksgiving a wax image of the child Jesus. Under the title the 'Infant of Prague', it was endlessly reproduced, and is still venerated all over the world as one of the most popular of all Catholic devotional images. In Rome a new church dedicated to St Paul was rededicated to Our Lady of Victories. Bernini would later place there his extraordinary image of St Teresa in Ecstasy.

Pope Paul V suffered a stroke during the thanksgiving celebrations for the victory in Rome, but his successor, Gregory XV (1621–3), bent all his efforts to maximising the advantage to the Church. Vatican subsidies continued to pour into the war-coffers of the Emperor and the League, and the Pope succeeded in ensuring that the devoutly Catholic Maximilian of Bavaria replaced the Protestant son-in-law of James I of England, Frederick, as elector palatine. In gratitude, Maximilian presented the fabulous library of Heidelberg, one of the most sumptuous pieces of war-loot ever, to the Vatican. On every front, the papal Counter-Reformation seemed triumphant, and the canonisation in Rome in March 1622 of the four great saints of the Counter-Reformation – the Carmelite mystic and monastic foundress Teresa of Avila, Ignatius Loyola, Philip Neri and Francis Xavier – set the seal on that triumph.

Within a generation, however, much of this had turned to ashes. The Thirty-Years War did indeed roll back the cause of the Reformation in central and eastern Europe. It ended in 1648, however, not with the hoped-for confessional triumph for Catholicism and the papacy, but with the institutionalising of Protestantism as a permanent presence within the empire. The fact is that none of the great powers of seventeenth-century Europe was prepared to tailor its foreign policy to purely confessional considerations. For France the Thirty Years War was as much about the containment of Habsburg domination in Europe as it was about religion. France therefore financed the armies of the main Protestant champion, Gustavus Adolphus of Sweden, and ignored papal calls to turn the war into a Crusade. The Pope might be revered as the figurehead of a renewed Catholicism, but his political interference was disregarded. Cardinal Richelieu summed the matter up when he declared that 'we must kiss his feet, and bind his hands'. The peace settlement which ended the war in 1648 had somehow to reconcile the interests of over 190 secular princes and rulers, many of them Protestant. There was therefore no chance of a simple 'Catholic' outcome to the war, and the terms of the Peace of Westphalia deliberately flew in the face of the repeated protests of the Papal Nuncio. The solemn bull issued by the Pope of the day, Innocent X (1644–55), in which he purported to 'condemn, reprove, quash, and annul' the treaty, was simply ignored.

These apparent contradictions in the position of the papacy – triumphant leader of militant Catholicism, and marginalised outsider in the *Realpolitik* of seventeenth-century Europe – are brought into sharp focus in the long and momentous pontificate of Urban VIII (1623–44). Maffeo Barberini was the product of a wealthy Florentine mercantile family, educated by the Jesuits, who had a successful career as a papal diplomat behind him. He had been nuncio in France, and was devoted to all things French. He was also devoted to the arts, on a scale and with a lavishness which rivalled any of the Renaissance popes. His early Roman career was spent in the midst of Sixtus V's ambitious replanning of the city. Under Paul V, the austere functionalism of much sixteenth-century papal art gave way to a love of surface, movement and colour. The young Cardinal Barberini watched while Pope Paul and his tasteless but fabulously wealthy nephew Cardinal Scipione Borghese poured money into palaces, churches, fountains and picture galleries. The completed façade of St Peter's was decorated with an immense and vulgar inscription which seemed to claim the church for Paul V rather than for the Apostle Peter. The papacy was set on a course of ostentatious display which Urban VIII would carry to new heights. Himself a gifted Latin poet, he patronised writers, musicians, painters and sculptors, above all the young Gian Lorenzo Bernini.

Bernini, the greatest sculptor of his age, was to create the unforgettable image of Baroque Rome, and of the seventeenth-century papacy. The fundamental commission here was the immense baldacchino Urban ordered to be placed over the high altar in St Peter's, which was begun in 1624, and which cost a tenth of the annual income of the Papal States. Modelled on the barley-sugar columns traditionally associated with the Constantinian shrine of Peter, the baldechino was a complete artistic success, instantly dominating and focusing the building on the tomb of the saint and the papal altar above it. Yet it was also a gross example of papal self-aggrandisement. The Barberini bees, monstrously enlarged, crawl up the columns, and the raw material for the commission was collected by stripping bronze girders from great classical buildings like the Pantheon, thereby provoking the observation that 'The Barberini have done what the barbarians never managed.'

That mixture of spiritual symbolism and vulgar ambition was characteristic of the entire pontificate. Urban's reign saw an immense flowering of Christian energy and a new phase of the Counter-Reformation, with the work of great pastoral reformers like the Frenchman Vincent de Paul. Urban himself took an eager interest in Christian missions, and founded the Collegium Urbanum to train clergy for the work of the Congregation for the Propagation of the Faith. Yet at the heart of the regime was a coarse secularism which inexorably eroded the spiritual prestige of the Baroque papacy. It was manifest in the autocratic absolutism of the Pope himself, who consulted no one and exercised the papal office as though he were an oriental khan. 'The only use of cardinals these days', wrote the Venetian Ambassador, 'is to act as a grandiose crown for the Pope.'

It was even more evident in the gross nepotism of the Pope, the endless promotion and enrichment of his family. There was nothing new about this, of course, but even by the standards of the period Urban carried nepotism to new heights. His favouritism to his family cost the papacy 105,000,000 scudi, and in old age would torment Urban with well-justified fears that he had squandered the patrimony of the Church. His nephews drew him into a disastrous war at the end of his pontificate with their hated rival Odoardo Farnese, who held the papal fief of Castro. This cynical war, undertaken to grab Farnese's possessions on a flimsy pretext, ultimately drew Venice, Tuscany and Modena into an anti-papal league, left the Papal States devastated, the papal coffers empty, and the ambition of Urban to assert an unchallenged secular power in Italy in shreds.

The war of Castro was not the only political catastrophe of Urban's pontificate, for his Francophile sympathies led to a steady alienation between the papacy and the Habsburgs in Spain and the empire. Urban understood the need for the Pope to preserve neutrality between Catholic nations, and genuinely struggled to do so. He was convinced, however, that Habsburg dominance in Italy was a greater danger to the papacy than any threat from France, and this assumption, coupled with his natural sympathy for France, consistently skewed his policy. When the Gonzaga line in the duchy of Mantua failed in 1627, therefore, Urban backed the French candidate for the succession. Since Mantua ran alongside the Spanish duchy of Milan, that decision permanently coloured Spain's attitude towards him.

The same pro-French sympathies coloured Urban's involvement in the Thirty Years War. Here again his intentions were basically good, for he wanted to settle the rivalry between Richelieu's France and Spain and the Habsburg empire, in the interests of a concerted front against Protestantism. It was a hopeless task. France worked to inflame the Pope's fears of Spanish ambition in Italy, and Spain took a high moral line on Urban's failure to condemn Richelieu's alliance with Protestant Sweden – as Philip IV wrote to the Pope in 1635, 'I trust that . . . your Holiness will deal with the King of France, who has allied himself with the Protestants, as the duty of a Pope demands.'[11] The failure of the Pope to achieve peace between the Catholic parties to the Thirty Years War was an eloquent – and for the papacy an ominous – indicator of the increasingly marginal place of religious considerations in determining the politics of Europe.

The rigidities of Urban's pontificate revealed themselves in other ways, above all in the Galileo affair. By the early 1630s Galileo was the most celebrated scientist in Italy. The Pope himself had written a Latin ode celebrating Galileo's discovery of sun-spots. The pioneers of early modern astronomy had met with papal encouragement. Nicholas Copernicus' epoch-making treatise outlining the revolutionary heliocentric hypothesis (that the earth and other planets revolved round the sun, not the sun round the earth) was dedicated to Paul III, and the Counter-Reformation popes had encouraged astronomy, Gregory XIII being credited with establishing the Vatican Observatory. The heliocentric theory was in apparent contradiction of the biblical account of creation, but it created no difficulties until 1616, when Galileo's own attempts to promote Copernicus' ideas triggered a belated condemnation of Copernicus. Despite this, Cardinal Barberini managed to prevent the inclusion of Galileo's name in the general condemnation of the Copernican system and its supporters. Galileo's own theories were freely discussed in Roman circles, and his attack on Aristotelian physics was tacitly approved. He was able to teach that the earth circled the sun under the thin pretext that he offered this as a way of making calculations, and not as a fact. Galileo was elaborately deferential to Church tradition, and careful to insist that he was an honest experimenter, who intended no invasion of the territory of the philosophers or theologians.

In 1632, however, he published a set of dialogues which clearly defended Copernicanism as true, and which made it clear that he thought his discoveries did indeed have theological implications. He was denounced to the Inquisition. The position was not helped by the fact that Galileo put in the mouth of a foolish character in the dialogues an argument which the Pope had once publicly defended. When it emerged that Galileo had been specifically warned by the Inquisition not to teach the heliocentric theory, the Pope's attitude to his erstwhile friend and client changed. Urban was an authoritarian. Error and conceit he could forgive: deliberate defiance of ecclesiastical authority was another matter. Galileo, he declared, 'has dared to meddle with matters beyond his competence ... it is an injury to religion as grievous as ever there was and of a perverseness as bad as could be encountered'. Galileo was forced to abjure the Copernican system, condemned to perpetual imprisonment (commuted in view of his age and eminence to house arrest) and forbidden to publish or teach. The contrast between the earlier toleration and indeed lionising of Galileo and the injustice of his condemnation was an eloquent sign of the rigidity of Baroque Catholicism. Underneath the extravagant architecture and showy surfaces was a deep uncertainty, which was resolved by the peremptory exercise of authority.

For the rest of the century the style established by Urban VIII determined the external face of the papacy. His successors Innocent X (1644–55) and Alexander VII (1655–67) continued Urban's patronage of Bernini, which bore fruit in a series of astonishing projections of the Baroque papacy's self-image – the Fountain of the Four Rivers in the Piazza Navona, the tombs of Urban and Alexander VII in St Peter's, and perhaps above all the great curved colonnade in the Piazza outside St Peter's, and the stupendous and theatrical shrine of the Chair of St Peter in the apse of the basilica itself. It is an unintended irony that this latter extravagant exaltation of papal power should have been built round a chair believed to be that of St Peter, but which was almost certainly the throne of the Frankish Emperor Charles the Bald.

Bernini's glorification of the Chair of Peter was hollow in more ways than one, for the principal legacy of Urban VIII was debt. He himself had inherited a debt of between 16,000,000 and 18,000,000 scudi, and within twelve years had added another 12,000,000 scudi to it. A huge proportion of papal income went into servicing this growing mass of debt. By 1635 the pope had only 600,000 scudi per annum available for current expenditure, and by 1640, when the debt had spi-

ralled to 35,000,000, this had shrunk to 300,000. Eighty-five per cent
of papal income was being swallowed up by interest repayments.

The political helplessness of the papacy became clearer with every
pontificate, and particularly so in the relations of the popes with
France. Urban's elderly and mistrustful successor Innocent X was as
hostile to France as Urban had been favourable. France's gain, Innocent considered, was inevitably the Roman Church's loss – 'only on
Spain could the Holy See rely with safety'. Cardinal Mazarin, chief
minister of France, seriously considered refusing to recognise Innocent's election (he had sent a veto which arrived too late) and French
hostility persisted into the pontificate of Innocent's successor
Alexander VII. The papacy's international role as peacemaker
between Catholic nations suffered as a result, for the French would
not permit papal mediation at the Peace of the Pyrenees between
Spain and France in 1659. French pressure on the papacy was relentless. In 1664 Louis XIV invaded the papal territory of Avignon and
forced the Pope into a humiliating treaty at Pisa. It had long been
accepted that a pope must defer to the Catholic monarchs by
appointing cardinals to represent their interests in the Curia. In 1675
the French tried to force the Pope to nominate a number of French
cardinals. When the Pope, for diplomatic reasons, delayed, the French
Ambassador in Rome, Cardinal d'Estrées, badgered the aged and frail
Clement X, pushing him back into his chair when Clement tried to
end the audience. Louis XIV put steady pressure on the papacy by
extending the exercise of the *régale*, royal control over episcopal
appointments in France, and over the revenues of vacant bishoprics
and benefices. Inexorably the church in France, as in other parts of
the Catholic world, was becoming a department of state.

The subordination of the papacy to the Catholic princes was not
confined within national boundaries. It reached out into the College
of Cardinals, and into the very process of papal election. In 1605
Henri IV of France was said to have spent 300,000 scudi on securing
the election of a Medici Pope (Leo XI), favourable to France. If so, it
was money badly spent, since the Pope survived only three weeks. In
the course of the seventeenth century the Emperor and the kings of
France and Spain established their title to a *jus exclusive*, a right of
veto on any candidate for the papacy whom they disliked, and by the
end of the century it had become routine for the ambassadors of the
great powers to attend the Conclave to make their wishes known.

Political considerations began to dominate the election of the Pope, and the required two-thirds majority became harder and harder to achieve. In 1669 during a conclave which dragged on for four months the French Ambassador vetoed Cardinal d'Elce, and the Spanish Ambassador blocked the election of Cardinal Broncaccio.

These political facts of life were accepted by many as part of the natural order of things, but at every conclave there was a strong party of *zelanti* who deplored all political interference. They were rarely able to secure their first choice for pope, but they were often decisive in preventing mere political appointments. Their interventions were admirable in principle, but not always happy in their outcome. The *zelanti* were responsible for the election of the pious and dedicated Pope Clement XI in 1700. A splendid administrator and a likeable man, he turned out to lack judgement and plunged the papacy into conflict with Spain, and with the church of France. His decision to outlaw the so-called Chinese Rites, by which Chinese missionaries had accommodated Christian practice to Chinese culture, effectively destroyed Christianity in China.

Pope Innocent XI (1676–89) tried to halt the slide in the prestige of the papacy. Benedetto Odescalchi was by any standards a very great pope. An experienced papal administrator, who had cut his teeth in Urban VIII's service, he became an exemplary and effective bishop of Novara in 1650, noted for his efforts to raise educational standards among clergy and laity, and for his lavish generosity to the poor. Ill-health led to his retirement into curial work in Rome, and he accepted election to the papacy with extreme reluctance, and only after forcing the cardinals to agree to a fourteen-point reform programme for the Church. His practical skills and personal integrity were soon demonstrated. As pope he inherited a debt of 50,000,000 scudi. By drastically reducing papal expenditure, abolishing useless honorary posts and introducing a raft of economy measures, he balanced his books and began to build up a financial reserve. He threw himself into promoting missionary activity all over the world, helped unite the King of Poland and the Emperor in a league against Turkish invasion of eastern Europe, and prevented influential Catholic rulers, including the Emperor, from marrying Protestants. Yet he strongly disapproved of religious persecution, condemned Louis XIV's treatment of the Huguenots, and tried to talk James II out of his aggressively Catholic policies in England.

Innocent's efforts to unite Catholic nations against the danger from the Turks in eastern Europe brought him into conflict with Louis XIV, for France welcomed Turkish pressure on the empire. While drawing back from actual alliance with the Turkish regime of the Grand Porte, Louis would not join the Pope's 'Holy League'. Innocent had other reasons for distrusting Louis. The Pope was determined to accept no further invasion of the Church's rights by secular rulers. In 1678 he called on Louis to abandon further extension of the '*régale*'. The King, declared the Pope, served the Catholic faith well by fighting heresy in his realms. Let him beware of angering God by undermining the Church. He hinted that Louis might die without heirs if he persisted (Louis was in fact pre-deceased by his son and grandson), and declared himself ready to endure persecution to defend the Church's rights.

Louis was unused to this sort of resistance, and a confrontation developed, in which Innocent's stand was presented as a breach of the rights of the Gallican church. Anti-papal feeling mounted in France, and in 1682 Louis mobilised the French Assembly of the Clergy against the Pope. The Assembly passed Four Articles which paid lip-service to papal primacy, while denying the Pope's temporal authority and the irreformability of his decrees even touching matters of faith, and making the Pope subordinate to a general council. Unsurprisingly, Innocent condemned these articles, and refused to ratify the appointment of any bishops for France till the matter was resolved. By the beginning of 1685, thirty-five French bishoprics were vacant. Relations steadily deteriorated, with Louis appealing to a general council against the Pope, and the Pope closing down the French quarter in Rome and refusing to receive a French ambassador. At the end of his pontificate Innocent was at loggerheads with Louis, and a schism between France and the papacy seemed inevitable. It would take the efforts of another two popes to heal the breach between Paris and Rome.

Gallicanism was not the only French challenge to papal authority in the seventeenth century. In the 1640s theological controversy erupted within the French church over the teaching of the posthumously published treatise *Augustinus* by a former bishop of Ypres, Cornelius Jansen. Jansen's immense and unreadable Latin treatise was in fact a manifesto for a party of devout Catholics alienated by the worldliness of much Counter-Reformation religion. They believed that too much insistence on human freedom in salvation had eclipsed the New Testament's teaching about grace. While rejecting Protestantism and placing great emphasis on the sacraments and the hierarchical Church, they also stressed the doctrine of predestination, taught that the grace of God was irresistible, and that therefore all who are damned are lost because God withholds his grace from them. By and large, they took a gloomy view of the average man or woman's chances of salvation. They shared the papacy's disgust at the opportunism of contemporary politics, and Jansen was also the author of *Mars Gallicus*, an attack on Richelieu's cynically opportunistic foreign policy.

Jansenism was therefore a hold-all term which included many of the most serious elements of French and Dutch Counter-Reformation Catholicism. On such matters as the need for a Catholic political alliance against Protestantism, Jansenists were ardent supporters of the papacy. They detested the Jesuits, however, whom they saw as the chief culprits in the spread of lax moral and sacramental teaching (they disapproved of too easy access to communion for 'worldly' lay people, and thought the Jesuits curried favour with rich patrons by granting cheap grace). Urban VIII had condemned Jansen's teaching, but the Jansenist debate really took hold under Innocent X. In 1653, responding to a formal request from eighty-five of the bishops of France, he condemned Five Propositions summarising Jansen's teaching in the bull *Cum Occasione*.

No one in France contested a solemn papal condemnation of doctrine. The Jansenist party, however, attempted to get round the bull by accepting that the Five Propositions were indeed heretical, while maintaining that the Pope was mistaken in thinking that they were to be found in Jansen's book. This distinction between 'right' and 'fact' was banned by Pope Alexander VII (1655–67), after which the Jansenists tried further evasive action by maintaining a right to 'respectful silence' in the face of papal condemnation. The papacy was now embroiled in a damaging debate about the nature of its own doctrinal authority, which would rumble on to the eve of the French Revolution. It was all the more damaging because the Jansenist party included some of the most serious and edifying clergy in France, and much of their practical teaching and devotional style could be traced back to the practice of Counter-Reformation models like Carlo Borromeo. Louis XIV set about suppressing Jansenism, because it damaged the unity of his realm. Papal condemnation of Jansenism was therefore seen by many Jansenist clergy as part of an unholy conspiracy between Pope and King against the Gospel. The only two bishops who protested on behalf of the church of France against Louis XIV's extension of the *régale* in the 1670s were Jansenists, one of whom, Nicholas Pavillon of Alet, had some claim to be the most outstanding French Bishop of the century. Many of those who sincerely accepted the Pope's teaching authority were alienated by the condemnation of men and women so patently dedicated to serious religion. The debate threatened the Pope's credibility as the guardian and leader of the Counter-Reformation.

The Jansenist quarrel came to a disastrous climax in 1713, when Clement XI (1700–21) issued the bull *Unigenitus*, condemning 101 propositions taken from the best-selling devotional treatise by the Jansenist Pasquier Quesnel, *Moral Reflections on the Gospels.* The publication of *Unigenitus* plunged the church of France into crisis. Fifteen bishops, led by Cardinal de Noailles, Archbishop of Paris, appealed against the bull, and of the 112 bishops who ultimately accepted it, many were reluctant, and published it with explanatory letters of their own – implying that episcopal approval and explanation was necessary before a papal bull carried authority in France. The Regency government of France, anxious to put an end to religious controversy, threw its weight behind the bull, but opposition persisted. In 1717 twenty bishops asked the Regent to appeal to the Pope for an explanation of the bull, and in the following year four bishops appealed against it to a general council. They were joined by twenty others and by 3,000 clergy, and there was widespread support for the Appellant cause among the lawyer class who staffed the regional Parlements. Slowly the dissidents were brought under control, but the last Appellant bishop did not die until 1754, and in the meantime the controversy had seriously damaged the papacy's authority in France. In Holland, the controversy led to the consecration of a schismatic Jansenist bishop and the creation of a breakaway Jansenist church.

By the beginning of the eighteenth century, the papacy had travelled far along the downward curve which would place it at the mercy of the great powers of Europe. Clement XI was the last Pope before the French Revolution to play a major role in European politics as a prince in his own right, and that role was an unqualified calamity for the papacy. Clement threw his weight behind the French candidate for the vacant throne of Spain in 1700. His intention was good. He thought Louis XIV was the most effective champion of the Catholic cause in Europe, and he knew that the Spaniards had a bad record in respecting papal territory in Italy. He judged it preferable to have a Frenchman in control of the Spanish territory of Naples, Milan and the coast of Tuscany. The result was an Austrian Habsburg invasion of Italy, a massive defeat of the papal armies in 1708, and a humiliating and damaging surrender to Austria in 1709 which led to Bourbon controlled Spain going into schism for six years.

Unworldliness, however, was no better protection for the papacy. The saintly Dominican Benedict XIII (1724–30) had resigned a dukedom to become a friar. He was elected pope in the stalemated Conclave of 1724 because everybody knew he was unworldly, and would preserve neutrality between France, Spain and the Austrian Habsburgs. He *was* unworldly, and he did try to be neutral. But he also refused to behave like a pope, instead behaving like a simple parish priest, living in a whitewashed room, visiting hospitals, hearing confessions and teaching children their catechism. Meanwhile, he put all the affairs of the papacy into the hands of his secretary, Niccolò Coscia. Coscia was totally corrupt, and surrounded himself with a disreputable parcel of cronies and profiteers. The administration of the Papal States became a public scandal. Nepotism had been formally abolished by Pope Clement XI, but now the Church had all the evils of nepotism without the nephew.

In 1728 Benedict provided more evidence that unworldliness can be a bad thing in a pope. He commanded the compulsory celebration of the Feast of St Gregory VII, formerly a local Italian observance, by the universal Church. The breviary lesson prescribed for the Feast was tactless in the extreme, and praised Gregory's courage in excommunicating and deposing Henry IV. The states of Europe set up a howl of anger. Venice protested to the Pope, Sicily (and Protestant Holland) forbade the celebration of the Feast at all, Belgium banned the offending lesson, the Parisian police prevented the breviary containing the service being printed. The ancient claim of the Pope to temporal power was no longer acceptable in 1728.

The eighteenth-century popes, therefore, found their room for manoeuvre more and more restricted, as the monarchs of Europe increasingly flexed their muscles and sought to bring the structures of the Church under state control. To secure as much liberty as possible for the Church, the popes adopted the expedient of making treaties or concordats which defined the Church's rights and role. But to define is also to confine, and successive rulers of France, Spain, Portugal and the empire whittled away at the terms of these concordats, and at the Church's freedoms and rights. The most genial, able and attractive practitioner of eighteenth-century papal statecraft was Prospero Lambertini, elected Benedict XIV (1740–58) after a blocked conclave of six months. A gifted theologian and lawyer, who wrote what remains the standard work on canonisation, Benedict was a supreme papal exponent of common-sense realism. Every inch an eighteenth-century man, Benedict strolled around Rome chatting to visitors, approachable, friendly, efficient, fond of slang. His long pontificate was filled with activity, all designed to streamline and modernise the traditional work of the papacy. He promoted seminary education and a whole range of practical Church reforms, protected the Italian religious reformer Ludovico Muratori against condemnation by the Spanish Inquisition, and the Jesuit editors of the *Acta Sanctorum*, whose rigorous historical investigation of the legends of the saints was causing offence to reactionary critics who thought them irreverent. He supported and encouraged Oriental-Rite Catholics of the Middle East who were being pressured to adopt Latin customs, raised papal revenues by improving agricultural methods in the Papal States, and won the affection of his subjects by reducing taxation. He was unflappable, amused. Stopped in the street one day by a fanatical visionary friar who told him that Antichrist had recently been born, Benedict asked interestedly, 'What age is he?' On being told that Antichrist was now three years old, the Pope smiled, sighed with relief and said, 'Then I will leave the problem to my successor to deal with.'[12]

Benedict was universally admired by Protestants as well as Catholics, and Voltaire dedicated one of his works to him. His own religious beliefs were conservative however, his piety sincere. He wanted an efficient, modern, active Catholicism, and thought that the Council of Trent had provided the blueprint for just that. Though he protected reform-minded historians and theologians and believed in the value of scholarship and science, he also drew up new rules for the Index of Prohibited Books. This was a revealing gesture, for Benedict, who thought the old Index trigger-happy and absurdly narrow, maintained the principle of censorship, but softened its impact by limiting the freedom of the Congregation of the Index to ban books without the Pope's express agreement. Above everything else a realist, he did what could be done to preserve as much of the Tridentine vision as was practicable in the age of absolute monarchies. He was the first Pope to make systematic use of the encyclical letter as a favoured form for teaching. Characteristically, recalling that it was the duty of the successor of Peter to 'feed [Christ's] lambs, feed [Christ's] sheep', he devoted his first Encyclical, *Ubi Primum*, to setting out the duties of bishops.[13]

Benedict avoided direct confrontation with secular rulers, but went to enormous diplomatic lengths to avoid surrendering even the temporal claims of the papacy. Where realism demanded the acceptance of uncomfortable reality, however, he did not flinch. He negotiated new concordats with Sardinia, Naples, Spain and Austria, making enormous concessions to the powers in the interests of practical working conditions for the Church. The Concordat with Spain in 1753, for example, conceded the right of presentation to 12,000 benefices in Spain to the Spanish crown, leaving the Pope with precisely fifty-two. There was a mass exodus from Rome of hopeful Spanish seekers for preferment. Up to 4,000 Spaniards were said to have left the city, causing a crisis for innkeepers and caterers, but providing an eloquent testimony of the massive transfer of patronage which had taken place.

The Concordat provoked an outcry from the Curia, who had mostly been kept in the dark while it was negotiated, and many felt that the Pope had betrayed the Church. Benedict was unmoved. He had secured 1,300,000 scudi in compensation for the transfer of rights, and was certain that, had he refused the Concordat, the Spanish crown would have taken matters into its own hands and gone ahead anyway, without any compensation to the Holy See. The same realism was in evidence over the Jubilee Indulgence which marked his accession in 1740. Benedict was an enthusiast for this Jubilee, personally overseeing the practical arrangements for pilgrims, and ensuring the provision of preachers and confessors to maximise the pastoral opportunities offered by the influx of pilgrims.

He was particularly anxious to have the Jubilee Bull proclaimed in France, because he hoped that the loyalty to Rome involved in the observances would constitute some sort of sign that the French church was still in communion with the Holy See. But he was concerned about whether or not the bull should specifically exclude Jansenist Appellants from its benefits. To do so would be to invite renewed resistance and controversy, and would probably lead to refusal to admit the bull by the Parlements. To remain silent would be seized on by the Jansenists as evidence that Benedict XIV did not approve of the bull *Unigenitus*. In the event he left the bull vague, but mentioned the exclusion of the Appellants in a covering letter to Louis XV. Even so the bull was not admitted, and in a second bull of 1744 he omitted any reference to the matter. His enthusiasm for the accession Jubilee and especially for the more solemn Holy Year of 1750 in itself demonstrates the fundamental continuity of his 'modern'-style papacy with what had gone before. For all his impeccable Enlightenment credentials Benedict was an enthusiast for 'old time religion', and he promoted and personally attended the revivalist preaching of the Franciscan Leonard of Port Maurice, who conducted spectacular open-air services in the Colosseum and the Roman squares throughout the 1750 Jubilee.

Benedict XIV did everything which high intelligence, boundless tact, bubbling geniality and civilised efficiency could do to hold back the rising tide of secular power. But everywhere secular rulers had set their hearts on controlling the Church. Tact, intelligence and geniality were not enough in the shark-pool of eighteenth-century power politics. Everywhere Catholic monarchs sponsored theologies which minimised papal authority, and which expounded the rights of national churches and the power of princes over those churches. Gallicanism had bred a host of these theologies, and Germany had produced its own version known as Febronianism, which exalted the power of the bishops (and therefore the King who appointed them) over against the Pope.

In 1768 the Duke of the tiny state of Parma, once part of papal territory and now a Bourbon fief, issued an edict forbidding appeals to Rome except by the Duke's permission, and banned all papal bulls or other documents which had not been countersigned by the Duke. To the pious but unworldly Pope Clement XIII (1758–69) this was an act of schism, subjecting the liberty of the Church to the tyranny of the prince. He declared the decree null and void, and justified his action by appealing to the bull *In Coena Domini*, with its anathemas against all who invaded the rights of the Church. The princes of Europe were outraged. Here was a priest presuming to annul the law of a prince. Portugal declared it treason to print, sell, distribute or make a judicial reference to *In Coena Domini*, and Naples, Parma, Monaco, Genoa, Venice and Austria followed suit. The Parlement of Paris banned the publication of the papal condemnation, the ambassadors of the Bourbon powers demanded its withdrawal. France occupied Avignon, Naples occupied Benevento and planned to divide the Papal States up among its Italian neighbours. Voltaire wrote a pamphlet arguing that the Pope should not rule a state at all.

But the humiliating reality of papal weakness was fully revealed in 1773, when Pope Clement XIV (1769–1774) caved in to pressure from the rulers of Spain, Portugal, France and Austria, and dissolved the Jesuit order. The Jesuits had long been the particular target of 'liberal' hatred in Enlightenment Europe, symbols of churchy obscurantism and clerical presumption. They had been the favourite butt of Jansenist pamphleteers, and Pascal's *Provincial Letters* pilloried them as self-seeking, half-pagan hypocrites. The real reasons for their unpopularity are complex, and the Society's sometimes obscure and suspect financial dealings had something to do with it. But they were also hated because they represented the strength and independence of the Church, and because their defence of the rights of 'native' peoples in South America had proved a thorn in the flesh of the great colonial powers. This powerful international organisation, like the Church itself, hindered the consolidation of the absolute rule of the monarch within his own domains. The Jesuits were the great bulwark of the Counter-Reformation papacy, their fourth vow of unquestioning obedience to the Pope a symbol of the centrality of the papacy in the renewal of the Counter-Reformation Church.

Everyone saw the dissolution coming. Already in the pontificate of Clement XIII hostile governments had acted to ban the Society in their own territories. The Portuguese Prime Minister, the Marquis de Pombal, confiscated the Society's assets in Portugal and its colonies, and deported all the Jesuits to the Papal States. France followed suit in 1764, Spain, Naples and Sicily in 1767. Clement XIII held out against this mounting pressure, and issued a bull in support of the Society in 1765, but he died suddenly in February 1769, and the ensuing Conclave was dominated by the question of the dissolution of the Society. The Austrian Emperor Joseph II visited the Conclave and pretended to be neutral, but made no secret of his contempt for the 'Blacks', as the Jesuits were called.

It became clear that the powers would veto any cardinal who was a friend of the Society. A promise by any cardinal that if elected he would dissolve the Society, however, would constitute simony, the purchase of the papacy. The Franciscan Cardinal Lorenzo Ganganelli, who emerged as Clement XIV (1769–74), gave no such promise, but let it be known that he thought the dissolution possible, and even a good idea. He was duly elected, and the destruction of the Society, therefore, was only a matter of time. Pope Clement delayed the evil hour as much as he could, by launching a series of placatory gestures towards the Catholic powers. These, however, only served to make it clear that he would dance whenever they pulled his string. The brother of the ferociously anti-clerical Prime Minister of Portugal, Pombal, was made a cardinal. In 1770 Clement dropped the annual reading of the bull *In Coena Domini*, and had it struck from the Roman liturgy. Though in theory still in force, it was never read again. Alongside all this, he made feeble attempts to mitigate the attack on the Jesuits, perhaps hoping that a simple ban on further recruitment might hold off further demands.

The monarchies, however, had scented blood, and would be content with nothing less. Clement at length surrendered, and the Society was formally abolished in 1773. In the interests of high politics, Father Ricci, the Jesuit General, a blameless and holy man who urged the Jesuits to accept the Pope's decision, was imprisoned in the Castel Sant' Angelo, where he spent the remaining years of his life. The Pope gave no explanation of his action, but indeed none was needed. The destruction of the order by the papacy it existed to serve was the clearest demonstration imaginable of the powerlessness of the Pope in the new world order. It was also the result of a lack of moral fibre in the occupant of the Chair of Peter, the unworthy successor of Gregory VII and Innocent III, even of Innocent XI. It was the papacy's most shameful hour.

CHAPTER FIVE

THE POPE AND THE PEOPLE

1774–1903

I THE CHURCH AND THE REVOLUTION

By the 1780s, every Catholic state in Europe wanted to reduce the Pope to a ceremonial figurehead, and most had succeeded. Kings and princes appointed bishops and abbots, dictated which feast days would be observed and which ignored, policed or prevented appeals to Rome, vetted the publication of papal utterances. This was a theological as well as a political phenomenon. Under the influence of Jansenism and a growing Catholic interest in the early Church many theologians emphasised the supremacy of the bishop in the local church. The Pope was primate, and the final resort in doctrinal disputes, but papal intervention in day-to-day affairs was considered usurpation, and the Christian prince fulfilled the role of Constantine in restricting it.

The powers and actions of papal nuncios focused some of these animosities. Everyone agreed that the Pope should have diplomatic representatives at the courts of Catholic kings. But the nuncios represented the spiritual as well as the temporal authority of the Pope, and had the powers of roving archbishops. They ordained, confirmed, dispensed, they heard appeals in the territories of the local bishops. These activities were resented. When Pope Pius VI (1775–99), at the invitation of the Elector of Bavaria, established a nuncio at Munich in 1785, the heads of the German hierarchy, the archbishops of Trier, Mainz, Cologne and Strasbourg, appealed to the Emperor to curtail the power of nuncios in Germany. The Congress of Ems in 1786 voted that there should be no appeals from Church courts to the nuncios, that the power to give marriage and other dispensations belonged to every bishop by divine right, so there was no need to apply to Rome, and that fees to Rome for the pallium and annates on the income of episcopal sees should be abolished.

Throughout Catholic Europe in the eighteenth century devout men looked for a reform of religion which would free it from superstition and ignorance, which would make it more useful, moral, rational. Many Catholics blamed the popes for upholding superstition. Men of the Enlightenment disliked relics and indulgences, and Rome was the main source of both. They disapproved of 'superstitious' devotions like the Sacred Heart, and the religious orders who propagated them, like the Jesuits; but the papacy was the friend of such devotion. They thought that the parish church and the parish clergy were useful, but that monasteries were a bad thing, refuges for men too lazy to work, or for girls who would be better off running homes and having babies. Yet the popes supported and privileged the monastic orders, and in the process undermined the authority of the local bishops and the parish clergy.

Joseph II of Austria, Holy Roman Emperor since 1765 and sole ruler of Austria from the death of his mother Maria Theresa in 1780, was a devout Catholic. He was fascinated by the smallest details of Church life, and he was painstaking and pious in discharging his role as the first Prince of Christendom. Frederick the Great of Prussia sneered at 'my brother the sacristan'. Joseph was an autocrat, though a benevolent one, who completed the liberation of the serfs begun by his mother, granted freedom of religion within his domains, and filled his kingdom with schools, orphanages, hospitals. He had no imagination, and had trouble grasping the contrariness of human nature. He was genuinely surprised that his edict forbidding the use of coffins and ordering the use of canvas sacks instead (to save on wood and nails) should produce so much resistance.

The Catholic Church was the special focus of Joseph's attempts at rationalisation and modernity, and he issued over 6,000 edicts regulating the religious life of his people. He had no doubts about his rights in such matters. Fundamental questions of doctrine fell within the jurisdiction of the Pope. Everything else in the life of the Church was for the Emperor to regulate. He was encouraged in these views by his Chancellor, Prince Kaunitz, a man with no real religious beliefs of his own, who saw the Church as a troublesome but crucial department of state.

Certainly the Church in Austria needed somebody's attention. In places it was dominated by immensely wealthy monasteries, where a handful of monks attended by liveried servants lived like princes on revenues originally designed to support hundreds. The parochial system was patchy and antiquated, with many communities far from the nearest parish church. Joseph established a central religious fund to provide new parishes, schools and seminaries, and raised the money he needed for these purposes by dissolving monasteries. In 1781 a decree dissolved religious houses devoted exclusively to contemplation and prayer, and preserved those that did 'useful' work like running schools or hospitals. More than 400 houses, a third of the total, disappeared. The Pope was not consulted.

Joseph thought that the provision of enlightened parish clergy was the job of the state, and he decreed that all clergy must train in one of six general seminaries established by him. There was more to this than a desire for better theological education. In the struggle to unite a scattered empire of many peoples, centralised training of key men for the localities would help make religion the cement of empire. The syllabus at the general seminaries included Jansenist works, and textbooks minimising papal authority.

Joseph's Church legislation offered rational solutions to real problems. It also fussed about petty details better left alone, and struck at dearly held beliefs. Special permission was needed for processions and pilgrimages, people were forbidden to kiss holy images or relics, a limit (fourteen) was put on the number of candles which could be burned about an altar, and Joseph forbade the dressing of statues in precious fabrics. All these measures were desperately unpopular.

Joseph's brother Leopold was Grand Duke of Tuscany, and he too aspired to dominate the Church in his own territories. His theological adviser was Scipio de Ricci, whom he made bishop of Pistoia and Prato in 1780. Ricci was earnest and devout. He was the great-nephew of the Jesuit General unjustly imprisoned by Clement XIV, and so he did not love the popes. Yet, though he had been educated by them, he also detested the Jesuits, for he was a Jansenist, in touch with excommunicated Jansenists in France and Holland, disapproving much that was most characteristic of Baroque Catholicism, determined to reform it. He was an extremist, a man with poor judgement and no antennae for popular religious feeling. His dining-room was decorated with a painting of the Emperor Joseph II ripping up a pious picture of the Sacred Heart. Ricci liked to talk of Rome as Babylon, the rule of Pope and Curia as outmoded tyranny.

In September 1786 Ricci held a diocesan synod at Pistoia, to an agenda supplied by Leopold, and with many of its decrees drafted in advance by a radical Jansenist professor from the Imperial University at Pavia, Pietro Tamburini. The acts of the Synod denounced the cult of the Sacred Heart, the Stations of the Cross, the abuse of indulgences and excessive Marian devotion. They recommended that statues be replaced in churches by paintings of biblical scenes, and they ordered tighter control of the cult of relics. Ricci wanted Mass in Italian, and many of the clergy agreed. The Synod thought this would be too far too fast, but ordered that the silent parts of the Mass, especially the central consecration prayer, the 'canon', should be recited in a loud clear voice, and that Italian translations of the missal should be provided for the laity to read. The people were to be encouraged to receive communion at every Mass. Bible reading was to be encouraged for all, feast days reduced, a new breviary produced which was purged of legendary material and with more scripture. All monasteries were placed under the direct jurisdiction of the local bishop, regardless of any papal privileges or exemptions, and all the religious orders were to be merged into one. Monasteries for men (maximum of one per town) should be outside the city, convents for women inside. Permanent vows were to be abolished for men, who would instead take vows for only one year at a time. Women might take permanent vows when past the age of childbearing. The Synod adopted the anti-papal teaching of the Four Gallican Articles.

Ricci received strong support from the clergy at the Synod, but the laity were outraged at the attack on ancient pieties. Reformed service-books were torn up, crowds rallied defiantly in defence of banished images. When rumours spread in May 1787 that he was about to destroy the relic of the Girdle of the Blessed Virgin venerated in the cathedral at Prato, rioting broke out, the Bishop's chair was dragged into the piazza and burned, and his palace looted. 'Superstitious' statues which he had removed were brought in triumph out of cellars, and crowds knelt all night in a blaze of candlelight before the condemned altar of the Girdle. Duke Leopold had to send in the troops.

The Prato riots shattered hopes for an anti-papal reform in Tuscany. News of the disturbances reached Leopold and Ricci during a national synod of the Tuscan bishops which they had hoped would adopt the Pistoia reforms for the whole region. Many of the bishops had been worried at the anti-papal tone of many of the measures, considered that radical changes in worship were outside the authority of individual bishops, and were unwilling to deny the Pope's prerogatives or to recommend condemned Jansenist works to priests and people. The riots confirmed their fears and frightened even the few radicals into caution. When Leopold succeeded to the Austrian throne in 1790 and left Tuscany, the reform movement collapsed. The Pistoian reforms and their doctrinal basis were solemnly condemned by the Pope in the Constitution *Auctorem Fidei* in 1794.

The Tuscan reform movement was inspired by theology. Many of its objectives, however pugnaciously and divisively asserted, were pastorally desirable, and would be realised two centuries later at the Second Vatican Council. Elsewhere in Italy anti-papalism took cruder forms. From the mid-1770s the Kingdom of the Two Sicilies had discontinued its traditional feudal payments to the papacy, and the government in Naples began to close down contacts with Rome, and with the international heads of the religious orders. The Inquisition was suppressed, the bishops were forbidden to use the sanction of excommunication, and from 1784 all direct contact with the Pope was forbidden on pain of banishment. Papal communications were made subject to state approval, and the crown asserted its right to appoint to all bishoprics.

Nobody could plausibly present these measures, which the bishops disliked but dared not resist, as being for the good of the Church. The Pope responded by refusing to institute any of the bishops nominated by the crown. By 1787 forty bishoprics were vacant, but the papacy was powerless in the face of government determination. In 1792, with almost half the sees in southern Italy vacant, the papacy caved in and instituted all the nominated bishops, leaving the Neapolitan crown triumphant.

Any pope would have found these challenges hard to handle. It was the Church's bad luck that the last Pope of the eighteenth century, Pius VI (1775–99), was a particularly poor specimen. Giovanni Angelo Braschi was an aristocrat who had worked his way with charm and efficiency through the papal civil service. He had been private secretary to Benedict XIV, and treasurer to Clement XIII, the latter a prestigious and profitable job which led to a cardinal's hat. He was not a man of deep spirituality, and was a latecomer to the priesthood, having been engaged to be married before hesitantly opting for a career in the Curia (his fiancée entered a convent). He was wholly without pastoral experience. After a conclave which dragged on for four months he emerged as the candidate acceptable to the Catholic monarchs. To secure his election he let it be known that he would rule in harmony with the monarchies and would not restore the Jesuits.

Braschi was tall, handsome and vain, proud of his elegant legs and noble mane of white hair. Despite the desperate state of papal finances he adopted a style reminiscent of Renaissance predecessors like Paul III, though he took the name Pius in honour of the austere St Pius V. He lavished money he did not have on raising Egyptian obelisks at key points in the city, on building an enormous new sacristy for St Peter's, on the creation of the modern Vatican Museum, and on a sustained but ultimately unsuccessful attempt to drain the Pontine marshes. He was a nepotist in the great Renaissance tradition, enriching his own nephews at the expense of the Church. In the mid-1780s Pius scandalised Rome by his involvement in a bitterly contested lawsuit over a legacy which he wanted to pass on to a nephew. A compromise solution was hammered out, and the nephew got his money, but the Pope appeared grasping, and the dignity and integrity of the papacy had been damaged.

For most of his pontificate, however, Pius rather specialised in dignity. Rome was now firmly established as the heart of the Grand Tour, and the age-old flood of pilgrims was augmented by a stream of tourists intent on seeing the sights. Pius' extension of the Vatican collections made the Vatican Museum an essential part of any tour, his patronage of artists like the sculptor Canova made Rome the model of taste. Almost as important, however, was the elaborate papal liturgy, over which he presided with a grave and reverent elegance which impressed Protestant onlookers, and did a good deal to soften their hostility to Catholicism.

None of this, however, could compensate for his growing powerlessness in the face of the determined anti-papalism of the Catholic states. Here Pius' vanity may have concealed from him the full seriousness of the situation. As relations worsened with Joseph II over imperial government of the Church in Austria and Milan, Pius determined to go himself to Vienna, hoping that Joseph would succumb to his personal fascination. The visit did indeed reveal a huge and perhaps unexpected popular reverence for the person of the

Pope. The Emperor received him with punctilious correctness and treated him with honour. Everywhere he went Pius was mobbed by yearning crowds, who queued for hours in the rain to catch a glimpse of him, to have their rosaries or scapulars blessed by him. But in hard terms he achieved nothing. Chancellor Kaunitz stunned him by shaking his hand instead of kissing it, and even while he was still in Vienna the relentless stream of government decrees for the reordering of the Austrian Church went on. When he left, Kaunitz gloated, 'He has a black eye.'

Joseph went on pressing his authority in Italy too, and by 1783 he and the Pope were at odds over the Austrian claim to appoint to all bishops in Milanese territory, a clear invasion of traditional papal prerogatives. This time Joseph reversed Pius' strategy, and arrived unannounced in the papal apartments in the Vatican by a back stair to talk the matter over. Pius conceded all his demands, saving face (and the theoretical rights of the papacy) by granting the nomination as a personal concession to Joseph as duke of Milan, and not a recognition of his rights as emperor. The papacy was dying the death of a thousand cuts.

In 1789 France was in financial and political crisis. Confidence in the monarchy had long been eroded by royal fiscal demands. It now dissolved altogether in the face of national bankruptcy, and bourgeois resentment of the stranglehold of the aristocracy over every aspect of national life exposed a deep rift in the heart of the French political system. On 4 May 1789 the Estates General met to confront and resolve the national crisis.

It was not, at first, a crisis of religion. Catholicism was an integral part of the French constitution. State persecution of Protestants had only recently been halted. The last pastor to be martyred had died in gaol in 1771, the last Protestant galley-slaves released in 1775. France's Prime Minister was the Cardinal Archbishop of Toulouse. But the nation was bankrupt and the Church was rich, and within the Church the gulf between aristocracy and commoners was writ large. Almost to a man the bishops were wealthy aristocrats, while a third of the parish clergy lived at or below subsistence level. In such circumstances resentments simmered, and it would not be long before the national crisis was replicated within the Church itself.

And, below the surface, Catholic Christianity in France had been eroded. The Cardinal of Toulouse was not in fact a Christian. Like many other fashionable clergy, he shared Voltaire's sardonic rejection of revealed religion, and when it had been proposed to promote him to Paris, Louis XVI had refused, on the ground that the Archbishop of Paris 'must at least believe in God'. Jansenist and Gallican views within the legal profession had created a widespread hostility to the papacy, while there was even wider dislike of the religious orders.

The key moment of the Revolution came in the last week of June, when after a period of agonising debate and uncertainty, the clergy, under mounting threats from the Paris mob, reluctantly threw in their lot with the commons of the Third Estate. The legal independence of the church of France was at an end. From August 1789 France was ruled by a single-chamber Constituent Assembly, which soon turned its attention to the reform of the Church. On 11 August 1789 the Assembly ended the payment of tithes. On 2 November, at the suggestion of Monseigneur Talleyrand, Bishop of Autun and another unbelieving aristocrat, the entire property of the French church was put 'at the disposal of the nation', and a massive sell-off began. The bankruptcy of the nation would be solved by confiscating the entire wealth of the church. The resulting alienation of Church property marked a new phase in the secularisation of the French national psyche. Nothing would ever be quite the same again: the sacred receded, anti-clericalism grew.

The attack on the Church's possessions inevitably spilled over into an attack on the most resented concentration of Church wealth, the religious orders. On 28 October 1789 the Assembly ended the taking of religious vows in France. Four months later, in February 1790, the suppression of the existing religious orders began. Before the Revolution, a monk or nun who abandoned the cloister thereby became an outlaw. Now, with the opportunity of liberty, there came a massive exodus, especially among men. Thirty-eight of the forty monks of Cluny walked away, and the greatest religious house of the Middle Ages came to an ignominious end. Within a few years the great abbey church would be no more, demolished and sold off as builders' rubble.

With the dismantling of the old financial machinery, the need for a reformed structure for the church of France became imperative. In July 1790 the Assembly enacted the Civil Constitution of the Clergy.[1] It imposed on the Gallican church a mixture of early-Church antiquarianism and eighteenth-century rationalisation. From now on all parish clergy and all bishops would be elected – the priests by the electors of the local districts, bishops by those of the civil Départements. All clergy became salaried officials, parishes of fewer than 6,000 souls were abolished or merged, and dioceses were reduced in number and brought into line with the civil Départements. Bishops were to rule in collaboration with a council of twelve vicars episcopal chosen from among the clergy. There was plenty to object to in all this, yet it was hard to maintain that the new arrangements were much worse than those which had produced unbelieving bishops like Talleyrand or the Cardinal of Toulouse, and the tide of revolutionary enthusiasm made clergy reluctant to resist the Civil Constitution.

Under the Constitution, the relations of the reordered church of France with Rome were to be more tenuous than ever. The Pope would no longer be asked for canonical institution of bishops. All that would be required would be that the new bishops should send the Pope a letter expressing unity of faith. In the previous year the Assembly had unilaterally abolished annates and other payments to Rome. The Pope had said nothing, and it was widely assumed that he would go along with the new arrangements, having little choice in the matter. All Europe knew of Joseph II's unilateral reforms, and the Synod of Pistoia. The Civil Constitution seemed just another step along the same road. In mid June 1790 the inhabitants of the papal enclave of Avignon threw off papal rule and asked for incorporation into France. The leaders of the Assembly were confident this gave them a bargaining counter with Rome which would ensure Pius VI's compliance.

On 22 July 1790 the King, reluctantly, sanctioned the Civil Constitution, having heard nothing from Rome. The very next day a brief arrived from Pius VI, condemning the Constitution as schismatical, and urging the King to reject it. The King suppressed the brief, but opened frantic negotiations with the Pope to try to reach some compromise. Most of the clergy were opposed to the Constitution, but many thought that some interim arrangements might make it tolerable – the Pope, it was thought, might institute the elected bishops without being asked, till the Constitution itself could be revised in a more Catholic direction. The bishops appealed to Rome to help them find a compromise.

At this fateful moment, Pius VI was silent. He detested the Civil Constitution, would not come to terms with schism. Yet he feared to speak out, in case he drove the church of France to re-enact the Anglican schism, two centuries on. While Rome dithered, however, anti-clerical feeling escalated. On 27 November the Assembly imposed an oath of obedience to the Civil Constitution on all office-holding clergy, setting 4 January 1791 as the final deadline for conformity.

The clergy of France were in an agonising dilemma. So far as anyone knew, the Pope had not spoken. Most clergy detested the new arrangements, but many were committed to the Revolution in broad terms, unwilling to destabilise it by rejecting its religious provisions. Many took the oath rather than starve, many took it out of a sense of duty to their people, many took it because the Pope had not condemned it, many took it with saving clauses 'as far as the Catholic faith allows'. When Pius VI finally did publish his condemnation in May 1792 there was a rush of conscience-stricken retractions. Only a third of the clergy in the Assembly took the oath. Of the clergy of France as a whole, about half of the parish priests and only seven of the bishops accepted the Constitution. Nevertheless, a schismatic Constitutional Church had come into existence, its newly elected bishops consecrated by the cynical Talleyrand, who then immediately resigned his own episcopal orders and returned to the lay state, eventually marrying an English Protestant divorcée.

In theory the 'refractory' clergy who had refused the oath should have been left unmolested, free to follow their own papalist form of Catholicism without hindrance, once the posts they had vacated had been filled up (often by ex-monks). In practice, as the Revolution became more radical, and fears mounted of an Austrian invasion to suppress it, refusal of the Constitutional Oath was equated with counter-revolutionary treason. By May 1792, with France at war with Austria, refractory clergy denounced by twenty citizens were liable to be deported. The King's refusal to sanction this decree hastened his own downfall. In July Prussia declared war on France; on 10 August the monarchy was abolished.

And now the persecutions began. Refractory clergy, however blameless, were forced into hiding, and massacres of the clergy imprisoned in Paris, Orleans and elsewhere took place. Over the course of the next year, 30,000 clergy, including most of the bishops, left France, to take refuge in the Papal States, in Switzerland, in Spain, in Germany, even in Protestant England, where Catholics had only recently been granted a modest amount of religious liberty, yet where 700 French priests and monks were maintained on the royal estate at Winchester alone. The Revolution, having called the Constitutional Church into existence, now turned against it. The Assembly had introduced clerical marriage. In September 1792 it took responsibility for registering marriages away from the Constitutional Church and handed it over to the local mayors. This apparently minor administrative change was in fact of enormous significance, for the same decree recognised civil divorce. The secular state had been born, the legal authority of the new Church fatally undermined.

By now the Revolution had turned on Christianity itself. As the guillotines of the Terror dealt with the enemies of the Revolution throughout the autumn and winter of 1793, an attack on Christianity was launched in the name of the republican religion of mankind. Busts of the tyrannicide 'saint' Brutus were solemnly dedicated in parish churches, sacred vessels and crucifixes tied to the tails of donkeys and dragged through the streets. In the Dechristianisation which followed, 22,000 clergy are thought to have renounced or simply abandoned their priesthood. The remaining 5,000 were increasingly subjected to the same persecution which the Refractories had endured. State funding of the Constitutional Church had been withdrawn in 1794. Now Christianity was abandoned altogether in favour of ersatz religions of Humanity and the Supreme Being. Pagan rituals of fertility and the fatherland were devised, the Christian calendar abandoned for a ten-day week and new months dedicated to a cycle of growth and renewal. 'Apostles of Reason', many of them ex-priests, were sent round the country to preach paganism.

The destruction of the church of France was watched in helpless horror at Rome. As revolutionary France went to war with Europe of the *ancien régime*, there was no doubt where the sympathies of Pius VI lay. In June 1792, while the royal family were still alive, the Pope sent Cardinal Maury as his special legate to the Diet of Frankfurt, to stir the new Emperor Francis II to the defence of the Church. Maury was a disastrous choice. A courageous non-juring French priest who had staged a dogged resistance to the Civil Constitution in the Assembly, he was a single-minded partisan against the Revolution, utterly lacking the political skills essential in a legate. At Frankfurt he threw caution to the winds in summoning the governments of Europe to war against France. The Pope, he declared, 'has need of their swords to sharpen his pen'. From now on, the Pope could only be seen in France as the implacable enemy of the Revolution, in league with European reaction against it.

During the next three years, despite his utter rejection of the Revolution, Pius VI held aloof from the European Coalition against France, anxious both to avoid giving the French an excuse to invade the Papal States and to preserve the tradition of papal neutrality in wars between Catholic nations. In May 1796, however, the young revolutionary General Napoleon Bonaparte advanced into Lombardy, establishing a republic at Milan and announcing his intention to 'free the Roman people from their long slavery'. Napoleon did not in fact advance on Rome, but he did annex the most prosperous part of the Papal States, the so-called 'Legations' (because ruled by papal legates) of Ravenna and Bologna. To secure Rome from invasion the Pope had to agree to a humiliating armistice which gave the French access to all papal ports, an immense ransom of 21,000,000 scudi, and the choice of any hundred works of art and 500 manuscripts from the papal collections. The Pope was also to urge French Catholics to obey their government. After further papal attempts at armed resistance failed, in February 1797 these humiliating conditions were confirmed and extended by the Peace of Tolentino. The Pope accepted the permanent loss of Avignon and the Legations, and the ransom was more than doubled. There followed an uneasy period of French occupation of Italy, and the establishment under French patronage of a series of Italian republics beginning in the Legations and Lombardy, and ultimately extending to Naples in 1799. Civil marriage and divorce were legalised, monasteries closed, Church property confiscated to fill the empty coffers of the new republics. This assault on Catholic values and institutions confirmed papal dread of the French.

But Napoleon was Corsican, not French, and though not a Christian he had a healthy sense of the power of religion. In Egypt he would toy with Islam, and he was to declare that if he ruled a nation of Jews he would restore the Temple of Solomon. He set about wooing the Italian clergy, emphasising his own respect for the Catholic religion. He prevented looting of the churches, protected clergy from Jacobin mobs, and told Cardinal Mattei, Papal Legate in Ferrara, that 'my special care will be to prevent anyone altering the religion of our fathers'. He tried to harness the bishops as allies in keeping law and order, and encouraged them to preach the compatibility of democracy and Christianity.

Some clergy thought that an accommodation was indeed possible. The future Pope Pius VII, Cardinal Chiaramonte, Bishop of Imola in the Legations (now the Cisalpine Republic), preached a long sermon on Christmas Day 1797 saying that God favoured no particular form of government. Democracy was not contrary to the Gospel. On the contrary, it required of citizens human virtues only possible with the help of divine grace. Liberty and equality were ideals only realisable in Christ. Good Catholics will also be good democrats. This careful utterance delighted Napoleon: 'The Citizen Cardinal of Imola preaches like a Jacobin.' The Cardinal used headed notepaper with the inscription 'Liberty, equality, and peace in our Lord Jesus Christ'.

Realists like Chiaramonte might look for an accommodation with democracy and republicanism, but to Pius VI matters seemed not so simple. Republicanism spelt the end of monarchy, and the Pope was a monarch. The Peace of Tollentino was a bitter pill to swallow, and many saw in it the beginning of the end for the temporal power of the popes, for the Legations which it had surrendered were in fact the only economically viable parts of the Papal States. The Pope was now an old and sick man. There were some even in Rome itself who hoped that he would have no successor.

In this fraught and expectant atmosphere a party of Roman republicans decided to plant a series of Liberty Trees round Rome. Tempers flared, rioting broke out, and in a skirmish on the morning of 28 December the young French General Duphot was killed. Joseph Bonaparte, the French Ambassador, at once left Rome, the papal Ambassador in Paris was arrested, and the order was given for the declaration of a Roman republic. French troops entered Rome on 15 February, the twenty-third anniversary of the Pope's coronation. The cardinals were arrested, the Pope ordered to prepare himself to leave Rome within three days. When he asked to be allowed to die in Rome the French commander, General Berthier, replied contemptuously, 'A man can die anywhere.' On 20 February the terminally ill 'Citizen Pope' was bundled into a carriage and taken north to Tuscany.

Lodged first in a convent in Siena, and then in a Carthusian monastery outside Florence, he rallied a little, but the French feared his presence in Italy as a focus for counter-revolution, and would not leave him be. Plans were made to take him to Sardinia, but he was too ill for the journey. In March 1799, despite his almost total paralysis he was once more pushed into a carriage and dragged through snow and ice across the Alps to France. He died in the citadel of Valence on 29 August 1799. The local Constitutional clergy refused his body Christian burial, and the town prefect registered the death of 'Citizen Braschi, exercising the profession of Pontiff'.

Pius VI had not been a good pope. He was weak, vain, worldly. While he built sculpture galleries and raised obelisks and fountains, the monarchies of Europe had hijacked the Church, and pressed religion into the service of the absolute state. For this Pius was not to blame. He had no more control over that process than his predecessors. Against the mounting demands of the monarchies neither the courage of an Innocent XI nor the skill of a Benedict XIV had availed.

At the crisis of religion in France, however, Pius had hesitated when decisive action was needed. Certain of his own divinely ordained leadership in the Church, he had failed to rise to the challenge of leadership, had allowed the situation to drift. At the last, however, he had endured, and the ignominies and wretchedness of his final months did more for the papacy than the whole previous twenty-four years of his pontificate, the longest and one of the most disastrous since the papal office had begun. Martyrdom wipes all scores clean, and in the eyes of the world Pius VI died a martyr. It remained to be seen what his successor – if he were to have a successor – would make of that inheritance.

II   FROM RECOVERY TO REACTION

In the late summer of 1799, Italy was uneasily free of the French. The Roman Republic had collapsed and Neapolitan troops occupied Rome. All over the peninsula improvised armies of 'Sanfedisti' (from 'holy faith') had arisen in defence of religion and against Jacobinism. Venice, the Legations and virtually the whole of the papal territories north of Rome were in the hands of the Austrians. Pius VI had favoured Venice as the most suitable location for a conclave, and many cardinals were already gathered there when he died. The Emperor Francis II, confident that the cause of the papacy and the interests of Austria were bound to be the same, offered to pay the Conclave expenses. The cardinals duly assembled in the Benedictine island monastery of San Giorgio there on 30 November 1799, the first Sunday in Advent. The newly appointed secretary of the Conclave, Ercole Consalvi, had announced the death of Pius VI to the monarchs of Europe in terms which underlined the links between throne and altar: 'Too many crowned heads, alas, in our times have seen that the princely power falls when the dignity of the Church decays. Restore the Church of God to her ancient splendour: then the enemies of the Crown will shake in terror.'[2] That assumed convergence of interests would dominate the election.

The Emperor, paying the bills, was clear in his requirements. The new Pope need not be a man of talent or ability – a pope, after all, was never short of advisers. But Austria needed a pope who would throw the moral weight of the papacy behind the forces of European counter-revolution, against revolutionary France. Though he did not say so, Austria in particular needed a pope who would surrender the Legations and the rest of Austrian-occupied papal territory, as Pius VI had surrendered them to France at the Peace of Tollentino. By contrast, Naples demanded a pope committed to the restoration of the Papal States, who for that reason would be willing to co-operate in driving Austria out of the peninsula.

With the whole of Europe in flux, the Conclave sat deadlocked for three months. Eventually, however, a compromise candidate emerged, and the cardinals unanimously elected the 'Citizen Cardinal of Imola', the sweet-natured monk, Barnaba Chiaramonte. From Austria's point of view this was a disaster. Chiaramonte, who took the name Pius VII (1800–23), was, like Pius VI, a native of Cesena in the Legations, and was bishop of the neighbouring see of Imola. He would never agree to Austrian sovereignty over this traditional papal territory. Moreover, everybody remembered his notorious 'Jacobin' Christmas sermon of 1797, in which he had baptised democracy. Here, in this mild-mannered man, who preferred to make his own bed and mend his own cassock, was a pope of decidedly unsound political views. To signal their displeasure, the Austrians refused the use of San Marco for the coronation, and Pius had to be crowned in the cramped monastery church, while the lagoon seethed with boatloads of spectators craning for a glimpse.

This was spiteful, but more than spite. The coronation of the Pope was a symbol of his temporal sovereignty. To co-operate in the coronation would be to recognise the integrity of the Papal States, including the Legations. The Emperor at once invited the Pope to come to Vienna. Pius, aware that once in Austria he would be pressured into conceding the Legations, politely but firmly declined, saying that his first duty must be to return to Rome. He was not permitted to travel overland, however, since this would certainly have provoked demonstrations of loyalty from the population of the Legations. Instead, he was taken to the Adriatic port of Malamocco, and put aboard the ancient tub *La Bellone*. There were no cooking facilities, and the journey south to the Papal States, which should have taken one day, stretched out to a nightmare twelve. It was just as well that Pius had refused to go to Vienna, however, for by the time he entered Rome in July 1800 the political situation had been transformed once more. Napoleon Bonaparte, having made himself First Consul of France, had defeated the Austrians at the Battle of Marengo, and was once more master of northern Italy.

There would be no re-run of the Jacobin attack on the Church, however. Napoleon had drawn his own conclusions from the religious chaos of revolutionary France, and he recognised that the claim to act in defence of religion against infidel France was one of the strongest cards in the hands of Austria and her allies. In December 1799 one of his earliest decrees as First Consul ordered funeral honours for the body of Pius VI, still lying unburied in a sealed coffin at Valence. Pius, Napoleon declared, was 'a man who had occupied one of the greatest offices in the world'. The Pope, to Napoleon, was 'a lever of opinion', his moral authority equivalent 'to a corps of 200,000 men'.

On 5 June 1800 Napoleon made a startling speech to the clergy of Milan. 'I am sure', he declared, 'that the Catholic religion is the only religion that can make a stable community happy, and establish the foundations of good government. I undertake to defend it always . . . I intend that the Roman Catholic religion shall be practised openly and in all its fullness . . . France has had her eyes opened through suffering, and has seen that the Catholic religion is the single anchor amid storm.'[3] All of this was intended for the Pope's ears. 'Tell the Pope', Napoleon declared, 'that I want to make him a present of 30,000,000 Frenchmen.' Bonaparte needed to pacify France, and the parts of Europe occupied by France. He recognised that an accommodation with the Catholic Church was a precondition for any such peace. The counter-revolution in the west of France, in the Vendée, was a Catholic counter-revolution, its banners adorned with the emblem of the Sacred Heart of Jesus, its leader a peasant priest, the Abbé Bernier. Only a religious settlement could still such unrest, and only the Pope could deliver a religious settlement.

France had two competing hierarchies – the pre-revolutionary bishops appointed by the Bourbon kings, most of whom had fled abroad, and the bishops appointed under the Civil Constitution. Some of the Constitutional bishops had apostatised from the faith during the Terror and its aftermath, but the Constitutional Church itself had held together under the leadership of the courageous Bishop Henri Grégoire, and it too had its martyrs. Napoleon was accustomed to speak scathingly about the Constitutional bishops – 'a bunch of brigands', he called them, at least when talking to Rome. He could hardly abandon them altogether, however, without appearing to repudiate the Revolution itself. Yet there was no reconciling these two groups of bishops. The only way out of this dilemma was to wipe the slate clean, and to start again with a new set of bishops (to include former bishops from both camps) appointed by Napoleon himself. To have any chance of being accepted, such an arrangement needed the backing of the Pope. In return, Napoleon promised that the clergy of France would be paid by the state (though there would be no question of the return of confiscated Church property), and he would do all in his power to restore the Papal States.

Negotiations for a settlement were to drag on for eight months, and to go through twenty-six different drafts. They were the focus of fierce hostility in both Rome and Paris. Many of Pius' cardinals rejected the thought of any accommodation with the Revolution, which had persecuted the Church, murdered its priests, stolen its property, and deposed and kidnapped a pope. Gregoire, leader of the Constitutional bishops, feared a sell-out. Committed Jacobins were revolted by the thought of the return of state-subsidised superstition and priestcraft. The French Foreign Minister was the former bishop of Autun, Talleyrand, with his English Protestant wife. He was determined that married priests must be left unmolested and their marriages validated.

Roman caution over the implications of every line and comma of the Concordat maddened Napoleon, feverishly concerned for a speedy resolution of the religious problem. He threw spectacular tantrums in Paris, threatening to turn Calvinist and to take Europe with him or, more worryingly because more plausibly, to imitate Henry VIII and establish a schismatic national church. In May 1801 the French Ambassador in Rome was instructed to deliver an ultimatum and then retire to Florence, where troops were waiting to march on Rome. Only prompt collaborative action between the Ambassador and the Cardinal Secretary of State, Ercole Consalvi, who hurried to Paris, rescued the negotiations. The Concordat was finally signed on 15 July 1801. It was to govern relations between France and the Holy See for a century, and to provide a pattern for the papacy's relations with the new international order of the nineteenth century.[4]

The Concordat recognised Catholicism as the religion of 'the vast majority of French citizens'. This comparatively weak statement was strengthened by a reference to the benefits the Church received from 'the establishment of Catholic worship in France', and from the profession of Catholicism by the Consuls. Catholicism was to be freely practised, though its public worship was to be subject to 'police regulations'. Predictably, this clause caused a good deal of worry in Rome, but in fact it represented a diplomatic triumph by Consalvi, for in reality it limited government interference to matters of public cult such as processions, leaving the Church's internal affairs and contacts with Rome otherwise unregulated. The Pope was to demand the co-operation of all existing bishops in reconstructing the French church, even if this involved 'the utmost sacrifice' of resignation. Within three months he was to institute new bishops to a streamlined diocesan system (ten archbishoprics and fifty bishoprics, in place of the pre-revolutionary 135).

The new bishops would be appointed by the First Consul along lines laid down for the crown in the Concordat of Bologna of 1516, the Pope granting canonical institution (authorisation to perform spiritual functions). The bishops would appoint parish priests, choosing only men acceptable to government. They could also establish cathedral chapters and seminaries. Confiscated Church property would be left in the hands of the present possessors, but churches and cathedrals needed for worship would be 'put at the disposal' of the bishops. The bishops and clergy would receive state salaries. There was no provision for any reconstruction of monastic life.

The Concordat bristled with difficulties for Rome. The Pope had failed to secure a declaration that Catholicism was the state religion of France. He had had to renounce for ever the plundered property of the wealthiest church in Christendom, and for the first time the clergy were to be salaried officials of the state. Consalvi and the Pope, determined to avoid charges of simony and anxious that the fate of the church of France should not appear to have been made a bargaining counter for the recovery of the Pope's temporal power, had not even raised the question of the return of Avignon or the Legations.

Nevertheless, the Concordat transformed the relationship between the Pope and the church of France in ways which would have been unimaginable even ten years earlier. The heart of this transformation was the reorganisation of the episcopate. During the negotiations, Consalvi himself had declared such an act impossible: 'To get rid of 100 bishops is something that just cannot happen.' Yet happen it did, by the sole exercise of papal authority. At his request, forty-eight bishops resigned. Thirty-seven others refused, on the grounds that they had been duly appointed by the crown, and to resign would be to recognise the Revolution. Pius declared their sees vacant, and most of them tacitly acquiesced in their own deposition. A few did not, and the resulting schismatic *petite église* would persist for the rest of the century. But this was the dying struggle of old Gallicanism, and it was largely an irrelevance. At a stroke, the entrenched resistance of the French church to papal authority was undone, the entire hierarchy reconstituted by an unprecedented exercise of papal power. Though few people grasped the full implications at the time, a new era in the history of the papacy, and the Church, had begun.

The new era, however, began stormily. As Napoleon pondered the terms which Consalvi had gained for the papacy, he became increasingly unhappy with the Concordat. Publication was delayed in France until February 1802, and when it came it was accompanied by seventy-seven 'Organic Articles', ostensibly spelling out the 'police regulations' mentioned in the Concordat, but in fact unilaterally imposing the very restrictions on the Church which Consalvi had struggled to fend off. No papal acts, briefs or bulls could be received or published in France without the *placet* of the state. No nuncio or legate could exercise jurisdiction without permission. No seminaries could be established without the express permission of the First Consul, and he was to approve their regulations. All seminary staff must sign the anti-papal Gallican Articles of 1682, which made a general council superior to the Pope. Civil marriage must precede any church ceremony.

The Organic Articles were deeply repugnant to the papacy, but, although he protested against them, Pius did not repudiate the Concordat. However hedged round with restrictions, it made possible the reconstruction of the devastated Church in France, and over the next few years Pius went out of his way to oblige Napoleon. At his request, the Pope sent a docile cardinal (Caprara) as *Legate a Latere* to France. In 1803 five Frenchmen, including Napoleon's uncle and former quartermaster, Monsignor Fesch, were made cardinals. The Vatican even accepted the establishment of a feast of 'St Napoleon' on 15 August, though it displaced a major Marian feast, the Assumption, and no one could come up with a convincing account of just who 'St Napoleon' was.

In May 1804 the French Senate decreed that Napoleon was emperor of the French. For Napoleon this was a step on the way to world domination. He dreamed of becoming a new and more glorious Charlemagne. Yet he was in the end only a soldier of fortune; he lacked the aura of legitimacy. Pius was invited to Paris to anoint Napoleon emperor. This invitation posed an enormous dilemma for Pius VII and Consalvi. The monarchies of Europe had deplored the Concordat and the legitimation it had given revolutionary France. Already the Pope was being referred to contemptuously as Napoleon's chaplain. The imperial coronation of this Corsican upstart would bring the Pope into disrepute from Moscow to London. In particular, the Austrian Emperor would be offended, and Austria had defended the Church from the Revolution.

Some of the cardinals thought that the Pope should refuse point-blank, most thought he should set stringent conditions before he agreed to go. Consalvi knew that any such conditions would be impossible to enforce. He was clear that the Pope must go to Paris, to secure whatever advantage to the Church could be won from the Emperor. It was a thousand years since a pope had gone to crown a king in France. The only precedent in living memory, Pius VI's fruitless visit to Vienna, was not encouraging. Nevertheless, Pius set out for Paris in the autumn of 1804.

The slow journey through northern Italy and France was a triumph, and a revelation. Wherever the Pope went, he was mobbed by emotional crowds. His carriage drove between lines of kneeling devotees, men pressed forward to have their rosaries blessed, women married by civil rites under the Revolution to have their wedding-rings touched by the Pope. It was clear to everyone that the papal office had gained more mystique than it had lost in the flux and turmoil of Revolution. Napoleon was not pleased. Throughout the

Pope's stay in France Napoleon inflicted on him a series of petty humiliations, which Pius had to swallow as best he could.

The coronation itself took place in Notre Dame in Paris on 2 December. There were hitches. Napoleon refused to receive communion, being unwilling to go to confession first, and he did not allow the Pope to place the crown on his head. Pius anointed the Emperor and Empress, and blessed the crowns, which Napoleon then took from the altar with his own hands. The Pope had however won a minor victory the day before. A tearful Josephine had come to him to reveal that she and the Emperor had never been through a rite of Christian marriage. The Pope refused to proceed with the coronation till this was rectified. In utter secrecy, and without witnesses, Napoleon's uncle Cardinal Fesch performed the ceremony in the Tuileries the day before the coronation.

There was little else tangible to show for the visit. Even the jewelled tiara presented to the Pope by Napoleon as a wedding-gift turned out to be a veiled insult, for it was decorated with stones looted from the Vatican in 1798. Napoleon was politely evasive about the question of sovereignty in the Legations, the Organic Articles remained in force, the religious orders were not restored. Yet Napoleon's bad grace and offensive behaviour only served to underline the fact that, however much he disliked it, he had *needed* the Pope to be there. The papacy's authority and holiness were still hard currency in the world of power politics. Indeed, the coronation, intended to underpin the authority of Napoleon, ultimately benefited the papacy more. Napoleon himself would bitterly complain of this. 'Nobody thought of the Pope when he was in Rome. Nobody bothered what he did. My coronation and his appearance in Paris made him important.'[5]

When Pius entered Notre Dame for the coronation, a choir of 500 voices had sung 'Tu es Petrus', 'Thou art Peter'. The kneeling crowds along his route back to Italy in April 1805 demonstrated that those words had not lost their power over the hearts and consciences of French men and women. It was perhaps symbolic that, as Pius passed through Florence in May 1805, the former bishop of Pistoia, Scipio Ricci, came to make his submission to the Pope, whose rule he had once denounced as Babylonian tyranny. The Synod of Pistoia and the Jansenist episcopalism it represented were now only a memory in Italy. The papacy had outlived its enemies.

In 1805 Napoleon was offered and accepted the crown of Italy, the northern Republic having been transformed into a kingdom. Italy, he declared, was a mistress he would share with no man. He began to style himself *Rex Totius Italiae*, King of All Italy, and he set about transforming that claim into reality. To secure the papal port of Ancona against British and Austrian forces, Napoleon annexed it in October 1805, a move which the Pope bitterly resented – he wrote to Napoleon calling for a French withdrawal, and speaking of his 'disillusionment' with Napoleon's behaviour since the coronation: 'We have not found in your Majesty that return of our goodwill which we had the right to expect.' It was a turning point – to Napoleon the Pope had begun to speak in the tones of Gregory VII.

In February 1806, using Ancona as a base, Napoleon annexed the kingdom of Naples and placed his brother Joseph on the throne. This was yet another insult to the Pope, for Naples was a papal fief, and the Pope had a right to be consulted about any transfer of rule. Finally, Napoleon wrote to the Pope demanding that he close all papal ports to the allies. He would not interfere with the freedom of the Papal States, he claimed, but 'the condition must be that your Holiness has the same respect for me in the temporal sphere that I have for him in the spiritual, and that he abandons useless intrigues with the heretic enemies of the Church [Russia and England] . . . Your Holiness is Sovereign of Rome, but I am Emperor. All my enemies must be his'.[6]

Here Napoleon had reached the Pope's sticking-point. To close the ports to the allies, Pius insisted, would be an act of war: 'We are the Vicar of a God of peace, which means peace towards all, without distinction between Catholics and Heretics.' He dismissed 'with apostolic freedom' Napoleon's demand for deference in the temporal sphere. The Pope 'has been such over so great a number of centuries that no reigning prince can compare with him in sovereignty'. Napoleon had no rights over the Papal States.

From this point onwards relations between Napoleon and the Pope deteriorated. Napoleon blamed Consalvi, whom he disliked, for Pius' stand: to keep lines of communication with France open, Consalvi resigned as secretary of state. This was a victory for Napoleon, but a self-defeating one, for the Pope now had to rely on the advice of extremist Italians, like the new Secretary of State, Cardinal Pacca, far less diplomatic and far more hostile to France than

Consalvi had ever allowed himself to be. Napoleon increasingly referred to the Pope as 'a foreign prince', and refused to allow French Catholics to travel to Rome to see him. The Pope must renounce all temporal power, and rely only on his spiritual authority.

In January 1808 French forces occupied Rome, and the Pope became effectively a prisoner within the Quirinal Palace, with eight French cannon trained on his windows. The Allies offered to rescue Pius in a British frigate, but the Pope feared that a flight under British protection would give Napoleon an excuse to renew a French schism, and he refused to leave Rome. On 6 July a French general presented himself before the Pope and demanded his abdication as sovereign of the Papal States. On his refusal, he was bundled into a carriage, still in his ceremonial robes and without so much as a change of linen, and taken north, on the route Pius VI had followed eleven years earlier. The Pope and his Secretary of State, Cardinal Pacca, padlocked into the coach in the summer heat, turned out their pockets. They had less than twenty sous between them, not enough for a single meal. Their laughter annoyed their gaoler.

Pius was taken to the episcopal palace at Savona, on the Italian Riviera, and isolated from his advisers, where it was hoped that, left to his own devices, he would give way. It was a shrewd judgement, for the Pope was prone to self-doubt and indecision. Pius retaliated in the only way open to him. He reverted to being the 'poor monk Chiaramonte', saying his breviary, reading, washing and mending his clothes. Above all, he refused to institute any bishops nominated by Napoleon. This was a serious matter. Many of the bishops appointed in 1801 had been elderly men, and they were now dying in droves. By the summer of 1810, there were twenty-seven sees without bishops.

In the meantime Napoleon had annexed Rome, declaring it the second city of the empire. French law and customs were introduced into the Papal States, and all the cardinals were removed to Paris. This move prepared the way for another confrontation. Napoleon wanted an heir for the empire, and Josephine had not provided one. He decided to marry the daughter of the Austrian Emperor, and so he needed a divorce. There was no chance of Pius granting a divorce, but the fact that the marriage celebrated the day before the coronation had been at the Pope's insistence, and without witnesses, provided an ideal pretext for annulment. It was duly granted by the obedient Church courts in Paris. In April 1810 Napoleon remarried. He invited the cardinals to attend, and more than half did. But thirteen absented themselves, including Consalvi. The 'invitation' had in fact been a command, and Napoleon stripped the absentees of their regalia and their stipends, and sent them into exile. These 'black cardinals' became a symbol for him of Roman intransigence, and his treatment of the Pope became more hostile. Napoleon appointed Cardinal Maury as archbishop of Paris. The Pope smuggled out a stinging rebuke, depriving Maury of all jurisdiction. Napoleon had the Pope's writing materials and books confiscated, and Pius' isolation increased.

The Paris divorce, however, had convinced Napoleon that the Pope could be circumvented. If Pius would not institute Napoleon's nominees to the vacant bishoprics (now mounting up all over French-occupied Europe), then the metropolitan archbishops could make good the Pope's neglect, granting institution after an interval of six months. He summoned a national council of the imperial bishops to Paris in June 1811 to approve this solution, but to his fury the Council, although led by his own uncle Cardinal Fesch, refused. Even Fesch resisted the anti-papal rhetoric of the Emperor's agenda, which the bishops thought was too redolent of the Synod of Pistoia and the Civil Constitution. They would not act in defiance of the Pope, who must approve any decision of the Council, and even its agenda, before it could be acted upon. Fuming, Napoleon dissolved the Council, imprisoned some of its ringleaders, and instead put pressure on the bishops individually. Deprived of the moral backbone provided by mutual support, eighty-five of them eventually agreed that institution by the Metropolitan was acceptable. Napoleon reconvened the Council, which now accepted the proposal, subject to the Pope's approval.

Armed with this vote, Napoleon despatched a deputation of bishops to Savona. They emphasised the Council's deference to his authority, the Emperor's concern for souls in the vacant dioceses, and the weight of episcopal opinion in favour of the proposal. The Pope, always ready to doubt his own opinion, reassured by the Council's protestations of loyalty and cut off from any advisers other than the Emperor's stooges, at last agreed. He insisted, however, on rewriting the Council's decree as his own, and he excluded the bishoprics of the Papal States from the arrangement.

Napoleon was furious. The exclusion of the Papal States touched a raw nerve, and the Emperor foolishly insisted the Pope must surrender on these bishoprics too. Saved from his own mistaken concession by Napoleon's truculence, Pius now refused to budge at all. The stalemate continued, but Napoleon announced that the Concordat was abrogated, and the powers of the papacy suspended. He determined to deal with the Pope himself, and ordered that he be brought to Fontainebleau. This time, however, there would be no kneeling crowds, no demonstrations of loyalty. Dressed as an ordinary priest, his white satin slippers blackened with ink, the Pope was whisked away from Savona under cover of night on 9 June 1812. The twelve-day journey became a nightmare to rival the worst sufferings of Pius VI. *En route* the Pope developed a chronic urinary infection. Crossing the Alps the carriage had to stop every ten minutes to allow him to relieve himself. His doctor feared the worst, and the Pope was given the last sacraments.

He reached Fontainebleau more dead than alive, only to find that the Emperor had already set out for Russia. As summer turned to autumn the Pope convalesced, relentlessly badgered by the 'red' cardinals and court bishops, allowed no news of the outside world, no contact with any adviser. When the Emperor finally came to Fontainebleau on 19 January 1813, he came as a defeated man, his army dead in the snows of Russia. But Pius knew nothing of this, and on his own he was no match for Napoleon. For six days the Emperor alternately wheedled and stormed at the Pope – he is said, somewhat improbably, to have smashed crockery, to have shaken Pius by the buttons of his cassock. And eventually the Pope gave in, and signed a draft agreement on a scrap of paper for a concordat which totally surrendered the temporal power. The Pope would be sovereign of Rome no longer, and the seat of the papacy remained to be decided, for Napoleon planned to move the papacy to France. Bishops henceforth would be granted investiture by the metropolitans within six months of nomination if the Pope declined to act, the Papal States alone excepted. In return, the Pope would receive financial compensation for the surrender of the patrimony, and the 'black' cardinals would be restored to favour.

Pius immediately regretted this surrender, but Napoleon, ignoring the fact that it was a only a draft, had it proclaimed as an achieved concordat, and ordered the singing of the 'Te Deum' all over the empire. Pacca and Consalvi, released at last, rushed to Fontainebleau, unable to believe the appalling news. They found the Pope a broken man, haggard and guilt-ridden, lamenting that he had been 'defiled', bitter against the red cardinals who had 'dragged him to the table and made him sign'. With Consalvi restored as secretary of state, and Pacca adding stiffening to his spine, Pius rallied. He defied the advice of the majority of cardinals, and wrote to Napoleon in his own hand, repudiating the so-called 'Concordat of Fontainebleau', declaring that his conscience now revolted against it. He had signed out of 'human frailty, being only dust and ashes'.

Napoleon suppressed the Pope's letter, but the writing was now on the wall for him and his dreams of empire. In January 1814 he offered the Pope full restoration to Rome and a peace treaty. It was clear, however, that Napoleon was no longer in a position to deliver any such thing. The Pope moved to Savona, and then to Rome, the journey increasingly taking on the character of a triumph as he went. On 12 April, Napoleon abdicated. On 24 May the Pope's carriage reached the gates of Rome. He was welcomed by King Carlos IV of Spain: the horses were removed from the shafts, and thirty young men from the best families of Rome drew him in triumph to St Peter's.

The reconstruction of Europe which was finalised at the Congress of Vienna in 1815 restored to the papacy almost all the lands it had lost. The sufferings of two successive popes at the hands of the Revolution, and Pius VII's dignified resistance to Napoleon, now stood the institution he represented in good stead. The papal negotiator at the Congress was Cardinal Consalvi, a consummate statesman, and, though he failed to recover Avignon, he persuaded the powers that it was to their advantage to return the Legations and the Marches of Ancona to the Pope, along with the territory immediately around Rome. The policy of papal neutrality so rigorously maintained by Pius VII and Consalvi now paid off, and Britain and France welcomed a strong papal presence in central and northern Italy, to prevent Austrian monopoly in the peninsula.

This restoration of the Papal States is the single most important fact about the nineteenth-century papacy. For more than a thousand years, since the time of Pepin, the security of the papal office had been linked to the defence of the Patrimony of Peter. In the nineteenth century, however, that link took on a new and all-devouring importance. As pressure built up for the unification of Italy, the Papal States, dividing the peninsula and enclosing its natural capital, became more and more of an anomaly. The papacy became the largest single obstacle in the way of the national aspiration of the Italian people. In the light of the Napoleonic era, however, it was entirely natural that the popes should identify the defence of the Papal States with the free exercise of the papal ministry. On the lips of Napoleon the call for the Pope to lay down his temporal sovereignty and to rely solely on spiritual authority had been blatant code for the enslavement of the papacy to French imperial ambitions. Without his temporal power, Pius VII had been reduced to saying his prayers and mending his linen, and he had come within a whisker of signing away even his spiritual authority. If the Pope did not remain a temporal king, then it seemed he could no longer be the Church's chief bishop. That perception coloured the response of all the nineteenth-century popes to the modern world.

There was an immense work of reconstruction to be done. All over Europe the structure of the Church of the *ancien régime* lay in ruins. Napoleon's conquests in Germany had redrawn the map. The great prince–bishoprics on the left bank of the Rhine – the electors of Cologne, Trier and Mainz, the prince-bishops of Speyer and Worms – had been swept away or reduced to powerlessness, and in 1806 the Holy Roman empire itself ceased to be the ancient elective office which had begun with Charlemagne, and was wound up. Henceforth, the Emperor was merely the hereditary ruler of Austria. As a result of all this, there was a massive transfer of German lands and political influence from Catholic to Protestant hands. And everywhere the religious orders had been decimated, dioceses lay empty, seminaries closed, priestly vocations dried up, Church property confiscated, communications with Rome destroyed. Wherever French rule had prevailed, civil marriage, divorce, a religiously free press and religious toleration remained as abiding – and to the papacy obnoxious – reminders of the apostasy of the state. Pius' determination to set this to rights was signalled by his restoration of the Society of Jesus on 7 August 1814.

If the churches of Europe were to be revived, however, the Pope would need more than the Jesuits to help him. He had to have the support of the rulers of post-Napoleonic Europe. Deals would have to be struck. The nineteenth century was to be the age of concordats, as the popes bargained with the monarchies of Europe and beyond to secure freedom for the Church's work: with Bavaria and Sardinia in 1817, with Prussia and with the Upper Rhine Provinces in 1821, with

Hanover in 1824, with Belgium in 1827, with Switzerland in 1828 and again in 1845, with the Two Sicilies in 1834, and so on into the rest of the century, more than two dozen such agreements.

These concordats sometimes secured more for the Church than anyone expected. In Bavaria, the Pope got guarantees of free contact with the bishops, security for surviving Church endowments, the reopening of monasteries and the establishment of seminaries, Church censorship of books and educational rights in schools. But the consistent feature of most of these concordats was the growing control of secular rulers over the appointments of bishops. Secular rulers in Bavaria had never appointed the bishops, but after 1817 they did. The Revolution had taught the rulers of Europe that they could not rule without the help of the Church: bishops and priests were needed to preach obedience and contentment. Bishops and priests cost money, however, and, because the Church had lost its endowments in the Revolution, it needed state funding to pay its ministers. The state valued the clergy, but demanded the right to appoint the men it paid, and Rome had no choice but to agree, even when the governments were Protestant (as in Prussia). By 1829, no fewer than 555 of the 646 diocesan bishops of the Roman Catholic Church were appointed by the state – 113 in the Two Sicilies, 86 in France, 82 in Habsburg Germany, 67 in Sardinia and the Italian duchies, 61 in Spain and its possessions, 35 in Spanish America, 24 in Portugal, 9 in Brazil, 9 in Bavaria. Another 67, in the USA, Ireland, Prussian Germany, the Upper Rhine, Belgium and Switzerland were locally elected by cathedral chapters or some similar arrangement. The Pope, acting as sovereign of the Papal States, not as bishop of Rome, appointed seventy bishops. As pope, he appointed directly only twenty-four, in Russia, Greece and Albania.

This massive transfer of episcopal appointments to the state had of course been well under way before the Revolution, but the Revolution altered the terms on which it was taking place. In the high Middle Ages the reform papacy had struggled to destroy the system of 'proprietary churches', by which laymen had appointed bishops, and since the Second Lateran Council (1139) the 'normal' method of episcopal appointment had been election by the cathedral chapter. For financial reasons, the later medieval papacy, especially at Avignon, had slowly eroded this situation by the use of 'provisions', to capture more and more episcopal nominations for itself. Theoretically, however, capitular election remained normative, and from 1814 until the 1860s, wherever the popes were free to do so, they preferred capitular election to other methods of appointment. But many cathedral chapters had been swept away in the storm after 1789, and, where they were restored, the concordats often ignored or removed their electoral powers. In effect, the concordats, and state payment of bishops, were recreating the proprietary system.

In post-Napoleonic Europe, religion was allied with reaction. The principles of 1789 – liberty, fraternity, equality – were inescapably associated with the guillotine, the pagan 'religion of humanity', the destruction of the Church. Bishops and preachers tumbled over themselves to emphasise the common foundations of throne and altar, and censorship, imprisonment of radicals, suppression of democracy, all had the blessing of churchmen. The situation was worst in France under the morbidly religious Charles X, and especially in Spain under King Ferdinand VII, who reintroduced the Inquisition. This meant that after the Revolution of 1820 liberal opinion in Spain would be violently anti-religious, the Church fatally compromised by its identification with coercion and tyranny.

The papacy did not mindlessly endorse these trends. The conservative Pope Leo XII (1823–9), for example, outraged Spain by circumventing the crown and appointing 'vicars apostolic' (missionary bishops) for areas of Latin America like Colombia and Mexico which were in revolt, befriending in the process rebel leaders like Simon Bolivar. Leo was acting on the advice of Cardinal Consalvi, who took the view that if legitimate monarchs could exert their authority in such areas within a reasonable time (he allowed fifteen years) well and good. But the Church could not leave bishoprics vacant for ever, for in the meantime the country might be 'filled with Methodists, Presbyterians and new Sun-worshippers'. Pastoral necessity came before political alliances.[7]

Yet there were ideological as well as pragmatic forces at work to impel the papacy into alliance with the conservative monarchy. Catholicism in the age of Enlightenment had no place in its heart for the papacy. The Pope's spiritual authority was acknowledged, but minimised, and it was imagined in juridical or administrative terms. It belonged to the ordering of the Church, not to the essence of the faith. Reform-minded Catholics saw nothing wrong in the prince or the state placing restrictions on the interference of popes.

The Revolution changed this. State control of the Church might look rational and benign in Joseph II's Austria or Leopold's Tuscany. It looked altogether different after the Terror, the government-induced schism of the Constitutional Church, and the attempts of Napoleon to turn Church and Pope into instruments of empire. Reforms based on reason now began to look like the disastrous blundering of a sorcerer's apprentice, unleashing forces which could not be controlled. All over Europe, thinkers reflecting on the solvent and destructive power of naked reason began to rediscover the value of ancient institutions, established authorities, tradition.

In 1819, the Sardinian Ambassador to St Petersburg, Count Joseph de Maistre, published his treatise *Du Pape*. Born out of an almost paranoid reflection on the horror of the Revolution, De Maistre's book argues for the absolute necessity of the papal office as the paradigm of all monarchic power. Historically, he claimed, the papacy had created the empire and the monarchies; it was the source from which all other authorities flowed. Since the sixteenth century, however, human society has been undermined by a rebellious questioning of legitimate authority. The symbolic focus of that challenge was first the Reformation, and now the Revolution. Once start to question, and there is no stopping: the stability of human society demanded the underpinning of an absolute authority. Catholicism provided just such an underpinning, and Catholicism needed an infallible pope: 'There can be no public morality and no national character without religion; there can be no Christianity without Catholicism; there can be no Catholicism without the Pope; there can be no Pope without the sovereignty that belongs to him.'[8] De Maistre exalted the papacy to provide a basis for conservative political society. He deplored Gallicanism and Josephism, not because he wanted to minimise royal authority, but because attempts to limit papal authority unwittingly subverted royal authority too. Yet, despite the political motivation of De Maistre's theory, his teaching had immense religious impact. As the century unfolded, the exaltation of the papacy as the heart of Catholicism, 'Ultramontanism' as it was called, would increasingly dominate Catholic thinking.

And here, once again, the Revolution helped. All over Europe, the Revolution destroyed the independent institutions of the clergy, and subjected them to the control of the state. Stripped of the local privileges, customs and rights which had given them autonomy, the clergy increasingly looked to Rome for protection. The Revolution had also swept away the great prince—bishoprics of Germany, the strongholds of episcopal resistance to papal power. Europe had now only one prince—bishop, the Pope, and he stood increasingly high as the visible centre of a Church which felt less local, more universal.

As ruler of the Papal States, however, king as well as bishop, the Pope himself embodied the combination of throne and altar. The government of the Papal States earned the popes the reputation of being the most reactionary prince in Europe. Consalvi had achieved the return of the most prosperous part of the patrimony, across the Apennines on the Adriatic, the Legations and the Marches, which included Ferrara, Bologna and Ravenna and the port of Ancona, in return for promises of a modernisation of papal government there. The promise was necessary. For twenty years the Legations had been out of papal control, and had experienced the modernising force of French government. Antiquated legal systems had been replaced by the Napoleonic Code, the civil service had been opened for the first time to laymen, local communities had been allowed representative government. This experience permanently altered the political consciousness of the people of the Legations. The areas round Rome, by contrast, were still archaic, ruled by priests, with no provision for elected lay involvement. To attempt to return the Legations to this mode of government would be folly, and Consalvi had undertaken to let the French innovations stand insofar as they were compatible with canon law.

In 1816 he introduced a modified French system of administration for the whole of the Papal States. They were divided into seventeen delegations, ruled by clerical delegates (cardinals in the case of the Legations) but assisted by nominated committees of lay people. All but the highest levels of the civil service were open to laymen, but they wore cassocks at work. This system pleased nobody. It was too brutally centralised and not clerical enough for the *ultras* in Rome, it put a ceiling on lay promotion within the system, and it made no provision for elected local bodies. In the Legations, in particular, it was a constant source of friction. Hostility to clerical government, and to the papacy which required it, grew.

Things might not have been so bad if that clerical government had not also been inefficient and reactionary. Consalvi's modest reforms were frustrated at every turn by vested interests, and the realism and moderation which he brought to all he did was swept away after the election of Annibale della Genga as Pope Leo XII (1823–9). Della Genga, a sickly sixty-three year old crippled by chronic haemorrhoids, disapproved of Pius VII's and Consalvi's policies, and wanted a stronger, more religious and more conservative regime in papal territory. He had been elected by the *zelanti*, the 'religious' cardinals, who were tired of seeing papal policy dictated by political prudence, and who wanted strong spiritual leadership. In 1814 della Genga had been humiliatingly sacked by Consalvi from the papal diplomatic service, after a spectacular row over his incompetence in negotiations over the return of Avignon. He now had his revenge, and Consalvi was dismissed as secretary of state. Leo came to appreciate Consalvi's brilliance before the Cardinal's death, but the reconciliation came too late for the Pope to derive much benefit from his political savvy.

Leo was a contrast with Consalvi in every way. Pious, puritanical (though he shocked the cardinals by his passion for shooting birds in the Vatican gardens) and confrontational, he lacked political realism. Naples had long owed the papacy the feudal tribute of a palfrey (saddle-horse). The feudal dependency of Naples on the Pope was a sore point, and the palfrey had not been presented for decades. Consalvi had wisely commuted it for a cash payment raised by a tax on clerical salaries. Leo demanded the palfrey.

The same lack of realism displayed itself in the internal government of the Papal States. Gaol sentences were introduced for people caught playing games on Sundays and feast days, tight-fitting dresses were forbidden for women. Encores and ovations in theatres were forbidden, since Leo and his advisers thought they provided the occasion for displays of seditious political feeling. For the same reason actors ad-libbing lines on current affairs were liable to imprisonment. The Roman bars were forbidden to serve alcohol, which instead had to be bought at grills fitted in the street, a disastrous and deeply unpopular measure which led to a huge increase in public drunkenness.

The Jews, liberated by the Revolution, became a particular target of the reaction. They were ordered back into ghettos, which were enlarged for the purpose and fitted with walls and lockable gates, and they were forbidden to own real estate. Three hundred Roman Jews were required to attend special Christian sermons every week, and the hiring of Christian proxies was forbidden. Business transactions between Jews and Christians were forbidden. The subsequent exodus of wealthy Jews from the Papal States worsened the Pope's already chronic economic problems.

A pope is no better than his advisers, and Leo's assistants within the Curia left a good deal to be desired. Cardinal Ravorolla, sent as legate to Ravenna, created a tyranny so extreme that he became a grim figure of fun. He closed inns, banned gambling, required any-one out at night after dark to carry a lantern before them, clamped down on freedom of speech, introduced imprisonment without trial, and installed a great iron-bound chest outside his residence into which people could put anonymous denunciations of their neigh-bours. In the south, Cardinal Palotta introduced martial law to deal with the huge numbers of brigands, abolished courts on the grounds that the judges might be intimidated, imposed huge fines on villages where bandits were discovered, and in 1824 introduced a decree per-mitting the summary execution of brigands within twenty-four hours of arrest. His policies were so hated that he was forced to resign within a month, and the local brigands paid for Masses of thanksgiving to be sung.

The extent to which the papacy had become locked into the alliance of throne and altar became clear with the election of the aus-tere Camaldolese monk, Dom Mauro Cappellari, as Pope Gregory XVI (1831–46). Cappellari, former Abbot of Gregory the Great's monastery on the Coelian Hill, had emerged as a compromise pope after a long and deadlocked conclave, in which the Spanish crown's veto had been exercised against one of the favoured candidates. He was in many ways a promising choice. A learned theologian, he was also an experienced administrator with a broad view of the Church and its needs. For the previous six years he had served as Cardinal Prefect of Propaganda, with immediate responsibility for the affairs of the Church in Great Britain, Ireland, the Low Countries, Prussia, Scandinavia, Africa, Asia, Oceania and the Americas. His choice of papal name was a gesture of homage both to Gregory XV, who had founded Propaganda, and to Gregory the Great, the first and greatest of missionary popes. He had been born in Venetia, in Austrian terri-tory, and was known for his conservative views. Predictably, his elec-tion was greeted with delight by the Austrian Chancellor, Metter-nich, though there is no reason to think Austria pulled any strings to have him elected.

Gregory's view of the papal office was both exalted and strictly monarchical. In 1799, the year of Pius VI's death in prison at Valence, he had published a work defiantly entitled *Il Trionfo della Sante Sede* ('The Triumph of the Holy See'). This was a vigorous attack on Josephism and Jansenist Episcopalism, arguing that the Church was a monarchy, independent of the civil power, and that the Pope is infallible when discharging his teaching office as chief pastor. The book made no great stir when it was first published, but it was rapidly reissued in a number of languages after his election, and it signalled to anyone who cared to read it a stern and uncompromisingly authoritarian cast of mind, and a view of the papacy which would brook no challenges.

Gregory's election came at a moment of grave political crisis. Radical discontent had been growing throughout Italy over the previous fifteen years, focused on a widespread secret organisation known as the Carbonari (Charcoal Burners). These societies were allied to Freemasonry, and were dedicated to the pursuit of political liberty and the unification of Italy. There was a strong strain of anticlericalism in them, though many clergy and devout Catholic laymen were also involved. The Carbonari had emerged as a formidable force in Naples in the wake of the Spanish Revolution of 1820, and had spread also to Piedmontese territory: they were ruthlessly suppressed by Austria.

The Revolution of 1830 in France, which overthrew the reactionary Bourbon regime of Charles X and replaced it with the 'bourgeois monarchy' of Louis Philippe, reactivated radical forces in many parts of Europe. The new regime issued a statement that it would not tolerate intervention in Italian affairs by other powers – a clear signal that it would hamper Austrian repression of any risings. By the summer of 1831 much of central Italy was in revolt, seeking the ejection of foreign powers and the creation of a unified Italian state. Out of these ferments, Giuseppe Mazzini's 'Young Italy' movement, and the national independence movement known as the Risorgimento, would emerge. More immediately, and within three weeks of Gregory's election, many of the cities of the Papal States had been occupied by rebel forces.

Gregory acted decisively. Ignoring the French non-intervention decree, he called for the help of Austrian troops to suppress the revolts. It was a fateful moment for the papacy, in which it threw its lot in with the big battalions, against a growing Italian desire for liberty and self-determination. The aftermath in the Papal States was disastrous. The papal prisons filled up, and liberal exiles schooled Europe in anti-papalism. The Secretary of State, Cardinal Benetti, raised a volunteer police force, in effect arming one element of the population against another, and the papal revenues were devoured by the machinery of repression. Gregory XVI was forced to negotiate a loan from the Rothschilds (which had at least the incidental benefit of easing conditions somewhat for the Jews). By his death the public debt was more than sixty million scudi.

These experiences determined the course of Gregory's pontificate, and his government became a by-word for obscurantist repression. Suspicious of all innovation, he would have nothing to do even with the railways ('infernal machines'), and the clergy and clerical concerns continued to dominate the secular administration of the Papal States. But the impact went far beyond the government of the Papal States. All over Europe, there were Catholics who had come to reject the alliance of throne and altar as a formula for tyranny.

In France, the priest Felicité de Lamennais had moved from an Ultramontanism derived from the teaching of De Maistre and a hatred of Enlightenment rationalism to a radical critique of the France of Charles X. To Lamennais the royalist church of France in the 1820s, staffed by state-appointed poodle bishops ('tonsured lackeys') was no better than the impotent state churches of eighteenth-century Europe, or even revolutionary France. For all its lip-service to Catholicism, the state, with its control of the episcopate, its restrictions on contact with the papacy and its monopoly of religious education, was manipulating religion for its own purposes, failing to allow it the freedom of expression and action which was fundamental to the Gospel. In the persisting Gallicanism of France, Lamennais saw not an ally of the Church but its opposite. The kings had had their day. To be itself, the Church must embrace the liberty which the Revolution had proclaimed, demand control of its own officers and its own affairs: 'The Church is being suffocated beneath the weight of the fetters which the temporal power has put upon it; and liberty which has been called for in the name of atheism must now be demanded in the name of God.'9 The Church, led by an infallible pope, must baptise the Revolution, and side with the people against the forces of reaction and revolution. Lamennais and his supporters launched a newspaper, *L'Avenir* ('The Future'), which had the slogan

'God and freedom' as its masthead, and which campaigned for the separation of throne and altar, a 'Free Church in a Free State'.

Lamennais was to a large extent inspired by events in Belgium, Poland and Ireland. In all these countries, Catholic populations lived under non-Catholic regimes: Poland partitioned between Orthodox Russia and Protestant Prussia; Belgium ruled by the Protestant King William I in the interests of Holland; Ireland ruled from Westminster. In such circumstances, 'throne and altar' politics were a recipe for oppression, and Catholics allied themselves with liberals in a common struggle. In Rome, such alliances appeared 'monstrous', as Cardinal Albani described the co-operation between Belgian Catholics and liberals. Freedom of religion meant freedom for irreligion: nothing good could come from slogans coined in the hell-hole of revolution. That perception led to the disastrous alienation of the papacy from Catholic aspiration in much of Europe, and the papacy had difficulty coming to terms with the successful Belgian Revolution of 1831, where Catholics accepted the separation of Church and state.

The great papal failure was in Poland. Since 1825, Tsar Nicholas I had been systematically undermining Catholicism in Poland, attempting to force Eastern-rite Catholics ('Uniates') into union with the Russian Orthodox Church, hindering contacts between Rome and the Latin-rite bishops, and deposing the Primate of Poland in favour of an elderly government stooge. Rome had protested, but bad communications and the Pope's overriding commitment to the support of monarchy meant that its protests were half-hearted and ineffective. In November 1830 Poland rose against Russia and briefly established a provisional government. By the autumn of 1831, however, the rebellion had been crushed, and Russia began a brutal campaign of reprisal without parallel anywhere else in Europe. In June 1832, while Poland was groaning under this savagery, Gregory issued the brief *Superiori Anno*, condemning the revolt, denouncing those who 'under cover of religion have set themselves against the legitimate power of princes', and warning the bishops to do their utmost 'against impostors and propagators of new ideas'.[10]

Gregory's heartless response to the agony of Poland was conditioned by the rebellion of the Carbonari on his own doorstep. To appear to condone rebellion against Russian misrule would be to legitimate rebellion in Italy. His rejection of liberal values received more considered expression in August 1832, in the encyclical letter

Mirari Vos, directed against Lamennais and the *L'Avenir* group. Lamennais' pugnacious attacks on the conservative alliance of throne and altar in France had been heightened by the July Revolution of 1830. He called on the Church to abandon nostalgia for the Bourbons and to join with the people in creating a new and freer world. These sentiments outraged the French bishops, and episcopal opposition to *L'Avenir* grew. Unwisely, Lamennais decided to suspend publication and to appeal to Rome for support and vindication. They would go 'to consult the Lord at Shiloh', to prostrate themselves at the feet of the Vicar of Christ: 'O Father, condescend to look down upon some of the least of your children, who are accused of being rebels against your infallible and mild authority . . . if even a single one of their thoughts deviates from yours, they disavow it, they abjure it. You are the rule of what they teach; never, no never, have they known any other.'[11]

Lamennais' extravagantly pro-papal writings had made him a popular figure at Rome under Leo XII: there had even been rumours of a cardinal's hat. But Lamennais had long since moved away from the papalist version of throne-and-altar legitimism which had first caught Roman attention. The decision to appeal to the papacy at this point was suicidal, given Gregory XVI's track-record and known opinions, and it would ultimately lead to Lamennais' condemnation and his eventual abandonment of Catholicism. He arrived in Rome at the beginning of 1832 against a background of frantic lobbying by the bishops and the French government, urging the Pope to give no comfort to such rebellious spirits. Gregory received Lamennais and his colleagues cordially, but studiously avoided any discussion of religious matters with them. He established a theological commission to report on their teaching, a report which formed the basis for the encyclical *Mirari Vos*.

The encyclical, when it finally came, was an out-and-out condemnation of everything the *L'Avenir* group stood for. Gregory repudiated 'the poisonous spring of indifferentism that has flowed from that absurd and erroneous doctrine or rather delirium, that freedom of conscience is to be claimed and defended for all men'. He denounced the 'detestable and insolent malice' of those who 'agitate against and upset the rights of rulers' and who seek 'to enslave the nations under the mask of liberty'. The Pope was particularly exercised by Lamennais' suggestion that the Church was in need of restoration and regeneration to meet the challenges of a new age. The Church, he insisted, 'has been instructed by Jesus Christ and his Apostles and taught by the Holy Spirit . . . It would therefore be completely absurd and supremely insulting to suggest that the Church stands in need of restoration and regeneration . . . as though she could be exposed to exhaustion, degradation or other defects of this kind.'[12]

Mirari Vos is a landmark document. Though its violent tone and resolute opposition to any hint of liberalism were not entirely new – Pius VIII had condemned Freemasonry in much the same tone – Gregory's encyclical set the register and to some extent the agenda for the key utterances of his successor, Pius IX. The papacy from now on was locked into an attitude of suspicious repudiation of modern political developments, and the current of ideas which underlay them. Gregory's hostility to the campaign for a 'Free Church in Free State' which underlay most liberal Catholic work on behalf of the Church coloured the rest of his pontificate. He was therefore less than supportive to liberal Catholics like Lamennais' former colleague Count Charles Montalambert and the French bishops who agitated for greater freedom of education in France in the 1840s, and he put up with the government's expulsion of the Jesuits from France in 1845, despite its disastrous impact on Catholic schools.

Elsewhere, the advent of liberal regimes more or less hostile to the Church moved the Pope willy-nilly towards the sort of independent action advocated by liberal Catholics. Throughout the 1830s and early 1840s Gregory was confronted by governmental action in Europe and beyond which threatened the liberties of the Church. His response was characterised at least as much by confrontation as co-operation. The most significant of these confrontations was the Cologne church struggle of 1837.

Prussian custom dictated that in marriages between Catholics and Protestants the sons took the religion of the father, the daughters the religion of the mother. The Catholic Church wanted all children brought up as Catholics. It would not permit Catholic priests to preside at marriages unless they got a guarantee to this effect. This made life impossible for Catholic women. As prefect of propaganda Gregory had been instrumental in the evolution of a compromise, promulgated by Pius VIII in 1830, which forbade priests to bless such weddings, but allowed them to attend as observers.

In practice, the German bishops co-operated with the Protestant government in stretching this papal directive, and they allowed priests to take an active part in the ceremonies. Rome was not informed. In 1837, however, the new Archbishop of Cologne, Clemens August Droste zu Vischering, announced that henceforth the papal directive would be followed to the letter. This was a red rag to an already anti-Catholic government, and in November 1837 the Archbishop was arrested and imprisoned without trial. Gregory issued a vehement protest, the conflict spread, and other bishops were suspended and arrested. The breakdown of relations between Church and government was healed only by the accession of a new king in Prussia, the romantically inclined Frederick William IV, whose fondness for the Middle Ages made him kindlier disposed to the Catholic Church. Gregory agreed to a compromise which involved the effective retirement of Clemens August. The conflict, however, served to raise Catholic consciousness all over Germany, hardened Catholics' sense of confessional identity, and led to a vast expansion of the Catholic press and the mobilisation of Catholic opinion. It also struck a death-blow at the remaining vestiges of Josephinism. A handful of anti-papal Catholics broke away to form a patriotic 'German Catholic Church' as a result of the Cologne struggle, but this served only to highlight the fact that a new and less docile Catholic identity had formed around loyalty to papal directives. Ultramontanism was no longer a theory, but was taking flesh in the life of the Church.

Outside Europe, too, the needs of the Church and the wishes of the monarchies came into conflict. Gregory cared passionately about Catholic missionary activity, and was not prepared to allow deference to governments to hamper the work of evangelisation. In 1831 he offended Spain by publishing the bull *Sollicitudo Ecclesiarum*, in which he formalised the policy of working with *de facto* rebel governments in Latin America and elsewhere. Between 1831 and 1840, in co-operation with revolutionary republican governments, whose principles he deplored, he filled all the vacant sees in Spanish America.

Gregory had a low opinion of the effects of state patronage in the Americas and the Far East. He condemned slavery and the slave trade in 1839, and backed Propaganda's campaign for the ordination of native clergy, in the face of Portuguese racism. His disapproval of the Portuguese misuse of the *padroado* (crown control of the Church) went further. In 1834 he subverted the *padroado* in India by establishing a series of apostolic vicariates, whose bishops were directly answerable to Rome, not to Portugal. In 1838 he suspended four *padroado* bishoprics in India and absorbed them into the new vicariates, and he correspondingly reduced the jurisdiction of the Archbishop of Goa. All this added to the growing focus of Church life on Rome. In the course of his pontificate Gregory created more than seventy new dioceses and vicariates (including ten for the USA and four for Canada) and appointed 195 missionary bishops. More and more extra-European churches owed their organisation and leadership to the papacy rather than to a colonial power. The world stature of the papacy grew.

III   Pio Nono: The Triumph of Ultramontanism

The cardinals meeting in Conclave to elect Gregory XVI's successor in June 1846 had a stark choice before them. They could continue Gregory's repudiation of liberal Catholicism and his policies of repression and confrontation with Italian political aspiration, by electing his Secretary of State, Cardinal Lambruschini, or they could seek a more conciliatory and open-minded pope. They chose the latter course, and elected the relatively unknown and, at fifty-five, unusually young Cardinal Giovanni Maria Mastai-Ferretti, who took the name Pius IX (1846–78). Mastai-Ferretti was a glamorous candidate. He was an ardent and emotional man (prone to epileptic fits when younger) with a gift for friendship and a track-record of generosity even towards anti-clericals and Carbonari. He was a patriot, who was known to have been critical of the reactionary rule of Gregory XVI in the Papal States, who disliked the Austrian presence in Italy, who used phrases like 'this Italian nation' and so was widely assumed to support the unification of Italy. Gregory XVI recognised his abilities, but distrusted him: even Mastai-Ferretti's cats, he declared, were liberals.

Pio Nono (as he was universally called) quickly justified the expectations raised by his election. He set up a commission to introduce railways into the Papal States, installed gas street-lighting in Rome, set up an agricultural institute to improve productivity and provide advice to farmers, introduced tariff reform to help trade, abolished the requirement for Jews to attend Christian sermons every week and admitted them to a share in the papal charities. He won golden opinions because of his edifying poverty (he had to borrow his travel money to the Conclave) and because as pope he immediately and very unusually established himself as a pastor, preaching, confirming children, visiting schools and hospitals, distributing communion in obscure city churches and chapels.

Above all, he introduced a measure of political reform. One of the earliest acts of his papacy was to declare an amnesty for former revolutionaries in the Papal States. Conservative Europe was horrified, and Metternich, who had been appalled by Pio Nono's election, predicted disaster. A liberal pope, he declared, was an impossibility, and Pio Nono was a fool to behave like one, for liberal reforms could in the end only mean the destruction of the Papal States. He was soon to be proved right. Meanwhile, Pio Nono went ahead with reform. In 1847 he introduced a consultative assembly with lay representatives to help govern the Papal States. When Austria occupied Ferrara, the Pope threatened Metternich with excommunication, told him Austria's presence in Italy could do no good, and secured the withdrawal of Austrian troops.

The Pope was in fact uneasy about all this, worrying about democratic concessions in the government of the Papal States which might give laymen unacceptable influence in spiritual matters and usurp the authority of priests. He was carried along with the tide of change, however, half approving, half fearful that to hold back might provoke a wave of hatred against the Church. And, whatever his private reservations, the Pope became the darling of Europe, congratulated by Protestant statesmen, celebrated in London, Berlin, New York as a model ruler. In Italy hopes for a federation of Italian states, with the Pope as president, grew. Mazzini wrote an open letter from England to tell him he was the most important man in Italy and the hopes of the people were in his hands, nationalist crowds chanted 'Viva Italia! Viva Pio Nono!'

Disillusion came in 1848, the year of revolutions all over Europe. In Rome, the Pope responded to the dangerous revolutionary fervour by establishing an elected municipal government, and in March agreed a new constitution for the Papal States with an elected chamber capable of vetoing papal policy. As the demand for the expulsion of Austria from Italy turned into a war, more and more Italians treated it as a Crusade, and called on the Pope to lead it. On 29 April 1848, Pius made a speech designed to clarify the nature of papal policy towards Italy. It was a douche of icy water on the overheated enthusiasm which had surrounded his first two years as pope. As father of all the faithful, he declared, he could take no part in making war on a Catholic nation: he would send no troops against Austria. He condemned the idea of a federal Italy led by the papacy, urging Italians to remain faithful to their princes.

This statement, in effect a clear return to the policy of Gregory XVI, provoked a universal sense of betrayal. Overnight, from being the most popular man in Italy, he became the most hated. Rome became increasingly ungovernable, and in November 1848 his lay Prime Minister, Pellegrino Rossi, was murdered on the steps of the Cancelleria. The Pope fled. Disguised as an ordinary priest, he left Rome by night on 24 November, and took refuge at Gaeta in Neapolitan territory. Rome erupted into revolution, and Garibaldi and Mazzini established themselves at the head of a fiercely anti-clerical republican regime. From Gaeta, Pio Nono called on the Catholic powers to restore him, and in July 1849 French troops duly took possession of Rome on his behalf. He himself re-entered Rome in April 1850. He never recovered from his exile of 1848, and for the rest of his life remained convinced that political concessions to democracy merely fuelled the fires of revolution. The liberal honeymoon was over.

For the next twenty years, Pio Nono's position as ruler of the Papal States depended entirely on the presence of French and Austrian troops to suppress rebellion. The Christian world was treated to the spectacle of the Father of all the Faithful seated on bayonets, and ruling, rather ineptly, 3,000,000 subjects, most of whom wanted to be rid of him. Leadership of the cause of Italian unity passed to the Piedmontese, under King Victor Emmanuel II. Pio Nono admired Victor Emmanuel, and found it hard to restrain his pride and delight at news of his victories over the Austrians. But the Piedmontese government at Turin, and its premier Cavour, pursued a systematically secularist policy, and through the 1850s introduced a series of hostile measures designed to reduce the influence of the Church. In 1854, all monasteries and convents in Piedmontese territory, except for a handful of nursing and teaching orders, were suppressed. This radical anti-clericalism, harking back to Josephinism and to the Civil Constitution, persuaded Pio Nono that the Risorgimento was hopelessly atheistic, a reincarnation of the spirit of 1789. Italy was witnessing an apocalyptic struggle between the forces of good, led by himself, and of evil, led by Turin.

The temporal power of the Pope over the Papal States was central to Pio Nono's religious vision. The Patrimony of Peter was 'the seamless robe of Jesus Christ', committed to each pope as a sacred trust, as the guarantee and defence of the Pope's universal spiritual ministry. The heroic resistance of Pius VII dominated Pio Nono's imagination, and those of his advisers. The absorption of papal territory into a united Italy therefore seemed to him a device of the devil to undermine the papacy itself. The issue came to a head in 1860, when the Legations and the Marches of Ancona were annexed to the kingdom of Piedmont, and the Papal States, reduced by two-thirds, shrank to a narrow strip of land on the western coast of Italy. The Pope refused to accept the loss of these provinces, and they were bravely but hopelessly defended by a volunteer international brigade, recruited from devout Catholics all over Europe. (Pio Nono had been doubtful about the Irish volunteers at first, because he feared the effects on Irishmen of the ready availability of cheap Italian wine.) Throughout the 1860s, as international pressure mounted on him to come to terms with the reduction and eventual eclipse of the temporal power, he remained serenely stubborn. As 'Vicar of a Crucified God' he was prepared to suffer, but never to surrender. If necessary he would take to the catacombs: God would vindicate him.

The conflict between the pope's perceptions and those of the secular world were starkly revealed in the late 1850s by the Mortara affair. Edgardo Mortara was a Jewish boy whose family lived in the papal territory of Bologna. When he was still only one, the child fell dangerously ill, and a Christian maidservant secretly baptised him by sprinkling water from a bucket while his parents were out of the room. When news of her action leaked out the Inquisition investigated, since it was contrary to Catholic law for a Christian – which the boy now technically was – to be brought up as a Jew. Eventually the six-year-old Edgardo was forcibly taken away from his parents, and placed under the direct protection of the pope in Rome. Despite the serious misgivings of many Catholics, including the pope's own Secretary of State, the appeals of the family, of the Roman Jews, the intervention of the Emperor of Austria and Napoleon III of France, and the protests of the anti-clerical press, Pio Nono resolutely rejected all pleas. He made a pet of Edgardo, escorting him into public audiences, playing hide and seek with him under his cloak. The pope's French protectors were so acutely embarrassed by the whole affair that the French ambassador seriously discussed with Cavour the possibility of kidnapping Mortara and returning him to his parents. For his part, the pope interpreted all criticism of his action as godless persecution, a veiled attack on religious conviction, and told the child 'My boy, you have cost me dearly, and I have suffered a great deal because of you'. The whole world, both the powerful and the powerless, he declared 'tried to steal this boy away from me' but 'by the grace of God I have seen my duty, and I would rather cut off all my fingers than shrink from it'. Mortara never returned to his family, but eventually became a happy enough Catholic priest, and lived on into the 1930s. His case was both a human tragedy and a demonstration of the gulf which had opened up between the thought-world of the papacy, and the secular liberal values which were now the common moral currency of Europe, even for many Catholics.

Paradoxically, the increasingly beleaguered position of the papacy in Italy added to its religious prestige. There were of course many Catholics, including some cardinals and curial clergy, who saw that the temporal power of the Pope was not in fact vital to his role as a spiritual leader, provided that conclaves and episcopal appointments were free from external pressures, that the Pope had uncensored communication with the local hierarchies, and that the Italian church was freed from harassment by the anti-clerical regime at Turin. Liberal Catholics in France, Belgium, Germany and England groaned at the confrontation between Pio Nono and the Risorgimento, and longed for an accommodation between the Church and political reality. Given the history of the papacy over the previous half-century, however, and the blatant animosity of Turin towards the Church, it was by no means obvious that such an accommodation was in the Church's best interests.

And there were many for whom the struggle in Italy was a microcosm of a greater confrontation between the anti-Christian spirit of the Enlightenment and of the Revolution on the one hand and God's revealed truth on the other. For them, Pio Nono's policy was not political obscurantism, but the last heroic stand of Christian civilisation against the forces of atheism and rebellion against God. The convert Anglican Henry Edward Manning, future Cardinal Archbishop of Westminster, declared that the temporal power of the Pope was the sign of 'the freedom, the independence, the sovereignty of the kingdom of God upon earth'. It was because the Papal States were 'the only spot of ground on which the Vicar of Christ can set the sole of his foot in freedom' that 'they who would drive the Incarnation off the face of the earth hover about it to wrest it from his hands'.[13] In a sermon at the requiem Mass for the Irish volunteers who had fallen in defence of the Papal States in 1860, Manning declared that the dead soldiers were martyrs for the faith; identifying the cause of the temporal power with 'the independence of the Universal Church', he denounced the attack on it as a 'falling away from the supernatural order, and a return to (merely) natural society', the end of Christendom.[14]

Manning was the spokesman for a new and ardent Ultramontanism which held the Pope in almost mystical reverence. This devout papalism was just one aspect of a devotional revolution within Catholicism, away from the sober decorum of eighteenth-century religion towards a more emotional and colourful religion of the heart, a new emphasis on ceremonial, on the saints, on the Virgin Mary. The reform Catholicism of the previous century had frowned on and played down such manifestations of popular religious feeling. Nineteenth-century Catholicism welcomed them. The romantic idealisation of the Middle Ages which was a feature of many of the artistic movements of the century led to a revived interest in the ancient Roman liturgy, in plainchant, in sacramental symbolism. In the 1830s Dom Prosper Guéranger revived the Benedictine life in France at the abbey of Solesmes, and led a reaction against the eighteenth-century rationalisation of liturgy advocated by French Jansenists. Guéranger pioneered the rediscovery of Gregorian chant, and adopted the Roman liturgy as the essential focus of a renewed liturgical life in the Church. Before he died, every diocese in France had adopted the Roman missal in place of the older Gallican books. Ultramontane piety was achieving a Roman uniformity which Trent had failed to impose.

Ultramontane piety, however, was not confined to the transformation of the liturgy. The cult of Mary blossomed, for this was the beginning of a great age of Marian apparitions. In 1830 Catherine Labouré experienced a vision of the Virgin crowned with stars which was popularised in the form of the so-called 'Miraculous Medal'. The cult was associated with the doctrine of Mary's perfect sinlessness, or Immaculate Conception, and the medal carried the prayer 'O Mary Conceived without Original Sin, Pray for us who have recourse to thee'. In 1846 two shepherd children in Savoy, at La Salette, had a vision of a beautiful weeping lady, who lamented the desecration of Sunday, the prevalence of swearing and blasphemy, and the spread of drunkenness. Revelations, miracles and healings followed, and a pilgrimage to the 'holy mountain of La Salette' became popular. In 1858 La Salette was eclipsed by the Marian visions of Bernadette Soubirous at the grotto of Massabielle, at Lourdes in the French Pyrenees, round which the greatest Christian pilgrimage site in the modern world rapidly developed.

This blossoming of the cult of Mary was intimately linked to growing loyalty to the papacy. Gregory XVI actively encouraged devotion to the Immaculate Conception, and in 1854 Pio Nono, who attributed his own recovery from epilepsy to the intercession of Mary, solemnly defined the once contentious doctrine of Mary's Immaculate Conception as part of the faith of Catholics. This definition was a momentous step in the development of the papal office, for although the Pope had consulted bishops beforehand, and the definition was widely desired, the doctrine was eventually proclaimed on the Pope's sole authority. The Pope's chamberlain, Monsignor Talbot, remarked that 'the most important thing is not the new dogma itself, but the way in which it is proclaimed'.[15] Heaven evidently approved, for four years later, at Lourdes, the visionary lady identified herself to Bernadette Soubirous by declaring, 'I am the Immaculate Conception.'

The same direct link between popular piety and papal authority was evident in the cult of the Sacred Heart of Jesus. This devotion had been particularly loathed by eighteenth-century Jansenists, who denounced it as 'cardiolatry'. In the nineteenth century it became the focus of an ardent devotion to the human nature of Christ, but it was never without a political dimension too. During the Vendée Rising in the 1790s it had been identified with popular Catholic repudiation of the Revolution, and its popularity among Ultramontane Catholics always carried this association. Pio Nono extended the Feast of the Sacred Heart of Jesus to the universal calendar of the Church in 1856, and in 1864 he beatified the seventeenth-century visionary who had first popularised it. In 1861, after the fall of Romagna and the Marches, Jesuits launched an 'apostolate of prayer' to secure the 'mystical subjugation' of the whole world to the Sacred Heart. The political dimension of the cult was well in evidence when in 1869 the Archbishop of Malines dedicated Belgium, with its liberal constitution, to the Sacred Heart, and when in 1873 Catholic deputies to the French National Assembly launched the first of a series of penitential pilgrimages of reparation to the Sacred Heart. The Sacré Coeur basilica in Montmartre was to become the focus of regular symbolic gestures of this sort. In 1876, Cardinal Manning made the links between the papacy and the cult of the Sacred Heart explicit in his best-selling sermon collection, *The Glories of the Sacred Heart*, where he presented Pio Nono's political difficulties as a sacramental embodiment of the pierced and suffering humanity of Jesus. The Pope, stripped of his 'temporal glory', was the living icon of the Sacred Heart.[16]

And indeed in the age of cheap popular print and the emergence of the mass media, the Pope himself became, quite literally, a popular icon. Catholic households from Africa to the Americas were as likely to display a picture of the Pope as a crucifix or a statue of the Virgin, and the face of Pio Nono was better known than that of any pope in history. Cheap books and mass-produced holy pictures spread and standardised the culture of Ultramontane Catholicism. In 1869 a book describing the first 200 miracles at Lourdes sold 800,000 copies. Lourdes itself was the product of the railway age, its pilgrims funnelled in from all over Europe and its offshore islands by steam packet and steam engine, in numbers and at speeds unimaginable in any previous century. The same mass transport brought pilgrims flocking to Rome to see and venerate the Pope, and, as his long pontificate stretched out, to celebrate his anniversaries.

This process was assisted by the charm of the Pope himself. Even his critics, exasperated by his stubbornness and unimpressed by his modest intellect, admitted that it was impossible to dislike him. He was genial, unpretentious, wreathed in clouds of snuff, always laughing. His sense of the absurd sometimes got the better of him, as when some earnest Anglican clergymen begged his blessing, and he teasingly pronounced over them the prayer for the blessing of incense, 'May you be blessed by Him in whose honour you are to be burned,' or when he scrawled at the bottom of a photograph of himself presented by a nun for an autograph the words of Christ in the storm, 'Fear not, for it is I.'[17] Above all, it was his human decency which impressed most, the open heart which made him exclaim on hearing of the death of his arch-enemy Cavour, 'Ah, how he loved his coun

try, that Cavour, that Cavour. That man was truly Italian. God will
assuredly pardon him, as we pardon him.'[18] The person of the Pope
became part of the fabric of Catholic piety, and was enshrined even
in the hymn-books:

> Full in the panting Heart of Rome,
> Beneath the Apostle's crowning dome,
> From pilgrim lips that kiss the ground,
> Breathes in all tongues one only sound,
> 'God bless our Pope, the great, the good.'[19]

However genial the Pope was in person, he had put himself at the
head of a party within the Church which was anything but genial. In
devotional terms Ultramontanism was a broadly based movement, in
touch with some of the most powerful religious energies of the age.
In doctrinal and institutional terms it was narrow, aggressive and
intolerant. In journals like the French *L'Univers*, edited by Louis
Veuillot, or the Jesuit *Civiltà Cattolica*, Ultramontanes extravagantly
vamped up papal authority, and denounced not only the secular
world which rejected the Church, but other Catholics whose opinions did not pass muster as sufficiently papalist. Everyone knew the
Pope favoured this school of thought, and in 1853 he even published
an encyclical, *Inter Multiplices*, defending Veuillot and *L'Univers*
against the French bishops. The result was a suffocating churchiness,
narrow, fearful and exclusive. The famous Anglican convert John
Henry Newman, now leader of the Oratory community in Birm-
ingham, and by Pio Nono's standards a liberal, deplored this Ultramontane tendency to create a 'Church within a Church', and the
failure of vision involved: 'we are shrinking into ourselves, narrowing
the lines of communication, trembling at freedom of thought, and
using the language of dismay and despair at the prospect before us'.[20]

The leading English Ultramontane was Henry Edward Manning,
whose main ally at Rome was Monsignor George Talbot, for many
years Pio Nono's most trusted confidant. Talbot ended his life in a
lunatic asylum, and was probably unbalanced for years before his
breakdown in 1869. He was certainly devious, feline, wreathed in
intrigue, his view of the world and the Church a perpetual game of
cowboys and Indians, heroes and villains. The villains included most
of the English bishops, whom he thought disloyal anti-papalists, and
Newman himself, in Talbot's view 'the most dangerous man in Eng-

land', still half a Protestant, and a leader of rebels – 'his spirit must be crushed'. Talbot had the Pope's ear, and was the key mover in the surprise appointment of Manning to succeed Cardinal Wiseman as archbishop of Westminster in 1865.

It was on the advice of men of this calibre that Pio Nono issued in 1864 the encyclical *Quanta Cura*, to which was attached the so-called *Syllabus of Errors*. As Pio Nono aged he became more responsive to Ultramontane pressure for strong, clear statements which would burn the bridges to the modern world that liberals like Count Montalembert were trying to build. The immediate trigger for the encyclical was the Catholic Congress held at Malines in Belgium in 1863, at which Montalembert had urged a reconciliation between the Church and democracy. The alliance of throne and altar was doomed, he argued, bringing the Church into discredit. It was better to tolerate error in order that the truth could speak freely, than to attempt to suffocate it by persecution and the Inquisition.

Monatalembert's speech was published under the headline 'A Free Church in a Free State', and the Ultramontanes flooded Rome with demands for his condemnation. In March 1864 the Pope instructed his Secretary of State Cardinal Antonelli to send letters of rebuke to Montalembert and the Archbishop of Malines, and in December, on the tenth anniversary of the definition of the Immaculate Conception, the encyclical itself appeared.[21] Much of it, though cast in the now familiar Vatican form of the Jeremiad, was a matter of rounding up the usual suspects – Indifferentism, Freemasonry, Socialism, Gallicanism, Rationalism were all condemned. It was the *Syllabus*, a list of eighty condemned propositions, which caused general consternation. Here again, many of the condemned propositions were uncontroversial. All Christians agreed that it was a bad idea to claim that Jesus Christ was a mythical figure, or that revelation could add nothing to human reason (Propositions 5, 7). No one can have been surprised to find Pio Nono condemning the view that the abolition of the temporal power of the Pope would be good for the Church (76). The final group of propositions, however, seemed designed to shock and offend, for example by denying that non-Catholics should be free to practise their religion (77). Above all, the last proposition seemed to sum up the Catholic Church's war against modern society, for in it the Pope condemned the notion that 'the Roman Pontiff can and should reconcile himself with progress, liberalism, and recent civilisation' (80).

The *Syllabus* was in fact a far less devastating document than it appeared at first sight. Its eighty propositions were extracted from earlier papal documents, and Pio Nono repeatedly said the true meaning of the *Syllabus* could be discovered only by referring to the original context. So, the offensive proposition 80 came from the brief *Iamdudum Cernimus* of 1861. Its apparently wholesale condemnation of 'progress, liberalism and modern civilisation' in fact referred quite specifically to the Piedmontese government's closure of the monasteries and Church schools. But in December 1864 matters struck nobody in this light. The *Syllabus* was intended as a blow at liberal Catholicism, and everyone knew it. The English government representative in Rome, Odo Russell, reported that liberal Catholics, the Church's 'ablest and most eloquent defenders', had been paralysed, 'because they can no longer speak in her defence without being convicted of heresy . . . Silence and blind obedience must henceforward be their only rule of life.' Russell was a sympathetic observer of Roman affairs, fond of Pio Nono, but even he thought that the Pope had put himself 'at the head of a vast ecclesiastical conspiracy against the principles of modern society'.[22]

He was not alone in thinking so. The French government, whose troops were the only bulwark between the Pope and the Risorgimento, banned the *Syllabus*; it was publicly burned in Naples; Austria considered a ban but decided that this would breach the Concordat. Montalembert's ally, Bishop Dupanloup of Orleans, wrote that 'if we do not succeed in checking this senseless Romanism, the Church will be outlawed in Europe for half a century'. He worked day and night to produce a pamphlet in mitigation of the *Syllabus*, claiming that it was not a prescription for the actual conduct of the Church's relations with society in the concrete, but an abstract outline of the ideal. This changeless 'thesis' needed – and, in the Church's actual agreements through concordats and the like, in fact received – modification to adapt it to actual circumstances: the 'antithesis'.

Dupanloup's pamphlet was a *tour de force* which went a long way towards defusing non-Catholic hostility to the *Syllabus*, and gained breathing-space for liberal Catholicism. Six hundred and thirty-six bishops wrote to thank him for it, and Montalembert called it 'a first-class verbal vanishing trick'. Pio Nono, daunted by the clamour the *Syllabus* had caused, also thanked him, but was privately unimpressed, and the Ultramontane juggernaut rolled on. On the feast of Sts Peter and Paul 1867, kept as the eighteenth centenary of the martyrdom of the Apostles, Pio Nono announced the summoning of a general council, to begin on 8 December 1869. Manning and other leading Ultramontane bishops took a solemn vow at the tomb of St Peter to work for the definition of papal infallibility at this, the First Vatican Council.

At first, however, infallibility was not on the agenda. The Pope had called the Council to tackle nineteenth-century unbelief and rationalism, which he thought were undermining Christianity, and to strengthen the Church in her stand against hostile societies and governments. As the date for the Council approached, however, it was clear to everyone that infallibility would be the dominating issue. Governments feared that the doctrines of the *Syllabus* would be made absolute, and thereby worsen the confrontation between Church and state. Liberal Catholics feared they were being edged out of the Church, and that an unlimited doctrine of papal infallibility would be imposed at the Council. All Catholics accepted that in fundamental matters the Church taught infallibly, and all accepted that solemn papal utterances spoke for the Church. Agreement ended there, however. Ultramontane enthusiasts like W. G. Ward attributed infallibility to almost every papal utterance. Ward thought that not only was the *Syllabus* infallible, but that every one of the other thirty encyclicals and allocutions from which the *Syllabus* quoted was thereby shown to be infallible. He wanted a new infallible statement from the Pope on the table every morning with *The Times*. Ultramontanes of this cast of mind imagined the Pope as permanently inspired, and were prone to statements like 'the infallibility of the Pope is the infallibility of Jesus Christ himself', or 'when the Pope thinks, it is God who is thinking in him'.[23]

Few nineteenth-century Catholics rejected out of hand the notion that the Pope might teach infallibly. But many thought that it was dangerous to try to define just how and when that might happen. They thought it unnecessary, for the infallibility of the Church had never been defined, yet all Catholics believed it. They also thought such a definition inopportune, likely to inflame anti-Catholic feeling, to alienate Protestants and Eastern Orthodox Christians, to antagonise governments. Some, like Bishop Dupanloup, thought that in any case such a definition would be almost impossible to get right. How, for example, could the Pope's teaching as an ordinary priest or theologian be distinguished from his solemn teaching *ex cathedra* ('from his throne')? This digging around in the roots of the Church's authority, he feared, might kill the whole tree.[24]

Seven hundred bishops attended the Council, 70 per cent of all those eligible. Italians dominated – all five of the presidents, all the secretaries and two-thirds of the consultors (expert advisers) were Italian. The key posts in the Conciliar bureaucracy were held by supporters of infallibility. The initial sessions were taken up with the formulation of the decree *Dei Filius*, a strong assertion of the rationality of faith and the uniqueness of the Christian revelation. Attention soon turned, however, to the draft document on the Church, a lengthy affair which dealt with everything from the nature of ministry to the relations of Church and state. Debate dragged on, and Manning and his colleagues persuaded the Pope that it would be dangerous to leave the question of infallibility unresolved. The chapter dealing with infallibility was moved to the head of the agenda.

The Council was polarised between two groups, the infallibilist majority, led by Archbishop Manning, and the inopportunist minority, which included all the Austrian and German hierarchy, and many of the French. Initially, the Pope preserved a scrupulous neutrality, greeting known opponents of infallibility with warmth and friendliness. He was offended, however, by a widely publicised letter by the dying Montalambert which said that the infallibilists were 'setting up their idol in the Vatican', and by the attempts of liberal Catholics to prevent infallibility being discussed. Dupanloup tried to persuade Napoleon III to intervene. The English Catholic layman Sir John Acton, who was a pupil of the German leader of theological opposition to the definition, Ignaz von Döllinger, organised a campaign to whip up public opinion and British, French and German action to prevent the definition. There was talk of the English Cabinet sending a gunboat.

Both sides lobbied and plotted frantically. Manning recorded that the inopportunist minority 'met often, and we met weekly to watch and counteract. When they went to Pius IX we went also. It was a running fight.'[25] The Pope's hand was decisively shown on 18 June, when the Dominican theologian Cardinal Guidi, Archbishop of Bologna, criticised the heading of the draft decree on infallibility, which ran 'On the infallibility of the Roman Pontiff'. This was erroneous, Guidi insisted: the *Pope* was not infallible, though his teaching might be. Infallible teaching is irreformable, the teacher is not. Guidi went on to argue that a condition of infallibility was that it should not be exercised rashly. The Pope teaches in consultation with other bishops, and this needed to be indicated in the decree. He proposed that the wording should state that the Pope is assisted by 'the counsel of the bishops manifesting the tradition of the churches'. This intervention was all the more powerful because Guidi was an infallibilist, basically in favour of the definition. His careful theological intervention, one of the weightiest of the whole Council, was designed to rule out any notion of an inspired or personally infallible Pope, and to protect the truth that the Pope taught not as an isolated monarch, but as first among the bishops. He was embraced by members of the minority as he descended from the podium. But Pio Nono was enraged. He summoned Guidi and berated him, as a cardinal and a bishop of the Patrimony, for treachery. Guidi replied that he had said only that bishops are witnesses to the tradition. 'Witnesses of tradition?' the Pope replied, '*I* am the tradition.'[26]

La tradizione son' io. Pius' magnificently arrogant aphorism laid bare both the attraction and the historical poverty of the infallibilist case. No controversy in the first thousand years of Christianity had been settled merely by papal fiat: even Leo I's Tome had been adopted by a general council. Agreement on the truth in early Christianity had emerged by convergence, consensus, debate, painful and costly processes which took decades and even centuries to crystallise. Manning and his associates wanted history without tears, a living oracle who could short-circuit human limitation. They wanted to confront the uncertainties of their age with instant assurance, revelation on tap.

They did not get it. Guidi had his bad half-hour with Pio Nono, but his words had their effect. The final decree, drafted by Archbishop Cullen of Dublin, took account of Guidi's arguments and was headed 'De Romani Pontificia infallibili magisterio' ('On the infallible teaching office of the Roman Pontiff'). The wording of the decree itself was carefully hedged around with restrictions. It declared that:

> The Roman Pontiff, when he speaks *ex cathedra*, that is, when, exercising the office of pastor and teacher of all Christians, he defines . . . a doctrine concerning faith and morals to be held by the whole Church, through the divine assistance promised to him

in St Peter, is possessed of that infallibility with which the Divine Redeemer wished his Church to be endowed . . . and therefore such definitions of the Roman Pontiff are irreformable of themselves, and not from the consent of the Church.[27]

Routine papal teaching, therefore, was *not* infallible. The Pope had to be speaking in a specially solemn form – *ex cathedra*. His teaching had to be on a matter of faith and morals (so not, for example, political denunciation of the kingdom of Italy, or instructions to Catholics about how to vote), and it had to be about fundamentals, a matter to be held 'by the whole Church' (so not addressed merely to some passing debate). Such solemn statements were indeed declared to be irreformable 'of themselves' – *ex sese* – a form of words designed specifically to refute the Gallican Articles of 1682, which said that papal definitions were only irreformable when they had been received by the Church. What the definition did *not* say, however, was that the Pope when teaching could or should *act* by himself, over against the Church rather than along with it. The wording avoided any comment on the processes by which such definitions emerge, and so did not concede the extreme Ultramontane case, in which the Pope need consult nobody, the idea implied in Pio Nono's 'I am the tradition.' In fact, though it was not at once apparent, the Vatican definition called a halt to the wilder Ultramontane fantasies about the papacy: it was a defeat for men like Ward and Viuellot. It is some measure of the effectiveness of these restrictions that, since 1870, only one papal statement has qualified as 'infallible', the definition of the Assumption in 1950.

All of that, however, would take time to emerge. The final vote on the infallibility decree took place on 18 July 1870. Fifty-seven members of the minority, including Dupanloup, having fought the definition to the last, had left Rome the day before so as not to have to vote against a measure they now knew would go through by an overwhelming majority. In the event, 533 bishops voted for the decree, only two against. One of these two was Bishop Fitzgerald of Little Rock, Arkansas in the USA. When the Pope finally read out the decree, Fitzgerald left his place, knelt at the Pope's feet and cried out, 'Modo credo, sancte pater' ('Now I believe, Holy Father'). The voting and the solemn definition itself, proclaimed by the Pope, took place in a devastating thunderstorm. Rain bucketed down on to the dome of St Peter's, and the dim interior was lit up by lightning flashes. Hostile commentators took the thunder as a portent – God, they said, was angry. Manning was scathing: 'They forgot Sinai and the Ten Commandments.'[28]

The Council's business was not finished, nor would it ever be. On 19 July, the Franco-Prussian War broke out, and the Council was prorogued *sine die*. In the event, it never reassembled, and the first business of the Second Vatican Council almost a century later would be to declare Vatican One closed. The outbreak of the war precipitated the crisis of the temporal power. Napoleon III now needed every soldier he could get. The French garrison was withdrawn from Rome on 4 August, leaving the Pope defenceless. Within a month, Napoleon's empire had come to an end, and King Victor Emmanuel had invaded the Papal States. On 19 September Pio Nono locked himself into the Vatican, instructing his soldiers to put up a token resistance to the royal troops, to make clear that he had not surrendered the city. The next day Rome fell, and within a year it would be declared the capital of a united Italy. A millennium and a half of papal rule in Rome was at an end.

The pontificate of Pio Nono ended in gloom and confrontation. In November 1870 Italy passed the Law of Guarantees, to regulate the new relations between Church and state. At one level, it was a generous settlement. Though now deprived of territory, the Pope was to have all the honours and immunities of a sovereign, including a personal guard and a postal and telegraph service. He was to have the exclusive use (not ownership) of the Vatican, the Lateran and the papal country residence at Castel Gandolfo. He was to receive 3,500,000 lire annually as compensation for his lost territories. And the state surrendered any claim to the appointment of bishops, though it retained its rights over clerical benefices.

The Pope refused to recognise this law, or to accept the financial compensation. In practice, however, he tacitly adopted many of the provisions as a working arrangement, allowing clergy to accept the revenues of their benefices from the state, and taking over the appointment of all Italian bishops. This last was a move of enormous significance. Italy had a greater concentration of bishoprics than any other part of Christendom, and, as new territories were annexed to the kingdom, Victor Emmanuel had accumulated immense powers of appointment, greater than those of any other king in Christian history. By 1870 he had the right to appoint 237 bishops. All these appointments now came into papal hands, and not only transformed the relationship of the Pope to the Italian episcopate, but shifted expectation in episcopal appointments generally. From now on, there was an increasing and quite new assumption that the Pope appointed bishops. Paradoxically, the loss of the temporal power enormously increased papal control over the Italian church.

Meanwhile, however, relations between the papacy and Italy worsened. Most Italians were Catholics, but a high proportion of Italy's tiny electorate (1 per cent of the population) were anti-clericals, and through the 1870s a series of anti-clerical measures were devised to reduce the Church's hold on Italian life. In 1868 Pio Nono had issued the decree *Non Expedit* forbidding Catholics to vote or stand in Italian elections, and this ban on political participation remained in force till after the First World War, further alienating Church and state. Pio Nono never again set foot outside the Vatican, and withheld the customary 'Urbi et Orbi' blessing of the city and the world, as a protest against his status as the Prisoner of the Vatican.

This confrontation with the Italian state was mirrored in Germany. The emergence of Prussia as the dominant European power after 1870 transformed the position of Catholicism in Europe, as the dominance of Catholic Austria was replaced by that of a strongly Protestant Prussia. The German church was extremely vigorous, with some of the best bishops of the age, like Archbishop Ketteler of Mainz, who had been a leader of the minority in the Council. In 1870 German Catholics organised themselves into a political party, the Centre Party, led by the brilliant tactician Ludwig Windthorst. The Chancellor of Prussia, Bismarck, detested and feared the Church as a potentially treasonous fifth column. Catholics in general wanted a larger pan-German state which would be less Protestant, and allied themselves with Liberal political critics of Bismarck's regime. In 1872, with the appointment of a new minister of cults, Dr Falk, there began a systematic harassment of the Church, under the so-called Falk Laws. Catholic schools and seminaries were subjected to state control, religious orders were forbidden to teach, the Jesuits and eventually all religious orders were expelled. The Franciscan nuns celebrated in Gerard Manley Hopkins' great poem 'The Wreck of the Deutschland' were refugees from this campaign. In 1874 imprisonment of 'recalcitrant priests' began, and in 1875 Pio Nono denounced the laws and excommunicated the few clergy who had submitted to them.

The *Kulturkampf* (struggle of civilisations) was devastating for the Church. More than a million Catholics were left without access to the sacraments, by 1876 all the sees in Prussia were vacant, and more than a thousand priests were exiled or imprisoned. Some German Catholics, led by Döllinger, had refused to accept the Vatican decrees. Bismarck systematically encouraged this schism, hoping to undermine Catholic unity. He also encouraged similar anti-Catholic campaigns elsewhere – in Italy, Switzerland, Belgium, though only Switzerland followed the Prussian example in launching its own *Kulturkampf*.

Bismarck's hostility to Catholicism predated the Vatican Council, but the Vatican decrees were of course a factor. Bismarck claimed that the Vatican definition had revived the most extravagant claims of Gregory VII and Boniface VIII: this time, however, he promised, 'We will not go to Canossa.' Ultramontanes expected this opposition and revelled in it, their language full of violent images of strife and confrontation. Louis Viuellot had written that 'Society is a sewer – it will perish – with the debris of the Vatican God will stone the human race.'[29]

Pio Nono died on 7 February 1878, after the longest pontificate in the Church's history. During those years the Church had been transformed in every aspect of its life. Almost the entire episcopate had been reappointed during his reign. The religious orders had experienced a renewal and growth which would have been unimaginable a generation earlier, not merely by the expansion of existing orders, but by the creation of new ones. Many of these new orders were dedicated to apostolic work in schools, hospitals and overseas missions, and they represent an astonishing flowering of Christian energy. In the three years from 1862, Pio Nono approved seventy-four new congregations for women religious. By 1877 there were 30,287 male religious and 127,753 women religious in France alone, many of them in brotherhoods and sisterhoods devoted to active works. The same vigour is in evidence in the spread of Christian missions outside Europe. After 1850 missionary orders multiplied, and men and women flooded into the mission field: by the end of the century there were in the region of 44,000 nuns alone working in mission territory.

Within established Catholic churches the same vigour is in evidence, and was deliberately fostered by Pio Nono. Responding to expanding Catholic numbers, he introduced new hierarchies into England (1850) and the Netherlands (1853) in the face of angry Protestant reaction. During his pontificate as a whole he created over

200 new bishoprics or apostolic vicariates. All this represented a massive growth of papal involvement and papal control in the local churches. The rapidly expanding church in the USA, in particular, whose bishops were effectively appointed in Rome, developed a strongly papalist character. That increased control was self-conscious. Pio Nono and his entourage saw to it that all these new religious energies were firmly harnessed to the papacy. Early on in his papacy he set up a special curial congregation to deal with religious orders, and he systematically encouraged greater centralisation, often intervening directly to appoint superiors for some of the orders – in 1850 for the Subiaco Benedictines and the Dominicans, in 1853 for the Redemptorists, in 1856 and 1862 for the Franciscans.

The drive to centralisation on Rome was seen at its starkest and least attractive in Pio Nono's treatment of the Eastern Rite Catholic churches, the so-called 'Uniates'. These local churches – in the Ukraine, India, the Middle East – were indistinguishable from the Eastern Orthodox in every respect: they used the Byzantine liturgy, had a married clergy, followed their own legal customs, elected their own bishops and held their own Eastern-style synods. They differed from the Orthodox, however, in recognising the Pope's authority. 'Uniate' Catholics had always had a difficult time, rejected by the Orthodox as traitors, suspect to the Latin authorities as half-schismatic.

Ultramontanism, however, had particular difficulty in accepting the value of these Eastern Rite Catholics. Ultramontanes identified Catholicism with *Romanitas*: they saw the unity of the Church as inextricably tied to uniformity. One faith *meant* one discipline, one liturgy, one code of canon law, one pyramid of authority presided over by a proactive and interventionist papacy. Rome paid lip-service to the value of the Eastern Rite communities and their traditions as signs of the Church's universality, and as potential bridges to Eastern Orthodoxy. In practice, however, it systematically undermined them. Latin missionaries were encouraged to wean congregations away from oriental rites, and pressure was brought to bear to phase out a married clergy. Rome tried to use patriarchal and episcopal elections to install pro-Latin candidates, and insisted on the presence of apostolic delegates at Eastern Catholic provincial synods, under whose pressure Latin customs were intruded. An attempt in 1860 to impose the Gregorian calendar on the Melkite Church (Syrian Christians under a patriarch at Antioch, who had been in communion with

Rome since the late seventeenth century) drove some of the Melkite clergy into communion with the Orthodox, and came near to splitting the Church. When they protested against this erosion of their distinctive traditions, the Melkite leaders were treated as disloyal, and during the celebrations for the anniversary of the martyrdoms of Sts Peter and Paul in 1867 the Pope issued the bull *Reversurus*, which rebuked the Eastern Rite churches for their schismatic tendencies, insisted that close papal supervision was for their good, and reorganised the machinery for episcopal and patriarchal elections to exclude involvement of the laity and the lower clergy. Unsurprisingly, the patriarchs of the Melkite, Syriac and Chaldean churches were among the minority bishops who left the Vatican Council early.

These tensions were inevitable, for Ultramontanism was a form of absolutism, revelling in what Cardinal Manning called 'the beauty of inflexibility'.[30] It could give no coherent or positive value to diversity and independence. Papal invasion of the prerogatives, authority-structures and rites of the Eastern churches merely highlighted a process which was far more highly advanced within the churches of the Latin West itself. In addition to defining papal infallibility, the Vatican Council had asserted that the Pope had 'immediate and ordinary jurisdiction' over every church and every Christian. 'Immediate and ordinary jurisdiction', however, is what bishops have over their flocks, and the Council never addressed the problem of how *two* bishops, the Pope in Rome and the local bishop, could have identical jurisdiction over the *same* flocks. Indeed, it is an issue which has still not been satisfactorily settled. Under Pio Nono, the problem was resolved by the steady papal erosion of the authority and independence of the local hierarchies. Bishops were increasingly thought of as junior officers in the Pope's army, links in the line of command which bound every Catholic in obedience to the one *real* bishop, the Bishop of Rome. The death of Pio Nono did little to halt or reverse these trends.

IV ULTRAMONTANISM WITH A LIBERAL FACE: THE REIGN OF LEO XIII

The Conclave which began on 19 February 1878 took only three ballots to choose a new pope, Gioacchino Pecci, Cardinal Bishop of Perugia, who took the name Leo XIII (1878–1903). Pecci was virtually unknown outside Italy. He was not a member of the Curia, and had been bishop of the relatively obscure see of Perugia since 1846. A protégé of both Leo XII and Gregory XVI, he had been a highly successful administrator in the Papal States, before being sent as nuncio to Belgium in 1843. He made a hash of this post, however, by wading into a complicated and delicate political situation and encouraging intransigent Catholic opposition to government educational measures, and he was withdrawn at the specific request of the royal family. This was the end of his career in the papal service: Perugia was his not very splendid consolation prize. Pio Nono made him a cardinal in 1853, but, for reasons which are still unclear, the coarse and worldly Secretary of State Cardinal Antonelli, distrusted him and saw to it that he stayed in obscurity. A year before his own death, however, Pio Nono made him Camerlengo, the Cardinal who administers the Roman Church between the death of a Pope and the election of his successor. It was a back-handed compliment, for there was a well-established tradition that the Camerlengo is not elected pope.

His election was probably based on three things: his impeccably conservative opinions (he had helped inspire the *Syllabus* and was an ardent defender of the temporal power), his success and popularity as a diocesan bishop, and the fact that between 1874 and 1877 he had published a series of pastoral letters which spoke positively about the advance of science and society in the nineteenth century, and which argued for reconciliation between the Church and the positive aspects of modern culture. Many of the cardinals felt that the apocalyptic denunciations of the world and political intransigence of Pio Nono had painted the Church into a corner. It was time for a little sweet-talk.

It was as if Cardinal Pecci had been waiting to be pope. Within hours of his election he declared, 'I want to carry out a great policy.' From his first day the new Pope displayed an astonishing sure-footedness in walking a tightrope, restoring the international prestige of the papacy without abandoning any of its religious claims. He would stand by the doctrines of the Vatican Council and the *Syllabus*, but he would abandon their shrillness of tone and confrontational manner. His first encyclical, *Inscrutabili Dei*, was typical. In it he laments the evils of the time – rejection of the Church's teaching, obstinacy of mind rejecting all lawful authority, endless strife, contempt for law. Out of this has sprung anti-clericalism and the theft of the Church's property. All this is misconceived, however, for the Church is the friend of society, not its enemy. It has led humanity from barbarism, abolished slavery, fostered science and learning, it is the mother of Italy. Italy must restore to the Pope what is his own, once more receive his authority, and society will flourish again. And Catholics everywhere, kindled by their clergy, must show 'ever closer and firmer' love for the Holy See, 'this chair of truth and justice'. They must 'welcome all its teachings with thorough assent of mind and will'. He recalled with approval Pio Nono's 'apostolic smiting' of error.[31]

The world noted both the content and the manner. The Italian journal *Riforma* declared that 'The new Pope does not ... curse, he does not threaten ...The form is sweet, but the substance is absolute, hard, intransigent.'[32] Italian perceptions of Leo's 'intransigence' were influenced by the continuing stand-off between the Pope and Italy. He had not given the blessing 'Urbi et Orbi' after his election (he had wanted to, but was prevented by the Vatican staff), he refused to recognise the King's title and did not notify him of his election as pope, he maintained Pio Nono's ban on political involvement in national elections, and he refused the income provided under the Law of Guarantees. Rome and the papacy, therefore, remained at odds. In 1881, when Pio Nono's body was moved by night to its final resting-place at San Lorenzo fuori le Mura, an anti-clerical mob almost succeeded in throwing the coffin into the river. The 1890s saw the erection of an aggressive monument to Garibaldi within sight of the Vatican, and a statue to the heretic Giordano Bruno in the Campo di Fiori, deliberate gestures of defiance and rejection. Leo was never in fact to abandon hope that he would recover Rome, and a good deal of his political activity outside Italy was undertaken in the hope of exerting external pressure to recover his temporal power. He was to establish himself as a great 'political' pope. To that extent, however, he never faced political reality.

Outside Italy, he was anything but intransigent. He inherited confrontations with Prussia, where the *Kulturkampf* still raged, with Switzerland, with Russia over the oppression of Polish Catholics, with some of the Latin American states where anti-clerical regimes were attacking the Church, and with France, where the republican government was fiercely anti-clerical. He set himself to defuse all these situations. The letters in which he announced his election to European heads of state were uniformly conciliatory, conceding nothing of substance, but expressing a strong desire for an accommodation.

His most spectacular success was in Bismarckian Germany. Bismarck was weary of the *Kulturkampf*, for it had backfired. The Centre Party, far from shrivelling away, had increased its representation with every election, and its tactical alliances with other opposition groups, like the National Liberals and the Social Democrats, were causing government defeats. The strong leadership of the German bishops was holding Catholic resistance to the Falk Laws steady, and Catholic public opinion was increasingly vocal. The conflict was also complicating Prussian rule in Poland. For his part, Leo hoped that Bismarck, now the most powerful statesman in Europe, might help him recover Rome, and he feared long-term damage to the Church if the confrontation persisted. Secret negotiations were initiated by the nuncios in Munich and Vienna, and, although these eventually broke down, Bismarck began to suspend the worst of the anti-Catholic legislation. Between 1880 and 1886 the Falk Laws were dismantled, though the Jesuits were not readmitted to Germany till 1917, and bishops remained bound to clear all appointments of priests with government.

It became clear, however, that Bismarck would do nothing to help Leo recover Rome. The Pope turned, therefore, to France. Most French Catholics were monarchists, sworn enemies of the principles of 1789. Most of the clergy were Ultramontanes, convinced that France should intervene to get the Pope his temporal power back. But from 1879 Republican anti-clericals were in the majority in the Senate and the Chamber of Deputies, and the government launched a campaign, like the *Kulturkampf*, to reduce the Church's influence in national life – restrictions on the religious orders, introduction of divorce, Sunday working permitted, prayers and processions abolished on state occasions, religionless funerals encouraged. Throughout the 1880s Church and government were at each other's throats, Church newspapers denounced the Republic, Catholics involved themselves in royalist plotting. It was the *Syllabus* given nightmare reality, and a total breach between the Church and French political culture seemed inevitable.

All through the 1880s, Leo did what he could to prevent this polarisation, and to conciliate the French state. He wrote a mild letter to the President in 1883, he published an encyclical to the bishops of France, *Nobilissima Gallorum Gens*, in 1884, expressing his love for France, recalling its ancient faithfulness to the Church, urging an end to hostilities, praising the Concordat of 1801, encouraging the bishops to stand firm on fundamentals but urging them to abandon extreme opinions for the sake of the common good. In 1885 he issued an encyclical on the nature of the state, *Immortali Dei*, arguing that Church and state are distinct but complementary societies, each with their own authority and freedoms. The state is truly free only when it supports the Church, and the Church is the best bulwark of a peaceful state. Liberty of religions, the press and oppression of the Church by the civil power are all damaging to society. But he insisted that no one form of government is privileged by the Church, and he urged Catholics to take a full part in the public life of their societies. With his eye on the ferocious divisions between liberal Catholics and Ultramontane royalists in France, he urged Catholics to put aside their differences in a common loyalty to papal teaching.[33]

Everyone thought the Church was the propaganda wing of the royalists, and papal utterances by themselves would not change that. The Pope made the Archbishop of Lyons and the Archbishop of Paris cardinals, and asked them to write a letter encouraging Catholics to support the Republic. Grinding their teeth, they wrote a diatribe against the government so bitter that he had to suppress it. So he summoned the great missionary Bishop Cardinal Lavigerie of Algiers, who had long believed that it was suicidal for the Church to make war on the state, and who needed French imperial support for his missionary efforts in Africa. On 12 November 1890, at a banquet for the mostly rabidly royalist officers of the French Mediterranean fleet, Lavigerie made an electrifying speech. To rescue the country from disaster, he said, there must be unqualified support for the established form of government (the Republic), which was 'in no way contrary to the principles ... of civilised and Christian nations'. He was certain, he went on, that he would not be contradicted 'by any authorised voice'.

The 'toast of Algiers' was a failure, and not merely in the eyes of the scandalised sailors who heard it. Everybody knew Lavigerie had been put up to it by Leo, and a few French Ultramontanes swallowed their horror and rage and said they would be loyal. Most, however, were too deeply alienated from the Republic to respond, and in any case the notorious Dreyfus affair was soon to unchain the worst of Catholic right-wing opinion and anti-Semitism, and further polarise French public life. Leo went on trying to force French Catholics into constitutional politics, but to little effect, for he was asking them to abandon attitudes and instincts rooted in a century of bitterness and conflict, and endorsed by several of his predecessors. His attempt to persuade the Catholics of France to 'rally' to the Republic, in fact, served only to demonstrate the limitations of papal influence, even over Ultramontanes.

Nevertheless, the Pope's campaign in favour of *ralliement* did help exorcise suspicions that Catholicism and democracy were incompatible. It evoked from him a series of encyclicals which registered the Church's acceptance of the legitimate autonomy of the state, and the compatibility of Catholicism with democratic forms of government. There was nothing strictly new about this teaching, and it did little more than codify the compromises with democracy which the popes had been making in practice since the Concordat of 1801. In many cases, his teaching repeats that of more uncompromising papal utterances like *Mirari Vos* or *Quanta Cura* and the *Syllabus*. But the tone of voice was utterly different and, having stated the ideal, he added the pragmatic qualifications. *Libertas Praestantissimum*, for example, the encyclical on liberalism published in 1888, reworks all that *Mirari Vos* and the *Syllabus* had to say in denunciation of freedom of religion, of conscience, of the press – and then goes on to say that the Church can nevertheless live with religious toleration, a free press, and the rest of the modern 'false liberties', 'for the sake of avoiding some greater evil'. It was as if Bishop Dupanloup had become pope.[34]

The papacy had a bad record on social reform. The posture of reactionary condemnation into which it had been frozen since the publication of *Mirari Vos* in 1832 made it suspicious of any schemes for the transformation of society. From the early years of Pio Nono socialism was a particular bogey. The call of Lamennais, Henri Lacordaire the Dominican priest and political activist, and of Count Montalambert to the popes to 'turn to the democracy' had been rejected. Papal rhetoric was concerned with the obligation of obedience, the rights of princes and popes, it had nothing to say to people whose lives were captive to the market forces of *laissez faire* capitalism, and who had no stake in the political process of the societies that fed off their labour.

Other Catholics, however, felt the urgency of the social question. Industrialisation and urbanisation had brought massive hardship for the proletariat of Europe, and a widespread and deepening alienation from organised Christianity in both its Catholic and its Protestant forms. In England, Germany, Belgium and France, sensitive Christians wrestled with the plight of working people, and with the need for the Church to move beyond exhortation and almsgiving, to questions of justice, and to a Christian vision of society. This sensitivity was found among both Ultramontanes and liberals. In Germany such movements were represented by Bishop Ketteler, in England by Cardinal Manning, in France by Count Albert De Mun and the industrialist Lucien Harmel.

Harmel was a practical visionary. He had launched an experiment in social partnership at his factory in Val-des-Bois, where he introduced model housing, saving-schemes, health and welfare benefits, and workers' councils to share in policy-making for the business. Harmel wanted other Catholic employers to follow suit, but was unable to persuade them. He decided to enlist the Pope. In 1885 he took 100 of his workforce on pilgrimage to Rome. Leo was impressed. Two years later 1,800 came, in 1889 10,000 came. These pilgrimages of working people, living proof that democracy and the Pope might shake hands, caught Leo's imagination, and helped persuade him that industrial society need not be conflictual, that social peace under the Gospel was a possibility.

Leo took a close interest in the American church, for there was a society where the 'liberal' doctrine of a free Church in a free state seemed not to be code for anti-Christian attacks on religion. In America, Catholic labour was organising in bodies like the Knights of Labour, which did not seem to be communistic or irreligious. Leo began to hope that in Europe, too, Catholic labour organisations might offset the communist unions.

From 1884 Catholic social thinkers from France, Germany, Austria, Italy, Belgium and Switzerland met annually at Fribourg to discuss the social question. The working papers of this conference accumulated as a summary of and stimulus to Catholic reflection on the condition of the working class. In 1888 Leo received members of the Union of Fribourg and discussed their ideas with them. Out of this conversation emerged the idea of a papal document which would address the social issue. The result was Leo's most famous encyclical, *Rerum Novarum*, published in 1891.[35]

Rerum Novarum opens with an eloquent evocation of the plight of the poor in industrial society, in which 'a small number of very rich men have been able to lay upon the teeming masses of the labouring poor a yoke which is very little better than slavery itself'. From this misery socialism offers an illusory release, fomenting class hatred and denying the right to private property. Defending this right to ownership, the Pope argues that class and inequality are perennial features of society, but need not lead to warfare. The rich have a duty to help the poor, and this duty goes beyond mere charity. Christianity is concerned with the healing of society as well as of individual souls, and in that healing the state must play a part. The state depends on the labouring poor for its prosperity, and must therefore protect the rights of labour, both spiritual and material. This protection extends to regulating working conditions, and ensuring that all receive a living wage, which will allow the worker to save and so acquire property and a stake in society. Labouring people have a right to organise themselves into unions, which ideally should be Catholic. Though the Pope thought strikes were sometimes the work of agitators, he thought they were often the result of intolerable conditions. He accepted the right to strike, but thought the state should legislate to remove the grievances that provoke strikes.

Rerum Novarum is one of those historic documents whose importance is hard now to grasp. Enough of what it had to say was couched in the traditional language of paternalism to allow conservatives to evade its radical thrust, and to pretend that nothing new had been said. Such people seized on passages like that in which Leo said suffering and inequality were part of the human condition, or exhorted the poor to be content with their lot. The Pope's social analysis was elementary, and what he had to say about the unions was timid, and wrapped up in romantic tosh about medieval craft gilds. The Anglican Christian Socialist Henry Scott Holland said the encyclical was 'the voice of some old-world life, faint and ghostly, speaking in some antique tongue of long ago'.[36] Many Christians, many Catholics, in the 1880s and 1890s were saying more penetrating and more challenging things.

For the successor of Pio Nono to say these things, however, was truly revolutionary. Leo's attack on unrestricted capitalism, his insistence on the duty of state intervention on behalf of the worker, his assertion of the right to a living wage and the rights of organised labour, changed the terms of all future Catholic discussion of social questions, and gave weight and authority to more adventurous advocates of Social Catholicism. Without being either a democrat or a radical himself, Leo opened the door to the evolution of Catholic democracy.

Rerum Novarum demonstrated that Leo was a more advanced social thinker than most nineteenth-century Catholics. With hindsight, he has come to be seen as a liberal pope, a courageous revolutionary transforming the Catholic intellectual and moral landscape, equipping the Church to deal with the modern world. As evidence for this view, one can put alongside *Rerum Novarum* a whole series of measures which reversed the policies of his predecessor, and nudged the Church out of the rigid posture into which the reign of Pio Nono had frozen it.

A clear case in point is Leo's reversal of papal policy towards the Eastern Catholic churches, and towards Orthodoxy in general. Leo called a halt to the drive to Latinisation and uniformity which had been such a feature of Pio Nono's treatment of Eastern Rite Catholics. In 1882 Leo stopped the offensive practice of naming Latin titular bishops to churches in Orthodox territory. In the same year he founded a Melkite seminary in Jerusalem, in 1883 an Armenian seminary in Rome. In 1894 he issued the encyclical *Praeclara Gratulationis*, which praised the diversity of churches and rites within a single faith, and the brief *Orientalium Dignitatis*, which emphasised the need to preserve the integrity and distinctiveness of the Eastern Rite churches. In the following year he regulated the relations between Eastern Rite bishops and patriarchs and the Apostolic Delegates, a matter which had been the source of endless friction and offence under his predecessor. Many of these measures were in fact frustrated by unrepentant Latinisers among missionaries, the papal diplomatic corps and the Curia. Leo's own intentions, however, were abundantly clear, and were the opposite of his predecessor's.

Theology had suffocated under Pio Nono. Great and original theological work was done far from Rome in the German Catholic universities, and by isolated and idiosyncratic figures like John Henry Newman in England. In Rome itself, however, a rigid, defensive and largely second-hand scholasticism dominated, and everything else was viewed with suspicion. Leo was determined to change this. In 1879 he made Newman a cardinal, an extraordinarily eloquent gesture given that Cardinal Manning believed, and often said, that Newman was a heretic. The Roman authorities disliked and feared modern historical enquiry, which they thought was anti-Catholic and sceptical. In 1881 Leo opened the Vatican Archives to historians, including Protestant historians. The scholarly world recognised the revolutionary nature of this step, and applauded a liberal pope.

But, above all, Leo believed that the key to a renewal of Catholic theology lay in a return to the greatest of the scholastic theologians, St Thomas Aquinas, and with the encyclical *Aeterni Patris* of 1879 he initiated a renaissance in Thomistic and scholastic studies to break the straitjacket of the Roman schools. He established an Academy of St Thomas in Rome, imported distinguished theologians, philosophers and textual scholars, and encouraged the establishment of Thomistic studies at the Catholic University of Louvain. From 1882 the future Cardinal Mercier was appointed to lecture on St Thomas at Louvain, where his classes became the focus for a theological renaissance in the university and beyond.

All these measures infused new life and confidence into Catholic theology, and the 1880s and 1890s saw a flowering of scholarship in biblical studies, Church history and philosophy which had all suffered from the paranoia and narrowness of Pio Nono's later years. The foundation of the Ecole Biblique under Dominican management in Jerusalem, the publication in 1893 of the encyclical *Providentissimus Deus*, which, however cautiously, accepted the legitimacy of scholarly study of the Bible using the resources of modern science and historical and textual criticism, and the establishment of the Pontifical Biblical Commission in 1902, with relatively liberal-minded personnel, all contributed to a sense of new openings.

Leo's preoccupation with St Thomas, however, points to the limits of his vision. St Thomas was indeed a transcendent genius, and the rediscovery of his teaching and his method opened a world of intellectual discourse and source-material which proved enormously fruitful. There were limits, however, to the usefulness even of Thomas in dealing with the intellectual problems of the late nineteenth century, yet Leo saw Thomism not as the starting point of theological enquiry, but as the end of it. In 1892 he sent a letter to all professors of theology, directing that all 'certain' statements of St Thomas were to be accepted as definitive. Where Aquinas had not spoken on a given topic, any conclusions reached had to be in harmony with his known opinions. Within a generation of the publication of *Aeterni Patris*, 'Thomism' had itself become an ossified orthodoxy in the Roman schools.

The limits of Leo's liberalism were shown also in the condemnation of Americanism. The intransigents and the party of *ralliement* in France had their counterparts in America. A substantial group of conservative

Catholics, led by Archbishop Corrigan of New York and Bishop McQuaid of Rochester, campaigned for a complete withdrawal of Catholics from the state educational system in America. Others, led by Archbishop John Ireland of St Paul, wanted a compromise which would allow continuing Catholic participation in the public schools. Archbishop Ireland's attitude reflected a more general openness to the distinctiveness of American social and religious culture, which was demonstrated by the participation of Cardinal Gibbons in the Chicago Parliament of Religions during the Exhibition there in 1892. For ten days Christian Churches and denominations took part with Buddhists, Hindus and Muslims in a public affirmation of 'basic religious truths'. Gibbons closed the proceedings by leading the assembly in the Lord's Prayer and giving the Apostolic Blessing – a sharing in public worship with Protestants and even non-Christians unheard of at the time, for which, remarkably, he had obtained permission directly from Leo XIII.

Such a display of 'indifferentism' would have been inconceivable in Europe, and many in America were disturbed by it. Leo himself condemned 'inter-Church conferences' in 1895. The continuing eagerness of 'progressive' Catholics to participate fully in American life and to integrate Catholic values as fully as possible into the 'American way' led many to fear a dilution of Catholic truth. Monsignor Satolli, the Apostolic Delegate in the USA, having initially supported Ireland and the progressives, came increasingly to feel that there was 'nothing of the supernatural' about the American church. In 1899 these tensions came to a head when a French translation appeared of a life of Father Hecker, founder of the Paulist order and a leading figure in the progressive wing of American Catholicism. The biography was prefaced by an enthusiastic essay by Father Felix Klein of the Institut Catholique in Paris, which 'out-Heckered Hecker' in recommending the adaptation of Catholic teaching to the modern world.

Critics fastened on this preface, and besieged Rome with demands for condemnation. The outcome in 1899 was Leo's letter *Testem Benevolentiae* addressed to Cardinal Gibbons, condemning the ideas that the Church should adapt her discipline and even her doctrine to the age in order to win converts, that spiritual direction was less important than the inner voice of the spirit, that natural virtues like honesty or temperance were more important than the supernatural virtues of faith, hope and charity, and that the active life of the virtues was more important than the contemplative and religious life.

Many Catholics, and many bishops, in America were grateful for this papal warning against the over-enthusiastic adoption of pluralist values, the 'false liberalism' which they believed threatened the integrity of the American church. Cardinal Gibbons, however, who had tried to fend off the condemnation, indignantly denied that any American Catholics held such views, and believed that the use of the word 'Americanism' to describe them was a slur on a great church. Certainly the condemnation had wider implications. There is no doubt that European tensions had a good deal to do with the condemnation of Klein's preface to the Hecker biography, and the condemnation was a sign that the liberalising forces released by Leo's own style of papacy were here being called to a halt, the limits of assimilation were being set. In America, the condemnation had a serious impact on American Catholic theological scholarship, inaugurating a phase of conservative anti-intellectualism which had a sterilising effect on American theology. In Europe, it was a straw in the wind which would turn to a gale in the pontificate of Pius X, and the Modernist crisis.

The fact is that however much Leo's tone of voice differed from that of his immediate predecessors, like them he believed that the Church – and therefore the Pope – had all the answers. If he thought less confrontationally, more historically, than Pio Nono, he had no doubt that the questionings and uncertainties of his age could all be resolved painlessly, by attention to what the Church, through St Thomas, through the popes, had long since taught. There is a numbing smugness about the insistence in many of his encyclicals that the Church is responsible for all that is good in human society, human culture. It is the voice of a man who has worn a cassock and lived among clerics all his life. In recommending the study of St Thomas, he was not calling Catholic scholarship to an open-ended encounter with historical and philosophical texts, but proposing a new standard of orthodoxy. It is no accident that the canonisation of St Thomas' writings was accompanied by the condemnation not only of the influence of Kant and Hegel, but of other, specifically Catholic, schools of thought, like the posthumous condemnation of the philosophy of Antonio Rosmini in 1887. He genuinely desired reunion with the Churches of the East, but could imagine such an outcome only in terms of their 'return' to Roman obedience. In the Churches of the Reformation he had no interest, and his condemnation of Anglican ordinations in 1896 as 'absolutely null and utterly void' was the inevitable outcome of ill-judged overtures by naively hopeful Anglo-Catholics.

He himself could not bear contradiction. When his Secretary of State once questioned his decision on some minor administrative matter he tapped the table and snapped at him, 'Ego sum Petrus' – ('I am Peter'). That authoritarianism is in evidence in everything he did. He insisted punctiliously on the style and ceremony of a sovereign, and he systematically exalted the papal office. His encyclicals are littered with paragraphs urging the faithful – and their pastors – to undeviating obedience to papal teaching. The sheer quantity of that teaching in itself testifies to his extraordinary commitment to a teaching office. Its quantity, however, was not its most significant characteristic. Until the time of Leo XIII, papal doctrinal interventions had been relatively rare, and their form generally reflected the papacy's role as a court of final appeal. Popes judged and, therefore, sometimes condemned. One of the attractions of Leo's encyclicals is that they rarely merely condemn, but we should not allow relief to blind us to the radical shift in the nature of papal teaching which his collected encyclicals represent. Here, for the first time, we have the Pope as an inexhaustible source of guidance and instruction. No pope before or since has come anywhere near his eighty-six encyclicals. Leo taught and taught, and expected obedience.

He expected obedience, too, in the day-to-day running of the Church. Despite his reversal of Pio Nono's centralising measures over the Eastern Rite Catholics, he himself tightened papal control over all the Church. He greatly increased the role of papal nuncios and apostolic delegates, insisting on their precedence over local hierarchies and other ambassadors as representatives of the Holy See. From 1881 the rise of international devotional rallies, known as Eucharistic Congresses, provided a platform for public manifestations of Catholic enthusiasm, in which the papacy played a growing role. From the late 1880s these events were routinely presided over by apostolic delegates or specially appointed groups of cardinals; in 1905 Leo's successor Pius X would personally preside over a eucharistic congress in Rome.

In negotiating with the *ralliement* and with Bismarck, Leo overrode the wishes of the local bishops and the leaders of the German Centre Party, in Germany even organising a secret settlement from which they were excluded. He kept a tight reign on episcopal conferences — the American hierarchy's momentous Third Council of Baltimore in 1884 was planned in Rome, and Archbishop Gibbons presided at it as the Pope's personal representative. The first Conference of Latin American Bishops was actually held in Rome under the Pope's personal chairmanship. Nor was his policy of support for the Republic an indication of liberal political views. He told the Bishop of Montpellier that if Catholics threw themselves into republican politics they would soon have the upper hand: 'If you follow my advice, you will have 400 Catholic deputies in France and you'll establish the monarchy. I'm a monarchist myself.'[37] His denunciations of socialism so delighted Tsar Nicholas II that he had them read out in Orthodox churches in Russia.

Leo's conception of the papacy, in fact, was no less authoritarian or Ultramontane than that of Pio Nono. He surrounded himself with the trappings of monarchy, insisted that Catholics received in audience kneel before him throughout the interview, never allowed his entourage to sit in his presence, never in twenty-five years exchanged a single word with his coachman. And all his actions tended to consolidate and extend papal involvement at every level of the Church's life. In a world in which the Church was increasingly being pushed to the margins, he retained grandiose ideas of the popes as arbiters of nations, elder statesmen at the centre of the web of world politics. Most of this was self-delusion: when Bismarck asked him to arbitrate in a territorial conflict between Prussia and Spain over the Caroline Islands he was offering a sop to Leo's vanity. Leo imagined he was being invited to give a ruling, and was dismayed when Spain insisted he was no more than a go-between.

Yet he lived long, and by the end of his pontificate the papacy had indeed recovered much of the prestige which it had forfeited in the fraught years between the Revolutions of 1848 and the Vatican Council. It had also become the unquestioned focus of policy-making and doctrinal teaching in the Church. Pio Nono had made the Vatican Council; Leo XIII was its principal heir and beneficiary.

CHAPTER SIX

THE ORACLES OF GOD

1903–1997

I THE AGE OF INTRANSIGENCE

At the end of the nineteenth century the fortunes of the papacy seemed at an all time low. The pope was beleaguered and landless, the prisoner of the Vatican. But, as if in compensation, his spiritual role and symbolic power had grown to dizzying heights. The pope was infallible, the unquestioned head and heart of the greatest of the Christian Churches, spiritual father of millions of human beings, revered from Asia to the Americas as the oracle of God.

In the nineteenth century, the popes had used their oracular powers to denounce secular thought, to present a siege mentality Catholicism which set the revelation of God in opposition to the godless philosophy of the modern world.

In the new century, the modern world would test this new papacy as it had never before been tested. New currents of thought in philosophy, in the physical sciences, in the study of history and in biblical criticism, would challenge ancient certainties, not from outside the Church, but from its own seminaries, universities and pulpits. How would an infallible papacy respond to these new modes of thought?

Furthermore, in place of the hostile liberal governments of Italy, France and Bismarkian Germany, the Church and the world would witness the rise of dictatorships more savage than any in human history. The nineteenth-century popes had first condemned and then struggled to come to terms with the industrial revolution. Now, all the resources of that revolution would be put to unimaginably terrible use, as the Nazi gas chambers and the camps of Stalin's Gulag harnessed modern technology, communications and bureaucracy, in the service of death. Pope after pope had denounced the anti-clerical activities of nineteenth-century governments. What would the oracle of God have to say to evil on this scale?

The twentieth-century papacy began, as was appropriate in this century of the common man, with a peasant pope, the first for three centuries. Giuseppe Sarto, who took the name Pius X (1903–1914), was the son of a village postman and a devout seamstress from northern Italy. He was chosen in deliberate contrast to the style of his predecessor, the remote and regal diplomat Leo XIII. The French curial Cardinal Mathieu later declared that 'We wanted a Pope who had never engaged in politics, whose name would signify peace and concord, who had grown old in the care of souls, who would concern himself with the government of the church in detail, who would be above all a father and shepherd'.[1]

This feeling was not universal: there had in fact been strong support for a continuation of Leo's policies, and the old pope's Secretary of State, Cardinal Rampolla, was a strong contender throughout the conclave. He was, however, vetoed by Austria, the last occasion in which one of the Catholic monarchies exercised a veto, and in any case he would probably not have won. After Leo's long and political reign Mathieu's views were widely shared, and the new pope could hardly have been less like his predecessor. Where Leo was cool, austere, detached, Sarto had a gusty humanity, a strong emotional piety and an eager sense of the priority of pastoral issues which had made him an extraordinarily effective diocesan bishop. Not one of his nineteenth-century predecessors had been a parish priest. Sarto, even as Bishop of Mantua and Patriarch of Venice, had never really been anything else. The positive reform measures of his pontificate sprang directly out of his own experience as parish priest and diocesan bishop, and he never lost the urge to function as such. One of his most startling innovations as pope was to conduct catechism classes himself every Sunday afternoon in the courtyard of the church of San Damaso.

His pontificate was therefore to be distinguished both by a personal approachability and warmth which contrasted absolutely with his predecessor, and by a series of important practical reforms. These included the reconstruction and simplification of the Code of Canon law, the improvement of seminary education for the clergy and of catechetical teaching in the parishes, the reform of the Church's prayer life through the breviary and missal, and a sustained campaign to get the faithful to receive communion more frequently, which included the admission of children to communion from the unprecedentedly early age of seven. These pastoral reforms, and espe cially the reform of the liturgy, modest in scope as they were, were to be picked up and extended in the mid-century by Pius XII, and would bear their full fruit at the Second Vatican Council.

All this, combined with his anti-intellectualism, his plump, hand some face and warm, open-hearted manner, won an immense popu lar following for the pope, a devotion which was to culminate in his canonisation in 1950. He was in many ways the first 'Pope of the people', a type which would become more familiar in the television age in the person of John XXIII and the short-lived John Paul I. But if Sarto's pontificate looked forward to a new populism, it also looked backwards to a nineteenth-century agenda.

For the choice of the name Pius X was no accident. The new Pope saw himself as a fighter against the modern world like Pio Nono, ready to suffer as he had suffered for the rights of the Church. He too was preoccupied with the Italian question, the confiscation of the Papal States and the temporal sovereignty of the Holy See, the issue which had made of Pius IX the voluntary 'Prisoner of the Vatican'. As Patri arch of Venice Pius X had cooperated pragmatically and tacitly with moderate liberal politicians, but this was mainly for fear of a growing socialism in Italy. He detested the Italian state, and distrusted even the modest advances towards other liberal regimes made by his diplomat predecessor. His first pastoral letter as Patriarch of Venice had empha sised this almost apocalyptic distrust of modern society:

> God has been driven out of public life by the separation of Church and State; he has been driven out of science now that doubt has been raised to a system.... . He has even been driven out of the family which is no longer considered sacred in its origins and is shorn of the grace of the sacraments.

His remedy for these ills was an undeviating devotion to papal directives, an absolute ultramontanism:

> When we speak of the Vicar of Christ, we must not quibble, we must obey: we must not...evaluate his judgements, criticise his directions, lest we do injury to Jesus Christ himself. Society is sick...the one hope, the one remedy, is the Pope.[2]

This exalted view of papal authority was directed, in the first place, to the renewal of the life of the Church, and the first five years of his pontificate saw the inauguration of a series of far-reaching reforms. Reacting to the interference of Austria during the conclave which had elected him, he abolished once and for all the right of any lay power to a voice in the electoral process. Though he had never worked in the Curia he had served for eighteen years as Chancellor of Treviso, and was an effective administrator. He restructured the Roman Curia, streamlining its thirty-seven different agencies and dicasteries to eleven Congregations, three tribunals and five offices, and redistributing its responsibilities on a more rational and efficient basis. His work at Treviso had also convinced him of the urgent need for a revision of the Code of Canon Law. He commissioned Monsignor Pietro Gasparri, former professor of Canon Law at the Institut Catholique, to coordinate this project, assisted by the young Eugenio Pacelli, the future Pope Pius XII.

The revised code was not finally approved until 1917, three years after Pius' death, but it was a project very close to his own heart and he personally drove it forward. It drew on a wide circle of expertise outside Rome, and its sections were sent out to the world's bishops for comment and approval. Its overall effect, however, was a massive increase in centralisation. It owed more to the spirit of the Napoleonic Code than to scripture or patristic tradition (scripture is rarely quoted in it), and it canonised as permanent features of church life aspects of the papal office which were very recent developments. Of these, the most momentous was the new canon 329, which declared that all bishops were to be nominated by the Roman pontiff, setting the seal of legal timelessness on a radical extension of papal responsibility which had taken place virtually in living memory.

These administrative and legal reforms were undertaken in the interests of greater pastoral effectiveness. That pastoral motive was evident in Papa Sarto's campaign for greater frequency of communion. The Eucharistic Congresses of the late nineteenth century had been designed as international demonstrations of Catholic fervour, and rallying points of Catholic identity. They had not been designed to encourage the laity to receive communion more frequently, but this had been a prime objective of Pius X as diocesan bishop and he now made it a priority of his pontificate. Many lay people received communion only a few times a year. Pius X believed that weekly and even daily communion was the key to a fully Catholic life. Between

May 1905 and July 1907 he issued a stream of initiatives, a dozen in all, to encourage more frequent communion, easing the fasting regulations for the sick, emphasising that communion was a remedy for shortcomings, not the reward of perfection. In 1910 he took these measures to unprecedented lengths in reducing the age of First Communion, conventionally administered at twelve or fourteen, to seven, laying it down that a child need only be able to distinguish the difference 'between the Eucharistic bread and common bread' to be eligible to receive it. The admission of children to communion was one of those relatively minor-seeming changes which profoundly transformed the religious and social experience of millions of Christians. Round these child-communions grew up a celebration of innocence and family – little girls dressed and veiled in white, little boys in sashes and rosettes, the gathering of kindred to celebrate, community processions and parades of first-communicants – which rapidly entered Catholic folk culture: Pius' own popularity as a pope of the people grew as a direct result.

He also pushed on a series of reforms within the structure of the liturgy itself. Nineteenth-century church music, especially in Italy, had been colonised by the opera house, and musical settings for Mass and Office often featured bravura solo and ensemble performances, and the use of orchestral instruments, which were often aggressively secular in character. In November 1903 the new pope denounced this decadent musical tradition and called for a return to the ancient tradition of plainsong, and the classical polyphony of the Counter-Reformation. The liturgical work of the Benedictine monks of Solesmes, who had pioneered the restoration of Gregorian chant, was given papal backing, and the result was the production of a new Kyriale, Graduale and Antiphonary, providing revised plainchant for all the solemn services of the Church.

He also set about the reform of the breviary, the daily prayer of the clergy. Over the centuries the ancient structure of the Divine Office, following the pattern of the liturgical year and drawing on most of the psalter, had been overlaid by the multiplication of saints' days and special observances. Pius commissioned an extensive revision of the breviary, simplifying its structure, reducing the number of psalms priests were expected to recite (from eighteen at Sunday matins to nine short psalms or sections of psalms), increasing the readings from scripture included in it and giving the ordinary Sunday liturgy priority over saints' days. There were critics of all these measures, but they were clearly and explicitly designed to encourage greater participation in the liturgy, and they were the first official stirrings of interest in the nascent liturgical movement.

Pius' other reform measures all show the same practical orientation – the improvement of seminary syllabuses to produce a better-qualifed pastoral clergy, the production of a new catechism which he hoped to see used throughout the world, and the closer scrutiny of the pastoral work of bishops through stricter enforcement of *ad limina* visits every five years. He cared passionately about the parish ministry, kept a statue of the patron saint of parish priests, the Cure d'Ars, on his desk, and on the fiftieth anniversary of his own ordination published an Apostolic Exhortation on the priesthood which is a classic of its kind. He was equally committed to raising episcopal standards, and devoted one encyclical, *Communium Rerum* (1909), to the qualities required in a good bishop. The increased emphasis on ad limina visits was designed to further this end. At these visits bishops had to submit circumstantial accounts of the condition of their diocese, based on a detailed questionnaire. The same growth of central supervision by the papacy was evident in Pius' measures to secure better episcopal appointments by personal scrutiny of the files of every candidate for promotion to the episcopate – papal absolutism in the service of Tridentine-style reform.

The dilemmas of a pastoral papacy in an age of intransigence are revealed in the relations of Pius X with the movement known as Catholic Action. The vigour of nineteenth-century Catholicism had produced a wave of Catholic activism and organisations devoted to good works, from charitable confraternities distributing old clothes to Catholic trade unions and youth organisations. Successive popes had encouraged such groups, but had also displayed a marked nervousness about the dangers of uncontrolled lay initiative within them. The popes were also anxious that the strictly confessional character of Catholic organisations be preserved, and Pius X was particularly emphatic about this. Catholic Action in Italy therefore had a strong 'ghetto mentality', aggressive towards the Italian state, strident and militant in tone. Since the 1870s Catholic voluntary organisations had been grouped together under the umbrella of the *Opera dei Congressi*, whose leader was appointed by the pope.

Here, as in so much else, Leo XIII, without radical intention, had caused a shift in ethos. The relatively open atmosphere of Leo's pontificate had encouraged the emergence of a Social Catholicism which engaged with the problems of modern society and sought solutions in social policies which had something in common even with socialism, and which did not flinch from calling itself Christian Democracy. In this more hopeful and upbeat atmosphere, and despite the condemnation of 'Americanism', Christian Democratic groups had emerged in France and Italy, which aimed to promote a new and more optimistic assessment of the relationship between the ancient faith and the new political order. These stirrings were reflected within even the traditionally hardline *Opera dei Congressi*, some of whose members now sought more direct political involvement in the Italian state, and greater freedom from clerical control. Tensions flared within the movement within a year of Pius X's election.

Pius X himself passionately believed in an active laity as the key to the success of the Church's mission in society, but he was deeply suspicious of all 'Christian Democratic' movements which were even remotely political. As Patriarch of Venice he had insisted that Christian Democracy 'must never mix itself up in politics', and that Catholics writing about the conditions of the working classes and the poor must never encourage class animosity by speaking 'of rights and justice, when it is purely a question of charity'.³ This was a definite retreat from the position mapped out in *Rerum Novarum*. He was equally clear that all lay action must be unquestioningly obedient to clerical direction. In July 1904 he dissolved the *Opera dei Congressi*, and in the following year issued an encyclical, *Il Fermo Proposito*, setting out the principles of Catholic Action. He encouraged Catholic organisations to pool their energies 'in an effort to restore Jesus Christ to his place in the family, in the school, in the community', but insisted that all such associations must submit themselves 'to the advice and superior direction of ecclesiastical authority'. As he wrote elsewhere, 'The Church is by its very nature an unequal society: it comprises two categories of person, the pastors and the flocks. The hierarchy alone moves and controls.... The duty of the multitude is to suffer itself to be governed and to carry out in a submissive spirit the orders of those in control'.⁴

THE ATTACK ON MODERNISM.

Encouraged by the freer atmosphere of Leo XIII's pontificate, Catholic theologians and philosophers in Germany, England, France and Italy had tried to adapt Catholic thought to a new age. Official theology seemed to many to have become locked into a rigid formalism, dependent on a biblical fundamentalism which had long since been discredited, insisting that the truths of Christianity were externally 'provable' by miracles and prophecies, and suspicious of the whole movement of 'romantic' theology and philosophy which pointed to human experience, feeling and ethical intuition as sources of religious certainty. In the last years of the nineteenth century Catholic biblical scholars and historians began to explore the early origins of Christianity with a new freedom, Catholic philosophers engaged creatively instead of defensively with the currents of thought which stemmed from Kant and Hegel, Catholic systematic theologians began to consider the nature of the Church not as a timeless and rigidly disciplined military structure centreing on the pope, but as a complex living organism subject to growth and change.

But the reign of Pius X was to see all these movements ruthlessly crushed. Deeply hostile to intellectualism of every kind, Pius X and the advisers he gathered round him saw in every attempt at the liberalisation of Catholic theology and social thought, nothing but heresy and betrayal. In his first pastoral as Patriarch of Venice he had declared that 'Liberal catholics are wolves in sheep's clothing: and therefore the true priest is bound to unmask them....Men will accuse you of clericalism, and you will be called papists, retrogrades, intransigents...Be proud of it!'[5] As pope, he acted on this obligation to 'unmask' the rot of liberalism which he saw everywhere in Catholic intellectual life.

Confrontation came over the work of the French priest and biblical scholar, Father Alfred Loisy, professor at the Institut Catholique in Paris. Loisy's book, *The Gospel and the Church*, was designed to defend the Catholic faith by demonstrating that the findings of radical biblical criticism dissolved traditional Protestant reliance on scripture alone, over and against the tradition of the Church, and made impossible any naive biblical literalism. In the New Testament, Loisy argued, we do not have a picture of Christ as he actually was, as many Protestants imagined, but as he was understood within the early

Church's tradition. There was therefore no getting behind the tradition of the Church to an unmediated Christ. We know him and can relate to him only through the developing life of the Church. Christ had proclaimed the Kingdom of Heaven, and what came was the Catholic Church.

Loisy's book was a sensational success. Many Catholics saw in it conclusive proof that modernity, in the shape of the latest theological scholarship, worked for and not against the Church. Even the pope himself remarked that here at any rate was a theological book that wasn't boring. But the remark implied no approval. He and his conservative advisers believed that Loisy's argument was based on a corrosive scepticism about biblical facts which would erode all religious truth and certainty. This subjectivism must be stamped on. Loisy was silenced, and in 1907 Pius issued a decree against the Modernist heresy, *Lamentabili*, and, two months later, the ninety-three page encyclical *Pascendi*, lumping a miscellaneous assortment of new ideas together under the blanket term 'Modernism', and characterising these new ways of thinking as a 'compendium of all the heresies'.[6] *Pascendi* had been drafted by Joseph Lemius, a curial theologian who had spent years obsessively collecting doctrinal propositions from the works of contemporary Catholic theologians, and assembling them into the elaborate anti-doctrinal system which he believed underlay all their works. There was more than a hint of fantasy and conspiracy theory behind all this, and the encyclical itself was characterised by extreme violence of language. The Modernists were denounced as not only mistaken, but as vicious, deceitful and disloyal: 'enemies of the church they are indeed: to say they are her worst enemies is not far from the truth…their blows are the more sure because they know where to strike her'. All Modernists are motivated by a mixture of curiosity and pride.

No one ever subscribed to all the views condemned by *Lamentabili* and *Pascendi*: at one level the Modernist heresy was a figment of the pope's imagination (or that of his ghost writer). Yet it cannot reasonably be doubted that the pope was responding to a genuine crisis within Catholic theology, as a host of thinkers wrestled, sometimes unsuccessfully, to appropriate for Catholicism new methods and discoveries in the natural sciences, in history and archaeology, and in biblical studies. To some extent, however, the crisis was of the papacy's own making. The increasingly narrow orthodoxy of the nineteenth-century Roman schools left Catholic philosophers and theologians little room for manoeuvre, and the enforced secrecy and isolation of much of the work being done meant that new thinking could not be properly integrated into the tradition. Despite the liberalising trends of Leo XIII's pontificate, many of the best theologians of the period felt themselves to be working as outcasts, against the grain of official Catholic theology. Inevitably there were casualties, and there were those whose work took them well beyond the limits of any recognisably Catholic or even Christian framework of thought. By the time he published *L'Evangile et L'Eglise*, for example, Loisy himself had long since ceased to believe in the divine character of the Church, or in any supernatural revelation.

In condemning Modernism, therefore, Pius X not unreasonably saw himself as exercising the papacy's traditional responsibility of vigilance on behalf of the Church, sounding a warning against the disastrous false direction in which he believed many theologians were leading the faithful. The trouble lay in the undiscriminating character of the condemnation, its unfocused severity and paranoia. If the pope had a duty to warn against error, he also had a duty to care for the erring, and to discriminate real error from legitimate freedom of reflection and investigation. No such discriminations were made, and little quarter was shown to those suspected of straying beyond the allowed limits. The encyclical was simply the opening shot in what rapidly became nothing less than a reign of terror. The pope's denunciation not merely of ideas but of motives unleashed a flood of suspicion and reprisal. Liberal Catholic newspapers and periodicals were suppressed, seminary teachers and academics suspected of flirting with new ideas were disgraced and dismissed from their posts. A secret organisation designed to winkle out theological deviants, the *Sodalitium Pianum*, ('The Society of St Pius V') led by Monsignor Umberto Benigni, was personally encouraged by the pope. It lied to, spied on and harrassed suspect theologians. Private letters were opened and photographed, clerical *agents provacateurs* lured unwary liberals into incriminating themselves and, ludicrously, over-zealous seminary professors even denounced their students for heresy, on the basis of essays written in class. The blamelessly orthodox Angelo Roncalli, future Pope John XXIII, taught church history in the obscure seminary at Bergamo. He was secretly denounced for encouraging his students to read a suspect book, the Vatican's informant even checking out the records of the local bookshop to see who was buying what (the book was Luis Duchesne's masterly *Early History of the Christian Church*). Roncalli, on a routine visit to the Vatican, was duly frightened out of his wits by a heavy warning from one of the most senior curial cardinals. Great scholars were sacked, compliant nonentities promoted. No one was safe, and distinguished bishops, even curial cardinals, found their every action and word watched and reported. Merry Del Val, the Cardinal Secretary of State, an uncompromising opponent of the new heresy often blamed for the campaign of repression, himself became alarmed by the extremism of these measures. He tried unsuccessfully to restrain Benigni, who in turn accused him of spineless over-caution.

The *Sodalitium Pianum* never had more than fifty members, but its influence and spirit was far more widespread than its mere numerical strength. A new intransigence became the required mark of the 'good' Catholic. 'Real' Catholics were 'integralists', accepting as a package deal everything the pope taught, not picking and choosing in the 'pride and curiosity' of their intellect. In September 1910 the general atmosphere of suspicion was institutionalised when a lengthy and ferocious oath was devised to impose a straitjacket of orthodoxy on suspects, and subscription to this oath became a routine and repeated part of the progress of every cleric's career, from the lowliest priest to the most exalted cardinal. The 'Anti-Modernist Oath' shattered public confidence in the integrity and freedom of Catholic academic standards. Only in Germany did the bishops succeed in having university professors exempted from subscription to the oath.

The worst features of the anti-Modernist purge were suspended at the death of Pius X in 1914. It was rumoured that one of the first documents across the desk of his successor, Benedict XV, was a secret denunciation of himself as a Modernist, which had been intended for Pius X's eyes. However that may be, the new pope's first encyclical formally renewed the condemnation of Modernism, but in fact dismantled the witch-hunt against it. He insisted on freedom of discussion where the Church had not formally pronounced on an issue, and called for an end to namecalling by the Integralists. When, a generation later, the cause of Pius X's canonisation was put forward, detailed evidence of the pope's personal involvement in this witch-hunt was published. It revealed his own passionate commitment to the campaign, shocking many Catholics who had admired Sarto's warmth and humanity. Some people, he had declared, want the Modernists 'treated with oil, soap and caresses: but they should be beaten with fists'.[7]

The canonisation went ahead. But the impact of the Modernist crisis on Catholic intellectual life was catastrophic, and persisted almost to the present. The anti-Modernist oath remained in force into the 1960s, a feature of the intellectual formation of every single Catholic priest, creating a stifling ethos of unjust and suspicious hyper-orthodoxy, and discouraging all originality. Catholic biblical studies withered, shackled to absurd and demonstrably false claims like the Mosaic authorship of the Pentateuch or the unity of authorship of the whole book of Isaiah. Catholic philosophers and theologians were forced into silence or into token parroting of the party line. Obedience, not enquiry, became the badge of Catholic thought. It was to be a generation before anything approaching an open and honest intellectual life was possible for Catholic theologians.

The confrontational attitudes which underlay the Modernist purges also informed Pius X's political actions. He had announced the motto of his pontificate as being 'To restore all things in Christ'. For him, though he denied he was a politician, that motto had an inescapably political meaning, for what he sought was a society which reflected Catholic values. The pope, he declared in his first papal allocution to the cardinals, 'is absolutely unable to separate the things of faith from politics'. The pope is 'head and first magistrate of the Christian Society', and as such he must 'confute and reject such principles of modern philosophy and civil law as may urge the course of human affairs in a direction not permitted by the restrictions of eternal law'.[8]

Within a few years, in pursuit of this mission to 'confute and reject' secular laws that conflicted with Church teaching, Pius had demolished the diplomatic achievement of Leo XIII. In contrast to his predecessor, Pius saw papal diplomatic activity not in terms of the art of the possible, of compromise, but in confrontational – or perhaps he would have said prophetic – terms. Professional papal diplomats were replaced as legates and nuncios by bishops and heads of religious orders, who would act as mouthpieces for the pope's fiery and apocalyptic views of the modern world. The problems of this policy of confrontation were laid bare in the collapse of relations between Church and State in France in 1905, and the subsequent confiscation by the Republican government of all Church property in 1907.

This disaster was not, to begin with at least, the pope's fault. Relations between the Church and the French state had been rocky for twenty years, growing anti-clericalism expressing itself in a succession of government measures of a depressingly familiar kind – the suppression of religious instruction in schools, attacks on and eventual expulsion of religious orders from France. Matters came to a head with the accession as Prime Minister in 1902 of Emile Combes, a rabid anti-clerical who had once been a seminarian, and was all the more bitter against the Church that had refused him ordination. Even the expert diplomacy of Leo XIII and his Secretary of State Cardinal Rampolla could do nothing to restrain Combes, who flouted the informal arrangements which had made the Concordat workable for a century, and he nominated unsuitable bishops without any consultation with Rome. By the time Pius X became pope, France and the Vatican were eyeball to eyeball over these bishops. The problem deepened when the pope demanded the resignation of two bishops accused of immorality and freemasonry. M. Combes refused to accept their resignations, on the grounds that the pope's action constituted an infringement of government rights.

This situation would have been hard for any pope to handle, but the political inexperience and clumsiness of Pius and his Secretary of State now proved fatal. When the French President paid a state visit to Rome in May 1904 and called on the King, Merry Del Val issued a routine diplomatic protest against this recognition of the Italian state in papal Rome. Foolishly and offensively, however, the Secretary of State circulated a copy of this protest to all governments, and these copies contained a sentence claiming that the papacy was only maintaining relations with France because the fall of the Combes Ministry was imminent. Here was a blatantly public political act by the papacy, apparently designed to bring about or at any rate speed up the fall of the French government. French public opinion was at frenzy pitch, the French ambassador was withdrawn from the Vatican, and, though Combes' goverment did indeed eventually fall, in December 1905 a law abrogating the Concordat of 1801 and separating Church and State was promulgated. The state would cease to pay clerical stipends, church buildings and property passed to the state, and would be managed for the use of the Church by religious associations of lay people, known as *Associations Cultuelles*.

The Law of Separation was unjust and arbitrary, and it unilaterally revoked an international treaty, the Concordat. Nevertheless, the overwhelming majority of French bishops believed that the Church had no choice but to accept it, if it was to continue its work in France. The pope took a different view. To accept the separation of Church and State anywhere was to acquiesce in robbing Christ of his crown rights over society, 'a grave insult to God, the Creator of man and the Founder of human society'. Moreover, the whole principle of the *Associations Cultuelles* was anti-Christian, for they challenged the hierarchical structure of the Church. Lay people, he considered, had no business 'managing' the Church's property or affairs. On 11 February he issued the encyclical *Vehementer*, denouncing the Law of Separation as a violation of natural and human law, contrary to the Divine constitution of the Church and her rights and liberty. A fortnight later he reiterated his rejection of the Law when he consecrated fourteen new bishops in St Peter's, chosen by himself, for the Church of France.

This condemnation left the French bishops almost no room for manouevre. They tried to modify it along the lines laid down in 1864 by Dupanloup in his pamphlet on the Syllabus, accepting the condemnation of the Separation in principle, but devising practical working arrangements so that church life could go on, the clergy be paid, the churches kept open. The *Associations Cultuelles* might be renamed *Associations Canoniques et Legales*, and put under the tacit supervision of clergy. Rome would have none of this. In August 1906 the pope issued another encyclical, *Gravissimo*, in which he seized on the bishops' dutiful endorsement of the papal condemnation of the Law, and under the pretence of supporting 'the practically unanimous decision of your assembly', ordered them to have no truck or compromise with the Law. When the plight of the French bishops was explained to the pope as part of a plea for political realism, he was unsympathetic and unyielding: 'They will starve, and go to heaven', he declared. [9]

As his canonisation in 1954 demonstrated, Pius X set a pattern of papal behaviour that went on influencing his successors. Since the definition of papal infallibility, the mystique of the papacy had intensified, though it manifested itself in different ways − in the regal detachment of Leo XIII, in the startling authoritarianism of Pius X's personal style. At the very beginning of his pontificate, the Swiss Guard, as was customary, went on strike for gratuities to mark the new reign: the new pope listened, and then abruptly announced the dissolution of the Guard, a decision from which he was only dissuaded with much pleading. His successors would emulate him, keeping their advisers and court standing round them while they sat, acting without consultation or consulting only an inner circle. Eugenio Pacelli, who became Pius XII in 1939 and a much gentler figure than either Pius X or Pius XI, declared that 'I do not want collaborators, but people who will carry out orders'. Now with the growing papal monopoly of episcopal appointments, the system of papal nuncios, sent to Catholic countries all over the world, directing policy, overriding local decisions, decisively influencing the choice of bishops, became an evermore powerful instrument of centralisation within the Church. In an age in which monarchies were tumbling everywhere, the popes had become the last absolute monarchs.

II THE AGE OF THE DICTATORS.

The election of Giacoma della Chiesa as Benedict XV (1914–22) to succeed Pius X, was as explicit a reaction against the preceeding regime as it was possible to get. Della Chiesa was a wisp of a man with one shoulder higher than the other – his nickname in the seminary had been 'Piccoletto', 'Tiny' – and none of the papal robes kept in readiness for the election was small enough to fit him. He was a Genoese aristocrat trained as a papal diplomat, who had served Cardinal Rampolla as Under-Secretary of State to Leo XIII. He had initially been retained in post under Merry Del Val and Pius X, but the pope distrusted him as a protégé of Rampolla's, and in 1907 he had been kicked upstairs as Archbishop of Bologna. The pope made clear the nature of this 'promotion' by witholding until 1914 the cardinal's hat that went automatically with the job, and Della Chiesa became a cardinal only three months before the conclave that made him pope. Della Chiesa was to have his revenge, for immediately after his election as Pope, Merry Del Val was sent packing from his post as Secretary of State without so much as time to sort his papers. The conclave took place one month into the First World War, and the choice of Della Chiesa was a recognition that blundering if saintly intransigence would not do in wartime.

War was to dominate and to blight Benedict's pontificate. He was a compassionate and sensitive priest, horrified by the realities of modern warfare, passionately committed to diplomatic solutions of international conflicts. He bent all his efforts to persuading the combatants to seek a negotiated peace. He refused to take sides, judging that the Holy See would only be listened to if it preserved a strict neutrality. In a war where public opinion was stoked by stories of atrocities of the 'babies-on-bayonets' type, he refused to condemn even documented outrages. The result was that each side accused him of favouring the other. Hurt but undeterred, he went on condemning the 'senseless massacre' and 'hideous butchery' being perpetrated by both sides. In 1917 he proposed a peace plan which involved all concerned agreeing to waive compensation for war damage. Most of this damage had been done by Germany in victim countries like France and Belgium, and they not unnaturally saw the pope's plan as favouring Germany. They also drew their own conclusions from the fact that Germany favoured the scheme, and had offered to help the pope recover Rome in the wake of the defeat of Italy. In France even the clergy spoke of him as 'the *Boche* Pope'.

The continuing confrontation with Italy over the Roman question further paralysed Benedict's efforts for peace. By a secret agreement in 1915 Italy persuaded her allies, including England, not to negotiate with the pope, for fear he would attempt to bring international pressure on Italy to recover Rome – as indeed he had hoped to do. To his bitter disappointment, he was excluded altogether from the peace negotiations of 1919, and he was highly critical of what he took to be the 'vengeful' character of the Versailles settlement. In hard terms, therefore, his contribution to the amelioration of war was confined to the money he lavished on relief work for the wounded, refugees and displaced people – 82,000,000 lire, leaving the Vatican safes empty.

In the aftermath of war, however, his diplomatic skills came into their own. He recognised that the war had thrown much of the political structure of Europe into the melting pot, and that the position of the Church everywhere from France to the Balkans, from Spain to Soviet Russia needed to be secured. He threw himself and his hand-picked helpers into a flurry of negotiation to secure new Concordats, sending the Vatican librarian Achille Ratti, destined to be his successor as Pius XI, to the newly resurrected Poland and Lithuania, and sending Eugenio Pacelli, the future Pius XII, to Germany.

Benedict XV was as conciliatory as his predecessor had been confrontational, and in many ways his policies can be seen as a resumption of the course drawn out for the papacy by Leo XIII. As we have seen, he dismantled the machinery of Integralist reaction, dissolving the *Sodalitium Pianum* and calling a halt to the anti-Modernist witch-hunt. He prepared the way for reconciliation with the state of Italy by lifting in 1920 the Vatican ban on visits by Catholic heads of state to the Quirinal. He tacitly lifted the 'Non Expedit' ban on involvement in Italian electoral politics for Catholics by giving his blessing to the new *Partito Popolare*, the Catholic political party led by the radical priest Don Luigi Sturzo. And in another reversal of Pius X's policy, he encouraged Catholics to join the trade union movement. Most spectacularly, he inaugurated a reconciliation with France. Ironically, he was helped here by the war he had hated so much. The abrogation of the Concordat had meant that French clergy and seminarians lost their immunity from military service. Twenty-five thousand French priests, seminarians and religious were called up and went to the trenches, and their participation in the national suffering – in sharp contrast to the non-combatant status of chaplains in the British army – did a great deal to dissolve inherited antagonisms between Church and nation. The pope signalled the new spirit of reconciliation by canonising Joan of Arc in 1920, a highly imaginative symbolic gesture: 80 French deputies attended and the French government sent official representatives. By the time of his death in 1922 Benedict had greatly increased the papacy's diplomatic standing, and twenty-seven countries had ambassadors or similar representatives accredited to the Vatican.

Nobody was ready for another conclave in 1922, for Benedict XV was still in his sixties and died after only a short illness. No one could predict the outcome of the election, and the outcome in any case was astonishing. Achille Ratti, who took the name Pius XI (1922–39) was a scholar who had spent almost all his working life as a librarian, first at the Ambrosiano in his native Milan, and then at the Vatican, where he replaced a German as prefect at the outbreak of the First World War. He was a distinguished scholar of medieval palaeography, and had edited important texts on the early Milanese liturgy. He was also a keen mountaineer, and the author of a readable book on alpine climbing. He had been mysteriously whisked out of his library by Benedict XV in 1919, consecrated titular Archbishop of Lepanto, and sent as nuncio to Poland, which had just emerged from Tsarist rule and where the Catholic Church was in the process of reconstruction. Why Benedict of all people should have given this delicate mission to a man like Ratti, utterly without any relevant experience, is a mystery. He was a gifted linguist, and his German and French proved useful, but he had no Slav languages at all. His time in Poland was extremely eventful, for Polish bishops resented and cold-shouldered him as a spy for a pro-German pope. The Revolution in Russia raised the spectre of a Bolshevik takeover of the whole of Eastern Europe. The nuncio, who refused to flee, was besieged in Warsaw in August 1920 by Bolshevik troops. The experience left him with a lasting conviction that communism was the worst enemy Christian Europe had ever faced, a conviction which shaped much of his policy as pope.

He returned from Poland to appointment as Archbishop of Milan, and the cardinal's hat, but he had been in office only six months when he was elected pope, on the fourteenth ballot in a conclave deadlocked between Benedict XV's Secretary of State, Cardinal Gasparri, and the intransigent anti-Modernist, Cardinal La Fontaine. Gasparri had been Ratti's immediate superior when he was nuncio in Poland, and when it became clear that his own candidacy could not succeed, he was instrumental in securing Ratti's election. It was certain, then, that the new pope would continue Benedict XV's (and Gasparri's) policies. Despite the new pope's choice of name, there would be no return to the Integralism of Pius X.

Benedict XV had been preparing the ground for a settlement of the Roman question, and Pius XI's first act as pope made it clear that he intended to carry this through. Having announced his papal name, he told the cardinals that he would give the blessing 'Urbi et Orbi' from the balcony in St Peter's square, and a window closed against Italy for fifty-two years was opened.

The instant announcement that he would use the balcony into the square for his blessing was characteristic of the decisiveness of the new regime, a decisiveness soon revealed as nothing short of dictatorial. From the moment of his election the mild and obliging scholar-librarian became pope to the utter degree. He remained genial, smiling, apparently approachable. The Vatican filled with visitors, especially from Milan, he spent hours in public audiences, he met and blessed thousands of newly-weds, he had expensive display-shelves built for the tacky gifts the simple faithful gave him. Nonetheless, an invisible wall had descended around him. He ruled from behind it and he would brook no contradiction. He accepted advice, if at all, only when he had asked for it, and he soon became famous for towering rages which left his entourage weak and trembling. Even visiting diplomats noted that the key word in the Vatican had become obedience.

The obedience was directed towards a vigorous development of many of the initiatives of Benedict XV. These included the rapprochement with France signalled by the canonisation of the Maid of Orleans. The way here, however, was blocked by the intransigent hostility of many Catholics to the French Republic. A key influence here was *Action Française*, an extreme anti-republican movement with its own eponymous newspaper, edited by Charles Maurras. Maurras, a cradle Catholic, had long since abandoned belief in God, but he admired the organisation of the Church and saw it as the chief and indispensable bastion of conservatism in society. Christianity, he thought, had fortunately smothered the 'Hebrew Christ' in the garments of the Roman Empire. Religion, he declared, 'was not the mystery of the Incarnation, but the secret of social order'. Royalist, anti-semitic, reactionary, Maurras had an immense following among Catholics, including some of the French episcopate. In 1926 the Catholic youth of Belgium voted him the most influential contemporary writer, 'a giant in the realm of thought, a lighthouse to our youth'. Maurras' views had long caused unease in the Vatican, but he championed the Church, and Pius X had protected him: he told Maurras' mother that 'I bless his work'. [10]

Pius XI was made of sterner stuff. Catholics excused Maurras' work on the grounds that it was politics pressed into defence of the Church. Ratti believed that in fact Maurras exploited religion in the service of his politics, and that in any case all politics went rotten unless inspired by true religion. Maurras was a barrier in the way of the political realism in France which Pius, like Benedict XV and Leo XIII, thought essential for the well-being of the Church. Despite stonewalling by the Vatican staff (the crucial file went missing, until the pope threatened all concerned with instant dismissal) in 1925 he took steps against Maurras and his movement, first by instigating episcopal condemnation in France, then by placing *Action Française* and all Maurras' writings on the Index, and finally, in 1927, by a formal excommunication of all supporters of the movement.

The suppression of *Action Française* was a measure of Pius XI's strength of character and singleness of mind. He was accused of betrayal of the Church's best friend, of siding with Jews, Freemasons, Radicals. From the French clergy he met with a good deal of dumb resistance. The Jesuit Cardinal Billot, who had been a key figure in the anti-Modernist purges and was the most influential theologian in Rome, sent *Action Française* a note of sympathy, which of course they published. Billot was summoned to explain himself to the pope, and was made to resign his cardinalate. Pius was equally ruthless with all who resisted the suppression. Support for Maurras was strong among the French Holy Ghost Fathers, one of whom was the rector of the French Seminary in Rome where the students had a strong *Action Française* group. Pius sent for the ancient, bearded superior of the Order, and told him to sack the rector. The old man replied, 'Yes, Holy Father, I'll see what I can do', upon which the Pope grabbed his beard and shouted 'I didn't say, see what you can do, I said fire him'.[11]

Pius also extended Benedict XV's concern with the renewal of Catholic missions. Benedict had published in 1919 an encyclical on missions, Maximum Illud, in which he had identified three priorities for future Catholic missionary activity: the recruitment and promotion of a native clergy, the renunciation of nationalistic concerns among European missionaries, and the recognition of the dignity and worth of the cultures being evangelised. These anti-imperialist guidelines became the basis for Pius XI's policy. He himself published an encyclical on missions in 1926, and in the same year put theory into practice by consecrating the first six indigenous Chinese bishops in St Peter's, and a year later the first Japanese Bishop of Nagasaki. He was later to ordain native bishops and priests for India, south-east Asia and China. Once again, this was a policy which met with widespread resistance, and once again Ratti doggedly persisted. At his accession not a single missionary diocese in the Catholic Church was presided over by an indigenous bishop. By 1939 there were forty, the numbers of local-born mission priests had almost trebled to over 7,000, he had created 200 Apostolic Vicariates and prefectures in mission territories, and missiology was an established subject for study and research in the key Roman Colleges. It was a dramatic internationalisation of the Catholic Church in an age of growing nationalism, and it was only achieved by the maximum exertion of papal muscle.

In diplomacy too, Ratti followed in his predecessor's footsteps. From his first year as pope a stream of new Concordats were concluded, to secure freedom of action for the Church in post-war Europe: Latvia in November 1922, Bavaria in March 1924, Poland in

February 1925, Romania in May 1927, Lithuania in September 1927, Italy in February 1929, Prussia in June 1929, Baden in October 1932, Austria in June 1933, Nazi Germany in July 1933, Yugoslavia in July 1935. Behind them all was a concern not merely to secure Catholic education, unhampered papal appointment of bishops, and free communication with Rome, but to halt as far as was possible the secularising of European life which the popes had been resisting under the lable 'Liberalism' for more than a century. So Ratti's encyclical of 1925, Quas Primas, inaugurating the new Feast of Christ the King, denounced the 'plague of secularism', and asserted the rule of Christ, not merely over the individual soul, but over societies which, precisely as societies, and not as aggregates of individuals, must reverence and obey the law of God proclaimed by the Church.

From the Vatican's point of view, incomparably the most important of these Concordats was that with Fascist Italy, the result of almost three years of hard bargaining with Mussolini, and finally signed in February 1929. The Concordat gave the pope independence in the form of his own tiny sovereign state, the Vatican City (at 108.7 acres, just one-eighth of the size of New York's Central Park), with a few extra territorial dependencies like the Lateran and Castel Gondolfo. He had his own post office and radio station (a guarantee of freedom of communication with the world at large), the recognition of canon law alongside the law of the state, Church control of Catholic marriages, the teaching of Catholic doctrine in state schools (and the consequent placing of crucifixes in classrooms, a weighty symbolic gesture) and finally a massive financial compensation for the loss of the Papal States – 1,750,000,000 lire, a billion of it in Italian government stocks, but still a sum which in the hungry 1930s enabled Pius XI to spend like a Renaissance prince.

This Concordat did not deliver all that the pope had hoped, and it horrified those committed to Catholic Action and the anti-Fascist struggle. Battista Montini, the future Pope Paul VI, was disgusted, and asked 'was it worth sixty years of struggle to arrive at such a meagre result?' Pius viewed it as a triumph, nonetheless, or it represented a decisive repudiation of the 'Free Church in a Free State' ideal of Liberalism. Moreover, Mussolini had not merely resolved the Roman question, he had also suppressed the Church's enemies, the Italian Communists and the Freemasons. In the first flush of enthusiasm, and against Gasparri's advice, Pius spoke publicly of Mussolini as 'a man sent by Providence'. In the elections of March 1929, most Italian clergy encouraged their congregations to vote Fascist. There is no such thing as a free Concordat, however, and the major casualty of the agreement was the increasingly powerful Catholic Partito Popolare. In the run-up to the Concordat Mussolini made it clear that the dissolution of this rival political party was part of any deal, and the Vatican duly withdrew support for the Popolare, and secured the resignation of its priest-leader, Don Luigi Sturzo, and his self-exile in London. Pius XI thereby assisted at the deathbed of Italian democracy. It is unlikely that he shed many tears, for he was no democrat. He disapproved of radicalism, above all radicalism in priests. And though he was passionately committed to Catholic Action, and devoted his first encyclical to the subject, like Pius X he envisaged it as being confined to what he rather chillingly described as 'the organised participation of the laity in the hierarchical apostolate of the church, transcending party politics'.

Nevertheless, the defence of Catholic Action in this broader sense was to bring him rapidly into conflict with Mussolini. One of the lesser casualties of the Concordat was the Catholic scout movement, which Mussolini insisted must be merged with the state youth organisations. This went against the grain with Pius XI, who valued Catholic youth movements as a prime instrument of Christian formation. Mussolini was bullish on the issue, bragging that 'in the sphere of education we remain intractable. Youth shall be ours'. Fascist harassment of Catholic organisations mounted, and in June 1931 the pope denounced the actions of the Fascist regime in the Italian encyclical *Non Abbiamo Bisogno*. This letter was primarily concerned to denounce the harassment of Catholic organisations, and to vindicate Catholic Action from the Fascist claim that it was a front for the old Partito Popolare, Catholic political opposition under another name. But the pope broadened his condemnation to a general attack on Fascist idolatry, the 'Pagan worship of the State'. He singled out the Fascist oath as intrinsically against the law of God.

Pius was not calling Italy to abandon Fascism. The encyclical was careful to insist that the Church respected the legitimate authority of the government, and was essentially a warning shot across Mussolini's bows to lay off Church groups. In this, it was largely successful. It was an indication nonetheless that the pope was aware of the need for a long spoon when dealing with totalitarian regimes, and that certainly applied to the Concordat with Hitler in 1933. That Concordat was negotiated by Eugenio Pacelli, Secretary of State from 1930. Pacelli had spent most of the 1920s in Munich as nuncio, and was devoted to Germany and its culture. He had no illusions about Nazism, however, which he recognised as anti-Christian, and indeed from 1929 a number of the German bishops were vocal in denouncing its racial and religious teachings, insisting that no Catholic could be a Nazi. From Rome, however, Nazism looked like the strongest available bulwark against communism, and the Vatican's overriding priority was to secure a legal basis for the Church's work, whatever form of government happened to prevail.

Pacelli in fact later claimed that he and the pope were primarily concerned to establish a basis for legal protest against Nazi abuses, and that they entertained no high hopes of establishing peaceful coexistence with what they both had rapidly come to feel was a 'gangster' regime. Between 1933 and 1936 Pius XI directed three dozen such notes of protest about infringements of the Concordat to Berlin. They were mostly drafted by Pacelli, and their tone is anything but cordial.

Once again, the price of this Concordat was the death of a Catholic political party. The Centre Party had been the major instrument of Catholic political advance in Germany since 1870, and it too was led by a priest, Monsignor Ludwig Kaas. The Centre Party helped vote Hitler in, but Hitler had no intention of tolerating a democratic rival, Cardinal Pacelli made it clear that the Vatican had no interest in the Centre's survival, and the Party did not last. Kaas was summoned to Rome, where he became keeper of the building works at St Peter's: it was to be Kaas's activities in reordering the crypt of St Peter's, to make space for Pius XI's coffin, which would lead to the discovery of the ancient shrine of St Peter. There was widespread dismay in Europe at the political castration of Catholicism in Hitler's Germany, and the removal of yet another buffer between the German citizen and the Nazi state, but article 31 of the Concordat protected Catholic Action, 'the apple of the Pope's eye', and Pius XI was content.

In his dealings both with Fascism and with Nazism, Pius XI staked the well-being of Catholicism in Italy and Germany in the development of a vigorous religious life, fostered not merely by the Church's liturgy and sacramental tradition, but through Catholic social organisations from boy-scouts to trade unions and newspapers: hence his enthusiasm for Catholic Action. He was also aware that in the age of the totalitarian state such organisations needed political protection if they were to survive. Unlike Benedict XV, however, he imagined that the papacy alone could provide that political protection. He failed to grasp that freedom could not be guaranteed merely by international treaties – which is what Concordats were. By sacrificing the Catholic political parties Pius assisted in the destruction of mediating institutions capable of acting as restraints and protections against totalitarianism.

This is all the more striking because in 1931 he published a major encyclical, *Quadragesimo Anno*, to commemorate the fortieth anniversary of Rerum Novarum. In it he extended Leo's critique of unrestrained capitalism, while emphasising the incompatibility of Catholicism and socialism. In the most remarkable section of the letter, however, he argued the need for a reconstruction of society, which was in danger of becoming stripped down to an all-powerful state on the one hand, and the mere aggregate of individuals on the other. What was needed were intermediate structures, 'corporations' such as guilds or unions, without which social life lost its natural 'organic form'. He sketched out the principles of 'subsidiarity', by which such groups would handle many social tasks which were currently left to the state. These suggestions seemed to many to have strong similarities with the Fascist 'corporations' established for trades by Mussolini. The pope, however, emphasised the need for free and voluntary social organisation, in contrast to the Fascist corporations, in which 'the State is substituting itself in the place of private initiative', and so imposing 'an excessively bureaucratic and political character' on what ought to be free social cooperation.

As these mild criticisms and the much stronger attack on socialism in *Quadragesimo Anno* indicate, however, all Pius' social thinking was overshadowed by hatred and fear of communism. He denounced the Bolsheviks as 'missionaries of antichrist', and spoke often of communism's 'satanic preparations for a conquest of the whole world'. In the late 1920s and early 1930s his fears seemed amply justified. To the murder of clergy and persecution of the Church in Russia, against which he openly protested in 1930, was added the savagely anti-Catholic regime in Mexico, which from 1924 seriously set about eradicating Christianity. From 1931 the new Republican regime in Spain was increasingly hostile to the Church. With the outbreak of the Spanish Civil War in 1936 hostility turned to active persecution, and refugees flooded into Rome with accounts of communist atrocities, the massacres of priests and seminarians (7,000 murdered within months), the rape of nuns. The Nationalist opposition, by contrast, though also guilty of atrocity, and not originally noted for their piety, increasingly saw the Church as integral to their vision of Spain. They received the endorsement of all but one of the Spanish bishops in a joint pastoral in 1937, and despite General Franco's murderous acts of repression, the papacy backed him.

There was no disguising Pius XI's softness towards the right. An authoritarian himself, he saw no particular evil in strong leadership, and he valued Fascism's emphasis on the family and social discipline. When Italy invaded Abyssinia in 1935 the pope did not condemn, and delivered speeches couched in such bewildering and lofty generalities that it was impossible to say what he thought – it seems likely they were written by Cardinal Pacelli.

Yet there were limits to this papal tendency to the right. Pius XI viewed with horror the claims of the dictatorships to the absolute submission of their subjects, and he detested the racial doctrine which underlay Nazism. With the Concordat safely achieved, Hitler discarded the mask of cordiality towards the Church, and the Nazi press began a smear campaign. The Archbishop of Baden, it was claimed, had a Jewish mistress, the Vatican was financed by Jews, the Catholic Church was profiteering on inflation. Press attacks gave way to physical intimidation. By 1936 the Vatican had accumulated a vast dossier of Nazi attacks on the Church's freedom in Germany, which, it was rumoured, it intended to publish. Cardinal Pacelli, on a visit to America, declared that 'everything is lost' in Germany. The pope was now a sick man, his energy ebbing fast, prone to doze off in audiences, uncharacteristically leaving more and more to his subordinates. But he was increasingly agitated by what was happening, and had come to feel that Nazism was little better than the Bolshevism he had hoped it would counteract. Always irritable, he horrified Cardinal Pacelli by shouting at the German ambassador that if it came to another Kulturkampf, this time for the survival of Christianity itself, the Church would win again. Mussolini comforted the German – he had had this trouble himself, there was no point arguing with the 'old man'.

In January 1937 key figures from the German hierarchy came to Rome on their *ad limina* visit. They told the pope that the time for caution had passed, and Pius XI decided to act. Cardinal Faulhaber, Archbishop of Munich, was commissioned to produce a draft encyclical, which was tidied up by Pacelli, and signed by the pope. In a triumphant security operation, the encyclical was smuggled into Germany, locally printed, and read from Catholic pulpits on Palm Sunday 1937. *Mit Brennender Sorge*, 'With Burning Anxiety', denounced both specific government actions against the Church in breach of the Concordat, and Nazi racial theory more generally. There was a striking and deliberate emphasis on the permanent validity of the Jewish scriptures, and the pope denounced the 'Idolatrous cult' which replaced belief in the true God with a 'national religion' and the 'myth of race and blood'. He contrasted this perverted ideology with the teaching of the Church in which there was a home 'for all peoples and all nations'.

The impact of the encyclical was immense, and it dispelled at once all suspicion of a fascist pope. While the world was still reacting, however, Pius issued five days later another encyclical, *Divini Redemptoris*, denouncing communism, declaring its principles 'intrinsically hostile to religion in any form whatever', detailing the attacks on the Church which had followed the establishment of communist regimes in Russia, Mexico and Spain, and calling for the implementation of Catholic social teaching to offset both communism and 'amoral liberalism'.

The language of *Divini Redemptoris* was stronger than that of *Mit Brennender Sorge*, its condemnation of communism even more absolute than the attack on Nazism. The difference in tone undoubtedly reflected the pope's own loathing of communism as the ultimate enemy. The last year of his life, however, left no one in any doubt of his total repudiation of the right-wing tyrannies in Germany and, despite his instinctive sympathy with some aspects of Fascism, increasingly in Italy also. His speeches and conversations were blunt, filled with phrases like 'stupid racialism', 'barbaric Hitlerism'. In May 1938 Hitler visited Rome. The pope left for Castel Gondolfo, and explained to pilgrims there that he could not bear 'to see raised in Rome another cross which is not the cross of Christ'. In September he told another group that the Canon of the Mass spoke of Abraham as 'our father in faith'. No Christian, therefore, could be anti-Semitic, for 'Spiritually, we are all Semites'. In the summer of 1938 an American priest, John LeFarge, the author of a recent study of American racial discrimination against black Americans entitled Interracial Justice, was summoned to a secret audience with the pope. Papa Ratti asked him to draft an encyclical against Nazi racial theories and their Italian imitations. The resulting draft, *Humani Generis Unitas*, was a product of its time whose primary focus was the well-being and work of the Church rather than any abstract philanthropy, and whose text grates again and again on a modern sensibility, for it reiterated centuries of Christian suspicion of the Jews, 'this unhappy people...doomed to wander perpetually over the face of the earth' because of their rejection of Christ. The encyclical stressed the dangers to Christian faith of excessive contact between Jews and Christians. Yet it also unequivocally asserted the unity of the whole human race, and denounced all racialism, and anti-Semitism in particular. *Humani Generis Unitas* was never to see the light of day, however, its progress through the Roman machinery slowed by shocked conservative resistance and by the pope's failing health. This 'lost encyclical' epitomises the contradictions of Papa Ratti's pontificate, showing everywhere a mindset which was the outcome of centuries of papal suspicion of the direction of modern religious, political and social developments, yet reaching out towards a larger and more inclusive understanding of humanity, and, for all its limitations, offering an absolute opposition to the root ideology of Nazism. That opposition became the all-absorbing preoccupation of the dying pope. In the last weeks of his life he drafted a blistering denunciation of Fascism and its collaboration with Nazi lies, which he had hoped to deliver to the assembled bishops of Italy: he begged his doctors to keep him alive long enough to make the speech, but died, on 10 February, with just days to go. 'At last', declared Mussolini, 'that stubborn old man is dead.'

He had not a liberal bone in his body. He distrusted democratic politics as too weak to defend the religious truth which underlay all true human community. He thought the British Prime Minister Chamberlain feeble and smug, and no match for the tyrannies he confronted. He loathed the greed of capitalist society, 'the unquenchable thirst for temporal possessions', and thought that liberal capitalism shared with communism a 'satanic optimism' about human progress.

He had even less time for other forms of Christianity. He hoped for reunion with the East, but envisaged it as the return of the prodigal to the Roman father. In 1928, in what is perhaps his least attractive encyclical, *Mortalium Annos*, he rubbished the infant Ecumenical

Movement, sneering at 'pan–Christians consumed by zeal to unite churches' and asking, in a characteristically tough-minded phrase, 'can we endure... that the truth revealed by God be made the object of negotiations?' The encyclical made it clear that the ecumenical message of the Vatican for the other Churches was simple and uncompromising: 'Come in slowly with your hands above your head'.

Yet that is not all there is to be said. Always a strong man and an energetic pope, in the last years of his pontificate he rose to greatness. The pope of eighteen Concordats ceased to be a diplomat, and achieved the stature of a prophet. British diplomats and French communist newspapers commented that the pope, of all people, had become a champion of freedom. When he died, the British Government's man in Rome, d'Arcy Osborne, not always an admirer, reported to the Foreign Office that Pius's courage at the end of his life had raised him to be 'one of the outstanding figures of the world', and that 'he may be said to have died at his post'.

This was the inheritance of Eugenio Pacelli, when he was elected Pope as Pius XII on the first day of the conclave on 2 March 1939. He was the inevitable choice. Immensely able, an exquisitely skilled political tactician, he had been groomed for the succession by Pius XI, who had sent him all over the world as nuncio. The pope told one of Pacelli's assistants in the Secretariat of State that he made him travel 'so that he may get to know the world and the world may get to know him'. The remark meant more than at first appeared. Pius XI's authoritarian regime had marginalised the cardinals as a body, and he had not held consistories. As a result, none of the non-Italian cardinals knew more than a handful of their colleagues. Most of them knew Pacelli, however, and that fact had a major bearing on the outcome of the conclave.

But he seemed born to be pope. Austere, intensely devout, looking like a character from an El Greco painting, Pacelli was everyone's idea of a Catholic saint. As nuncio in Germany he had struck Kaiser Wilhelm II as the 'perfect model' of a high-ranking Roman prelate. As a young man he stammered slightly. The deliberate and emphatic speech he adopted to cope with this gave his words a special solemnity, which he himself came to believe in. He was fond of dramatic devotions and expansive gestures, raising his eyes to heaven, throwing his arms wide, his great and beautiful eyes shining through round spectacles. Despite the austere persona and the hieratic poise, he responded to people's emotion, smiled and wept in sympathy with his interlocutor. As pope, he had a mystical, overwhelming sense of the weight and responsibility of his own office, going down into the crypt of the Vatican by night to pray among the graves of his predecessors. In every photograph he seems poised in prayer, preoccupied with another world. Vatican staff were expected to answer the phone from his apartments on their knees.

He was elected, as everyone knew, to be pope in time of total war, a role for which everything about his career – his diplomatic skills, his gift of languages, his sensitivity and intelligence – equipped him. But there were complications. He had been nuncio for many years in Germany, spoke fluent German for preference with his own household, and although he loathed and despised Nazi racial theory, he loved German music and culture. Moreover, like Pius XI he saw Soviet communism, not Nazism or Fascism, as public enemy number one. He had been in Munich in 1919 during the communist uprising there, and had been threatened by a group of communist insurgents armed with pistols. He had faced them down, but the experience marked him for life with a deep fear of Socialism in all its forms.

The allies therefore would be suspicious of his pro-German as well as his pro-Italian sympathies. Deeply committed to the papacy's role as spiritual leader of all nations, he spent his first months as pope in a hopeless effort to prevent the war. As he declared in an impassioned speech in August 1939, 'Nothing is lost by peace: everything may be lost by war'. Once it began, he would struggle to avoid taking sides, to promote peace at every opportunity, to seek to prevent atrocities and inhumanity, yet to avoid sprinkling holy water on the arms of either side. In a war which came increasingly to be seen as a crusade against tyranny, that balanced stance became daily more difficult, and came to seem less and less tolerable in the leader of Catholic Christendom. Pacelli himself was not entirely consistent. Longing for a negotiated peace, and recognising that this was impossible while Hitler was alive, in 1940 he personally acted as intermediary between the allies and a group of army plotters in Germany who were planning to murder Hitler. He anguished over the morality of this, and concealed his actions from even his closest advisers. And at the heart of all his actions was an increasingly timid indecisiveness, a diplomatic sophistication in which the weighing of every contingency seemed to paralyse action.

His difficulties came to focus on the question of Nazi genocide against the Jews. The Catholic Church had a bad record on the Jews, particularly in Central and Eastern Europe. Many Catholics thought of the Jews as the murderers of Christ, and Hitler had learned a good deal about the political appeal of anti-Semitism from early twentieth-century right-wing Catholic parties in Austria and Germany. But official Church teaching ruled out the racial theories which underlay Nazi policy, and as the war progressed the Vatican built up an appalling dossier on Nazi atrocities against the Jews. Pressure mounted on the pope to speak out, not only from the Allies, who wanted a papal denunciation as propaganda for the war effort, but from his own advisers. He was operating Benedict XV's policy, but in a different war, and a different world. To many of those around him, the moral circumstances seemed qualitatively different, and Pacelli himself sometimes felt it. It took, he told the Archbishop of Cologne 'almost superhuman exertions' to keep the Holy See 'above the strife of parties'.

By temperament, training and deep conviction, however, Pacelli flinched away from denunciation. In his peace broadcast of August 1939 he wrote into his typescript a direct reference to Germany – 'Woe to those who play nation against nation...who oppress the weak and break their given word'. But he thought better of it, and crossed it out again, and never spoke the words. He was a diplomat and, like his first mentors Cardinal Gasparri and Benedict XV, believed that prophetic denunciations closed doors, narrowed room for manoeuvre. Vatican funds were poured into rescue measures for Jews, and he did what he could to protect the Jews of Rome, offering to supply fifteen of the fifty kilos of gold demanded as a ransom for the safety of the Roman Jews by the German head of police there in 1943. As pressure on the Italian Jewish community mounted, he ordered the opening of the Roman religious houses as places of refuge – 5,000 Jews were sheltered there and in the Vatican itself. After the war, the chief Rabbi of Rome became a Catholic and took the baptismal name Eugenio.

But a denunciation, the pope believed, would do nothing to help the Jews, and would only extend Nazi persecution to yet more Catholics. It was the Church as well as the Jews in Germany, Poland and the rest of occupied Europe who would pay the price for any papal gesture. Moreover, given his horror of communism, he was not prepared to denounce Nazi atrocities while remaining silent about Stalinist brutality. Yet how could the oracle of God remain dumb in the face of sins so terrible, so much at odds with the Gospel of the Incarnate?

At the end of 1942 Pius at last gave in to the mounting pressure, and in his Christmas address included what he believed to be a clear and unequivocal condemnation of the genocide against the Jews. He called on all men of good will to bring society back under the rule of God. This was a duty, he declared, we owe to the war dead, to their mothers, their widows and orphans, to those exiled by war, and to 'the hundreds of thousands of innocent people put to death or doomed to slow extinction, sometimes merely because of their race or their descent'.

Both Mussolini and the German Ambassador, von Ribbentrop, were angered by this speech, and Germany considered that the pope had abandoned any pretence at neutrality. They felt that Pius had unequivocally condemned Nazi action against the Jews. But not everyone agreed. To the Allies, and not only to them, but to some in the Vatican, it seemed a feeble, oblique and coded message, when what was demanded by the horrifying reality was something more fiery and direct. Pius XI, they were certain, would have acted differently. This feeling was largely silent in Pius XII's lifetime, and immediately after the war it was the Vatican's immense humanitarian efforts – Vatican officials had processed no fewer than 11,250,000 missing persons enquiries – which attracted attention and gratitude. It erupted, however, in public controversy over Rolf Hockhuth's play *The Representative* in 1963, which portrayed an avaricious and anti-Semitic Pacelli as refusing to make any efforts on behalf of the Jews of Rome in 1943, and controversy has raged since.

For many people, the moral credibility of the papacy and the Catholic Church had been radically compromised. Pius XII's actions were vigorously defended by those closest to him, including Cardinal Montini, who had been his closest adviser on such matters during the war, and the integrity and humanity of whose own role in the matter was accepted by everyone. But clearly the accusations of moral failure cut deep, and in the wake of Hockhuth's play the Vatican took the unprecedented step of appointing a team of Jesuit historians to publish everything in the archives that bore on Vatican involvement with the war and especially with the Jewish question. The resulting eleven volumes of documents decisively established the falsehood of Hockhuth's specific allegations, but did not entirely exorcise the sense that the troubling silence and tortuous diplomacy of the Vatican had more to do with Pius XII's oblique and timid sensibility than with rational prudence.

Controversy revived in the 1980s with suggestions that the 'Ratline' from Rome to Latin America, down which Nazi war criminals such as Klaus Barbie and possibly even the Gestapo chiefs Martin Borrmann and Heinrich Mueller had escaped, was a Vatican network. There can be no doubt that pro-Nazi Austrian and Croatian clerics in Rome, and right-wing Catholic circles in France, actively concealed war criminals and did assist in such escapes. Everything we now know about Vatican policy towards Nazism and Fascism, however, about the Pope's own attitudes, and above all about the anti-Fascist convictions and impeccable integrity of Monsignor Montini, who would have had to know about any such network, make accusations of papal complicity unlikely in the extreme.

Even while Europe was plunged in total war, however, theological renewal had begun within the Catholic Church. Despite the stifling intellectual atmosphere inherited from the anti-Modernist era, there had emerged in Germany and France, particularly in the intellectual orders of Dominicans and Jesuits, a movement away from the rigidly hierarchical understanding of the Church which had prevailed since the First Vatican Council. These new movements emphasised the spiritual character of the Church, rather than its institutional structure, and pointed to the liturgy of the mass and breviary as a rich source of understanding of the nature of Christianity. There was a renewal of interest in the writings of the Early Christian Fathers, with a consequent downplaying of the 'timeless' authority of the more recent theological orthodoxies dominant in seminaries and textbooks. The Jesuit Henry de Lubac pointed the Church back to the writings of the Greek Fathers in particular, while the French Dominican Yves Congar urged the importance of the corporate dimension of the Church, and the active role of every Christian within it, not simply as obedient footsoldiers under the military rule of the hierarchy.

These currents of thought began to appear in papal utterances. Between 1943 and 1947 Pius XII published three theological encyclicals, each of them in different ways opening up new and hopeful avenues for Catholic theology. In *Mystici Corporis* the pope proposed an organic and mystical model of the Church as the Body of Christ, supplementing the political model of the 'perfect' (meaning 'complete

and self-contained') society in which the pope was general or chief
magistrate, which had dominated Catholic thinking for three centuries. In *Divini Afflante* Pius reversed the suspicion of biblical scholarship which had stifled Catholic theology since 1910, recognising the
presence in the Bible of a variety of literary forms which made any
straightforward 'fundamentalist' reading of scripture inadequate. And in
Mediator Dei, published in 1947, he placed the renewal of a more par-
ticipatory liturgy at the heart of the renewal of Catholicism.

These documents had their limitations. *Mystici Corporis*, despite its
emphasis on the organic nature of the Church, identified the Church
of Christ absolutely with the visible Roman Catholic Church (to the
implicit exclusion of all other Christian bodies), and remained dispro-
portionately preoccupied with the hierarchical dimension and the
centrality of the papacy. *Mediator Dei* warned against overeager 'litur-
gisers', and showed how long Roman memories could be by including an attack on the 'pseudo-synod' of Pistoia of 1786, and its liturgical
reforms. Nevertheless, their cumulative effect as the world emerged
from total war was an almost miraculous liberation for theology
within the Church. The intellectual and imaginative freeze which had
set in in the wake of the campaign against Modernism began to thaw.
Pius himself followed up these initiatives in the early 1950s through
practical reforms such as permission for evening masses, the relaxing of
the need to fast from midnight before receiving communion, and
above all by reforming and restoring the heart of the ancient liturgy,
the moving and powerful ceremonies of Holy Week, which for centuries had been in abeyance.

But this was a false dawn. Pius at heart was deeply conservative,
increasingly fearful of the genie he had let out of the lamp. His early
papal utterances had often called for 'audacia', daring, in action. In
the last ten years of his life that word virtually disappears from his
vocabulary. In August 1950 he published another encyclical, *Humani
Generis*, in which he warned against the dangerous tendencies of the
new theology, attacking the historical contextualising of dogma as
leading to relativism, and warning also against a 'false irenicism'
towards other Christian traditions which would lead to compromise
over fundamentals of the faith. He called on bishops and the superiors of religious orders to prevent the spread of these new and dangerous opinions. No one was named, but that made the impact of the
condemnation all the worse, widening the net of suspicion to anyone

whose views were considered unconventional. A new attack on theologians began, and many of the most distinguished of them, like the great French Dominicans Yves Congar and Marie-Dominique Chenu, were silenced and forbidden to teach or publish.

The last years of Pius XII's reign increasingly resembled the regime of Pius X, as new initiatives in theology and pastoral work were suppressed, against the background of the all-consuming struggle with the universal enemy, communism. Catholics in the Soviet Union, Poland, Lithuania, Slovakia, Hungary, Yugoslavia and Romania lived under Communist rule, and papal denunciations could make life harder for them. But this struggle had a particular urgency in post-war Italy, where communists were reaping the benefits of having led the anti-Fascist resistance. In Emilia between 1944 and 1946 fifty-two priests had been murdered by communists.

The Vatican did not forget. The pope believed that the freedom of the Church would be at an end in an Italy ruled by communists, he talked gloomily about being ready to die in Rome, and he did everything he could to ensure that communists would not win elections. The Vatican pumped funds into the Christian Democratic Party, and promoted links between Italy and America. In 1949 Pius excommunicated anyone who joined the Communist Party or supported communism in any way. The ruling unleashed a flood of anti-Catholic measures in Eastern Europe. Mgr Alfredo Ottaviani, head of the Holy Office (the Inquisition) boasted that people could say anything they liked about the divinity of Christ and get away with it, but that 'if, in the remotest village in Sicily, you vote communist, your excommunication will arrive the next day'. In 1952, the Vatican encouraged an anti-communist political alliance between Italian Christian Democrats and neo-Fascist and other extreme right-wing groups. Catholic politicians unhappy about this 'opening to the right' were elbowed aside. Pius watched in anguish the arrest, torture and show-trial of Cardinal Jozsef Mindszenty by the communist regime in Hungary in 1948–9. When the Russians sent in the tanks to suppress the Hungarian Revolution in 1956 he published three encyclicals of denunciation in ten days. 'If we were silent', he insisted in his Christmas message for 1956, 'we would have to fear God's judgement much more'. The contrast with the silences of the war years was striking.

In France the most exciting Catholic experiment for generations, the Worker Priest movement, fell victim to this growing hatred and fear of communism. The movement had begun from the war-time recognition by clergy like Cardinal Suhard, Archbishop of Paris, that huge tracts of urban France were effectively dechristianised mission-territory as much in need of evangelisation as anywhere in Africa or the Far East. Suhard and other bishops authorised a small group of priests to shed clerical garments and lifestyle, to take jobs as factory workers or dockers, and to explore a new type of ministry. The French Dominican Order was closely associated with this movement, and provided its theological rationale. Many of the priests became involved in union activities, many developed communist sympathies. A few were unable to sustain their vocation to celibacy. In 1953, the year in which it signed a new Concordat with Franco's Spain, the Vatican ordered the suppression of the Worker Priest experiment.

In the Vatican an atmosphere of suspicion and denunciation of the modern world flourished, feeding off the inflated rhetoric of a century of papal condemnation of modernity. Under the prompting of Mgr Alfredo Ottaviani at the Holy Office and Cardinal Ruffini of Palermo, the pope toyed with the idea of calling a General Council which would denounce modern errors like existentialism and polygenism (the view that the human race evolved from more than a single pair), and define the doctrine of the Virgin Mary's bodily Assumption into heaven. The Conciliar plan was abandoned, but its condemnations reappeared in 1950 in Humani Generis, and in the same year the pope, for the first time since the definition of papal infallibility in 1870, exercised the infallible Magisterium and defined the doctrine of the Assumption in his own right. The definition embarassed many Catholic theologians, since it was unsupported in scripture and was unknown to the early Church, and it was a disaster for relations with other Churches, even those which, like the Orthodox Churches, believed the doctrine but rejected the unilateral right of the pope to define articles of faith. And in 1954, too, Pacelli canonised the anti-Modernist Pope Pius X, whose embalmed body, enshrined in glass, was sent on a sacred tour of Italy.

The pope himself retired into ever more remote isolation. Giovanni Battista Montini, one of his two closest assistants during the war, and widely tipped as the next pope, fell under suspicion of holding dangerously liberal sympathies. A sensitive, warm and highly intelligent man, Montini, though himself impeccably loyal and sharing something of Pius XII's mystically exalted view of the papacy, sympathised with the new theology and disliked the reactionary ethos which Pius had let loose. In an age when Vatican attitudes to other churches were characterised by hostility or dismissiveness, he was an ecumenist, cultivating friends among Anglicans and Protestants, seeking to make and maintain contacts in other Churches. He did what he could to protect potential victims of the new ultraorthodoxy, and even rescued stocks of condemned books by the French Jesuit Henri de Lubac. He had specially close links with the Church in France, and sympathised with the Worker Priest experiment. He strongly disapproved of the Vatican-backed political alliance between Christian Democracy and neo-Fascists.

In 1954 the inevitable happened. The pope's mind was poisoned against Montini by a whispering campaign, and he was dismissed from his Vatican post and kicked upstairs to be Archbishop of Milan. This post invariably carried with it a cardinal's hat, but Pius XII held no consistory for the making of new cardinals in his last years. The omission was probably not aimed specifically at punishing Montini, but was taken by many at the time as a signal of Pius XII's displeasure. Deliberate or not, the withholding of the red hat from Montini, who was increasingly being seen as the inevitable choice as next pope, excluded him from the succession which was now imminent.

Surrounded now by ultra-conservative advisers, his privacy jealously guarded by his German nun-housekeeper, Sister Pasqualina, Pius XII retreated into a suffocating atmosphere of exalted piety exacerbated by hypochondria. His health, always a subject of acute anxiety to himself, visibly deteriorated. A quack remedy designed to prevent softening of his gums, tanned and hardened his soft palate and gullet: he developed a permanent uncontrollable hiccup. As he weakened, his doctor tried to keep him alive with injections of pulverised tissue taken from slaughtered lambs. Rumours circulated of visions of the Virgin and participations in the sufferings of Christ granted to him. He cultivated his role as Vatican oracle. Teaching gushed from him, unstoppable, a speech a day. Since the pope was the Church's hotline to God, everything he had to say must be of interest. Pius himself came to believe that he had something valuable to contribute on every subject, no matter how specialised. He lived surrounded by encyclopedias and monographs, swotting up for the next utterance. Midwives would get an update on the latest gynaecological techniques, astronomers were lectured on sunspots. One of his staff recalled finding him surrounded by a new mountain of books in the summer of 1958. 'All those books are about gas', Pius told him – he was due to address a congress of the gas industry in September. The notion of pope as universal teacher was getting out of hand.

III THE AGE OF VATICAN II

Pius XII died on 10 October 1958. As always at the end of a long pontificate, the conclave that met two weeks later to replace him was deeply divided between an old guard committed to continuing and extending Pacelli's policies, and a group of younger cardinals disillusioned by the sterility, repression and personality cult of the last years of Pius XII's regime. The 'youth' of these men was relative. Pius XII had held only two consistories during his long pontificate, and although for the first time Italian cardinals were outnumbered almost two-to-one, nearly half the Sacred College were in their late seventies or eighties. The ideal pope of those who hoped for change, however, was Archbishop Montini, electable in theory, even though he was not a cardinal (he got two votes during the conclave), but in practice ruled out by his absence. Deadlocked, the cardinals looked around for an interim seat-warming pope. Their choice fell on the fat seventy-seven year old Patriarch of Venice, Angelo Roncalli, a genial Vatican diplomat who had been made Patriarch as a retirement job, with a reputation for peacable holiness and pastoral warmth, and who clearly did not have long to live. He was too elderly to rock any boats, and everyone believed that a few years of King Log inactivity would give the Church time to take stock before choosing a younger and more vigorous man to set the Church's agenda for the second half of the century. Human calculation has seldom been more spectacularly mistaken.

Roncalli, even more than Pius X, was a peasant pope, the son of poor farming people from Bergamo who shared the ground floor of their house with their six cows. He had spent an entire life in the papal diplomatic service, mostly in obscure posts, in wartime Bulgaria and Turkey. In the process he had come to know a good deal about the Eastern Churches, about Islam, about the non-Christian world of the twentieth century. A keen student of Church history, he had a special interest in the career of San Carlo Borromeo, the great sixteenth-century Archbishop of Milan, and he arranged his coronation as pope for San Carlo's feast day. Antiquarian interests of this sort seemed harmless enough: no one noticed that what he valued about San Carlo was the fact that he was above all things a pastoral bishop, translating into action the reforming programme of an ecumenical council, the Council of Trent.

As pope, he took the name John partly because it was his father's name, and that human gesture set at once the keynote of his pontificate, his transparent goodness and loveableness. He was certainly no radical: his own theology and piety were utterly traditional. As nuncio in France, during the early stages of the troubles over the Worker Priest experiment, he showed some sympathy but little real understanding of the issues, and as pope he was to renew Pius XII's condemnation of the movement. He was also to issue an encyclical demanding the retention of Latin as the language of instruction in seminaries. Yet under the stuffy opinions was a great human heart. He had managed to live a long life in the papal service without making any enemies, winning the affection and trust of everyone with whom he came in contact, Catholic and non-Catholic, Christian and non-Christian. After the arctic and self-conscious sanctities of Pius' reign, the world awoke to find a kindly, laughing old man on the throne of Peter, who knew the modern world and was not afraid of it. In part it was because he had the freedom of an old man. Announcing his name, he had jokingly pointed out to the cardinals that there had been more popes called John than any other name, and that most of them had had short reigns.

He was unconventional: he hated the white skullcap popes wear and which would not stay on his bald scalp, so he reinvented and wore with aplomb the red and ermine cap seen in portraits of Renaissance popes. He cut through papal protocol, and was a security nightmare, sallying out of the Vatican to visit the Roman prisons or hospitals. Disapproving of Marxism, he welcomed communists as brothers and sisters, and was visited in the Vatican by the daughter and son-in-law of the Russian Premier, Nikita Kruschev. He sent stamps and coins for Kruschev's grandchildren, and asked their mother to give a special embrace to the youngest, Ivan, because that was the Russian form of John. Under the warmth of his overflowing humanity the barriers which had been constructed between Church and world melted away.

The personal warmth was also matched by a willingness to rethink old issues. His first encyclical, *Mater et Magistra*, published in

1961, broke with Vatican suspicion of lurking socialism by welcoming the advent of the caring state, and it insisted on the obligation of wealthy nations to help poorer ones. The CIA thought the pope gave comfort to communists. His last encyclical, *Pacem in Terris*, published on Maundy Thursday 1963, was characteristically addressed not to the bishops of the Church but 'to all men of good will'. It welcomed as characteristic of 'our modern age' the progressive improvement of conditions for working people, the involvement of women in political life, and the decline of imperialism and growth of national self-determination. All these were signs of a growing liberation. He declared the right of every human being to the private and public profession of their religion, a break with the systematic denial of that right by popes since Gregory XVI. Above all, he abandoned the anti-communist rhetoric of the Cold War. He denounced as 'utterly irrational' the nuclear arms race, declaring that war in an atomic age was no longer 'a fit instrument with which to repair the violation of justice', as near as a pope could get to repudiating the value of just war theory in a world of nuclear weapons. Even the Russians were impressed, and the Italian Marxist film director, Pasolini, dedicated his masterpiece, the film *The Gospel according to St Matthew*, to Pope John.

One of the earliest acts of the new pope was to make Archbishop Montini a cardinal, the first of his reign. It was a clear signal that a new regime had arrived, that there would be no more of Pacelli's later policies. And then, staggeringly, less than three months after his election, on 25 January 1959, John announced the calling of a General Council. King Log was going to disturb the pond after all.

There had in fact been some discussion of a Council under Pius XII. What had been imagined, however, was a continuation of the First Vatican Council, a docile assembly which would denounce secularism and communism, compile a new list of heresies in the spirit of the Syllabus of Errors, wipe the floor with the Ecumenical Movement, and perhaps define infallibly the doctrine that Mary was the Mediatrix of all Graces, a favourite belief of Pius XII which would have further alienated the Protestant and Orthodox churches. John, however, had different ideas. He conceived his Council not as one of defiance and opposition to the world and the other Churches, but as a source of pastoral renewal and of reconciliation between Christians, and with the wider world. It was time, in his word, for 'aggiornamento', bringing up to date, a word that to conservative ears sounded suspiciously like Modernism.

Recent studies of the origins of the Council have made clear just how opposed to it the Vatican old guard were. The whole drift of Pacelli's pontificate had been to subordinate the local churches and their bishops to the papal central administration, the Curia. The thought of assembling the world's three thousand bishops and letting them talk to each other, and maybe even have new ideas, was horrifying. It was suggested, apparently seriously, that there was no need for the bishops to gather in Rome at all, but that copies of papally approved 'Conciliar' documents should be posted to them for assent. Another Vatican adviser even suggested that no one but the pope should be allowed to speak during the Council. Even Cardinal Montini, exiled in Milan, was alarmed: he told a friend that 'this holy old boy doesn't realise what a hornet's nest he's stirring up'.

Vatican officials did what they could to block the preparations, and when it became clear that they could not prevent the Council going ahead, tried to hijack its proceedings, to stack the preparatory committees, determine the agenda and draft the Conciliar documents. At the Holy Office, Cardinal Ottaviani refused all cooperation with other bodies, insisting that doctrine was his department's sole responsibility, and 'we are going to remain masters in our own house'. Lists of doctrines to be condemned mounted up, and seventy-two draft schema were prepared, all of them destined to be rejected by the Council. Theologically they were firmly rooted in the integralism of the last hundred years. The draft declaration of faith drawn up for the Council contained no scriptural citations whatever, reiterated the condemnations contained in *Pascendi* and *Humani Generis*, and quoted no theological text earlier than the Council of Trent.

John's determination that this should be a pastoral Council devoted to opening up the Church, not to barricading it in, was absolutely vital, strengthening bishops to reject the prepared texts and to demand a real voice in the deliberations of the Council. Without his encouragement the Council would have become a rubber stamp for the most negative aspects of Pius XII's regime. And it was his personal insistence that the Council was not to be a Council against the modern world. There were to be no condemnations or excommunications. Yet he himself had no clear agenda, and there was a desperate danger that lack of clear guidance from the pope would either lead to a demoralising lack of achievement, or allow the direction of the Council to fall into the hands of curial officials opposed to the very notion of a Council.

For guidance John turned to Cardinal Montini and the Belgian Cardinal Suenens. They saw that the Council must centre on the nature and role of the Church, that it must be ecumenical in character, must present a pastoral not a bureaucratic vision, and that it must renew the liturgy and restore the notion of collegiality in the Church, that is, the shared responsibility of the bishops with the pope, no longer an isolated papal monarchy. It must also engage with the relationship of the Church to society at every level, freedom of conscience, peace and war, the relationship of Church and State, the world of work and industrial society, and questions of justice and economics. All these issues had preoccupied popes since the mid-nineteenth century, but always in a spirit of confrontation and suspicion. The time had come for the Church to consider all these issues afresh, in the confidence of faith and with a discerning eye for what Pope John called 'the signs of the times'.

The pope's inaugural address at the Council, *Gaudet Mater Ecclesia*, contrasted strikingly with most papal utterances since the 1830s. For over a century the popes had confronted the modern world in the spirit of Jeremiah, as a place of mourning, lamentation and woe. John urged a different spirit, and challenged the 'prophets of misfortune' who saw the world as 'nothing but betrayal and ruination'. The Church had indeed to keep the faith, but not to 'hoard this precious treasure'. The Church could and should adapt itself to the needs of the world. There was to be no more clinging to old ways and old words simply out of fear: it was time for 'a leap forward' which would hold on to the ancient faith, but reclothe it in words and ways which would speak afresh to a world hungry for the gospel, 'for the substance of the ancient deposit of faith is one thing, and the way in which it is presented is another'.

From the perspective of the late twentieth century, there seems about John's rhetoric a note of over-optimism, a confidence in progress which was a characteristic of the 1960s. He spoke confidently and perhaps naively of providence guiding humanity towards 'a new order of human relationships', which the years since have not delivered. It was his language about the possibility of recasting the substance of Catholic teaching in new forms, however, that alarmed conservative forces in the Church. This was the language of Modernism, and there were many who believed that they now had a Modernist pope. When the Latin text of his speech was published, it had been heavily censored to remove any hint that the teaching of the Church might change, and recast in words borrowed from the anti-Modernist oath.

John lived to inaugurate his Council, but not to guide or conclude it. While battles raged between the forces of conservatism and reform within the Council, his life ebbed away in cancer. He had reigned for only five years, the shortest pontificate for two centuries, yet he had transformed the Catholic Church, and with it the world's perception of the papacy. When he died on 3 June 1963 the progress of his last illness was followed by millions of anxious people across the world, and throughout his last hours St Peter's square was thronged with mourners for this, the most beloved pope in history.

The Council he had called, with no very clear notion of what it might do, proved to be the most revolutionary Christian event since the Reformation. Despite the divided state of Christendom, it was, geographically at least, the most Catholic Council in the history of the Church: 2,800 bishops attended, fewer than half of them from Europe. Orthodox and Protestant observers attended the sessions, and substantially influenced the proceedings. The monolithic intransigence which had been the public face of the Catholic Church since 1870 proved astonishingly fragile, and over the four sessions of the Council, between 11 October 1962 and 8 December 1965, every aspect of the Church's life was scrutinised and transformed. As at Vatican I, the Council rapidly polarised (with the help of sensational media coverage), but this time the intransigent group with curial backing were in a minority, and one by one, often with considerable bitterness, the curial draft documents were swept aside and replaced with radically different texts, more open to the needs of the modern world, and more responsive to pastoral realities. By a supreme irony, the most influential theologians at the Council were men like Yves Congar and Karl Rahner who had been silenced or condemned under Pius XII, and their ideas shaped many of the crucial Conciliar decrees.

The central document of the Council was the Decree on the Church, *Lumen Gentium*. It moved far beyond the teaching of *Mystici*

Corporis, abandoning the defensive juridical understanding of the Church which had dominated Catholic thought since the Conciliar movement, and placing at the centre of its teaching the notion of the People of God, embracing both clergy and laity. This concept moved understanding of the nature of the Church out of rigidly hierarchic categories, and enabled a radical and far more positive reassessment of the role of lay people in the life of the Church. The decree also moved beyond *Mystici Corporis* and all previous Roman Catholic teaching by refusing to identify the Roman Catholic Church with the Church of Christ, stating instead that the Church of Christ 'subsisted in' the Roman Catholic Church, and not that it simply 'was' the Roman Catholic Church. This apparently fine distinction opened the way to the recognition of the spiritual reality of other Churches and their sacraments and ministries. The decree's use of the image of the 'pilgrim people of God' also opened the way to a new recognition of the imperfections and reformability of the Church and its structures. And in one of its most crucial and contested chapters, the Decree sought to correct – or at any rate complete – the teaching of Vatican I on papal primacy and the episcopate, by emphasising the doctrine of collegiality, and placing the pope's primacy in the context of the shared responsibility of all the bishops for the Church.

But *Lumen Gentium* was not the only revolutionary document produced by the Council. *Gaudium et Spes*, the 'Pastoral Constitution on the Church in the Modern World' (the Latin actually says 'in this world of time'), represented a complete overturning of the Conciliar and papal denunciations of the 'Modern World' which had been so regular a feature of the ultramontane era. Setting out to 'discern the signs of the times', the Constitution embraced the journey of humanity in time as a place of encounter with the Divine. It emphasised the need of the Church 'in the events, needs and the longings it shares with other people of our time' to discern in faith 'what may be genuine signs of the presence or the purpose of God'. Faith is thereby presented as something which completes and seeks to understand our common humanity, not a matter of exclusive concern with a supernatural realm set over and against a hostile world. The religious pilgrimage towards the 'heavenly city' is claimed to involve 'a greater commitment to working with all men towards the establishment of a world that is more human'. In the wake of the

Council, this emphasis would provide the charter for the development of theologies of social and political engagement, like Liberation Theology. It was one of the Council's most profound acts of theological reorientation, and one which transcended the somewhat glib optimism of the *Gaudium et Spes* itself, which, it must be admitted, in its concern to affirm the worth of human culture, shows little sense of the tragedy and brokenness of human history.

Its central emphasis, nevertheless, lay at the heart of the Council's rethinking of Catholic theology, and was worlds away from the aggressive, hard certainties of the age of Vatican I. Then Catholics had felt that they, and they alone, knew exactly what both Church and world were. By contrast, six months before his own election as Pope Paul VI, Cardinal Montini told the young priests of his diocese that in the Council

> the Church is looking for itself. It is trying, with great trust and with a great effort, to define itself more precisely and to understand what it is...the Church is also looking for the world, and trying to come into contact with society...by engaging in dialogue with the world, interpreting the needs of society in which it is working and observing the defects, the necessities, the sufferings and the hopes and aspirations that exist in human hearts.

Lumen Gentium and *Gaudium et Spes* were great acts of theological reorientation, reshaping the parameters of Catholic theology. The Council's work on specific issues was hardly less revolutionary. The decree on the liturgy established a series of principles which would transform the worship of Roman Catholics, introducing the vernacular in place of Latin, encouraging greater simplicity and lay participation. The decree on revelation abandoned the sterile opposition between scripture and tradition which had dogged both Catholic and Protestant theology since the Reformation, and presented both as complementary expressions of the fundamental Word of God, which underlies them both. The decree on Ecumenism broke decisively with the attitude of supercilious rejection of the ecumenical movement which Pius XI had established in *Mortalium Annos*, and placed the search for unity among Christians at the centre of the Church's life. The decree on other religions rejected once and for all the notion that the Jewish people could be held responsible for the death of Christ, the root of the age-old Christian tradition of anti-

Semitism. Perhaps most revolutionary of all, the decree on religious liberty declared unequivocally that 'the human person has a right to religious liberty', and that this religious freedom, a fundamental part of the dignity of human beings, must be enshrined in the constitution of society as a civil right.

This was truly revolutionary teaching, for the persecution of heresy and enforcement of Catholicism had been a reality since the days of Constantine, and since the French Revolution pope after pope had repeatedly and explicitly denounced the notion that non-Catholics had a right to religious freedom. On the older view, error had no rights, and the Church was bound to proclaim the truth, and, wherever it could, to see that society enforced the truth by secular sanctions. Heretics and unbelievers might in certain circumstances be granted toleration, but not liberty. The decree was opposed tooth and nail, especially by the Italian and Spanish bishops (the decree flew in the face of the Concordat which regulated the life of the Spanish church, and which discriminated against Protestants). Another opponent was Archbishop Marcel Lefebvre, who, after the Council, would eventually form his own breakaway movement committed, not only to the pre-Conciliar liturgy, but to the intransigent integralism and rejection of religious liberty which had flourished under Pius X and the last years of Pius XII.

The decree on religious liberty was largely drafted by the American theologian John Courtney Murray, another of those under a cloud in the pontificate of Pius XII. It was strongly pressed by the American bishops, who felt that a failure to revise the Church's teaching on this issue would discredit the Council in the eyes of the democratic nations. A lead had been given by the new pope, Paul VI, during a flying visit to the United Nations in October 1963, when he spoke of 'fundamental human rights and duties, human dignity and freedom – above all religious liberty', a clear endorsement of the new teaching. Key support for the change also came from the Archbishop of Cracow, Karol Wojtyla, the future Pope John Paul II, who saw in the decree's assertion of the fundamental human right to freedom of conscience, a valuable weapon in the hands of the Churches persecuted under communism.

On every front, then, the Council redrew the boundaries of what had seemed until 1959 a fixed and immutable system. For some Catholics these changes were the long-awaited harvest of the new theology, the reward of years of patient endurance during the winter of Pius XII. For others, they were apostasy, the capitulation of the Church to the corrupt and worldly values of the Enlightenment and the Revolution, which the popes from Pius IX to Pius XII had rightly denounced. And for others, perhaps the majority, they were a bewildering stream of directives from above, to be obeyed as best they could. Many of the older clergy of the Catholic Church found themselves sleepwalking through the Conciliar and post-Conciliar years, loyal to an authority which called them to embrace attitudes which the same authority had once denounced as heresy. Pope John's successor would have to deal with all this.

With a sort of inevitability, Giovanni Battista Montini, middle-class son of a Partito Popolare politician from Brescia, was elected to succeed John on 21 June 1963, taking the name Paul VI (1963–78). Everyone knew how crucial Montini's insight and determination was to the shaping of the Council and the forcing through of its reforms. John had often felt outflanked by the Vatican bureaucracy, his peasant shrewdness no match for the complexities of curial phili-buster and red tape. Montini, by contrast, who had worked in the Secretariat of State from 1922 to 1954, knew every inch of the Vati-can and its ways, and could fight fire with fire. While still a young man he had toyed with the idea that the pope of the future should break away from St Peter's and the claustrophobia of the Vatican City, and go to live among his seminarians at the Cathedral Church of Rome, the Lateran, to take the papacy once more to the people. He never in fact had the daring to put this vision into practice, but it says much about his understanding of the tasks and challenges that con-fronted the pope and the Council that he entertained it at all.

Yet he was emphatically no radical, and could hold the confidence of all but the most diehard reactionaries. It was up to him to steer the Council to the successful completion of its work, to oversee the implementation of its reforms, and to hold together conservatives and reformers while he did so. In the turbulent sixties and early sev-enties, when religious reform and social and moral revolution flowed together, the task was almost impossible. No pope since the time of Gregory the Great has had so daunting a task. The societies of the West were passing through a period of general questioning of struc-tures and authority, a crisis of confidence in old certainties and old institutions which was far wider than the Church. The reforms of

Vatican II flowed into this general flux and challenging of values, and were often difficult to distinguish from it.

A century and a half of rigidity had left the Church ill-equipped for radical change. An institution which had wedded itself to what Manning had called 'the beauty of inflexibility' was now called upon to bend. The transformations of Catholicism which flowed from the Council were drastic and to many inexplicable. A liturgy once seen as timeless, beautiful and sacrosanct, its universality guaranteed by the exotic vestments and whispered or chanted Latin in which it was celebrated, was now reclothed in graceless modern vernaculars to the sound of guitars and clarinets. Previously, the Council Catholics had been forbidden even to recite the Lord's Prayer in common with other Christians: they were now encouraged to hold joint services, prayer groups, study sessions.

The reform was experienced by many as the joyful clearing away of outmoded lumber, by others as the vandalising of a beautiful and precious inheritance. In addition to the signs of renewal and enthusiasm, there were signs of collapsing confidence. Thousands of priests left the priesthood to marry, nuns abandoned the religious habit, vocations to the religious life plummeted. In the exhilaration – or the horror – of seeing ancient taboos broken, prudence, a sense of proportion and the simple ability to tell baby from bathwater were rare commodities. Both the enthusiasts and the opponents of reform looked to the papacy for leadership and support. To hold this strife of voices in some sort of balance was a daunting task. Montini, who took the name Paul to signify a commitment to mission and reform, rose to the challenge, signalling both continuity and change from the very moment of his election. He allowed himself to be crowned according to custom, but then sold the papal tiara which had been used for the ceremony, and gave the money to the poor.

Not everyone liked Paul's methods. Determined that the Conciliar reforms should not be thrown off course, he was also determined that no one should feel steamrollered. There was to be, he declared, no one who felt conquered, only everyone convinced. To achieve this he tried to neutralise conservative unease by matching every reform gesture with a conservative one. In a series of deeply unpopular interventions, he watered down Conciliar documents which had already been through most of the stages of Conciliar debate and approval, notably the decrees on the Church and on Ecumenism, to accommodate conservative worries (which he himself evidently shared). He gave to Mary the title 'Mother of the Church' which the Council had withheld because it seemed to separate her unhelpfully from the rest of redeemed humanity. He delayed the promulgation of the decree on religious liberty.

This balancing act was not confined to his interventions at the Council. In 1967 he published his radical encyclical on social justice, *Populorum Progressio*, which advanced beyond the generalities of *Gaudium et Spes* and denounced unrestrained economic liberalism as a 'woeful system', and called for the placing of the 'superfluous wealth' of the rich countries of the world for the benefit of the poor nations. This encyclical delighted the theologians and pastors of the Third World, and established Paul's credentials as a 'progressive' on the side of the poor. In the same year, however, he reiterated the traditional teaching on priestly celibacy, alienating many of the same people who had acclaimed the encyclical. These contradictory gestures earned him, unjustly, the title 'amletico', a waverer like Hamlet.

Yet steadily he pushed the essential changes onwards: the reform of the mass and its translation into the language of every day so as to involve ordinary people more deeply in worship; the establishment of the notion of episcopal collegiality along with the pope, and the creation of the Synod of Bishops, which was to meet regularly to embody it. To increase efficiency and to break the stranglehold of Pius XII's cardinals and bishops over the reform process, he introduced a compulsory retirement age of seventy-five for bishops (but not the pope!) and decreed that cardinals after the age of eighty might not hold office in the Curia or take part in papal elections. This was a drastic measure. The average age of the heads of the Vatican dicasteries was seventy-nine: ten of the cardinals were over eighty, one was over ninety. Two of the leading curial conservatives, Cardinal Ottaviani and Cardinal Tisserant, made public their fury at their disenfranchisement.

To make the central administration of the Church more representative Paul hugely increased the membership of the College of Cardinals, including many Third World bishops, thereby decisively wiping out the Italian domination of papal elections. In the same spirit he established a series of bodies to carry out the work of the Council. In particular he confirmed permanent secretariats for Christian unity, for non-Christian religions and for non-believers as permanent parts of the Vatican administration. Paul was deeply committed to Christian unity, going to Jerusalem to meet the Greek Orthodox leader Patriarch Athenagoras in 1964. In the following year they lifted the age-old mutual excommunication of the Eastern and Western Churches. In 1966 he welcomed the Archbishop of Canterbury, Michael Ramsay, on a formal visit to Rome, to whom in a warmly personal but shrewdly dramatic gesture he gave his own episcopal ring. With calculated theological daring, he spoke of the Anglican and Roman Catholic Churches as 'sister Churches'.

Paul began to travel, a new development for the modern papacy, addressing the United Nations in 1963 in a dramatic speech which greatly enhanced his standing as a moral leader – 'no more war, war never again' – and visiting the World Council of Churches in Geneva in 1969, the first pope to set foot in Calvin's city since the Reformation. In 1969 he also became the first pope to visit Africa, ordaining bishops and encouraging the development of an indigenous Church. In 1970 he visited the Philippines (where there was an assassination attempt) and Australia (where the Anglican Archbishop of Sydney boycotted the visit).

The character of Paul VI's pontificate was perhaps most clearly revealed in the emergence under him of a new Vatican 'Ostpolitik', to ease the condition of the Churches behind the Iron Curtain. Despite his apprenticeship under Pope Pacelli, Paul believed that the Church's confrontational attitude to communism was sterile and counter-productive, and he went far beyond Pope John's personal warmth, to a new policy of realpolitik and accommodation to communist regimes. There were casualties. The symbol of the old confrontational attitude which had dominated the pontificate of Pius XII was the heroic and intransigent cold warrior Cardinal Josef Mindszenty. He had been living in the secular 'sanctuary' of the American embassy in Budapest since the failure of the Hungarian Revolution in 1956, refusing every offer of rescue, a permanent witness against and thorn in the side of the Hungarian communist authorities. In 1971 the Americans told the pope that Mindszenty was an embarrassment to them, preventing rapprochement with the Hungarians. The pope ordered him to leave, and he settled in Vienna, writing his memoirs and denouncing the Hungarian regime. The Hungarian bishops told the pope the denunciations were making life harder for the Church in Hungary. In 1973 the Pope asked Mindszenty to resign as bishop of Esztergom. He refused, on the grounds that the new Vatican arrangements with the Hungarian government would give communists the final say in appointing his successor. Paul declared the see vacant, and in due course a replacement was appointed. The cardinal never forgave this 'betrayal', and denounced Paul in his Memoirs. Mindszenty, like Archbishop Marcel Lefebvre, was the ghost of the pontificate of Pius XII, haunting the Church of the Second Vatican Council.

In all this, however, aspiration went further than achievement. Paul himself was often frightened by the runaway speed of change and was afraid of sacrificing essential papal prerogatives. However much he believed in the Church of the Second Vatican Council, however sincerely he fostered episcopal collegiality, he had been formed in the Church of Vatican I and never abandoned the lofty and lonely vision of papal authority which underlay the earlier Council's teaching. Six weeks after becoming pope, Paul jotted down a private note on his new responsibilities. 'The post', he wrote

> is unique. It brings great solitude. I was solitary before, but now my solitariness becomes complete and awesome... Jesus was alone on the cross...My solitude will grow. I need have no fears: I should not seek outside help to absolve me from my duty; my duty is to plan, decide, assume every responsibility for guiding others, even when it seems illogical and perhaps absurd. And to suffer alone....Me and God. The colloquy must be full and endless.

This is a papacy conceived as service, not as power, but it is not a papacy conceived in terms of partnership with others. Given such a vision, and for all his good intentions, there were severe limits to the sharing Paul thought possible with his fellow bishops. Between him and them was the awesome gulf of that lonely vision, an absolute difference in responsibility and authority. The international synods of bishops would increasingly turn into talking shops, with little real power, where even the topics for discussion were carefully chosen by the Vatican. And in 1968, within three years of the end of the Council, his pontificate was profoundly damaged by the furore provoked by his encyclical on artificial birth control, *Humanae Vitae*.

In the face of growing unhappiness with the Church's total ban on all forms of artificial birth control, even within marriage, Paul had taken the radical step of removing the question of contraception from the jurisdiction of the Council and remitting it to an advisory commission of theologians, scientists, doctors and married couples. The commission prepared a report recommending modification of the traditional teaching to allow birth control in certain circumstances, and it was widely expected that the pope would accept this recommendation. In the event, he could not bring himself to do so, and the encyclical reaffirmed the traditional teaching, while setting it within a positive understanding of married sexuality. To his horror, instead of closing the question, *Humanae Vitae* provoked a storm of protest, and many priests resigned or were forced out of their posts for their opposition to the pope's teaching.

Paul never doubted that he had done what had to be done, but his confidence was shattered. He never wrote another encyclical, and the last ten years of his pontificate were marked by deepening gloom, as he agonised over the divisions within the Church and his own unpopularity, the mass exodus of priests and religious, and the growing violence of the secular world, signalled for him in 1978 (the last year of his life) by the kidnap and murder of his close friend, the Christian Democratic politician Aldo Moro.

Paul was a complex man, affectionate, capable of deep and enduring friendship, yet reserved, prone to fits of depression, easily hurt. He was passionately committed to the Council and its pastoral renewal of the Church, yet he ardently believed also in the papal primacy and was fearful of compromising it. Hugely intelligent and deeply intuitive, he saw and was daunted by difficulties which others could brush aside, a fact which sometimes made him appear indecisive where another would have acted first and reflected later. He felt criticism deeply, and was acutely conscious of the loneliness and isolation of his position. His last years as pope were a sort of slow crucifixion for him, and he was often to identify himself with the suffering servant of the prophet Isaiah, unloved, bearing the world's woes. He did not despair. In 1975, a weary seventy-eight year old, he jotted down a series of notes on his isolation:

> What is my state of mind? Am I Hamlet or Don Quixote? On the left? On the right? I don't feel I have been properly understood. My feelings are "Superabundo Gaudio", I am full of consolation, overcome with joy, throughout every tribulation'.

Tribulation had indeed become the element he moved in, yet he held the Church together during a period of unprecedented change, and there was no doubting his deeply felt Christian discipleship or his total dedication to the Petrine ministry as he understood it. More than anyone else, he was responsible for the consolidation of the achievements of the Second Vatican Council and the renewal they brought to the Church. His funeral was conducted in the open air of St Peter's square, his simple wooden coffin bare of all regalia except the open pages of the gospel book blown about by the wind. It was a fitting symbol of one of the greatest but most troubled pontificates of modern times.

He was succeeded by another peasant pope, Albino Luciani, son of a migrant worker who had risen to become Patriarch of Venice. Luciani was a pope in the mould of Roncalli rather than Montini, a simple, good-humoured pastoral bishop chosen to lift the gloom that had descended during Paul's last years. He signalled his commitment to the Council by taking the composite name John Paul, and established himself at once as a pastoral figure, opposed to all pomp, refusing, for example, to be crowned. There was universal enthusiasm for his appointment, despite his lack of experience, and the English Cardinal Hume was unwise enough in the euphoric aftermath of the conclave to call him 'God's candidate'. There are in fact signs that the responsibilities of the papacy might have overwhelmed him, but there was no time to discover whether he had the stamina to cope with them or not, for just one month after his election he was found dead of a coronary embolism in the papal apartments. Sensational rumours, later shown to be groundless, suggested that he had been murdered to prevent him exposing and cleaning up financial corruption in the Vatican bank.

IV The Way We Live Now

Once more the shocked cardinals assembled. They had elected a simple good man to be a pastoral pope, and the Lord had whisked him away. Was there a message in all this? General opinion called for another pastoral choice: but who? The choice of the cardinals, an overwhelming 103 votes out of 109, staggered every commentator. For the first time since 1522 they elected a non-Italian. He was a Pole, Karol Wojtyla, Archbishop of Krakow and at fifty-eight the youngest pope since Pius IX. He took the name John Paul II. Though not widely known to the general public, he had established himself during the Vatican Council as a coming man, and had attracted some votes at the conclave which had elected John Paul I.

A former university professor of philosophy and a published poet and playwright, a practised mountaineer and skier, a skilled linguist in French, German, English, Italian and Russian, Wojtyla was by any standards a star, with a remarkable career behind him. Son of a retired army officer widowed while Karol was still a child, he was a student at the outset of the Nazi occupation of Poland, and had served as a labourer in a quarry and a chemical factory. He was the first pope for two centuries to have had anything approaching an ordinary upbringing – if such an upbringing counts as ordinary – and even a girlfriend. When he decided to become a priest he had to commence his studies in secret. His priestly and episcopal career had been under communist rule. He understood and was able to confront and handle the communist system. His philosophical interests were in the field of ethics and human responsibility, and he was deeply read in existentialist thinkers such as the Jewish philosopher and theologian Martin Buber. Paul VI greatly admired him, and had drawn on his book *Love and Responsibility* in drafting *Humanae Vitae*.

From the outset John Paul II pledged himself to continue the work of the Council and his immediate predecessors, whose names he took. But it was equally clear from the outset that his agenda was quite distinctive, and marked both by his philosophical concerns and his Slav identity. Much preoccupied with the so-called 'Church of silence' suffering under communism, he set himself to strengthen it in its struggle with materialist regimes. He visited Poland in June 1979, addressing a rapturous third of the nation at meetings up and down the country. Polish television was instructed never to show these crowds, but to keep the cameras trained on the pope himself. All in vain. The visit rallied national confidence in the face of a crumbling communist regime, and was a major factor in the emergence of the independent union Solidarity in the following year. Papal support, both moral and, it was plausibly said, financial, played a crucial role in the success of the Solidarity movement, and Poland's eventual transition to self-government and the end of communism there. Lech Walesa, the Solidarity leader, would pointedly sign the agreement with government which legalised Solidarity with a souvenir pen of the 1979 papal visit, sporting a portrait of Wojtyla. When, after a crackdown on the new freedoms by the Polish leader

General Jaruzelski, Wojtyla paid a second visit to Poland in 1981, the General's knees, to the delight of the nation, visibly and violently trembled throughout his televised meeting with the pope at the Belvedere Palace in Warsaw. This Polish triumph marked the emergence of a new phase in Vatican Ostpolitik, more upbeat and assertive than the conciliatory approach of Paul VI's years. The Slav pope's insistence on the centrality of the Church as a champion of human freedoms, and the renewed credibility this gave to its institutions and spokesmen in countries seeking to liberate themselves from totalitarianism, contributed to the erosion of communism which would culminate in the collapse of the Soviet Empire in 1989.

Like Pius XII, Wojtyla saw the pope as first and foremost a teacher, an oracle. In 1979 there appeared the first of a series of teaching encyclicals, *Redemptor Hominis*, setting out his vision of a Christian doctrine of human nature, in which Christ is seen not merely as revealing the nature of God, but revealing also what it is to be truly human. From this first encyclical, which picked up themes from *Gaudium et Spes*, in the drafting of which Wojtyla had played an important part, the distinctive character of the new pope's Christian humanism was in evidence. He based his teaching on human dignity and responsibility, not on natural law, but on the mystery of love revealed in Christ – as he wrote 'the name for [our] deep amazement at man's worth and dignity is the Gospel'. The profundity of John Paul's thought was quickly recognised, but so also was its markedly authoritarian cast, and *Redemptor Hominis* contained a stern call to theologians to 'close collaboration with the Magisterium' which foreshadowed tighter papal control over theological freedom within the Church.

This concern with orthodoxy showed itself especially in the field of sexual ethics. From the start of his pontificate, Wojtyla campaigned tirelessly against birth control and abortion, which he invariably linked, and there were recurrent rumours of a solemn statement which would endorse infallibly the teaching of *Humanae Vitae*. No such statement was in fact forthcoming, but his most formidable encyclical, *Veritatis Splendor*, published in October 1993, insisted on the objective reality of fundamental moral values, and asserted the existence of 'intrinsically evil' acts, which purity of intention could never make licit. Contraception was cited as one such act. Like *Humani Generis*, the encyclical was designed to reject, without naming names, a range of current theological approaches to morality. His concern with the evil of abortion expressed itself in 1995 in the encyclical *Evangelium Vitae*, in which he called for 'a new culture' of love and reverence for life, and attacked the 'culture of death' which he saw as characteristic of materialist societies, and of which abortion and euthanasia are the principle expression.

John Paul's attitude to Liberation Theology was to become one of the most controversial aspects of the pope's theological stance. During the 1960s and 1970s theologians in Europe and the Americas increasingly gravitated towards an account of Christian salvation which emphasised the liberating effect of the Gospel not merely in the hereafter, but wherever human beings are enslaved by economic, social or political oppression: they were able to appeal for justification both to *Gaudium et Spes* and to Paul VI's *Populorum Progressio*. The Exodus account of the deliverance of Israel from slavery, and the celebration in biblical texts like the Magnificat of a God who 'puts down the mighty from their thrones' and 'lifts up the humble and meek', were developed into a theological critique of the political and economic order which had particularly direct application in polarised societies like those of Latin America. Theologians like the Peruvian priest Gustavo Guttierez pressed into service Marxist notions such as 'alienation', and emphasised the evils of sinful economic and social structures as a form of institutionalised violence against the oppressed. In Nicaragua, Liberation Theology played a part in the Sandanista revolution, and five Catholic priests took their place in the Sandanista cabinet, including the poet Fr Ernesto Cardenal.

These emphases were taken up by many bishops and priests in Latin America during the pontificate of Paul VI, and became central to much rethinking of the nature of the Church's mission, not least in the Society of Jesus. They alarmed Pope John Paul, however. Profoundly hostile to communism, he was deeply suspicious of the emphases of Liberation Theology, which he believed subordinated Christian concerns to a Marxist agenda. He was deeply opposed, also, to the direct participation of priests and bishops in politics, and he viewed the activities of bishops like Oscar Romero, Archbishop of San Salvador, or Evaristo Arns, Archbishop of Sao Paulo, who had thrown themselves into the defence of the poor against their governments, with a marked lack of warmth. When Romero was murdered by government assassins while saying mass in 1980, he was acclaimed throughout Latin America as a martyr. The pope, who had cautioned him not long before on the need for prudence, spoke of him only as 'zealous', and, addressing the Conference of Latin American Bishops in 1992, removed from the agreed text of the speech a reference to Romero's martyrdom. Arns was undermined by having his huge diocese subdivided without his agreement, and the five new suffragen sees created filled with conservative bishops hostile to his social commitment.

Yet this reserve about Liberation Theology went alongside a profound suspicion of Western capitalism, signalled in a series of powerful and distinctive social encyclicals, like the denunciation in *Dives in Misericordia* (1980) of the 'fundamental defect, or rather a series of defects, indeed a defective machinery...at the root of contemporary economics and material civilisation', defects which trap the 'human family' in 'radically unjust situations' in which children starve in a world of plenty. Even more explicitly, in his remarkable *Sollicitudo Rei Socialis*, published in 1988 to commemorate Paul VI's *Populorum Progressio*, John Paul II excoriated both 'liberal capitalism' and 'Marxist collectivism' as systems embodying defective concepts of individual and social development, both of them in need of radical correction, and both contributing to the widening gap between North and South, rich and poor. He saw Catholic social teaching as something quite distinct from either, offering a critique of both, and even found space to praise the use of the concept of liberation in Latin American theology. The encyclical, which echoed the call for a 'preferential love for the poor', caused consternation among conservative American theologians and social theorists, used to seeing papal utterances as valuable underpinning for Western economic and social theory.

Nevertheless, for all these signs of ambivalence, under his pontificate conservative theological forces have reasserted themselves in the Church, producing a series of confrontations between theologians and the authorities, especially the Congregation for the Doctrine of the Faith (the old Holy Office or Inquisition renamed) headed by the Bavarian Cardinal Joseph Ratzinger. Ratzinger had a distinguished record as an academic theologian, and in an earlier incarnation was one of the theological architects of the reforms of Vatican II. He had been profoundly shocked by student radicalism and the sexual revolution in Germany in the sixties, however, as well as by what he regarded as the hijacking of genuine reform by essentially irreli-

gious Enlightenment values. The flexibility and openness of his earlier writings gave way to a harshly pessimistic call for 'restoration'
which suggested strong reservations about the legacy of the Council.
Poacher turned gamekeeper, he presided over the silencing or dis-
owning of a string of theologians, beginning with Hans Kung in
1979, and the reconstruction of a tight and increasingly assertive
orthodoxy which was to become one of the hallmarks of the pontificate. A few of those acted against had indeed placed themselves outside any reasonable understanding of Catholicism, but a number of
loyal theological explorers, like the blameless and distinguished Jesuit
theologian of inter-faith dialogue, Jacques Dupuis, would fall foul of
the Congregation of the Doctrine of the Faith. The contrast with the
pontificate of Paul VI, when even the traumatic aftermath of
Humanae Vitae produced no papal denunciations or excommunications of theologians, was striking.

John Paul actively assisted in this process, most notably in his issuing of the apostolic letter *Ordinatio Sacerdotalis* in 1995, declaring that
the debate about the ordination of women (hardly begun in the
Catholic Church outside North America, and hardly an issue in most
of the Third World, where the majority of Catholics live) was now
closed. Christ had chosen only men as apostles, and so only men may
be priests. In order that 'all doubt may be removed', therefore , 'in
virtue of my ministry of confirming the brethren', he declared that
'the Church has no authority whatsoever to confer priestly ordination to women and that this judgement is to be definitively held by
all the Church's faithful'. The form in which this statement appeared
– an 'apostolic letter' – was several notches down in the hierarchy of
authoritative papal utterances, below that of an encyclical, for example. Its phrasing, however, hinted at something more weighty – just
what might be meant by 'definitively held', for example? In a subsequent gloss, Cardinal Ratzinger actually attempted to claim infallibility for the pope's statement, evoking widespread protest at a blatant attempt to stifle discussion of an issue which many considered
not yet ripe for resolution.

Pope John Paul, intensely conscious of his Slav inheritance from
the start of his pontificate, also looked East more consistently than
any pope of modern times. His strong sense of Slav identity
expressed itself in the conviction that the religious schism between
East and West had left the Church breathing 'through only one lung',

desperately in need of the spiritual depth and wisdom born of suffering which the Churches of the East could bring. The 1995 encyclical *Ut Unum Sint*, on Christian unity, contained an extended and hopeful discussion of the fundamental unity of the 'Sister Churches' of East and West (unlike Paul VI, John Paul has been careful never to apply this phrase to any Church of the Reformation). The encyclical left no doubt about the Pope's ardent commitment to reconciliation with the Orthodox churches. Paradoxically, however, his own exalted understanding of papal authority, combined with the reintroduction or strengthening of Catholic hierarchies of both the Latin and Byzantine rites into the countries of the former Soviet Union, has done a good deal to set back relationships with the Orthodox world. *Ut Unum Sint* recognised the barrier presented by the Petrine ministry, but asserted its permanent and God-given role as a special 'service of unity'. The pope, in a remarkable gesture, invited the leaders and theologians of other churches to enter into a "patient and fraternal dialogue" with him to discover how the Petrine ministry might be exercised in a way which 'may accomplish a service of love recognised by all concerned'. Rueful Catholic hierarchies and theologians wondered if he wanted a similar dialogue with them.

For Wojtyla, it was clear from the start, believed passionately in a hands-on papacy. As soon as he was elected, the flood of permissions for priests to leave the priesthood and marry dried up. Priests might leave the ministry, but with difficulty, and the pope would not release them from their vows of celibacy: there was no mistaking in this change of policy Wojtyla's own stern convictions. More broadly, the role of the pope and his nuncios became absolutely central once again in Catholic thinking, and in the running and staffing of the local Churches. John Paul II understood his role as universal bishop with a startling immediacy and directness. Within months of his appointment he launched on an extraordinary series of pastoral visits to every corner of the world, carrying his message of old-fashioned moral values and fidelity to the teaching authority of the hierarchical Church, yet with a personal energy and charisma which brought the faithful out in their millions like football fans or zealots at a rally. Asked by a reporter why he intended to visit Britain in 1982 he explained, 'I *must* go: it is my Church'. Critics deplored these paternalist visitations as disabling and absolutist: he saw them as a distinctive and necessary feature of the modern Petrine ministry.

His interventions extended to every aspect of the Church's life, not least that of the religious Orders. He became alarmed by the spread of radical theological opinions among the Jesuits under Paul VI's friend, the saintly and charismatic General Pedro Aruppe. In 1981 Aruppe had a stroke, and Pope John Paul suspended the constitution of the Society of Jesus, thereby preventing the election by the Jesuits of a successor. Instead, the pope, in an unprecedented intervention, imposed his own candidate, the seventy-nine-year-old Fr Paolo Dezza, a Vatican 'trusty', theologically conservative and almost blind. The move was seen as an attempt to impose a papal puppet on the Society, and strained Jesuit loyalty to the limit, evoking a letter of protest from the venerable Jesuit theologian Karl Rahner. The pope subsequently allowed the Order to proceed to a free election and publicly expressed his confidence in their work, but the intervention was recognised as a shot across the bows of an Order which he felt was in danger of politicising the Gospel by over-commitment to the Theology of Liberation.

In his later years, therefore, John Paul II has seemed at times more like the successor of Pius IX, Pius X or Pius XII than of John XXIII or Paul VI. An ultramontane, filled with a profound sense of the immensity of his own office and of his centrality in the providence of God, he was convinced, for example, that the shot with which the deranged Turkish communist Mehmet Ali Agca almost killed him in St Peter's Square in 1981 was miraculously deflected by Our Lady of Fatima. There were resonances behind this conviction that went beyond mere piety. Fatima is a Portuguese shrine where the Virgin was believed to have appeared in 1917. The apparitions and the Fatima cult rapidly became drawn into the apocalyptic hopes and fears associated with the Bolshevik Revolution and the communist attack on Christianity. During the cold war years Fatima became a devotional focus for anti-communist feeling, and the ageing Pius XII was rumoured to have received visions of the Virgin of Fatima. Agca's bullet was later presented to the shrine at Fatima, where it was set in the Virgin's jewelled crown. During the Jubilee year 2000 Papa Wojtyla beatified two of the three child visionaries of Fatima (one was still alive in a Spanish convent) and published the long suppressed 'Third Secret of Fatima'. This turned out to be a lurid but hazy vision of a bishop in white labouring uphill past a ruined city and through piles of corpses until he was himself shot with bullets and arrows by a group of soldiers. The vision was a readily intelligible product of early twentieth-century Portugal, where the Church was face-to-face with a violently anticlerical government, in a period when murdered popes were in any case the common currency of the ultramontane imagination, like the murdered English pope in Fr Rolfe's fantasy-romance *Hadrian VII*. Pope John Paul, however, clearly understood the vision as a direct prophecy of the failed assassination attempt of 1981. A theological commentary on the Third Secret by the Congregation of the Doctrine of the Faith compared the Fatima visions to the visions of scripture, and was deplored on that account by theologians worried by the authority thereby bestowed on what they saw as dubious and dangerously irrational forces within the Church. The commentary was in fact a careful damage limitation exercise by Cardinal Ratzinger's Congregation to generalise the meaning of the 'Third Secret' into an unexceptionable meditation on the difficulties of the Christian life in the modern world. The assassination attempt was not the only event interpreted by John Paul as a manifestation of his mystical vocation. In 1994, when, like many another old man, he fell in the shower and broke his thigh, he saw the accident as a deeper entry into his prophetic calling: the pope, he declared, must suffer.

Suffering, one may feel, offers the key to his character: the death of his mother when he was nine, of his beloved elder brother when he was thirteen, the harshness of his wartime experience as a labourer in a quarry and a chemical factory, the years of concealment, resistance and confrontation as seminarian, priest and bishop under Nazi and then communist rule. All these combined to shape an outlook half grieved by and half contemptuous of the self-indulgence of the West, dismissive of the moral and social values of the Enlightenment which, he believes, have led humanity into a spiritual cul-de-sac and have more than half-seduced the Churches.

He is a hard man to measure. Sternly authoritarian, he abandoned the use of the royal plural in his encyclicals and allocutions: he is the first pope to write not as 'we', but in his own persona, as Karol Wojtyla. He was also a passionate believer in religious liberty, and at Vatican II played a key role in the transformation of Catholic teaching in that area. Often seen as dismissive of other faiths, he has an intense interest in Judaism, born out of a lifelong friendship with a Jewish boy from Krakow: he was the first pope to visit the Roman synagogue, and in 1993 he established formal diplomatic relations with the State of Israel. His openness to other religions extends to the non-Abrahamic traditions. In October 1986 at Assisi he initiated acts of worship involving not only Muslims, but Hindus, the Dalai Lama and assorted Shamans. When praying by the Ganges at the scene of Ghandi's cremation he became so absorbed that his entourage lost patience and literally shook him back into his schedule. The uncompromising defender of profoundly unpopular teaching on matters such as birth control, he became nevertheless the most populist pope in history, the veteran of nearly seventy international tours, an unstoppable tarmac-kisser, hand-shaker, granny-blesser, baby-kisser. Convinced of his own immediate authority over and responsibility for every Catholic in the world, he went to the people, showing himself, asserting his authority, coaxing, scolding, joking, weeping and trailing exhausted local hierarchies in his wake. Everywhere he has gone too, he has canonised or beatified droves of local saints, more than all the popes in history put together, often waiving the traditional requirement for proven miracles in the process, so that outraged conservatives complained of the Vatican becoming a 'saint-factory'. For Wojtyla, however, this unique exercise of papal authority went to the heart of the Petrine ministry, his way of encouraging and recognising the life of the spirit in the local Churches, by providing them with their own exemplars and heavenly intercessors. And despite, or perhaps on account of, the uncompromising character of his moral teaching, his encyclical *Veritatis Splendor* reached far beyond the ranks of the converted and attracted the attention and praise of many non-Christians concerned about the nature of moral commitment and the ordering of society.

The titanic energy of this pontificate has had momentous consequences for the Church, not all of them good. The endless journeys, designed to unite the Church around the pope, sometimes seemed rather to highlight divisions. The rhetoric of shared responsibility with other bishops was often belied by increasing Vatican intervention in the local Churches, not least in some disastrous, and disastrously unpopular, episcopal appointments, like that of Mgr Wolfgang Haas to the Swiss diocese of Chur. Haas, deeply conservative and very confrontational, was widely believed to have been introduced by the Vatican to promote 'restorationist' theological views and pastoral policies. He rapidly alienated clergy and laity alike, priests applied in large numbers for transfers to other diocese, and there were public demonstrations against him: the Canton of Zurich voted to cut off all payments to the diocese. Haas attributed all this to the fact that he was a defender of orthodoxy: 'If one fully accepts the magisterium of the Church, an essential condition for Catholics, then one comes under fire'. In 1990 the other Swiss bishops went to see the pope to secure Haas's removal. He was not in fact removed. Instead, in 1997 the Vatican adopted the extraordinary face-saving device of creating a new Archdiocese for the tiny principality of Liechtenstein (formerly part of the diocese of Chur), and transferred Haas into it.

Under John Paul the authority of local hierarchies has been systematically whittled away. Vatican theologians challenged the theological and canonical status of the National Conferences of Bishops, arguing that episcopal 'collegiality' is only exercised by the bishops gathered round the pope, never acting independently. Joint decisions of Conferences of Bishops – like those of Latin America, or the North American bishops – represented merely 'collective' decisions, introducing inappropriate 'democratic' structures into the hierarchy of the Church which have no theological standing. In all this, critics saw the reversal of trends inaugurated by his predecessors, like the devolution of authority to local Churches which was so striking a feature of Paul VI's pontificate.

For despite his patent commitment to the implementation of the Second Vatican Council, John Paul II has increasingly thrown his weight behind movements and energies which seemed to sit uneasily with the spirit of the Council. He has given strong personal endorsement to lay movements like *Communione e Liberazione*, a renewal of Catholic Action in the style of Pius XI and to clerical movements of a strongly conservative character, like the 'Legionaries of Christ' founded by the Mexican Marcial Maciel. In particular, he gave his protection and the unique canonical status of a 'personal prelature', and hence exemption from local episcopal authority, to the secretive organisation Opus Dei, founded in pre-Franco Spain by Jose Maria Escriva. Wojtyla went to pray at Escriva's tomb in Rome just before the conclave which elected him Pope in 1978. Escriva's rapid beatification in 1992, against strong and vocal opposition, and the announcement of his imminent canonisation at the beginning of 2002, made clear the pope's identification with the spirit and objectives of the Opus Dei movement. Its conservative pastoral influence and growing backroom control over many official Church events and institutions, including even episcopal meetings and synods, was causing considerable unease to some local hierarchies.

John Paul II is the very embodiment of a particular and high vision of papacy, and so a sign of strife as well as of unity. Hailed by some as God's reply to the Second Vatican Council, he was denounced by others as an oppressor of women. The unpopularity which his stance on a host of issues brought him has troubled him not a whit. In the solemn and silent moment of his episcopal ordination in Poland, a former workmate from the chemical plant shouted out the pope's nickname. 'Lolek', he cried, 'don't let anyone get you down'. For good or ill, he never has done.

John Paul's last years have been dogged by visibly advancing illness which reduced the former athlete to a painfully stooped and frail figure. Parkinson's disease froze his charismatic face into an immobile mask, incapable of smiling: his left hand trembled uncontrollably. He has refused to be defeated. Despite increasingly explicit discussion in the media of the possibility of a papal resignation, he has soldiered on, permitting no let-up in the gruelling regime of roving evangelist he had evolved for himself. The international visits go on – by the end of the Jubilee year 2000, more than ninety trips to over 120 countries, covering a million miles, every trip a punishing round of receptions, mass-meetings and liturgies. Some, like that to Castro's Cuba in January 1998, were of major international significance: a deal which helped Cuba in its efforts to lift the American-led blockade against it, and which, from the pope's point of view, gave him an opportunity to secure new freedoms for the Cuban church and to carry his unswerving campaign for religious and human liberties into the last outpost of Soviet-style communism in the West (Wojtyla secured from Castro the release of 200 political prisoners). Kept on his feet by injections administered in the sacristy before long ceremonies, the ageing pope was often visibly exhausted, stunned or dozing as his illness overcame him, yet capable of summoning his strength in astonishing returns of the old magic. The Bimillennial Holy Year 2000 was a series of such surprises: Wojtyla drew a flood of pilgrims to Rome, and packed the year with far-reaching initiatives, like the Day of Pardon he presided over, against the advice of more cautious voices in the Vatican, at the start of Lent in March 2000. In the course of this ceremony in St Peter's, designed to initiate a 'Purification of Memory' for the Church in the Third Millennium, he solemnly acknowledged and apologised for the Catholic Church's past sins against human and religious freedoms, against the dignity of women, against the Jews. He reiterated this public act of repentance during an historic visit to the Holy Land later the same month, in an eloquent address at the Yad Vashem memorial for the dead of the Shoah, and, even more touchingly, when the stooped and trembling old man inserted into a crevice in the Wailing Wall a prayer of penitence for Christian sins against the Jews. The Holy Year had begun, too, with spectacular gestures, notably the ceremony for the opening of the Holy Doors at St Paul's outside the walls in January, when Wojtyla was assisted in swinging back the door by the Protestant evangelical Archbishop of Canterbury, George Carey, an ecumenical gesture unimaginable in any previous pontificate, and a testimony to Wojtyla's continuing ability to draw imaginative and generous responses from other Christian leaders.

He was to continue such gestures after the Holy Year had ended, for example in his remarkable visit to Greece in May 2001, which initially evoked a storm of protest from Orthodox ecclesiastics, but in the course of which the pope simply and humbly apologised before the Archbishop of Athens for Roman Catholic sins against the Orthodox Churches, especially the Sack of Constantinople during the Fourth Crusade, an episode which for many Orthodox epitomised the evils of Latin Christendom. Wojtyla's trip in June that year to the Ukraine, where historic tensions between the Orthodox Church and the five million Byzantine-rite Catholics had worsened since the collapse of communism, heartened the Catholic faithful there, but was less successful ecumenically.

In such journeyings the pope's frailty itself became an instrument of his mission, almost a weapon, a reproach to his opponents and an eloquent sign of the total dedication and abandonment to the will of God which he saw as the core of the Christian and above all the priestly life. But it was also a source of anxiety to many in the Church, who admired Wojtyla's courage and fidelity, but who feared that his growing weakness left control of the central administration of the church in the hands of the Vatican bureaucracy. Always on the move, he had never given much attention to administrative detail or the structures of the Church, leaving that largely to his staff. The lack

of concern for detail was evident in the new procedures he authorised in 1996 for future papal conclaves, which made provision for
the abandonment of the traditional two-thirds majority in the event
of deadlock, and permitted election by a simple majority. Many
viewed such a change as placing a weapon in the hands of any well-
organised faction determined to impose a particular candidate rather
than work for consensus, and thus a recipe for disaster: a more experienced papal administrator would never have agreed to it. In his old
age, the authority of the Vatican Congregations has grown, above all
that of Cardinal Ratzinger's Congregation for the Doctrine of the
Faith, always the single most influential Vatican department and now,
rightly or wrongly, widely perceived as empire-building. A case in
point was the publication by the Congregation for the Doctrine of
the Faith in September 2000 of a declaration on the unity and universality of Christianity, *Dominus Iesus*. Markedly different in tone
and rhetorical impact from *Ut Unum Sint*, the pope's own encyclical
on this subject, *Dominus Iesus* was an emphatic assertion of the centrality of Christ for salvation, and hence of the imperfection and
incompleteness of all other religions. Within Christianity it insisted
on the centrality of the Roman Catholic Church. A 'note' on the
usage 'sister churches' seemed designed to reverse a trend inaugurated by Paul VI, by forbidding the application of the phrase to the
Church of England and other Reformed or Protestant Churches.

This document was widely understood as a restorationist attempt
to halt creeping relativism in the Catholic Church's relations with
other Churches and other faiths. It was issued, however, without
proper consultation with the two Vatican bodies charged with direct
responsibility for Ecumenism and inter-faith dialogue, and was
accordingly resented. Cardinal Walter Kaspar, head of the Pontifical
Council for Promoting Christian Unity, considered the document
ecumenically disastrous, and issued a statement criticising, explaining
and correcting its emphases: he described it as 'perhaps too densely
written', a phrase which in Vatican-speak was as near to a howl of
protest as protocol allowed. Kaspar later let it be known that when he
went to the pope with a file full of protests about *Dominus Iesus* from
spokesmen and leaders of the other Christian Churches, Papa
Wojtyla seemed uncertain of the exact content of the document. The
implication was clear: the Pope was no longer in charge of major
statements and policy decisions issued under his authority.

John Paul II's pontificate, the longest for more than a century, will also be judged one of the most momentous, in which a pope not only once more reasserted papal control of the Church, and thereby sought to call a halt to the decentralising initiated as a result of the Second Vatican Council, but in which the pope, long since a marginal figure in the world of *realpolitik*, once more played a major role in world history, the downfall of Soviet communism. John Paul's own contradictions defy easy categorisations. Passionately committed to the freedom and integrity of the human person, he was the twentieth century's most effective ambassador for such freedoms, setting his own country on a path to liberation and thereby helping trigger the collapse of the Soviet empire. Two of his major encyclicals, *Veritatis Splendor* and *Fides et Ratio*, celebrate the ability of the free human mind to grasp fundamental truth and to discern the will of God which is also the fulfilment of human nature. Yet under his pontificate the last quarter of the twentieth century saw a revived authoritarianism in the Catholic Church, in which, in the judgement of many, theological exploration was needlessly outlawed or prematurely constrained. Passionately committed to reconciliation with the Orthodox, his pontificate saw an expansion of Catholicism within the former Soviet Union which outraged Orthodox leaders and hardened the ancient suspicions he so painfully and sincerely laboured to dispel. This Polish pope has done more than any single individual in the whole history of Christianity to reconcile Jews and Christians and to remove the ancient stain of anti-Semitism from the Christian imagination: his visits to the Roman synagogue and above all to the Holy Land in 2000, and his repeated expressions of penitence for Christian anti-Semitism, were imaginative gestures whose full implications and consequences have yet to appear. Yet he canonised Maximillian Kolbe, the Polish Franciscan who voluntarily took the place of a married man in a Nazi concentration camp death cell, but who had edited an anti-Semitic paper between the Wars. Wojtyla also canonised Edith Stein, the Jewish convert to Catholicism who became a Carmelite nun and died because she was a Jew in Auschwitz in 1942. The pope saw Stein as a reconciling figure. Jews saw her as an emblem of proselytisation and, like Kolbe, an attempt to annex the Shoah for Catholicism. Wojtyla was not deflected from his purpose, and despite protests both canonisations went ahead. The making of saints has also been used to send equally ambivalent messages in other areas too. On 3 September 2000 Wojtyla beatified Pope John XXIII, the much loved pope of the Council. This was an immensely popular move – John's tomb in the Vatican crypt had been constantly surrounded by kneeling pilgrims since the day of his burial, and his raising to the altars of the Church was seen by many as an overdue endorsement of Papa Roncalli's Council and the changes it had brought. But in the same ceremony Wojtyla also beatified Pio Nono, the pope of the *Syllabus of Errors* and the First Vatican Council, and the symbol of an infallible papacy intransigently at odds with modernity and with secular Italy. It had originally been planned to beatify Roncalli alongside his very different predecessor, Eugenio Pacelli, Pius XII. Controversy over Papa Pacelli's alleged silence about the treatment of the Jews during the Nazi era made this pairing impossible. Pio Nono's cause had been in process long before Roncalli's, but canonisations are public statements, and inevitably there were many who were bound to see the linking of these incongruously contrasting popes as an attempt to offset any advantage pro-Conciliar forces in the Church of the Third Millennium might have derived from the raising of Pope John to the altars.

If such apparent contradictions made Papa Wojtyla suspect to liberal and secular opinion, equally he has defied annexation by the religious and political Right. A passionate opponent of communism, he was almost as vehement in his criticism of Western capitalism, and in protest against the exploitation of the world's poor by the developed world. Denouncing the 'culture of death' which legitimated the 'liberalisation' of abortion laws, he has consistently included in his condemnations of the same culture of death the use, or threatened use, of nuclear weapons, and the exercise of the death penalty, papal positions with which conservative 'pro-life' lobbyists were often much less at ease.

At the start of a new millennium, convinced of his providential mission to lead the Church into the twenty-first century, this 261st successor of St Peter commands a papacy whose credibility has been damaged in some quarters by its recurrent hostility to modern opinion and modern mores, yet with a spiritual status and prestige greater than at any time since the high Middle Ages. This standing was based in large part on the personality and patent Christian goodness of so many of the recent popes, and on the manifest greatness of Wojtyla himself. The energies released by the Second Vatican Council seemed to point the Church in the direction of greater cultural and theological pluralism, more lay participation, less hierarchy, more dialogue. But the years since that Council, now fading from the Church's collective memory, have not delivered all the transformations once hoped for. The abilities and inclination of the last pope of the twentieth century, and first of the twenty-first, point elsewhere, to a more exalted, lonely and hierarchic vision of the papal office and the Church it serves – or rules. With its emphasis on obedience and conformity to the *magisterium* – a concept which in Roman usage often seems to boil down to what the Pope says – it is a vision uncomfortably like that promoted in the aftermath of the Modernist crisis. Whether it can command adherence in the post-Conciliar age, in which the cultural dominance of Latin liturgy and thought patterns has been decisively broken, remains to be seen. To many people Pope John Paul has seemed a backward looking figure, a man engaged in forcing a champagne cork back into the bottle. To others, his pontificate pointed the way towards a recovery of balance, a restoration of order and true faith in the flux of time. Only time, and the next conclave, will reveal which of these directions in their long walk through history the heirs of St Peter will take.

APPENDIX A

CHRONOLOGICAL LIST OF POPES AND ANTIPOPES

Dates for the first fifteen popes are approximate, and for the first five (excluding Clement) are arbitrary. Following the convention of the most ancient lists, the Apostle Peter is not reckoned as a pope.

The names of popes are given in capital letters, preceded by a number giving their place in the succession. The names of the antipopes are indented, without number, and in plain type. Where a pope assumed a new name on election, his baptismal name is given in square brackets.

1	St Linus	
2	St Anacletus	
3	St Clement I	c. 96
4	St Evaristus	
5	St Alexander I	
6	St Sixtus I	c. 116–c. 125
7	St Telesphorus	c. 125–c. 136
8	St Hyginus	c. 138–c. 142
9	St Pius I	c. 142–c. 155
10	St Anicetus	c. 155–c. 166
11	St Soter	c. 166–c. 174
12	St Eleutherius	c. 175–c. 189
13	St Victor	c. 189–c. 199
14	St Zephyrinus	c. 199–c. 217
15	St Callistus I	c. 217–222
	St Hippolytus 217–c. 235	
16	St Urban I	c. 222–230
17	St Pontian	21 July 230–28 Sept. 235
18	St Anterus	21 Nov. 235–3 Jan. 236
19	St Fabian	10 Jan. 236–20 Jan. 250
20	St Cornelius	Mar. 251–June 253
	Novatian	Mar. 251–258
21	St Lucius I	25 June 253–5 Mar. 254

22	St Stephen I	12 May 254–2 Aug. 257
23	St Sixtus II	Aug. 257–6 Aug. 258
24	St Dionysius	22 July 260–26 Dec. 268
25	St Felix I	3 Jan. 269–30 Dec. 274
26	St Eutychian	4 Jan. 275–7 Dec. 283
27	St Gaius (Caius)	17 Dec. 283–22 Apr. 296
28	St Marcellinus	30 June 296–?: died 25 Oct. 304
29	St Marcellus	c. 308–309
30	St Eusebius	18 Apr.–21 Oct. 310
31	St Miltiades (Melchiades)	2 July 311–10 Jan. 314
32	St Sylvester I	31 Jan. 314–31 Dec. 335
33	St Mark	18 Jan.–7 Oct. 336
34	St Julius I	6 Feb. 337–12 Apr. 352
35	Liberius	17 May 352–24 Sept. 366
	St Felix II	355–365
36	St Damasus I	1 Oct. 366–11 Dec. 384
	Ursinus	366–7: died 385
37	St Siricius	17(?) Dec. 384–26 Nov. 399
38	St Anastasius I	27 Nov. 399–19 Dec. 401
39	St Innocent I	21 Dec. 401–12 Mar. 417
40	St Zosimus	18 Mar. 417–26 Dec. 418
	Eulalius	418: died 423
41	St Boniface	28 Dec. 418–4 Sept. 422
42	St Celestine I	10 Sept. 422–27 July 432
43	St Sixtus III (Xystus)	31 July 432–19 Aug. 440
44	St Leo I (the Great)	29 Sept. 440–10 Nov. 461
45	St Hilarus (Hilary)	19 Nov. 461–29 Feb. 468
46	St Simplicius	3 Mar. 468–10 Mar. 483
47	St Felix III (II)	13 Mar. 483–1 Mar. 492
48	St Gelasius I	1 Mar. 492–21 Nov. 496
49	Anastasius II	24 Nov. 496–19 Nov. 498
50	St Symmachus	22 Nov. 498–19 July 514
	Laurence	498–499, 501–506: died 508
51	St Hormisdas	20 July 514–6 Aug. 523
52	St John I	13 Aug. 523–18 May 526
53	St Felix IV (III)	12 July 526–22 Sept. 530
	Dioscorus	530
54	Boniface II	22 Sept. 530–17 Oct. 532
55	John II [*Mercury*]	2 Jan. 533–8 May 535
56	St Agapitus I	13 May 535–22 Apr. 536
57	St Silverius	8 June 536–11 Nov. 537: deposed, died 2 Dec. 537

58	Vigilius	29 Mar. 537–7 June 555
59	Pelagius I	16 Apr. 556–3 Mar. 561
60	John III	17 July 561–13 July 574
61	Benedict I	2 June 575–30 July 579
62	Pelagius II	26 Nov. 579–7 Feb. 590
63	St Gregory I (the Great)	3 Sept. 590–12 Mar. 604
64	St Sabinian	13 Sept. 604–22 Feb. 606
65	Boniface III	19 Feb.–12 Nov. 607
66	St Boniface IV	15 Sept. 608–8 May 615
67	St Deusdedit I (Adeodatus)	19 Oct. 615–8 Nov. 618
68	Boniface V	23 Dec. 619–25 Oct. 625
69	Honorius I	27 Oct. 625–12 Oct. 638
70	Severinus	28 May 640–2 Aug. 640
71	John IV	24 Dec. 640–12 Oct. 642
72	Theodore I	24 Nov. 642–14 May 649
73	St Martin I	5 July 649–17 June 653: deposed, died 16 Sept. 655
74	St Eugenius I	10 Aug. 654–2 June 657
75	St Vitalian	30 July 657–27 Jan. 672
76	Adeodatus II	11 Apr. 672–17 June 676
77	Donus	2 Nov. 676–11 Apr. 678
78	St Agatho	27 June 678–10 Jan. 681
79	St Leo II	17 Aug. 682–3 July 683
80	St Benedict II	26 June 684–8 May 685
81	John V	23 July 685–2 Aug. 686
82	Conon	21 Oct. 686–21 Sept. 687
	Theodore	687
	Paschal	687: died 692
83	St Sergius I	15 Dec. 687–9 Sept. 701
84	John VI	30 Oct. 701–11 Jan. 705
85	John VII	1 Mar. 705–18 Oct. 707
86	Sisinnius	15 Jan.–8 Feb. 708
87	Constantine I	25 Mar. 708–9 Apr. 715
88	St Gregory II	19 May 715–11 Feb. 731
89	St Gregory III	18 Mar. 731–28 Nov. 741
90	St Zacharias	3 Dec. 741–15 Mar. 752
91	Stephen II (III)*	26 Mar. 752–26 Apr. 757

* In March 752 an elderly presbyter, Stephen, was elected pope, but died before he was ordained bishop. His successor, confusingly, was also called Stephen. Under modern canon law, however, a man is pope from the moment of election. Some modern Roman Catholic lists therefore count the first of these two Stephens as Pope Stephen II, with a consequent disturbance of the numbering of all subsequent Stephens. He is *omitted* from our list, but the variant numberings are noted.

92	St Paul I	29 May 757–28 June 767
	Constantine	767–768
	Philip	768
93	Stephen III (IV)	7 Aug. 768–24 Jan. 772
94	Hadrian I	1 Feb. 772–25 Dec. 795
95	St Leo III	27 Dec. 795–12 June 816
96	Stephen IV (V)	22 June 816–24 Jan. 817
97	St Paschal I	24 Jan. 817–11 Feb. 824
98	Eugenius II	5/6 June 824–27 Aug. 827
99	Valentine	Aug.–Sept. 827
100	Gregory IV	end of 827–25 Jan. 844
	John	844
101	Sergius II	Jan. 844–27 Jan. 847
102	St Leo IV	10 Apr. 847–17 July 855
103	Benedict III	29 Sept. 855–17 Apr. 858
	Anastasius Bibliothecarius	855
104	St Nicholas I (the Great)	24 Apr. 858–13 Nov. 867
105	Hadrian II	14 Dec. 867–Dec. 872
106	John VIII	14 Dec. 872–16 Dec. 882
107	Marinus I (Martin II)	16 Dec. 882–15 May 884
108	St Hadrian III	17 May 884–Sept. 885
109	Stephen V (VI)	Sept. 885–14 Sept. 891
110	Formosus	6 Oct. 891–4 Apr. 896
111	Boniface VI	Apr. 896
112	Stephen VI (VII)	May 896–Aug. 897
113	Romanus	Aug.–Nov. 897
114	Theodore II	Nov./Dec. 897
115	John IX	Jan. 898–Jan. 900
116	Benedict IV	May/June 900–July/Aug. 903
117	Leo V	July/Aug.–Sept. 903: murdered 904
	Christopher	903–904
118	Sergius III	29 Jan. 904–14 Apr. 911
119	Anastasius III	April/June 911–July/Aug. 913
120	Lando	Aug. 913–Mar. 914
121	John X	Mar./Apr. 914–May 928: deposed, murdered 929
122	Leo VI	May–Dec. 928
123	Stephen VII (VIII)	Dec. 928–Feb. 931
124	John XI	Feb./Mar. 931–Dec./Jan. 935/6
125	Leo VII	3(?) Jan. 936–13 July 939
126	Stephen VIII (IX)	14 July 939–Oct. 942

127	MARINUS II (Martin III)	30 (?) Oct. 942–May 946
128	AGAPITUS II	10 May 946–Dec. 955
129	JOHN XII	16 Dec. 955–14 May 964
130	LEO VIII*	4 Dec. 963–1 Mar. 965
131	BENEDICT V	22 May–23 June 964: deposed, died 966
132	JOHN XIII	1 Oct. 965–6 Sept. 972
133	BENEDICT VI	19 Jan. 973–July 974
	Boniface VII	June–July 974, Aug. 984–20 July 985
134	BENEDICT VII	Oct. 974–10 July 983
135	JOHN XIV [Peter Canepanova]	Dec. 983–20 Aug. 984
136	JOHN XV [John Crescentius]	Aug. 985–Mar. 996
137	GREGORY V [Bruno of Carinthia]	3 May 996–18 Feb. 999
	John XVI	Feb. 997–May 998: died 1001
138	SYLVESTER II [Gerbert of Aurillac]	2 Apr. 999–12 May 1003
139	JOHN XVII [John Sicco]	16 May–6 Nov. 1003
140	JOHN XVIII [John Fasanus]	25 Dec. 1003–June/July 1009
141	SERGIUS IV [Pietro Buccaporca: 'Pig's snout']	31 July 1009–12 May 1012
	Gregory VI	May–Dec. 1012
142	BENEDICT VIII [Theophylact II of Tusculum]	17 May 1012–9 Apr. 1024
143	JOHN XIX (Romanus of Tusculum]	19 Apr. 1024–20 Oct. 1032
144	BENEDICT IX [Theophylact III of Tusculum]	21 Oct. 1032–Sept. 1044, 10 Mar.–1 May 1045, 8 Nov 1047–16 July 1048: deposed, died 1055/6
145	SYLVESTER III [John of Sabina]	20 Jan.–10 Mar. 1045: deposed, died 1063
146	GREGORY VI [John Gratian]	1 May 1045–20 Dec. 1046: deposed, died 1047
147	CLEMENT II [Suidger of Bamberg]	24 Dec. 1046–9 Oct. 1047
148	DAMASUS II [Poppo of Brixen]	17 July–9 Aug. 1048
149	ST LEO IX [Bruno of Egisheim]	12 Feb. 1049–19 Apr. 1054
150	VICTOR II [Gebhard of Dollnstein-Hirschberg]	13 Apr. 1055–28 July 1057
151	STEPHEN IX (X) [Frederick of Lorraine]	2 Aug. 1057–29 Mar. 1058
	Benedict X [John Mincius]	1058–59: died 1074
152	NICHOLAS II [Gérard of Lorraine]	6 Dec. 1058–July 1061
153	ALEXANDER II [Anselm of Baggio]	30 Sept. 1061–21 Apr. 1073

*Because John XII was deposed by the Emperor Otto I, the validity of Leo VIII's election has been contested, and he is included as an antipope in many lists. The Roman Catholic Church's official list of popes, as printed in the *Annuario Pontificio*, recognises him as a true pope.

	Honorius (II) [*Peter Cadalus*]	1061–64: died 1072
154	ST GREGORY VII [*Hildebrand*]	22 Apr. 1073–25 May 1085
	Clement III [*Guibert of Ravenna*]	1080, 1084–1100
155	BL. VICTOR III [*Desiderius of Monte Cassino*]	24 May 1086, 9 May–16 Sept. 1087
156	BL. URBAN II [*Odo of Lagery*]	12 Mar. 1088–29 July 1099
157	PASCHAL II [*Rainerius of Bieda*]	13 Aug. 1099–21 Jan. 1118
	Theoderic	Sept. 1100–Jan. 1101: died 1102
	Albert	1101/2
	Sylvester IV [*Maginulf*]	1105–11
158	GELASIUS II [*John of Gaeta*]	24 Jan. 1118–29 Jan. 1119
	Gregory (VIIII)	1118–21: died c 1140
	[*Maurice Burdanus – 'the donkey'*]	
159	CALLISTUS II [*Guido of Burgundy*]	2 Feb. 1119–14 Dec. 1124
160	HONORIUS II [*Lambert Scannabecchi*]	21 Dec. 1124–13 Feb. 1130
	Celestine II [*Teobaldo*]	1124: died 1126
161	INNOCENT II [*Gregorio Papareschi*]	14 Feb. 1130–24 Sept. 1143
	Anacletus II [*Pietro Pierleoni*]	1130–38
	Victor IV [*Gregorio Conti*]	1138)
162	CELESTINE II [*Guido di Castello*]	26 Sept. 1143–8 Mar. 1144
163	LUCIUS II [*Gherardo Caccianemici*]	12 Mar. 1144–15 Feb. 1145
164	BL. EUGENIUS III [*Bernardo Pignatelli*]	15 Feb. 1145–8 July 1153
165	ANASTASIUS IV [*Conrad of Rome*]	8 July 1153–3 Dec. 1154
166	HADRIAN IV [*Nicholas Breakspear*]	4 Dec. 1154–1 Sept. 1159
167	ALEXANDER III [*Orlando Bandinelli*]	7 Sept. 1159–30 Aug. 1181
	Victor IV [*Ottaviano of Monticelli*]	1159–64
	Paschal III [*Guido of Crema*]	1164–68
	Callistus III [*Giovanni of Struma*]	1168–78
	Innocent III [*Lando of Sezze*]	1179–80
168	LUCIUS III [*Ubaldo Allucingoli*]	1 Sept. 1181–25 Nov. 1185
169	URBAN III [*Uberto Crivelli*]	25 Nov. 1185–20 Oct. 1187
170	GREGORY VIII [*Alberto di Morra*]	21 Oct.–17 Dec. 1187
171	CLEMENT III [*Paulo Scolari*]	19 Dec. 1187–Mar. 1191
172	CELESTINE III [*Giacinto Boboni*]	30 Mar. 1191–8 Jan. 1198
173	INNOCENT III [*Lothar of Segni*]	8 Jan. 1198–16 July 1216
174	HONORIUS III [*Cencio Savelli*]	18 July 1216–18 Mar. 1227
175	GREGORY IX [*Ugolino dei Conti di Segni*]	19 Mar. 1227–22 Aug. 1241
176	CELESTINE IV [*Goffredo da Castiglione*]	25 Oct.–10 Nov. 1241
177	INNOCENT IV [*Sinibaldo Fieschi*]	25 June 1243–7 Dec. 1254
178	ALEXANDER IV [*Rainaldo dei Conti di Segni*]	12 Dec. 1254–25 May 1261
179	URBAN IV [*Jacques Pantaléon*]	29 Aug. 1261–2 Oct. 1264
180	CLEMENT IV [*Guy Foulques*]	5 Feb. 1265–29 Nov. 1268
181	BL. GREGORY X [*Tedaldo Visconti*]	1 Sept. 1271–10 Jan. 1276

182	BL. INNOCENT V [*Pierre of Tarantaise*]	21 Jan.–22 June 1276
183	HADRIAN V [*Ottobono Fieschi*]	11 July–18 Aug. 1276
184	JOHN XXI* [*Pedro Juliano, 'Peter of Spain'*]	8 Sept. 1276–20 May 1277
185	NICHOLAS III [*Giovanni Gaetano Orsini*]	25 Nov. 1277–22 Aug. 1280
186	MARTIN IV [*Simon de Brie (or Brion)*]	22 Feb. 1281–28 Mar. 1285
187	HONORIUS IV [*Giacomo Savelli*]	2 Apr. 1285–3 Apr. 1287
188	NICHOLAS IV [*Girolamo Masci*]	22 Feb. 1288–4 Apr. 1292
189	ST CELESTINE V [*Pietro del Morrone*]	5 July–13 Dec. 1294: resigned, died 1296
190	BONIFACE VIII [*Benedetto Caetani*]	24 Dec. 1294–11 Oct. 1303
191	BL. BENEDICT XI [*Niccolo[2] Boccasino*]	22 Oct. 1303–7 July 1304
192	CLEMENT V [*Bertrand de Got*]	5 June 1305–20 Apr. 1314
193	JOHN XXII [*Jacques Duèse*]	7 Aug. 1316–4 Dec. 1334
	Nicholas (V) [*Pietro Rainalducci*]	1328–30
194	BENEDICT XII [*Jacques Fournier*]	20 Dec. 1334–25 Apr. 1342
195	CLEMENT VI [*Pierre Roger*]	7 May 1342–6 Dec. 1352
196	INNOCENT VI [*Etienne Aubert*]	18 Dec. 1352–12 Sept. 1362
197	BL. URBAN V [*Guillaume de Grimoard*]	28 Sept. 1362–19 Dec. 1370
198	GREGORY XI [*Pierre Roger*]	30 Dec. 1370–27 Mar. 1378
199	URBAN VI [*Bartolommeo Prignano*]	8 Apr. 1378–15 Oct. 1389
	Clement VII [*Robert of Geneva*]	1378–94
200	BONIFACE IX [*Pietro Tomacelli*]	2 Nov. 1389–1 Oct. 1404
	Benedict XIII [*Pedro de Luna*]	28 Sept. 1394–26 July 1417: died 1423
201	INNOCENT VII [*Cosimo Gentile dei Migliorati*]	17 Oct. 1404–6 Nov. 1406
202	GREGORY XII [*Angelo Correr*]	30 Nov. 1406–4 June 1415: abdicated at Council of Constance, died 18 Sept. 1417
	Alexander V [*Pietro Philargi*]	1409–10
	John XXIII [*Baldassare Cossa*]	1410–15: died 1419
203	MARTIN V [*Odo Colonna*]	11 Nov. 1417–20 Feb. 1431
	Clement VIII [*Gil Sanchez Munoz*]	1423–29: died 1446
	Benedict (XIV) [*Bernard Garier*]	1425–?
204	EUGENIUS IV [*Gabriele Condulmaro*]	3 Mar. 1431–23 Feb. 1447
	Felix V [*Amadeus of Savoy*]	1439–49: died 1451
205	NICHOLAS V [*Tommaso Parentucelli*]	6 Mar. 1447–24 Mar. 1455
206	CALLISTUS III [*Alfonso Borgia*]	8 Apr. 1455–6 Aug. 1458
207	PIUS II [*Aeneas Silvio Piccolomini*]	19 Aug. 1458–15 Aug. 1464
208	PAUL II [*Pietro Barbo*]	30 Aug. 1464–26 July 1471
209	SIXTUS IV [*Francesco della Rovere*]	9 Aug. 1471–12 Aug. 1484

*Because of a mistake in the medieval numbering, no pope has ever borne the title John XX

210 INNOCENT VIII [*Giovanni Battista Cibo*]   29 Aug. 1484–25 July 1492
211 ALEXANDER VI [*Roderigo de Borgia*]   11 Aug. 1492–18 Aug. 1503
212 PIUS III [*Francesco Todeschini*]   22 Sept.–18 Oct. 1503
213 JULIUS II [*Giuliano della Rovere*]   1 Nov. 1503–21 Feb. 1513
214 LEO X [*Giovanni de' Medici*]   11 Mar. 1513–1 Dec. 1521
215 HADRIAN VI [*Adrian Dedel*]   9 Jan. 1522–14 Sept. 1523
216 CLEMENT VII [*Giulio de' Medici*]   18 Nov. 1523–25 Sept. 1534
217 PAUL III [*Alessandro Farnese*]   13 Oct. 1534–10 Nov. 1549
218 JULIUS III [*Giovanni del Monte*]   8 Feb. 1550–23 Mar. 1555
219 MARCELLUS II [*Marcello Cervini*]   9 Apr.–1 May 1555
220 PAUL IV [*Giovanni Pietro Caraffa*]   23 May 1555–18 Aug. 1559
221 PIUS IV [*Giovanni Angelo Medici*]   25 Dec. 1559–9 Dec. 1565
222 ST PIUS V [*Michele Ghislieri*]   8 Jan. 1566–1 May 1572
223 GREGORY XIII [*Ugo Buoncompagni*]   14 May 1572–10 Apr. 1585
224 SIXTUS V [*Felice Peretti*]   24 Apr. 1585–27 Aug. 1590
225 URBAN VII [*Giambattista Castagna*]   15–27 Sept. 1590
226 GREGORY XIV [*Nicolo[2] Sfondrati*]   5 Dec. 1590–16 Oct. 1591
227 INNOCENT IX [*Giovanni Antonio Fachinetti*]   29 Oct.–30 Dec. 1591
228 CLEMENT VIII [*Ippolito Aldobrandini*]   30 Jan. 1592–5 Mar. 1605
229 LEO XI [*Alessandro de' Medici*]   1–27 Apr. 1605
230 PAUL V [*Camillo Borghese*]   16 May 1605–28 Jan. 1621
231 GREGORY XV [*Alessandro Ludovisi*]   9 Feb. 1621–8 July 1623
232 URBAN VIII [*Maffeo Barberini*]   6 Aug. 1623–29 July 1644
233 INNOCENT X [*Giambattista Pamfili*]   15 Sept. 1644–1 Jan. 1655
234 ALEXANDER VII [*Fabio Chigi*]   7 Apr. 1655–22 May 1667
235 CLEMENT IX [*Giulio Rospigliosi*]   20 June 1667–9 Dec. 1669
236 CLEMENT X [*Emilio Altieri*]   29 Apr. 1670–22 July 1676
237 BL. INNOCENT XI [*Benedetto Odescalchi*]   21 Sept. 1676–11 Aug. 1689
238 ALEXANDER VIII [*Pietro Ottoboni*]   6 Oct. 1689–1 Feb. 1691
239 INNOCENT XII [*Antonio Pignatelli*]   12 July 1691–27 Sept. 1700
240 CLEMENT XI [*Gianfrancesco Albani*]   23 Nov. 1700–19 Mar. 1721
241 INNOCENT XIII [*Michelangelo de' Conti*]   8 May 1721–7 Mar. 1724
242 BENEDICT XIII [*Pietro Francesco Orsini-Gravina*] 27 May 1724–21 Feb. 1730
243 CLEMENT XII [*Lorenzo Corsini*]   12 July 1730–8 Feb. 1740
244 BENEDICT XIV [*Prospero Lorenzo Lambertini*]   17 Aug. 1740–3 May 1758
245 CLEMENT XIII [*Carlo della Torre Rezzonico*]   6 July 1758–2 Feb 1769
246 CLEMENT XIV [*Lorenzo Ganganelli*]   19 May 1769–22 Sept. 1774
247 PIUS VI [*Giovanni Angelo Braschi*]   15 Feb 1775–29 Aug. 1799
248 PIUS VII [*Barnaba Chiaramonte*]   14 Mar. 1800–20 July 1823
249 LEO XII [*Annibale della Genga*]   28 Sept. 1823–10 Feb 1829
250 PIUS VIII [*Francesco Saverio Castiglione*]   31 Mar. 1829–30 Nov. 1830

GLOSSARY

AD LIMINA: Latin for 'to the threshold', meaning a visit to the house of the Apostle Peter, i.e. Rome or St Peter's Basilica. The phrase applied originally to all pilgrimage to the shrine of the Apostle. In modern usage it applies especially to the five-yearly visits bishops are required to make to Rome to give an account of their dioceses to the Pope. Currently seen as an expression of the COLLEGIAL responsibility of the bishops with the Pope, historically it has been a way of enforcing and underlining papal authority.

ANTIPOPE: rival claimant to the papacy, elected or appointed in opposition to the incumbent subsequently recognised officially as the 'true' Pope. A complete list will be found in Appendix A.

APOCRISIARY: papal ambassador to the Byzantine Emperor.

ARCHBISHOP: the senior bishop of a region. Since the early Middle Ages the authority of the Archbishop over the subordinate or 'suffragan' bishops has been symbolised by the gift of the PALLIUM from the Pope.

ARIANISM: Christian heresy preached originally by the Alexandrian presbyter Arius (died 336), denying the full divinity of Jesus Christ, and teaching that as 'Son of God' Christ was subordinate to God the Father, by whom he had been created before the beginning of the world. The teaching seems to have sprung from a concern to protect the sovereignty and unchanging nature of God from the limitations implied in the doctrine of the INCARNATION.

BEATIFICATION: the solemn papal authorisation of religious cult in honour of a dead Christian; a step on the way to full CANONISATION or declaration that the canonised person is a saint.

BISHOP: from Greek *episcopos* ('overseer'); the senior pastor ('shepherd') and focus of unity within a Christian church: probably originally indistinguishable from the 'elders' (Greek 'presbyter', from which the word 'priest' is derived). Within the first hundred years of Christianity the bishops emerged as the chief ministers, to whom the government of the churches, and the right to ordain other ministers, was confined. The territory over which bishops rule is called a DIOCESE, though early bishops probably presided over the church in a single town. The Pope is Bishop of Rome.

BRIEF: an official papal letter, less solemn than a papal bull.

BULL: solemn papal document or mandate announcing a binding decision, and carrying a formal seal.

BYZANTIUM, BYZANTINE: Byzantium was the Greek town on the Bosphorous where Constantine established the new capital of the Roman empire in 330, when it became Constantinople. It gave its name to the empire as a whole, to the state Church and to the distinctive liturgy of the Church. In contrast to the Latin Church, where the Pope's authority came to be seen as supreme, the Byzantine Church paid special reverence to the Christian authority of the Emperor. After the Turkish conquest of 1453 Byzantium was renamed Istanbul.

CANON: CANON LAW: (i) Formal item of Church law. (ii) A decree of a council or synod.

CANONISATION: solemn declaration that a deceased Christian is a saint, to whom prayers and other religious honours may be paid. Originally canonisation was a matter for the local church, and was usually signalled and formalised by the 'translation' (transfer) by the bishop of the relics of the saint to a visible shrine, and the insertion of their feast day into the calendar of the local church. The first known papal canonisation was of Ulrich of Augsburg in 993; since the late twelfth century the power of canonisation has been reserved to the Pope alone.

CARDINAL: from the Latin word *cardo*, a hinge. At first, any priest attached to a major church, later restricted to the parish clergy of Rome, the bishops of the SUBARBICARIAN DIOCESES, and the district DEACONS of Rome. The special advisers and helpers of the Pope and, since 1179, the exclusive electors of a new pope. Since 1970 they have been excluded from voting in a CONCLAVE after the age of eighty.

Since the pontificate of Paul VI all cardinals have had to be ordained bishop, but historically they needed only to be in 'minor orders', and many of the most famous cardinals of history were never priests.

COLLEGIALITY: the co-responsibility of all bishops, in communion with the Pope and with each other, for the whole Church. Emphasised in the teaching of early theologians like Cyprian of Carthage, it was obscured by the growth of the papal monarchy, but re-emphasised at the Second Vatican Council.

CONCILIARISM, CONCILIAR THEORY: the doctrine that supreme authority in the Church lies with a GENERAL COUNCIL, rather than with the Pope: Conciliar theory had widespread support during the period of the Great Schism, and was only finally rejected by the definition of papal INFALLIBILITY in 1870.

CONCLAVE: from the Latin *con clave*, 'with a key'. Since 1271, the closed place into which the assembly of cardinals is locked to elect a new pope and, by extension, the assembly of cardinals themselves. Regulations until recently emphasised the need to make conditions in the Conclave as uncomfortable as possible, to speed the process of election.

CONCORDAT: an agreement between the Church and a civil government to regulate religious affairs.

CONSISTORY: the assembly of cardinals, convoked by the Pope and presided over by him, to advise the Pope or witness solemn papal acts.

COUNCIL, ECUMENICAL COUNCIL, GENERAL COUNCIL: a solemn assembly of bishops to determine matters of doctrine or discipline for the Church. Councils called for the whole empire, the *Oecumene*, were called 'ecumenical' or general councils, and their solemn teaching was believed to be INFALLIBLE. The first of these general councils was Nicaea, called by the Emperor Constantine in 325 to settle the Arian controversy. In Catholic theology, no general council can meet without papal agreement.

CURIA: Latin for 'court': the papal court and central administration of the Roman Catholic Church, organised in a number of separate congregations each presided over by a cardinal known as the 'Prefect'.

DEACON: Christian minister appointed to assist the Bishop in the liturgy, and in Church administration and especially charitable activity. Often considered the most junior of the three traditional grades of ministry, in antiquity and the Middle Ages the deacons of Rome were often more powerful than any of the city's priests or assistant bishops. Because of their administrative experience and close association with papal government, the Pope was often chosen from among the deacons.

DECRETALS: papal letters, usually in response to requests for guidance or rulings. Collected in the Middle Ages as the basis for CANON LAW.

DICASTERY: Vatican department.

DIOCESE: the district governed by a bishop. The word, and the areas covered, were originally taken over from units of Roman civil government.

DONATISM: schismatic puritanical African movement in the fourth century and afterwards, which rejected the ministration of any clergy who had lapsed under persecution, and which taught that the sacraments of such clergy contaminated the churches within which they were performed. It took its name from the third-century Numidian Bishop Donatus.

ENCYCLICAL: a solemn letter addressed by the Pope to the bishops, the clergy, the whole Christian people or, more recently, to 'all people of goodwill'. Encyclicals came into use under Benedict XIV, and have become the favoured form of papal teaching since the early nineteenth century. Individual encyclicals are known by the first two or three words of their opening paragraph – normally in Latin.

EXARCH: the representative or 'viceroy' of the Byzantine Emperor in Italy and in Africa.

EXCOMMUNICATION: the sentence by which a bishop or pope excludes an individual or group from a share in the sacraments and prayers of the Church. In the Middle Ages excommunication effectively deprived an individual of all civil rights.

FILIOQUE: Latin word meaning 'and from the Son': a clause inserted into the Nicene Creed in sixth-century Spain, and later adopted throughout the Western Church. It is part of the Western version of the doctrine of the Trinity, and it teaches that the Holy Spirit proceeds from the Son as well as the Father. The Eastern Churches reject the formula, and it was one of the principle reasons for the breaking off of communion between East and West in the Middle Ages. Some

Eastern theologians, however, agree that, although the inclusion of the word in the Creed is illicit, the teaching contained in the *Filioque* is acceptable if rightly interpreted.

GALLICANISM: from the Latin name for France, Gallia: the teaching, current especially in France from the later Middle Ages, that local or national churches have independence from papal control.

GNOSTIC, GNOSTICISM: from the Greek word *gnosis*, knowledge. Blanket term for widely differing forms of heretical Christian teaching, current from the second century onwards, making a sharp distinction between spirit and matter, and claiming that only spirit can be redeemed.

HERESY: from the Greek word *haeresis*, choice or thing chosen: the formal denial or doubt of Catholic doctrine; a term of disapproval for religious error.

ICONOCLASM: Greek term meaning 'image-breaking': applied especially to the reaction against religious images in the Eastern Church in the seventh and eighth centuries.

INCARNATION: the teaching that in the life of the man Jesus of Nazareth, the second person of the Trinity, God himself, took human flesh (Latin *carnis*) and became a human being.

INDULGENCE: the remission by the Church, and especially the Pope, of the temporal punishment due to sins already forgiven. In medieval Western theology, sin was conceived of as leaving behind it a temporal 'debt' or scar, even when it had been confessed and forgiven. This 'debt' could be wiped away by acts of penance such as fasting or pilgrimage. As part of the 'power of the keys' to bind and loose in matters of sin and forgiveness, bishops had the power to remit the need to perform such acts. Theologians explained this by interpreting 'indulgences' as the dispensing to sinners of a 'treasure of merits' acquired by Christ and the saints, on the analogy of transfers from a full bank account to an overdrawn one. In the late Middle Ages, it was believed that these indulgences could be extended to the souls suffering in PURGATORY, and so could hasten their translation to heaven. Indulgences could be partial, i.e. equivalent to a fixed period of penance, such as forty days or a year, or 'plenary', i.e. unlimited, and remitting all the temporal punishment due to sin.

INFALLIBLE, INFALLIBILITY: Latin word meaning free from error. From early times it was believed that the Church could not fall into error about the fundamental truths of the faith. A negative concept, this infallibility does not mean that the Church or any of its teachers are inspired, but that in certain circumstances they will be protected from fundamental error. Infallibility was attributed from earliest times to the collective teaching of the Church, and hence to the decrees of general councils. In 1870 the First Vatican Council in its decree *Pastor Aeternus* laid down that the *ex cathedra* or most solemn teaching of the Pope possessed the infallibility which Christ had willed for the Church.

INTERDICT: solemn ecclesiastical sentence cutting off a whole community or country from the sacraments of the Church.

JANSENISM: named after Cornelius Jansen, its founder: a religious and doctrinal- movement within the Catholic Church from the seventeenth century onwards, which emphasised human sinfulness, the doctrine of predestination and the sovereign grace of God. Because of successive papal condemnations and the interest it took in the early history of the Church, Jansenism became associated with anti-papalism and an emphasis on the independent authority of the bishops; it was therefore often allied with GALLICANISM and JOSEPHINISM.

JOSEPHINISM: named after the Emperor Joseph II of Austria: a form of Gallicanism, which emphasised the independence of local churches and bishops from papal control. Josephinism was a doctrine propagated by secular rulers anxious to control the church in their territories, and keen therefore to restrict the supranational influence of the popes.

JUBILEE OR HOLY YEAR: a year during which the Pope grants a plenary Indulgence to all who visit Rome on pilgrimage and fulfil certain conditions. Instituted in 1300 by Boniface VIII, it was originally intended to occur once a century. The interval was reduced to fifty years by Clement VI, to thirty-three (the supposed age of Christ at the Crucifixion) by Urban VI, and to twenty-five by Paul II. The most important ceremony associated with the Jubilee is the opening of the Holy Door into St Peter's, which is bricked up between Jubilees.

LEGATE: clerical representative of the Pope, exercising extensive papal powers.

LEGATIONS: the prosperous parts of the Papal States in the north west of Italy and the Adriatic coast, governed by cardinal legates.

MAGISTERIUM: Latin for 'teaching'. Term currently used to signify the official teaching, and the teaching office, of the Catholic Church, and especially of the Pope and bishops. In the Middle Ages theologians were widely thought of as exercising a parallel and complementary magisterium – hence HenryVIII consulted the theological faculties of the European universities when refused a divorce by the Pope.

METROPOLITAN: title given to senior bishop (always an archbishop) possessing authority over the other bishops of a region. From the early Church down to the early nineteenth century metropolitan and papal authority frequently came into conflict. In the Roman Catholic Church, no metropolitan can function without the bestowal of the PALLIUM by the Pope.

MONOPHYSITISM: from the Greek words for 'only one nature': the teaching that in Jesus Christ there was only one nature, which was divine, or an amalgam of divine and human exactly corresponding to neither. Orthodox Christianity insisted that Jesus Christ was a single person composed of two natures, human and divine. In him these two natures were united but not confused. Monophysitism, which was rejected as a heresy, was an attempt to protect the divine nature from suggestions of change or limitation in the INCARNATION.

MONOTHELITISM: a Greek word for the teaching that there was in Jesus Christ only one will: it arose from the dangerous religious divisions of the Byzantine empire in the seventh century, and was a politically inspired attempt to win over monophysite Christians by softening the teaching that Christ had two natures.

NESTORIANISM: the teaching that in Jesus Christ there were two distinct persons, the God and the man, and not merely two natures. The doctrine takes its name from Nestorius, Patriarch of Constantinople, who died c. 451, though it is now believed that he did not himself hold this teaching, which was condemned at the Council of Chalcedon, 451.

NUNCIO: permanent diplomatic representative of the Pope to a sovereign state, who is also an instrument of papal authority over the local church.

PALLIUM: circular white stole of lamb's wool, embroidered with crosses, given by the popes to other bishops, originally as a special mark of honour and communion, now as a formal sign of metropolitan authority in their region. Since the papal reform era, successive popes have summoned archbishops to Rome to receive the pallium, as a sign of papal sovereignty over them.

PAPAL STATES: the areas of Italy and southern France which acknowledged the Pope as sovereign. Also known as the Patrimony of St Peter, or the States of the Church. Derived originally from the gifts of Constantine, the Roman imperial family and aristocratic converts to Christianity, they were formally recognised by Pepin and Charlemagne, who undertook to protect them on behalf of St Peter, and were finally abolished in 1870, when Italy confiscated the last of the papal territories.

PATRIARCH: from the fifth century, title given to the bishops of the five senior sees of the universal Church – Antioch, Alexandria, Constantinople, Jerusalem and Rome. The Patriarch exercised authority over his whole region and had the right to ordain the metropolitans; from the Middle Ages the title has been extended to other bishops in East and West – e.g. Venice – though without the powers originally associated with the title.

PATRIMONY OF ST PETER: *see* PAPAL STATES.

PENTAPOLIS: the area of the Papal States in Italy containing the 'five cities' of Rimini, Pissaro, Fano, Senigallia and Ancona.

PONTIFF, SUPREME PONTIFF: Latin pagan title (*pontifex* = a bridge-builder) for priests and the supreme priest of the Roman religion, the Emperor, eventually taken over by bishops and by the Pope.

POPE: Latin term of endearment and respect, 'papa', meaning 'daddy'. Widely applied in the early Church to bishops (the Bishop of Carthage was called 'pope'), and in the Orthodox churches of the East given to parish priests, from the early Middle Ages in the West its use was restricted to the Bishop of Rome.

PURGATORY: in Western Catholic theology, the place or state of cleansing in which redeemed but imperfect souls are believed to await after death the beatific Vision of God. It is believed that the prayers of the living, and the ecclesiastical privileges known as INDULGENCES, can assist the souls in purgatory through this process of cleansing.

SACRED COLLEGE: the collective body of the CARDINALS.

SCHISM: Greek word meaning tear: applied to formal divisions within the Church for doctrinal or other causes.

SIMONY: from Simon Magus, a magician who attempted to buy magical powers from the Apostles. The name given to the sin of paying or receiving money or favours in return for spiritual office or promotion. In the period of the reform papacy it was thought of as a heresy.

SUBARBICARIAN BISHOPRICS: the seven ancient dioceses round Rome whose bishops were senior members of the College of Cardinals.

SYNOD: a local assembly of clergy under their bishop, or of a number of local bishops, and possessing less authority than a GENERAL COUNCIL.

ULTRAMONTANISM: Latin term meaning 'the other side of the mountains', i.e. the Alps, hence the doctrine that lays great emphasis on the supreme authority of the Pope on the Church as a whole outside his own diocese: the opposite of GALLICANISM. By extension, the style of piety and churchmanship associated with the nineteenth-century papacy and Italian church.

VATICAN: the modern centre of the papacy, made up of the basilica church of St Peter and the buildings round it, occupying the ancient Roman *mons Vaticanus*, Vatican Hill. Outside the ancient city of Rome, the Vatican was not the original papal residence, and St John Lateran not St Peter's is the cathedral church of Rome. Since the annexation of Rome to the state of Italy in 1870, however, the Vatican has been the Pope's main residence and the administrative centre of the Church. By the Lateran Treaty of 1929 the Vatican City was recognised as an independent state, of which the Pope is the sovereign.

HOW A NEW POPE IS MADE

The papacy can be vacated only by the resignation or the death of a reigning pope: there is no provision in canon law for the deposition of a pope, even in the event of lunacy or incapacity. No pope has voluntarily resigned since St Celestine V in 1294, although in resolving the Great Schism by deposing all three claimants to the papacy, the Council of Constance in 1415 permitted the 'real' (Roman) Pope Gregory XII the face-saving fiction of resignation. The provisions for the election of a new pope were last revised in February 1996 by Pope John Paul II, in the Apostolic Constitution *Universi Dominici Gregis*, which introduced some revolutionary changes into a process which in essentials had been standardised for centuries.

On the death of the pope all the heads of the various Vatican Congregations are immediately suspended from their offices: only the Cardinal Camerlengo (Chamberlain, the head of the Papal household), the Cardinal Major Penitentiary (responsible for the adjudication of grave cases of conscience), the Cardinal Vicar of Rome (who administers the diocese) and the Cardinal Archpriest of St Peter's (where the Pope will be buried) remain in office. If there is no Camerlengo at the time of the pope's death, the Cardinals present in Rome elect one. The Camerlengo is responsible for ascertaining and certifying that the pope is in fact dead (traditionally this was done in a ritual in which he tapped on the dead pope's forehead with a small ivory mallet, calling him three times by his baptismal name, but this custom has now lapsed). The Camerlengo also ritually smashes the Fisherman's Ring, the gold signet-ring with which papal documents were once sealed, and which is made fresh for each pope and engraved with his name. The Cardinal Dean (the senior cardinal) then summons the whole college of cardinals, and all the routine powers of the papacy are exercised in the vacancy by them collectively, meeting daily in the Vatican in General Congregations. The curial departments continue their ordinary business under their deputy prefects or secretaries.

Nine days of mourning are observed for the pope, whose funeral is held in St Peter's. Popes are traditionally buried in a triple coffin, the inner shell of cypress, the next of lead and the outer one of plain elm. Not sooner than fifteen days, nor later than twenty, after the announcement of the pope's death the cardinals must assemble in conclave to elect a successor. In preparation for the conclave the cardinals are addressed by two preachers, chosen for their orthodoxy and wisdom, who reflect on the Church's needs and the considerations which the cardinals should bear in mind in making their choice. The conclave begins with a solemn mass invoking the aid of the Holy Spirit in St Peter's, and takes place in the Sistine Chapel within the Vatican Palace itself, into which the cardinals process while a hymn to the Holy Spirit is sung. In the past, provision of adequate accommodation in the Vatican for the cardinals and their staff during the conclave has been a recurrent problem, and conditions have often been primitive in the extreme. For the future, cardinals will live during the conclaves in a specially constructed and comfortable hostel in the Vatican grounds, the Domus S Marthae (the House of St Martha), opened by John Paul II in May 1996. The Domus S Marthae normally serves as a conference centre and residence for selected Vatican officials, but it was built with conclaves specifically in mind. It has 130 suites and single rooms for the cardinal electors and their attendants – who include priests from the religious orders able to hear confessions in all the languages of the cardinals – and two medical doctors, together with the catering staff needed to feed them. The number of cardinal electors was set at 120 by Pope Paul VI, and this number was confirmed by John Paul II in 1996, cardinals losing the right to take vote in a papal election when they reach the age of eighty. However, restricting the number of electors to 120 is likely to prove impossible in practice, since the pope's concern to make the College of Cardinals as inclusive and representative as possible of a world Church has inexorably inflated numbers. The consistory of February 2001, at which 37 new cardinals were created (the largest number ever announced at a single consistory), took the total number of cardinals at that time to 178, and the number of qualified electors to 128. There is no procedure in place for selecting the 120 entitled to vote, nor, if these numbers are maintained or increased, is it at all clear where the extra numbers would be accommodated during the conclave.

Once the cardinals have entered the conclave, the Domus S Marthae and the Sistine Chapel are sealed off, all contact with the outer world is forbidden, and the cardinals and their assistant staff take an oath of secrecy about the proceedings of the conclave. Conclave means 'with a key', and they have always been surrounded with rules designed to ensure that external pressure is not brought to bear on the cardinals as they make their choice. Under the current rules, however, electors who unavoidably turn up late have to be admitted, even if the conclave has already begun its work (before the days of air travel, American and other non-European cardinals often arrived too late to exercise their rights as electors, a matter which caused immense and understandable resentment).

For more than 800 years the normal mode of election of a pope has been by secret written ballot. Nowadays the election takes place in the Sistine Chapel, from which all assistants are excluded during voting, leaving only the cardinals. Three 'scrutineers' are chosen at random from the cardinals to oversee the voting. The cardinals are given a small supply of rectangular voting forms which say in Latin 'I elect to the Supreme Pontificate', below which is a blank space in which to write a name. Each elector writes a name in the space provided, and folds the form once length-ways so as to conceal their choice. Cardinals are also encouraged if possible to disguise their handwriting. Taking the folded form between thumb and index finger of the right hand, the cardinals then approach the altar of the Sistine Chapel in order of seniority, each one announcing in a clear voice 'I call as my witness Christ the Lord who will be my judge, that my vote is given to the one whom, before God, I think ought to be elected.' On the altar is a large chalice covered with a metal plate or paten. The cardinal places his ballot paper on the paten, and tips it into the chalice, watched by the other electors. He then returns to his place. Elderly or infirm cardinals have their votes collected from their places by a scrutineer. Cardinals confined to their rooms by illness place their votes in a sealed ballot box, carried to their room by three randomly chosen 'Cardinal Infirmarians', who ensure that no malpractice takes place during this procedure.

In theory the cardinals may vote for any adult male Catholic, and need not confine their choice to a member of the College of Cardinals. In practice, every pope since 1389 has already been a cardinal, and the election of a non-cardinal is nowadays almost unimaginable.

When each round of voting is complete, the three scrutineers count the ballot papers into another chalice. If there is a discrepancy between the number of papers and the number of electors, all the ballots are burned unopened and the whole procedure is repeated. If however all is in order, counting begins. Each of the three scrutineers in turn looks at each ballot paper and records the name there in writing: the third scrutineer calls out the names so that all the cardinals can make their own record. The votes are totalled for each person nominated, and each bundle is sown together with a thread through the word 'eligo', 'I elect'. The outcome is announced formally, and then checked by three 'cardinal revisers', again randomly chosen at the outset of the conclave. Since the eighteenth century, if the outcome has been indecisive the bundles of votes are taken to a specially constructed stove with a chimney visible in St Peter's Square, and burned along with a chemical which turns the smoke a dense black. This is a signal to the outside world that the vote has not produced a pope. If the vote has been successful, the chemical is omitted and the smoke is white.

To elect a pope, there must be a two-thirds majority plus one (in case a cardinal has voted for himself). There are normally two ballots each morning, and two in the afternoon, but on the first day of the conclave there is normally only a single ballot. If after three days of voting no election has been made, the cardinals pause for prayer and reflection, for not more than a day. Voting resumes for another seven ballots, with another pause if no pope has been elected. After thirty ballots, the Cardinal Camerlengo invites the cardinals to suggest some method of resolving the deadlock. When they then resume voting, the requirement for a two-thirds majority lapses and a simple majority suffices. This is a truly startling change in the procedures in operation since the twelfth century, and, on the face of it, an unwise one. The international composition of the Sacred College and the large number of electors involved means that the cardinals may take time to familiarise themselves with potential candidates, and makes a prolonged election by no means unlikely. There is a risk that this 'emergency' relaxation of the two-thirds majority rule might in fact happen frequently, and result in the election of popes who do not command the consensual support of the College of Cardinals as a whole. There is room in the new rules for abuse: a determined (and unscrupulous) group of cardinals could block the necessary two-thirds majority for thirty ballots, and then shoe in their own man by a simple majority (all forms of partisan coordination and plotting of this kind are absolutely forbidden in papal elections, on pain of excommunication: they are nevertheless by no means unknown).

Once an election has successfully taken place, the secretary of the conclave (not a cardinal) and the papal Master of Ceremonies are summoned to the Sistine Chapel. The Cardinal Dean approaches the elect and asks him 'Do you accept your canonical election as Supreme Pontiff'. If he accepts, the Cardinal Dean asks, 'By what name do you wish to be called', upon which the new pope chooses and announces his papal name. (With very few exceptions, for the last thousand years all new popes have chosen a name different from their baptismal or Christian name). If he is not already a bishop (cardinals are normally ordained archbishops, but a new cardinal may not have been so ordained, and some choose to remain priests) he is immediately ordained by the Cardinal Dean. The new pope is then robed in white cassock and sash and white skull-cap, red slippers, a lace rochet or episcopal surplice, and a short red cape. (Three cassocks small medium and large are kept in readiness). The pope then sits on a stool before the altar, the Camerlengo gives him the Fisherman's Ring, and the cardinals come in order of seniority and kneel to pay homage to him. The proceedings conclude with the singing of a solemn hymn of thanksgiving, *Te Deum Laudamus*, We Praise Thee O God.

While all this is proceeding, crowds have gathered in St Peter's Square, alerted by the white smoke. The Senior Cardinal Deacon goes to the balcony overlooking the Piazza, and declares 'Annuntio vobis Gaudiam Magnam, habemus Papam', 'I announce to you a great joy: we have a Pope', and he informs the crowd of the pope's old name and his new papal name. The new pope then appears and gives his blessing 'Urbi et Orbi', to the City and the World. It is not customary for the new pope to make a speech at this point: when Karol Wojtyla did so, an impatient cardinalatial voice was clearly audible over the loudspeaker system muttering 'Basta! Basta!', 'That's enough, that's enough'.

Up to and including the pontificate of Paul VI, new popes were inaugurated by being solemnly crowned with the triple tiara in St

Peter's basilica, to which they were carried on the *Sedia Gestatoria*, the ceremonial throne carried on the shoulders of members of the old Roman aristocracy, accompanied by two great ostrich-feather fans, relics of Byzantine court ritual. Pope John Paul I renounced this ceremony, which had come to seem too reminiscent of the medieval papacy's conflicts with emperors and inappropriate claims of the popes to temporal dominion. Popes now are simply inaugurated at a special mass in or outside St Peter's, at which the pope is invested with the white woollen stole, known as the Pallium, by the Senior Cardinal Deacon: the mass concludes with a repetition of the blessing 'Urbi et Orbi'.

NOTES

CHAPTER ONE: UPON THIS ROCK

1   Most of the early texts bearing on the history of the papacy up to the reign
    of Damasus I are conveniently collected and translated into English in J.T.
    Shotwell and L. R. Loomis, *The See of Peter*, New York 1927, reprinted in
    1991. The passage from Irenaeus' *Contra Haereses* III cited in the text will be
    found at pp. 265–72.
2   For these passages, ibid., pp. 72, 236–9, 265–72.
3   Ibid., pp. 266–7.
4   Eusebius, *History of the Church*, ed. A. Louth, Harmondsworth 1989, pp.
    170–4 (V/24).
5   Shotwell and Loomis, *See of Peter*, p. 267, but following here the better
    translation in J. Stevenson, *A New Eusebius*, London 1963, p. 119.
6   The cult of Peter and Paul at San Sebastiano poses many problems, not least
    that of whether at any stage the Apostles' bodies were buried there. It has
    been suggested that the shrine was originally a schismatic one, independent
    of any grave, set up by the supporters of the Antipope Novation in opposi-
    tion to the official Vatican cult, but there is no clear evidence for this claim.
    More plausibly, it has been suggested that the shrine at San Sebastiano was
    an unofficial 'folk' shrine, which the authorities were forced to adopt to
    prevent it spiralling out of the Bishop's control: either way, the cult demon-
    strates the growing importance of the two saints. Description and plans of
    the site at San Sebastiano, D. W. O'Connor, *Peter in Rome*, New York 1969,
    pp. 135–58; helpful discussion and examples of the inscriptions quoted in
    the text, in H. Chadwick, 'St Peter and Paul in Rome', in his *History and
    Thought of the Early Church*, London 1982, pp. 31–52.
7   Shotwell and Loomis, *See of Peter*, pp. 252–3.
8   Quoted in K. Schatz, *Papal Primacy from its Origins to the Present*, Col-
    legeville, Minnesota, 1990, p. 6.
9   Shotwell and Loomis, *See of Peter*, pp. 334–7.

10 Ibid., pp. 267, 294.

11 All the texts on the disputes gathered in ibid., pp. 399–420.

12 Ibid., p. 415.

13 R. Davis (ed.), *The Book of Pontiffs (Liber Pontificalis)*, Liverpool 1989, pp. 14–26.

14 Documents for Sardica in Shotwell and Loomis, *See of Peter*, pp. 503–34.

15 Ibid., pp. 561, 571.

16 Ibid., pp. 572–6.

17 Ibid., p. 686.

18 R. B. Eno, *The Rise of the Papacy*, Wilmington, Delaware 1990, pp. 80–4.

19 Davis, *Book of Pontiffs*, p. 29.

20 Shotwell and Loomis, *See of Peter*, p. 633.

21 Chadwick, 'St Peter and Paul in Rome', pp. 34–5; R. Krautheimer, *Rome: Profile of a City, 312–1308*, Princeton 1980, pp. 39–41.

22 Krautheimer, *Rome*, p. 41.

23 The whole letter is printed in Shotwell and Loomis, *See of Peter*, pp. 699–708.

24 Eno, *Rise of the Papacy*, p. 94.

25 Ibid., p. 100.

26 Quoted in Schatz, *Papal Primacy*, p. 35.

27 Eno, *Rise of the Papacy*, pp. 102–9.

28 J. Tillard, *The Bishop of Rome*, London 1983, p. 91; R. B. Eno (ed.), *Teaching Authority in the Early Church*, Wilmington, Delaware, 1984 pp. 161–2.

CHAPTER TWO: BETWEEN TWO EMPIRES

1 Text of Gelasius' letter in S. Z. Ehler and J. B. Morall, *Church and State through the Centuries*, London 1954, p. 11 (translation slightly altered).

2 P. Brown, *The World of Late Antiquity*, London 1971, pp. 146–8.

3 Latin text in C. Rahner (ed.) *Henrici Denzinger, Enchyridion Symbolorum*, Barcelona, Freiburg, Rome 1957, no. 171–2.

4 R. Davis (ed.), *The Book of Pontiffs (Liber Pontificalis)*, Liverpool 1989, p. 49.

5 Quoted in K. Schatz, *Papal Primacy from its Origins to the Present*, Collegeville, Minnesota 1996, p. 54.

6 J. Richards, *Consul of God: The Life and Times of Gregory the Great*, London 1980, p. 36.

7 P. Llewellyn, *Rome in the Dark Ages*, London 1993, p. 90.

8 Jeffrey Richards, *The Popes and the Papacy in the Early Middle Ages, 476–752*, London 1979, p. 283.

9 J. Barmby (ed.), *The Book of the Pastoral Rule and Selected Epistles of Gregory the Great*, Library of Nicene and Post-Nicene Fathers, end Series vol. 12, New York 1895, p. 176.

10 Ibid., p. 176.

11 Richards, *Consul of God*, p. 31.

12 Barmby, *Selected Epistles of Gregory the Great*, pp. 140–1.

13 Ibid., p. 179; Richards, *Consul of God*, pp. 64–8.

14 R. W. Southern, *Western Society and the Church in the Middle Ages*, Harmondsworth 1970, p. 172.

15 Barmby, *Selected Epistles of Gregory the Great*, p. 170.

16 Ibid., pp. 166–73 for a series of letters on the dispute about the 'Ecumenical' title: the letter cited is ibid., pp 240–1, but I have preferred the translation in J. Tillard, *The Bishop of Rome*, London 1983, pp. 52–3 (Latin text pp. 203–4).

17 Barmby, *Selected Epistles of Gregory the Great*, p. 88.

18 Bede, *The Ecclesiastical History of the English Pope*, i 27, para. III, ed. Judith McClure and Roger Collins, Oxford 1994, p. 43.

19 Ibid., iii 25, p. 159: for King Oswiu's smile, Eddius Stephanus, *Life of Wilfred*, in J. F. Webb and D. H. Farmer (trans and eds), *The Age of Bede*, Harmondsworth 1983, p. 115.

20 Davis, *Book of Pontiffs*, p. 72.

21 Ibid., p. 85.

22 R. Davis (ed.), *The Lives of the Eighth-Century Popes*, Liverpool 1992, p. 13.

23 W. Ullmann, *A Short History of the Papacy in the Middle Ages*, London 1974, p. 72; Southern, *Western Society and the Church*, p. 59.

24 Davis, *Eighth-Century Popes*, pp. 26–7; Llewellyn, *Rome in the Dark Ages*, pp. 202–3.

25 Text in Ehler and Morall, *Church and State*, pp. 15–22.

26 Text in J. Wallace-Hadrill, *The Frankish Church*, Oxford 1983, p. 186.

27 This is the interpretation of Charlemagne's reservations offered by Notker the Stammerer: L. Thorpe (ed.), *Two Lives of Charlemagne*, Harmondsworth 1969, p. 124.

28 Ullmann, *Short History of the Papacy*, pp. 105–8; R. Davis (ed.), *The Lives of the Ninth-Century Popes*, Liverpool 1995, pp. 201–2; H. K. Mann, *The Lives of the Popes in the Early Middle Ages*, London 1902–32, vol. 3, pp. 58–61.

29 R. W. Southern, *The Making of the Middle Ages*, London 1987, pp. 131–2.

CHAPTER THREE: SET ABOVE NATIONS

1 Text of Cluny's foundation charter printed in R. C. Petry (ed.), *A History of Christianity: Readings in the History of the Church*, Grand Rapids 1981, vol. 1, p. 280–1.

2 Quoted in G. Tellenbach, *The Church in Western Europe from the Tenth to the Twelfth Century*, Cambridge 1993, p. 170.

3 For a translation of the Dictatus, S. Z. Ehler and J. B. Morall, *Church and State through the Centuries*, London 1954, pp. 43–4.

4 Tellenbach, *Western Church*, pp. 206–7.

5 Text of Henry's letter printed in Petry, *Readings in the History of the Church*, vol. 1, p. 237.

6 Text in H. Bettenson (ed.), *Documents of the Christian Church*, Oxford 1954, pp. 144–5.

7 Letter to Bishop of Metz 1081, in ibid., pp. 145–53.

8 Quoted in C. Morris, *The Papal Monarchy: The Western Church from 1050 to 1250*, Oxford 1991, p. 125.

9 Quoted in R. W. Southern, *Western Society and the Church in the Middle Ages*, Harmondsworth 1970, p. 105.

10 J. D. Anderson and E. T. Kennan (eds), *St Bernard of Clairvaux: Five Books of Consideration: Advice to a Pope*, Kalamazoo, Michigan 1976, p. 121.

11 Ibid., pp. 66–8.

12 Ibid., pp. 57–8.

13 Morris, *Papal Monarchy*, p. 213.

14 R. W. Southern, *The Making of the Middle Ages*, London 1987, pp. 147–8.

15 Quotations on Crusade and indulgences, I. S. Robinson, *The Papacy, 1073–1198*, Cambridge 1993, pp. 326–30.

16 Ibid., p. 299; W. Ullmann, *A Short History of the Papacy in the Middle Ages*, London 1974, pp. 182–3.

17 Robinson, *Papacy*, p. 24.

18 Quoted in Morris, *Papal Monarchy*, p. 431.

19 Southern, *Western Society and the Church*, pp. 144–5.

20 Morris, *Papal Monarchy*, p. 440.

21 My translation from Dante, *Inferno*, XVIII 25–33.

22 Edited texts of both *Clericos Laicos* and *Unam Sanctam* in Bettenson, *Documents of the Christian Church*, pp. 157–61.

23 Kenelm Foster and Mary John Ronayne (eds), *I, Catherine: Selected Writings of Catherine of Siena*, London 1980, p. 94.

CHAPTER FOUR: PROTEST AND DIVISION

1 L. Pastor, *History of the Popes from the Close of the Middle Ages*, London 1912–, vol. 2, p. 30.

2 C. B. Coleman (ed.), *The Treatise of Lorenzo Valla on the Donation of Constantine*, New Haven 1922, p. 179.

3 Pastor, *Popes*, vol. 2, p. 166.

4 Ibid., pp. 125–37.

5 A. Grafton (ed.), *Rome Reborn: The Vatican Library and Renaissance Culture*, New Haven and London 1993, p. xiii.

6 L. C. Gabel (ed.), *Memoirs of a Renaissance Pope*, London 1960, p. 81.

7 J. C. Olin (ed.), *The Catholic Reformation: Savonarola to Ignatius Loyola*, Westminster, Maryland 1969, p. 9; Pastor, *Popes*, vol. 6, p. 17.

8 J. A. Froud, *Life and Letters of Erasmus*, London 1895, p. 158.

9 Ibid., p. 165.

10 P. Partner, *Renaissance Rome, 1500–1559: A Portrait of a Society*, Berkeley 1976, p. 158.

11 Pastor, *Popes*, vol. 28, p. 348.

12 M. Walsh, *An Illustrated History of the Popes*, London 1980, p. 181.

13 *Sanctissimi Domini Nostri Benedicti Papae XIV Bullarium*, Tomus Primus, Venice 1777, pp. 4–7.

CHAPTER FIVE: THE POPE AND THE PEOPLE

1 Text in S. Z. Ehler and J. B. Morall, *Church and State through the Centuries*, London 1954, pp. 236–49.

2 Consalvi's letter and the details of the Conclave in F. Nielsen, *The History of the Papacy in the XIXth Century*, London 1906, vol. 1, pp. 191–218.

3 Owen Chadwick, *The Popes and European Revolution*, Oxford 1981, p. 484.

4 Printed in Ehler and Morall, *Church and State*, pp. 252–4.

5 A. Dansette, *Religious History of Modern France*, Edinburgh and London 1961, vol. 1, p. 152.

6 E. E. Y. Hales, *Revolution and Papacy*, Notre Dame, Indiana 1966, pp. 180–1.

7 Nielsen, *Papacy in the XIXth Century*, vol. 2, pp. 10–11.

8 Quoted in K. Schatz, *Papal Primacy from its Origins to the Present*, Collegeville, Minnesota 1996, pp. 148–9.

9 A. R. Vidler, *Prophecy and Papacy: A Study of Lamennais, the Church and the Revolution*, London 1954.

10 E. E. Y. Hales, *The Catholic Church and the Modern World*, London 1958, pp. 93–4.

11 Vidler, *Prophecy and Papacy*, pp. 184–220.

12 K. O. von Aretin, *The Papacy and the Modern World*, London 1970, pp. 64–6.

13 H. E. Manning, 'Roma Aeterna', a lecture to the Roman Academy in 1862, printed in *Miscellanies*, New York 1877, p. 22.

14 'Occisi et Coronati' in *Sermons on Ecclesiastical Subjects*, Dublin 1863, pp. 273–5.

15 F. Heyer, *The Catholic Church, 1648–1870*, London 1969, pp. 186–7; see also H. E. Manning, *The True Story of the Vatican Council*, London 1877, pp. 42–3.

16 H. E. Manning, *The Glories of the Sacred Heart*, London nd, pp. 167–88, 'The Temporal Glory of the Sacred Heart'.

17 E. E. Y. Hales, *Pio Nono*, London 1954, pp. 278–9, 329.

18 Ibid., p. 227.

19 [W. S. Bainbridge, (ed.)] *The Westminster Hymnal*, London 1941 no. 226 (words by Cardinal Wiseman).

20 S. Gilley, *Newman and his Age*, London 1990, p. 344.

21 Extract from the encyclical, and the whole of the *Syllabus*, in C. Rahner (ed.), *Henrici Denzinger, Enchyridion Symbolorum*, Barcelona, Fribourg, Rome

1957, pp. 477–90 (nos 1688–1780); translated extracts from the *Syllabus* in Ehler and Morall, *Church and State*, pp. 281–5.

22 N. Blakiston, *The Roman Question*, London 1962, p. 303.

23 C. Butler, *The Vatican Council*, London 1962, pp. 57–61.

24 Ibid., pp. 101–7; Hales, *Pio Nono*, pp. 286–7.

25 E. R. Purcell, *Life of Manning*, London 1896, vol. 2, p. 453.

26 Butler, *Vatican Council, p. 355.*

27 *Denzinger,* Enchyridion Symbolorum, p. 508 (no. 1839).

28 Manning, *True Story*, p. 145.

29 Butler, *Vatican Council*, p. 50.

30 Manning, *Glories of the Sacred Heart*, p. 183.

31 H. Parkinson (ed.), *The Pope and the People: Select Letters and Addresses on Social Questions by Pope Leo XIII*, London 1920, pp. 15–27.

32 L. P. Wallace, *Leo XIII and the Rise of Socialism*, Durham, North Carolina 1966, p. 92.

33 Parkinson, *The Pope and the People*, pp. 71–100.

34 Ibid., pp. 101–30.

35 Ibid., pp. 178–219.

36 A. R. Vidler, *A Century of Social Catholicism*, London 1964, p. 127.

37 J. McManners, *Church and State in France 1870–1914*, London 1972, p. 74.

CHAPTER SIX: THE ORACLES OF GOD

1   Quoted in H. Daniel Rops, *A Fight for God, 1870–1939*, London 1965, p. 51.

2   I. Giordani, *Pius X, a Country Priest*, Milwaukee 1954, p. 47.

3   R. Bazin, *Pius X*, London 1928, pp. 162–9.

4   R. Aubert (ed.), *The Church in a Secularised Society*, London 1978, pp. 129–43.

5   Bazin, *Pius X*, p. 104.

6   Extracts from Modernist texts, and from *Lamentabili* and *Pascendi*, in B. Reardon (ed.), *Roman Catholic Modernism*, London 1968.

7   C. Falconi, *Popes in the Twentieth Century*, London 1967, p. 54.

8   Quoted in ibid., p. 73.

9   J. McManners, *Church and State in France, 1870–1914*, London 1972, pp. 158–65; well-illustrated summary of Pius' point of view in Bazin, *Pius X*, pp. 192–30; Falconi, *Popes in the Twentieth Century*, pp. 75–7.

10 A. Rhodes, *The Vatican in the Age of the Dictators, 1922–1945*, London 1973, pp. 103–11.

11 F. X. Murphy, *The Papacy Today*, New York 1981, p. 51.

12 P. Hebblethwaite, *Paul VI*, London 1993, p. 102.

13 J. Derek Holmes, *The Papacy in the Modern World*, London 1981, p. 80 (from Pius' first encyclical).

14 Rhodes, *Vatican in the Age of the Dictators*, p. 49.

15 Text in S. Z. Ehler and J. B. Morall (eds), *Church and State through the Centuries*, London 1954, pp. 457–84.

16 Text in ibid., pp. 407–56.

17 H. Stehle, *Eastern Politics of the Vatican, 1917–1979*, Athens, Ohio 1981, pp. 151, 169.

18 Text in Ehler and Morall, *Church and State*, pp. 519–39.

19 Ibid., pp. 545–78.

20 Despatch quoted in W. O. Chadwick, *Britain and the Vatican during the Second World War*, Cambridge 1986, p. 28.

21 H. Jedin and J. Dolan, *History of the Church*, vol. 10, London 1981, p. 80.

22 Stehle, *Eastern Politics of the Vatican*, pp. 193–4.

23 Chadwick, *Britain and the Vatican*, p. 218.

24 P. Blet, R. A. Graham, A. Martini and B. Schneider (eds), *Actes et documents du Saint Siège relatifs à la Seconde Guerre Mondiale*, 11 vols, Vatican City 1965–78.

25 Hebblethwaite, *Paul VI*, p. 245.

26 Stehle, *Eastern Politics of the Vatican*, p. 296.

27 Hebblethwaite, *Paul VI*, p. 284.

28 P. Hebblethwaite, *John XXIII, Pope of the Council*, London 1984, pp. 430–3.

29 A. Flannery (ed.), *Vatican Council II: The Conciliar and Post-Conciliar Documents, Leominster 1981*, pp. 350–432.

30 Ibid., pp. 903–1001.

31 Cited in A. Stacpoole (ed.), *Vatican II by Those Who Were There*, London 1986, pp. 142–3.

32 Flannery, *Vatican Council II*, pp. 1–56 (Liturgy), pp. 452–70 (Ecumenism), pp. 738–42 (Other Religions), pp. 799–812 (Religious Liberty).

33 Hebblethwaite, *Paul VI*, p. 339.

34 Cited in A. Hastings (ed.), *Modern Catholicism*, London 1991, p. 48.

35 J. M. Miller (ed.), *The Encyclicals of John Paul II*, Huntington, Indiana 1996, p. 59.

36 Ibid., p. 137.

37 Ibid., pp. 442, 472.

38 Ibid., pp. 914–77.

BIBLIOGRAPHICAL ESSAY

This is not an exhaustive bibliography of the papacy. It is intended as a guide to further reading on the main periods and issues discussed in the text. The emphasis is on books in English, but some fundamental works in other languages have been included where appropriate.

A. GENERAL SURVEYS AND REFERENCE WORKS

The best general history of the papacy, to the end of the eighteenth century, is unfortunately available only in German: F. X. Seppelt, *Geschichte der Papste*, Munich 1954–9: the same applies to J. Schmidlin, *Papstgeschichte der neuesten Zeit*, Munich 1933–9, which takes the story on from the pontificate of Pius VII. There is a modern one-volume survey, from a respectful Roman Catholic point of view, with up-to-date bibliographies, edited by Yves-Marie Hilaire, *Histoire de la Papaute: 2,000 ans de mission et de tribulations*, Editions Tallandiers, Paris 1996. Horst Fuhrmann's *Die Papste: von Petrus zu Johannes Paul II*, Munich 1998, is a stimulating survey by a distinguished medievalist, though its episodic structure reflects its origin in a series of radio broadcasts. There are now two full and excellent one-volume dictionaries: P. Levillain, *Dictionnaire Historique de la Papaute*, Paris, Fayard, 1994, and J. N. D. Kelly, *The Oxford Dictionary of the Popes*, Oxford 1986. F. J. Coppa, *Encyclopedia of the Vatican and the Papacy*, London 1999, is briefer than either, but useful. The Istituto della Enciclopedia Italiano celebrated the Jubilee Year 2000 with the publication of a major three-volume *Enciclopedia dei Papi*, Rome 2000, which offers extended coverage of every pontificate. Though some of the individual entries were originally written for other reference books, and are already showing their age, overall it is a tremendous resource, specially to be recommended for the bibliographies, the invaluable concluding 'cronotassi' of the popes by Mgr Charles Burns, and for the handsome and sometimes unusual illustrations.

For individual popes, in addition to the above, the entries in the following encyclopedias are generally reliable, though of course not every pope is included: *The New Catholic Encyclopedia*, NewYork 1967 + supplements: *Encyclopedia Cattolica*, Vatican City 1949–54. For canonised popes, the entries in the Italian *Bibliotheca Sanctorum*, Rome 1961, are often outstandingly good.

For general reference, *The Oxford Dictionary of the Christian Church*, 3rd edition, E.A. Livingstone (ed.), Oxford 1997, provides concise articles and excellent bibliographies.

There are many general histories of the Church: the ten-volume *History of the Church*, originally published in German and edited by H. Jedin and J. Dolan, London 1965–81, is sometimes densely written but is packed with information. For English readers a disadvantage is that its bibliographies rely heavily on works in German: note that volumes 1 and 3 appeared under the original German title *Handbook of Church History*. The French multi-volume history, still in progress, edited by Jean Marie Mayeur, Charles & Luce Pietri, André Vauche and Mark Venards, *Histoire du Christianisme des origines à nos jours*, Paris 1990, is excellent. Briefer, but still very good and more user-friendly is R. Aubert, D. Knowles and L. J. Rogier, *The Christian Centuries*, London 1969–78, of which only volumes 1, 2 and 5 appeared, covering the Early Church, the Middle Ages, and the mid-nineteenth and twentieth centuries: the bibliographies are now in need of updating.

Three general works provide useful introductory treatments of the theology of the papacy: T. G. Jalland, *The Church and the Papacy*, London 1944 (Anglican): J. Tillard, *The Bishop of Rome*, London 1983 (Roman Catholic): K. Schatz, *Papal Primacy from its Origins to the Present*, Collegeville Minnesota 1996 (Roman Catholic). For a range of theological and ecclesiological reflections on the papacy after the Second Vatican Council, Robert Markus and Eric John, *Papacy and Hierarchy*, London 1969 (two gifted historians call for the repudiation of the legacy of GregoryVII and the papal monarchy): Patrick Granfield, *The Limits of the Papacy*, London 1987 – cautious exploration by a canonist: H. UrsVon Balthasar, *The Office of Peter and the Structure of the Church*, San Francisco 1986 – attempt at reconstruction by the most influential theologian of the era of John Paul II.

B. SPECIFIC PERIODS

CHAPTER ONE: 'UPON THIS ROCK'

General histories of the Early Church provide basic introductions to the history of the papacy in the first four centuries. Despite its age, Louis Duchesene's masterly *The Early History of the Christian Church*, 3 vols, London 1909, remains in many ways the best of these. A short and lively survey in H. Chadwick, *The Early Church*, Harmondsworth 1993. R. B. Eno, *The Rise of the Papacy*, Wilmington Delaware 1990, focuses on the texts and theology.

Most of the ancient texts bearing on the history of the papacy up to the reign of Damasus I are collected and translated into English in J. T. Shotwell and L. R. Loomis (eds), *The See of Peter*, Columbia University Press 1927, reprinted 1991. Supplementary texts up to the time of Leo I will be found in J. Stevenson (ed.), *Creeds, Councils and Controversies, Documents illustrative of the History of the Church 337–461*, London 1966. A fundamental source is Eusebius, *The History of the Church from Christ to Constantine*, Harmondsworth 1989. The Clement and Ignatian epistles can be found in M. Staniforth (ed.), *Early Christian Writings*, Harmondsworth 1987: they are included along with 'The Shepherd of Hermas', Greek text and translation, in J. B. Lightfoot (ed.), J. R. Harmer, *The Apostolic Fathers*, London 1898.

On the background of Christianity and the Empire, Peter Brown, *The World of late Antiquity*, London 1971, and the early chapters of the same author's *The Rise of Western Christendom*, Oxford 1996: Robin Lane Fox, *Pagans and Christians in the Mediterranean World from the second century AD to the conversion of Constantine*, Harmondsworth 1988: R. L. Markus, *Christianity in the Roman World*, London 1974.

Survey of the treatment of Peter in the New Testament by an ecumenical team of scholars in R. E. Brown, K. P. Donfried & J. Reumann, *Peter in the New Testament*, London 1974: Oscar Culmann, *Peter, Disciple, Apostle, Martyr*, London 1962: T. V. Smith, *Petrine Controversies in Early Christianity*, Tubingen 1985. There is a huge literature on Peter's presence in Rome and the supposed tomb of St Peter, much of it unreliable. A start can be made with L. Hertling and E. Kirchbaum, *The Roman Catacombs and their Martyrs*, Milwaukee 1956: E. Kirschbaaum, *The Tombs of St Peter and St Paul*, London 1959: J. Toynbee and J. W. Perkins, *The Shrine of St Peter and the Vatican Excavations*, London 1956: D. W. O'Connor, *Peter in Rome*, New York 1969. For the developing cult of Peter in Rome and the shrine at San Sebastiano, see also H. Chadwick, 'St Peter and Paul in Rome' in *History and Thought of the Early Church*, London 1982, pp. 31–52.

The Jewish community in Rome is the subject of H. J. Leon, *The Jews of Ancient Rome*, Philadelphia 1960.

Some of the older treatments of the Church in 1st and 2nd-century Rome retain value, notably G. La Piana, 'The Roman Church at the end of the 2nd Century', *Harvard Theological Review*, vol. 18 (1925), pp. 201–77. But all modern discussion of the issues must now start from the exhaustive and persuasive analysis by Peter Lampe, *Die Stadsromische Christen in den ersten beiden Jahrhundetern*, Tubingen 1987, which is, unfortunately, not yet available in English translation. The late evolution of a single Roman episcopate is controversially explored in Allen Brent's *Hippolytus and the Roman church in the third century*, Leiden and New York 1995. On the architectural setting of the early Christian community in Rome, R. Krautheimer and S. Curcic, *Early Christian and Byzantine Architecture*, New Haven and London 1986: G. Snyder, *Ante-Pacem. Archaeological evidence of Church Life before Constantine*, Macon, Georgia 1985.

On persecution and the Early Church, in addition to Lane Fox, *Pagans and Christians*, ch. 9, W. H. Frend, *Martyrdom and Persecution in the Early Church*, Oxford 1965. For Cyprian's treatise on unity, and his relations with the papacy, Jalland, Eno (above), and M. Bevenot (ed.), *St Cyprian, the Lapsed, and the Unity of the Church*, London 1957.

The best account of Constantine's religious beliefs, N. H. Baynes, *Constantine the Great and the Christian Church*, London 1929: A. H. M. Jones, *Constantine and the Conversion of Europe*, Harmondsworth 1962: R. MacMullen, *Constantine*, London 1970.

On Donatism, W. H. Frend, *The Donatist Church*, London 1952. On Arianism, R. D. Williams, *Arius: Heresy and Tradition*, Oxford 1987: R. P. C. Hanson, *The Search for the Christian Doctrine of God: the Arian Controversy 318–381*, Edinburgh 1988. The rationale and strategy behind the Constantinian settlement of Christianity as the religion of the Empire is explored in H. A. Drake, *Constantine and the Bishops: the politics of intolerance* (Johns Hopkins, U P 2001).

Fundamental work on Rome in the Constantinian and post-Constantinian era, and on popes Liberius and Damasus, in C. Pietri,

Roma Christiana: Recherches sur l'Eglise de Rome...de Miltiade a Sixte III (311–440), Rome 1976, reissued 1994. R. Krautheimer, *Profile of a City 312–1308*, Princeton University Press 1980, deals with far more than architecture: John Beckwith, *Early Christian and Byzantine Art*, New Haven and London 1979.

On Milan and Ambrose, R. Krautheimer, *Three Christian Capitals*, Berkeley 1983, pp. 69–92: N. B. McLynn, *Ambrose of Milan: Church and Court in a Christian Capital*, Berkeley 1994. Papal relations with Africa explored in J. E. Merdinger, *Rome and the African Church in the time of Augustine*, New Haven 1997. On Leo the Great, T. G. Jalland, *The Life and Times of Leo the Great*, London 1941: P.A. McShane, *La Romanitas et le Pape Leon le Grand*, Paris 1979: W. Ullmann, 'Leo I and the theme of Papal Primacy', *Journal of Theological Studies*, New Series, vol. 11 (1960), pp. 25–51. English translation of Leo's sermons and letters in C. L. Feltoe, *Library of Nicene and Post Nicene Fathers of the Christian Church*, 2nd Series, vol. 12.

CHAPTER TWO: 'BETWEEN TWO EMPIRES'

Surveys of the period: Peter Llewellyn, *Rome in the Dark Ages*, London 1993: Peter Brown, *The World of Late Antiquity* and *The Rise of Western Christendom*, (above): Judith Herrin, *The Formation of Christendom*, London 1989: the older study by H. St L. B. Moss, *The Birth of the Middle Ages 395–814*, Oxford 1935, remains worth reading. Jeffrey Richards, *The Popes and the Papacy in the Early Middle Ages 476–752*, London 1979, is fundamental, and should be read alongside Walter Ullmann, *A Short History of the Papacy in the Middle Ages*, London 1974 – over-schematic but packed with ideas. Bernard Schimmelpfennig, *The Papacy*, New York 1992, is a questioning survey by a distinguished Roman Catholic scholar – but this English translation from the German leaves a good deal to be desired. G. Barraclough, *The Medieval Papacy*, London 1968, is the best short narrative.

On the Goths and other Barbarians, J. M. Wallace-Hadrill, *The Barbarian West 400–1,000*, London 1967: P. S. Barwell, *Emperors, Prefects, Kings. The Roman West 395–565*, London 1992: C. Wickham, *Early Medieval Italy*, London 1981. R. McKitterick (ed.), *The New Cambridge Modern History*, vol. 2, *c. 700–900*, Cambridge 1995, contains many essays of direct relevance. One-volume survey of the religious background of the period in D. Knowles and D. Obolensky, *The Christian Centuries* vol. 2:

the Middle Ages, London 1969, good on Byzantine/Latin relations. C. Mango, *Byzantium. The Empire of New Rome*, London 1980: for fuller treatment of the Byzantine church and its relations with the West, survey and good bibliographies in J. M. Hussey, *The Orthodox Church in the Byzantine Empire*, Oxford 1986: J. Pelikan, *The Christian Tradition vol. 2: The Spirit of Eastern Christendom 600–1700*, Chicago 1977 – excellent on theology and spirituality. L. Duchesne's *l'Eglise au VIe siecle*, Paris 1925 is strong on the often bewildering theological controversies of the sixth century, and the role of the popes in them.

The fundamental source for the popes of the period is the *Liber Pontificalis*, the great papal chronicle which provides contemporary biographies of the popes from the sixth to the ninth centuries. The Latin text with splendidly full French notes was edited by L. Duchesne, *Le Liber Pontificalis, Texte, introduction et commentaire*, Paris 1886–92, reissued with third supplementary volume, C. Vogel (ed.), 1955–7. A good English translation from Duchesne's edition, incorporating much of the material from his notes, has been published in three volumes by Raymond Davis, *The Book of Pontiffs (Liber Pontificalis)*, Liverpool 1989; *The Lives of the Eighth-Century Popes (Liber Pontificalis)*, Liverpool 1992; *The Lives of the Ninth-century Popes (Liber Pontificalis)*, Liverpool 1995.

The fullest narrative history of the popes for this period is H. K. Mann, *The Lives of the Popes in the Early Middle Ages*, 18 vols, London 1902–32. Mann was a Roman Catholic priest and Rector of the English College in Rome. His book was solidly grounded in the available sources, and wears its prejudices on its sleeve. It is uncritical, but readable and (mostly) factually reliable.

On Ravenna, Rome, and the Empire, R. A. Markus, 'Ravenna and Rome 554–604', *Byzantion*, 51 (1981): T. S. Brown, 'The Church of Ravenna and the Imperial administration in the seventh century', *English historical Review*, 94 (1979), pp. 1–28: G. Bovini, *Ravenna Mosaics*, Oxford 1978: L. Von Matt and G. Bovini, *Ravenna*, Cologne 1971: J. Meyendorf, *Imperial Unity and Christian Divisions*, New York 1989.

On Monophysitism, A. A. Luce, *Monophysitism, Past and Present*, London 1920: W. H. C. Frend, *The Rise of the Monophysite Movement*, Cambridge 1972.

On Gregory the Great, F. H. Dudden, *Gregory the Great, his place in history and thought*, 2 vols, London 1905 (still valuable): Jeffrey Richards, *Consul of God: the life and times of Gregory the Great*, London 1980: R.A.

Markus, *From Augustine to Gregory the Great*, London 1983, (important for English mission), and the same author's *Gregory the Great and his World*, Cambridge 1997: C. Straw, *Gregory the Great. Perfection in Imperfection*, Berkeley 1988: C. Dagens, *Gregoire le Grand. Culture et Experience Chretienne*, Paris 1977. His letters and the *Pastoral Rule* have been translated into rather stiff English by J. Barmby (ed.), *The Book of the Pastoral Rule and Selected Epistles of Gregory the Great*, Library of Nicene and post-Nicene Fathers, 2nd series, vol. 12 & 13, New York 1895: his dialogues were translated by E. G. Gardner, *The Dialogues of St Gregory*, London 1911, and by O. J. Zimmermann, *Dialogues of St Gregory the Great*, New York 1959. The best treatment of the patrimony remains E. Spearing, *The Patrimony of the Roman Church in the time of Gregory the Great*, Cambridge 1918, but see also Jeffrey, *The Popes and the Papacy*, ch. 18.

For the Church in Ireland, K. Hughes, *The Church in Early Irish Society*, London 1966, and a survey of recent literature in Daibhi o Croinin, *Early Medieval Ireland 400–1200*, London 1995.

For 'micro-christendoms' in the age of Gregory, Herrin, *Formation of Christendom*, and Brown, *Rise of Western Christendom*.

For Anglo-Saxon Christianity, H. Mayr-Harting, *The Coming of Christianity to Anglo-Saxon England*, London 1972: discussion of Rome and England in Eamonn o Carragain, *The City of Rome and the World of Bede*, Newcastle upon Tyne 1994: for the Lindisfarne Gospels lectionary and Southern Italian influence, J. Backhouse, *The Lindisfarne Gospels*, London 1981, ch. 3. Essential sources in J. F. Webb and D. H. Farmer (trans and eds), *The Age of Bede*, Harmondsworth 1983 (includes Eddius Stephanus 'Life of Wilfred') and J. McClure and R. Collins (eds), *Bede, The Ecclesiastical History of the English People*, Oxford 1994.

For the anti-Gregorian reaction in Rome, Peter Llewellyn, 'The Roman Church in the seventh century: the legacy of Gregory the Great', *Journal of Ecclesiastical History*, 35 (1974), pp. 363–80.

For the rise of Islam, F. Gabrieli, *Muhammed and the conquests of Islam*, London 1968: H. Kennedy, *The Prophet and the Age of the Caliphates*, London 1986.

For Iconoclasm, Herrin, *Formation*, ch. 8, Brown, *Rise*, ch. 14 and 'A Dark Age Crisis: aspects of the Iconoclastic controversy', *English Historical Review*, 88 (1973), pp. 1–34; Hussey, *The Orthodox Church in the Byzantine Empire*, pp. 30–68. For Roman pilgrimage, Debra J. Birch, *Pilgrimage to Rome in the Middle Ages*, Woodbridge 1998: a delightful exploration of English pilgrimage, mostly focused, however, on later periods, is Judith Champ, *The English pilgrimage to Rome, a dwelling for the soul*, Leominster 2000.

For the emergence of the papal state, L. Duchesne, *The Beginnings of the Temporal Sovereignty of the Popes AD 754–1073*, London 1908: P. Partner, *The Lands of St Peter*, London 1972: T. F. X. Noble, *The Republic of St Peter, the Birth of the Papal State 680–825*, Philadelphia 1984.

For the popes and the Franks: Noble, *Republic*: R. McKitterick, *The Frankish Kingdoms and the Carolingians 751–987*, London 1983: J. M. Wallace-Hadrill, *The Frankish Church*, Oxford 1983: D. Bullough, *The Age of Charlemagne*, London 1973: L. Wallach, 'The Roman Synod of 800 and the alleged trial of Leo III', *Harvard Theological Review*, 49 (1956), pp. 123–42. Sources in L. Thorpe, *Two Lives of Charlemagne*, Harmondsworth 1969: B. W. Scholz and B. Rogers (eds), *Carolingian Chronicles*, Ann Arbor 1970: C. H. Talbot (ed.), *The Anglo-Saxon Missionaries in Germany*, London 1954 (contains a selection of the correspondence of St Boniface with a series of eighth-century popes, which throws a flood of light on attitudes to the papacy, and the self-understanding of the popes of the period).

On Nicholas I and the East, F. Dvornik, *The Photian Schism, history and legend*, Cambridge 1948. Much of Dvornik's scholarship was distilled into the brief and readable *Byzantium and the Roman Papacy*, New York 1966: F. A. Norwood, 'The Political Pretensions of Nicholas I', *Church History*, vol. 15 (1946), pp. 271–85: Y. Congar, 'S Nicolas Ier: ses positions ecclesiastiques', *Rivista di storia della chiesa in Italia*, vol. 21 (1967), pp. 393–410.

There is no satisfactory overview of the 'Dark Century'. A detailed picture can be built up from the relevant volumes of Mann's *History* (embarrassed) and the third volume of F. Gregorovius, *History of the City of Rome in the Middle Ages*, 8 vols, London 1894–1902, (censorious), while the early chapters of Peter Partner, *The Lands of St Peter*, provide an overarching political narrative. Helpful brief discussion of the Ottonian revival in C. N. L. Brooke, *Europe in the Central Middle Ages 962–1154*, London 1994, pp. 211ff. The greatest gossip of the tenth century was the chronicler and diplomat Liudprand of Cremona, the source for some of the most entertaining and discreditable stories about the popes of this period. His observations on the papacy, on an embassy to Byzantium, and on the reign of Otto the Great, are translated by F. A. Wright, *The Works of Liudprand of Cremona*, London 1930.

CHAPTER THREE: 'SET ABOVE NATIONS'

Mann, *History*, Gregorovius, City of Rome, Krautheimer, *Rome*, Barraclough, *Medieval Papacy*, and Ullmann, *Short History*, all remain valuable for this period. Two books by R. W. Southern provide profound introductions to the medieval world and the place of the Church within it: *The Making of the Middle Ages*, London 1987, and *Western Society and the Church in the Middle Ages*, Harmondsworth 1970 (particularly good on the evolution of papal institutions). Brooke, *Europe in the Central Middle Ages* provides general political context and a strong emphasis on the religious dimension, with up-to-date reading lists. For the rest of the period two books in the same series, J. H. Mundy, *Europe in the High Middle Ages 1150–1309*, London 1991, and (specially) D. Hay, *Europe in the Fourteenth and Fifteenth Centuries*, London 1989, are invaluable.

Two surveys of the reform papacy provide essential and complementary coverage, Colin Morris, *The Papal Monarchy: the Western Church from 1050 to 1250*, Oxford 1989 – beautifully written and very comprehensive, with exhaustive bibliographical essays, and I. S. Robinson, *The Papacy 1073–1198*, Cambridge 1990, an in-depth exploration of institutional and ideological transformation. Also valuable but drier is G. Tellenbach, *The Church in Western Europe from the tenth to the early twelfth centuries*, Cambridge 1993.

On Cluny and monastic reform, B. Bolton, *The Medieval Reformation*, London 1983: C. H. Lawrence, *Medieval Monasticism*, London 1984: H. E. J. Cowdrey, *The Cluniacs and Gregorian Reform*, Oxford 1970: N. Hunt, *Cluny under St Hugh*, London 1967: N. Hunt (ed.), *Cluniac Monasticism in the Central Middle Ages*, London 1971.

On celibacy of the clergy, A. L. Barstow, *Married Priests and the Reforming Papacy*, New York 1982: C. N. L. Brooke, *Medieval Church and Society*, Cambridge 1971, pp. 69–99 (on Norman England).

On the Normans in the South, R. H. C. Davis, *The Normans and their Myth*, London 1976: D. C. Douglass, *The Norman Achievement*, London 1969, and *The Norman Fate*, London 1976: D. Mack Smith, *Medieval Sicily*, London 1968: J. J. Norwich, *The Normans in the South 1016–1130*, London 1967, and *The Kingdom in the Sun 1130–1194*, London 1970 – compulsively readable popular accounts. On Byzantium and Rome, Hussey, *Orthodox Church*, and C. M. Brand, *Byzantium confronts the West*, Cambridge Mass. 1968.

On the cardinals, Robinson, *Papacy*, ch. 2, and S. Kuttner, 'Cardinalis: the history of a canonical concept', *Traditio*, vol. 3 (1945), pp. 129–214.

There are extended discussions of Gregory VII, in Ullmann, Morris, Robinson and Brooke: magisterial biography by H. E. J. Cowsrey, *Pope Gregory VII 1073–1085*, Oxford 1998: the best short life is that in the *Bibliotheca Sanctorum*: a survey of modern interpretations is provided by I. S. Robinson, 'Pope Gregory VII: bibliographical survey', *Journal of Ecclesiastical History*, vol. 36 (1985), pp. 439–83: a selection of his letters has been edited by E. Emerton, *Gregory VII: a selection of the letters*, Columbia 1932, and see also H. E. J. Cowdray (ed.), *Epistolae Vagantes of Pope Gregory VII*, Oxford 1972. Gregory's great opponent has now found a worthy English biographer in I. S. Robinson, *Henry IV King of Germany 1056–1106*, Cambridge 1999. For the papacy after Gregory, one of the best treatments is H. E. J. Cowdrey, *The Age of Abbot Desiderius*, Oxford 1983, which covers the pontificate of Blessed Victor III, and much more.

On the Investiture controversy, see B. Tierney (ed.), *The Crisis of Church and State*, New Jersey 1964 (documents): K. Morrison, *Tradition and Authority in the Western Church 300–1140*, Princeton 1969: I. S. Robinson, *Authority and Resistance in the Investiture Contest*, Manchester 1978, and W. Ullmann, *The Growth of Papal Government*, London 1970. Y. Congar, *Eglise et Papaute: Regards Historiques*, Paris 1994, collects some important papers on the theology of the papacy by a great historical theologian: chapter 6 deals with the seminal influence of St Bernard of Clairvaux. St Bernard's instructions to Pope Eugenius III have been translated by J. D. Anderson and E. T. Kennan, *St Bernard of Clairvaux: Five Books on Consideration, Advice to a Pope*, Kalamazoo, Michegan 1976.

For the Crusades, Jonathan Riley-Smith, *What were the Crusades?* London 1992, with bibliography, and the same author's *The First Crusade and the Idea of Crusading*, London 1986: C. Erdmann, *The Origin of the Idea of Crusade*, Princeton 1977 (classic discussion): H. E. Mayer, *The Crusades*, London 1972: S. Runciman, *History of the Crusades*, 3 vols, Cambridge 1951–4: Robinson, *Papacy*, chapter 9 is also important.

For Hadrian IV, E. M. Almedingen, *The English Pope: Adrian IV*, London 1925: W. Ullmann, 'The Pontificate of Adrian IV', *Cambridge Historical Journal*, vol. 11 (1953–5), pp. 232–52: R. W. Southern, *Medieval*

Humanism and other Studies, Oxford 1970, pp. 234–52: my discussion of the papacy, the Normans and Ireland is based on F. X. Martin, 'Diarmaid MacMurchada and the coming of the Anglo-Normans' in A. Cosgrave (ed.), *A New History of Ireland vol. 2, Medieval Ireland 1169–1534*, Oxford 1987, pp. 43–66. The standard life of Barbarossa in English is by P. Munz, *Frederick Barbarossa*, London 1969, though its reading of Barbarossa's policy is widely rejected.

On the twelfth and thirteenth-century papacy in general, K. Pennington, *Pope and Bishops: the Papal Monarchy in the Twelfth and Thirteenth centuries*, Pennsylvania 1984: Agostino Paravicini Bagliani, *Il Trono di Pietro: l'Universalità del papato da Alessandro III a Bonifacio VIII*, Rome 1996. R. Brentano, *Rome before Avignon*, London 1974 is unfailingly fresh and challenging. On Innocent III, the standard life is by H. Tillmann, *Pope Innocent III*, Amsterdam 1980: briefer study with useful bibliographies by J. Sayers, *Innocent III, leader of Europe 1198–1216*, London 1994: selection of essays and issues James L. Powell (ed.), *Innocent III: Vicar of Christ or Lord of the World?*, Washington 1994: C. R. Cheney, *Pope Innocent III and England*, Stuttgart 1976: D. P. Waley, *The Papal State in the Thirteenth century*, London 1961. The legend of Pope Joan is searchingly analysed in Alain Boureau, *The Myth of Pope Joan*, Chicago 2001.

On repression of heresy, R. I. Moore, *The Origins of European Dissent*, London 1977: B. Bolton, 'Innocent III's treatment of the Humiliati', in D. Baker (ed.), *Studies in Church History*, vol. 8 (Oxford 1971), pp. 73–82: J. R. Strayer, *The Albigensian Crusade*, New York 1971: B. Hamilton, *The Medieval Inquisition*, London 1981 (for later developments): E. A. Synan, *The Popes and the Jews in the Middle Ages*, New York 1965: on the Fourth Crusade, D. E. Queller, *The Fourth Crusade: The Conquest of Constantinople*, Leicester 1978, and J. Godfrey, *1204: the Unholy Crusade*, Oxford 1980: Byzantine/Roman relations more generally are treated in J. Gill, *Byzantium and the Papacy 1198–1400*, New Jersey 1979: theological study from a sympathetic Roman point of view, Aidan Nichols, *Rome and the Eastern Churches, a Study in Schism*, Edinburgh 1992. On the friars, R. M. Brooke, *The Coming of the Friars*, London 1975: C. H. Lawrence, *The Friars*, London 1994.

For Frederick II and the papacy, T. C. Van Cleve, *The Emperor Frederick II of Hohenstaufen*, Oxford 1972: D. Abulafia, *Frederick II: a Medieval Emperor*, London 1988: for papal provisions, G. Barraclough, *Papal Provisions*, London 1935 (throwing light on papal government and authority more generally). Papal finance is illustrated by the collection of documents with commentary by W. E. Lunt, *Papal Revenues in the Middle Ages*, 2 vols, New York 1934. For a fascinating account of an incident illuminating the role of the papacy in thirteenth-century Italian politics, S. Runciman, *The Sicilian Vespers*, Cambridge 1958.

The unfortunate Celestine V has found a splendid biographer in Paolo Golinelli, *Il Papa Contadino: Celestino V e il suo tempo*, Firenze 1996. For Boniface VIII, T. S. R. Boase, *Boniface VIII*, London 1933, has weathered well and remains the only full-scale life: F. M. Powicke, 'Pope Boniface VIII', *History*, vol. 18 (1934), pp. 307–29: C. T. Wood, *Philip the Fair and Boniface VIII*, London 1971: the French dossier of accusations against Boniface VIII edited, explored and (mostly) dismissed in Jean Coste (ed.), *Boniface VIII en procès: Articles d'accusation et depositions des temoins (1303–11)*, Rome 1995: for the Jubilee, H. Thurston, *The Holy Year of Jubilee: An Account of the History and Ceremony of the Roman Jubilee*, London 1900, which has relevance for subsequent chapters also: H. L. Kessler and J. Zacharias, *Rome 1300, On the Path of the Pilgrim*, New Haven and London 2000, offers an imaginative and beautifully illustrated evocation of the city during the first Jubilee. Apocalyptic hopes and fears centred on the papacy are explored in Marjorie Reeves, *The Influence of Prophecy in the Later Middle Ages*, Oxford 1979, Part 4.

The artistic and architectural setting of the papacy of the high Middle Ages is discussed in Krautheimer, *Rome*, chapter 8: John White, *Art and Architecture in Italy 1250–1400*, New Haven and London 1993, chapters 4, 7, 10: P. Hetherington, *Pietro Cavallini, a Study in the Art of Late Medieval Rome*, London 1979: W. Oakeshott, *The Mosaics of Rome*, London 1967: E. Hutton, *The Cosmati: the Roman Marble Workers of the XIIth and XIIIth Centuries*, London 1950.

On the Avignon papacy, B. Guillemain, *Le Cour Pontificale d'Avignon 1309–1376*, Paris 1962: G. Mollat, *The Popes at Avignon*, Edinburgh 1963: Y. Renouard, *The Avignon Papacy 1305–1403*, Hamden, Connecticut 1970. The first Avignon pope is subjected to close scrutiny in Sophia Menache, *Clement V*, Cambridge 1998. An invaluable sidelight on the papacy of the Avignon period is thrown by J. Gardner, *The Tomb and the Tiara: Curial Sculpture in Rome and Avignon and Rome in the later Middle Ages*, Oxford 1992.

On the Great Schism and the Conciliar Movement, W. Ullmann,

The Origins of the Great Schism, London 1948: J. H. Smith, *The Great Schism 1378*, London 1970: B. Tierney, *Foundations of Conciliar Theory*, Cambridge 1955: E. F. Jacob, *Essays in the Conciliar Epoch*, Manchester 1963: H. Jedin, *A History of the Council of Trent*, vol. 1, London 1949: J. Gill, *The Council of Florence*, Cambridge 1959, and his *Eugenius IV: Pope of Christian Union*, Westminster, Md., 1961: J. W. Stieber, *Pope Eugenius IV, the Council of Basle and the Secular and Ecclesiastical Authorities in the Empire*, Leiden 1978: G. Alberigo (ed.), *Christian Unity: the Council of Ferrara/Florence 1438–9*, Louvain 1991. The best general textbook on the Church in the period is E. Delaruelle, E. R. Laband and P. Ourliac, *L'Eglise au temps du Grande Schisme et la crise conciliaire*, Paris 1952–5: there is a short but excellent book in English by F. Oakley, *The Western Church in the Later Middle Ages*, Cornell 1979. Documents in C. M. D. Crowder, *Unity, Heresy and reform 1378–1460: the Conciliar Response to the Great Schism*, London 1977, key theoretical writings in J. H. Burns and T. M. Izbicki (eds), *Conciliarism and Papalism*, Cambridge 1997. For Italy and the Papal State, Partner, *Lands of St Peter*, and the same author's *The Papal State under Martin V*, London 1958: excellent discussion of the impact of the schism on the papacy and the Italian Church in D. Hay, *The Church in Italy in the Fifteenth Century*, Cambridge 1977, pp. 26–48.

CHAPTER FOUR: PROTEST AND DIVISION.

The Renaissance has generated an immense literature of its own, which cannot even be touched on here. J. Hale, *The Civilisation of Europe in the Renaissance*, London 1993, is a good introduction. The Italian background is sketched in D. Hay and J. Law, *Italy in the Age of the Renaissance 1380–1530*, London 1989. The religious history of the period is covered in all the standard histories (see General section, above), in Oakley, *Western Church*, and in Hay, *Church in Italy*. John Bossy's *Christianity in the West 1400–1700*, Oxford 1985, has little on the papacy but crackles with ideas. The art and architecture of the period are comprehensively surveyed in F. Hartt, *The History of Italian Renaissance Art*, London 1987.

The fundamental quarry for any account of the papacy from the fifteenth to the late eighteenth centuries is L. Pastor, *History of the Popes from the close of the Middle Ages*, 40 vols, London 1912–1952. Pastor was an ultramontane Austrian Catholic who wrote from a strongly papalist point of view, but his immense and detailed work is based on profound acquaintance with the sources. It is the starting place for any study of the Catholic Church in the period, and in most cases Pastor's biographies of individual popes remain the most thorough treatment available. Readers with Italian can now supplement and update Pastor with the lives in the *Enciclopedia dei Papi*.

Survey of the institutions and activities of the Renaissance popes in J. A. F. Thompson, *Popes and Princes 1417–1517: Politics and Policy in the Late Medieval Church*, London 1980: further exploration of the political dimension in P. Prodi, *The Papal Prince*, Cambridge 1987 and K. P. Lowe, *Church and Politics in Renaissance Italy*, Cambridge 1993.

For Rome on the eve of the Renaissance, P. Partner, *Renaissance Rome 1500–1559: a Portrait of a Society*, Berkeley 1976: Loren Partridge, *The Renaissance in Rome 1400–1600*, London 1996, sketches the art and architectural patronage.

On Nicholas V and the replanning of Rome, C. W. Westfall, *In this most Perfect Paradise: Alberti, Nicholas V and the Invention of Conscious Urban Planning in Rome 1447–55*, Pennsylvania 1974: P. A. Ramsey (ed.), *Rome in the Renaissance, the City and the Myth*, Binghampton, New York 1982: On Bernardino of Sienna, Iris Origo, *The World of San Bernardino*, London 1963.

On the Renaissance and the papal court more generally, C. L. Stinger, *The Renaissance in Rome*, Bloomington Indiana 1985: J. F. D'Amico, *Renaissance Humanism in Papal Rome: Humanists and Churchmen on the Eve of the Reformation*, Baltimore and London 1983: E. Lee, *Sixtus IV and Men of Letters*, Rome 1978: A. Grafton (ed.), *Rome reborn: the Vatican Library and Renaissance Culture*, New Haven and London 1993: J. W. O'Malley, *Praise and Blame in Renaissance Rome: Rhetoric, Doctrine and Reform in the sacred orators of the Papal Court 1450–1521*, Durham NC 1979.

On the Sistine Chapel, C. Pietrangeli et al, *The Sistine Chapel. The Art, the History and the Restoration*, New York 1986, and Pietrangeli is also the editor of the lavishly illustrated Paintings in the Vatican, Bulfinch Press, Boston, New York, Toronto and London 1996: L. D. Ettlinger, *The Sistine Chapel before Michaelangelo: Religious Imagery and Papal Primacy*, Oxford 1965: C. F. Lewine, *The Sistine Chapel Walls and the Roman Liturgy*, Pennsylvania 1993.

On Pius II the old work by C. M. Ady, Pius II, London 1913, remains useful: his entertaining autobiographical *Commentaries* were translated in an abridged form by F.A. Gragg, *Memoirs of a Renaissance Pope: the Commentaries of Pius II*, London 1960. For Julius II there are two good modern lives: C. Shaw, *Julius II, the Warrior Pope*, Oxford 1988, and I. Cloulas, *Jules II*, Paris 1990: for Callistus III and Alexander VI, M. Mallet, *The Borgias*, London 1969.

On the papacy and Crusade, N. Housley, *The Later Crusades*, Oxford 1992: C. A. Frazee, *Catholics and Sultans: the Church and the Ottoman Empire 1453–1923*, Cambridge 1983.

On the Renaissance cardinalate and the Curia, P. Partner, *The Pope's Men: the Roman Civil Service in the Renaissance*, Oxford 1990: Lowe, *Church and Politics*, pp. 46–52: A. V. Antonovics, 'Counter-Reformation Cardinals 1534–1590', *European Studies Review*, vol. 2 (1970), pp. 301–27: D. S. Chambers, *Cardinal Bainbridge in the Court of Rome 1509–1514*, Oxford 1965, and the same writer's 'The economic predicament of renaissance cardinals', *Studies in Medieval and Renaissance History*, vol. 3 (1966): B. M. Halma, *Italian cardinals, Reform, and the Church as property*, Berkeley 1985.

For papal finance, J. Delumeau, *Vie economique et sociale de Rome dans la seconde moitie du XVIe siecle*, 2 vols, Paris 1957–9: some of Delumeau's conclusions summarised in his article 'Rome: political and administrative centralisation in the Papal State in the sixteenth century' in E. Cochrane (ed.), *The Late Italian Reniassance 1525–1630*, New York 1970, pp. 287–304: F. Gilbert, *The Pope, his Banker and Venice*, Cambridge Mass. 1980, deals with the funding of Julius II's pontificate. The most important recent contribution to the understanding of the economics of the early modern papacy is P. Partner, 'Papal Financial policy in the Renaissance and Counter-Reformation', *Past and Present*, 1980, pp. 17–60.

For Savanarola, R. Ridolfi, *The Life of Girolamo Savanarola*, New York 1959: D. Weinstein, *Savanarola and Florence: Prophecy and Patriotism in the Renaissance*, Princeton 1970. Catholic reforming texts in J. C. Olin (ed.), *The Catholic Reformation: Savanarola to Ignatius Loyola. Reform in the Church 1495–1540*, Westminster MD. 1969.

There are hundreds of books on Erasmus: R. H. Bainton, *Erasmus of Rotterdam*, New York 1969, is a basic narrative: see also R. J. Schoek, *Erasmus and Europe: the making of a Humanist*, Edinburgh 1990: A. G. Dickens and W. R. D. Jones, *Erasmus the Reformer*, London 1994. In some ways the liveliest introduction is still the delightfully prejudiced and vivid Victorian life, copiously illustrated from the letters, by J. A.

Froude, *Life and Letters of Erasmus*, London 1895. There is an English translation of the *Julius Exclusus* by J. Kelley Sowards, *The Julius Exclusus of Erasmus*, Bloomington Indiana 1968.

On Lateran V and Trent, H. Jedin, *History of the Council of Trent*, London 1957 – though only two of the five volumes have been translated into English: they are available in French and Italian, as well as German.

There are hundreds of books on Luther. A good introduction is E. G. Rupp, *Luther's Progress to the Diet of Worms*, London 1951: good biography by R. M. Bainton, *Here I Stand, a Life of Martin Luther*, New York 1950: the German context (and anti-papalism) explored in A. G. Dickens, *The German Nation and Martin Luther*, 1974. Overviews of the Reformation in S. Ozment, *The Age of Reform*, New Haven and London 1980: H. J. Grimm, *The Reformation Era, 1500–1650*, London 1973. German pictorial propaganda dealt with in R. W. Scribner, *For the Sake of Simple Folk: Popular Propaganda for the German Reformation*, Cambridge 1981.

On the Sack of Rome, J. Hook, *The Sack of Rome*, London 1972: A. Chastel, *The Sack of Rome 1527*, Princeton 1983: the account in Pastor, *History of the Popes*, vol. 9, is vivid and remains worth reading.

On the Counter-Reformation in general there are a number of good general surveys: Robert Bireley, *The Refashioning of Catholicism 1450–1700*, London 1999: R. Po-Chia Hsia, *The World of Catholic Renewal 1540–1770*, Cambridge 1998: M. D. W. Jones, *The Counter-Reformation: Religion and Society in Early Modern Europe*, Cambridge 1995 presents a well-chosen anthology of documents: J. Delumeau, *Catholicism Between Luther and Voltaire*, London 1977, is brilliant and gripping, but extreme in its interpretation of the 'newness' of Counter-Reformation Catholicism: O. Evenett, *The Spirit of the Counter-Reformation*, Cambridge 1968, is a set of brilliant interpretative lectures, but not very useful for beginners.

The best treatment of the 'Spirituali' is D. Fenlon, *Heresy and Obedience in Tridentine Italy*, Cambridge 1972, of the Jesuits by J. W. O'Malley, *The First Jesuits*, Cambridge Mass. 1993. In some ways, and until John Bossy's volume on the Counter-Reformation in Italy, and Dermot Fenlon's biography of Philip Neri appear, the best work on the religion of sixteenth-century Rome is L. Ponelle and L. Bordet, *St Philip Neri and the Roman Society of His Times*, London 1932. The crucial final phase of the Council of Trent has been treated briefly and brilliantly by H. Jedin in *Crisis and Closure of the Council of Trent*, London 1967. For Borromeo, the papacy and the Council, J. M. Headley and J. B. Tomaro, *San Carlo Borromeo: Catholic Reform and Ecclesiastical Politics in the Second Half of the Sixteenth Century*, Washington 1984, pp. 47–63. A fascinating and indispensable contemporary assessment of Rome in the years immediately after the Jubilee of 1575 is Gregory Martin's *Roma Sancta*, ed. G. B. Parks, Rome 1969.

Surprisingly few of the Counter-Reformation popes have evoked good biographies, and, apart from the relevant volumes of Pastor, there is nothing recent in English: N. Lemaitre, *Saint Pie V*, Paris 1994: I. de Feo, *Sisto V: Un grande papa tra Rinascimento e Barocco*, Milan 1987. For the Counter-Reformation reconstruction of Rome, R. Wittkower, *Art and Architecture in Italy 1600–1750*, Harmondsworth 1980: Torgil Magnusson, *Rome in the Age of Bernini*, 2 vols, Stockholm and Atlantic Heights, NJ 1982, 1986: G. Labrot, *L'Image de Rome. Une arme pour la Contre-Reforme 1534–1677*, Champ Vallon, Seyssel 1987: H. Gamrath, *Roma Sancta Renovata*, Rome 1987 (on Sixtus V's projects): S. Ostrow, *Art and Spirituality in Counter-Reformation Rome*, Cambridge 1996: J. Freiberg, *The Lateran in 1600: Christian Concord in Counter-Reformation Rome*, Cambridge 1995: L. Rich, *The Altars and Altarpieces of New St Peter's: Outfitting the basilica 1621–1666*, Cambridge 1997. Irene Polverini Fosi, 'Justice and its image: political propaganda and judicial reality in the pontificate of Sixtus V', *Sixteenth-century Journal*, 24 (1993), pp. 75–95, powerfully questions the propagandist claims of one of the most forceful post-Tridentine popes to have rid the Papal States of banditry, and in the process illuminates the objectives and self-understanding of the Counter-Reformation papacy: the article summarises her book, *La Societa Violenta: il bandito nello stato pontificio nella seconda meta del Cinquecento*, Rome 1985. A. D. Wright's *The Early Modern Papacy: from the Council of Trent to the French Revolution 1564–1789*, London 2000, is an invaluable overview of the workings of the papacy in the ancien régime. A valuable survey of recent work on the Counter-Reformation papacy is provided by Simon Ditchfield in 'In search of local knowledge: rewriting early modern Italian religious history', *Cristianesimo nella Storia*, vol. 19 (1998), pp. 255–296. The Papal Court is discussed in H. D. Fernandez, 'The Papal Court at Rome *c.* 1450–1700' in John Adamson (ed.), *The Princely Courts of Europe*, London 1999, pp. 141–63.

On the religious situation in the Empire in the age of the Counter-

Reformation, R. J. W. Evans, *The Making of the Habsburg Monarchy 1550–1700*, Oxford 1979. For Venice, W. J. Bouwsma, *Venice and the Defence of Republican Liberty*, Berkeley 1968, and P. F. Grendler, *The Roman Inquisition and the Venetian Press*, Princeton 1977. For the confessional polarising of politics and the Thirty Years War, J. Lecler, *Toleration and the Reformation*, 2 vols, London 1960: C. C. Eckhardt, *The Papacy and World Affairs as Reflected in the Secularisation of Politics*, Chicago 1937: G. Parker (ed.), *The Thirty Years War*, London 1984 (good political narrative and interpretation): R. Bireley, *Religion and Politics in the Age of the Counter-Reformation: Emperor Ferdinand II, William Lamormaini SJ, and the Formation of Imperial Policy*, Chapel Hill 1981.

On Propaganda Fide and papal missionary involvement, Delumeau, *Catholicism*, and R. H. Song, *The Sacred Congregation for the Propagation of the Faith*, Washington 1961: see also the invaluable commemorative collection, *Sacrae Congregationis de Propaganda Fide Memoria Rerum*, (3 vols in 5) Freiburg 1971–6.

On the pontificate of Urban VIII and Baroque Rome, Wittkower, *Art and Archtecture*: F. Haskell, *Patrons and Painters: Italian Art and Society in the Age of the Baroque*, London 1963: A. Leman, *Urbain VIII et la rivalité de la France et de la Maison d'Autriche de 1631 a 1635*, Lille 1920: J. Grisar, *Papstliche Finanzen, Nepostismus und Kirchenrecht unter Urban VIII*, Rome 1943: brief treatment of the Galileo affair, with bibliographies, Stillman Drake, *Galileo*, Oxford 1980: documents in M.A. Finnochiaro, *The Galileo Affair: a Documentary History*, Berkeley 1989: Vatican symposium in G.V. Coyne (ed.), *The Galileo Affair: a meeting of Science and Faith*, Vatican City 1985.

Papal involvement in the Jansenist debates is best followed through successive volumes of Pastor, but an overview of the issues can be gained from N. J. Abercrombie, *The Origins of Jansenism*, Oxford 1936: L. Cognet, *Le Jansenisme*, Paris 1961: A. Sedgwick, *Jansenism in Seventeenth-century France*, Charlottesville 1977: on *Unigenitus*, there is a useful overview by J. M. Gres-Gayer, 'The *Unigenitus* of Clement XI: a Fresh Look at the Issues' in *Theological Studies*, vol. 49 (1988), pp. 259–82 and an older work, A. le Roy, *La France et Rome de 1700 à 1715*, Paris 1892. On Innocent XI, J. Orcibal, *Louis XIV contre Innocent XI*, Paris 1949: L. O'Brien, *Innocent XI and the Revocation of the Edict of Nantes*, Berkeley 1930.

For the eighteenth-century Church and papacy, apart from the general works indicated in Section A, and Wright's *Early Modern Papacy*, three books in English provide basic orientation and flesh out the detail: W. J. Callahan and D. Higgs (eds), *Church and Society in Catholic Europe of the Eighteenth Century*, Cambridge 1979 – excellent essays with good bibliographies: Owen Chadwick, *The Popes and European Revolution*, Oxford 1981, a wonderfully detailed and entertaining book which despite its title is mostly devoted to the eighteenth century: Hans Gross, *Rome in the Age of Enlightenment: the Post-Tridentine Syndrome and the Ancien Régime*, Cambridge 1990, particularly good on social context. C. M. S. Johns, *Papal Art and Cultural Politics: Rome in the Age of Clement XI*, Cambridge 1993, throws light on ideology and papal patronage in the early eighteenth century: F. Heyer's *The Catholic Church from 1648 to 1870*, London 1969, is brief and sometimes innaccurate, but has a good deal of material on papal relations with Germany which is not otherwise easily available in English. Volume I of an older work, F. Nielsen, *The History of the Papacy in the Nineteenth-Century*, London 1906, is devoted to the later eighteenth-century popes. S. J. Miller, *Portugal and Rome c.1748–1830: an aspect of the Catholic Enlightenement*, Rome 1978, provides a useful case study. For Benedict XIV, Pastor's account in vols 35–6 is full and very good: R. Haynes, *Philosopher King: the Humanist Pope Benedict XIV*, London 1970, is lightweight. There is a valuable collection of papers delivered at a convention on Benedict XIV in Bologna in December 1979, dealing with every aspect of his work, as canonist, bishop and pope, in M. Cecchelli (ed.), *Benedetto XIV (Prospero Lambertini)*, 3 vols, Ferrara 1981.

On the dissolution of the Jesuits, Pastor, vol. 38, on Clement XIV is the fullest and fairest account, Chadwick, *Popes and European Revolution*, chapter 5, is a balanced and compassionate survey, and W. J. Bangert, *A History of the Society of Jesus*, St Louis 1986, chapters 5 and 6, covers the affair from a Jesuit perspective.

CHAPTER FIVE: THE POPE AND THE PEOPLE

In addition to the multi-volume histories recommended in Section A, there is good coverage of the papacy in the late eighteenth and early nineteenth centuries in F. Nielsen, *The History of the Papacy in the Nineteenth Century*, London 1906: E. E. Y. Hales' *Revolution and Papacy*, Notre Dame, Indiana 1966, is a lively and judicious narrative, and

Chadwick's *The Popes and European Revolution* is also indispensable. Chadwick has continued his overview of the papacy in his delightful and weighty *A History of the Popes 1830–1914*, Oxford 1998. F.J. Coppa's *The Modern Papacy since 1789*, London 1998, is a little colourless in its judgements, but is based on a wide range of interesting material. The best biography of Pius VI is that in the final volumes (39 & 40) of Pastor, but see also A. Latreille, *L'Eglise Catholique et la Revolution Française*, Paris 1946–50. On Josephism, in addition to Chadwick and Hales, T. C. W. Blanning, *Joseph II and Enlightened despotism*, London 1970: S. K. Padover, *The Revolutionary Emperor: Joseph II of Austria*, London 1967: M. C. Goodwin, *The Papal Conflict with Josephinism*, New York 1938: on Scipio Ricci and the Synod of Pistoia, C. A. Bolton, *Church Reform in Eighteenth Century Italy*, The Hague 1969.

On the French Revolution and the Church, Latreille, *L'Eglise Catholique*, (above), A. Dansette, *Religious History of Modern France*, vol. I, Edinburgh and London 1961 (good for the whole Napoleonic episode): J. McManners, *The French Revolution and the Church*, London 1969. For Pius VII, in addition to Hales, *Revolution and Papacy*, (above), J. Leflon, *Pie VII: Des Abbayes Benedictines à la Papaute*, Paris 1958.

Apart from the general histories and the material in Nielsen, Hales and Chadwick, there is no specialist study of the pontificates of Leo XII or Gregory XVI in English. J. D. Holmes, *The Triumph of the Holy See: a Short History of the Papacy in the Nineteenth Century*, London 1978, is slight but covers the ground. For the Liberal Catholic Movement and its condemnation, A. R. Vidler, *Prophecy and Papacy: a Study of Lamennais, the Church and the Revolution*, London 1954. The theological basis of Ultramontanism is studied in Bernard Reardon, *Liberalism and Tradition: aspects of Catholic Theology in Nineteenth-century France*, Cambridge 1975. For a fascinating and illuminating contemporary source, N. Wiseman, *Recollections of the Last Four Popes and of Rome in their times*, London 1858 (the popes concerned are Pius VII, Leo XII, Pius VIII and Gregory XVI).

For Pius IX, on whom again Chadwick should be consulted, there are three good specialist studies, one of which is in English. The fullest biography is by G. Martina, *Pio Nono*, 3 vols, Rome 1974–90: the most readable, specially good on the political context, is E. E. Y. Hales, *Pio Nono*, London 1954: the best integrated into an overview of the nineteenth-century Church is R. Aubert, *Le Pontificat de Pie IX*, Paris 1952. Aubert edited volume 5 of *The Christian Centuries* (above, section A) under the title *The Church in a Secularised Society*, covering all aspects of the Church in the period. Hales' *The Catholic Church and the Modern World*, London 1958, provides a brisk and readable survey of the century. A fascinating perspective on the Roman Question is offered by the despatches of the British Government's man in Rome, Odo Russell, recording many interviews with Pio Nono. They were edited by N. Blakiston, *The Roman Question*, London 1962. For a vivid picture of Rome under Pio Nono, R. de Cesare, *The Last days of Papal Rome 1850–1870*, London 1909. For a poignant episode in the fall of the Papal States, G. F.-H. Berkeley, *The Irish Battalion in the Papal Army of 1860*, Dublin and Cork 1929. For the First Vatican Council, the best account remains C. Butler, *The Vatican Council*, London 1962: for a hostile and tendentious account, containing some interesting material, A. B. Hasler, *How the Pope Became Infallible: Pius IX and the Politics of Persuasion*, New York 1981. For an account by a key player at the Council, H. E. Manning, *The True Story of the Vatican Council*, London 1877. Manning's correspondence with Pio Nono's confidant Mgr George Talbot makes up much of volume 2 of E. R. Purcell's notorious *Life of Cardinal Manning*, London 1896, and throws a flood of light on Ultramontane attitudes. The essays 'The Forgotten Council' and 'The primacy: the small print of Vatican I' by Garrett Sweeney in A. Hastings (ed.), *Bishops and Writers*, Wheathamstead 1977, offer helpful theological comment on Ultramontanism and the First Vatican Council: the statistics on papal appointments of bishops in my chapter are taken from Sweeney's essay 'The Wound in the Right Foot', in the same collection. The Mortara affair is the subject of David I. Kertzer's *The Kidnapping of Edgardo Mortara*, New York 1997.

For the *Kulturkampf*, in addition to the material in volume 9 of Jedin and Dolan, *History of the Church*, G. Goyau, *Bismark et l'Eglise: Le Kulturkampf 1870–78*, 4 vols, Paris 1911–13: M. L. Anderson, *Windhorst*, Oxford 1981, pp. 130–200: David Blackbourn's study *Marpingen: Apparitions of the Blessed Virgin Mary in Bismarkian Germany*, Oxford 1993, offers wonderful insight into the frictions between ultramontane Catholicism and the Prussian state. R. J. Ross, *The Failure of Bismark's Kulturkampf: Catholics and State Power in Germany 1871–87*, Washington, DC 1998. E. Helmreich (ed.), *A Free Church in a Free State?*, Boston 1964, is a collection of source material and essays which juxtaposes the *Risorgimento* and the *Kulturkampf*. The standard treatment of the Roman question after 1870 is A. C. Jemolo, *Church and State in Italy 1850–1950*, Oxford 1960.

There is no adequate biography of Leo XIII. Those by C. de T'Serclaes, *Le Pape Leon XIII*, 3 vols, Lille 1894–1906, and by E. Soderini, *Il Pontificato di Leone XIII*, Milan 1932–3, are more or less 'official' lives with little critical distance from their subject (Leo XIII read the proofs of T'Serclaes book), though both present much valuable material. The first two volumes only of Soderini have been translated into English. Lillian P. Wallace, *Leo XIII and the Rise of Socialism*, Durham, NC 1966, is an intelligent study of wider interest than the title suggests: E. T. Gargan (ed.), *Leo XIII and the Modern World*, New York 1961, a valuable collection of essays. For Catholic social teaching, Paul Misner, *Social Catholicism in Europe*, London 1991: M. P. Fogarty, *Christian Democracy in Western Europe 1820–1953*, London 1957: A. R. Vidler, *A Century of Social Catholicism*, London 1964: P. Furlong and D. Curtis (eds), *The Church Faces the Modern World: Rerum Novarum and its impact*, Hull 1994. Useful selection of Leo XIII's encyclicals H. Parkinson (ed.), *The Pope and the People: Select Letters and Addresses on Social Questions by Pope Leo XIII*, London 1920, and a fuller selection (thirty, including *Apostolicae Curae*) was edited by J. J. Wynne, *The Great Encyclical Letters of Pope Leo XIII*, New York 1903. For a survey of the alienation between the Church and the working classes in nineteenth-century Europe, H. McLeod, *Religion and the People of Western Europe 1789–1970*, Oxford 1981.

For France and the *Ralliement*, A. Dansette, *Religious History of Modern France*, vol. 2, and especially J. McManners, *Church and State in France 1870–1914*, London 1972. For the opening of the Vatican archives, W. O. Chadwick, *Catholicism and History, the Opening of the Vatican Archives*, Cambridge 1978: for intellectual liberalisation and Americanism, Jedin and Dolan, *History of the Church*, vol. 9, pp. 307–34, and Hales, *Catholic Church in the Modern World*, pp 179–88: for the condemnation of Anglican orders, J. J. Hughes, *Absolutely Null and Utterly Void: the Papal Condemnation of Anglican Orders 1896*, London 1968.

CHAPTER SIX: THE ORACLES OF GOD

For every aspect of the twentieth-century papacy, Jedin and Dolan, *History of the Church*, vols 9 and 10 are invaluable, as is Aubert, *Christian Centuries Volume 5: the Church in a Secularised Society*, J. D. Holmes,

The Papacy in the Modern World 1914-78, London 1981, is a reliable short survey. Carlo Falconi's *The Popes in the Twentieth Century*, London 1967, is acerbic and sometimes bilious, but very well-informed and consistently challenging. R. A. Graham, *Vatican Diplomacy: a Study of the Church and State on the International Plane*, Princeton and London 1960, covers an area of relevance for the whole century, while H. E. Cardinale, *The Holy See and the International Order*, Gerard's Cross 1976, is an account of the rationale of papal diplomacy by a senior papal diplomat. F. J. Coppa, *Controversial Concordats: the Vatican's relations with Napoleon, Mussolini and Hitler*, Washington 1999, explores a vital facet of papal diplomacy.

There is as yet no satisfactory life of Pius X. R. Bazin, *Pius X*, London 1928, and I. Giordani, *Pius X, a Country Priest*, Milwaukee 1954, both have a good deal of material swamped in cloying piety. C. Ledre, *Pie X*, Paris 1952, covers most of the features of the pontificate but is uncritical, as is H. Dal-Gal, *Pius X*, Dublin 1953. I have not seen G. Romanato, *La Vita di Papa Sarto*, Milan 1992.

On Modernism, J. Riviere, *Le Modernisme dans l'Eglise*, Paris 1929: E. Poulat, *Histoire, Dogme et Critique dans le Crise Moderniste*, Paris 1979: A. R. Vidler, *The Modernist Movement in the Roman Catholic Church*, Cambridge 1934, and *A Variety of Catholic Modernists*, Cambridge 1970: good anthology of source material, including large selections from *Pascendi* and *Lamentabili*, in B. M. G. Reardon, *Roman Catholic Modernism*, London 1970. The most searching theological analysis (strongly anti-papal), is G. Daly, *Transcendence and Immanence: a Study of Catholic Modernism and Integralism*, Oxford 1980. For the anti-modernist campaign and the pope's part in it, E. Poulat, *Integrisme et Catholicisme Integral*, Tournai-Paris 1969.

For the separation of Church and State in France, McManners, *Church and State*, and H. W. Paul, *The Second Ralliement: The Rapprochement between Church and State in France in the Twentieth Century*, Washington 1967, chapter I.

For Benedict XV there is now a valuable brief study by J. F. Pollard, *The Unknown Pope, Benedict XV and the pursuit of peace*, London 1999: there are older and still useful biographies by H. E. G. Rope, *Benedict XV: the Pope of Peace*, London 1941: W. H. Peters, *The Life of Benedict XV*, Milwaukee 1959, and F. Hayward, *Un Pape méconnu: Benoit XV*, Tournai 1955: Falconi, *Popes in the Twentieth Century*, pp. 89–150, is a sympathetic sketch.

For Pius XI there is no satisfactory biography: the two best are R. Fontenelle, *His Holiness Pope Pius XI*, London 1939, and P. Hughes, *Pope Pius XI*, London 1937. The latter is reverential and was written while its subject was still alive, but is accurate and reasonably comprehensive up to and including the great encyclicals of 1937. It sheds no light on the personality, for which see E. Pellegrinetti, *Pio XI, l'uomo nel Papa e il Papa nell'uomo*, Rome 1940. There is a collection of essays sponsored by the diocese of Milan, *Pio XI nel trentesimo della morte*, Milan 1969. A. Rhodes, *The Vatican in the Age of the Dictators 1922–45*, London 1973, has a good deal on Pius XI himself. For the Roman Question and the Fascist state, Jemolo, *Church and State*: D.A. Binchy, *Church and State in Fascist Italy*, Oxford 1941: J. F. Pollard, *The Vatican and Italian Fascism, 1929–32, A Study in Conflict*, Cambridge 1985. *Humani Generis Unitas*, Pius XI's lost encyclical on the Jews, is reconstructed and discussed in Georges Passelecq and Bernard Suchecky, *The Hidden Encyclical of Pius XI*, New York and London 1997.

The best lives of Pius XII are by O. Halecki, *Pius XII: the Pope of Peace*, London 1954, and N. Padarello, *Portrait of Pius XII*, London 1956, though both are uncritical. D. Tardini, *Pio XII*, Vatican City 1960, is a testimony by one of Pacelli's pro-secretaries of state. A. Riccardi (ed.), *Pio XII*, Rome–Bari 1985, is a collection of essays in Italian on various aspects of the pontificate. W. A. Purdy, *The Church on the Move*, London 1966 is a wise insider's reflection on the differences in style and substance between the pontificates of Pius XII and John XXIII, illuminating about both. Owen Chadwick's *Britain and the Vatican during the Second World War*, Cambridge 1986, is the best treatment of a fraught issue, full of insight on the characters of Pius XII and the future Paul VI. Chadwick's lengthy review article 'Weizsacker, the Vatican and the Jews of Rome', *Journal of Ecclesiastical History*, vol. 28 (1977), pp. 179–99, gets to the bottom of the incident round which Hockhuth based his play. The case for the prosecution against Pius XII is presented by John Cornwell, *Hitler's Pope, the Secret History of Pius XII*, London and New York 1999: Cornwell attributes Pius XII's disastrous dealings with the German Church to a defective theology of the Church obsessively preoccupied with the papacy and its prerogatives. The Vatican's wartime dealings with the Jews are surveyed with somewhat distorting hostility by Susan Zuccotti in *Under his Very Windows: The Vatican and the Holocaust in Italy*, New Haven and

London 2000. For the most part, the defences of Pius XII, such as P. Blet, *Pius XII and the Second World War*, Hereford 1999, which essentially recycles the editorial material to the *Actes et Documents du Saint Siege* noticed below, or M. Marchione, *Pope Pius XII: Architect for Peace*, New Jersey 2000, have been unconvincing or have not engaged with the specific concerns of his critics: G. Miccoli, *I dilemmi e I silenzi da Pio XII: Vaticano, seconda guerra mondiale e Shoah*, Milano 2000, which I have not seen, is reputedly more balanced. For the Nazis and the Church more generally, G. Levy, *The Catholic Church and the Nazi Regime*, New York 1964, and J. S. Conway, *The Nazi Persecution of the Churches 1933–45*, London 1968. The Vatican's activities during the Second World War have been exhaustively documented in P. Blet, R. A. Graham, A. Martini and B. Schneider (eds), *Actes et Documents du Saint Siege relatifs à la Seconde Guerre Mondiale*, 11 volumes, Vatican City 1965–78. For post-war attitudes, Owen Chadwick's *The Christian Church in the Cold War*, Harmondsworth 1993. E. O. Hanson, *The Catholic Church in World Politics*, Princeton 1987, is an important analysis, with a strong American emphasis. H. Stehle, *Eastern Politics of the Vatican 1917–79*, Athens, Ohio 1975, surveys the shifts in Vatican Ostpolitik (highly critical of Pius XII). The *Memoirs* of Cardinal Joseph Mindszenty, London 1974, are a fascinating testimony by a key figure in the confrontation with communism.

For the development of Catholic theology before the Council, surveys in Jedin and Dolan *History of the Church*, vol. 10, pp. 260–98 and (especially) Aubert, *Church in a Secularised Society*, pp. 607–23: E. O'Brien, *Theology in Transition: A bibliographical evaluation of the 'Decisive decade' 1954–1964*, New York 1965: A. Nichols, *The Shape of Catholic Theology*, Edinburgh 1991, pp. 321–48, esp. 335ff.

For John XXIII there is a good biography by Peter Hebblethwaite, *John XXIII, Pope of the Council*, London 1984. Edited selections from his diaries appeared as *Journal of a Soul*, London 1980, and of *Letters to his Family*, London 1969.

For Paul VI, once again there is a first-class biography by Peter Hebblethwaite, *Paul VI, the first modern pope*, London 1993. The documents of Vatican II, and many of Paul's most significant post-Conciliar utterances, including *Humanae Vitae*, have been edited by Austin Flannery as *Vatican Council II: The Conciliar and Post-Conciliar Documents*, Leominster 1981, and *Vatican Council II: More Post-Conciliar Documents*, Northport, New York 1982. Highly influential contemporary reporting of the four sessions of the Council by 'Xavier Rynne' (Fr F. X. Murphy) in *Letters from Vatican City*, 4 vols, London 1963–6: H. Vorgimler (ed.), *Commentary on the Documents of Vatican II*, 5 vols, Freiburg and London 1967–9: G. Alberigo and J. A. Komanchak (eds), *History of Vatican II*, 5 vols in progress, Maryknoll and Leuven 1995– is absolutely indispensable: G. Alberigo, J.-P. Jossua and J. A. Komanchak, *The Reception of Vatican II*, Washington 1987: A. Stacpoole (ed.) *Vatican II by those who were there*, London 1986: A. Hastings, *Modern Catholicism: Vatican II and After*, London 1991, presents a valuable if somewhat uneven collection of essays on most aspects of post-Conciliar Catholicism, and a useful review of the work of the Council and its documents.

For the brief pontificate of John Paul I, P. Hebblethwaite, *The Year of Three Popes*, London 1978: John Cornwell, *Thief in the Night: the death of Pope John Paul I*, Harmondsworth 1990, disposes convincingly of near-paranoid conspiracy theories about murder in the Vatican, replacing them with a sad tale of neglect and panic.

For John Paul II, all earlier biographies have been superceded by George Wiegel, *Witness to Hope, the biography of Pope John Paul II*, New York 1999, massively full if uncritically laudatory. J. Michael Miller has edited *The Encyclicals and Post-Synodical Apostolic Exhortations of John Paul II*, Huntingdon, Indiana 2001. Other key writings of Karol Wojtyla are *The Acting Person*, Dordrecht 1979: *Sources of Renewal: The Implementation of the Second Vatican Council*, New York 1980: *Sign of Contradiction*, New York 1979: *Collected Poems*, London 1982: *Collected Plays and Writing on Theater*, Berkeley 1987: *Crossing the Threshold of Hope*, London 1994 (prepared 'interviews' with the Italian journalist Vittorio Messori). For his thought, G. H. Williams, *The Mind of John Paul II: origins of his thought and action*, New York 1981: J. M. McDermott, (ed.), *The Thought of John Paul II*, Rome 1993: Avery Dulles, *The Splendour of Faith, the theological vision of Pope John Paul II*, New York 1999.

For John Paul's involvement in the reordering of Eastern Europe, Stehle, *Eastern Politics of the Vatican*, and P. Michael, *Politics and Religion in Eastern Europe*, Oxford 1991. On Liberation Theology, A. T. Hennelly, (ed.), *Liberation Theology: a Documentary History*, Maryknoll, NY 1990: P. E. Sigmund, *Liberation Theology at the Crossroads: Democracy or Revolution?*, New York and Oxford 1990: for Oscar Romero, J. R. Brockman, *Romero, a life*, Maryknoll and London 1989: Jon Sobrino, *Archbishop Romero, Memories and reflections*, Maryknoll 1990. The politics of canonisation are robustly and entertainingly handled in Kenneth L. Woodward, *Making Saints: how the Catholic Church determines who becomes a saint, who doesn't, and why*, New York 1996.

There is a clear and concise exposition of the process of electing a new pope in the pamphlet by Mgr Charles Burns, *The Election of a Pope*, London, 1997.

PICTURE CREDITS

INDEX